THE LAW OF CHRIST

THE LAW

Volume One:

GENERAL MORAL THEOLOGY

For the law of the Spirit of the life in Christ Jesus has delivered me from the law of sin and of death. (ROM 8:2)

Moral Theology
for Priests and Laity

OF CHRIST

by Bernard Häring, C.SS.R.

Translated by EDWIN G. KAISER, C.PP.S.

THE MERCIER PRESS
4 BRIDGE STREET, CORK

This translation was made from the fifth edition of
Das Gesetz Christi, published by Erich Wewel Verlag,
Freiburg im Breisgau, Germany, in 1959.

Imprimi potest: Very Rev. John E. Byrne, C.PP.S.
Provincial
June 13, 1960

Nihil Obstat: Frederick J. Hunnefeld, C.PP.S.,
S.T.D.
Censor Librorum

Imprimatur: John J. Carberry, D.D.
Bishop of Lafayette, Indiana
June 13, 1960

TO THE MEMORY OF MY
DEAR PARENTS
first to bring to me
the Good News of God's Love
through an unforgettable
example
of authentic Christian love

FOREWORD

THE principle, the norm, the center, and the goal of Christian Moral Theology is Christ. The law of the Christian is Christ Himself in Person. He alone is our Lord, our Saviour. In Him we have life and therefore also the law of our life. Christian life may not be viewed solely from the point of formal enactment of law and not even primarily from the standpoint of the imperative of the divine will. We must always view it from the point of the divine bounty: God wills to give Himself to us. In Christ, the Father has given us everything. In Him and through Him the Father manifests the profoundest depths of His love. In the love of Christ and through the love of Christ for us He invites our love in return, which is a life truly formed in Christ. The Christian life is following Christ, but not through mere external copying, even though it be in love and obedience. Our life must above all be a life in Christ. The essential orientation in this moral theology, as indicated by Magnus Jocham, is toward "the mysteries of the children of God." It is mystical identification of our whole being in Christ through the sacraments, a manifestation of the divine life in us.

The existence of man cannot be explained historically except through Christ, who is the ideal according to which we have been created and re-created. Christian morality must be explained and formed in the light of the eternal realities. We are created in the eternal image of the Logos, the Word of God, and re-created by the Redemption through Christ Jesus. Christian morality is life flowing from the victory of Christ, the hopeful anticipation of the Second Coming of the Saviour in the glorious manifestation of His final triumph on the great day of judgment. All men are called to share in this union with Christ through imitation of Him. To be mystically identified with Christ, to live in Christ, means to be a member of His Body, to be made a subject of His kingdom. Therefore Christian morality in its totality is salutary and apostolic in character. In all its parts it must reveal an organic unity directed to life in and through Christ, and to the final triumph with Him.

The author is well aware that any exposition of Catholic Moral Theology will betray a preference for one of many diverse approaches or perspectives in relation to the wealth of the truths of faith. The study of these under various aspects leads to a diversity of types in moral theology. The present work attempts to expound the most central truths in the light of the inspired word of the Bible. The effort is one of many, none of which should exclude the others. All should prove mutually helpful and complementary to one another.

A textbook or manual of moral theology is written primarily to suit the purpose proposed by its author. One author endeavors primarily or exclusively to provide the confessor with solid and comprehensive doctrine and procedure for the discharge of his duties as judge in the tribunal of penance. He will adapt his work to such an end and purpose. It will differ from the work of another writer who aims to present the Christian life as flowing uniquely from divine grace and truth, and hence expressly attempts to write a moral theology of the Christian message for enlightened teaching and instruction of all the faithful. Nothing is so far from the writer's mind as theological polemics. He has not the slightest desire to exclude other types of moral theology. He is quite content if with God's help he is able to fulfill his chosen task as faithfully and effectively as the purely casuistic textbooks have discharged their particular function in their chosen area of concentration. Our purpose is an integration and synthesis of various systems, as the following brief summary shows.

First, we shall endeavor to describe the perfect ideal of the life in Christ and with Christ. This is the ideal of radical conformity with Christ through the exercise of the Christian virtues. In other words, we take up and discuss the Christian virtues which make us like to Christ.

Secondly, in conjunction with the treatment of the virtues, we shall point out the limits of the law beyond which lies the dread realm of death and loss of the life in Christ. But it should be made plain that even this part of our work does not constitute a simple "morality of law." Rather, from a central point of vantage we indicate those limits beyond which our conduct becomes a contradiction to the life in Christ and a hazard to the imitation of Christ. Law may be described as an expression or manifestation of the reality of creation and redemption. It is the reverse side of the loving divine bounty. It may be compared to an off-limits warning of the abyss of death! But it also points to the golden summit of constant progress in love and urges us forward toward this ideal! All this clearly implies that the doctrine of virtue and the delineation of the limits of the law in Christian moral theology are not unrelated, as though there might be a statistical summary of doctrine on the virtues and parallel to it a statistical summation of law, nothing more. In fact, the two are intimately connected. Christian morality is life and progress in life. This leads to our third point.

Moral theology must reveal how the good, like an arch resting on solid foundation, has its sound basis in law, but reaches to the summit of perfection. The dynamic character of morality is explicitly treated in the special chapter on conversion placed between the chapters on sin and virtue, but it is implicit in all the chapters of our work. Wherever and whenever one discusses limits and bounds together with the ideal of fulfillment and perfection, the dynamics of growth and progress in relation to the persistent imperfection and incompleteness of the Christian, the earthly pilgrim and sojourner (*viator*), must be in evidence.

The subtitle, suggested by the work of J. M. Sailer, reveals the intent and hope of the author that his effort will be profitable to the educated laity as well as to theologians or students of theology preparing for the clerical state. However, the scientific character proper to a true work of theology is not in any way sacrificed. Nor is the traditional scholastic terminology slighted. Nevertheless the endeavor to provide a text which conforms to the ideals of a theology of the Christian message is constantly kept in mind. With this end in view, the author attempted to keep the technical terminology at a minimum and to provide a text within the grasp of the earnest layman and also suitable for ready use by preacher and confessor for whom it should lighten the burden of presenting the eternal truths in a manner befitting our times. The very fact that a moral theology has been adapted to the capacity of the interested non-theologian may prove to be its best recommendation to the theologian and director of souls. The extent to which the author has attained his own ideals must be left to the kindly judgment of his readers.

Moral theology proclaims the eternal truth, but in each age the manner varies to meet the needs of the times. It must penetrate and illumine the problems and tasks of each period in the light of eternity. Moral theology attempts to serve the age. It is service in the kingdom of God. As such, moral theology can be of help to the layman in understanding his Christian duty in the world. It can furnish him with an insight into the problems of his private and public life in all the breadth and depth of their relation to the imitation of Christ, problems which can be solved by an earnest study of the law of Christ.

The theologian, for his part, should be able to find in this moral theology—such is the earnest hope of the author—not only the essential materials for instruction in moral doctrine, but also what he may need as confessor and director of souls. For the confessor and director is not merely judge, but also pastor and guide of souls. His first duty is to bring the glad tidings of the kingdom of God to each particular soul. This message of the Gospel is a summons and an invitation to complete conversion to God with total renunciation of sin. As teacher of the divine truth he must lead and direct souls toward the perfection of Christian life in all its breadth and depth.

It is a matter of supreme concern to the author to forestall any misunderstanding regarding one important point: if our text presents the full dimension of the Christian moral ideal in all its awesome and blissful height, this should never be viewed as any justification for rigorism in the administration of the sacrament of penance. Whenever the question arises regarding granting or refusing absolution in this holy tribunal, the supreme rule to be followed is to demand in the spirit of great mildness no more than the minimum required by the law. But with equal emphasis one must caution against the opposite extreme of laxness, which is no less fatal than the worst severity. If occasionally the manuals for confessors written by the mildest authors in the Church lay down the minimum requirement of the law, this must be understood to be for the guidance of the confessor as judge of souls and not at all the complete norm set up as a standard for everyone under any and every circumstance. Obviously, such misunderstanding is not likely to be encouraged by the perusal of the present work.

Our arrangement is very largely in the traditional manner. Under general moral theology the moral foundations are first explained. Then, in a kind of Christian anthropology, we give the teaching on the subject and bearer of moral value. There follows the doctrine on the law which governs the disciple of Christ and the role he must play in the Christian task, the teaching on sin, conversion, and virtue.

At first blush it may seem a serious departure from the exalted theological plan in the concept of Saint Thomas to place the cardinal virtues before the theological, as we do. The *Summa* of the Angelic Doctor has the treatise on the theological virtues in his II–II, before the tract on the cardinal virtues. This arrangement is altogether sound, and our arrangement is not at all an implied criticism. Our presentation has the practical purpose of placing all possible emphasis on the life in grace and the theological virtues. Therefore, the fundamental attitudes (cardinal virtues) are treated in general moral theology, where they are described as general attitudes or dispositions in the following of Christ.

Special moral in its entire content is presentation and explanation of the three theological virtues. Significantly, the tract on the virtue of religion immediately follows the treatment of the theological virtues, since the divine virtues demand and require the exercise of religion. Under the latter the traditional materials related to the first table of the decalog are dealt with. Then follows the doctrine on Christian love of neighbor, which is the second great ideal and pattern for our life with God. Finally, in the sequence of the decalog, the various walks of life are taken up and discussed under the aspect and pattern of the "realization of love." The reader of the text need scarcely be reminded that the point of departure in our study is not the decalog, but the life of Christ. The contents as presented not only fit in well with the ideal of Christian love, which is central to the whole Christian life, but they should serve admirably for practical use in the day-by-day service of God.

Deliberately the author abstained from including the materials of ecclesiastical law and civil law in the content of this text, in order to avoid all semblance of equating law and moral or of reducing moral theology to forms of law. Since, however, the morality of law is of tremendous importance in moral theology and may not be ignored, the moral-theological basis of canon law and the moral-theological coordination of civil law, as well as typical problems bearing on the relation between moral and law, are expressly taken up and discussed. They are presented in the light of that inner bond between the human law, particularly the law of the Church, and the "law of the Spirit of the life in Christ Jesus" (Rom 8:2).

The author's primary purpose of presenting theological truth in its full depth and coherence of meaning could not be attained without a degree of repetition. Each individual truth should be presented in the light of the whole truth, in so far as this is possible. The present work attempts to combine completeness of doctrine with balance and coordination of particular teaching.

The bibliography for each chapter goes beyond the strictly scientific works of research, for it is intended not only for the expert or specialist who is engaged in further research or teaching, but also for the director of souls and the layman. In consequence, the bibliography includes very much that pertains to the "theology of popular instruction." The reader will note that many of the older standard works are not listed. He is directed to the well-known handbooks for a copious listing: Aertnys-Damen, Noldin, Mausbach, Schilling, and Tillmann. We usually refer to particular tracts in the manuals only when they were a source to which the writer is indebted. The student should find no difficulty orientating himself in the sources through careful use of the table of contents and index found in most authors.

The author is grateful to God for any success which crowns his efforts. He prays that his work will prove useful to students of theology, to those engaged in the care of souls, to spiritual directors, to many laymen devoted to the divine truths and the Christian life. He will be especially grateful if his work will be allowed to find a place, modest though it may be, among the outstanding moral theologies. He is quite conscious that his own achievement is modest by comparison with the work of noted theologians to whom he is so greatly in debt. Particularly influential in forming his mind and shaping his entire endeavor in moral theology are Augustine, Cyril of Jerusalem, Thomas Aquinas, and Alphonse Liguori, and among moral theologians of more recent times, Sailer, Hirscher, Tillmann, and Steinbuechel.

TRANSLATOR'S PREFACE

THE work of Bernard Häring, the noted Redemptorist moral theologian, was enthusiastically received in many countries and widely acclaimed as a unique enrichment of moral theology. It is here presented to English-speaking readers in a translation which is faithful to the thought and order of the original without being slavishly bound to it. The reader who may wish to compare it with the French translation-adaptation, *La Loi du Christ,* which proved something of a bestseller in France, will note an occasional reliance on that splendid version. If this English version will be welcomed with even a slight measure of enthusiasm in a day of numerous translations of varying quality, the translator will be highly gratified.

The Law of Christ, if the caution be necessary, is not simply another text designed to supplant the seminary manuals; nor is it a *vade mecum* for the busy priest who seeks the answer to many problems of a practical nature which clamor for an immediate solution. It is rather a new and rich approach to the whole field of moral theology, as the reception of the work in many parts of the world testifies. The Archbishop of Toulouse, in his Foreword to Volume One of *La Loi du Christ,* speaks of it as a grand and beautiful work, the work of a master. The Cardinal of São Paulo recommended the work very highly in his Foreword to the Portuguese version recently published by Herder of São Paulo. The papal Secretary of State, Domenico Cardinal Tardini, addressed the following message of appreciation to the French publishers, Desclée of Tournai, after a bound volume of *La Loi du Christ* had been presented to the Holy Father: "The Holy Father realizes the vastness of this excellent undertaking. He hopes it will prove of great help to Christians in our day to bring them to a better recognition of the moral demands of their faith, and a life according to the Law of Christ, so that they are truly children of God." The confidence of the Holy See is further indicated by the recent appointment of Father Häring as consultor of the theological commission for the Second Ecumenical Council of the Vatican.

The translator wishes to express his deep appreciation to all who have helped him in his immense task. He is particularly indebted to the Reverend Frederick Hunnefeld of the St. Charles Seminary theological faculty in Carthagena, Ohio, who reviewed the entire manuscript, checked the bibliography and the notes. If the translator has any sense of confidence in the accuracy of his work in an area of theology in which he is far from expert, it must be ascribed to the painstaking criticism of Father Hunnefeld. Fathers Joseph Smolar, Raymond Cera, Aloysius O'Dell, and Mr. Louis Gatto of the St. Joseph's College faculty were very helpful in preparing the work for publication.

The bibliography in the present translation lists all the authors and works found in the fifth German edition. Wherever a particular work has been translated into English, however, the latter alone is mentioned. A number of works cited in their German translations from the French are here listed under their original French titles. Moreover, at the end of the parts a number of titles in English have been added by the translator. It is hoped that the addition of the name of the publisher of the works in English will prove useful to the student. For his benefit asterisks were placed before the names of the non-Catholic authors of the works written in English.

In some few instances the translator has made a considerable variation in the text and added notes of his own. The pages on abnormal psychology were completely revised and are largely the work of Father Hunnefeld.

EDWIN G. KAISER, C.PP.S.

St. Joseph's College
Rensselaer, Indiana

CONTENTS

PART TWO:

THE SUBJECT OF MORAL VALUES
THEOLOGICAL ANTHROPOLOGY

PART THREE:

THE MORAL DUTY OF THE DISCIPLE OF CHRIST

PART SIX:

GROWTH AND PERFECTION IN THE FOLLOWING OF CHRIST: THE CHRISTIAN VIRTUES

ABBREVIATIONS

AAcSt	*Acta Academiae S. Thomae*
AAS	*Acta Apostolicae Sedis*
ABR	*American Benedictine Review*
AER	*American Ecclesiastical Review*
AGP	*Archiv fuer gest. Psychologie*
AmCl	*L'Ami du Clergé*
AnalGreg	*Analecta Gregoriana*
Ang	*Angelicum*
ARP	*Archiv fuer religioese Psychologie*
BGCP	*Bulletin of the Guild of Catholic Psychiatrists*
BM	*Benedictinische Monatschrift*
BoZ	*Bonner Zeitschrift fuer Theologie und Seelsorge*
BullThom	*Bulletin Thomiste*
Cath	*Catholica*
CC	*Civiltà Cattolica*
CiTo	*Ciencia Tomista*
ClerRev	*Clergy Review*
CMQ	*Catholic Medical Quarterly*
ColGand	*Collationes Gandavenses*
ComR	*Commentarium pro Religiosis*
CrossC	*Cross Currents*
CrossCr	*Cross and Crown*
DivThom (F)	*Divus Thomas (Freiburg)*
DivThom (P)	*Divus Thomas (Piacenza)*
DR	*Downside Review*
DSp	*Dictionnaire de Spiritualité*
DTC	*Dictionnaire de la Théologie catholique*
DubRev	*Dublin Review*
EphThLov	*Ephemerides theologicae Lovanienses*
EtCar	*Études Carmelitaines*
FLR	*Fordham Law Review*
FranzStud	*Franziscanische Studien*
GeistLeben	*Geist und Leben*
Greg	*Gregorianum*
HerderKorr	*Herder-Korrespondenz*
Ho	*Hochland*

HPR	*Homiletic and Pastoral Review*
HS	*Hispania Sacra*
IER	*Irish Ecclesiastical Record*
ITQ	*Irish Theological Quarterly*
JP	*Jus Pontificum*
JPP	*Jahrbuch fuer Psychologie und Psychotherapie*
JPpF	*Jahrbuch fuer Philosophie und phaenomenologische Forschung*
LebS	*Lebendige Seelsorge*
LumVie	*Lumière et Vie*
MedST	*Medieval Studies*
MélScRel	*Mélanges de science religieuse*
MiscCom	*Miscelánea Comillas*
MisMor	*Miscellania Moralia*
MThZ	*Muenchener Theologische Zeitschrift*
NewSchol	*New Scholasticism*
NO	*Die Neue Ordnung*
NRTh	*Nouvelle Revue Théologique*
OrCh	*Orientalia Christiana*
PhJahrb	*Philosophisches Jahrbuch*
PhT	*Philosophy Today*
PRM	*Periodica de re morali*
RACh	*Reallexikon fuer Antike und Christentum*
RAM	*Revue d'Ascétique et de mystique*
RazFe	*Razón y Fe*
Rb	*Revue biblique*
REsDo	*Revista Española de Derecho Canonico*
RevEspir	*Revista de Espiritualidad*
RevEspT	*Revista Española de Teologia*
RevNeoscolPh	*Revue Néoscholastique de Philosophie*
RevR	*Review for Religious*
RevSR	*Revue des Sciences religieuses*
RevThom	*Revue Thomiste*
RHT	*Revue d'histoire et theologie*
RoemQschr	*Roemische Quartalschrift*
RPol	*Review of Politics*
RThP	*Revue théologique et philosophique*
Sal	*Salesianum*
SC	*Scuola Cattolica*

ScEccle	*Sciences Ecclésiastiques*
Schol	*Scholastik*
So	*Sophia*
StimmenZeit	*Stimmen der Zeit*
StTh	*Studia Theologica*
ThD	*Theology Digest*
ThG	*Theologie und Glaube*
ThLitZtg	*Theologische Literaturzeitung*
ThPrQschr	*Theologisch-praktische Quartalschrift*
ThQschr	*Theologische Quartalschrift*
ThSt	*Theological Studies*
ThW	*Theologische Woerterbuch zum Neuen Testament*
ThZ	*Theologie der Zeit*
ThZschr	*Theologische Zeitschrift*
TrThZ	*Trierer theologisches Zeitschrift*
Univ	*Universitas*
VieInt	*La Vie Intellectuelle*
VieSpir	*Vie Spirituelle*
VieSpirSupp	*Supplément de la Vie spirituelle*
WissWeish	*Wissenschaft und Weisheit*
WW	*Wort und Wahrheit*
ZAM	*Zeitschrift fuer Aszese und Mystik*
ZKathTh	*Zeitschrift fuer Katholische Theologie*
ZKG	*Zeitschrift fuer Kirchengeschichte*
ZNtWiss	*Zeitschrift fuer die neutestamentliche Wissenschaft und die Kunde der aelteren Kirche*
ZSystTh	*Zeitschrift fuer systematische Theologie*

Part One:

INTRODUCTION

CHAPTER ONE

HISTORICAL SURVEY OF MORAL THEOLOGY

I. THE MORAL TEACHING OF JESUS

THE moral teaching of Jesus is contained in its totality in the glad tidings of salvation. The tremendous *Good News* is not actually a new law, but the Sovereign Majesty of God intervening in the person of Christ and the grace and love of God manifesting itself in Him. In consequence, all the precepts of the moral law, even the most sacred, are given a new and glorious orientation in divine grace and a new focus, the Person of the God-man. There is nothing novel in the call to repentance for all sin. What is new is the glad tidings announcing that *now* the time for the great conversion from sin and the return to God is at hand.

Nor is the commandment of love new. The most enlightened minds of the Old Testament were well aware of the law of love as a summary of the law. What is new is the full revelation of the nature and the meaning of the love of God: "God so loved the world that he gave his only begotten Son" (Jn 3:16). The consequence is something tremendously new in the old and abiding commandment of love. Jesus' own love is the basis and measure for the commandment of love: "A new commandment [or a commandment as something new] I give you, that you love one another: that as I have loved you, you also love one another" (Jn 13:34; 15:12ff.). This is new in the commandment of love, that in an entirely new form we "have learned from God to love one another" (1 Thes 4:9). As John, the disciple whom Jesus loved, expresses it, this is new, namely that "the darkness has passed away and the true light is now shining" (1 Jn 2:8).

As Christ fulfilled the Old Covenant in the new covenant of His love, so also did He fulfill the old law. He broke down the hedge which separated the people of Israel from all other peoples. (This is especially evident in Paul and the Apostolic Council of Jerusalem.) But He did not abolish or suppress a single letter of the will of God manifested in the Old Testament, but fulfilled it perfectly (Mt 5:17ff.). The plenitude of salvation appearing in Him, bringing to man a new heart, a new life, demands also a purer disposition. What Moses conceded to the Israelites only because of the hardness of their heart (Mt 19:8), what was not permitted from the beginning, surely cannot be lawful in the time of the fulness of God's sovereignty and the plenitude of His grace.

3

The law of the Old Covenant in the decalog establishes minimum requirements in the form of prohibitions, but Christ as the sole teacher of the New Covenant founded in His sacrifice on Calvary establishes a new law sealed with the Blood of the New Covenant. This incomparably great law is life in Him; it is the following in His footsteps; it is loving service, bearing the cross, humility, love of enemies (cf. MT 5: Sermon on the Mount). What is new in the moral preaching of Jesus is not antithesis to the Old Testament, but its fulfillment. It is cast into still sharper relief by contrast with the externalistic and legalistic righteousness of the Pharisees.

The moral sermons of Jesus as found in the Gospels are not at all a scientific and systematic presentation, much less a doctrinaire explication. The Gospel preaching of the Saviour is the announcement of the divine message of salvation and the summons in an actual concrete situation presented with unique dramatic vividness. And yet there shines forth from it, from its very heart, more clearly than from any scientific system of teaching, the great reality: His person, His love, the grace of following in His footsteps, the "truth and the life!" (JN 14:6).

II. THE MORAL PREACHING OF THE APOSTLES

The moral preaching of the Apostles—we notice especially the insistence of Paul and John—re-echoes the glad tidings of Jesus. Their message is an urgent, beatifying imperative of divine love: "The love of Christ impels us" (2 COR 5:14). "The charity of God is poured forth in our hearts by the Holy Spirit" (ROM 5:5). "It is now no longer I that live, but Christ lives in me. And the life that I now live. . . . I live in the faith of the Son of God, who loved me and gave himself up for me" (GAL 2:20).

The simple message of the Apostles is the teaching of their Master, His life and the new life of grace given us in and through Christ. They preach the word, all that they have seen and heard; and the ideal they proclaim is also evident in their own lives which are an imitation of the Master's. "Be imitators of me as I am of Christ" (1 COR 11:1). The moral impulse springs primarily from the ineffable influence of divine grace and from the power of the kingdom of God in our midst. With profound love for the crucified Saviour who had risen in glory the Christians awaited His second coming to judge all men.

As was to be expected, when Christianity entered the cultural world of Greek and Roman paganism and simultaneously broke with the synagogue, many individual problems clamored for solution. Not satisfied with the immediate practical way out of the difficulty for peace of conscience, the Christian leaders studied the problems theoretically and in principle. Already the Apostle Paul took up the question of the relation between the Old Testament law and the new law of grace in Christ, as we notice particularly in the letter to the Romans and in the letter to the Galatians. The Apostle shows the relation existing between the law of nature given to all men, including the pagans, and the law revealed in the Old Covenant and in Christ (ROM 1ff.). He investigates the problem of the binding force of the ritual law, not merely to ascertain its validity after the promulgation of the new law, but above all to solve various particular problems in the light of the new law of love (ROM 14). The same fundamental principles shed light on the perplexing dietary problem regarding the meats sacrificed to idols and then offered for sale in the markets (1 COR 8). Paul likewise has a brief summary of the principal mortal sins in the so-called "catalog of vices." In the table of domestic duties (COL 3:18ff.; EPH 5:22ff.) he lists the domestic and vocational virtues. Under pressure of circumstances many other problems are taken up and solved, as, for example, that of the Christian's relation to the state and civil authority (ROM 13).

III. THE MORAL TEACHING OF THE FATHERS

In moral questions, as in all others, the Fathers of the Church faithfully transmit the Christian heritage. But they do not attempt at all to present complete systems of doctrine. Often they merely arrange in summary and sketchy form the moral instructions of the Old Testament and the New Testament or the words of the Lord handed down by oral tradition. An example is the *Didache,* the oldest part of which may date as far back as the year 75. The Christian ideal of virtue presented against the ugly background of pagan vice particularly by the Apologetes is very effective. Singularly charming is the account of the two ways in the *Didache,* the way of the good and the way of evil. Here we have initial phases of the basic outlines of later moral theology: the teaching on virtue as the way of salvation and the catalog of sins.

Special monographs expressly take up the burning moral questions of the time, usually treating them in their basic relation to the imitation of Christ. Realization of an incomparably lofty Christian morality in the morass of a perverted pagan world and a heathen state posed innumerable problems, which today would be comprised in the concept of "material cooperation." Such was the question regarding the stand to be taken by the Christian in connection with pagan worship and the fashioning of idols by Christian craftsmen. It was likewise asked what the Christian attitude should be toward the theatre, the fashions, military service in the pagan army (Tertullian, Clement of Rome, Clement of Alexandria, Cyprian, and others). Such problems were not solved on the mere basis of escape or evasion through flight into the desert, but in the more profound sense of escape from the evils of the world by not being "of the world," though remaining in the world (Jn 17:14ff.).

Widely discussed was the problem of martyrdom and flight from persecution (Origen), and the question of the reconciliation of public sinners, particularly those who had proven weak in time of persecution (Cyprian). The problems of obedience of the Christian to ecclesiastical authority were pondered by Ignatius of Antioch, Clement of Rome, Cyprian, and other Fathers of the Church.

In the scale of values in the primitive Church, virginity is unique. Alongside martyrdom it is the supreme testimony of faith and love. It is the characteristic manifestation of the new life of salvation. Monographs on virginity are still extant, by Tertullian, Cyprian, Methodius of Philippi, Athanasius, Basil, Gregory of Nyssa, Ambrose, Jerome, Augustine, and other Fathers. Even more numerous are the treatises on prayer.

The moral teaching of Saint John and Saint Paul which views morality from the standpoint of life in and with Christ is taken up by Ignatius of Antioch. Very effectively he shows the moral imperative as deriving from grace, from the life in Christ, from the unity of the Body of Christ, the Church. His passionate yearning for martyrdom in order to be united with Christ, his burning desire for the salvation of the Christian communities, arise from one source, the consciousness that the Christian is a "temple of God," a "bearer of Christ" (*Ad Ephesios* 9, 1), and must manifest himself as such in all things. To be a Christian means to follow Christ in loving, in suffering, in dying. Source and center of the Christian life is the altar, the communion of all in the Eucharist.

We think it correct to say that Clement of Alexandria (died before 216) made the first bold effort to construct a truly systematic moral theology. The principal problem of the teacher (*Lógos paidagogós*) is the problem of Christianity in the world. With astonishing largeness of vision and greatness of heart he depicts the ideal of the true Christian. Even under the most trying conditions of metropolitan life he can and must follow Christ. The noted monograph, "What Rich Man Can be Saved?"

(*Quis dives salvetur?*), does more than point out the perils of wealth and extol poverty; it offers constructive suggestions for the right use of wealth in the attainment of salvation. The *Strómata* (*The Carpet*) are a series of sketches and outlines which deal with many problems basic to a scientific moral teaching and the perfect Christian life.

The chief preoccupation of Clement was to show the intimate relation between the positive values of heathen philosophy and morality on the one hand and supernatural revelation and morality on the other. For Clement, genuine Christian life is imitation of God in Christ. Indeed, wherever authentic morality is found, there Christ the teacher is at work. Since the pagans have gathered up whatever genuine truths they possessed as "so many seeds strewn about by the Logos," we who have ourselves been taught by the Logos-made-man, the Word Incarnate, may without any reproach accept the truth found in their lives and their philosophical systems. In some instances, Clement may have fallen short of the critical discernment we expect of a man of his intelligence, as we note in his appraisal of the Stoical and Platonic-Greek ethical ideals, particularly regarding the extinction of passion, the *"apatheia,"* and the "genuine gnosis" which he stresses so sharply. But he never fails to maintain a genuine Christian attitude. With truly pastoral zeal he endeavored to open the treasure of Christian moral teaching to the cultured classes in the philosophical idiom of their own cultural circle so that they would not fall prey to a false gnosis.

With the most delicate sympathy he defends the way of salvation in the married state against the Gnostic hostility to marriage. But he completely shuns the opposite error of disparagement of virginity. He in no wise condemns those who forsake marriage "for the kingdom of heaven's sake" (MT 19:12). He demands of the married that they strive to please the Lord in a community of love and together think on the things of the Lord, as does the virgin (*Stromata,* lib. III, cap. XII).

Origen (died about 253), successor of Clement in the catechetical school of Alexandria, devotes the third book of his *Origins* (*Perì archón, De Principiis*) to the fundamental themes of a moral theology: freedom of will, sin, restoration of all things in God. He is less open to the world than Clement, his teacher, but in many ways more realistic. One of his central thoughts is the imitation of God in the contemplative as well as in the practical life. Moreover, Origen, as Clement before him, made strenuous efforts to enlist pagan wisdom in the service of theology.

The book *De Officiis* of Saint Ambrose (339–397), giving the doctrine regarding moral duties (written for the clerics of his diocese), may be looked upon as the first systematic work of moral theology of a casuistic nature. Ambrose does not share the optimism of the great Alexandrine writers regarding pagan wisdom, and yet this very work on duties reflects the Stoic philosophy and borrows particularly from Cicero's work of the same title. Still it is quite evident that Ambrose is at great pains to animate the Stoic concepts with the Christian spirit. We have a clear example of such an effort in his scheme of the cardinal virtues, which Origen had already introduced into the Christian moral teaching. Ambrose is particularly insistent regarding the essential difference between Christian morality and pagan philosophy, and the superiority of the Christian moral ideal. Though one is astonished at his predilection for the Old Testament and his admiration for the exalted morality of the patriarchs, the preference may be explained by his penchant for concrete examples in pastoral instruction.

A great original spirit influencing all subsequent moral theology is Saint Augustine (354–430). He did not compose a grand systematic work in moral theology after the manner of the *Secunda Secundae* of the *Summa Theologiae* of Saint Thomas and still less in the manner of Saint Alphonse and the modern moral theologians. Nevertheless, he is one of the greatest, if not the very greatest, moral theologian of all time. This judgment is not based merely on the importance of his individual writing in the spheres of moral or pastoral theology (note the titles: *De agone christiano* or *The Christian Combat; De bono conjugali* or *The Good of Marriage; De sancta virginitate* or *Holy Virginity, De bono viduitatis* or *The Good of Widowhood; De continentia* or *Continence; De mendacio, Contra Mendacium* or *On Lying, Against Lying; De patientia* or *Patience; Speculum* or *The Mirror; Enchiridion sive de fide, spe et caritate* or *Summary on Faith, Hope, and Charity*), but on his work as a whole. Precisely those doctrinal problems are placed in the foreground which are fundamental to moral theology: grace and freedom; faith and good works; faith and love; original sin and restoration in grace; grace and law; the *lex aeterna* or eternal law in God, the natural law manifested in the order of creation, and the revealed law; the works of the pagans and the works flowing from faith and grace; divine love and its antithesis, the "natural" desires or concupiscence; the kingdom of God and the history of salvation and the opposing camp of Satan and the great duel between them in the history of the world. The splendid conception of Aquinas as found in the second part of the *Summa,* which is the point of departure for moral theology, plays an important role in Saint Augustine's work: the loving union with God in eternal beatitude as the end and Christian morality as the way and the means.

Augustine is master and model in exploiting the sacred text. For this very reason his moral theology is centered in faith and love, and its *élan vital* is divine grace. He is not less notable for casting into a Christian mould the permanent values of a profound pagan heritage. Throughout his whole life he held fast to the values he had absorbed from the teaching of Plotinus and Plato and from the ethics of the Stoics, though this influence wanes as he grows older, and the pagan thought is increasingly purged and purified in the Christian sense.

A psychologist of the first rank, Augustine elaborates a moral psychology which deals with the spiritual way of life, with the spiritual order of becoming, with the dynamic. As a Christian philosopher he looked upon the moral imperative as a manifestation of truth, being, life. According to this teaching there is profound unity and harmony between the imperative imposed on the will, the "must," and the genuine desire for happiness; both are fulfilled in the end of man. With all possible insistence he focused attention on the singular worth of interior disposition, on conduct regulated by conscience and springing from faith and love. "Not the external conduct but the moral disposition of heart is decisive."[1] But at the same time Augustine makes it very plain that this interior disposition of love cannot be genuine unless it is rooted in obedience and remains in harmony with the divine law. "The genius of Augustine is unique in its versatile mastery of all the literary genres in his ethical writings: vivid description; profound handling of principles; captivating manifestation of emotions; practical moral exhortation; epistolary admonition and direction of souls. Even the diverse methods found within Catholic moral theology, the scholastic and mystic, the ascetic and casuistic find their models in his works."[2]

Gregory the Great (died in 604) is also a moralist, but altogether different in genius. He is a genuine Roman taken up entirely with the practical Christian life. Practical also are his study and use of the Scriptures, in which he finds constant illustrations and exhortations for the moral life. Classic examples of this type of use of the inspired sources are his *Moralia in Job* and his homilies. None of the earlier great patristic theologians, not Chrysostom, Basil, Athanasius, or any of the others, is so dedicated to the primacy of the moral imperative as is Gregory.

A classical example of systematic sacramental orientation is found in

Cyril of Jerusalem (died in 386). His moral instruction is woven entirely from the sacred mysteries, a form of instruction which was the dominant ideal in the East at least throughout the patristic period and in the West to the time of Augustine and beyond. Viewed as a whole, the moral direction was rather a supplement, though, of course, a very important supplement, to the instruction in the faith. The moral imperative was evidently characterized as the development and consequence of the life of Christ.

IV. MORAL THEOLOGY FROM THE SEVENTH
TO THE TWELFTH CENTURIES

The period from 600 to 1200 was barren. In moral theology there was little activity beyond the compiling of summaries. Materials handed down from the earlier Fathers were collected and coordinated for practical uses (note particularly Isidore of Seville). A veritable treasure-trove for the research into moral theology of this period, and the same is true for any other period, are sermons and the decrees of Popes, bishops, and councils, which, at least in their condemnation of the moral excesses of the age, uphold the ideals of Christian morality in all its purity.

Original and creative in this period and of singular significance for the later development of moral theology are the penitential books, the *libri poenitentiales*. These penitentials appeared first in Ireland, then in Germany and France. They were composed to aid and direct the confessor in determining the character and degree of sacramental penance he was to impose on his penitent. Since nothing was to be left to the discretion of the particular confessor, the various species of mortal sins were examined in the most minute detail. The penitential of Burchard[3] is a pertinent example; it lists no less than twenty varieties of homicide, each with its own appropriate penance.

As might be expected, there were ceaseless complaints about the mechanical character of the penitential books and their use and application from the time of the Carolingian renaissance.[4] And still no one seems to have thought of searching in these *"libelli sacerdotum"* for a Catholic moral theology. In consequence, the very absence of a positively developed moral theology placed these works in a position of primary practical importance in the task of spiritual direction, although the disregard of fundamental problems and the excessive emphasis on satisfaction to the neglect of the other elements of the sacrament of penance distinguish the penitentials from the casuistic texts of later moral theology. If the neglect of the fundamental problems was almost complete in this barren period, the greatness of the effort of the classical period of the Middle Ages is all the more significant.

V. MORAL THEOLOGY IN THE HIGH MIDDLE AGES

The high Middle Ages are significant not merely for classical theology as a whole, but particularly for notable achievement in moral theology. Bernard of Clairvaux, Hugh and Richard of Saint Victor, Eckhart, Tauler, Gerson, Thomas à Kempis are noted representatives of the moral theology with an ascetical-mystical orientation.

Since the great scholastics preceding Thomas do not distinguish a special branch of moral theology in their systems, they take up the moral problems in connection with the teaching on creation, the fall of man, the Incarnation, the sacraments. This is true of Peter Lombard and his commentators up to the time of Albert the Great (1193–1280).

Though Albert composed a philosophical commentary on the Nico-machean Ethics of Aristotle, he never devised a plan to construct a special theological discipline after the analogy of the Aristotelian ethics. In this, the teacher of Thomas pursues the same essential line of thought as the great teachers of the Franciscan school, Alexander of Hales (died in 1245) and Bonaventure (1221–1274). For them the whole of theology is indivisible doctrine on God, and on man only in the sight of God; in all its truths it is the "teaching of wisdom"; this means that by their very nature all revealed truths are to be studied in theology so as to stimulate fruitfully our faith and our love. Theology exists not merely "to serve contemplation, but also to make us holy; in fact, its first purpose is to make us holy."[5]

Christian morality for the Seraphic Doctor was so completely the consequence of the mysteries of the faith that the thought of constructing a distinct discipline of moral theology along the lines of the scientific principles of moral philosophy and growing out of dogmatic theology never occurred to him. Equally foreign to his mind was the thought of a moral theology constructed entirely within the framework of dogma. True as this may be, we may not conclude that moral theology is entirely absent in the writing of Bonaventure.

We are indebted to Saint Thomas Aquinas (died in 1274) for a magnificent synthesis of all that the theological tradition of the previous ages had handed down, as well as for notable beginnings in moral theological science. For him Christian moral teaching is a part of the one undivided science of theology. Its object is not man, but God. As known through natural and supernatural revelation, God is also central to the scientific presentation of the Christian life. The intellectual bond which unites moral theology (this term is not used by Saint Thomas, who speaks only of the teaching of faith, etc.) with the whole Thomistic theological system is, first, the idea of man in relation to his creation and to his last end, and, secondly, the idea of man as made in the image and likeness of God, so that, in the last analysis, when we treat of man we can say nothing essential about him except in relation to the divine model and in the presentation of this image always refer to God, its ultimate cause and pattern. The third basis of unity, which synthesizes and embraces the whole system, is the concept of the humanity of Christ as our way to God.

Like mighty columns these three ideas support the whole unified edifice of the theology of Saint Thomas: "Because the chief aim of sacred doctrine is to teach the knowledge of God not only as He is in Himself, but also as He is the beginning of things and their last end, and especially of rational creatures . . . therefore, in our endeavor to expound this science, we shall treat: 1) of God" (Part I of the *Summa Theologica*); "2) of the rational creature's movement toward God" (Part II); "and 3) of Christ who as man is our way to God"[6] (Part III). "Man is made in the image of God in so far as he is patterned after God through intellectuality, freedom of will, and self-determination. Hence, after the discussion on the exemplar, namely God, and those things which came forth from the power of the divine will, there remains to be studied His image, namely man, in so far as he too through his free will is the principle of his own works."[7] "Our Lord and Saviour Jesus Christ, saving His people from their sins, showed us the way of truth in Himself, through which after our resurrection we can attain to the blessedness of immortal life. Hence it is necessary . . . that after we have treated the ultimate end of human life, and of virtues and vices, there follow our consideration of the Saviour of all and of the salutary benefits bestowed by Him on the human race."[8]

The second part of the *Summa* is a systematic synthesis of human morality on the sacred level of the divine image in man. But it is not at all presented as a closed and independent system of moral theology which one can remove from the whole work as something final and complete. Nor is the doctrine of eternal happiness, introduced in the *Prima Secundae*, the one dominant theological theme which comprehensively synthesizes the whole of the moral teaching. What is really ultimate is the doctrine on

God Himself, Creator and Finisher, and the doctrine on Christ, Saviour and Master, in whom our likeness to God is supernaturally founded. Here we have the basic foundation for our whole edifice of theology. Only if we tear asunder what Thomas held to be inseparable, can we fail to see in his moral teaching the theocentric and Christocentric orientation. The thought of the following of Christ flowing from the sacramental bond of grace in Christ is essential to the moral doctrine of Saint Thomas, which always remains an inseparable part of the teaching of faith, of the glad tidings of salvation.

In his methodology Saint Thomas was particularly influenced by Aristotle: the study of the Nicomachean Ethics clearly revealed the positive importance of natural reason, or, more specifically, the importance of natural revelation, through creation, for the moral life of man. In this area Saint Thomas gave the final answer to the age-old question which had intrigued and disturbed Clement of Alexandria and Ambrose and all the great theological minds of previous ages: the question of the relation between natural and supernatural morality, between reason and faith in the moral life. Nevertheless, in content and ultimate intention the moral doctrine of Thomas draws its nourishment much more from the roots of the traditional theology (Augustine, Dionysius the Areopagite) than from Aristotle. In Aristotle happiness centers in man and in this world. For Thomas happiness is *"beatitudo"* or the blessed community with and in God through participation in His knowledge and in union of love. Accordingly, the Aristotelian virtues underwent a radical transformation in the theology of Thomas. Virtues cease to be man's perfection of himself; they no longer center in man, within the reach of his own power. Now love, openness to the loving will of God, docility to the movement of grace, to the word and example of Christ, all these give the virtues their orientation, their center of meaning, even though the formulas which prevail are derived from Aristotelian categories.

The I–II of the *Summa* is properly a species of moral theology. It treats the doctrine of last end, of freedom of will, of the passions and the "basic attitudes" (*habitus*), of the virtues in general,[9] of sins, of law and grace. The entire first part of the second part of the *Summa* is orientated toward grace. This is the heart of the "new law." "That which is preponderant in the law of the New Testament and whereon all its efficacy is based is the grace of the Holy Spirit, which is given to those who believe in Christ. Consequently the New Law is chiefly the grace itself of the Holy Spirit, which is given to those who believe in Christ. . . . The

New Law contains certain things that dispose us to receive the grace of the Holy Spirit, and pertain to the use of that grace. Such things are of secondary importance, so to speak, in the New Law."[10]

The II–II may be looked upon as special moral theology. It treats the whole realm of moral life comprehended in the three divine virtues and the four cardinal virtues. These latter, as they are treated, were not derived in the first instance from Aristotle. Thomas got them from the ancient Christian tradition and its concept of them, even though in many incidental points regarding them he refers to "the Philosopher."

Down to our own time Thomas has had a succession of noted commentators and continuators. Especially eminent were the writers of the scholastic renaissance of the sixteenth century. But Bonaventure and his school also had great successors. Duns Scotus (died 1308) is specially noteworthy. The primary difference between the Scotistic and the Thomistic school in the basic concept of moral theology, the former holding to the primacy of will or love, the latter to the primacy of intellect, is perhaps often exaggerated. In fact, Thomas also holds that ultimately love is decisive, and neither Bonaventure nor Scotus deny that human love must be clearly grasped and guided by reason. The "practical reason" of Thomas is not far removed from love; in fact, it is potential love. Nevertheless, it would be wrong to slight the difference between the diverse points of view and approach in the two great trends of thought. Only if we view them as complementary do we see the unity of theology in all its richness and splendor.

VI. MORAL THEOLOGY IN THE FOURTEENTH AND FIFTEENTH CENTURIES

1. *Nominalism*

In the work of the Angelic Doctor the science of moral theology reaches the summit of theological science. But unfortunately his successors could not carry on the great tradition, and the Ockhamists were responsible for the fateful decline in moral theology. At the fountainhead of the development of the moral theology of the fourteenth century is the baneful metaphysics of William of Ockham (died in 1359). The fundamental intuition of Nominalism is the unique value of the singular, the individual. The only true reality is the individual. Only the particular man, the human individual, really exists.

What characterizes the moral act of the individual is its absolute un-prepossession, particularly in regard to the habit (this means what is already in possession, the basic attitude). Here we have a moral system of individual acts in contradistinction to a morality of the Thomistic habits (the *habitus,* the permanent, constant, the pre-decided). A further characteristic is the typically biased concept of the good viewed as a conformity of action with will. This conception of the good paved the way for voluntarism and legalism. But the influence for good was also significant. There was a tremendous encouragement of the study of moral theology and especially of its methodology. Particularly significant was the analysis of the moral act in its singularity and uniqueness, and in its subjective and objective presuppositions!

Among the moralists associated with Nominalism were the following: in France, John Buridan (died in 1350); in Germany, Albert of Saxony (died in 1390), Henry of Langenstein (1340 to 1390), Henry Totting of Oyta (1330–1397), Nicholas of Dinkelsbuehl (1360–1433), John Nider (1380–1438).

Works dealing with the virtue of justice are multiplied in this period. Because of the precipitous economic progress toward the end of the fifteenth century, the Nominalists showed a special interest in problems of justice. From this time date the comprehensive studies on justice, *"de justitia,"* such as we find in the tracts "On Contracts" by Henry of Langenstein, Henry Totting, John Nider, and particularly by Conrad of Summenhart (died in 1502). The influence Conrad had on the moral teaching regarding finance was very considerable.

If the impact of Nominalism on the speculative thought in the Church was nothing less than disastrous, there was something positive and con-structive to counterbalance the evil in the field of practical theology. Thorough-going research into concrete problems by the moralists of the period furnished an immense mass of data and observations which could be embodied in a sounder system, with the result that moral teaching would assume a more vital and realistic character. But meanwhile the baneful heritage of Nominalism had its effect also on the mind of the Reformers, who developed a positive hostility to the very concept of law.

2. *The Golden Age of the Penitential Books*

Parallel to the commentaries on the *Book of Sentences* and the great monographs was the progressive development of the penitential literature.

The penitential summas of the fourteenth and fifteenth centuries had their origin in the Irish penitential books, which catalogued penances according to the gravity of sin in the period of the revival of private penance. The penitential summas were spread among the clergy from the thirteenth century. Among the first were the *Summa* of Robert of Flamesbury and the treatises of John, Lector of Fribourg, on the capital sins and confession. In the fourteenth century we have the *Summa Pisana* of Bartholomew of Pisa (died in 1347), the *Summa Astesana* of Astesanus of Asti. The fifteenth century is the period of the great summas. Notable are the *Summa Angelica* of Angelo Carletti di Chivasso and the *Rosella Casuum* of Baptista de Salis. The most important penitential summa is that of Saint Antonine, which presents a complete picture of the moral life of the fifteenth century. Its influence on subsequent summas was immense. At the beginning of the sixteenth century the *Summa Sylvestrina* of Sylvester Prierias (died in 1523) appeared. It went through at least fourteen editions and ranks with the *Summula* of Cardinal Cajetan as the best summa of the sixteenth century.

All these penitential summas have general tracts; most of them are arranged in alphabetical order; some are quite methodic, as is the *Summa* of Saint Antonine. But none can lay claim to be moral theology in the sense of the moral theological works of the seventeenth century. Nor are they manuals or texts for instruction in the sense of our current textbooks or handbooks of instruction, our *Institutiones Morales.* They are plain and simple *Lexica theologiae moralis,* a kind of dictionary of moral theology. They contain the ready information necessary for the priest engaged in the care of souls, moral, law, liturgy, pastoral instruction on the sacraments. The arrangement is according to significant key words, after the manner of a dictionary. A work of this kind is a genuine *vade mecum,* but not a handbook of moral theology. At that time the moral teaching remained embodied in the whole Christian doctrine, which constituted the one undivided theology.

VII. MORAL THEOLOGY IN THE SIXTEENTH CENTURY

1. *The Thomistic Revival*

In the course of the fifteenth century the first stirrings of a Thomistic revival made themselves felt. The movement began in the German universities. In fact, it was at Cologne that Henry of Gorkum (died in 1431) wrote the first commentary on the *Summa* of Saint Thomas. But only at the beginning of the next century did the *Summa* replace the *Book of Sentences* of Peter Lombard as a text in the schools. The consequences were tremendous. In the *Book of Sentences* moral themes were not assigned their own distinct and independent position. The object of moral theology did not occupy its own logical place in relation to the rest of the work. The consideration and study of the virtues, to cite one example of methodology, is attached to the doctrine of the Incarnation. The *Summa* of Thomas, on the other hand, is so constructed as to provide a well-organized and comprehensive treatment of moral problems. The revival of moral theology took place within the framework of the theological summas. The Thomistic renaissance is largely a blossoming of moral theology.

The *Secunda Secundae* of Saint Thomas interested the greatest number of commentators. Among the notable moralists of the early sixteenth century whose works introduce a long series of Thomistic moral theologies is Conrad Koellin, O.P. (died in 1536). A German, he produced the first complete commentary on the I–II. In Italy, Thomas de Vio, Cardinal Cajetan (died in 1534), wrote a commentary on the *Summa,* which together with his *opuscula* in moral theology and his *Summula* constitutes a comprehensive achievement in moral theology of primary importance. In Spain the Dominican Francis of Vitoria (died in 1546) is undoubtedly the most imposing figure of the Thomistic renaissance. His commentaries, recently published (Salamanca: 1932 seqq.), are very comprehensive. His *Relectiones* have merited for him the title of founder of scholastic teaching on international law. He is the first of a long line of scholars of the Salamancan school, among whom we note the highly important moralists, Melchior Cano, O.P. (died in 1560), Dominic Soto, O.P. (died in 1560), Bartholomew Medina, O.P. (died in 1581), Dominic Banez, O.P. (died in 1604). In its great classical period in moral theology this school embodied within the framework of Thomistic moral teaching the fruits of Nominalistic research, the sense of objective reality, and conformity to the needs of the modern age in method. Notable are the great commentaries on Saint Thomas. And of singular merit is its achievement in the study of justice and of the rights of nations.

2. Origin of "Moral Theology"

The Thomistic revival in Christian moral theology in the sixteenth century was marked by profound adjustments in the development of moral teaching. Speculative and practical united to form a splendid synthesis but were soon disturbed by the penchant for the practical which made of moral theology an autonomous science with a practical orientation, leaving to dogmatic theology the entire area of the speculative. The reasons for this estrangement of the two are numerous; we can mention only a few: the decrees of the Council of Trent regarding the administration of the sacrament of penance: the council clearly enunciated the norm requiring the confession of all mortal sins, according to their number, species, and circumstances. A deeper research into the whole area of moral problems was indicated. The individualistic tendency of the age, however, led to a progressively greater concentration on examination of conscience and reception of the sacrament of penance. Let us add to this individualistic tendency the greater need and urgency for a thorough-going pastoral care of souls on the part of the clergy as a whole, as revealed by the Counter Reformation. Nowhere was this need more evident than in the administration of the sacrament of penance and in its devout reception. It became imperative, therefore, that the priest and director of souls acquire a more precise knowledge of Christian morality, particularly in its practical and positive phases. The Society of Jesus was the center of this activity throughout the sixteenth and seventeenth centuries.

The *ratio studiorum* (order of studies) of the Society of Jesus determined that in the houses of study the professors who were charged with lecturing on the *Summa* of Saint Thomas should limit their courses to the more basic principles of moral teaching. On the other hand, certain professors of moral doctrine were assigned the task of dealing professedly with "cases of conscience" in moral matters. The theological activity of these latter professors of moral theology was different from that of the summas for confessors (*summae confessorum*) of the earlier period previously referred to. The goal of this present effort was to determine the doctrinal principles underlying the correct solution of cases. The result was a gradual development of an independent and self-sufficient moral discipline.

But since the study was no longer centered in the master ideas of Saint Thomas (such as the last end of man), because this area of concentration was assigned to speculative theology, the entire endeavor was placed on the level of the tract on conscience (*de conscientia*). The practical problem to be solved is expressed in the question: has this penitent sinned? Yes or no? In such "moral theology" the primacy of honor was accorded to the probabilistic systems. The new order of questions led to the rise and rapid development of the problematique of "theological opinion" and personal opinion, which is actually a problem of morality. The other treatises are coordinated with this problem in such a manner as to form a complete unity, with the result that all the necessary sources for the solution of any case of conscience which can arise are immediately available in the text. Herein lies a partial explanation for the incorporation of canon law into the discipline of moral theology. Certain tracts, in fact, are treated almost exclusively from the perspective of canon law, for example the treatises on matrimony and penance.

There are four distinct groups among the theologians of the Society of Jesus. First are the commentators on the *Summa,* who do not differ radically in method from the commentators of the school of Salamanca. Notable are: Cardinal Francisco de Toledo (1532–1596) and Gregory of Valencia (1541–1603), who lectured at Dillingen and Ingolstadt. Among the very great commentators on the *Summa* are Gabriel Vasquez (died in 1604) and Francis Suarez (died in 1617). Distinctive about these writers is the legal approach. Arguments and methods from ecclesiastical law are embodied in their work. Because of a certain independence from the word of Thomas, the writings of these two commentators would form an integral and autonomous text even if they stood alone.

A second group of Jesuit writers devoted their efforts to a study of select questions, particularly in the field of the morality of law. Louis Molina (1545–1600) in his *de justitia et jure* investigates the development of trade and finance especially in Spain and Portugal. Leonard Lessius (1554–1623) makes a study of the industrial and social politics with emphasis on the trade area of Antwerp and Frankfurt on the Main. Cardinal John de Lugo (1583–1660) is author of the classic *de justitia* and *de poenitentia.* Within the very shadow of the Council of Trent Thomas Sanchez (1550–1610) wrote his massive work on marriage, *de matrimonii sacramento,* which comprises the whole traditional theology of marriage and also the matrimonial legislation.

The third group is noted for the theological manual. Foremost among the many thorough-going and comprehensive studies of moral theology is the handbook *(Institutiones Morales)* by John Azor (1536–1603). It is a pioneer work, forerunner of the type of "moral theology" which has prevailed down to our own day. The pattern established itself so firmly that subsequent moralists make scarcely any change in the form used by Azor. The first part gives the general principles, which are followed in order by the commandments of God and the Church, the sacraments, censures and indulgences, and finally the particular obligations of the various states of life. The first edition of the moral theology of John Azor appeared in the period of 1600–1611. In its wake similar comprehensive works comprising the whole of moral theology appeared. Apart from de Lugo and Sanchez (*Opus morale in praecepta decalogi*), already mentioned, we note Vincent Filliuci (1566–1622), Paul Laymann (1575–1635), Ferdinand de Castropalao (1581–1633), and Herman Busenbaum (1600–1668).

Finally the fourth group is concerned with the handbooks for the confessor, which are practical and convenient successors of the penitential summas of the fourteenth and fifteenth centuries. We can only mention the *Instructio Sacerdotum* or *Summa Casuum* of Cardinal Francisco de Toledo (died in 1596) and the *Praxis paenitentialis* of Valerius Reginaldus (1543–1623).

Obviously the activity in this vast field of moral theology is not at all limited to the Jesuits. Many writers outside the Order also represent the "new theology." Nevertheless, the work centers in the Society of Jesus, just as the other tendency centers in the school of Salamanca.

VIII. MORAL THEOLOGY IN THE SEVENTEENTH AND EIGHTEENTH CENTURIES

Divorced from dogmatic theology, moral theology pursued its own course of development along the lines indicated. With attention focused on the tract on the judgment of conscience, the theologians were principally concerned with the well-known problem of probabilism. So thorough-going was the effort that the history of moral theology throughout these two centuries is basically little more than the history of probabilism. It is also true that such a limited perspective leads to a type of abstract casuistry bereft of vital nourishment. For over a century moral theology enshrouded itself in its own problems.

Among the authors who enjoyed the melancholy reputation of devoting themselves exclusively to casuistry and of veering rapidly toward laxism we mention: Antonine of Diana, Theatine (died in 1663), who solved more than 20,000 cases in his *Resolutiones Morales;* Anthony Escobar, whose work, *Universae theologiae moralis receptiores absque lite sententiae* (1652), soon attained great fame; Thomas Tamburini, S.J. (died in 1675), and John Caramuel, Cistercian (died in 1682), called the "prince of laxists."

Reaction against laxism was exceedingly sharp: the Jansenists in their opposition went to the extreme of attacking every kind of casuistry. Their moral teaching was set forth principally in the following works: *Morale pratique des Jésuites* (1643) by Anthony Arnauld; *Essais de morale* by Pierre Nicole (1625–1695); *Lettres Provinciales* (1656) by Blaise Pascal. There were others who shared to a greater or lesser degree the rigorism of the Jansenists and followed their approach in the solution of moral problems. We note only Louis Habert and his *Theologia Dogmatica et Moralis* (1709) and the *Theologia Moralis* of Gaspar Juenin (1741).

The Carmelites of Salamanca remained aloof from the heat and bitterness of theological quarrels. In addition to the famous *Cursus Theologicus,* they composed the *Cursus Theologiae Moralis* (1665–1724), which is beyond doubt the most significant work in moral theology of the time. Remote from the controversy, likewise, was Charles René Billuart, O.P. (1685–1757), who aimed at a synthesis of moral and dogmatic teaching, and Paul Gabriel Antoine, S.J., who published his *Theologia Universa* in 1726.

The controversies over probabilism finally led to the sterility of the whole moral theological endeavor and to a rather general disregard of the unique character of Christian morality. It is the special merit of Saint Alphonse Liguori to have found the golden mean between the extremes of laxism and rigorism in the solution of moral problems. The probabilioristic attitude of the saint soon made way for a moderate probabilism, which ultimately assumed the more precise form of equi-probabilism. This solution best suited the spiritual realism of the great director of souls. In his moral theology as a whole, the understanding and appreciation of the concrete circumstances of moral action always prevails over a mechanical employment and application of a formula, no matter how correct and justifiable the formula may be. But it still must be conceded that the Alphonsian moral teaching is to be classified with the moral theologies prevalent since the end of the sixteenth century, partaking of their vigor and also of their weakness. However, it would be unfair to the great saint to study the *theologia moralis* as though it were his exclusive and complete presentation of Christian morality, to the neglect of his writing on the perfection of Christian life, which is much more comprehensive and much more widely read. From the abundance of such literature we should single out his *Practica di amar Gesù Cristo,* a precious little book which views the Christian life from the profound and radical aspect of the divine love in the light of the thirteenth chapter of the first letter to the Corinthians.

The most important "casuistic" works of Saint Alphonse are the following: the *Theologia moralis,* which appeared in 1748, was originally a complement and commentary on the extraordinarily popular work of Herman Busenbaum, S.J., entitled *Medulla Theologiae Moralis.* Later, 1753–1755, it appeared as an independent work and after the saint's death went beyond 70 editions.[11] The *Homo Apostolicus* appeared first in Italian under the title, *Istruzione e practica per un confessore.* Probably the most mature of the saint's works, it went through 118 editions. The *Praxis confessarii* and *Il confessore diretto per le confessione della gente di campagna (Confessor of Country People)* are compendious manuals for the confessor. He also wrote numerous monographs which attempt to solve the knotty problem of probabilism.

Even a hasty review of his great work makes clear that the merit of Alphonse, to use a phrase of M. Labourdette, O.P., consists in paving a secure way through the maze of opinions. The Church's great concern was to preserve by means of her teaching office the integrity of doctrine regarding the Christian life. And probabilism seemed for a long time to be bound up with laxism. In the confusion of "probable, more probable, safe, more safe *(tutiores),* less safe, lax and dangerous" opinions, the doctrinal opinions of Saint Alphonse are always practically reliable. On this level of practical conduct rests the true genius of the saint, the great director and pastor of souls, whose extensive literary effort is directed entirely to this same noble end.

IX. MORAL THEOLOGY IN THE NINETEENTH AND TWENTIETH CENTURIES

The controversy regarding the moral systems continued after the death of Saint Alphonse. But the most serious misgivings in this delicate area were resolved so that the distinction between moderate representatives of probabilism on the one hand and the representatives of probabiliorism on the other over against equi-probabilism were no longer of such tremendous consequences.

The texts of the Redemptorist theologians Wouters, Konings, Marc-Gestermann, Aertnys-Damen, are essentially a condensation of the moral teaching of the founder of their Congregation. But there is also an earnest endeavor on their part to follow the developments in the law of the Church and make use of them in practical application in the received text. Likewise, without departure from the established forms, there is some adaptation to the changes which have taken place in social conditions. Increasing prominence is also given to the dogmatic basis of many problems in the manual of Aertnys-Damen,[12] even though the work as a whole is orientated toward fruitful administration and reception of the sacrament of penance.

In the same category are the much used manuals of the Jesuits, Scavini, Gury, Ballerini-Palmieri, Genicot, Lehmkuhl, Noldin, Vermeersch, and also Tanquerey, Goepfert, Jone, and many others. They are primarily concerned in their theology with the pastoral care of souls. Though they usually adhere to a line of simple probabilism, the question of the so-called "moral systems" does not play a great role in these works. The manuals of instruction composed by the Dominican theologians (for example, Merkelbach, Pruemmer) tend toward probabiliorism. Though they retain more of the speculative elements of the moral teaching of Saint Thomas, they belong to the class of textbooks which explain moral doctrine primarily with a view to the sacrament of penance.

Such pastoral-mindedness may not be made a matter of reproach. It will always be a matter of primary importance for the moral theologian to direct his attention toward forming enlightened confessors and to direct the faithful to fruitful reception of the sacrament of penance. Surely success in this matter will contribute very much to the guidance of the faithful in the life of virtue.

John Michael Sailer and John Baptist Hirscher were pioneers in a vital renewal of moral theology. They realized very keenly that the casuistic moral teaching of this period of rationalism and enlightenment had as its primary purpose the establishment of fixed limits of precept and obligation, particularly with regard to the many positive laws which were constantly changing. The consequence was an inevitable slighting of the eternal law resting in the very nature of things and written in the heart of the Christian man.

These pioneer theologians felt the urgent need of shaping—over and above the casuistic moral of the age—a moral theology whose primary concern should be to restate the perfect ideal of the whole Christian life and to underline the means of attaining it. Since the basis of their moral teaching is the Gospel, the method and approach differ radically from the procedure and technique of jurisprudence, and the language is closer to the word and spirit of the Gospel. In all these efforts, however, these two eminent theologians lost nothing of their loyalty to the Church and were thoroughly imbued with her spirit. Not in the slightest inclined to disparage obedience to positive ecclesiastical law, they made every effort to clarify and awaken the true Christian spirit which alone makes correct observance of all individual precepts possible. Such efforts could not result in lessening esteem for the Church or for her law. We may, in fact, use the present day term, "kerygmatic theology," of their writings. As we note in our own time, such an approach is all the more essential and urgent the more completely our civilization becomes de-Christianized.

At the height of intellectual and spiritual maturity, Sailer (1751–1832) wrote his *Handbuch der christlichen Moral zunaechst fuer kuenftige katholische Seelsorger und dann fuer jeden gebildeten Christen* (Munich: 1817). As the title indicates, this is a handbook primarily for the formation of the priest who is to guide and direct souls and also for the educated Catholic layman. Quite evidently it purports to be more than pastoral advice for the future confessor in his administration of the sacrament of penance. It is really an introduction "to virtuous and Godly living" for the Christian.

Both in the aim he set for himself and in the spirit and unction of his language, Sailer resembles the sainted writer whom he so much loved and admired, Francis de Sales. But he does not content himself with imparting practical advice for progress in virtue in the spirit of the masterly ascetical treatises of Francis. His purpose and plan include the entire edifice of teaching on the Christian life, a systematic presentation of the perfect ideal of the Christian way. He does not aim exclusively and primarily at describing the particular ways to attain perfection in the various states of life or the individual stages of progress in virtue. The strange notion that moral theology should busy itself only with delineating the minimal requirements or obligations of the Christian, while leaving the doctrine of full perfection of Christian virtue in conformity with the Sermon on the Mount to ascetic theology, was simply incomprehensible to Sailer.

The reproach frequently made that Sailer neglected the scientific method is not altogether justified and rather redounds to the discredit of the critic. Of set purpose he enters the lists against those who attempt to transpose the ideal of rationalization taken from modern mathematics and natural science to the area of theology. In the sharpest contrast to the frigid and sterile thought of the Enlightenment, Sailer cultivates the ideal of a theology of the heart, a *theologia cordis*.

Sailer must be studied in the light of his times. He belongs to the Romantic period, and his ideal of personality is of the period: the use and development of all individual gifts of God in manifestation of the perfection of the whole Mystical Body of Christ. Though his youth was not altogether free from the taint of the Enlightenment, he is rightly numbered among its most notable and successful adversaries.

As one might expect, his first work in moral theology fell far below the high standard of his subsequent labors, which truly effected a renewal of theology of the heart. Despite all their spirit and warmth, these first efforts still bear the stamp of the philosophy of the age. The titles themselves betray this weakness: *Vernunftlehre fuer die Menschen, wie sie sind, Glueckseligkeitslehre aus Vernunftgruenden mit Ruecksicht auf das Christentum* (*Rational Doctrine for Men as They Are, Doctrine of Beatitude Based on Principles of Reason in Relation to Christianity*). This youthful attitude of Sailer partially explains the bias of Saint Clement Hofbauer against him, despite the fact that the two were really kindred spirits engaged in the same struggle against the superficial and sterile Enlightenment.

The second great pioneer in moral theology in the nineteenth century was J. B. Hirscher (1788–1865). The nature of his work is indicated by the title, *Die christliche Moral als Lehre von der Verwirklichung des Reiches Gottes* (*Christian Moral Teaching as Realization of the Kingdom of God*) (Tuebingen: 1835 seq.). His moral theology is based entirely on the central biblical concept of the Kingdom of God, which because of his depth and breadth of vision proved extraordinarily fruitful. He does not yield to Sailer in theological depth, though he singles out the profundity of his great predecessor as most characteristic and worthy of special praise.[13] But Hirscher is greater in psychological insight. More realistic, more aware of the age in which he lives, he presents a more rigorously closed and completed system of thought, though he occasionally falls short of Sailer's mystic loftiness.

Sublime in conception and happy in execution, the moral theology of Hirscher suffered from the defects which are inevitable in the enterprise of pioneers. The first edition was marred by certain dogmatic defects which the author later corrected. Regrettable also was his lack of familiarity with the moral theology of the great scholastics and his opposition to the methods of the neo-scholastics, which he carried to excess. But despite all this his merit is outstanding.

If we judge him in the light of his age, as we already noted for Sailer also, we can arrive at a more adequate appraisal of his true worth. The "Enlightened" theology of the previous decades in Germany was frigid and rationalistic, based on a rationalistic concept of faith and a concept of science alien to the ideal of the true science of faith. If we view Sailer and

Hirscher against such a background, their merit as great and successful pioneers in moral theology is apparent. Their influence is still strongly felt in the subsequent period, as is noticeable in the very considerable independent theological activity to which they gave the spiritual impetus.

Ferdinand Probst (1816–1899), entirely a product of the Tuebingen school, is more Thomistic than the two preceeding thinkers. His work *Katholische Moraltheologie* (1848–1850) purposes "to combine the constructive and positive approach of previous works in moral theology and their correct theological attitude with the psychological organic development of the moral life which is characteristic of the more recent period."[14]

The Tuebingen school stresses the notion and doctrine of development. It places theology on the level of the psychological-dynamic, and in this Probst is distinctly of the school. The dogmatic influence of Moehler should not be overlooked, nor that of Hirscher in this area. And even before him, Sailer made the concept of progress and conversion a formal element of his moral theology. The moral theologians, Deutinger, Werner, Fuchs, Jocham, and Linsenmann also must be placed here. Their point of departure is the life of grace, which they present as the very root of Christian morality and the summons to a perfect Christian life. They do not look upon the moral life as mere static reflection of universal norms, but as a dynamic struggle with the darksome forces of evil dragging man down to the abyss, in response to the challenge of grace which calls man to the height of good. Likewise, freedom for them was essentially the freedom of the children of God. It was not, as rationalistic thought would have it, a great and glorious immutable thing, but a gift ever fresh with a spiritual summons ever new, a spiritual gift with a spiritual challenge.

Over and above the writers just mentioned, a significant group must be included among the eminent moral theologians of the past century who preferred a more static presentation of the norms and duties of Christian life. Let us simply note such men as Simar, Martin, Pruner, Schwane, Mausbach, Schilling. Though these men were thoroughly imbued with the Thomistic concept of virtue and all steered completely clear of the hazards of legal minimalism, there were some individual representatives of this same group who came dangerously close to a moral science of mere legal forms. Such an attitude betrays itself rather plainly when discussion arises concerning points transcending the minimal requirement of the law. These are taken up as something more or less incidental. As appendage of the essential and required we have, it is very significant to note, "the work of supererogation." The Sermon on the Mount and the counsels are not accorded their rightful place of honor in moral theology as such.

In 1852 a profound theological work entitled *Moraltheologie oder die Lehre vom christlichen Leben,* by Magnus Jocham (1808–1893), appeared. Unfortunately the adverse conditions of the time and a certain tendency to overgeneralize on Jocham's part conspired to rob the work of the success it deserved.[15] But it is moral theology based on the concepts of grace as found in Saint John and Saint Paul. Written in the spirit of Hirscher and Sailer, the work of Jocham has for the master idea of its moral teaching the "competence of the children of God sanctified by the sacraments."[16] "The mysteries of the children of God"[17] are actual norms for their entire inner life in God. Jocham was far in advance of his age in his forceful emphasis upon the Mystical Body of Christ as norm and formative power of genuine Christian life. However, it must be conceded that he is somewhat excessive in his aversion for what he considered the flaunting display of philosophy and the "dead dry bones of concepts."

Bernard Fuchs (1814–1854) in his *System der christlichen Sittenlehre (System of Christian Moral Teaching)* (1851) makes much of the "mind of the Church" in the sense of the Tuebingen school. As forcefully as Jocham, he presents the ideal of life in the Mystical Body, life as member of the Mystical Christ. Rebirth in God, growth in grace, development of freedom through union with God—these are his master ideas. Unmistakable traces of the influence of German idealism are found in his presentation of the New Testament theological bases of Christian morality.

Martin Deutinger (1789–1864) is a philosopher, an outspoken independent mind, who attempts to unfold a personalism of love suitable to Christianity in his *Moralphilosophie* (1848). Human freedom at its profoundest depths is rooted in God's love and in man's capacity to love God in return. The true freedom of man, "the power to act (morally) manifestly consists in the possibility of loving what is most exalted and therefore it can find its perfection only in the actual love of it."[18] "The highest power of man obviously resides in the union of his will with the transcendent will which is free by its very essence, which creates, conserves, governs."[19] "Man can become one with the love of God for His creatures through the will to love God."[20] "It is not necessity of reason which binds man with God and the world, but freedom itself. It is love which leads man to God, makes man like to God. We are like to God not as beings who know, but as beings who know how to love."[21] Deutinger's fundamental ideas about grace and love and the law of progress of the

Christian life through grace and in love are expressed still more vividly in his later work, *Das Reich Gottes nach dem Apostel Johannes* (*The Kingdom of God According to the Apostle John*) (1867).

Karl Werner (1821–1888) is outspokenly anti-Thomistic in his *System der christlichen Ethik* (*System of Christian Ethics*) (1850–1852). Though he labors more or less under the influence of the philosophy of the times (Guenther, Schleiermacher), his basic theological conception is outspokenly Christocentric; and despite all the defects arising from the spirit of the times it is truly profound. Werner proposes a religious moral teaching of love, of the cross, of conformity to Christ. "Thus, penetrated with the Christian idea of sacrifice, the way of love constitutes the highest synthesis of all moral activity."[22] "The idea of sacrifice is the highest moral idea."[23] Orientated in this manner, the moral teaching of Werner reserves for the virtue of humility a position of preference. In his system Christian anthropology is highly developed, as is the principle of progress and growth arising from it. Growth implies the necessity of incessant struggle for perfection.

The most important continuator of Sailer and Hirscher in the last century is Francis Xavier Linsenmann (1835–1898) of the Tuebingen school. In his *Untersuchungen ueber die Lehre von Gesetz und Freiheit*[24] (*Study of the Doctrine of Law and Liberty*) we sense a genuine Pauline spirit. Energetically he counters the tendency to center moral teaching in jurisprudence with the basic concept of the freedom of the children of God. "Only a tiny portion of our duties is circumscribed by 'laws.' An immense area of free moral activity lies open before us."[25] Wherefore, Linsenmann considers it one of the major tasks of moral theology to reveal the deeper meaning of our freedom through union with God regarding the things which are, generally speaking, matters of mere counsel and not of law. As this freedom in God develops, the child of God perceives more clearly than ever the deeper binding force of the divine call. The *Lehrbuch der Moraltheologie* (1878) (*Manual of Moral Theology*) is a happy synthesis of speculative and practical method applied to the problems of the age, a harmony of static normative science with the dynamic concept of progress. Too lofty and noble to stoop to any anti-scholastic bias, Linsenmann also perceives the value of casuistry and the study of law despite his opposition to the legalistic orientation of moral theology. It is to be deplored that his work did not meet with the recognition and success it deserved in his time.

The moral theology of Anthony Koch, *Lehrbuch der Moraltheologie* (1905) continues the work of Linsenmann. Written in the spirit of the Tuebingen school, it adheres to the patristic and scholastic tradition, though there are traces of a Eudaemonistic tendency in the Aristotelian sense.

We should also call attention to an important group of independent moral theologians (Martin, Simar, Schwane, Pruner, Mausbach, Schilling) whose interests centered in a theology suitable to the moral needs of the times. They held fast to Thomistic principles, though they endeavored to employ and apply the casuistic method of Saint Alphonse. But the tracts on canon law were almost totally excluded from their texts.

An exception in this regard is the *Moraltheologie* (1860–1865) of Francis Friedhoff (1821–1878), who embodies the entire canonical legislation on censures in his moral teaching. Though he belongs to the class of dogmatic-centered moralists, he places special stress on our obedience to the Church. The moral life is the development of the supernatural life bestowed on us in grace. "The shortest and best summary of the whole Catholic moral teaching may be expressed thus: Preserve the sanctifying grace you have received and make progress in it until death."[26] "The whole of moral theology revolves about these two concepts: to obtain and to preserve sanctifying grace."[27]

He sees the basic concept of our relation to the Church, not in the sacramental life, in community of grace in and with the Mystical Body of Christ, but in the relation of obedient action toward the Church in her hierarchy. This explains his stress on the Church's legislation in his moral as the essential part, and also enables us to appreciate the position of duty in Friedhoff and in many other Thomistic-minded moralists, who substitute the "doctrine of duty" or, more specifically, the ethic of duty for the teaching on the virtues as found in Aquinas.[28]

Conrad Martin (1812–1879) in his *Lehrbuch der katholischen Sittenlehre* (1850; 5th edition, 1865) (*Manual of Catholic Moral Teaching*) is a very thorough and clear writer, possessed of a true Catholic sense. As Mausbach after him, he strives for a synthesis of the rich heritage of tradition found in Augustine, Thomas Aquinas, and Alphonse Liguori.

Theophilus Hubert Simar (1835–1902), in contrast to the theologians mentioned thus far, distinguishes sharply throughout his work "between the obligatory exercise of virtue and mere counsel."[29] In this feature he is followed by Joseph Schwane (1824–1892), a forceful systematic Thomist whose *Moraltheologie* (1873–1885) is almost a complete departure from the psychological dynamism of the Tuebingen school. Even the positive doctrine of Saint Thomas in this area is almost entirely ignored. One of Schwane's primary interests is the achievement of natural reason in the area of Christian morality and the position of natural ethics in the framework of moral theology.

For these representatives of German moral theology in the nineteenth century the central mysteries of the Christian religion, grace, love, and, in a measure at least, the sacramental life itself, were the formative basis of scientific moral theology. But John the Evangelist Pruner (1827–1907) in his *Lehrbuch der Moraltheologie* (1875) reverts to the principle of external authority almost exclusively: "the will of the legislator penetrates into the very heart."[30] On such a level the sacraments simply become a part of the duties dictated by the will of the lawgiver. Typical of such moral teaching is the almost complete absence of discussion of the virtue of humility.

Similar in many ways to Pruner is Francis Schindler (1874–1922), although his *Lehrbuch der Moraltheologie* (1907–1910) draws from both Augustine and Thomas for speculative thought and relies on Saint Alphonse for solid casuistic method. But the Sermon on the Mount is slighted somewhat, and the evangelical counsels with personal accountability for doing good are not adequately stressed. Schindler seems to reduce the spiritual disposition to "an inner readiness to fulfill the work of the law."[31]

Joseph Mausbach and Otto Schilling are illustrious pioneers in the formation of a more profound systematic moral theology in our own day. Thoroughly conversant with the whole field of patristic and scholastic literature, open to the needs of the times, these two expert critical minds not only were endowed with sharp insight into the particular tendencies of Catholic moral theology, but also proved themselves ardent defenders of the whole edifice of Catholic morality itself.

Joseph Mausbach (1861–1931), author of *Die Ethik des Hl. Augustinus* (1909), *Die katholische Moraltheologie und ihre Gegner* (1901; 5th edition, 1921) (*Catholic Moral Theology and its Adversaries*), *Katholische Moraltheologie* (since 1915–1918 this work has gone through new editions, been expanded and deepened) explains the supreme rule of morals as "the glory of God,"[32] supplemented by the ideal of the perfection of being. His presentation of the doctrine of special moral theology follows the order of the decalog, but is far more than a simple moral of precepts. It is, in fact, a true theology of the virtues which must be practiced in the principal spheres of Christian life. The order of the Ten Commandments appealed to Mausbach as intrinsically the most sound and also as practically the most useful for pastors and directors of souls.

Otto Schilling (*Moraltheologie:* 1922; 2nd edition, 1952) carries on the work and the ideals of the Tuebingen school, which saw in moral theology an expression of the genuine Christian spirit rather than the mere orderly summation of precepts. For the content of his work he is principally indebted to Saint Thomas and Saint Alphonse. In fact, Schilling ranks among the best of the recent German moral theologians and is rated as one of the foremost Thomistic scholars of the Tuebingen school. He maintains uncompromisingly that divine love (*caritas*) is the formal principle of moral theology, and his approach is above all through the Thomistic concept of the end of man. Hence it is not altogether incomprehensible that he should view Tillmann's concept of the imitation of Christ as somewhat antagonistic to his formal principle of love.

But surely the imitation of Christ centers in love. The force of love and loving response in the disciple to the loving call of the Master has love at its very core. Its sole ideal is love.

It is somewhat surprising that Schilling, the Thomist, should organize his subject matter through a division based on the three cycles of duty, toward God, toward self, toward one's neighbor. (This may be partially explained as due to the perspective in which charity is viewed. It is not primarily personal and dynamic, not a response. It is measured by goals and its object. Perhaps the approach followed by Linsenmann may have been decisive in the example it set for Schilling.)

This arrangement cannot avoid the pitfall of frequent repetition, if one area of obligation is treated adequately under the aspect of Christian love of self and then studied again under the aspect of relation to one's neighbor and the community. (The same is true of Tillmann, in whose work it is even more evident.) Schilling's special merit consists in the thoroughness with which he studies the social-ethical phases of Christian moral and in the significance of his presentation of concrete social problems.

A century after Sailer and Hirscher, a rich counterpart to their early genius is found in the work of Fritz Tillmann (died in 1953), whose moral teaching is based entirely on the inspired word. In his *Handbuch der katholischen Sittenlehre* (*Handbook of Catholic Moral Teaching*) the third volume is *Die Idee der Nachfolge Christi* (*Idea of the Imitation of Christ*) and the fourth is *Die Verwirklichung der Nachfolge Christi* (*Realization of the Imitation of Christ*) (4th edition, 1950). The ethos of Christian love, the ethos of the Sermon on the Mount, is presented very specifically and definitely as obliging all Christians. In this system the often stressed antithesis between a morality of minimal requirement or legal minimum, between the morality of law on the one hand and an asceticism for the perfect on the other, is radically eliminated on Biblical grounds and on the basis of the noble concept of the imitation of Christ by all men.

In view of the moral teaching of M. Jocham, treated above, and particularly in view of the current flowering of sacramental piety and formation of Christian life, it is a matter of some surprise that sacramental unity with Christ is not brought out in strong relief as one of the constructive elements in the imitation of Christ. Likewise, we are somewhat shocked to note the treatment of the sacraments under the title: *Duties toward Oneself in the Religious Sphere*. For a manual or handbook of doctrine, casuistry is dismissed somewhat too cavalierly. Yet in defense of Tillmann it should be noted that he limited the sphere of his work in this matter of set purpose and design. Nor does he deny the merit of books of casuistry for the care and direction of souls.

Likewise we should note that he left to others certain basic approaches to his own work. He was able to forgo the more thorough speculative and psychological research since this was provided in the series by Theodore Steinbuechel and Theodore Muencker, who wrote the first two volumes respectively, *Die philosophische Grundlegung* (*The Philosophical Basis*) and *Die psychologischen Grundlagen* (*The Psychological Foundations*). These furnish a truly contemporary and profound study for the whole work of Tillmann.

Steinbuechel (1888–1949) is a forceful representative of the Tuebingen school in its efforts to free moral theology from the extreme bias of its juridical approach. His voluminous work is largely posthumous. He concentrated more and more on the actuality of the moral judgment in the concrete situation and under the influence of grace. Nevertheless, no one who is familiar with his work as a whole will accuse him of constructing a "situation ethics" hostile to law. He views moral life as an organic whole and is particularly concerned with the area not hedged in by specific law and lying beyond legal enactment, but not beyond the exigence of love and the call of grace. Consequently, at least at his deepest, he is very remote from all antinomian moral teaching. With a unique appreciation for the good which in the philosophy of our age awaits redemption, he absorbs the values inherent in existentialism and personalism to use them profitably in a Christian theology of liberty, grace, and love. In all this a profound sense of tradition constantly keeps him safely in the sound Catholic center.

CHAPTER TWO

ESSENTIAL CONCEPTS OF MORAL THEOLOGY

I. MORALITY OF RESPONSIBILITY

RELIGION truly lived must have as essential characteristic the element of response. Response, responsibility, dialogue belong to religion essentially. We have religion only if man conceives of the Holy as a Power which advances toward him and to whom he can turn in dialogue. Religion and morality are not simply synonymous. Some elements of morality may well survive after religion has lost its vitality. Within the religious-ethical we can distinguish two grand types: the first springs from religion which animates it essentially; the second is given form and sanction by religion which is rather accessory and superimposed from without.

If religion essentially has the character of response and responsibility, it must follow that an ethic is truly religious only to the extent that it bears the mark of response. The pure type of religious ethic is of the nature of response, in which moral conduct is understood as response to the summons of a person who is holy, who is absolute. The prototype of the non-religious ethic is monologue rather than dialogue, and all moral tasks, norms, laws have their center and meaning in the human person and its perfection. Systems of religious ethics which in any way are centered in man himself are at best systems in which religion is superimposed. By setting up this standard of relation to religion, we can acquire a true insight into the type of the religious-ethic systems which prevail. Accordingly, we shall undertake the task of measuring and judging the essential nature of every religious ethic by the standard of the essential religious form which affects it.

1. *Religion as Community of Person in Word and Response*

For the Christian, religion is infinitely more than any sentiment. It is more than any need or experience, even more than "saving one's soul," striving for "happiness." It is fellowship with the living God. The reality of religion is not reached merely through concern for one's soul nor through profound self-absorption of the devout. Not even the glory and majesty of God give us religion. We come to the heart of religion only at the point of encounter between the word of God and the response of man.

35

God and man in fellowship, in community, *Deus et anima* (God and the soul) in the trenchant phrase of Augustine, this is the essence of religion.

Religion is supported by two immovable pillars: God, the infinite personal God, and the finite created person, which is man. Religion also comprises two essential themes: God in the glory of His love and man in the favor of God's grace. True community of persons is possible only if two persons commune seriously, in deadly earnest. God takes man seriously, He speaks to man. This makes religion possible. The tremendous earnestness of God regarding man even to the point of sacrificing His only-begotten Son for him on the cross—this constitutes the superabundant treasure, the ineffable mystery of the true religion. In turn, man must take God seriously, God all-holy—this is the first demand of religion upon man.

Religion lies between two poles, man and God—an infinite distance between them. Where this essential diversity, this infinite distance between man and God is lost sight of and with it the transcendent holiness of God is made to disappear from our view, the essence of religion is lost, for where there is no encounter with the "Holy" there is no true religion. But religion ceases to exist also as soon as either of the two poles, even though it be the human one, is no longer taken seriously. For with this earnestness personal fellowship stands or falls.

As soon as the soul really encounters God, it reflects the splendor of His holiness. It has worth before God, a value which indeed is intimately entwined with this fellowship with God. The soul exults before the majesty of the all-holy God, not only in adoration, but also in astonishment at the glance of divine love resting upon it. God is the soul's salvation. All the great dogmas of creation, Incarnation, and Redemption have as their theme, besides the glory of God, the salvation of the soul. When we chant and pray: *"Qui propter nos homines et propter nostram salutem descendit de coelis"* ("Who for us men and for our salvation descended from heaven"), we sing the jubilant hymn of our participation in the loving glory of God. God reveals His glory to us in the condescension of His love, His *agápe,* and His holiness in the work of our salvation.

Deus et anima, God and the soul, the terrifying and beautifying mystery of the I–Thou communion between God and the soul is also the mystery of the Word of God. In the Word, the Logos, through the Word, and in the image of the Word we are created. In Christ the Word-made-man God comes to us and we to Him. (Man's likeness to God is the significant key word of moral theology!)

God speaks to us in words comprehensible to us. From the truth that our objective I–Thou intimacy with God flows from the Person, who is the Word of God, all the words which God directs to us, whether in the natural or supernatural revelation, assume an ineffable splendor and earnestness. Every word of God that is addressed to us comes from His will to establish the bond of fellowship and ultimately from the divine mystery of the Trinity. Every answer on our part affects our bond of unity with Him and the formation of the divine image in us.

2. Fundamental Rôle of Prayer

All of this sheds a light on the fundamental rôle of prayer as an essential manifestation of religion. To pray is nothing less than to harken reverently to the Word of God and to attempt, however falteringly, to respond to it. Religion thrives on prayer because *religio* (bond with God) cannot exist without the Word of God and our power to respond. In the Second Person of the Trinity, the Word of the Father, religion has its source, and in the Word and our response it is exercised. The more deeply the religious man enters into the Word of God addressed to him and the more his life bears the stamp of response to God's Word, the more is his religion (*religio*), the bond with God, perfected and the divine likeness manifested within him.

Man is only then fully religious when the fellowship of his word with God has penetrated to that depth in which he regards his own person and his own salvation only from the standpoint of the loving will of God. And the concern for one's own salvation is no longer anything but the response, inspired by the breath of divine love, to the gracious offer of God's favor and beatitude. It follows, therefore, that Christian personalism does not culminate in the cult of one's own personality, but rather in the relation—the word-and-response relation between God all-holy and the soul called to salvation. Christian personalism is altogether different from any form of religion centering in the I. Ever open and receptive to the word of love, true personalism exists only in man's fellowship with God.

We can realize the true meaning of human personality only in the light of man's likeness to God. The more intimate the bond between man and God, the word-response relation, so much the more is the personality enriched and perfected as "image and likeness of God," who imparts in word and in love the glory of the intimate life of the Trinity. Religion as community with God is also the foundation of the human community, the genuine fellowship of persons. True community of men rests on word and love, and perfects itself in the dialogue of love. The capacity for word and love, which centers in the very heart of the Thou, is fulfilled in us, however, only in so far as we are caught up by the word and love of God and give to God our response and love in return. Fellowship with God in word and love develops and fulfills our individual personality (the image of God in us) and at the same time reveals our essentially social nature. Therefore religious living, if it develops its own sound dynamic, places us necessarily in the human community—the word-love fellowship with our fellow men.

The expression "God and the soul," *Deus et anima,* must not be construed in an individualistic sense. It is a monstrous error on the part of Kierkegaard and many others with him to maintain that the religious life looses the bonds of community and places the individual naked and alone before God! To be pierced by the word of the divine love obviously means to be liberated from the masses, from the namelessness and anonymity of the flux of life. For in truth God calls us personally, each by his own name. In His presence we find ourselves, but we also find our neighbor and the way to fellowship and community. To come to God we must renounce chatter with men. But in accepting the word of God directed to us we find the way opened to the word-love relation with our neighbor. The Father created all things in the Word (JN 1:3). We enjoy community with the Father in Christ the Incarnate Word. To be in Christ means necessarily to be bound up with all those who have fellowship in Christ, who are called by Christ. Hence it belongs to the essence of religious living that it place us in the community with our neighbor because it is a life in Christ, the Incarnate Word of God.

II. MORALITY AS FELLOWSHIP:
CHALLENGE AND RESPONSIBILITY

Our moral life must be nourished entirely and utterly on the religious relation to God. Religion must not be looked upon as a mere external aid and sanction to morality, but as its very spirit. Only if it is imbued with religion, centered in the religious, can morality be correctly judged. The more fully it conforms to the basic laws of the religious, the more it is animated by the essential spirit of the religious, the more sound and wholesome will it be. In the following pages therefore we shall examine the most significant of the central moral concepts and key terms in the light of this criterion.

1. Morality of Self-Perfection and Religious Ethics

Although the only rational basis and foundation for true morality is religion, there have been moral efforts and there are moral systems not primarily centered in religion or at least not based on the divine fellowship. What characterizes all these systems?—We immediately discard all "scientific" systems of ethics and all pragmatic methods of shaping human conduct which sacrifice the human person to the collective or to any other impersonal end, for they cannot form any serious basis of morality at all. They rather destroy morality. We can take up for serious consideration only the systems which recognize the value of the human person. They all agree in making it the duty of man to perfect himself. For Aristotle, for the Stoic, for Kant and Schleiermacher (to mention only a few), man himself and his own greatness form the foundation of ethics and constitute its goal.

Even though in many instances the existence of a personal God is not formally denied, nevertheless the human person and moral life are not centered in Him. To a degree these systems preserve the earnestness of morality, since they place man in a comprehensive framework of meaning, value, and law to which he must conform. But the ultimate in meaning and goal is always man and his own development and perfection: "The truly noble man never forgets his dignity. He never loses it in things which are inferior to him." The value of all values for him is his own soul, the preservation and development of the worth of his own person. Center of all these ethical systems is man himself. His moral obligation is self-perfection.

If religion exerts influence upon a previously accepted ethical attitude of this kind, the soul is raised to a higher realm of values. Once we have entered into the sphere of the religious, we no longer speak of mere self-perfection, but of salvation of our soul. No matter how extreme the difference between the Indian religious concept of self-purification and the Stoical ethic of self-perfection, the Hindu and all kindred religious orientations are basically nothing more than a projection of the anthropocentric ethic of self-perfection into the sphere of religion.

It is a simple fact that man must think in terms of "person." If God is not thought of as a person or at least if no fellowship is sought with Him, it must inevitably follow that the human person alone can occupy the center of attention. And this is true even when man seeks salvation in the escape from the personal, as in Indian pantheism. Whether the Indian seeks Nirvana as a positive beatitude of a soul which survives after death, or whether he seeks its extinction, the motivation and central meaning of all his asceticism and virtue is man, his own salvation.

Obviously, salvation of soul in the Christian sense is something altogether different. It is not a blessed solitude of existence nor a blissful absorption into an impersonal essence, but loving community with the living God. For this very reason even the Aristotelian or Stoic concept of self-perfection cannot consistently remain projected into an essentially Christian morality. This means that concern for one's salvation may not be centered in self-perfection. The Christian religion as personal fellowship with God cannot tolerate man as center and focal point of ethics.

Viewed in the perspective of religion, the human person can be understood only from the standpoint of personal community and fellowship with God. Nevertheless, as a matter of fact, at least at the beginning of the religious life things are usually different. Particularly the man who at first directed his moral efforts predominantly toward his own perfection is all too readily inclined, once he turns to religion, to seize on it as a means to perfect himself and save his soul. Instead of viewing religion in the proper perspective as first of all a loving community with God and seeking this in fellowship, he sees in it and seeks in it the furtherance and assurance of his own salvation, which flows from such fellowship. If one continues in this attitude, consciously or unconsciously, he closes to himself the surest and deepest approach to God. He disregards the keystone of religion, the holiness of God, which can never be a means to anything, only the end. He loses the sense of loving communion which leads us to eternal bliss only if we seek it first and above all else.

Some may object: it is evident that God's glory and loving homage to Him are central in our religious relation to God, but our moral effort is simply directed to man and his salvation! In reply we stress that the effort is indeed concerned with man. This we cannot deny. But must not this very concern for man ultimately be also a concern about God, about obedience to Him, abiding in His love, the coming of His kingdom?

The greatest hazard to genuine religious life arises from making man its center, from viewing all divine worship and all communion with God primarily from the standpoint of the profit it brings to man. But even in the strictly religious activity where such hazard is avoided, there still lurks the danger of a fatal dichotomy between worship and the moral life. Prayer and sacrifice on the one hand have their center and meaning in the divine fellowship, and the moral life is more or less independent— something parallel to or alongside of it—with its ultimate goal man and his salvation. Inevitably the religious and moral life will be estranged and divorced or the man-centered moral orientation will lead to anthropo- centric orientation of religion.

The efforts of non-religious man to perfect himself, we must note, are not worthless. They have, in fact, a positive value, at least as long as religion is not dismissed as meaningless. And this positive value can be coordinated with the religious orientation, but not without being re- formed, Christianized. In some manner it must be removed from its previous non-religious moorings. To be truly embodied in the realm of the sacred, it must be placed in the service of holiness.

Ultimately morality and religion must have the same center: com- munity and fellowship with God. This is true both for the scientific presentation of the Christian moral doctrine and for popular instruction and preaching. But unfortunately both the one and the other were too often, especially after the days of the Enlightenment, a continuation of Aristotle (self-perfection) rather than of the Gospel (the sovereignty of God).

We cite only one example chosen from among many: Anthony Koch, a highly esteemed moralist of the Tuebingen school, makes the following significant remark in his moral theology: "Whereas dogmatic theology concerns itself with the nature of God and His external works, with Christ and His Redemptive work, moral teaching has man for its object in as much as it shows him the way prescribed by God to reach his eternal goal."[33] "The aim of moral life is consequently the eternal perfection and the beatitude flowing from it."[34] "According to Catholic moral theology happiness is the goal of all moral endeavor."[35] It is true that this view is poles apart from that of Aristotle, for the simple reason that the Christian cannot attain happiness through his own unaided efforts, but depends for it entirely on God and community of life with God. But precisely because this is presented as something merely accessory or even in a measure extrinsic, or we might say as an afterthought, as though the living friend- ship with God was only an essential means for the full attainment of the moral purpose—it is evident that the concept of self-perfection or external happiness and salvation cannot be the sound and appropriate foundation for a religious moral system.

Instead of having as its foundation the dialogue between God and man, this system is on the level of the monologue—man to himself and within himself—scheme of morality. Or it is at best, when measured by the standard of the essence of true religion, imperfect dialogue. Dialogue between man and God, word and response, is not basic and essential in this system, but accessory and secondary, something super-added to the monologic morality centering in man.

2. Commandment, Law, and Ethics of Response

Commandment and law are and always must be central ideas in the Christian moral teaching. The sermon or instruction on the commandments must be God-centered and at the same time dialogical; this is to say, essentially based on the dialogue between man and God, on the word and response, for the simple reason that *commandment* is an entirely religious concept. God Himself prefaced the promulgation of the commandments on Sinai with the twofold theme of religion: His sovereign majesty and His revelation of love: "I am the Lord thy God, who brought thee out of the land of Egypt, out of the house of bondage" (Ex 20:2). The commandments of God are words of the divine Love addressed to us, expressed in the great command of love. And true fulfillment of the command is the obedient response of love, obedient love.

As the ethic of commandment, so the ethic of law in its very concept is religious, founded on the response of man to God. It is true that the concept of natural law as the expression of the order of creation is directly borrowed from the moral philosophy of the Stoics. But Christian ethics, above all in the thought of Augustine, purged it of all impersonal and fatalistic elements. For Augustine, law is the expression of the all-holy essence and will of God. It is engraved in every human heart by God Himself as appeal and invitation, altogether personal and addressed to every man. Nevertheless, the explanation and enunciation of Catholic moral doctrine in sermon and instruction did not altogether escape the influence of the Nominalistic interpretation of commandment nor of the rationalistic-Kantian concept of law. We must conclude that, since the commandment in the Nominalistic doctrine is not based on the all-holy nature or essence of God, but only on the sovereign will of God, all inquiry into its intrinsic foundation and beauty is devoid of meaning. In fact, such inquiry would bear the obvious and dangerous implication that the less evident the intrinsic value of the commandment, the more meritorious and praiseworthy it would be to obey it.

We do not at all deny that particular instances of this type of obedience can be fruitful, provided of course that the superior's authority and intent are evident. An example is the Biblical instance of the obedience of Abraham! But what if we were to make a rule of the exception? The result would be incalculable loss in the sphere of value, which ultimately would be discerned exclusively in the light of obedience. And eventually even this very virtue of obedience itself would be lost, since it would no longer enter into the sphere of all values and influence them. Such obedience places man in the presence of God, surely, but not in the full fellowship of the word and of love. For such fellowship is granted only when the summons of the divine word is accepted lovingly with all its wealth of meaning by man and lovingly answered. But it would be really hazardous, constituting an extreme danger to true morality, if a Nominalistic conception of law would lead us to exact blind obedience to mere men without concern for the right order of things to which all commandments and commands must conform.

A conception of this kind demanding obedience to commandment is sometimes found linked with the subjectivistic ethic of self-perfection (though not correctly nor legitimately). Sometimes unreflecting and implicit obedience is extolled as the best and safest means of perfecting one's self. It does not appear too disturbing that in the process objective right and good may be lost through the act of blind obedience: "How happy the obedience which assures our salvation of soul and absolves us from all responsibility!" But what of the Kingdom of God in all this? It is quite clear that such a development of the doctrine of obedience to authority is not imbued with the spirit of loving fellowship. It is not based on the word of God with the loving response, not on the loving community with God and fellowman.

It is characteristic of our present day moral teaching that, by contrast with the "ethic of law," it shows a marked preference for the subjective correctness of interior disposition rather than the pure and simple objective observance of the commandment, but—we make the point—do we not often forget that subjective correctness consists precisely in the endeavor to do with all devotion that which is right and good in itself? Ethic of right disposition and inner spirit must be wedded to the ethic of commandment. In this way both preserve their true and genuine dialogue. On the one hand, an ethic of disposition which is not truly genuine because it labors under the spell of a subjective ideal of self-perfection will poison morality more completely than any system which combines self-perfection with obedience of the kind just described. Still, such obedience, since it is not pervaded with the sense and beauty of what is prescribed, cannot bear the stamp of personal responsibility or at least is little affected by it.

The Kantian-rationalistic way of thinking robs the morality of law of its dialogical mould in another way. Under the spell of the universal validity of the law, the man of the Kantian cast of mind overlooks the force of law as affecting the individual in each instance. He views law as an abstract absolute which dominates the whole order of creation. He ignores the particular powers and endowments of each individual and the circumstances of each situation, although God manifests His will through these just as truly as He does through universal law. The law in its most universal form is presented as the sole and adequate expression of the divine will. But in reality the laws of reason are only abstractions which are totally incapable of reflecting the richness of the concrete individual. Even the positive divine laws, for the greatest part, embody only the minimum requirements. Their very prohibitive and negative formulation is ample evidence of this point. As far as they have reference to the call to virtue in each individual, they are only the first step to right understanding which is the exclusion of error and misconceptions. A moral system content with a morality of law which is exclusively abstract and universal leads to impoverishment of morality, implicit legal minimalism, and moral sterility.

Under the influence of Kantian theory, conscience descends to the level of logical function. Just as the moral life is confined to observance of universal law, so conscience is reduced to a mere syllogistic application of universal to the particular instance. No one denies, of course, that the individual instance reflects the universal norm and is bound by it. But it is surely deplorable if the concrete particular realities and possibilities for good are scorned. The deeper and richer the moral life of a man, the more he is brought to a realization and appreciation of concrete individual and personal values with the obligation they impose. He learns that the talent given us by God may not be buried nor hidden. It must be used.

In genuine personal religious morality, man is not confronted by universal law (though, of course, it exists). But God calls man personally, as he is able to perceive from the special gifts and endowments and from the circumstances of the particular situation in which he lives. Obviously knowledge of the universal law must preserve him from seeing his own self-interest in the law. But vital morality demands more than mere acquaintance with the norms of law; it demands the fine delicacy of tactful conscience, the sense for the particular and special, which goes beyond mere knowledge of law. This is prudence.

Law in the Kantian concept intervenes as an impersonal power between God and the human conscience. Indeed it is unfortunate that there is a melancholy reality within us which corresponds to this rationalistic ethic of law. Deep down within fallen man is a radical tendency to conceive of himself and his existence, not in relation to God, not after the manner of dialogue with God, but entirely in relation to self, after the manner of monologue. To be redeemed means to live in intimacy with God, to know and love the will of God our Father. But for the "unredeemed," God is a "stranger." And God's law is alien, dead!

In fact, God finally becomes so much a stranger to him that he no longer sees God, but only the law. There remains only the "alien," impersonal law. In this fashion the law of the "alien" God is transformed into an impersonal principle. Enslaved by the dead law, which he himself brought to its death, the unredeemed seeks his salvation in this, he endeavors to adopt as his own law this alien law which still, though remotely, refers to God. He seeks to make his own law, a law indeed which looks only to man.

True personalism and authentic moral of law are in living dialogue with God. The "personalism" of fallen man and his law do not transcend the "monologue" of the I itself. In consequence, the law no longer leads to the living God of religion, but comes between God and the soul. An ethic of law in the "Kantian" sense will inevitably increase this peril lurking in original sin.

3. Morality of Responsibility

The foregoing should be sufficient evidence that in our work the terms *salvation of soul, commandment* and *law* do not suffer any loss of meaning. Such terms and their concepts will retain their full value. However, none of them is the focal center of Catholic moral teaching. To our mind

the term *responsibility* understood in its religious sense is the more apt; even from the mere standpoint of etymology the word designates the personal-essential characteristic of religion. This is the relation of dialogue, word and response, in a community. It apparently is the most apposite to express the personal relation between God and man—which is the I and Thou relation—of word and response—specifically God's word calling and inviting man and the human decision in response of acceptance. The word also refers directly to man's likeness to God. Hence responsibility means that in a community between man and God, man responds to God's word with the responsibility of his personal decision and action. But we must make a point of the distinction between the purely religious and the religious-moral relation between man and God. This is necessary to preserve the distinctive character of morality as responsibility.

a. Religious Life as Response to the Word of God

Religion consists of word and response. In the eternal Word, God draws nigh to us. In Christ the Incarnate Word we enter into community with God. Only in the light of the word and response relation with God in such fellowship can we understand the three divine virtues. For they are surely more than a turning to God Himself. Essentially they are also a drawing nigh to His Word given to us, to all the words of truth, of the promises, of love. Since in this world God does not reveal Himself to us through vision, face to face, but "only" in His Word, so it is that only progressively do we develop in our response to His Word, through growth in Christ, the Word, and thereby in fellowship with God.

The virtue of religion is our response to the majesty of God, our Creator and Father revealing Himself to us in the word (Jn 1), to the glory of Redemption which envelops us in Christ, in the Church, in the sacraments. This virtue is differentiated from the theological virtues in that it includes external acts. But it is focused on these divine virtues because by its very existence it must turn to God. It looks to the moral virtues because it is responsible for something of our true pattern of life. In fact, that which is most essential in the fabric of our living depends on the virtue of religion, namely, whether the worship of God is accorded its rightful place in our private and public life. Is the divine cult afforded the time and place for its correct formation and manifestation so that all visible creation is directed to the glory of God?

b. Moral Life as Responsibility

The other moral virtues are more sharply differentiated from the theological virtues than is the virtue of religion. They do not essentially and necessarily,[36] and never immediately or directly, look to God, respond to God. They have to do with the fulfillment of created order, with created persons, goods, and values. Since they are directly concerned with created order, they are not in the full religious sense of the word response and responsibility. Response assumes that there is a person to whom response is made. The character of dialogue, response and responsibility to God, comes only when they penetrate through created order to God.

The believer detects in the order of creation the message of the Lord and Creator; the child of God hears in all things the word of His Father. He is sustained by the inner vital bond of the three divine virtues with the inner word and response. In community and fellowship with God through this word and response of the divine virtues, his responsibility to God is expressed in religious response to God. From this it is evident that the term *respons*-ibility is best suited to express the interpenetration and formation of the moral through the religious, and also the distinction of the two.

To bring this distinction into clearer relief, we must stress the following points: the moral order is concerned with the fulfillment of the order of creation. It is response to God, the correct response precisely to the extent that man takes his terrestrial tasks seriously, and earnestly accepts created values.

The very core of moral decision is the spirit of obedience to God. It is saying yes to God's will. But this decision is essentially more than a simple or lighthearted saying yes or no to God. It proceeds much further in a personal effort to discover the proper response which should be made to God. It is the hazard and venture of response itself, or, shall we say, it is daring to answer God. The moral decision requires humble and docile attention to the will of God our Creator and Father from the very beginning, but often it is completed by faltering or bold hazard of choice among a multitude of possibilities that lie open before us. In this manner man bears the responsibility for his free decision in his own particular situation. His response is his responsibility.

One cannot evade this responsibility toward God through recourse to human authority. One is accountable for his obedience as well as for his disobedience, though in a different manner. No one has the right to shoulder the responsibility of outright refusal of the assistance which God offers through authority, through community, through prudent counselors in seeking to discover the divine will. But even the seeking of counsel and the actual obedience to authority can never serve as excuse for shirking personal responsibility. These cannot be viewed as exemption from responsibility, but only as the exhausting of all available possibilities in preparation for the decision for which one is altogether accountable. Naturally one is particularly responsible for non-obedience to lawful authority. One must carefully probe his own motives to assure himself that he is truly disinterested and unselfish in any such decision. Moreover, one must carefully weigh the consequences of the decision in so far as they concern and affect the community. Refusal to obey can never be justified without a clear perception of all that is involved in the case. Particularly important in obedience to human authority is this very bearing on community and the responsibility to society. This should always be a matter of serious reflection, most particularly when there is justification for non-compliance.

Every moral act involves accountability before God and responsible cultivation of a value which has an appeal for some individual. But it is much more. The moral act is always in greater or less measure weighted with responsibility toward our neighbor and toward the natural and supernatural community in which we live and upon which our individual moral decisions and our whole religious-moral life react. The mystery of the Mystical Body of Christ makes us fully conscious of this truth. To be in fellowship with God through the Word, to be in Christ the Incarnate Word, implies that we are immediately united with all the other members of the Body of Christ and act in immediate communion with them.

In every moral decision and, above all, when his moral integrity is endangered, man senses that his response to God involves his very existence, his salvation. Moral conduct can never be loosed from the moorings of obligation; moral action can never be freed from the bond of obligation; for one cannot respond to God all-holy without the bond of obligation. In the moral act the person must be answerable to himself. The final judgment will be the eventual revelation in the presence of God of this very responsibility of the individual to himself. This aspect of responsibility, of course, belongs to the actual religious act in the same way. In fact, in the religious act man is more immediately aware that his salvation depends on giving the right response to the Word of God all-holy. Both areas belong to moral theology. It has as its object the religious life and activity as well as the whole sphere of religious moral responsibility.

4. *Responsibility and Personal Salvation*

Even though we refuse to see in self-perfection and salvation of soul the central concept of Christian morality, but place it rather in the idea of "responsibility," nevertheless we should not forget that under a certain aspect our personal salvation occupies the first place in our responsibility. It takes precedence absolutely over all the impersonal values for which we are accountable, though not over the Kingdom of God as a whole and the salvation of our neighbor. However, we are more responsible for our own salvation than for that of others. Responsibility of each individual for himself exceeds in a measure his co-responsibility for his neighbor, because he has immediate free control of his own will alone. Responsibility and freedom of will, however, are in close interdependence. So we are most accountable for what is most subject to our own voluntary acts. Hence we may and must take direct and immediate care of the salvation of our own souls. And a great number of acts may be subordinated and directed to this goal, for example, discipline of will and ascetic exercises.

Our occupation with all the passing things of this life may be viewed at least partially under this aspect (even though it is not the supreme aspect). But it would be an error to subordinate our co-responsibility for our neighbor and the Kingdom of God to ourselves and to the care for our own personal worth and value. Because the former are not intrinsically inferior in value to our own personal salvation, it follows that our moral endeavor ought not to subordinate, but rather coordinate them and hold them equal to our salvation in striving for eternal happiness (cf. the first section in volume three). However, it must never be overlooked that the common center of all values is God, the love of communion with Him, responsibility before Him.

In the hierarchy of values in the Christian moral teaching, as just outlined, the thought of our own salvation and personal sanctification may not appear so prominently as in the popular instruction and preaching on the moral life. However, the urgency of our own salvation is merely increased by being viewed in relation to the more central idea of morality. Finally, one very important point should not be lost sight of. The formation of the moral-religious takes place by slow degrees and continuous growth. The great masters of the spiritual life attribute this progress precisely to the progressive subordination of self, with the I viewed more and more in the light of its proper position in the whole scale of values. From the very outset the spiritual director must have a clear view of the absolute hierarchy of values. But he must also take into consideration the actual spiritual condition of the soul he directs: what is its present degree of perfection? What forces and motives are available in each concrete instance for the most effective promotion of spiritual advancement?

The moral sermon or moral directive intended for beginners, or even for those estranged from God, which neglects the prudent appeal to man's craving for happiness and his legitimate concern for his own salvation, may well prove a tragic failure! Desire for happiness and morality are not identical—we hope that we have made the point clear—but they do belong to each other. Desire for happiness is the grand ally of the moral *ought;* often no other appeal can be heard in the desolation and abyss of sin into which the soul has been plunged. Or should we say it is the last faint echo of God's call to obedience and love?

In the moral sermon as well as in our personal moral effort we must keep the entire goal in mind from the very beginning: our total conversion to God. But in each instance we must present the motives which are calculated to prove the most effective in the concrete circumstances. The clarion call to "save your soul" may not be perverted into an invitation to egotistic and egocentric moral-religious effort. It must be the true call to response and responsibility in God's sight. The call to salvation must be an appeal to the entire breadth and depth of the soul's moral endeavor. But it must be clearly understood that the immediate legitimate interest in self, the unrest of the soul far from God, is like a tiny crevice through which the heavenly light can penetrate to the soul imprisoned in sin.

Finally, it is scarcely possible for us pilgrims in this earthly sojourn to attain a degree of perfection in love in which the innate desire for happiness need not be called upon to assist our progress as the ally of our love.[37] The unrest in our souls is not yet love of God but rather the mainspring which tautens the powers of the soul for the movement of love. God Himself sets this force to work by drawing the soul to divine love through a holy fear and hope. Happiness and self-perfection constitute a moral goal, but not the sole and ultimate one. Legitimate interest in one's own salvation is like the lever of Archimedes. It can raise the soul from the false basis of self to the true and lofty level of hope whence it can turn to God. But from the very outset it must be clearly realized that we are concerned with an important aim indeed, though not with the final goal. The fulcrum is only the means of reaching the higher level! The alarm is only to alert one to the danger and should not be confused with the actual message it calls to our attention.

III. RESPONSIBILITY AND IMITATION OF CHRIST

The object and purpose of moral theology is not involved in the philosophical analysis of "responsibility" nor in the explanation of the term. And it is equally certain that it is not the function of the moral sermon or instruction to offer such an analysis. Their purpose is to present the rich and vital content of the history of salvation and our loving fellowship with God in Christ. The word *responsibility* merely reflects something essential in all this. All the requirements arising from the foregoing considerations on responsibility are abundantly fulfilled in a moral teaching which has our community with Christ as center, in a moral teaching on the Kingdom of Christ and on the imitation of Christ. In a moral teaching based on the imitation of Christ, the essential characteristics of religion as fellowship with God, and morality as responsibility before God, are entirely in the foreground.

The foundation for the imitation of Christ is the incorporation of the disciple in Christ through grace. Imitation of Christ in our lives is accomplished through activity of love and obedience in objective union with Christ. Imitation binds us to the word of Christ: in His grace, in the gift of love, Christ binds us to Himself. In love we unite ourselves with His Person, the Incarnate Word. Our obedience unites us with Him through the following of His example eloquently inviting us to imitate Him. In obeying Him, we make of every word flowing from His sacred lips a bond of union with Him. For the true disciple receives the word of Christ, actively fulfilling it in his life on his own responsibility and in his own time. This means that he must imitate the example of Christ in his own individuality, according to his own unique possession of particular gifts and endowments bestowed on him with all self-accountability in the sight of God.

To be in Christ means to be incorporated into His Kingdom. To be a member in the Kingdom of Christ (in the Body of Christ) demands of us the responsibility of active participation. We in our own person, with all our individual powers, must assert ourselves for the Kingdom of Christ, for our neighbor. Imitation of Christ bears with it the concept and notion of responsibility. We cannot speak of the imitation of Christ without implying responsibility for every soul redeemed by Christ, without proclaiming responsibility for service in the Kingdom of Christ.

Commandment and law also retain their place and their validity in the imitation of Christ. But for those who follow Christ, they cease to be mere impersonal forces intervening between God and the soul. They are the living words of Christ addressed to us. They are an ever new appeal of Christ through His grace to us, holding us responsible for fulfillment of His "great command" according to the measure and standard of the grace He has given us. Such a standard obviously is far higher than the minimal requirement of the Law of Sinai and infinitely above the standard of the natural law.

Neither the natural ideal of personal perfection nor the supernatural ideal of personal salvation is simply central for the disciple of Christ, but they are best attained through following the Master. It is true that the disciple does not see in the imitation a mere means to save his soul. Yet when seen in the light of our Saviour's love, salvation becomes a matter of tremendous importance. The disciple who at first looked to the promises of the Master rather than to His immense love learns in following Christ to see his own soul in a new light, to love his soul in a new way, namely, in the love for the Master. Now our love for ourselves rests in the love of the Master for us and in our love for Him. Salvation of souls now appears in the splendor of God's loving glory and the beauty of His kingdom.

Christian moral teaching, it is evident, is not anthropocentric. It does not center in man. Nor is it theocentric in a sense alien to man and foreign to his world. It centers in grace-endowed fellowship of man with God, in the dialogue of word and response, in "responsibility." Only if it is centered in Christ does our moral life possess the worth of response made to God, for Christ is the Word in whom the Father seeks and calls us. Our loving obedience in the imitation of Christ is the echo, the image, the participation in the triune, eternal life of God, in the Word and the response of love.

It is possible for us to follow Christ, to imitate Him, because He is the "Word" in whom our likeness to God rests and through whom it has been wonderfully restored by the Redemption. In the fulfillment of the imitation, our likeness to God becomes manifest. And just as all discussion about an image refers back to the original or prototype which has been copied, so too must moral theology direct the Christian life in all points to the Word or Logos, the divine pattern in whom and through whom man made to the divine image lives and to whom he can respond.

BIBLIOGRAPHY

AERTNYS, J., AND DAMEN, C.A., C.SS.R. *Theologia moralis secundum doctrinam S. Alfonsi.* 17 ed. Taurini, 1956–58.

ALSZECHY, Z., S.J. *Grundformen der Liebe. Die Theorie der Gottesliebe bei dem hl. Bonaventura.* Romae: Universitas Gregoriana, 1946.

AMMER, J. *Christliche Lebensgestaltung nach der Ethik Johann Michael Sailers* (Abhandlungen aus Ethik und Moral, Band 17). Duesseldorf, 1941.

ANDREWS, M. *The Ethical Teaching of Paul. A Study in Origin.* Chapel Hill, 1934.

ARREGUI, A. A., S.J. *Compendio de teologia moral.* 19 ed. Bilbao, 1950.

ASTING, R. *Die Heiligkeit im Urchristentum.* Goettingen, 1930.

BAEUMKER, CL., AND GRABMANN, M. *Beitraege zur Philosophie und Theologie des Mittelalters.*

BARDY, G. *La vie spirituelle d'après les Pères des trois premiers siècles.* Paris, 1935.

BAUMGARTNER, CH., S.J. *La morale chrétienne.* Paris, 1952.

BERG, L. *Die Gottebenbildlichkeit im Moralsubjekt nach Thomas von Aquin.* Mainz, 1948.

BLAESER, P. "Glaube und Sittlichkeit bei Paulus," *Festschrift fuer Meinertz* (Muenster, 1951), 114–121.

BOECKLE, FR. "Bestrebungen in der Moraltheologie," *Fragen der Theologie heute* (Einsiedeln-Zuerich-Koeln, 1957), 425–446.

BOELEN, B. J.M. *Eudaimonie en het wezen der ethiek.* Leuven, 1949.

BONSIRVEN, J. *Les enseignements de Jesus.* Paris, 1946.

BUYER, C. *San Augustin, Sus normas de moral.* Buenos Aires (Excelsa), 1945.

BRICKA, C. *Le fondement christologique de la morale paulinienne.* Paris, 1923.

BRUNNER, A. *Eine neue Schoepfung. Ein Betrag zur Theologie des christlichen Lebens.* Paderborn, 1952.

*BRUNNER, E. *Das Gebot und die Ordnungen.* Zuerich, 1939.

———. *Divine Imperative.* Philadelphia: Westminster Press, 1947.

BURI, FR. *Klemens von Alexandrien und der paulinische Freiheitsbegriff.* Zuerich-Leipzig, 1939.

BUYS, L., C SS.R. "Onze moraaltheologie en de bergrede," *Festschrift fuer G. C. van Noort* (Utrecht, 1944), 34–59, 278–281.

CALVERAS, J., S.J. "Los 'Confessionales' y los Ejercicios de San Ignacio," *Archivum Historicum S.J.,* 17 (1948), 51–101.

CAPITAINE, W. *De Origenis ethica.* Muenster, 1889.

———. *Die Moral des Klemens von Alexandrien.* Goettingen, 1902.

CARPENTIER, R., S.J. "Vers une morale de charité," *Greg.,* 34 (1953), 32–55.

CARRO, V. "De Pedro de Soto a Domingo Bañez," *CiTh,* 37 (1928), 145–178.

———. *Domingo Soto y el derecho de Gentes.* Madrid, 1930.

———. *El Maestro Fray Pedro de Soto, Confesor de Carlos V y las controversias político-teológicas del siglo XVI.* Madrid, 1927.

CECHINI, L. *Il problema morale in S. Agostino.* Reggio Emiliae, 1934.

CERIANI, G. "La Compagnia di Gesù e la Teologia Morale," *SC* (1941).

The Church Teaches, documents of the Church in English Translation. St. Louis: Herder, 1955.

CLARK, F., S.J. "The Challenge to Moral Theology," *ClerRev,* 38 (1953), 214–223.

CONNELL, F., C.SS.R. *Outlines of Moral Theology,* Milwaukee, 1953.

CONSIGLIO, A. "Il limite come principio della vita morale," *So*, 53, Fasc.1.

DAFFARA, M., O.P. "Tommaso de Vio Gaetano interprete e commentatore della morale di S. Tommaso," *RevNéoscolPh*, Suppl. to volume XXVII (Marzo, 1935), 75–102.

DAVIS, H., S.J. *Moral and Pastoral Theology* (four volumes). New York, 1943.

DE BLIC, J., S.J. "L'intellectualisme moral chez deux aristotéliciens de la fin du XIIIe siècle" *MisMor* (Louvain, 1948), 45–76.

DEININGER, F. *Der Kampf der Loewener Fakultaet gegen den Laxismus.* Duesseldorf, 1928.

DELERUE, F. *Le système moral de S. Alphonse.* S. Etienne, 1929.

DELHAYE, PH. "L'enseignement de la philosophie morale au XIIe siècle," MedSt, 11 (1949), 77–99.

————. *Florilegium morale oxoniense.* Texte publié et commenté par Ph. Delhaye. Louvain, 1955.

————. "Die gegenwaertigen Bestrebungen der Moral-Wissenschaft in Frankreich," *Moral probleme im Umbruch der Zeit* (Muenchen, 1957), 13–39.

————. "La théologie morale d'hier et d'aujourd'hui," *RevSR*, 27 (1953), 112–130.

————. "Dogme et morale. Autonomie et assistance mutuelle," *MélScRel*, 11 (1954), 49–62.

DEMAN, TH., O.P. *Aux origines de la théólogie morale.* Paris, 1951.

DEMPF, A. *Die Ethik des Mittelalters.* Muenchen and Berlin, 1927.

DER GROSSE HERDER, BAND 10, *Der Mensch in seiner Welt.* Freiburg, 1953.

DESCAMPS, A. "La morale des Synoptiques," *Morale Chrétienne et requêtes contemporaines* (Tournai, 1954), 27–46.

DEWAR, L. *An Outline of New Testament Ethics.* Philadelphia, 1950.

DIEBOLT, J. *La théologie morale catholique en Allemagne au temps du philosophisme et de la restauration 1750–1850.* Strasbourg, 1926.

DIETTERLE, J. "Die *Summae confessorum sive de casibus conscientiae* von ihren Anfaengen an bis zu Silvester Prierias," *ZKG*, 25–27 (1903–1906), continued series.

————. *Die Franziskanischen Summae Confessorum und ihre Bestimmungen ueber den Ablass.* Doebeln, 1893.

DIRINK, A. *Sancti Basilii Magni de divitiis et paupertate sententiae.* Muenster, 1921.

DITTRICH, O. *Geschichte der Ethik* (4 Bde). Leipzig, 1926/33.

*DODD, C. H. *Gospel and Law. The Relation of Faith and Ethics in Early Christianity.* New York: Columbia University Press, 1951.

DOELLINGER, IG. AND REUSCH, R. *Geschichte der Moralstreitigkeiten in der roemischkatholischen Kirche.* Noerdlingen, 1889.

EBERLE, A. *Ist der Dillinger Moral-professor Christof Rassler der Begruender des Aequiprobabilismus?* Freiburg, 1951.

————. "Am Ende des Probabilistenstreits," *Neues Abendland*, 8 (1953), 725–736.

EGENTER, R. *Gottesfreundschaft. Die Lehre von der Gottesfreundschaft in der Scholastik und Mystik des 12. und 13. Jahrhunderts.* Augsburg, 1928.

ELERT, W. *Das christliche Ethos, Grundlinien der lutherischen Ethik.* Tuebingen, 1949.

ERMECKE, G. "Die Stufen der sakramentalen Christusebenbildlichkeit als Einteilungsprinzip der speziellen Moral," *Festschrift fuer F. Tillmann* (Duesseldorf, 1950).

————. "Die katholische Moraltheologie heute," *ThGl* (1951), 127–142.

ERNESTI, K. *Die Ethik des T. Flavius Klemens von Alexandrien oder die erste Zusammenhaengende Begruendung der christlichen Sittenlehre.* Paderborn, 1900.

EUGÈNE, R. P. "La conscience moral à cinq siècles de distance. Autour de Saint Antonin," *RevThom*, 18 (1935), 211–236.

FANFANI, L. J. *Manuale theorico-practicum theologiae morǎlis ad mentem D. Thomae* (four volumes). Rome, 1951.

FECKES, C. *Die Lehre vom christlichen Vollkommenheitsstreben.* Freiburg, 1949.

FISCHER, G. *Johann Michael Sailer und Immanuel Kant.* Freiburg, 1953.

FOGLIASSO, E. "Circa la rettificazione dei confini tra la teologia morale e il diritto canonico," *Sal,* 13 (1953), 381–413.

FRASSINETTI, G. *Compendio della teologia morale di S. Alfonso de Liguori* (two volumes). Torino, 1947.

GAUDE, L. *De morali systemate S. Alphonsi M. de Liguorio.* Rome, 1894.

GEISELMANN, J. R. *Die theologische Anthropologie Johann Adam Moehlers.* Freiburg, 1954.

GENICOT, E., S.J. AND SALSMANS, J., S.J. *Institutiones theologiae moralis* (17 ed. by Gortebecke, 2 Vols.). Brussels and Bruges, 1951.

GIET, ST. *Les idées et l'action sociales de saint Basile.* Paris (Gabalda), 1941.

———. "Le rigorisme de saint Basile," *RevSR.,* 23 (1949), 333–342.

GILLEMAN, G., S.J. *The Primacy of Charity in Moral Theology.* Westminster, Md.: Newman, 1959.

GILSON, E. *The Spirit of Mediaeval Philosophy.* London: Sheed and Ward, 1936.

———. *Moral Values and the Moral Life.* St. Louis: Herder, 1931.

———. *Saint Thomas d'Aquin.* Paris, 1925.

GORCE, M. M. "A propos de B. de Medina et du probabilisme," *EphThLov,* 7 (1930), 480 ff.

GRABMANN, M. "Das Weiterwirken des moraltheologischen Schriftums des hl. Thomas von Aquin im Mittelalter," *DivThom* (*F*), 24 (1947), 3–28.

———. "Albert von Brescia, O.P. (†1314) und sein Werk 'De officiis sacerdotis,'" *DivThom(F)* (1940), 1–38.

———. *Mittelalterliches Geistesleben.* Muenchen, 1926.

GRAIL, A., SCHMITT, J., GIBLET, J., TREMEL, Y. B., SPICQ, C. "Grandes lignes de la morale du Nouveau Testament," *LumVie,* Nr. 21 (1955), 3–123.

HADROSSEK, P. *Die Bedeutung des Systemgedankens fuer die Moraltheologie in Deutschland seit der Thomas-renaissance.* Muenchen, 1951.

HÄRING, B. *Das Heilige und das Gute, Religion und Sittlichkeit in ihrem gegenseitigen Bezug.* Krailing vor Muenchen, 1950.

HARVEY, J. F. *Moral Theology of the Confessions of Saint Augustine.* Washington: The Catholic University Press, 1951.

HAUSHERR, I. "L'imitation de Jésus Christ dans la spiritualité byzantine," *Mélanges offerts au R.P. Cavallera* (Toulouse, 1948), 231–259.

HEARD, G. *Morals since 1900.* New York, 1951.

HEINEN, W. *Die Anthropologie in der Sittenlehre Ferdinand Geminian Wankers* (1758–1824). Freiburg, 1955.

HEITMANN, AD. *Imitatio Dei. Die ethische Nachahmung Gottes nach der Vaeterlehre der ersten zwei Jahrhunderte.* Rome, 1940.

HEMPEL, J. *Das Ethos des Alten Testamentes.* Berlin, 1938.

HILDEBRAND, D. VON. *Christian Ethics.* New York, 1952.

HILLER, J. A. *Albrecht von Eyb. A Medieval Moralist.* Washington, 1940.

HOERMANN, K. *Leben in Christus. Zusammenhaenge zwischen Dogma und Sitte bei den apostolischen Vaetern.* Vienna, 1952.

HOMMEL, F. *Nosce teipsum. Die Ethik des Peter Abaelard.* Wiesbaden, 1947.

HUERTH, F., S.J. AND ABELLAN, P. M., S.J. *Notae ad praelectiones theologiae moralis* (two volumes). Rome, 1948.

HUNSCHEIDT, W. *Sebastian Mutschelle 1749–1800. Ein Kantianischer Moraltheologe.* Bonn, 1948.

IZAGO, L. "Luis de Molina, internacionalista," *RazFe,* 110 (1936), 43–55, 192–206.

JAFFA, H. *Thomism and Aristotelianism. A Study of the Commentary by Thomas Aquinas on the Nicomachean Ethics.* Chicago, 1952.

JANVIER, A., O.P. *Exposition de la morale catholique* (16 Vols.). Paris, 1903/1919.

JEROME DE PARIS, P. *La doctrine morale de S. Laurent de Brindes.* Paris, 1933.

Jorio, Th. *Theologia moralis* (3 Vols.). Neapolis, 1946–47.

Junker, A. *Die Ethik des Apostels Paulus* (2 Bde.). Halle, 1904/1919.

Kaup, J. *Die theologische Tugend der Liebe nach der Lehre des hl. Bonaventura*. Muenster, 1927.

Kern, E. *Das Tugendsystem des hl. Bernhard von Clairvaux*. Freiburg, 1934.

Keusch, K. *Die Aszetik des hl. Alfons Maria von Liguori* (2 Aufl.). Paderborn, 1926.

Klein, J. *Tertullian, Christliches Bewusstsein und sittliche Forderungen. Ein Beitrag zur Geschichte der Moral und ihrer Systembildungen* (Abhandlungen aus Ethik und Moral, Band 15). Duesseldorf, 1940.

Klotz, Ph. *Johann Michael Sailer als Moralphilosoph. Ein Beitrag zur Geschichte der christlichen Ethik im 19. Jahrhundert*. Paderborn, 1909.

Kraus, J. "Zum Problem des christozentrischen Aufbaus der Moraltheologie," *DivThom* (F), 30 (1952), 257–272.

Krautwig, N. "Entfaltung der Herrlichkeit Christi," *WissWeish*, 7 (1940), 73–99.

————. "Die christliche Lebensaufgabe," *ZAM*, 18 (1943), 1–16.

LaGrange, M. J. *La Morale de l'Évangile*. Paris, 1931.

Lanza, A. *Theologia moralis* (tom. I).

————. *Theologia moralis fundamentalis*. Torino, 1949.

Lauer, H. *Die Moraltheologie Alberts des Grossen*. Freiburg, 1911.

Le Bras, G. "Pénitentiels," *DTC*, XII, 1160–1179.

Lebreton, J. *La vie chrétienne au premier siècle de l'Eglise*. Paris, 1927.

Leclercq, J. *L'enseignement de la morale chrétienne*. Paris, 1950.

————. *Christliche Moral in der Krisis der Zeit*. Einsiedeln, Zuerich, Koeln, 1954.

————. *Essais de morale catholique* (4 vol., 3 ed.). Tournai, 1950.

Le Senne, R. *Traité de morale générale* (2. ed.). Paris, 1947.

*Lewis, H. D. *Morals and the New Theology*. New York: Harper, 1948.

Lopez, Ulpiano, S.J. "Il metodo e la dottrina morale nei classici della Compagnia di Gesù, in La Compagnia di Gesù e le Scienze Sacre," *AnalGreg* (Romae, 1942), 83–111.

Losskij, W. *Essai sur la théologie mystique de l'Eglise d'Orient*. Paris, 1944.

Lottin, O. *Morale fondamentale*. Paris-Tournai, 1954.

————. *Psychologie et morale aux XIIe et XIIIe siècles*. Louvain, 1942/54.

————. "Pour une réorganisation du traité thomiste de la moralité," *Scholastica rationalis, historica, critica* (1951), 307–371.

————. *Psychologie et morale aux XIIe et XIIIe siècles* (Vol. II, Problèmes de morale. Louvain and Gembloux, 1948.

————. *Au coeur de la morale chrétienne. Bible, Tradition, Philosophie*. Tournai, 1957.

McGregor, G. *Les frontières de la morale et de la religion*. Paris, 1952.

Marc, Cl.-Gestermann, F.-Raus. *Institutiones morales Alphonsianae* (two Volumes, 20 ed.). Lyon-Paris, 1939–43.

Maritain, J. *Neuf leçons sur les notions premières de la philosophie morale*. Paris, 1951.

Marshall, L. H. *The Challenge of New Testament Ethics*. London, 1946.

Mausbach, J. *Die Katholische Moral, ihre Methoden, Grundsaetze und Aufgaben*. Koeln, 1902.

————. *Die Ethik des hl. Augustin* (2 Bde. 2 Auflage). Freiburg, 1929.

————. *Katholische Moraltheologie* (9 Aufl. bearbeitet von G. Ermecke). Muenster, 1953–1955.

————. *Catholic Moral Teaching and Its Antagonists* viewed in the light of principle and of contemporaneous history. New York: Wagner, 1914.

————. *Thomas von Aquin als Meister der christlichen Sittenlehre*. Muenchen, 1925.

Mayer, A. *Das Gottesbild im Menschen nach Klemens von Alexandrien*. Rome, 1942.

Meffert, Fr. *Der hl. Alfons von Ligouri*. Mainz, 1901.

Mersch, E., S.J. *Morale et corps mystique* (3 ed.). Bruxelles, 1949.

———. "La morale et le Christ total," *NRTh*, 68 (1946), 633–647.

MOHR, R. *Die christliche Ethik im Lichte der Ethnologie.* Muenchen, 1954.

———. *Moral and Pastoral Theology, A Summary.* New York, 1952.

MORAN, S. A., O.P. "La rectificación de los confines entre la theología moral y el derecho canónico," *Rev. Españ. de Derecho Canónico* (1952), 695–699.

NOELKENSMEIER, CH. *Ethische Grundfragen bei Bonaventura.* Leipzig, 1932.

NOLDIN, H. S.J. *Summa theologiae moralis* (30 ed., three Volumes). Innsbruck, 1952.

ODDONE, A., S.J. "La morale cristiana come intera e perfetta moralità" *CC*, 101 (1950), I, 129–143.

PEETERS, H., O.F.M. *Manuale theologiae moralis.* Macau, 1950.

PEINADOR, A., C M.F. *Cursus brevior theologiae moralis ex Divi Thomae principiis inconcussis* (two Volumes). Madrid, 1950.

PELSTER, F. "Eine Kontroverse ueber die Methode der Moraltheologie aus dem Ende des 16. Jahrhunderts," *Schol*, 17 (1942), 385–411.

PELZER, A. "Les cours inédits d'Albert le Grand sur la Morale à Nicomaque et rédigé par saint Thomas d'Aquin," *RevNéoscolPh*, 24 (1922), 333–361, 479–520.

PETIT, F., O.P. "Le décadence de la morale, jalons d'histoire," *VieSpirSupp*, 4 (1951), 144–152.

PETROCCHI, M. *Il problema del lassismo nel secolo XVII.* Roma, 1953.

PIESCH, H. *Meister Eckharts Ethik.* Luzern, 1949.

PREGER, F. *Die Grundlagen der Ethik bei Gregor von Nyssa.* Wuerzburg, 1897.

PREISKER, J. *Das Ethos des Urchristentums* (2 ed.). Guetersloh, 1949.

PRUEMMER, D. M., O.P. *Vademecum theologiae moralis* (6 ed. by Muench, E. M., O.P.). Freiburg i. Br., 1949.

RAUCH, W. *Lexikon des katholischen Lebens.* Freiburg, 1952.

RAUSCHEN, G. *Eucharist and Penance in the First Six Centuries of the Church.* St. Louis: Herder, 1913.

REDING, M. *Der Aufbau der christlichen Existenz.* Muenchen, 1952.

———. *Handbuch der Moraltheologie.* Band 1: *Philosophische Grundlegung der katholische Moraltheologie.* Muenchen, 1953.

REGATILLO, E. F., AND ZALBA, M., S.J. *Theologiae moralis summa.* Matriti, 1952.

REUL, A. *Die sittlichen Ideale des Hl. Augustinus.* Paderborn, 1928.

RIETTER, A. *Die Moral des hl. Thomas von Aquin.* Muenchen, 1858.

ROLAND-GOSSELIN, B. *La morale de saint Augustin.* Paris, 1925.

RUETHER, TH. *Die sittliche Forderung der Apatheia in den beiden ersten christlichen Jahrhunderten, besonders bei Klemens von Alexandrien.* Freiburg, 1949.

RUEVE, S. J. *Francis Suarez and the Natural Law.* Ann Arbor, 1940.

SCHARL, J. *Gesetz und Freiheit. Die theologische Begruendung der christlichen Sittlichkeit bei J. B. Hirscher.* Muenchen, 1941.

SCHILLING, O. "Das Prinzip der Moral," *ThQschr*, 99 (1938), 419–426.

———. *Handbuch der Moraltheologie* (2 Aufl). Stuttgart, 1952.

SCHMITZ, H. J. *Die Bussbuecher und die Bussdisziplin der Kirche.* Mainz, 1883.

SCHNACKENBURG, R. *Die sittliche Botschaft des neuen Testamentes.* Muenchen, 1954.

SCHOLZ, FR. *Benedikt Stattler und die Grundzuege seiner Sittlichkeit unter besonderer Beruecksichtigung der Lehre von der philosophischen Suende.* Freiburg, 1957.

SCHUELER, A. *Verantwortung. Vom Sein und Ethos der Person.* Krailing vor Muenchen, 1948.

SCHUHMACHER, H. *Kraft der Urkirche. Das "neue Leben" nach den Dokumenten der ersten zwei Jahrhunderte.* Freiburg, 1934.

SCHULZE, P. *Die Entwicklung der Hauptlaster- und Haupttugendlehre von Gregor dem Grossen bis Petrus Lombardus.* Greifswald, 1914.

SEMERIA, G. *La morale e le morali.* Firenze, 1934.

SERTILLANGES, A. D., O.P. *La philosophie morale de S. Thomas d'Aquin.* Paris, 1942.

Söe, N. N. *Christliche Ethik* (translated from the Danish by W. Thieman). Muenchen, 1949.

SOEHNGEN, G. "Die biblische Lehre von der Gottebenbildlichkeit," *MThZ,* 2 (1951), 52–76.

SOUKUP, L. *Grundzuege einer Ethik der Persoenlichkeit.* Wien, 1951.

SPICQ, C. "La morale paulinienne," *Morale chrétienne et requêtes contemporaines* (Tournai, 1954), 47–70.

STEINBUECHEL, TH. *Der Zweckgedanke in der Philosophie des hl. Thomas.* Muenster, 1912.

―――. *Religion und Moral im Lichte christlicher Existenz.* Frankfurt a. M., 1951.

―――. *Der Zerfall des christlichen Ethos im 19. Jahrhundert.* Frankfurt a. M., 1951.

STELZENBERGER, J. *Anton Joseph Rosshirt, Eine Studie zur Moraltheologie der Aufklaerungszeit.* Breslau, 1937.

―――. *Die Beziehungen der fruehchristlichen Sittenlehre zur Ethik der Stoa.* Muenchen, 1933.

―――. *Moraltheologie, Die Sittlichkeit der Koenigsherrschaft Gottes.* Paderborn, 1953.

SWITALSKY, B. *Neoplatonism and the Ethics of St. Augustine.* Vol. I, *Plotinus and the Ethics of St. Augustine.* New York: Polish Institute Series n. 8, 1946.

TEETAERT, A. "Un compendium de Théologie Pastorale du XIIIe-XIVe siècle," *RHT,* 26 (1930), 66–103.

TER HAAR, F. *Das Dekret des Papstes Innocenz XI. ueber den Probabilismus.* Paderborn, 1904.

TERNUS, J. *Zur Vorgeschichte der Moralsysteme von Vitoria bis Medina.* Paderborn, 1930.

THAMIN, R., S. *Ambroise et la morale chrétienne au IVe siècle.* Paris, 1895.

THIELICKE, H. *Theologische Ethik,* 1 Band. *Dogmatische und kontroverstheologische Grundlegung.* 2 Band, *Entfaltung.* Tuebingen, 1955.

THILS, G. *Tendences actuelles en Théologie moral.* Gembloux, 1940.

TILLMANN, F. *Handbuch der katholischen Sittenlehre.* (This work in four volumes was written in collaboration with Th. Steinbuechel and Th. Muencker.) 4 ed. Duesseldorf, 1950.

―――. *Der Meister Ruft. Die katholische Sittenlehre gemeinverstaendlich dargestellt.* Duesseldorf, 1949.

TYSKIEWICZ, S., S.J. *Moralistes de Russie.* Romae, 1951.

URDANOZ, T., O.P. *Estudios ético-juridícos en torno a Vitoria.* Salamanca, 1947.

UTZ, A. F. *Wesen und Sinn des christlichen Ethos.* Muenchen-Heidelberg, 1942.

VAN DER HAGEN, J. *De Clementis Alexandrini sententiis oeconomicis, socialibus, politicis.* Triecti ad Rhenum, 1920.

VAN KOL, A., S.J. *Christus' plaats in S. Thomas' moralsysteem.* Roermond-Maaseik, 1947.

VAN OYEN, HENDRIK *Evangelische Ethik l. Grundlagen. Die Anwaltschaft des Geistes.* Basel, 1952.

VILLER, M., AND RAHNER, K. *Askese und Mystik in der Vaeterzeit.* Freiburg, 1939.

Vindiciae alphonsianae seu S. Alphonsi doctrina moralis vindicata . . . cura quorumdam theologorum e C.SS.R. Rom und Doornik, 1874.

VOELKER, W. *Das Vollkommenheitsideal des Origenes.* Tuebingen, 1931:

―――. *Der wahre Gnostiker nach Clemens Alexandrinus.* Berlin, 1952.

VOLLERT, W. *Die Lehre Gregors von Nyssa vom Guten und vom Boesen und von der schliesslichen Ueberwindung des Boesen.* Leipzig, 1897.

WAGNER, W. *Der Christ und die Welt bei Klemens von Alexandrien.* Goettingen, 1903.

WAGNER, F. *Der Sittlichkeitsbegriff in der Heiligen Schrift und in altchristlichen Ethik.* Muenster, 1931.

―――. *Der Sittlichkeitsbegriff in der christlichen Ethik des Mittelalters.* Muenster, 1936.

WEBER, L. *Hauptfragen der Moral theologie Gregors des Grossen. Ein Bild christlicher Lebensfuehrung.* Freiburg i. Br., 1947.

WEHRUNG, G. *Welt und Reich, Grundlegung und Aufbau der Ethik.* Stuttgart, 1952.

WEILNER, I. *Gottselige Innigkeit. Die Grundhandlung der religioesen Seele nach Johann Michael Sailer.* Regensburg, 1949.

WINTER, F. J. *Die Ethik des Klemens von Alexandrien.* Leipzig, 1882.

WITTMANN, M. *Die Ethik des hl. Thomas von Aquin.* Muenchen, 1933.

ZEIGER, IVO, S.J. "Katholische Moraltheologie heute," *StimmZeit,* 134 (1938), 143–153.

ZIERMANN, B., C.SS.R. "Die Eigenbedeutung des hl. Alfonsus von Liguori in der Moraltheologie," *ThPrQschr,* 93 (1940), 199–214.

ZWICKER, H. *Reich Gottes, Nachfolge und Neuschoepfung.* Bern, 1948.

Additional Works in English

KELLY, G., S.J., AND FORD, J., S.J. *Contemporary Moral Theology.* Vol. 1, *Questions in Fundamental Moral Theology.* Westminster, Md.: Newman, 1958. Cf. Chaps. 4–6, pp. 42–103.

———. *Man and His Happiness* (Theological Library, Vol. 3). Chicago: Fides, 1956. Cf. pp. 1–24.

SLATER, T., S.J. *A Short History of Moral Theology.* New York: Benziger, 1909.

Part Two:

THE SUBJECT OF MORAL VALUES
THEOLOGICAL ANTHROPOLOGY

W E UNDERSTAND moral theology as the doctrine of the imitation of Christ, as the life in, with, and through Christ. Therefore its starting point cannot be man, as might be tenable in the science of natural ethics. The point of departure in Catholic moral theology is Christ, who bestows on man a participation in His life and calls on him to follow the Master. Our moral theology is consciously a dialogue. And since such dialogue is possible only if God first speaks to us, and since He speaks to us in Christ, the Word of God, it follows that the person of Christ, His word, His example, and His grace must be the focal center of moral teaching.

Not anthropology in itself alone, but Christology breathes the spirit of life into the theme of moral theology. The grace comes from Christ. From Him comes the call. "You have not chosen me, but I have chosen you" (JN 15:16). So deep is our conviction that the doctrine about man in moral theology (anthropology) must be studied in the light of Christology that it seems to us to be in a measure an actual part of Christology. Let us note that if we are to understand man who is called by Christ, this is possible only in the light of Him who calls. Our study of man is not just man, but man as created in the Word of the Father, who is Christ, and in Christ wonderfully renewed.

Anthropology studies the whole man with all that he is and has from the standpoint of the call of Christ to man. The present chapter, therefore, forms an inner unity with the subsequent extensive chapter which deals with the moral task of the disciple of Christ from the standpoint of the creative and redemptive love of God. Created in the Word of God and renewed in Christ, we all bear within us the law of Christ, the very same law which is revealed to us naturally in creation and still more clearly and more gloriously supernaturally in the word and example of Christ and through the teaching of the Church. The following chapters on general moral (sin, conversion, virtue) explain man's response to the divine call of Grace in Christ.

CHAPTER THREE

CHRIST INVITES MAN TO FOLLOW HIM

C HRIST's message is addressed to the whole man, to all that is essential in man: to man as body-and-soul totality (I), to man as an individual unique person and as social being (II), man in his historic dimensions (III), and, above all, as devoted to prayer and cult (IV).

I. MAN IN HIS TOTALITY, BODY AND SOUL

Man's likeness to God is rooted in his spiritual nature. Only in virtue of his spiritual nature is man capable of becoming a child of God and of hearing the call which God in His paternal love deigned to make to him. But it would be a fatal error to see in man, the image of God, and the person capable of receiving the divine call, only the spiritual element and to limit to it our moral concepts. The inevitable consequence would be a narrow spiritualistic notion of moral duty reserved to cultivation of the spirit alone. The whole man is the image of God formed in the likeness of the essential image of the Father. The whole man is fallen and also redeemed and called to eternal community of love with God.

Nothing is further from the truth than the view that bodily things are the principle of sin and temptation, and the spiritual the principle of the good and the subject of redemption. We are warned against such misconception by the very dogmas of the Incarnation ("The Word was made flesh." Jn 1:14) and of the resurrection of the body and, not least, by the essential nature of the holy sacraments as material signs of grace. The sacraments with all the freshness of created nature in their use of material elements to manifest and signify spiritual meaning, and by reference to the visible body of man as well as to the spiritual soul, express most concretely and graphically the great truth: we in our whole present existence of body and soul stand before God and must respond to Him with the responsibility of our whole being.

1. Sin and the Whole Man, Body and Soul

Augustine held that original sin consisted primarily in concupiscence, even though he looked upon estrangement from God (loss of the divine sonship) as the greatest evil in fallen man. Unfortunately, in popular preaching, bodily concupiscence is often depicted as the most grievous consequence of original sin and the root of all evil. In reality it is only one of the chief sources of evil in our fallen state. A greater and more perilous source of evil is the pride rooted in our spiritual nature. This may be called spiritual concupiscence. Both the carnal and the spiritual concupiscence seize upon the whole man and can be overcome only by the full power of the whole man. Only by disciplining the spirit and curbing the senses through voluntary self-denial can bodily concupiscence be kept under control. Only through exercise of humility before God even in matters affecting his bodily nature, only through crucifixion of the flesh, can man conquer the pride which reigns in his spirit.

The whole man, body and soul, functions as one in human activity. And body and soul cannot be kept in order without a spirit in which order reigns. On the other hand, the body cannot lapse into disorder affecting the whole man as long as the spirit is subject to discipline. We may go a step farther. The spiritual is in great part incapable of manifesting and expressing itself at all without the coordinate activity of the bodily powers. "There are instances in therapy in which the physiological expression of any spiritual power of reaction, for instance, anxiety, can be so effectively repressed that the corresponding emotional movement cannot take place at all. This plainly shows that the emotional movement or act is dependent on its expression of bodily resonance. A closer interdependence of body and soul can scarcely be conceived."[1]

At any rate, the so-called *Zweiseitentheorie* (the theory of the irreconcilable antinomy existing between soul and body) proposed by Jaspers and many other writers cannot be accepted. In this we are in agreement with Hedwig Conrad-Martius. Nevertheless, no matter how great the bond of unity, the diversity should not be ignored. The relation of the two is that of a mutual "causality of impression and expression."[2] We must particularly caution against any view of the total composite which blinds us to the possibility of the existence of the spiritual soul without the body, and any view which denies that within certain limits the spiritual powers can react against disorders. In that higher part of its spirituality, its freedom, the soul can rise above and shape and rule the bodily elements. But it cannot simply isolate itself and remain aloof from the agitation of this bodily counterpart. In order to rule, it must press into service the powers of both body and soul.

2. *"Instinct" (Sensuality) and Spirit*

Fundamentally Max Scheler is correct when he defines the relations between instinctive tendency or sensuality and spirit in the well-known critical formulas: Human instinct (as comprising all the body-soul drives and impulses) divorced from the spirit and viewed as a whole is without direction; but the spirit on its part, when divorced from instinct, is weak and powerless.[3] "We know that all activity of man, action as well as neglect of action, his genuine love as well as his worst excesses, are linked with instinctive forces of passion."[4] But the spirit with its insight into value and its power of free decision assumes responsibility. The free decision of the spirit determines whether the instinctive drives and urges are to turn perverse and erupt into sin, or, properly channeled, serve the purest and noblest love. Even in the very work of guidance and leadership the human spirit cannot function effectively in this mundane order of things without these psychophysiological forces and energies.

Thomas Aquinas is unequaled in his insight into the moral values of the soul-body unity in man. In his general moral teaching he devotes an extensive tract[5] to the passions or body-soul powers (*passiones*). Thomas does not treat them, as later writers do almost exclusively, primarily as a hazard endangering moral freedom or as occasions of sin, but as essential and indispensable forces in the service of man's moral activity. He rejects decisively the Stoic concept of the passions, which looked upon the passions as essentially evil and harmful, a disorder of the good. Even though he stresses with all vigor that the moral life is actually rooted in the spirit, he immediately adds that the moral action acquires an increase in perfection through the coordinated effort of body-soul powers, the passions. "It belongs to moral perfection that man be moved not only according to the will, but also according to the sensitive appetite (*appetitus sensitivus*)."[6]

Good must proceed from the whole man, for only the good of the whole man is fully human good. This basic insight of Aquinas has been frequently obscured by the ascetic injunction to war against one's inclinations basically and on principle (*agere contra*), as though every inclination were something perverted! Such a notion is diametrically opposed to the Catholic concept of man and his nature! The caution and warning that we must distrust our inclinations, though practically necessary, may never be perverted into sweeping condemnation in principle of all human inclinations and passions. Equally bizarre is the notion that there is an essential conflict or opposition between the spirit and the senses in man, as though a pure spirit in man chafes under carnal restraint and is constrained to war against the bodily element of his nature or even that it could do so.

But there is a conflict. There must be a counterattack issuing from the higher realm of the spirit, the citadel of moral freedom, against every disorder arising from the senses. This is the genuine impulse against evil (the genuine *agere contra*). But even this necessary counter-offensive can be successful and meaningful only if it is genuinely human. In a truly human way the spirit must function in coordination with the soul-body powers and through the power of its free decision recruit the forces of the senses in its service. By way of example, we note that bad thoughts and vile fancies are not driven from the mind by a mere fiat of the will, but only through the free determination of the will to substitute wholesome thoughts and images which turn the attention from evil by fixing it on the good.

Therefore resistance to inclinations and passions may never degenerate into an attempt to throttle or even to destroy the passions as such. The effort must rather be directed toward bringing the emotional life under the guidance of the spirit, with the result that it will participate in the moral ideals and dignity of the spiritual. Hence we must aim, not at suppressing the passions, but at cultivating and restraining them in accordance with the standard of practical reason. Such guidance is orientated toward sound values.[7]

False spirituality cannot fail to impoverish and enervate the spirit itself. By way of illustration, let us note the following: feelings of sorrow are not of the essence of contrition. But there is no sorrow genuinely and fully human in which the spiritually motivated act of contrition does not affect the senses and overflow into feelings of grief. In other words, one cannot be sorry for sin in a fully human way without some expression of emotion. Human sorrow cannot be manifested without some trace of the passion of grief. Similarly, one cannot possess spiritual joy, joy in God, intensively and in a genuine way without the emotional element of the passion of joy, without the thrill which affects our entire sensitive nature. And this in turn cannot fail to be reflected in the countenance. Perfect and pure love of God (*caritas Dei*) cannot at all be permanently sustained without the coexistence of the natural love with its emotional affection (*amor sensitivus*).

It goes without saying that man cannot actually approach God through the senses or by means of sense activity, but only through spiritual acts. But these spiritual acts of love are not genuinely human unless in some fashion they affect the sphere of the emotions by arousing or manifesting the passion of love.

Naturally we are not speaking here of sexual love, though it should not be overlooked that sexual love can be true love between human persons only if it is integrated in the context of the totality of love, hence, sustained by the spiritual motivation of love.

The supernatural acts of hope and fear, under the influence of divine grace, also require scope for emotional expression and resonance in the corresponding passion of hope and, of course, also of fear. According to the psychological laws governing man in the totality of his nature, joy, grief, fear, hope, and love concerned with spiritual things must necessarily wither away if such emotional expression and resonance is violently withdrawn, if the domain of the passions is suppressed rather than cultivated.

In many difficulties of life the spiritual faculty of the will needs the noble passion of anger to surmount the mountainous obstacles which obstruct our path. Obviously the fuming temper which dissipates itself in senseless impatience and fretting is of no profit to the spirit. But wherever the spirit scorns the passions and fails to direct them through wise and prudent motivation, they will run amuck and exhaust their forces in meaningless and futile hostility to the spirit.

A careful study of the various stages of the life of prayer and moral development will reveal a certain variation of the stress of the passions. This variation in value and importance exists despite the essential uniformity of the laws governing them. The imagination likewise does not always play the same role in meditation and prayer, although it cannot be absent altogether without a complete loss of progress in meditative prayer. And even in the highest degree of contemplative prayer, contemplation must be actuated by the images of the imagination. As to the affections, they leave their own impress on a specific kind of prayer (affective prayer). But they also have a part to play in all the other stages. It is always the whole man who is active, even though the individual powers may vary considerably in importance and significance in their relation to the various stages of spiritual development.

At this point we can do no more than refer to the theory of Aloysius Mager,[8] who holds that it is essential for certain transitional stages of the mystical life to be kept altogether free of affective activity. But according to this same psychologist the stages of mystical progress are such that the spiritual tends more and more to draw the emotional and affective into the mystical occurrences. Genuine "spiritualization" necessarily embraces a parallel or corresponding "bodilization."

3. The Body, Essential Companion of the Soul

Nothing could be more alien to the spirit of revelation than the Greek-Gnostic conception of the body as the prison of the soul, or the Hindu doctrine of metempsychosis, or transmigration of souls, according to which souls are condemned at death to live imprisoned in other bodies and pass through successive existences of this kind. The Old Testament offers no justification for any such teaching. It always views man in his totality. Nowhere does it speak of the body as inferior in dignity and value or as alien in nature to the soul. The marked dichotomy of body and soul so characteristic of Greek thought is entirely foreign to the Old Testament. The Hebrew notion of *Sheol* (where the shades of the dead dwell), so baffling to our minds, is comprehensible only if we bear in mind how thoroughly the Old Testament takes the unity of body and soul for granted. The artless manner in which the Old Testament speaks of bodily things springs from this same attitude. The inspired writer presents the most exalted spiritual and religious truths concretely and graphically by means of bodily images. This is particularly evident in the Song of Songs. But on the other hand, the Old Testament does not ignore the disorder which sin introduced into the whole man and which is particularly experienced in the flesh. "And the eyes of them both were opened: and . . . they perceived themselves to be naked" (Gn 3:7). Likewise the sermons of our Saviour, though they develop the thought of what is central to man, the "heart," do not reveal the slightest trace of hostility to the body of man.

The body is not the prison of the soul. But man, the whole man, can make it such if his spiritual soul makes itself a serf and enslaves the body. It becomes a slave from the ultimate theological point of view, not directly by abandoning itself to the cravings of the flesh, but through false emancipation from its heavenly support, from God. If the soul in an effort to achieve an illusory independence seeks to disown its true Lord and Master, it will inevitably fall under the sway of a tyrant, quite often the tyrant of unrestrained passion. Indeed man, the whole man, has but one choice: between the freedom of the children of God and the freedom of slaves.

And the body becomes either a partner in slavery or a companion in the freedom of true service. Fundamental basis for this union is the substantial union of body and soul which constitutes the very nature of man.

The Thomistic doctrine of individuation within the species sheds light on the whole area of body and soul relation. According to this teaching, the body is not "this" body without the individual soul which animates it, and the soul is not "this" individual soul without the individual body.

"Man is an organic whole with diversity of members on various levels" (T. Steinbuechel). This unity in organic diversity is the imperishable structure of man's nature and the basis for tasks and duties ever confronting man in new forms. Accordingly, man must shape his life in conformity with the totality of his nature and with the laws governing it and in agreement with its scale of values. He must "become what he is" (Pindar).

Recent theories of typology in the field of personality study have shed considerable light on many phases of our knowledge of the whole man formed in the unity of soul and body. Attempts have been made to determine and differentiate the pathological as well as the sound normal personality by means of bodily criteria.[9] Extensive research has been employed tending to show that determinate physiques, e. g., of the pyknic or the asthenic, correspond invariably to a determinate temperament, and even that the development of the capacities inherent in our dispositions produce distinctive physical modifications.[10] The essential and perennial beauty of the plastic arts consists in their capacity to express the characteristics of the spiritual through a material medium. Nevertheless, the confessor and director of souls is well advised to proceed with great caution in forming judgment based on such externals. Most misleading is the judgment regarding moral or spiritual qualities which is not based on the careful study of the entire conduct of the individual.

The true nature of man's substantial unity in soul and body structure is further confirmed by the scientific investigation of what are called psychogenetic disorders: an entire series of diseases apparently corporeal have their origin in the spiritual element in man. Conversion hysteria is the best known type in this series. Present-day medical science, anthropologically inspired as it is, concludes from these findings that it is not sufficient to treat diseases solely with pharmaceutical prescriptions in conformity with chemical laws. It aims at a therapy of the whole man looking to body and soul. Conversely, in spiritual direction and pastoral care, the director should not look to the soul alone, but keep both soul and body in mind.

Above all it must be realized that psychopaths cannot be cured by the simple expedient of "moral" directives!

From the above we draw the following basic rule for all moral conduct: there is a moral obligation to develop and use all the powers of man, of the body-and-soul composite, all the powers of his spirit in right order and harmony. The neglect, the perversion or abuse of a part to the detriment of the whole order of the human person is sin. Nevertheless, the higher parts of our nature may and must demand the sacrifice of the lower under certain circumstances (cf. Mt 16:26). But genuine sacrifice is always for the benefit of the whole man.

4. The Individual Act as Manifestation of the Whole Person

As we shall see later, in the specifically human act (actus humanus) the whole person expresses himself. However, from the phenomenological point of view a distinction must be made between certain acts and others. Some are simply the expression of moral excellence or moral depravity of the whole person. Others appear rather as the still lingering effects of a previous state or attitude already repudiated, though not entirely abandoned; or more specifically, they may be either the first hint of a defection that will follow or the indication of incipient stages in preparation for a higher moral value as a whole. Acts of this kind do not leave their mark on the whole person on all levels. In any case, every free act tends to lay hold of and express the fulness of our being, whether there is question of progress or decline.

Even the absolutely new beginnings which arise from the inmost depths of our personality (conversions) are not possible without the activity of all the forces of the whole man, body and soul and all their powers. Still there is a very marked difference between the chaste conduct of an entirely pure man, whose purity is reflected in his very countenance, and the isolated act of chastity performed by someone who succeeds just in this instance in suppressing violent tendencies to impurity, still rooted deep within him and not completely overcome. According to Kant, a pure act of the latter kind would be the Ideal Type of the morally good. For us, however, the pure act which springs up like a flower from the chaste soul as an expression of the whole man is a manifestation of higher moral value. In this way the question is answered: is the "good will alone" (Kant) the bearer of moral good or is it rather in a much higher sense the whole person?

An act as such has worth and merit in proportion to its power to harness all available energies of the will and contribute to a greater enrichment of the entire person. But the personal value which ennobles the act manifests itself in it as all the greater the more the moral act springs from the perfection of the whole person. Finally, the value and merit of a particular act will be reckoned all the greater the more completely it belongs to the whole person, the deeper and richer the permanent (habitual) moral source from which it springs. The ultimate valid criterion is the degree of love (of habitual charity) from which the act flows.

To return to the example of the pure act: under certain circumstances an act of purity which is the result of a decisive victory after a desperate struggle may prove for the individual concerned the realization of a supreme triumph of virtue. But his effort, no matter how noble, does not possess the same deep intense purity as the act of a thoroughly and perfectly pure person, e.g., the Virgin Mother of God. If for no other reason than that he does not possess the same deep realization and intimate grasp of the excellence of purity, he cannot give to the virtue the same fervent and profound approval. Therefore chastity flowing from a heart that is profoundly chaste and not constrained to wrestle with temptation, by comparison with purity resulting from the painful struggle with lust, absolutely speaking, is more excellent in moral worth. But it must also be borne in mind that the valiant combat for virtue has its special merit.

When viewed in this light, it is an error to represent the ideal of moral life as a persistent and toilsome struggle, a counterattack against evil (in the sense of the *agere contra*). The painful wrestling with evil is obviously a result of original sin and of our own moral imperfection in the beginning of the life of perfection, but it should be viewed as a necessary transitional stage of moral development rather than as the valid measure of true worth. It is true that as long as we are earthly sojourners still in exile (*in via*), the labor and effort to succeed, the painful resistance to stubborn tendencies to evil, will in some measure always haunt us. Such is our spiritual freedom and such the bounty of more abundant grace that we must constantly inch forward, for we always can and must attain a nobler status in our moral perfection as a whole. But it is evident that in this progress there is no question of an encounter between one essential part of our nature and the other, but of advance and cooperation in a mutual effort toward moral growth, with our habits fruitful in virtuous acts.

If the "Kantian" conception is supported by an appeal to the word of our Lord, "The kingdom of heaven has been enduring violent assault" (Mt 11:12; Lk 16:16), we may promptly refer to that exegesis of the passage which explains the violence endured by the kingdom of heaven as meaning the violence of the enemies of God. The stern injunction of our Lord regarding the self-denial which is an indispensable part of the imitation of the Master (Mt 16:24) and which obviously also means a doing of violence to self, does not at all signify that the Christian must or even may do violence to his body or to the body-soul composite, but that the whole man must summon all his energies and totally suppress all perverse instincts and tendencies and, above all, his spiritual pride, and forge ahead toward the goal of moral perfection.

The Christian attains to harmonious unity and integrity of soul and body, of corporeal and spiritual existence only by means of asceticism, self-denial, assimilation to the crucified Christ. Even though we are constrained "to put off the old man" (Rom 6:6; Eph 4:22), our goal is not a perpetuation of the struggle (the *agere contra*), but conformity with Christ, Ideal and Model of the whole man.

5. *Moral Perfection of the Whole Man through Imitation of Christ*

Complete dedication to the good and the sound development of the whole man which follows from it is assured through the following of Christ. Christ stands before us as perfect man, fully spiritual and devoted to the Father, entirely humane and open to His brethren, to all the joys and sorrows of the world, absorbed in the majesty of the Father and filled with wonder over the lilies of the field. He also calls to us with all our powers. He appeals to all that is in man: intellect and will, heart and spirit. Christ who lives on in history, Christ who is the Church mystically does the same. She is visible and at the same time invisible, supra-terrestrial and fixed in space and time. To this corresponds the ecclesial piety in sacraments and sacramentals and in the Eucharistic Sacrifice. There the whole man and the whole of creation are invited to the chorus of divine praise. Any mystic way that seeks to approach God directly by ignoring the devotion to the Sacred Humanity of Christ and the visible worship of the Church is very suspect.

There is no surer way to the full perfection of the whole man than the perfect following of Christ in the communal life of the Church. In the light of all this, the conscious care and deliberate discipline in the cultivation of our entire moral effort and all its spiritual forces must play a secondary role. The inner harmony of man is realized very largely "astride the action" (Scheler); we might say it spontaneously follows the well-ordered fulfillment of all that is demanded of him as incidental favor of the total imitation of Christ in its full perfection. On the other hand, the well-ordered following of Christ is not possible without the exercise of moral self-control and self-denial (asceticism) in order to counteract any disorder in regard to objective values manifesting itself in our moral acts. Our very impotence and failure, despite sincere efforts, reminds us that we must exert all our God-given powers. We must discipline them or foster them, lowly though they be, for they are always basic and essential to moral endeavor.

II. THE INDIVIDUAL, THE PERSON, THE COMMUNITY
AS SUBJECTS OF MORAL VALUE

We noted above that moral value is not restricted to "the good will alone." It belongs to man in the integrity of his nature, body and soul in their entirety. But to understand man fully, one cannot be content to concentrate on the mere union of essential and component parts. Man must be viewed in the entire context of being and life, in the texture of relations which enrich his life and which offer him the opportunity to develop his inner capacities fully. Man is not an isolated monad, but both individual and member of community.

1. *Individuality*

Human individuality implies uniqueness, realization of an essence in unique, unrepeatable, incommunicable existence. Even according to Thomas, in whose philosophy the concept of the universal dominates, the individual is not an impoverished incorporation of the universal, but actually possesses primacy of value over it.[11] Philosophical idealism, based in this instance on rationalism, dissolves the individual entirely in the universal idea. Interest in the individual and concern for the individual, on the contrary, is a profoundly Christian attitude, and in this sense we understand the solicitude of Kierkegaard for the individual existence.

Individuality and existence are correlative concepts, just as universal and essence. Exclusive preoccupation with the universal is a consequence of pantheistic thinking or of the philosophical attitude which envisages God as pure thought. But the individual flows from the creative will, the loving will of God, who holds the individual dear, who, we well know, creates all things according to the pattern of ideas eternally conceived in the divine Mind. Every individual is God's own thought actualized, for God does not think in universal ideas, as man does. If it is true that each individual being actually reflects the radiance of the creative love of God within itself, surely this is true in an altogether special way of each individual person. Every individual has his own name before God. He exists because God has called him by name. And that name with which God called him is a filial name, the name of God's own child. The person is beckoned by God with ineffable paternal love. For our created intelligence it is in the profoundest sense true: *individuum ineffabile,* the mystery of the individual person, is unfathomable to us.

Every individual man, therefore, possesses the fulness of a unique and singular existence given by the creative will of God. And with the gift of existence is given the task of fostering and cultivating it. Each individual person is given the task of attaining that stature and perfection of moral value which responds to his own uniqueness and incommunicability before God. He must be truly his individual moral self. He must respond to the unique name with which God calls him.

The individual is not a mere "singular instance" of the universal, but a true embodiment of universal nature with the special richness of his own personality. In consequence, his moral life must be the fruition of all the essential and the individual values as well. The person is able to realize his individual potentialities only if he is supported by the universal values and laws which are manifested through the common bond of real community of all who share the same nature. Hence, the following norm is inferred from the relation of individuality to the universal nature: in the fulfillment of his own proper moral task, each individual must be supported by the community, in which alone the universal laws and values of nature are made comprehensible to him.

2. *Individuality and Personality*

Individuality is the expression of the singular being which, though distinct from the universal, at the same time embodies the universal. Personality presupposes the singularity of being in individuality, but implies more. Individuality as such is the valid expression of the richness of existence. But the person must have a clear realization—vital and active —of his own individual being and his relation to the universality and make this the source and focal center of his life activity. To be a person means to have the capacity of removing one's self from all else, to preserve the peculiar and unique "being-oneself" in true inwardness, in order to know the "intimate sphere" (Scheler) in its profoundest depths. The person must, in order to live as a person, be present to himself intimately. Otherwise he could not approach and encounter the Thou, which is the other person.

But it is most richly rewarding to note that the person is never more fully present to self than when giving self generously and unselfishly to another, when the I with its own insight and decision gives itself to the Thou. And conversely, the Thou can be found only in the preservation of that inner intimate sanctuary of both the I and the Thou, in veneration and awe for the Thou, which is infinitely more than a mere "object," more than the subject-matter or term of one's knowledge and desires. To be a spiritual person means to be able to take an objectively universal view of other things, of the "not-I," of that which confronts him. When confronting a Thou, this position of objective regard is called respect.

But being a person does not mean merely being able to hold in regard. It also means to be able through the wonder of knowledge to open one-self to that which is not I (*fieri aliud inquantum aliud,* to be another in so far as it is other). Such grasping of self can be meaningful for the Thou, the unique person, but not if it fails to go beyond conceptual knowledge (which really refers only to essences). It is truly meaningful only if it is concrete sympathetic appreciation, if it is "understanding" in the sense of fulfillment of meaning which is possible only through acts of love and devotion. From this it appears that the relation of one person to another is like that of two poles of reverence and love, the aloofness of respect or reverence and the submission or devotion of love.

The I and the Thou can open themselves to each other, bestow themselves on each other with mutual enrichment, because every individual person is the subject of the wealth of his own individuality. Each is possessed of the "intimate sanctuary" of his own personal individual existence. From the rich depths of genuine individuality flows the power of "seeking self" in aloofness and submission. It is also true that only in the submission to the Thou and in the deference for the Thou does the individual attain to its full maturity of perfection.

The inference is evident: we see that individuality and personality are not ultimately reduced to isolation, but are enrichment of the I-Thou fellowship whose ultimate source is God. Because the God of love has called us by name and at the same time permits us to utter His own name, we are endowed with individuality and personality and can turn to one another as persons.

3. Person and Personality

A person is a spiritual substance in actual and concrete existence. Possessed of spiritual mastery over his own acts, the human person in virtue of human nature itself has the duty to be open to his fellows, to the Thou of his fellow man. Personality then implies fulfillment of this task. Personality means self-mastery lived in all its intimate richness and authentic openness to the world around us, to the Thou of others. If we ask how and wherein the person attains to personality, experience and the nature of person refer us, not merely to the particular Thou of our fellow man, but ultimately to the Thou of God and the fellowship with Him in Christ.[12] And they refer us equally and in all instances to the human community—family, religious community, state—in which man progresses and develops: from person to personality. The question then naturally arises: what is community?

4. Community, Distinct from Mass, Organization, Collective, Society

In the mass the individual merits no special rating. In fact, he does not have special tasks. Absorbed like an atom in the field of mass activity, he is carried away by a system of forces of which he himself is a part, without deliberate will and decision of his own. The leader of the mass has no need for persons, each with the contribution of his own individual nature and particular worth, but for units of force and energy, which allow themselves to be propelled by the dictate of his will. The chief motive force of the mass is psychic contagion. "For the process of infection no spiritual function is required. Still the contagion which affects mental attitudes and leads to mental persuasion always presupposes some degree of intellectual life."[13]

Frequently, however, mass suggestion is bereft of genuine intellectual conviction altogether. And if there should be, whatever minimal thought content may be present is scarcely grasped inwardly by the mind. For the individual absorbed in the mass there is no true acceptance of the mind with the personal conviction of the self holding firmly to the truth. There is rather an infection of the mind produced extrinsically through propaganda. The mass lacks "the fount which lies in the inner depth of soul, the deep positive convictions which the person cherishes for himself and the enrichment of others."[14] Mass is dominated by uniformity, absence of reflection, crassness of standards, hysterical impressionability to the contagion of ideas which inundate groups and individuals in a tide of propaganda.

In organization the individual does not rate as this particular man with an individuality of his own, for he is simply a functionary. The organization, machine-like, does not inquire into the value of the person or about his convictions. It is concerned only with the discharge of his functions. "Functional societies" are dominated by the spirit of organization. They depend for their existence, not on any principle intrinsic to their nature, but on the free choice of goal and purpose made by a group of individuals who create the organization with this in mind. And no member is more important than his contribution toward attainment of the goal arbitrarily established by the group itself. No one is indispensable. Should a member of the group die, he simply ceases to count. At best some forms of legal obligation may still remain in effect regarding him and the group. It is different in the true community: a deceased father or mother remains a tremendous reality in the bereaved family. Family is meaningless without them.

Should the purpose of association be intellectual and cultural, it cannot be achieved through mere pragmatic methods. The associational spirit alone is not equal to the task. In consequence, the association must be transformed into a "community" in order to attain the end sought by such a group. The state, for example, must necessarily adopt the organizational form of an "association," but it can thrive only if in its deepest roots it functions as "community." If the state is reduced to a mere "pragmatic association," it becomes a mere caricature of the true state.

The collective is nothing less than such a caricature, the perversion of community into mere organization, degrading it to the level of mere "association." To this we must add that its mode of operation is identical with that of the mass. Psychic contagion replaces authentic community spirit.

Genuine community is not constituted by the mere pursuit of common objectives, nor is it achieved solely by organization. Community is something presupposed and given, with its roots deep in the very nature of man. Only in community can man attain to the full measure of individuality and personality (that is, become a personality with the fulness of personal values). Community means more than the union of two persons in a relationship of I-Thou. (Exclusive friendship between two individuals is therefore not the model or prototype of community.) True community can be understood only in the light of an intimate grouping of members who refer to themselves as We, and to which each person is drawn by the closest ties of loving solidarity. But this in no way implies that the community life is lived as abstract relationship of the individual person with the community as a whole. Community life is meaningful only if members enjoy the intimate relationship expressed by the personal forms of speech, I and Thou. The bond of love between the individual member and the community, the I and the We, also embraces each individual member in a tender I and Thou relationship, so that each individual in his affection for the whole community loves each and every other member (at least virtually!).

But the Thou must also be met and experienced in the relation of respectful aloofness and loving openness. And in some measure against the background of the Thou there always must be seen the comprehensive We of community, whose individual members are the I and the Thou. In every Thou the I also confronts the whole community, of which they both are parts and in which they are united. The I and the Thou love each other in the We, and in turn love the We through their own mutual love for each other. They dedicate themselves to the community; they realize their responsibility toward it; they are aware that they are supported by the community and at the same time that they are called to support and sustain the community.

The solidarity of the individuals is in the highest degree community-centered. It is characteristic of community, in contradistinction to mass and collective, that in it "individuals are open to each other, that the intellectual attitudes and convictions of the one will not repel the other but rather penetrate into his mind and influence him. . . . Without such a community of thought, true community is not possible."[15] These convictions of the individual in the community are fully community-forming only when they reveal a sense of responsibility, not merely for the individual fellow member, but also for the bond of unity which holds all the group together, the unity of the We. This is what is implied by solidarity.

Community is not a mere plurality of individuals, many I's united by their acceptance of a common obligation. It possesses its own proper nature, its own distinctive ethos, and its own way of life. But it does not have the power of intellectual reflection because it is not a person. It has no I as its center. (Later we shall see in what sense we may say that Christ is the "I-Center" of the Mystical Body.) We infer that the community can be conscious of itself and exercise conscious influence only in the individual members and through the individual members.

5. Person and Community as Bearers of Moral Value

The fact that it is not centered in an I and in consequence is really not what is called a "collective person" (as Scheler would have it) does not prevent the community as such from being the subject of special values and with its members participant in their moral values. The moral worth of the community is manifested in a certain "objective spirit" (apparent in works of art, fiction, poetry, et al.), and it is embodied particularly in the community-minded members imbued with this spirit.

Not only the average man in his spiritual immaturity, but also the mature and advanced person is largely sustained and moulded in moral worth by the community. In fact, the support is mutual. "Not only is the community incapable of fully developing its powers if it does not number among its members individual personalities truly responsive to its needs, but the converse is also true. Only through growth within the community, already existing or created for this express purpose by the personality and suited to the basic needs of its nature, can a personality develop fruitfully."[16] If this holds true of the mature individual, it is all the more valid for the developing personality of the child and the morally immature adult. Many of the good acts of children and even of adults spring not from personal and independent appreciation of moral values, but rather from the moral riches of the community as a whole.

Should authentic values prevail in the life of the community, then social conformity even without personal insight into the values involved has some worth and cannot be equated with the conformity to the perverse conduct in the milieu. Above all, it may not be confused with the contagion of the baser instincts of the masses. More is at stake here than making the simple and obvious distinction between waters drawn from polluted cisterns and the stream flowing from a pure spring. Good behavior of a purely social origin (therefore, not based on direct and conscious personal conviction) is often the experience of the individual, even though it be quite rudimentary, reflecting the current values of the community, so that his moral conduct is still ultimately based on his own good will and intention. At any rate even the purely associative conformity in matters of good conduct offers the individual the most opportune occasion and the most favorable approach to personal contact with true values. The virtuous conduct of an entire community naturally enkindles a true appreciation of good, whereas the associative conformity to a debased social standard will indeed engender evil morals, but never appreciation of true moral values.

If this be true, there can be no disagreement with Bergson when he says that morality has also a social source.[17] Social conformity to the worthy conduct of the group, in sharp contrast with psychic contagion, already implies an orientation toward true values and to a degree also harbors a presentiment of their worth. Here we have appreciation in the intentional order, for there is a sense of true value. Even though such awareness may not be in the mind of the conforming subject, it is very definitely and effectively communicated through the activity of the community itself with its sense of values. Through this sense of values the group tends to influence the social conformist. It strives to penetrate to the very center and core of his moral being—and unlike the procedure of mass psychosis, it does not contact merely the flammable area of sense and emotion from without through the contagion of mass suggestion.

In order to perceive the extent to which our moral values are sustained by the community, it is sufficient to compare a morally zealous individual in a noble community with a member of a base and degenerate one. Despite the most earnest personal initiative and the most strenuous effort, the latter will not be able to make the same fruitful, profound and comprehensive contact with the world of moral values as the member of an ideal community. (Here we abstract altogether from the question of the degree of individual merit and recompense in the sight of God.) But we must say that a member of a good community, assuming equal effort, will be better than one in a base environment. His élan in moral value (that is, the acts which manifest the élan) is his own, but it is sustained more by the community than by himself.

6. Individual Person and Mystical Body as Subjects of Moral Goodness

All that we have established so far regarding personality and community finds its highest fulfillment in the membership of the Christian personality in the Mystical Body of Christ. It is true of the supernatural community of the Mystical Body in an altogether singular manner that it possesses a nature of its own which is distinct from the sum of its members. It is a reality which stands before God as a totality and is loved by Him. Though it is loved in an altogether singular way because of the members who are united in it, the ultimate reason is Christ Himself. Similarly to other communities, the Mystical Body is unified under directive control of one of its members; but this is not all, for Christ Himself is the native center of leadership and at the same time its source of inner power. Christ operates in each member of His Mystical Body, first of all, in fashioning the varied hierarchical structure of the sacred community: His love beckons to the love and obedience of each member. He is united with this community in the loftiest possible solidarity. He thinks and feels with all the members, works for all, suffers for all. His solidarity with us in the expiatory sacrifice of the cross is truly transcendent; it is simply incomprehensible. Christ beholds Himself persecuted or beloved in His members: "Why dost thou persecute me?" (ACTS 9:4); "As long as you did it for one of these, the least of my brethren, you did it for me" (MT 25:40).

Here we have a solidarity immeasurably superior to any mere solidarity of dispositions; we have a true interior, intimate togetherness. Our good actions are ultimately sustained by Christ (and through Him and in Him by His whole Mystical Body). In Him they have their source of grace, their vital center, their power and merit. He is also the source of our knowledge of values. For through word and example He opens our eyes to the good. As the Eternal Truth it is ultimately He who makes it possible for us to have any knowledge of value at all.

Christ lives and acts in us, not merely individually as from I to Thou, but also constantly in the community of the Mystical Body through the We of supernatural fellowship: in the sacraments, in the doctrine, in the guidance and example of the Church. Christ accepts as His own all that we on our part do through Him. And He accepts it and augments its value in the fulness of the Mystical Body in which it continues its effectiveness. Therefore Saint Paul could say that "what is lacking of the sufferings of Christ I fill up in my flesh for his body, which is the Church" (COL 1:24). In virtue of the suffering of Christ the Church even now possesses the absolute fulness as far as her Head is concerned. But only by means of our suffering does she also possess the fulness in so far as this can be attained solely in and through the members themselves. Not only does Christ wish to awaken through our love a continual response of love in the community; He wishes to augment through our meritorious acts the plenitude of grace in the Church and therefore in a certain sense His own plenitude.

Still, the term *collective person,* as applied in the strict sense to the Church by Scheler, is not admissible. Christ is person in His own unique I even apart from the Church. But only in a strictly analogical sense can we speak of the Church as an extension of this "I" of Christ, even though a certain species of "communication of properties" from Christ to His Mystical Body is justified. Obviously such a use is not the same as the communion of idioms of which theologians speak in reference to the two natures in the hypostatic union, in the one divine person of the Word.

According to Gerda Walther, person implies possession of "a center of will and a center of autonomous I." To be centered in the will means that the person possesses interior self-determination. No other person can affect his inner center except through the influence of attitudes from without, for instance, through example, words, and love. But no influence of attitudes can be such as to merge the center, which is the will, with the will of another person, or to transform the will of one into that of another, even through the most intimate union of love. For the only union possible is through mutual exercise of the wills, which remain independent and distinct in their own focal center of personality. Moreover, all influence of Christ's will within His Mystical Body is directed to other centers of will distinct from His. There is even such personal relationship between each member and Christ in the Mystical Body in the performance of supernatural good works under the motion of grace flowing from Christ.

From this we must conclude that Christ as center and source of power in the Mystical Body is not at all the center of will or the center of an autonomous I in His Mystical Body as He is in His own unique divine person. Without doubt He is infinitely more to His Mystical Body than a center of influence and direction. The relation is so singular that it has no analogy in the whole natural order. For Christ acts not only as the historic Leader and Founder through an influence from without, but also from within as Head of the Mystical Body. His influence from within is from His own center of power in virtue of His plenitude of grace, which is inwardly bound up with His personal life and will. Indeed, from His plenitude of grace as Head (*gratia capitis*) of the Mystical Body, Christ not only transforms us into the likeness of His own nature, but constantly beckons to us with His loving will. For the operation of the grace of Christ is not at all a natural impersonal activity like the flow and flood of the tide: grace is distributed by Christ, the Head, according to His own free choice through action of the center which is His own "will" and "I." It does not operate in the soul after the manner of something self-imposed from an autonomous center of power, since the persons who are members of the Mystical Body themselves freely accept or refuse grace through a decision that emanates from their own center—of will and autonomous "I"—although ultimately their freedom, in some mysterious way, is a participation in the freedom of Christ.

In Christ, it is true, there are two distinct centers of decision, two wills, the divine and human, united in one person. Consequently there is but one center of person, one "I," whereas in the moral union of the will of Christ with that of the member of His Mystical Body two wills, two centers of will and I, confront each other.

Undergirded by grace, the disciple of Christ is in a measure united even physically (through an accidental union) to the autonomous center of power of Christ in the Mystical Body; indeed, he does participate in the power of Christ, but he is not united with the autonomous center which is the "I" of Christ. He can say truly that Christ lives in him, but he would consider it blasphemy to equate his own center of being, the "I," with the "I" of the person of Christ. Nor does the Church as the Mystical Body of Christ live simply as such in the center—the "I"—of Christ, but rather in the centers, the "I" of the Head and of each individual member.

All the supernatural values of His Mystical Body (hence, all the good actions of the members) are sustained by the person of Christ; but the actions of the members are not posited by the center, which is the "I" of Christ. They are only moved or stimulated by the center which is the will of Christ, made possible by the center which is His power, but always posited by the center which is the will and the autonomous center, the "I," of the individual member. We must, therefore, distinguish between the subject of merit, the source of power, and the center of decision, the "I" which posits the act.

Christ the Head and His Mystical Body, the Church, are in distinct ways the subjects of our good and our unworthy actions. Our bad acts do not derive from the Christ-center of power and certainly not at all from His person, from the center which is His "I." Evil acts are never a yes to the word of Christ, but always a no. Nevertheless, since they are response to His word and proceed from a member of His Mystical Body, they do not affect Christ as the actions of a person who is stranger to Him: they affect Him as the Head of the member. "He bears our iniquities," not, of course, as though He were guilty of them, for guilt derives exclusively from the center of the person, from the "I" which performs the act. But He bears the burden of them as His own.

The Church as the historic manifestation of the Body of Christ in the diversity of her members shares the guilt and the burden of the sins of the individual members to the extent that the failure of the one arises from the guilt of others. In this sense of the term Christ cannot share in any guilt, because He, the very Fount of all good, can never be a source of sin. When we say the Church shares the guilt of one of her members in so far as it is rooted in the guilt of many others who share the responsibility for the sin, again it must not be thought that the Church herself commits sin and incurs guilt. The Church by her very nature is holy and can never commit sin. Sin is always the act of the individual, and the primary source of guilt is the sinful member of the Church to the degree of his responsibility. But perhaps many others by their sinful deeds and neglect of the good contribute to his guilt and even more toward his indeliberate faults which lower the moral tone of the community.

There is something profoundly mysterious about the interrelation of the various subjects of the morally good and the far-reaching and comprehensive contagion of moral evil within the community. A realization of these facts awakens in us a profound sense of gratitude toward the community which makes the good possible for us, namely, the Church. And we should be singularly grateful to Christ, grateful and profoundly humble. But at the same time, whenever we rejoice over the wide diffusion of the good, the dreadful extension and deep corrosion of moral evil ought to inspire us with great horror. The ravages of evil penetrate to the very center of mankind. They reach even to Christ who permits Himself to be crushed beneath the weight of our guilt, although He Himself is totally incapable of any sin.

7. The Concept of Collective Guilt and Moral Responsibility in the Social Order

The post-war discussions regarding the collective guilt of whole nations focused attention on one particular phase of this complex and thorny problem: to what extent does the individual share the collective guilt of his environment? In order to answer this question, we must distinguish between the moral guilt in the sight of God and the judgment of the individual's conscience, on the one hand, and the juridical concept of guilt on the other. The latter must be clearly understood in so far as it may be the basis for punishment, in the strict sense of that term, and for juridical responsibility and liability before the law.

We have already referred to the various ramifications of guilt, how in some manner it can have its source in the community, how the guilt of the individual in the Mystical Body of Christ affects the whole community, together with the individual, to such a degree that even Christ allows Himself to be burdened by the guilt of the individual sinners and led to the death on the cross. To measure the full extent of the responsibility, we must also take into account the neglect of good acts, in fact, of heroic acts of virtue which singular gifts of grace could oblige some individuals to perform even though there may not be any obligation according to the general norms of law. Precisely the failure to do the heroic, to perform acts of heroic virtue at critical junctures in the social or political order may result in tremendous loss to the community.

Current research in the sociology of religion clearly shows what far-reaching evils do result from failure in the exercise of social responsibility. It is also evident that only through an active and concerted effort for the good can the individual himself and the social groups as such be preserved permanently from the contamination of the surroundings. Whoever fails to close ranks in the united struggle for the kingdom of God delivers himself over to the baneful solidarity of evil. Particularly the élite, those who have received the "five talents" from God, must bear great responsibility for a sound social order and for the whole community.

But it is not the concern of the human community to pass judgment on such individual endowments and the culpable neglect of them. It has no competence in these matters. The Church herself, in the sacred forum of the sacrament of penance, does not pass sentence (even though it be to pardon) in these matters. Only God can call us to account for this failure and in the day of judgment open our eyes to the havoc wrought in the community by our neglect of grace. Even where there is question of a fault which can be judged by men, its subsequent effect in the community falls under human judgment only in so far as the culprit had the capacity to foresee and the obligation to take into account the social consequences of his action (e.g., seduction, scandal). One may with good reason defend himself before men by maintaining that he did not anticipate these consequences, and yet pray fearfully to God: *ab alienis parce servo tuo* (pardon thy servant for the sins of others), have mercy on me, Lord, if by neglect of cooperation with the fulness of your grace, I shared in the guilt of another's sin!

Purely human societies concerned with temporal matters (e.g., states) do not have the competence to judge the matter of responsibility of the individual for the internal consequences of his guilty act. Moreover, in the instances just referred to, there was question of individual, not of a collective guilt, of individual, not of collective centering of will in a sinful decision. Finally, if it should be verified in a particular instance that the crime of one individual, by force of necessity leads to the failure of others, it follows that the guilty man may deserve sharp condemnation, whereas the others cannot be condemned at all, for absence of freedom excuses from all guilt, individual or collective.

Juridically only the crime deliberately committed either by a particular individual or by a group acting in concert merits punishment. Only those who voluntarily cooperate in the actual commission of a crime can be held juridically guilty. Only if each individual member of the community incurs guilt through the one common reprehensible action can there be collective guilt. "Collective guilt" is therefore due to the guilt of each individual and is the sum of individual culpable acts.

Should a community contract obligations or inflict damage culpably through its official ruling authority, then according to principles universally regarded as valid, it can be held jointly responsible for the fulfillment of the obligations and for reparation of the damage. But the imposition of the burden of reparation may not be coupled with discrimination against any particular individual, unless there is evidence that he was actually responsible in some criminal cooperation. Collective guilt in the sense of the post-war indictments does not exist.

Every subject of a nation is obliged to acknowledge the crimes of its leadership and its misguided masses, even before foreign nations and powers. He must also be prepared to cooperate in a coordinate effort to repair the damage inflicted in so far as he is able to do so. But the enemy states, on their part, cannot evade the responsibility for their own acts of injustice. If there is a reckoning of reparations due, this damage which they have inflicted cannot be left out of account. But each individual has the right to repudiate the charge of collective guilt unless his own culpable acts made him accessory to the crime of which his nation is accused. Nevertheless, he should examine himself humbly, in the divine presence, whether he could have prevented much of the dreadful evil if he had been entirely responsive to the call of grace. Finally, a nation as a whole must always beware of the danger of exculpating itself before God when it rejects the indictments of human authority as beyond the competence of any earthly tribunal to sit in judgment. And one might also add that the accusers should fear the guilt of the Pharisee, who thanked God that he was "not like the rest of men" (Lᴋ 18:11).

III. MAN IN HISTORY

The foregoing study viewed man in the dimension of community, which conditions and influences his acts and which in turn is subjected by them to a most profound and far-reaching influence. Now we are to view man in the dimension of history: the past meets the future at the focal point which is the present, the "now" in the historic moment of a man, which is his hour of grace and trial. Amid the forces that lie between the beginning and the end of time he decides his destiny at each temporal moment in the light of the great ages of salvation.

1. *The Historicity of Man*

"Historicity is the polarity in man between being and becoming."[18] Man is subject to history as long as he has not yet reached his eternal immutable goal. He attains it by a process of becoming, of growth, in the direction of good or of evil. "The first law of our human state is the law of finite becoming: man is always orientated toward the complete and perfect expression of himself and of all being."[19] This becoming of man is not effected by the exclusive and immediate actualization of the inner potentialities of man, but through growth in a given historic context of space and time. In each historic moment (in the *kairos*) man is summoned to a realization of his whole self and likewise is brought face to face with the supreme significance of history.

History is to be viewed from the standpoint of the "now" in relation to beginning and end. The historic present (in the language of the Holy Scriptures it is the *kairos,* the hour of grace and trial granted to us by God) reaches out into past and future. The entire past enters the present as destiny. The past has its heritage (biological, cultural, moral-religious) which may be compared to the warp and woof of a rich fabric constantly redesigned into marvelously new and alluring shapes and forms. This treasure inherited from the past is a summons or invitation, and a challenge as well, to the free will of man in the historic moment of the present. Always in the historic present, in the "now," the destiny fashioned in the past summons us, challenges us. We must accept the destiny by our own free decision and within the limits it imposes set our wills to the good.

Freedom can exercise itself only on the materials of the past, on the "destiny" of the historic heritage. The free will must seize this destiny and within its limits render its own unique decision.

To make a decision in the *kairos,* however, means again to pass on the historical heritage of the past new-formed, as fruit of one's own freedom, to the future. Accordingly, in the Now of history man must mould anew his own past and that of his forebears and be responsible for it anew. In this very way he is responsible to the future. The heritage of the past always bears within it the decision of the present, the Now. In the present the call to man is always concrete and particular. But the decision of the Now also anticipates the future and establishes a pattern for the decisions which will follow.

The virtue of penance offers us an illustration. Man as he actually exists historically and concretely, not merely abstractly, cannot without further ado turn from his past and forge ahead into the future. In every instance he must remould the past. Only by a new and present effort to remove the obstacles that have beset his path in the past does he clear the way for a better future. Of course it is also true that only by the right orientation toward the future can we succeed completely in correcting the mistakes of the past. Contrition and purpose of amendment belong together.

Living in history demands of man a realization of his entire space-time position. Because his days are confined to a particular period of historic time, he must be aware that he is conditioned by space and time. But he must also realize that he has the power to mould and fashion the conditions of his surroundings and of the past and in this way in turn form a pattern for the future. History can be grasped only in the light of the coordination of creative individuality, uniqueness of the providential hour, the *kairos,* with the universal laws of nature, with the grand synthesis of the past and future in the Now. Just as the present, the Now, lacks all meaning and force of history without the spiritual power of man to survey past and future, so creative individuality can fashion history only through its incorporation in the universal laws of nature. Without the uniqueness of the present moment, the Now and creative individuality, there would be no history, but mere similarity of before and after and an endless unfolding of events. Without any permanence in the current flowing from past to future, without any constancy of essential forms, we should have sheer discontinuity, and, in consequence, the dissolution of history into unrelated fragmentary instances of time.

2. Historicity and Transcendence

In each of his actions man extends over a span of time from the past into the future and yet in every single moral act he transcends the mere span of time. For every act places him in the dialogue with the eternal God, for each says yes or no to the call of the Eternal. God sends His invitation through history as an appeal to historic activity. But the response to the invitation ultimately is addressed to the Lord of History who transcends history. Thus history in every instance of the present, in every Now, in the *kairos,* is confronted by transcendence. In fact, history taken as a whole becomes history truly only because it is rooted in the transcendent.

History is not true and does not become human until we study its beginning and its end. If the beginning is chance or deterministic evolution without the design of a lawgiver, if at the end again there is only chance or an eternal cycle of recurrent events, then history is no more than the child of chance or a dreadful process of incessant becoming. The transformation of the events bearing on man and his own activity into intelligible history arises from their beginning in the Word of God and their end in the General Judgment. "In the beginning was the Word. . . . All things were made through him, and without him was made nothing that has been made" (JN 1:1ff.). This gives history its dynamic power. It was fashioned by the creative Word of God and entrusted to man to be formed and moulded by him. In every historic event man must, therefore, seek to understand the word which God speaks to him. To be attentive to the message of history is to harken to the Word of God.

The Word of God launched the course of history, which in its entirety lies before Him and can be brought to its conclusion only through Him. This tremendously deep dimension of history is transcended in incomprehensible manner through the entry of the Word of God into history, through the Incarnation, the *In-carnatio,* the becoming man: "And the Word was made flesh, and dwelt among us" (JN 1:14).

3. The Historicity of Jesus Christ

We cannot take the reality of Christ in history too literally. Jesus Christ really became man at a providential moment in history, in a *kairos,* prepared by the Father, and in the historical context of free human cooperation. He became man in the midst of an historical people and subject to all the conditions of space and time. Christ entered into world history as a momentous reality which no historical decision can ignore.[20] Every historical moment must be judged in the light of its relation to this central fact, which is the very heart of history. Even the desire or attempt to slight this most stupendous historical event implies that one has already taken a position of tremendous and far-reaching importance regarding it.

Christ in His glory by means of His grace acts interiorly in the souls of men in our historic present, in the Now of history, hence, in a manner that transcends history. But just as truly does He constantly act upon us, upon our Now, in a manner entirely subject to history in and through His historical Church. And at the end of time Christ Himself will conclude the course of history through His coming and His judgment. Then He will deliver all things to the Father (cf. 1 Cor 15:24). As He entered into history, so Christ also remains ever the Lord of history. As He began history, so shall He end it, so shall He finish and perfect it.

The momentous significance of the entry of Christ into history is evident from the fact that He took upon Himself the burden of the sin of Adam. It was this sin, the fall of our first parent, which had the most dire consequences for the whole human race throughout all its history. And it was the burden of this sin, the consequences of this enormous event, that Christ accepted through His entry into the history of the children of Adam. He permitted Himself to be involved in the horror of this tragic historic occurrence and thus bore, as His own destiny, the fearful burden of the past with all its dreadful effects for the present. And by his acceptance He transformed it and triumphed over it, with the result that the past was given an entirely new meaning through the dolorous relation of Christ to it. Nevertheless, despite the acceptance of its effects by Christ, the reality of the sin of Adam continued its evil influence, although in an altogether new dimension of meaning: basically it was vanquished. Now every Christian has the power to conquer it. In this sense the evil which Christ has conquered and which every Christian can overcome is the Christian's "destiny." His historic act was so enormous and affected his descendants so radically as to become the destiny of every mere son of Adam. In consequence, no individual member of his family could essentially undo it. But Christ triumphed over it, though in an altogether "historic" manner; this is to say that the sin was not simply eliminated from the future history of man, but that, as transformed and as a reality utterly different in import, it entered future history as the "destiny" of man.

4. *Son of Adam and Disciple of Christ*

In his whole temporal existence, in every moment of historic time, in the Now of history, man confronts the immensity of the past and the future, but above all he faces the two most fundamental historic realities, the fall of mankind in the sin of Adam and Redemption through Christ. In every historic moment he is the son of Adam, but much more the child redeemed by Christ and called to follow Him. In union with Christ who both submits to history and transcends history, the son of Adam is able to transform the evil heritage transmitted to him from his first parents. He transforms it by vanquishing the evil in its profoundest depths.

The clash between the first and second Adam in history creates an enormous tension which is at once fearful and fruitful: to gain mastery in this struggle is to render special homage to the Lord of History. This is the task which mankind together with its Head, Christ, must fulfill. And each individual according to his own station and talent must share in the task.

5. *Eschatological Orientation of History*

For a mastery of history man must turn back to that initial instant in which the Creator by His Word laid its foundations and through the order of creation gave mankind its historic potentialities and its role in the course of history. Man must take into account, not only the great possibilities inherent in creation, but also the form and shape into which they were moulded in the past through Adam and Christ, through all the followers of Adam and the disciples of Christ. Man must grasp the Now of the situation as *kairos* (the providential moment of decision given with the grace of God) and in it prove himself before God. This test means more than the mere preservation of the order of creation and the full acceptance of the historical heritage. It also opens to man the opportunity for the encounter with God through the historic and trans-historic union with Christ.

Even profane history, as it is usually called, is to be viewed in this same light, because the *Heilsgeschichte* has entered into the world history through Christ. "The way of salvation is within the bounds of history, never a departure from it, until the final summons by death. But it is the critical test within history. History is a genuine category of reality and the whole of reality in all its categories must be brought under the sway of the

Lord."[21] "History is not a meaningless interlude between beginning and end. If it were no more than a mere interlude, beginning and end could not be taken seriously. And our Saviour would not have appeared in its midst."[22] History has reference not solely to beginning and the past. It is also linked with the future, with the growth and development of the Kingdom of God which is to continue until the day of the Lord, in fact, until the end of all history, the *Eschata*. At the end of all history and accordingly at the end of the Now there will be the second coming of Christ, the general judgment, the new heaven and the new earth. All that we do on earth, our whole activity in the setting of history, is good only if it is orientated toward these "last things," the *Eschata*. And this orientation is impossible without an ever recurring reflection on these last things, without contemplation of our *kairos* in the light of the day of the Lord. Just as the first coming of Christ, His *kairos,* considered as the fulness of time, can be understood only in the light of His second coming, the completion of time, so also our historic existence must be viewed in the context of the first and second coming.

As our moral activity becomes a part of the texture of history from the beginning through the creative Word, woven into the heritage of the first and second Adam, so too must the total reality of the present moment be moulded and fashioned with a view, not only to the immediate future, but also to the end, the *Eschata,* which already looms on the horizon, for the Saviour is coming.

IV. MAN AND WORSHIP

1. *Man's Vocation to Worship*

The first meaning and purpose of creation is the glory of God. Man as intermediary between mere matter and pure spirit, man as microcosm, should lend to the voiceless jubilation of creation the rational utterance of praise, and in adoration and thanksgiving raise his voice to God. As long as man carried out this priestly role in paradise, God dwelt in the garden of the earth among men as in a temple of His glory. Adam's fall was disobedience to God and also rejection and abandonment of his priestly task and vocation to worship God. Through disobedience man became profane, henceforth incapable of offering acceptable adoration and praise to God. Thereupon the world also, though still remaining entirely God's own property, was profaned by man who had fallen from his priestly vocation. It became entirely subservient to human ends and purposes and no longer served man, as it should, in the adoration of God. Since man had profaned his "natural" priestly dignity, all creation under him also failed to fulfill its mission of worship.

2. Restoration of Man and the World to Cult through Christ

What mankind lost in Adam was abundantly restored in Christ. In Him the whole of creation was crowned with the most sublime dignity of priesthood. Mankind was consecrated anew (at least radically and in vocation). If the Incarnation was priestly consecration of Christ through the anointing in the Holy Spirit, then His sacrificial death was the supreme act of priesthood and the preparation for the consecration of the Church as a whole, as well as of the individual man for priestly activity with Him. Our union with Christ, the High Priest, is effected in the sacraments, in which the Holy Spirit continues the work He initiated in the anointing of the Messias.

Christ is the supreme sacrament: through Him and in Him we have the most evident and perceptible sign and pledge of the divine favor; in Him mankind is consecrated and admitted to filial cult in adoration and love and is assured of the acceptance of its worship. The seven sacraments unite us with Christ the supreme sacrament and the High Priest. For the individual and the Church as a whole, the sacraments are the fulfillment of the unique consecration of mankind in Christ. Especially the sacraments which imprint a character (baptism, confirmation, Orders) assimilate the recipient to Christ, the High Priest, and confer the special priestly rank and power essential to the exercise of the divine cult. Just as Jesus is made High Priest through the anointing in the Holy Spirit (the Messias, Christ), so are the faithful anointed in the Holy Spirit through the sacraments and thereby assimilated to Christ the anointed one, the High Priest. As a result, all the activity of sacramental man, even the fulfillment of his mission in the world, bears the seal of the divine cult in the most exalted sense of the word. It partakes of his worship of God. For to be anointed by the Holy Spirit ultimately means nothing less than to be made to share the inner divine jubilation with which the Father and the Son eternally rejoice in the Holy Spirit (the jubilee of divine love).

By the very nature of things a deep abyss separates the "profane" from the "holy," all created things from the uncreated God, who by contrast to all creation (despite any analogy of being) is "totally other" (Rudolph Otto), before whom all creatures must tremble in awe, even though at the same time they feel themselves drawn to Him from the primordial depths of their being. Though sacramental consecration in no wise erases the essential distinction between creature and Creator, sacramental man ceases to be "profane"; he is admitted to the intimacies of divine love; he is encompassed with the radiance of the holiness of God. Indeed, anointed by the Holy Spirit, he shares in the mystery of God's own inner love.

3. Sacramental Piety and "Sacramental" Morality

Through the sacraments we are granted participation in the holiness of God. This is immediately only a sacral sanctification (note the antithesis between profane and sacral). Distinct from the sacral is the so-called ethical holiness (analogous to the Old Testament distinction between Levitical or legal holiness and moral purity). Through sacramental consecration the Christian is admitted into the intimate circle of divine holiness and cult, not merely externally through some fictitious device and declaration, but by inner assimilation to Christ in His priesthood, which, however, is not yet full and perfect union with Christ, Head and Redeemer, and the initiation into the life of the triune God through sanctifying grace. Without the grace the Christian can surely be validly consecrated for the cult (*sacer, not sanctus;* sacral, not holy), although the very consecration becomes a reproach to one who receives it unworthily or lives in contradiction to it through mortal sin. From this it is evident that sacral holiness as given in the sacraments demands also the holiness of grace, which is impossible without some measure of moral or ethical rectitude.

Moral rectitude is moral holiness (*sanctitas*) if it is more than the achievement of man's struggle, if it looks beyond his own perfection, if it springs from the sacral consecration through the efficacy of divine grace.

Moreover, the whole moral duty of man in the secular order must be looked upon as participation in the divine cult. The entire edifice of sacramental-cultal morality must rest on the foundation of sacramental piety. The sacraments are not intended as mere episodes or interludes in the life of the Christian. They are rather the leaven for his whole mission on earth, imparting to it its true and full meaning. It is more than a casual call which invites the Christian to praise God in the holy of holies from time to time. He is called to Christ and to divine cult as to the constant source of his vocation and power. From this center he receives the summons and the vigor, in an ever newer and deeper sense, to bring to the service of God, in fact, into the temple of the triune God, himself with all his activity and the world entrusted to him.

Viewed in this light moral disobedience is more than mere transgression of law or disorder in creation. It is a refusal of worship, profanation of the world destined to give glory to God, attack on the high priesthood of Christ, to which the disobedient man still remains intimately bound, if not indeed by free decision of will, still by reason of his whole being.

Because man to the innermost depths of his being is destined for divine cult, because the entire mundane order and the order of salvation are orientated toward the divine worship, therefore the moral disobedience of man is not only apostasy from the true cult, but it is always false worship, inauguration of rival cult. Perhaps in the light of this truth we can best understand the elemental dynamism of superstition and the fanatical dedication of sinful man to his false ideals, to idolatry, money, power, honor. Man is either a priest of God with Christ through the anointing of the Holy Spirit or in his sin a "priest" of the fallen Angel of Light.

4. Sacrifice of Christ: Supreme Expression of Worship

The supreme manifestation of cult is the sacrifice of Christ on the cross. The sacrifice of Calvary is the cultal act of perfect obedience and loving devotion to God the Father. It is the most perfect restoration of man and the universe in the temple of divine glory. In the performance of our duty to offer worship to God, we are nourished by union with the sacrifice of Christ on the cross, a duty which is fulfilled and completed in bearing the cross and suffering with Him. The suffering and hardship of the Christian's toil must bear the stamp of the Eucharistic sacrifice. Then it has the dignity and value of a cultal (priestly) act.

All the seven sacraments are fruit of the sacrificial death of Christ, issuing from the riven side of the Saviour. Through His supreme priestly act the Lord redeemed the world, rededicated it to the divine cult, consecrated mankind anew, and made the universe a temple for the adoration of God. The sacraments communicate to the Church and to her members individually the consecratory power of Christ's death. Therefore they all require of man that he constantly unite himself anew to Christ carrying the cross. And they give him the power to do so. The sacraments manifest their full meaning and efficacy in the divine cult only when the Christian receives them as summons to the imitation of Christ crucified and as source of the grace to follow Him on the way to Calvary, as means to bring glory to the Father. Through the grace of the sacraments and the union with the sacrifice of Christ every trial and joy of the Christian shares in the cultal value of the sacrifice of Christ on the cross and in His high priestly prayer and in the jubilee of His praise of God the Father.

5. Man's Comprehensive Vocation to Worship

The diverse aspects of human nature which we explained in the second chapter are not without their bond of inner unity. They are mutually interdependent and form a synthesis. For this reason we can rightly appraise the whole depth and breadth of the cultal character of man only by a comprehensive survey of all the essential traits hitherto discussed.

The sacraments affect the whole man in all the dimensions of his being. The whole man is taken up in the sphere of the divine cult and influenced by the efficacy of the sacraments. The sacramental sign consecrates all of inanimate nature and especially man's own senses. The invisible grace signified by the sacramental sign affects the whole human person. Man in the profoundest depths of his being possesses a capacity to become like God. This potentiality is actuated by the grace of the sacrament which assimilates him to the death and Resurrection of Christ. It unites him most intimately with Christ, who is the substantial image of God the Father.

The sacraments do not lay hold merely on the individual person. By their inmost nature they are sacraments of the community, of the Mystical Body of Jesus Christ. Through the sacraments the human person grows into the community of the Church. Especially is this true of the three sacraments which imprint a character. Baptism and confirmation make men Christians through membership as citizens and soldiers in the Church. The sacrament of Orders is entirely at the service of the cultal community of the body of Christ. Penance is reconciliation not only with God, but also with the Church. The Eucharist is union with Christ and at the same time *agape,* banquet of love, the bond of love in the community. Sacramental marriage forms a perpetual bond between two human beings by uniting them in a singularly intimate manner with Christ and the community of His Mystical Body. Marriage creates in the Church a "church in little" (*ecclesiola* or miniature church) as a community member in the universal Church and thus provides for her natural growth and expansion. Extreme Unction as completion of penance prepares man for union with the Church triumphant and eternal resurrection.

The sacraments encompass man in the entire dimension of his historic and trans-historic existence. They embrace the whole span of man's life on earth.[23] Every sacrament links man with the High Priest, risen and glorified, and also with His death and Resurrection as historic reality and source of grace. As types of things to come they have an eschatological meaning and direct the Christian to the end of history and the celestial realm transcending history. Particularly the sacraments introduce the Christian into the profound and significant depths of history opened to us by the Incarnation of the Word of God. The sacraments effect in us the historic and trans-historic triumph over the sin of Adam and bring us into contact with the center of all history, with the fulness of time between the death of Christ and the second coming.

Moral decision is always rendered by the entire man, who is both individual and member of community, living within the context of history, dedicated to the divine worship. And every moral decision enters into all these dimensions and affects man under all these aspects, a point to be borne in mind when we study the place which the moral decision of man occupies in his freedom and knowledge of values in the following pages.

CHAPTER FOUR

THE TRUE BASIS OF MORALITY

IN THE previous section we surveyed the setting of moral activity. We presented the background of tremendous dimensions which provides the setting for moral decision and personal moral growth and development. Moral responsibility embraces both body and soul. Its roots are sunk deep in every sphere of the social order; its effects are experienced in every social area. Its source and effects can be traced to the past, into the depths of history and the *eschata* of history. Man with full moral responsibility stands in the shadow of the divine majesty through the obligation of divine cult. However, the direct and immediate source of moral responsibility is the free will of man which can be considered morally free and responsible only in the light of man's knowledge of values, his own inner disposition and spirit, his own conscience.

I. HUMAN FREEDOM AS BASIS OF MORALITY

1. *The Essence of Freedom*

We recognize the true nature of our freedom when we perceive values and experience the challenge of the morally good. Often we are brought to the keenest realization of our freedom by the very revolt of evil which we confidently trust we can resist and master. Freedom is not enunciated in the necessity of the Must, but in the Ought of the good, not in the triumph of sin, but in the temptation to embrace it. Freedom exists only in those profound depths of personality where the convictions are formed and positions taken, accepting the divine summons or revolting against it. In essence freedom is the power to do good. The power to do evil is not of its essence. Freedom is present only where there is the power to overcome evil. Indifference to good or evil is not a quality of liberty as such, but only of the finite and limited liberty of man. The power to do good, however, derives from the likeness of man to God, from the created participation in the divine freedom. When man is infallibly preserved from sin through the action of efficacious grace, he suffers no loss of liberty, but attains a superior power of freedom, which in itself transcends the normal condition of his finite nature.

a. Human Freedom in the Divine Image

Just as God is the Lord of the entire universe because He created it, so is man the ruler of the universe because God created him in His own likeness and placed him over it. "God created man to his own image: to the image of God he created him: male and female he created them. And God blessed them, saying: 'Increase and multiply and fill the earth, and subdue it, and rule over the fishes of the sea, and the fowls of the air, and all living creatures that move upon the earth.'" (Gn 1:27f.). God is Lord and Creator of the world. He does not spend Himself in creation and governance of the universe, but He celebrates His eternal Sabbath rest, His absolute blessedness apart from the world. In like manner the freedom of man is not spent in the task of ruling the world. If he is not completely absorbed in this mundane effort, if he is not taken up altogether in things of the world, but constantly raises his eyes to the Sabbath joy of God, then his freedom is safeguarded and preserved.

God's liberty is absolutely circumscribed only by His own great glory, for there can be no motive for His free acts outside Himself. Analogously God's creature, man, made in the divine image, is constrained by nothing beyond his own freedom, for nothing altogether extrinsic to himself can determine or force his will.

Just as God transcends the world and yet preserves and governs it immanently, so in an analogous manner the free will of man transcends the composite of soul and body (only analogously, for there is no complete independence), and yet governs the entire body-soul structure with all the human urges and drives through the most intimate coordination with them. Similarly in the pattern of the divine causality, as God is the First Cause and has no cause outside Himself moving Him, so it is with man, though in an analogous and limited manner. Always dependent on God in all his acts, he is still a kind of first principle, a manner of "first cause." "He in himself is the cause that in one instance he becomes grain, in the other chaff."[24]

Freedom is always fresh and new, always a creative beginning. It pertains to its essence that the free act is never univocally predetermined. But the free act itself, though on an entirely distinct level, is the first determining cause of the still undetermined movement of the will. It is really a new beginning, which is truly "creative" in so far as it is posited new and for the first time by the will. But it is not blind and irrational. Rather, as God creates according to the pattern of ideas, so also the creative new beginning in the free act decides according to motives, according to guiding ideas.

b. Human Freedom, Participation in the Divine

Human freedom is the capacity to take one's stand in accepting or rejecting God's call to us, but only by virtue of a participation in the divine freedom. The free human act produces itself, is a cause of itself (*causa sui*), though always dependently, for it depends on the First Cause. Even though absolutely speaking man himself in his voluntary act is the cause of his sin and the "first cause of the fall from grace,"[25] he can be so only by force of the actuation of his freedom to do good through the exercise of the causality which comes from the First Cause, God. Sin as defeat of freedom is a diminution of the sharing of divine freedom and therefore a lessening of human freedom itself. Conversely, the highest participation in the divine freedom is acting entirely under the influence of divine grace.

Altogether incomprehensible, especially to the science which relies solely on principles of natural causality, human liberty remains ever a great mystery, for it rests on the still greater mystery of God's own freedom. Most obscure in this mystery of human freedom is its participation on the one hand in the divine freedom and its profound inviolability on the other. It partakes of God's freedom and yet is so highly esteemed by God Himself and so utterly and inviolably its own that man can say no to God by force of the very freedom God grants him.

The grandeur of human freedom is manifested in the most exalted fashion when it surrenders entirely to the guidance of grace and thus becomes capable of saying yes to God, in filial obedient love in and through Christ. The dizzy height of freedom towering over the abyss of evil manifests itself in the terrifying and incomprehensible power of decision against Christ, which expels the Spirit of God, the loving source of liberty itself.

2. *Degrees of Freedom*

The power of freedom is effective on many levels, highly diversified in breadth and depth. Human freedom is greatly restricted in its scope by our biological and spiritual heritage and by our environment through the attraction of motives or ideals and the suggestion of lines of action. It is also circumscribed in many ways by the effects of our previous conduct and former free decisions.

The power of freedom is granted us only in germ. Its seeds implanted in us must grow from within through the development of person into personality. This growth and expansion is through the full exercise of the inherent capacity of the will tending to the good. Freedom in man is the power by which he transcends himself in his own act, attaining thereby— albeit gradually and progressively—a new and higher freedom. But neglect of the practice of true freedom (freedom in omission) or failure to exploit it fully will result in atrophy of liberty. If practiced only in the failure which is sin, it is progressively reduced to impotence for the good and ultimately impotence for true freedom altogether. On this point it is necessary to caution against any delusion arising from the force of passion in doing evil. It is true that freedom, if it is not to become impotent, must press the passions into its service. But the characteristic power of human freedom is to guide and direct them; its deepest impotence is to be over- come by them. Even though the utmost force of passion is manifested in evil, still the power of freedom itself is no greater than its practical capacity to channel the forces of passion into the good.

Freedom can be so far lost that the spirit becomes entirely the slave of base drives, free and responsible in its enslavement only because of prior voluntary decisions made when the capacity to choose the course of good was not yet vitiated. But still we must hold fast to the conviction that, so long as we are pilgrims on earthly sojourn, God will never deny the grace of returning to Him. To everyone still possessed of normal mind and will He graciously grants the power to take the first step toward conversion. But a new guilt is always incurred if the sinner delays his conversion.

Freedom can also attain the stage in which man surrenders entirely to the guidance of the Spirit. "Now the Lord is the spirit; and where the spirit of the Lord is, there is freedom" (2 Cor 3:17). There is no greater freedom than that of the children of God, who have freely risen above the impotence of sin, thrown off the shackles of the slavery of Satan, and voluntarily submitted to the law and yoke of Christ; who have liberated themselves from the selfish quest of self and from the law as a mere instrument of self-righteousness, and instead have placed themselves entirely in the service of the Kingdom of God. They have freed themselves from the universal law as the sole and ultimate norm of morality and without constraint of law have accepted the joyous responsibility of seek- ing what is most perfect in the situation in which God has placed them;

they have cast aside all desire of resisting the guidance of the Holy Spirit and have thus arrived at the very summit of freedom in obedient service to God.

Freedom is both a gift from the divine bounty and a divinely imposed task; it is both gift and burden. It is like a bud with the urge to blossom forth and ripen into rich fruit of virtue. But like the bud it can wither away, fail to blossom and ripen. Then the power of virtue is lost, and freedom becomes impotent. Freedom which makes man responsible for his actions is itself a noble trust committed to man, a tremendous responsibility.

3. *Freedom and Law, Freedom and Motive*

God's freedom knows neither law nor limitation outside Himself, but it would be rash to hold that it is in the slightest capricious or arbitrary. It is governed by the inviolable law of the sanctity of the divine essence. God's free will is under the sovereign law of divine love. Similarly human freedom, if it is true freedom in action, is not submission to the coercive pressure of external force, but self-fulfillment through inner love of the good in accordance with the pattern of the divine holiness which is the eternal law (*lex aeterna*) reflected in man's own nature (*lex naturalis*). Obviously God's freedom is infallibly effective in accordance with the law of His sanctity, whereas man on his earthly sojourn is in constant danger of lapsing from the lofty eminence of obedience to law and thereby marring the integrity of his liberty. But he is still free even in his defection from the integrity and ideal of freedom, free in breaking the hedge of freedom which is the law and lapsing into the slavery of license. The law is the warning which safeguards liberty. It grants liberty and imposes a task upon it: law is both gift and summons to duty. The more the Christian grows to maturity in the liberty of God's children, the more does the law of God unfold itself to him as a living safeguard of love. It is the hedge that encircles the golden center of love. Only those who possess the liberty of the children of God have real insight into the true nature of law, which in its depths is loving dialogue with God.

In the divine activity God's creative freedom is in accord with the pattern of his eternal ideas. Therefore human freedom, fashioned in the divine image, is all the greater the more man's activity is motivated by clear and evident ideals. Just as God Himself cannot act outside Himself without the light of His own love, so too man cannot exercise his freedom without motives. And as God in His free creative activity chooses from the infinite treasure of His eternal ideas, so man (analogously) within certain limitations chooses among a diversity of motives. He can elect from among various good motives, preferring one to another. He can choose between the evident good and the enticement of darksome passion, choose the illusory allurement of sheer pleasure and profit or follow the attraction of the morally good motives pleasing to God, often obscured by the vain pleasure of sense.

The crucial point in question regarding liberty is not whether the external act flows freely from the inner source (from the *actus elicitus,* the elicited act), but whether this inner source itself is pre-determined by the free will itself or by something else. The decisive question is this: is freedom unequivocally determined by the motives which press upon it, or does it transcend these very motives and remain free in choosing (though it cannot make any choice without motive)? The will is not necessitated. It determines itself in making its own final or ultimate decision, whether it permits itself to be drawn to the basically good and lofty or abandons itself to the illusive splendor of self—self-glory or self-seeking. Once this final or ultimate decision has been made (i.e., the willed choice of what shall be the ultimate and decisive goal of life), the motives directing one's particular actions still leave room for freedom within their own area and according to their own scope of influence, so that the will is not necessitated by them, but itself selects from among them and directs them in accordance with the ultimate goal (assuming, of course, the limitations imposed by psychological laws).

If a motive thrusts itself upon the spirit of man with such insistence as to create an abnormal psychological tension which diverts the free will from every other possible alternative, then psychic coercion has removed the conditions of freedom. It is quite a different matter if the will with undivided force of freedom is motivated by a clear and lofty incentive. The more profound the motivation, the more potent is the freedom. In the choice and nurture of true ideals lies the final decision of freedom.

4. *Education to Freedom*

From what we have just said, it is evident that any formation in obedience which merely domineers by means of imperatives, without furnishing insights and motivation, breaks the free will, at best "breaks it in," but does not truly educate it. Though liberty is in part a matter of exercise and use (of true freedom), it is still much more a matter of fostering motives with insight and love. This throws light upon the importance of meditation in the spiritual life. Education to obedience springing from the inmost source of liberty must be based on motivation rather than command. Even though at first the mind cannot provide an insight into the inmost nature of the good itself, still there must always be the wholesome motivation of noble authority and the gradual clarification of the intrinsic values and a growing perception of the worth of the commandment.

Genuine formation in obedience is without doubt also education in the law (in the established norm of the good), but it is even more initiation into liberty which goes beyond the universal law, into that liberty which is born of the insight into the good and of love for the good and for that which is always more perfect. Freedom unfolds its capacity as it exercises itself in obedience, but it must be obedience of the spirit. And this is impossible without the true spirit of independence and self-mastery. The spirit of true independence (virtue of freedom) reigns when the Christian acts even without bidding, when he possesses the disposition and will to obey even though there may be no mandate or precept. The spirit of obedience is marked by free initiative and acceptance of responsibility even without command.

5. The Limit and Extent of Liberty

Man's liberty is relatively narrow in the scope of its activity, though, as explained above, this scope can be significantly and gradually broadened. But it can likewise be restricted and narrowed through our own fault. Scope, impress, limit of freedom are all determined by one's own individual temperament, by the historic heritage, by the moral level of environment, by the surrounding communities. The "destiny" of man sets the bounds of his liberty, but it also determines the tasks and duties and broadens the scope of the free actions. Man must accept his destiny in freedom, bear up with it, and at the same time master it.

Freedom is effective not merely on the immediate level of decision or in actual intention (*intentio actualis*). In every moral act, besides the present actual free decision, in some way the prior decisions, the predeterminations, the prejudices make themselves felt. The virtual intention (*intentio virtualis*) is the prolongation of previous decisions which are still effective in their influence until they are revoked or completely lose their dynamic power. Even in conversion, which is the act of renouncing or repudiating the past and revoking the prior false decisions of the will, they still may exert a very considerable influence as false attitudes or dispositions (examples are the lowering of esteem for true values due to mental dullness or partial blindness in this important area, superficiality in positive value judgments). Only steadfast and determined personal intervention will enable us to deprive these prior decisions of their force and render them impotent.

It is likewise true that previous decisions of our will often exert no influence on subsequent series of acts either because their effectiveness is suspended for the moment, even though the past may not have been actually repudiated or renounced, or—and this is usually the case—because they are not our present concern. However, for this very reason they can reassert themselves when occasion arises, since the disposition and tendency (*habitus*) still persist.[26] The unrevoked prior intention or attitude of mind which does not influence the subsequent acts is a habitual intention (*intentio habitualis*). But should it again become efficacious, it is no longer merely a habitual, but a virtual intention by which we again influence the subsequent acts.

We speak of a presumed intention or readiness of will (*intentio interpretativa*) in those instances of doubt when we have no evidence that the intention was ever actually made, but reasonably presume that it was. From the entire attitude of the individual concerned we have reason to assume that he would have made such an act (the actual intention) if the matter had been placed before him for decision, or that he actually did so. An interpretative intention is real and effective in so far as it is rooted in this attitude of the Christian and is expressed in acts corresponding to it.

6. *Extent of Responsibility in Free Decision*

Man is directly accountable for the entire object of his free decision, whether it be through positive act or through failure to act. In fact, the consequences of omission can be as important and as far reaching as the effects of the positive acts, or acts of commission. Man is responsible, not merely for what he directly chooses or decides upon, but also for the other objects which are mediately or indirectly within his choice. In this way they fall within the scope of his intention. Responsibility, in fact, extends to much which is not included in his particular intention as means or end (*voluntarium in se* or *voluntarium directum*), but which is foreseen as a mere result of the act intended without being directly intended or sought (*voluntarium in causa* or *indirectum*).

An example: a drinker knows how he will act when he is under the influence of drink. He may indulge in profanity, resort to quarreling or fighting, engage in immoral conversation. Despite his attempt to assure himself as he takes his drinks, "I just want to enjoy a drink or two," he is still the voluntary cause responsible for all the resultant deviations in moral conduct precisely because he voluntarily makes himself their cause. He freely does the act and foresees, in a general way at least, the effects which will ensue. The guilt, however, and it is important not to overlook this point, is not so serious as the guilt of the premeditated offense. One who consciously seeks after a sinful object is far more culpable than one who is guilty as cause. The malice is greater in the former instance because there is a greater freedom of will in the choice of evil.

The mature man must have a keen realization of the profound and far-reaching influence of his moral conduct on his own personality as a whole and on the community, both in the immediate present and in the future. And if he does good or evil with this background of general knowledge, he also assumes the responsibility for his act and its consequences. He must bear the burden of blame for his bartering with evil and is responsible for the evil consequences of his acts, even though he may deplore them. However, the difference between deliberate choice of evil and the conscious but regretful acceptance of it in this form of package deal is quite apparent.

Responsibility for the consequences of such decisions is all the weightier the more certain and immediate is the consequence or effect which is foreseen, though not intended. The certainty is greater if the cause is direct (*causa per se*) than if it is indirect (*causa per accidens*). The effect is more immediate if the cause is a proximate or immediate cause (*causa proxima vel immediata*) than if it is only mediate or remote (*causa mediata vel remota*). There is a vast difference between an act which physically and necessarily produces an effect as its efficient cause and a moral impulse given to the free act of another.

One cannot entirely prevent one's own good or even one's obligatory acts from accidentally (*per accidens*) or remotely (*remote*) producing many evil effects. Some of these are physical, such as suffering and hardship; others are moral, as vexation and scandal to others (actions with double effect). Still there is an obligation in conscience to prevent the evil effects if one can do so without offending against what is right in the

particular situation in which one is placed, or against the good which one
is obliged to do. If the act as such and immediately (*per se et proxime*)
produces an undesired evil effect, then only proportionately serious reasons
(fulfillment of an obligation, attainment of a higher necessary good) can
justify the act despite the evil effects. But all the circumstances must be
seriously pondered. And under no condition may evil effects which in
themselves are unlawful as ends of our action, be employed as means even
for the attainment of a good end. Nor is it licit to will them or approve
of them subsequently in the completion of the action. Moral evil may
never be made the direct object of the deliberate free act of our will.[27]

7. *Diminution and Destruction of Liberty*

a. Interference with Liberty: Violence

A purely physical intervention proceeding from some external agent
can destroy the freedom to perform an external action (*actus imperatus*),
but not the liberty of interior decision. Violence or force, in any instance,
if it is bound up with the refined cruelty of present-day methods of
psychological torture, can constitute a serious temptation and often also
contribute toward a notable diminution of inner freedom.

An example of violence is that of the sinful attack on a virtuous girl:
by firm exercise of her freedom she can adhere steadfastly to chastity in
her mind and heart and also shun every wilful word and deed contrary
to the virtue. The result of the violence to which she is shamefully subjected is not really a human act (*actus humanus*) on her part, but passive
sufferance. Therefore, it is neither voluntary nor imputable (*actus imputa-
bilis*) except in so far as the inner decision of her will may not have been
sufficiently firm and the external resistance may have fallen short of the
vigor possible and necessary in the particular circumstances.

b. Diminution of Freedom: Fear

Fear which arises entirely from without (*metus ab extrinseco*) can
weaken or destroy freedom of the will only to the extent that it produces a
partial or total paralysis of the powers of the soul (*metus ab intrinseco*). In
some instances sheer exterior force or the threat of force can so completely
unsettle man inwardly that he is no longer master of his own inner acts
and still less of his external actions.

Fear which is overcome by freedom (*metus concomitans*) reveals the power of free will. Fear which precedes decision of will (*metus antecedens*) does not in itself lessen liberty and accountability. Surely it is possible that extreme fear stifle freedom and responsibility temporarily and yet not destroy imputability for the simple reason that guilt may have been incurred through the prior failure to control incipient fear when mind and will were still capable of facing the menace.

The new psychology distinguishes between fear and anxiety: fear knows exactly the reason for fright and is in direct proportion to the cause producing it, neither greater nor less. Consequently, control over it is more readily within man's grasp. But anxiety is the haunting formless fear in which the individual does not know what he fears, but is just afraid.[28] Fear becomes anxiety when one succumbs entirely to it, so that the feeling of anxiety (acute anxiety) is out of all proportion to the cause of fear.

Anyone who violates a commandment binding him in conscience because of fear of temporal loss or of punishment is guilty of sin. Even the menace of torture or death can never justify any act in itself sinful, such as apostasy from the faith or denial of the faith. But if fear arising from anxiety totally or partially unbalances the mind, then freedom is destroyed or diminished and consequently the guilt is entirely absent or is diminished. Fear of a great evil or loss out of all proportion to the gravity of the law itself excuses from any positive law, for such laws do not bind so strictly as to require their observance even at a great loss or under great difficulty.

What is true of fear holds also for the other passions—sadness, joy, anger.[29] But the passion which is controlled and channeled properly by the free will increases the force of the free action.

c. Diminution of Freedom: Unbridled Concupiscence

In so far as inordinate concupiscence precedes the free decision of the will (*concupiscentia antecedens*), it can diminish liberty, but it is a constant challenge to the full assertion of freedom and the mastery of passion. When passion disturbs the mind (above all, through the imagination) to the extent that the use of reason is entirely lost, it also destroys freedom altogether. But passion to which the will has freely consented (*concupiscentia consequens*) strengthens the voluntariness of the action through its organic drive. Because the degree of freedom at the moment of decision is above all the determining factor in the gravity of sin, the sins of weakness committed under spell and lure of passion are not so grave as sins of malice to which the will freely consents with cold and dispassionate calculation. We must differentiate between the force of will as such (*voluntarium*) and the power of free decision (*liberum*), which stand in inverse relationship to each other under the abnormal conditions referred to. Moreover, in drawing the line between sins of malice and sins of weakness, the distinction of motives is highly significant, for the motive largely determines the merit or demerit of the act.

The impulses of passion and concupiscence which precede the free decision of the will are devoid of all moral guilt. But there may be a degree of culpability, for the very passion in evil concupiscence is often the effect of previous sinful conduct. Similarly evil impulses are frequently voluntary in their source or cause. In the language of the schools, impulses which have not been brought under the discipline of reason and free will are "non-deliberate impulses" (*motus primo primi*). Disordered impulses which are not fully deliberate because distraction or confusion of mind disturbs the attention or because they lack the full and complete approval of the will (*motus secundo primi*) can never be more than venial sin. For every grave sin is a perfectly free act. Only the deliberate evil concupiscence and disordered passion (*motus secundi*) which the free will fully approves are mortal sins, always assuming that the object is a matter of moment.

d. Diminution or Loss of Freedom through Ignorance

If there is no conscious advertence to law or value on the part of the mind, there can be no question of violation of law. Quite often, however, lack of advertence and ignorance is the fault of the free will in so far as there was some realization of the obligation to be more attentive to duty. Thus, for example, a physician or a priest who has seriously neglected to continue his professional studies, cannot be excused on the ground of ignorance if he blunders in the performance of his tasks. In the language of the law, culpably serious neglect of the truth and of the necessary effort to inform oneself regarding it is called crass or supine ignorance (*ignorantia crassa seu supina*). Ignorance arising from direct and deliberate refusal to inform oneself is called pretended ignorance (*ignorantia affectata*). Most particularly this latter type of ignorance does not diminish accountability, but rather displays the enormity of the irresponsibility.

e. Diminution of Freedom through Inveterate Habits

A good habit (*habitus*), as consequence of the repetition of many prompt and ready acts which say yes to the morally good, augments the power of freedom. An evil habit, as expression and result of a multitude of voluntary evil acts, bears within itself the weight of these previous free decisions, with responsibility for all their after-effects and manifestations until the habit is entirely repudiated. Should it still recur in individual unworthy acts, despite the basic good resolutions to the contrary, the resultant evil acts are less culpable because the evil habit has lessened the individual's freedom.

Example: so long as one who is in the habit of swearing or cursing or indulging in profanity does not in any way give up his sin by true repentance for dishonoring the divine name or bestir himself to counteract the habit, all his acts of profanity constitute a kind of unity. They flow like a current from his evil freedom. In fact, by the very lack of effort to combat the vice, the man takes a position, voluntarily and permanently, which imparts its evil character to all his individual acts of profanity. But should he repent of his sins and resolve to fight against them, the individual evil words themselves, which at any time may crop up despite his most resolute good intentions, are basically removed from the current of freedom, at least to the extent of the genuineness of his sorrow and desire to rid himself of the bad habit. Through sorrow the individual acts of profanity which still occur are torn from the evil root of voluntary culpability and no longer partake of sin, in the sense of conscious and actually willed offense, though perchance there is some culpability in the remissness of effort in the struggle which the conquest of bad habits requires.

f. Loss of Freedom through Hypnosis and Narcotics

Anyone who voluntarily submits to hypnosis subjects his use of freedom to the hypnotist's influence as long as the spell of hypnotic dependence lasts and deprives himself of the power of insight into values and the ability to make decisions, which are the bases of freedom. Acts performed in this condition in which liberty is diminished or destroyed are morally accountable in virtue of the free cause which was responsible for the loss of liberty. It is beneath the dignity of man to surrender to the dictation of any hypnotist who may misuse or abuse him or lead him into morally evil ways.[30]

The persistent use of narcotics readily produces addiction or the drug habit. The addict deprives himself of his freedom directly and immediately only in the sphere of the abnormal craving for the drug. But as the craving and dependence become more insistent and insatiable, the loss of will power and eventual total loss of freedom in this sphere will gradually affect the entire domain of free decision. If, despite his better knowledge and the freedom still in his possession, the addict refuses to take the necessary therapeutic and other measures to cure his habit, he incurs additional guilt and is accountable for the persistence of the abuse and the progressive deterioration of his will power. All the evil effects in any way foreseen as resulting from such impaired freedom of will, including the corresponding wrong attitudes and evil actions, are radically voluntary. They are voluntary indirectly and in cause.

g. Loss of Freedom through Suggestion: Mass Suggestion

It is a serious duty to resist the insidious influence of evil suggestion, either by actively fighting against it or by publicly exposing it or at least by attempting to escape from it by flight. Certain types of individual are endowed with such power of suggestion that weaker men fall irresistibly under their spell, so that escape from the evil is possible only through flight or extreme reserve, if this power of suggestion is turned to vile purposes. Friendship or marriage between immoral and skeptical men or women with great suggestive power and weak and susceptible individuals must result in a far-reaching surrender of moral freedom on the part of the latter.

In our time propaganda by means of mass suggestion or mass hypnosis is one of the greatest hazards to our freedom. Its effect is not only acute and deep, but extends to the broad masses like an epidemic. It may affect the groups massed in assemblies, the workers in industry, the members of legislative bodies, men in the armed forces, in fact, an entire people. The result is such that men of weak will are almost totally defenseless against the contagion, and even morally mature men and women may be perceptibly hampered in the free and independent exercise of their moral responsibility. Pestilential outbursts of fanatic nationalism and hatred for other nations and races, the rash of superstition, anti-Semitism, kangaroo and "lynch" justice, must be studied and to a great degree appraised in the light of mass psychology and mass hypnotism.

Though there are cases on record in which criminal elements cynically exploited the extreme caducity of certain men and by the vilest calculation achieved their base ends, it often happens that the leaders and spokesmen of causes are themselves the prey. Caught in the net of psychic illusions, irresistible mass movements, propaganda of hate, they become victims of the very forces they exploit and direct. But those who succumb to the violent force of mass suggestion are no worse off than the chronic victims of the moral deception and perversion of mass thinking. The evils are equally grave. The development of true moral freedom is nothing less than the gradual emancipation of self and the human person from the fraud and delusion of the herd.

Existentialism in serious minds touches a nerve in its analysis of "coming to oneself," "coming to the truth." It focuses attention on a very essential point, even though it largely fails to grasp the real meaning of the antithesis between community and impersonal man, between the value of community and the value of man as a mere individual.

The supreme hazard of being caught up with the herd and being led by the unproved ideals of the mob demands constant self-examination: do I permit myself to be influenced by the notion that "men think thus"; "men act thus," or do I decide on the basis of moral principles, which I have made my most sacred possession? To regain our moral independence, we must escape from the masses and the cultural mass production with its outpouring of syndicated news and reports, its daily and weekly press, its pamphlets, magazines, books, movies, broadcasts, telecasts, its multiple appeal to indulgence and even sin. This moral independence demands that we throw off the serfdom of "impersonal man." And no means is more suited to this effort toward moral freedom than the manful intervention for the cause of the true faith and sound morals. No means is more effective than bold engagement for the good when the masses withhold their applause. The strangle hold of the masses on our freedom cannot be broken without the support of the true community of the good, the community of faith and love, which is the Church, and the invigoration of the natural communities. The evils of an unspiritual climate of thought and opinion in which freedom is imperiled are most effectively combatted by the concerted apostolic effort of the community of the good with all its force of counterattack. Encouraging examples are evident all about us: one instance is the "circles of young families" formed for mutual encouragement in the maintenance of the Christian ideal of marriage in the pagan surroundings of our time.

h. Restriction of Freedom through Psychic Defect or Illness[31]

Some mental abnormality is permanent and due to structural deviations of the brain or to physiological malfunctions traceable to embryonic life or to infancy. Such abnormalities are all classified as mental deficiency or amentia.[32] They may range in severity from mild feeble-mindedness to imbecility and idiocy.

The psychoses are severe mental illnesses in which the subject has little or no insight into his affliction and from which issue extremely aberrant thought and behavior. The term *psychosis* is usually restricted to severe illnesses of psychogenic origin (such as schizophrenia, manic-depressive psychosis, paranoia, and involutional melancholia), but it may at times be extended to include illnesses due to impairment of brain tissue function (such as general paresis and the alcoholic psychosis). The psychoses tend to pervade the total personality and generally mean extremely poor contact with reality. There is generally serious intellectual impairment or deterioration, and the subject is often dangerous to himself and to society. The psychotic almost always requires hospitalization.

Certain personality types display symptoms and traits that can be likened to those of schizophrenia or the manic-depressive psychosis. This is not to say that persons with such symptoms or traits tend to become schizophrenic or manic-depressive. They may be and usually are quite normal individuals who are simply characterized by one or the other pattern of traits. Persons of schizoid type are shy, close-mouthed, incapable of overt emotional display, and not particularly interested in social or group activity. Some are hostile and easily given to suspicion and jealousy. Others are apathetic, passive, and unresponsive. The cycloid type of person is boisterous, emotionally unstable, has marked swings in mood between elation and depression, is interested in social events, and is in general outgoing in behavior. Such a person tends to be generous with help and with gifts. But he will wish—and even demand—a return in kind for his generosity.

Mental deficiency and the psychoses may and often do entirely exclude moral responsibility in those afflicted. It is nevertheless the duty of society to hinder these unfortunates from performing evil actions as far as possible. Above all, it is the duty of society to bestow loving care upon them in the effort to provide necessary scientific treatment for their afflictions, provided there is still hope for a cure. If relatives, despite ample financial resources, fail to furnish the necessary medical assistance for the mentally retarded and disturbed as long as there is reasonable hope, they sin gravely against love and piety.

The psychoses are to be differentiated from the psychoneuroses. In the latter form of mental illness, character and personality are basically intact. The subject is able to live in society and maintains fairly good contact with the real world of persons and events. He can usually perceive the deviation from the normal pattern of behavior in his fancies and urges or at least can be made to realize it by others. He is still in possession of a wholesome sphere of knowledge of values and a sound area of freedom available in his struggle to master mental suffering or at least to bear up with it in Christian patience.

Some authorities think there is a previous basis for all psychic disorders rooted in personality structure or physical constitution. We cannot hold that the disorder itself is innate, but that there is an inborn predisposition to any of a wide variety of mental and emotional deviations. It has become increasingly evident to students of psychotherapy and psychiatric medicine that in these matters the determining factors are not merely somato-biological. Total environment, especially in early childhood, is of supreme importance in the whole process of ideational and affective development. Heredity, physical constitution, health or sickness, social and economic status, interpersonal relationships, educational and cultural patterns, and last, but not least, the moral-religious training together with its discipline of personal responsibility and self-determination are decisive factors in the development or the prevention of serious neurotic traits or out-and-out psychotic aberrations.

Becoming a neurotic is far more than suffering a simple weakening of nerves. It is rather induced by an extremely unfavorable milieu, which has a gradual disorganizing effect on behavior. Characteristic in the origin of neurosis is a weakness in coping with reality and a more or less un-conscious effort to escape responsibility. It often arises from a subconscious attempt to find an escape from a difficult situation in life through various possible reactions (for example, anxiety, hysteria, phobias, obsessions and compulsions, depression) instead of employing the forces of mind and will to master it. The morbid reactions of the nervous system which formerly were simply called nervousness often have a psychogenic origin. Mutual interaction of the psychical and the corporeal clearly revealed in current studies in neurosis, together with the sharp stress laid on psychic origins of illness in modern medicine, serve to teach us, among other things, how profoundly not only health but also freedom depends on the spiritual attitude of man himself and his interpersonal relationships. This points up our moral obligation, not only to have a rational concern for our health, but also to gain the right attitudes of mind and heart toward conscience and its obligations in order to prevent or to offset the restrictions which neurosis imposes on freedom.

Those who have charge of the mentally ill and those around and about them must do their part through kindly understanding and through patient and sympathetic realization of their needs in order to help them come to a wholesome insight into their own condition and to unhampered use of their freedom and, if necessary, to assist them in obtaining therapeutic care.

The organ neurosis reaction is the development of any one of a number of diverse physical symptoms (cardiovascular, intestinal, urinogenital) interfering with specific organic functions; it is appropriately termed psychosomatic. Other neurotic reactions, on the other hand, like the obsessive-compulsive reaction or phobias, produce painful psychic disturbances. On the basis of the psychic area in which the obsessive-compulsive symptoms are evidenced, we distinguish obsessive images and compulsive urges. Basically they are the same kind of reaction, i.e., they are involuntary and compelling. The same may be said of phobias. Because of their domination of consciousness, obsessions lead to indecision, hesitation, and uncertainty, while resistance to compulsive acts may give rise to severe anxiety. This results in what is sometimes called abulia, or lack of volition, but it should not be confused with the abulia or generic irresoluteness of simple neurasthenia (chronic fatigue). The obsessive-compulsive person may not readily do anything evil despite images and urges, but his affliction leads him to fail to do much good.

One who is tortured by psychic compulsion bears some resemblance to certain cases of psychosis. But unlike the latter, he has a real perception of the irrationality or immorality of his fancies, impulses, restraints, or anxiety complexes, and the very realization causes him acute suffering. At times persons of culture and lofty moral character suffer from psychic compulsions. In fact, psychoneurotic traits in any sphere are not at all incompatible with lofty cultural (especially artistic) and moral endowments. At times they seem to be simply the counterpart of these gifts, the reverse side of a precious coin.

Compulsive ideas or impulses do not manifest themselves exclusively in the area of the ethical. Of frequent occurrence are phobias concerning disease in all conceivable forms. The compulsive ideas may be concerned with personal cleanliness, with numbers, with endless self-analysis. In religious natures there is a predilection for fancies and impulses diametrically opposed to the religious attitude and moral earnestness. Galling persistence of blasphemous thoughts in the minds of those who love nothing so much as to honor God is a clear instance of the image compulsion.

As in many ills of a psychic nature, so particularly in cases of psychic compulsion, calm perception of the nature of the illness, the detection of the hidden origin and cause, and resignation to the will of God are the first steps toward recovery. Convulsive attacks on these defects and fretful wrath over them are likely to create fixation of ideas and only to aggravate the evil. Far more prudent is it to go about one's daily tasks, disregarding the troubles with the gentle humor of the Christian who may heartily laugh at all that is not sinful. Impulses that contravene Christian morals may never be deliberately approved. However, the opposite extreme is no less to be eschewed; to defend oneself by all sorts of assurances against temptation can only lead to secondary compulsive acts and to a general aggravation of the evil. There is scarcely any danger of moral deviation when the individual's conduct is objectively lawful (simple rejection of sin, cheerfulness, tranquil resolution not to yield to impulse, buoyant use of energies for the good in other areas).

Another well-known type of neurosis is hysteria. This term, however, is very inclusive in scope and for that reason difficult to define or even adequately describe. In conversion hysteria, psychological disturbances are "converted" into physical complaints, the physical symptoms replacing in this manner the emotionally charged ideas and ensuing inner conflicts. The symptoms may involve practically any organ or function of the body. Among the more frequent symptom categories are the loss of sensory function (anesthesias, blindness, deafness), the loss of motor function (paralysis), and autonomic disturbances (tachycardia, shortness of breath, constipation, nausea). The individual suffering from conversion hysteria is usually rather childish in personality and desirous of gaining attention. He is talkative, sociable, and inclined to dramatize himself (noticeable in the character of his complaints). His numerous physical complaints appear, disappear, and shift to other forms without any demonstrable organic basis. He is not, however, a malingerer or faker, as he does feel the symptoms, although he is unaware of their basis and meaning. His symptoms may definitely serve the purpose of helping him to escape some uncomfortable or disagreeable situation or to keep him from doing something he feels he should not do, but has an urge to do. He himself is not conscious of any such motivation.

Other hysterical symptoms (now referred to as dissociation symptoms) take the form of amnesia, fugue states, multiple personality, or other trance states. These symptoms are functional, not organic. They unconsciously serve the purpose of escaping an intolerable situation or conflict.

Obviously hysteria in all its forms implies a typical loss of freedom and of the conscious mastery of life. The hysterical person can hardly be held responsible for his behavior, influenced as it is by unconscious desires. But the failure to struggle against infantile self-will and selfishness must bear some of the burden of blame for his condition.

Among personality disorders the most noteworthy is the so-called psychopathic personality, today usually referred to in official circles as the sociopathic personality. Included under this term are those cases involving antisocial or asocial behavior, deviant morality (especially sexual), and addiction to drugs or alcohol. Psychopathic persons invariably return to their disturbing behavior and constantly distress their families and society, but seldom if ever themselves. Their deviant behavior usually starts in childhood and is now believed to be due predominantly or even exclusively to familial and social factors prejudicing adequate moral development. They are often intellectually normal and perfectly logical and reasonable in conversation, but they behave according to impulse, quite often of an aggressive type. They say what they do not mean; or if they mean it, they immediately forget it. Once psychopathic behavior is well established, neither praise nor punishment works as a corrective. Drug or alcoholic addiction is distinctive by reason of its compulsiveness, but this is more often due to long-standing abuse of drug or intoxicant. Sometimes addictive abuse of drugs or alcohol is merely a symptom of deeper disturbances of a neurotic character. Today there is more hope for helping psychopaths (and particularly drug and alcohol addicts), provided they can be made to want help. Unlike neurotics, the psychopath seldom wants help and scarcely listens to suggestion.

In serious cases of neurosis and personality disorders, the sick man must consult a specialist in the field of psychopathology. The treatment of psychic aberrations and mental disorders which under certain conditions gravely endanger moral freedom is a much more pressing obligation than the care for mere bodily health. Even though the major part of mankind is not seriously affected by mental disorder, nevertheless most men show some symptoms or traits which can develop into neurosis or into some great handicap to the practice of virtue. This is a serious matter for men who become slaves of passion and do not exercise themselves in the discipline of will power or fail to meet the test of severe trials of life in the spirit of faith. Each individual can profit from a realization of his own frailties. True humility not only gives him an insight into his weakness, but to a degree indicates its origin as well (for example, organic deficiency or profound failures and disappointments in life have a correspondingly deteriorating effect on the mind).

Every defect and every mental illness which hampers moral freedom is a cross. To bear it patiently makes us like to Christ in His passion. But both the individual who is afflicted and those connected with him must do all they can to safeguard the liberty imperiled by his condition and attempt to extend the scope of his moral freedom ever more widely.[33]

i. The Church's Doctrine on Human Liberty

The Church has defined as a dogma of faith that the children of Adam even after the fall are still in possession of moral freedom of choice.[34] This means simply—neither more nor less—that the normal human being, at least in the decisive stages of his moral life, has at his disposal the measure of freedom of will necessary to decide for or against God, with such validity and earnestness that by God's own sanction eternal happiness or eternal loss depends on his free choice. As far as each particular action is concerned, however, we are often perplexed. Does it or does it not have this measure of freedom? It is impossible to form a clear and certain judgment on the moral maturity of many individuals of extremely elemental mentality or of the mentally ill or feeble-minded persons: are they sufficiently free to make a deliberate decision, such as is required for mortal sin? In other words, is the restricted scope of their free will such that they are still able to take a deliberate position in opposition to God, a position which God will judge with such stern disapproval as to respond to it by eternal rejection? Ultimately, only God can judge the individual. Our study and knowledge of psychology can and should serve to teach us to be mild and cautious in our judgment of our neighbor. It should help us to do all we can by way of understanding and correcting ourselves and also others. We must make every effort to broaden the scope of moral freedom through control or elimination of the psychic disorders that hamper it. In the fundamental problem of the nature and degree of freedom essential for moral responsibility, the Church, not experimental psychology, has the authority to make the final decision.

We learn about the transcendent splendor and mystery of our liberty only through revelation: it is the exaltation of our freedom to a supernatural likeness to God in the liberty of His children. It is the divine dowry of Christ's own obedience unto death on the cross and the incipient revelation of Christ risen in His glory. It is the power to follow Christ, which is perfected and preserved in filial obedience to God, whose message of command to His children is expressed only through His deeds and gifts of love.

The freedom of the children of God is His noblest gift and therefore it is also our most sacred obligation and bond of love.

II. KNOWLEDGE OF GOD AS BASIS OF VALUE

1. Our Likeness to God through Moral Knowledge

That man is created in the "image and likeness of God" implies not only that his liberty is patterned on the divine, that it is participation in the divine freedom, but also that man's knowledge is like to God's and partakes of its splendor. Indeed, God's freedom is not blind, but essentially lucid and splendid. According to the measure in which man shares this infinite lucidity and splendor of divine knowledge, in the measure of his enlightenment by the divine knowing, can he be like to God through participation in His freedom. Man's likeness to God manifests itself in every conception of truth and every act of knowing, for there can be no truth except through participation in the eternal truth. A mere theoretic grasp of contingent realities, which is not directed to any action, is on the lowest rung of similarity to God. Next follows the knowledge of practical truth with power, a "power-conscious knowing" [hence patterned on God's creative mandate: "have dominion!" (Gn 1:26)]. Higher is the philosophical knowledge of essences which with true insight into supreme causes and principles points to the ultimate source of all things, God, and shows how they all lead to God. Essentially the loftiest level of divine likeness in our knowledge is attained only through love. The summit is knowledge penetrated with love, engendering love, made dynamic in love. Such in its innermost reality is God's knowledge, for God is love! The second person in the most Holy Trinity is "not just any word, but the Word breathing forth love."[35] We can enunciate nothing more pertinent on the essence of the Word of God than this: the Word in eternal and necessary *élan vital* breathes forth the Spirit of love in union with the Father.

Moral religious knowledge, salutary knowledge or "science of salvation," therefore, reaches a singular depth of assimilation to God and participation in God. This cannot be said of the most exalted scientific understanding of the profane sciences unless their essential relation to God shines forth from them and awakens love for God. As a matter of fact, a simple peasant mother with her loving knowledge of God and of good has a much nobler cultural formation (in conformity with the image of God) than a "learned" sceptic. Moral-religious knowledge elevates man in the hierarchy of the divine likeness in proportion to the degree with which it is animated by the spirit of love and inspires us to love. The most brilliant theoretic moral knowledge is not on the same high level as the simple understanding of a saint who may be altogether illiterate.

2. *Knowledge of Good the Basis of Moral Freedom*

In God, the Word is the second person, Love is the third. This means that the Holy Spirit, the personal love, proceeds from the Father and the Son. Here we have the divine pattern showing that the free acts (moral obedience and love) must have their essential source in knowledge. The free decision of our will in the image of God is in proportion to our knowledge in the image of God. Our decision can reach no further than the light of the knowledge which is in the divine image. Where understanding is absent, there freedom is absent, there responsibility is lacking. The more comprehensive and profound the understanding the greater the responsibility before God. Thus the Lord says: "If I had not come and spoken to them, they would have no sin. But now they have no excuse for their sin" (JN 15:22ff.). "If you were blind, you would not have sin. But now that you say, 'We see,' your sin remains" (JN 9:41).

As long as we recognize the good, we must live according to it. Otherwise the light could be lost through our fault and we would not be capable of doing good any longer: "Walk while you have the light, that darkness may not overtake you" (JN 12:35). All knowledge of God and the good is an appeal to us to choose God and His law. A clear and practical knowledge places our decision in an altogether different light than does mere conceptual or speculative knowledge. (It is immensely important for the preacher and teacher of the divine word to realize this.) But the eternal "Word of the Father, breathing forth love" transcends this distinction of practical and speculative. He is indeed the eternal Concept, but also the living person, infinite knowing. Since we are all created in the Word and after the pattern of the Word, no one may make the excuse that he has acquired only a theoretic understanding of the good.

There can be no knowledge of God and the good which is not in some degree dynamic, moving us to love in the divine image, since there can be no normal man who does not feel in his inmost likeness to God the dynamic force of the known good, impelling him to action.

To frustrate the theoretic knowledge of the good by making it sterile and void of all fruit is a fault fraught with the direst consequences, which profoundly deforms the divine image in man. But the very possibility that man possessed of the knowledge of good can fail to make the decision for good or to do the good action, reveals most clearly, despite all resemblance to God, his created dissimilarity.

3. Goodness of Person Preliminary to True Moral Knowledge

Even though in the Holy Trinity the Word is the second and Love is the third person, nevertheless in the intimate divine life (*perichoresis*) which is the Trinity, love is not in any way just a term or conclusion. It is also the source and center of the *perichoresis*. In love, from love, and to love, the Father speaks His consubstantial Word. Accordingly there must also be a mutual relation of moral knowledge and moral decision (attitude) in man. "Will and knowledge can be conceived only in the mutual interrelationship of priority, not as unilinear relationship of direction."[36] Only in so far as knowledge of good is sustained by the goodness of the subject, infused or acquired, can it provide the impulse to the good and the highest perfection of virtue. Through the power of grace infused by God this impulse ceaselessly carries the subject beyond the status of moral perfection already attained. From the psychological point of view, we can say that moral knowledge is not a torch which merely sheds light without heat or warmth. Indeed, it must first glow with warmth before it can rightly and thoroughly shed its light. Often, however, the circle of light is cast much farther than the warmth of its glow.

That moral-religious attitude and conduct serve as the basis for the ethico-religious knowledge and understanding is evidently set in the clearest light in the doctrine of the primacy of love over knowledge in the Augustinian-Franciscan theology. But Thomas, though he holds the primacy of the intellect, is far from ignoring the mutual interdependence of the two. The noted Thomist, the philosopher Maritain, says on this point: "Here (that is, in the moral knowledge and specifically in prudence) Saint Thomas has correctness of understanding depend on the uprightness of the will and this indeed by reason of the existentiality, no longer speculative, but practical, of the moral judgment. The practical judgment can be right only if actually here and now the dynamism of my willing is right and strives for the true goods of human life. It is plain, therefore, that practical wisdom, prudence, is indivisibly a moral and at the same time an intellectual virtue."[37]

In the Sacred Scripture, especially in Saint John, there is the clearest evidence, not only that the basis of moral decision is in knowledge, but also reciprocally that the basis of knowledge is in love. Perhaps the clearest and profoundest passages are those in which the Lord calls the promised Holy Spirit the "Spirit of Truth" (Jn 14:17; 15:26). Only through the "Spirit of Truth," only when they are filled with charity in the Holy Spirit, will the disciples know the truth fully. "Let the anointing which you have received from him, dwell in you, and you have no need that any one teach you. But as his anointing teaches you concerning all things, and is true and is no lie, even as it has taught you, abide in him" (1 Jn 2:27). "But you have an anointing from the Holy One and you know all things" (1 Jn 2:20). Through the anointing of the Holy Spirit, that is, through love, we are confirmed in the truth. "He who does not love does not know God; for God is love" (1 Jn 4:8; cf. Jn 8:47; 18:37).

The more love grows in us, the more will God manifest Himself to us, the more shall we also understand the morally good. Knowledge of God and moral knowledge are intimately bound together. "He who loves me will be loved by my Father, and I will love him and manifest myself to him" (Jn 14:21). Profound authentic understanding of God and the moral good is possible only for one who possesses love and manifests it practically in his conduct. One who constantly neglects good and turns to evil deeds will grow vile and sinister. "He who says that he is in the light, and hates his brother, is in the darkness still. He who loves his brother abides in the light" (1 Jn 2:9f.).

An understanding of values is in itself a treasure of moral values. To welcome the light of truth beckoning us is surely a morally worthy act, a profound moral decision. To accept the truth and not shun the burden and hardship of its claims is itself a great good.

Knowledge of values (here we do not have in mind purely speculative or theoretical knowledge of the good!) expresses and reveals the whole moral value of the person. Not only in our morally good actions (JN 14:21) is our virtue manifest. Even the clear perception and depth of moral understanding reveals the good in us, manifests our love for God. Who does not keep the commandments does not love God. But it is also true that one who breaks the commandments can lay no claim to "knowing" God. "He who says that he is in the light, and hates his brother, is in the darkness still" (1 JN 2:9). (Obviously the word *light* means more than the simple light of reason; it means the total splendor of grace proceeding from the light of knowledge in the Word.) A life of sin is unthinkable in one who actually "knows" God, and the good is incompatible with this "knowledge." "No one who sins has seen him, or has known him" (1 JN 3:6). Thus the observance of the commandments is not merely a sign that we love God, but also that we "know" Him. "And by this we can be sure that we know him, if we keep his commandments. He who says that he knows him, and does not keep his commandments, is a liar and the truth is not in him" (1 JN 2:3f.).

Are the statements contradictory? On the one hand, we say we cannot love what we do not know. We cannot do the good before we know it. On the other hand, we cannot know what we do not already love. Surely it is true that we must have some knowledge in order to do good, otherwise our neglect of it would not be culpable. But to know the good as it should be known implies that one is already good. "He who knows God listens to us" (1 JN 4:6). A study of the diversity and degrees of moral knowledge should clear up any difficulty arising from such paradoxical statements. To these we now turn our attention.

4. *The Species of Moral Knowledge*

a. Knowledge of Law and Experience of Value

There is a profound difference between theoretically clear conceptual knowledge and the concrete and practical perception of the good one has experienced. The most radical difference in moral knowledge is between mere legal knowledge that something must be done or avoided and the insight into the value itself which is the basis of obligation. The science of law provides a strict norm and determines the limits for action in general or gives an imperative for particular action. In one way or other one who knows the law must possess the basic realization that the "ought" is good. Otherwise there would be no moral knowledge at all. But this reference to the good is, in the first place, only in the background. Secondly, it is not a clear and evident intuition of the good or the experience of it from within, but only a kind of extrinsic knowledge. There is another entirely essential distinction in the science of the law. The imperative character of law may be viewed primarily from the standpoint of sanction (reward or punishment) or under the aspect of recognition of the lawmaker's authority which is recognized as good. In this latter case there is an approach to the awareness of value.

Knowledge of value (as distinct from knowledge or science of law) on its part again comprises a diversity of species and degrees: there is a simple and basic abstract intuition, conceptual understanding of something as good and perception of the intrinsic reason why it is good. This knowledge, however, suffers from a certain frigidity. It arouses no personal enthusiasm, lacks concreteness, color, warmth, unless it is bound up with direct appreciation of values. Then there is the practical perception of value: value is plainly discerned in its clarity and splendor and its concrete worth and claim to our acceptance. Next we note what we may call a sense of value:[38] one experiences the value not merely in the full radiance of its beauty and exaltation, but also with ardent devotion to it. In fact, the sense of value attains perfection only in the total response to its word of love, only when the attitude of the one who perceives it measures up to the essential attraction of the good, in so far as this is possible. For ultimately the essence of the good is its appeal to love. Finally, there is the knowledge of value arising from a kind of intimate conaturality with the good. Not only does one see and experience value concretely in particular situations, but one possesses a bond and contact with it, an actual and most intimate affinity with it which transcends every particular instance and situation. This exalted knowledge of value is altogether within the reach of virtuous men who do not have the capacity to explain its object in conceptual and philosophical terms.

It is precisely these two latter kinds of value-experience which justify the assertion of Scheler: "There are more men who grasp God familiarly through love than there are men who familiarly conceptualize Him."[39] But the sense and the knowledge of values as just explained should not be construed as being opposed to the conceptual grasp or science of values, nor should it be explained as irreconcilable with them. Precisely the authentic sense and knowledge of values provide the basis for a flawless conception of value, always assuming the maturity of reasoning power with adequate capacity for abstractive thought.

Whereas capacity for abstraction or conceptualization has its limits, concrete perception and sense and knowledge of value are capable of ever greater development in depth according to the total moral worth of the person. And this is not an endowment limited to privileged individuals, though we do say that the morally perverted or even the morally immature individual lacks moral endowment. But the reason is that such an individual here and now is no longer capable or is not yet capable of any noble moral conduct.

Whereas a knowledge of the law, in fact, even some perception of value is also within the reach of one who is morally very immature, authentic vital experience of value demands a far greater moral sensibility. "*Conditio sine qua non* of the perfect experience of value is the endowment of a clear intuition. But this is not sufficient guaranty to preserve it; an inner competence of the subject must be added in order to make possible the acceptance of value."[40]

We must make a clear distinction between knowledge and appreciation, between possessing knowledge of value and assuming a position toward it. We must distinguish between the appeal and summons in the awareness of value which is in the intellect and the response which is in the will. However, the sense of value and the knowledge of value, as we have used the term, strictly and typically, are characterized by an inner presence and participation of a loving will.

Saint John uses the term *knowing* in its religious sense. In this "knowing" there is a loving will supporting the "knowledge," and therefore the right response of will to God's appeal is assured. "He who knows God listens to us" (1 Jn 4:6). On the contrary, one who does not have love, who is not entirely and utterly devoted to the good, cannot have any such knowledge of it. "He who does not love does not know God" (1 Jn 4:8). In this sense the Socratic aphorism that it is sufficient to know the good in order to do it, is justified. But to arrive at this knowledge there must be some antecedent good acts based on a less intimate esteem for the good, a point which seems to have escaped Socrates.

b. Basic Value, Type of Value, Particular Values

All particular values and all types of value rest in basic value: in the "good" (ultimately in God, the fulness of all good). But it does not follow that knowledge of basic value always guarantees the right understanding of all types of value and all particular values. Obviously a perfect and comprehensive grasp of the basic value of the "good" would include within it the full knowledge of all the values contained in the concept. However, one may possess a general knowledge of the good with a vital awareness of good and evil, together with some understanding of significant types of value, and still have only a meager knowledge and appreciation of the value of certain virtues. There are many people, for example, who understand and appreciate the virtue of justice. And they also have a knowledge and a sense of the evil of injustice. With this sense of virtue and the inner conviction of its value, they earnestly strive to promote justice. But the inner dignity and beauty of chastity and particularly of virginal chastity escapes them altogether. For them it is an alien value. But this does not imply that they are ignorant of the precept of chastity and could not fulfill it!

The fact is that the value of many virtues is more difficult to attain because they are so exalted; we might say that they are qualitatively finer and loftier. Such are unselfish kindness, simple humility, purity. It is well to bear in mind also that many a one is quite aware of the worth of chastity, and not only because of extrinsic knowledge through precept, through warning against violation of the sixth and ninth commandments. And yet under stress of temptation and its enticement and lure he no longer realizes that now and for him this value of chastity is at stake. Such is the power of temptation to deceive and blind men, especially if they fail to pray and struggle nobly against it. For man also has the power to resist temptation. Though we cannot enter into a detailed explanation of the conditions and circumstances under which temptations have this blinding effect, the underlying basis is evident: in the deeper level of one's character there is a basically defective moral attitude.

Corresponding to the three objects of moral knowledge (basic value, type of value, particular value) are three species of blindness to value: comprehensive blindness to value, partial blindness to value, and blindness in the application to value. The first of these, comprehensive blindness to value, is found in various degrees of obscurity in various individuals. There may be an incapacity for vital perception and appreciation, for clear intuition, for right realization of the basic value, the "good," or even for the proper acceptation of legal obligation. But incapacity for knowledge of the precept of the good is never absolute as long as moral freedom and responsibility are still present.

Partial blindness to value has as its object a particular type of value or perhaps even a group of these. The loftier types of value are most likely to be affected where there is no profound and ceaseless effort to attain the good. But again we must insist that even the lack of such vital effort does not necessarily exclude the very basic knowledge of precept necessary for an incipient fulfillment of good.

As to the third kind of blindness, it is concerned with the application of moral principles to concrete instances: one recognizes moral value in general, but fails to discern the particular instance in the light of the general moral principle which should apply. More or less unconsciously one shies away from those values which might pain or grieve. The danger of blindness to value, particularly in the application of principles, is not so great if we ourselves are not directly concerned. One is not so likely to err regarding the obligations which bind others. Obscurity more readily blinds one to a realization of his own duty, for the element of personal interest very conveniently destroys true objectivity.

Blindness to value usually assumes one of two possible forms which correspond to the diversity of its source: hostility and insensibility. Hostile to value is the malicious man who has set for himself an ultimate goal which is irreconcilable with the good as such, especially, however, with certain specific or particular values in virtue. Perhaps he can still discern the values, but in the depth of his soul he does not care to notice them. They are an accusation against his false attitude, a disparagement of his autonomous self-glorification. This is the aspect of value he actually perceives, whereas the true dignity of the value itself is something alien to him. The proud man is actually hostile to value. And the summit of such pride is diabolical malice. Satan has knowledge of values. But he is totally hostile to them. He does not penetrate into value itself, but looks only to the hostile aspect turned to him. This attitude of hostility toward value gradually makes a complete fraud of man as he develops a mastery in the vile art of obscuring and scorning disagreeable values, even though he cannot totally disavow them. Still the very hatred of the good shows that one cannot altogether evade the verdict of the good.

One who is insensible to value is not thereby necessarily hostile to an equal degree or in the same manner. A common type of insensibility toward value is the "Don Juan" voluptuary or bon vivant. Totally bent on enjoyment, he has no desire to "harm" any one, though he plays fast and loose with all the virtues where enjoyment is concerned. The source of this insensibility is not so much pride as self-indulgence and lust.

When the blindness is only partial, the attitude of hostility or insensibility is directed, not against the good as such, but only against that realm of values which is in opposition to the still potent pride or lust. But it is not incompatible with an incipient will to do good.

The ultimate root of all man's moral blindness is sin, although not every sin invariably leads to moral blindness in its evil domain. Only the sin which is not erased by repentance has this dire consequence, for it gains the mastery over the acts of man and over his personality as well. In our teaching on conscience we shall probe more deeply into much of this, in so far as conscience is connected with the dynamic of the ontic unity of knowing and willing. If the movement of the will does not follow the knowledge of the intellect, it will recoil against the intellect. Then the unity for which nature clamors will be forced into a reverse, with inevitable darkening of the mind through malice of will.

Only too often knowledge outdistances moral performance. Unless humility bridges this gap which imperils unity, a deceptive pride will assume control of our powers and totally destroy the inner harmony. Thus defect of obedience in the face of the challenge of the good will conspire with defect of humility to effect moral blindness. Psychologically the blinding force of pride or indulgence has its source in the normal ontic tendency toward unity in knowing and willing. Both the dynamic of conscience with its tendency to good in the case of the obedient will and the blinding power of sin in the case of persistent disobedience spring from this same source. Merely partial blindness in application to particular instances has its special source in the striving of the "I," at once proudly passionate and yet in some way attached to the moral, in the endeavor to erase the moral conflict. On the one hand frivolous hostility or indifference to value is absent. The basic position in favor of the good or at least in fear of evil still remains. On the other hand, "there is no intimate resolution or decision to renounce whatever is pleasant or agreeable even though it is bound up with moral evil."[41] It is possible that actually the will is inclined to acknowledge value, but still on a deeper, more or less unconscious, level an obstacle exists and a deviation occurs. This is due to the fact that one seeks the good in a general way indeed, but not at the price of every sacrifice.

Blindness to value ceases to exist only after a profound and universal orientation toward the good replaces it; this means serious and total conversion to God. Unless we are ready to deny that the person must and can convert, we must concede that the person is responsible for this sort of blindness to value even though the forces that blind operate mainly on the level of the unconscious. He is aware of the existence of these forces, for he can discern the false tendencies. As to the particular act arising from this attitude influenced by the blindness to value, it is not here and now a responsible act of the human agent, but it is in some manner the effect of a prior responsible free decision.

Conversion does not bear with it the perfection of an immediate intimate sense of value or even the perfect "knowing" of the good in the sense of the text of Saint John. For this, love must first develop and exercise itself in the good. For such growth and self-exercise simple insight into values or the right application of the knowledge of precept to one's own case is sufficient.

The blindness to value due to a will which blanches in fear of moral conflict and will not hear of it is called, in the language of the Schools, *ignorantia affectata,* pretended ignorance. It is a deliberate not wanting to know. But this ignorance embraces very diverse degrees of knowledge or lack of it and, consequently, of responsibility. In one instance it can arise rather from a genuine fear of the menace of conflict with moral principles, the while one cannot muster the courage to break away from the occasion of sin and hazard to salvation, from objects one wishes were still (and in consequence of the wish, also believes they are) morally permissible. But this type of pretended ignorance may also be caused by a calculating will seeking the excuse of ignorance before the lawgiver with his sanction of punishment. Though these two kinds of ignorance are quite different and also admit of many intermediate variations and shades, it is this latter calculating type which is the usual concern of jurists when they deal with ignorance.

5. *Depth of Value Knowledge*

We must distinguish a twofold depth of moral knowledge: the first is on the level of individual value; the second, on that of the person, already discussed in the preceding paragraphs. As the mere novice in moral effort does not possess the same depth of will as the saint, so they are unequal in moral knowledge. (Obviously the comparison is far from perfect.) On the part of the subject, the depth essentially depends on the radical nature of the "basic intention." If the good does not derive from the universal resolve to do the good always and under all circumstances, the essential depth is lacking. And this absence of depth is associated with a parallel deficiency in knowledge as long as particular values and whole types of value are excluded from the recognized fundamental values.

From the standpoint of value, the saint who does not merely perceive the particular value in its own dignity and in the moral seriousness of its demand of his acceptance, but who also knows all moral values in the splendor of the divine sanctity, is on a much profounder level than the man of stern moral fiber who is not a saint. Even an irreligious man can see and sense the value of justice, but he does not perceive the profound interior depth which belongs to the value of justice: it is founded in the depths of the divine justice and holiness and reaches the heights of the divine attributes. There is also a profound diversity between the man of faith who does no more than hold fast to faith—firmly but coldly—and the saint whose faith is vitalized in love, and who sees in every moral value the splendor of sanctity which is God, the Lawgiver, the source of all good.

We may not conclude from all this, however, that slighting of particular values can ever be justified. Just as the values are resplendent in the light of the divine holiness as a harmonious whole, in unity and multiple diversity, so the genuineness and depth of man's knowledge of values is preserved and safeguarded only through the insight into and earnest acceptance of each particular value. How superficial are we if we fail to cultivate the spirit of love and warm appreciation for the particular value entrusted to us! If, instead, we do no more than formally direct our acts to the will of God! (As for example: "Objectively I am indifferent in the matter, but since it is the will of God. . . .") Surely all things center not only in the will of God, but also in the eternal intelligence of the divine essence. Each particular value has its corresponding task in the creative manifestation of the one infinitely simple all-holy essence of God.

Mere knowledge of law, mere legal science, is obviously superficial. But when the holy Legislator is seen in His law, the knowledge of law rises inestimably above the mere sense of legal values. It has a profound assurance that makes it superior even to the intimate sense of values which perceives God only as ultimate source of all good.

6. Sources of Moral Knowledge

a. Objective Sources

The objective sources are community and divine revelation. It is the great service of community to propose moral ideals to the developing personality through doctrine, precept, and example. Particularly significant and important is the service of a superior association, of the community, of the people, of the cultural circle, especially of the holy Catholic Church. She leads us to virtue through her teaching and precepts, which she presents to us in the living example of her saints. All this is of inestimable value for the moral orientation of the individual. But the quality of this service is very diverse according to the times, for there are periods of lofty moral achievement, with their noble heroes and saints, and periods of moral decline and decadence. The moral man as a rule owes his inner formation in the good to the family in which he was born and raised.

The good has been revealed to us by God naturally in the order of creation, from which we can learn the hierarchy of natural values and the design of the good. But because of original sin our minds were darkened. We no longer saw the light which "shines in the darkness" (JN 1:5). Then God in His mercy gave us the Law and the Prophets and finally His only begotten Son as teacher.

In the order of His creation and more particularly in His Covenant with the Chosen People, God gave man more than arid legal knowledge, more than the dead letter of Law. He taught us through the works of His love. The Covenant with the Chosen People was made the foundation and motive of the law. It was a covenant and alliance of love. (Indeed, motivation in the order of value transmutes science of law to science of value.) Still more gloriously did God exalt this divine instruction and orientation through Christ, who teaches His precepts with words of infinite tenderness, with words filled with impressive and loving earnestness, and not least through acts of His love. Christ gave us a new commandment, the commandment of love. He presented it to us as He Himself lived it, so that we can penetrate into the profound depths of its value and meaning.

Christ is the universal teacher of moral as well as of religious knowledge. "One is your Master" (MT 23:10). "I am the way, and the truth, and the life" (JN 14:6). "I have given you an example, that as I have done to you, so you also should do" (JN 13:15). "Have this mind in you which was also in Christ Jesus" (PHIL 2:5).

It is our duty to study incessantly in the school of the Master. And basic to that study is meditation, which is therefore essential for every true Christian. But meditation is far more than mere acquisition of abstractive or theoretical knowledge. Only through the love of our hearts, that is, in loving meditation, are we actually formed in the knowledge of the school of Christ. Just as the Master teaches the good in His love, so we can learn from Him only through the "anointing of the Spirit" and "in the Spirit of truth," who is Love.

To go to the school of the Master means above all to seek to enter into the mind and heart of Christ. Imitation of Christ is obviously not a mere copying of His acts, unique and inimitable as they often are, not a mere mechanical fulfillment of His words and law. Only if we are united to the Person of Christ in love, through profound submission of heart, will we become docile disciples of Christ with true perception of values and right application of them to ourselves.

Not merely the historic Christ as He is depicted in the Gospels is our teacher, but the whole Christ, the historic and the mystical Christ, who lives on in His Church. Through the Church in every age He makes known to us our personal tasks and places before us concrete and varied illustrations of His own example in the lives of the great saints.

In the ultimate analysis, if we are to arrive at a clear understanding of the true import of community, authority, law, and example of Christ for our moral development, we must reflect again on the various steps or degrees of knowing, from simple knowledge of law to the lofty spiritual "knowing" of the good which we have just discussed. How can beginners in the moral life or souls blinded by the obscurity of sin find an opening to the good? Or how can they be brought to enlightenment if there is no brother to admonish them, no superior to direct them, no authority to lay down laws and norms for their conduct? How can we enter the intimate sanctuary of the good unless the word and example of Christ and His saints clearly and plainly point the way. The school of Christ is adapted to the novice in virtue, and equally as well to the more advanced, since Christ employs all motives, all forms of teaching, so that even the dullest of minds can harken to it with some understanding and the most intellectual does not exhaust it. Christ is not just one teacher among many. He teaches us as the eternal Truth, and not merely externally. He teaches us as the "true light that enlightens every man" (Jn 1:9). "He wakeneth my ear, that I may hear him as a master" (Is 50:4). He has given us the "Spirit of truth" through whom alone we become docile disciples of the eternal Truth.

b. Subjective Sources

Our knowledge of values is based essentially and primarily on our affinity for the good, which is a kind of second nature (*connaturalitas*).

We are good in the depth of our being and created for the good. Only because "our eye is made for the light" can it see the light of goodness. Only because we are created for love by Eternal Love itself are we challenged by the force of love in the good and inflamed by it. This natural affinity of ours for the good (ultimately for God) can be disturbed by habits of sin, so that we become partially blind spiritually, but the seed of the good is not destroyed. It still remains in our nature, and the warmth of divine love like rays from the sun can quicken it with life. The heavenly physician offers the remedy and makes possible the beginning of recovery from the blindness of sin through the warm love of His heart. The great spiritual preventives and remedies for moral blindness are: vigilance and mortification of the disordered appetites, humility and purity, prompt repentance after every fall, conversion and earnest penance after the failures of an evil life.

The motivating power of our moral knowledge is the firm and inviolable resolution to submit to God in all matters, cost what it may. Where moral obedience has attained self-mastery by shuffling off the caprice of contingency and relativity, where it rests and relies on an absolutely good interior disposition, a true knowledge of law will develop. There will be a conscious appreciation of fundamental value rightly directed as source of this knowledge of law, which will enter all realms of virtue and attain the surest and clearest awareness of value on that summit of true knowledge mentioned by Saint John when he spoke of the understanding of divine things. This inner dynamism of moral knowledge can be developed by obedience only when it is animated by a love transforming the servile obedience under law into filial obedience in liberty under God. The freedom of the children of God can exist only where the child lovingly harkens in every command to the loving voice of God. Loving obedience, obedient love in the school of the divine Master, is attended by zeal and vigilance, on the strength of which one is not merely aware of the good in general, but also harkens to the direct invitation of the good appealing to the person in each and every situation, even when it summons to arduous and painful tasks.

Only the accomplishment of the good gives us that intimate conaturality with the good, from which we are able to grasp it with true interiority and "know" it. "He who does the truth comes to the light" (Jn 3:21). This passage surely does not primarily mean the light of evidence, but that light which "has come into the world" (Jn 3:19). To come to Christ, the "light" of eternal truth, also means to arrive at a profound understanding of the good.

One of the principal sources of moral knowledge has already been mentioned, prayer. Meditative prayer is nothing more than instruction in the school of the Saviour. Prayer of petition must incessantly beseech God for the "anointing of the Spirit," for "the Spirit of the truth," without which we can never become docile disciples of Christ.

We add by way of practical comment for confession: although it is true that the penitent is obliged to confess only what he recognized as sinful at the actual moment when the sin was committed, still we must also realize how wholesome is the attitude of those Christians who, after their conversion, when their eyes are opened, react with horror to their past acts and accuse themselves of many faults which they had previously committed without any thought of sin. Since these material faults are fruits of an evil tree, planted and nurtured in the state of fallen liberty, it is spiritually profitable to expose in confession the tree with all its fruits. However, it surely would be sufficient in itself to make known one's evil state and those evil fruits of conscience of which one was actually guilty.

III. THE MORAL FACULTY: CONSCIENCE

1. Significance of Conscience in the Imitation of Christ

Conscience, man's moral faculty, with its knowledge of values and freedom, is the subjective source of moral good. As intimate monitor of moral good, conscience manifests through its firmness and delicacy the ethical worth and dignity of the moral person. Sharp in its warning, unmistakable in its reproach after the most calamitous fall, after sin, conscience at least reveals the values which have been lost and the capacity for value still available. Within us conscience re-echoes the call of the Master inviting us to follow Him. It receives and accepts the invitation, but only with the help of grace. In the depth of our being, conscience makes us keenly aware that our inner self is linked with Christ; and it in turn is enlightened and formed through the imitation of Christ. Conscience has a voice of itself, but not a word of its own; it is the word of Christ (spoken in creation, in the Incarnation of the Word, through the influence of grace) which speaks through this voice. Of itself conscience is a candle without a flame, but Christ, the Light, shines forth with His brightness and warmth from it.

a. Conscience in the Consciousness of Peoples

It is the conviction of all peoples that in his heart man can harken to the good and to the voice of God. Within him man possesses an organ or power or sense, his conscience, concerned with the good. It is more than his own good will or witness to the good, for it is not altogether silenced even if the malice of man has all but extinguished the light of reason. It is not merely the voice of the good admonishing from without. It is the monitor in man's own heart, calling him to God, binding him to the good, even when he seeks to escape from it or evade it. The primitives and all civilized peoples speak of conscience or its equivalent. Socrates speaks of *Daimonion* which admonishes him to do good. People of the late cultures tending more to reflection and introspection than to objective reality speak of a spiritual disposition or power. Their explanation of conscience is on the psychological plane. The primitive peoples, however, who accept the objective world with less self-reflection than we, do not speak of the subjective disposition of conscience, but simply of the voice which calls them, of God within them, of God who exhorts them, of the spirits of vengeance which give the guilty no rest until they atone for their sin.

Among the ancients the philosophers of the Stoa have left us psycho-philosophical speculation on conscience of singular interest. Conscience (*syneidesis, conscientia*) is a knowledge about the good and about oneself in relation to the good. For Chrysippus conscience is the urge or instinct for self-preservation (*conservatio*) of the spiritual person, the instinct which takes even reason (*hegemonikón*) under its protection. Conscience binds man to the spirit of world order (the *nous*). It is *deus in nobis* (God in us—Ovid). In the sense of most Stoics the divinity which expresses itself in conscience is not the living personal God, but the impersonal cosmic power of design and order, the world's divine "principle," its eternal law and harmony (the Stoic *lex aeterna*). Conscience is participation in this *lex aeterna,* in the eternal law. It—not the terrestrial city, the *polis*—is the "supreme guide" (Epictetus) in moral decisions.[42] Seneca speaks of God, "God stands by you, God is with you, God is in you." "In us dwells a holy spirit, the observer of our good and our bad deeds." The fundamental demand of conscience is: "live according to nature."[43]

b. Conscience in Holy Scripture

The book of Wisdom (17:10ff.) employs the Greek concept of *syneidesis* in a pejorative sense (stressing a bad conscience). If not in so many words, at least as to meaning, the doctrine of conscience throughout the entire Old Testament is much more comprehensive and profound than the teaching of the Stoa. "The spirit," "the soul," "that which is within," "the heart" admonishes man; it cries out to God. God "searches heart and reins." Sin committed greatly distresses the inner being of man. "You, with sad hearts, cry aloud, groan in the heaviness of your spirits" (Is 65:14 [Knox translation]). The heart praises or blames our deeds. "My heart doth not reprehend me in all my life" (Jb 27:6). "But David's heart struck him after the people were numbered" (2 Sm 24:10).

In contradistinction to the Stoa, the inspired teaching throughout the entire Old Testament sees conscience in the light of an appeal addressed to man by a personal God. Through conscience God speaks to man, as is especially evident in the characteristic example of Cain's remorse for his crime: "Cain said to the Lord, 'My punishment is too great to bear ... from your face I shall be hidden. And I shall be a fugitive and a wanderer on the earth' " (Gn 4:13f.).

Holy Scripture views the testimony of the good conscience and the remorse of a bad conscience from the standpoint of God's supreme knowledge. Man's examination of conscience becomes a matter of tremendous earnestness because it takes place in the sight of God, under the scrutiny of His all-seeing eyes. For man's conscience tells him that he is called by God and must stand judgment before the divine tribunal. Both the Old and New Testament writers portray conscience as inexorable, but they also recognize the phenomenon of the hardened conscience. The psalmist is amazed and shocked at the (apparent) composure of the sinner who says in the depth of his folly, "There is no God!" Most earnestly Christ Himself warns against the danger of the hardening of heart, against the obscuring of conscience. "If the light that is in thee is darkness, how great is the darkness itself!" (Mt 6:23; Lk 11:33ff.). But conscience still abides in the sinner, in the unbeliever, in the heathen. It reveals also to the heathens what is good and what is bad. It reveals to them "through their nature" (compare the Stoic "life according to nature") the demands of the law (Rom 2:14ff.). Conscience deprives the heathens of any excuse for their great sins, as it does the Jews (*ibid.*).

The New Testament adopts the Stoic term *syneidesis* (it is found 31 times in the New Testament, 19 times in Paul alone). The concept and term conscience occurring so frequently among the pagans offer the missionary a point of contact, an avenue of approach in the work of evangelization. But the deeper reality of conscience is now revealed through the light of Christian thought. By force of conscience everyone (pagan included) is capable of harkening to the call of God and is responsible, before God, for saying yes or no to sin.

Conscience is not suppressed by faith, but ennobled. Illumined by faith, it itself becomes light. Paul recognizes "conscience bearing . . . witness in the Holy Spirit" (ROM 9:1). For the Christian to act according to the faith and to act according to conscience are one and the same (cf. ROM 14:23 and the pastoral letters throughout). "Conscience and faith are very closely related in their mutual interaction."[44] Faith enlightens and clarifies conscience; "good conscience" shields and safeguards the faith. The mystery of faith is well preserved "in a pure conscience" (1 TM 3:9; cf. 1 TM 1:19). In the pastoral letters the relation of conscience to faith is most clearly expressed, whereas the letter to the Romans and the letters to the Corinthians display a preference for the general moral function of conscience and bring it to the fore. But conscience is always understood as bearing on religion with God as its source. It must bow to the decree of the divine judge.

Paul declares that the judgment of conscience is binding upon men, even though it has not reached the high level of Christian enlightenment (1 COR 8, and 10; ROM 14:20–23). But it is contrary to the ideals of our faith to insist that one's own conscience (one's own insight into the good) is the court of last resort. To act according to conscience means to take into consideration, not merely what is lawful in itself, but also the concrete circumstances, particularly the effect of our actions on the salvation of others. Only in the fulfillment of the law of love does the Christian conscience stand the test (cf. especially 1 COR 10:28f.).

Résumé: moral conscience is the instructor of the Gentiles, in so far as it binds them to the law of God as manifested in creation, in so far as it reproaches them if they act against their reason. Conscience is the focal point where Christ as Logos also instructs the Gentiles who do not yet know Him. Conscience becomes clear and certain when it admits the light of faith. It is the strong inner force which presses us to accept the teaching of Christ and preserve it in its purity. To stray from the teaching of Christ is a sign of a "conscience branded" (1 Tm 4:2). The perfect conscience is enlightened by faith and animated by love.

2. Conscience as Spiritual Disposition

What new element is displayed in the phenomenon of conscience over and above that which we have just described in our previous section on the knowledge of value? In fact, is there anything at all in conscience beyond what we have just described? Does not the good of its very self, when it is rightly understood, with all its energy and inexorability demand of us the morally good? It pertains to the very nature of value in its moral significance to express a universal ideal "ought" to us and in the concrete "situation" an actual "ought." Genuine knowledge of value arises only with the acknowledgment of this demand. And yet conscience essentially does more than practically grasp or lay hold of value which enunciates such an "ought" to us. It is a disposition of the soul which assures this imperative of the necessary response. Conscience produces the vital conviction in one's inner self that the attitude assumed toward the good is bound up with one's own salvation or damnation.

a. Distinction between Conscience as Power (*Synteresis*) and as Act (*Conscientia*)

Already in his time Saint Augustine made a profound theological study of the *synteresis*. In his doctrine on conscience he adopts the Stoic conception of participation in the eternal law through conscience, but places it on the exalted level of the divine clarity and majesty of the personal God and the participation of man created in the divine likeness. God's light enters the most intimate recesses of the heart of man, which knows no rest until man finds God. For from the inmost depths of his being the heart of man yearns for the love of God and the good.

Scholastic theology distinguished clearly between synteresis and con- scientia, that is, between conscience as permanent power or disposition and its activity in the particular dictate of conscience. The term *synteresis,* which is often written *synderesis,* is probably due to a slip of a copyist in writing the word *syneidesis* in Saint Jerome's Commentary on Ezechiel. The scholastic explanation of *synteresis* is often associated with the Stoic concept of self-preservation (*conservatio*). In this connection conscience is looked upon as the innate urge of the spiritual person to preserve himself

Man conserves his being as spiritual person when he acts according to his spiritual nature (*secundum naturam, id est secundum rectam rationem,* according to nature, which means according to right reason). Ultimately, when man renders God the service his nature requires, it is the service demanded by all the natural and supernatural endowments of his being.

The special seat of the conscience, according to many scholastics, especially the great mystics, is the *scintilla animae,* the inmost center of the soul, or the spark of the soul, which is least accessible to the contamination of sin. As regards the rôle attributed to reason (the practical intellect) or the will inclined to good, there is a division of opinion found in the various scholastic explanations of this matter.

b. Theories regarding Conscience

(1) *Intellectualistic Theories (Albert the Great, Thomas Aquinas)*

Synteresis is the permanent treasure of the highest moral principles (*habitus primorum principiorum*) which need not be reduced to principles still more basic (and indeed are not reducible) and are immediately perceived by the practical understanding. The most universal principle of *synteresis* is that "the good is to be done" (*bonum est faciendum*). (This, in the language of value ethics, means that the obligatory character of the moral value, the "ought" springing from the morally meaningful, is immediately evident.)

The decision of conscience may be considered the conclusion of a syllogism. In this syllogism (which may be merely implicit) the proposition of the *synteresis* is the major premiss. The minor premiss is a proposition expressing the practical judgment made in a concrete instance by prudence. The judgment of conscience, in the sense of the act of conscience, is the actual conclusion. Because this conclusion, the final practical judgment, is contained in the major premiss (the *synteresis*), it derives from it its imperative character.

"To understand this point we must bear in mind that according to Thomas the natural inclination of the will is always bound up with the knowledge of the practical reason. Thus by the very nature with which it is created there is in the will a disposition which permits it of itself to strive for the good conceived by reason."[45] "To command the act of moral value, the will ultimately needs the right judgment of the understanding, for by its nature it presses toward the good as known by reason (*bonum rationis*)."[46] Moreover, as to the view—

so harshly criticized—that the judgment of conscience is the result of a syllogism, we must observe what Saint Thomas says about prudence and the gifts of the Holy Spirit, which according to his teaching are essential to a mature judgment of conscience. What we treat in the doctrine on the judgment of conscience in the situation (the "act of conscience") is found in Thomas for the most part in the tract on prudence.

(2) The Voluntaristic Theory (Alexander of Hales, Bonaventure, Henry of Ghent)

Synteresis is that lofty essential quality of the will binding it inseparably and unto its inmost depths (according to many, this is the *scintilla animae*) to the known good. What is recognized as right reason (*recta ratio*) receives its dynamic force in each particular instance through the moral power of the will (*synteresis*), through the will manifesting the loving nature of the soul.[47] Thus right reason becomes the voice of conscience (*conscientia*). The will created for love possesses this dynamic urge to love in the inmost depths of its nature (the little spark of love), because it is touched by God, the source of all love. Conscience is all the more alert the more active God is in the depth of the soul and the more He draws to Himself the power of love in man. Here the religious depth of this theory of conscience is revealed.

There is no thought of contesting the presence of the intellectual aspects which the proponents of the Thomistic explanation of conscience stress in their exposition, since the will is never a blind force, but a power drawn to the known good. Just as Thomas, without expressly incorporating the will into his exposition of conscience is far from ignoring the true nature of will pressing forward toward the good, so the great representatives of the voluntaristic theory reveal the most profound insights into the meaning of moral knowledge. This they explain partially in the Augustinian manner as the effulgence of eternal truth. But the actual phenomena of conscience seem to them sufficiently well explained through the nature of the will.

(3) False "Historical Evolutionistic" Theories

The biological theory of conscience of the evolutionists sees in conscience no more than the vital pragmatic adjustment to environment. Such is the intellectually impoverished antithesis to the exalted Stoic conception of the spiritual urge for self-preservation, its lowering to the biological level, since the spirit and its eternal laws were ignored. Concept of conscience corresponds to the concept of man.

The sociologistical theory sees in conscience no more than the manifestation of adjustment to society, the vitally necessary balance between egoism and social interest. According to Sigmund Freud this adjustment of the immediately asocial driving force of men to the rules of the game of the social group takes place through the "super ego" which signifies a bond with parental authority.

Criticism: no matter how favorably or unfavorably the example of parents and the adjustment with the evaluations of society may affect the development of the phenomenon of conscience in adolescents, they still cannot in any way explain the binding force of the judgment of conscience felt in the very depths of personality, a judgment which often enough makes itself felt in actual contradiction to the demands of environment. The absolute bond with the image of father or mother or even with the spirit of one's surroundings not only fails to explain conscience, but indicates a morbid stricture of conscience and the whole personality.

(4) *Comprehensive Theory of Conscience*

The comprehensive concept of conscience which we adopt and propose is built on the double foundation of the practical intellect seeking truth and the natural yearning of the will and heart of man for the true good. It is Thomism which stresses the practical intellect as likeness to God, whereas the Augustinian-Franciscan tradition lays greater stress on heart and will tending toward the good. The comprehensive theory of conscience aims at a synthesis of the two, for the ultimate dynamism of conscience is explained, not from the distinct nature of intellect and will viewed in isolation, but from the profound unity of the two in the depths of the soul. We view them in the light of their profound likeness to God as He is active in the depths of the soul in a rich and wonderful harmony of its whole being.

In God, He who knows and loves (the Father), His knowing (the Son who is the Word), and His loving (the Holy Spirit) are united in the one divine essence, three persons in one sole nature. The soul in its totality (the soul itself which is the substance, the intellect, the will, all in unity) is the most profound image of the divine Trinity. Even though in man soul, intellect, and will are really distinct, they cannot really thrive without each other. At any rate, intellect and will—such is the mark of the finite nature—can part ways in their activity, but not without unleashing the most profound grief in the depths in which they are united, not without creating a rift in those very depths. And this wound in the soul cries out to be healed. And the deep cry from this wound is a summons to heal the wound, to close the dreadful gap of dissension through restoration of the unity and harmony which makes men like to God.

Because of the profound harmony of intellect and will in the depth of the soul (in the substance), the intellectual power must be shaken to those very depths when the will struggles against it because of deep and sinister motives. Therefore, the will in its turn must tremble in agony when it combats the clear knowledge of understanding and allows itself to be fascinated and deceived by a mere mirage of the good. The most agonizing cry wells up from the depth of the soul itself, for as root and source of unity of the powers, it is directly wounded by their dissension. Here is the profound reason for the first elemental agony of conscience, a spontaneous unreflecting pain. The image of the Trinity within us recoils in horror at the menace of distortion of the divine likeness in our souls.

As to conscience, there is more at stake than the inner unity and completeness of the psychic powers. To the moral equipment belongs also the total alignment of the human spirit with that which is objectively true and at the same time objectively good, so that man can be perfectly one in himself only if he is in accord with the world of both true and good. Nor can the imperative of the true and the good be felt within the human heart unless the intellectual power is most intimately bound up with them both. The will would not be magnetically drawn to the known good if it were not actually created for it, if from the value known and from the nature of will there did not issue the same mutual message of love. Not only has the knowing intellect a kinship with the true, but it also has an innate basic love for the true good. The will in turn is not simply made to love, but through the union with mind in the same depth of soul to love the true value.

It follows that conscience must be looked upon as the spiritual instinct for self-preservation arising from the urge for complete unity and harmony. The soul craves this inner unity within herself, which is possible only through unity with the world of the true and the good.

If the soul is to possess a true inner unity and harmony with the consequent healthy integrity and soundness, the mind must be open to the true value and devoted to it, the will must be open to the known good and dedicated to it. But this is not sufficient. The soul in the profoundest depths of the person must be attracted by the living source of all truth and all goodness. In the uttermost depths of its being the soul must be one with the living God, for it is created in His image. Through Him it is preserved in the truth, in the good, and in the unity of being.

3. Conscience as Moral and Religious Phenomenon

a. Relation of Conscience to the "I" and to Value

The first reaction of a morally wounded conscience (the "evil conscience") is a cry, a cry of torment over a deep wound, not an expression of a concept or a proposition. But if we were to formulate in a proposition what takes place, it would be couched in such terms as, "O, I am in danger," or "How dreadful! I feel I am torn asunder deep down!" Progressively we would come to a realization of the appeal which conscience makes for a cure of its ills, which might also be expressed in such words as, "I want to be restored to the inner harmony which I have lost." This cry and this appeal arise from the depths of the soul. And in the cry, will and knowledge first begin to tremble in their roots. The will has shaken the soul's harmony. If it now permits itself to be flooded with sorrow, if it shuns the cold darkness of the refusal of grace, it will turn anew with the beginnings of love toward appreciation of moral value. It could shut out the light of understanding only by allowing itself to be beguiled by the sinister light of error. Only if it welcomes the lamp of understanding already beginning to glow from the soul's depths will it attain to clear knowledge of conscience and form a new contact with value through the craving which afflicts it and which is satisfied only by true worth. And the reproach of moral awareness becomes clear: "You have failed to grasp the values within your reach! You are guilty!"

The first movements of conscience refer to the I (they are not "egotistic"). The wounded I simply cries out. But as soon as man, disturbed by the first qualm of conscience, renews his appreciation of the value he has violated, there issues forth from it not merely the torment of the gaping wound. Terrified by his lapse, man harkens to the trumpet of the angel of judgment. He becomes aware of a new admonition arising from the obligation inherent in value. Reproach and warning to repent mingle in the agony of the tortured soul—of the I—which by its disobedience, specifically by its aversion from value, weakened its capacity to harken to the voice inviting it to love. But it is attuned to the loving voice of value through its own hurt and pain.

Here the approach to good must begin. We cannot picture offended value as simply saying without further to-do: "I am the remedy you can use to restore your moral health." But the value violated suggests much on such points as this: through it one sickens or grows well morally; the soul is torn by moral disobedience, remains morally sound through obedience. But as soon as the spastic grip of sin upon the will is broken or in some measure weakened, so that we can turn again to the light and knowledge of value, then the good makes its appeal. From the lofty summits of its majesty it calls to man: "You must! I possess dignity and authority over you!" Obviously conscience in its distress perceives most acutely the essential consequence of the good. It is a matter of life or death, and the decision rests with conscience; to choose the good means life; to reject it, death.

The good moral conscience is faced with a different situation. Just as a man in good physical condition usually reflects little on the state of his health, despite all his vigor and energy, so the man who is entirely dedicated to moral values is not in the habit of turning back in self-reflection on the wholesome effects of spiritual good health. He rather rejoices in good, does good under the impulse of the most intimate love for it. And this bears with it the obvious consequence, the greatest vigor of spiritual health, that is the intimate unity and harmony of soul and the rich abundance of good flowing from it.

The following results are particularly evident: the conscience possesses a legitimate function centering in the person, in the I, a function, however, which is truly meaningful only when it leads to function centering in value. Sorrow centering in the person, the I, to cite an example, has the inner dynamic to summon up all the forces of the soul tending toward unity, and turn them to the offended and violated value again. If the offense has brought illness to the soul, a return to the value offended alone can restore spiritual health. The more fully the elemental torment of conscience has attained its purpose, the more the conflict of conscience is resolved and the craving which afflicts it is satisfied by return to the value violated. The more value assumes new forms of love and is sheathed in sorrow by the will, so much the more is the hurt of conscience, centering in the I, healed as the torment of conscience diminishes and recedes into the background.

Personal health and harmony of inner unity, psychic wholeness of the I, arising from recognition of value, is no less a reality than the personal disruption, the disorder of the I, which follows in the wake of sin. Unity and disorder of soul are inevitable results, the one of moral good, the other of moral evil. But disorder (illness of soul) is more obvious and more readily recognized than unity (health of soul) and consequently we are more conscious of it. This is only natural and normal.[48] The sharp realization of the distinction between good and bad conscience should not lead us to ignore the reality of good conscience. Nor should we underestimate the good conscience by contrast with the evil, for the good conscience is the dynamic force of spiritual health pressing forward to new good. For the Calvinists there is only an "evil conscience," resting on a false concept of man and leaving no room in the innermost depth of the soul for any soundness, but only for the dismal ruin of concupiscence.[49]

b. Conscience: Confronting a Principle or God?

If on the loftiest level of personality the living person feels so firmly bound to the good that obedience to duty arising from the exigence of value means life for him, and disobedience means disruption and supreme peril, then the challenge is inescapable: What is the nature of such an imperative placed upon me? What is the nature of this vital force penetrating my nature? The human spirit cannot rest satisfied with the answer, "That is simply a principle." The more man lives from the depths of his personality, the more surely and inescapably will his spiritual intuition assure him: it is not an abstraction, not an absolute principle, but a living person, who sustains all the demands of values. Our basic philosophy and theology of life show that this is certain and even self-evident. Conscience itself, which furnishes us with our most profound experiences of the attachment to the good and of the perils arising from resistance to it, summons us with clarion call to the search for that which can challenge us so mightily.

For our age with its practical problems of life, conscience must be studied as a moral phenomenon, for the simple reason of its universal presence. Even those who have no realization of its religious depth recognize its existence. Here we have a point of contact with those who are not religious-minded at all. The greater the dimension of moral depth within conscience, the more significant its religious foundation appears. Inevitably the religious must reveal itself as the ethical deepens and develops, for conscience is in the very roots of its being a religious phenomenon with its ultimate origin in man's likeness to God.

The profound depth of conscience is revealed to man only if he transcends value and its challenge, only if he harkens to that which is beyond, to the Person, holy, insistent, source of all value, only if he discerns in the loud cry of his own soul the echo of a genuine summons from the person who calls. Only one who wants to make a god of himself prefers an impersonal value, an abstract legal principle to the Person who sustains both law and principle. Anyone whose pride has not corrupted his conscience with all its experience will turn to the Person with absolute confidence and certainty. Beyond the majesty of judgment and the warning call to repentance and conversion there is the Person who calls and invites, a Judge, living, absolute, the source of the summons and the law.

c. Conscience as the Voice of God

Ultimately beyond the voice of conscience we see God, all-holy. But it would be going too far to look upon each single judgment of conscience as a direct act of divine intervention. God has endowed us with moral faculties. He established the order of nature which by use of the natural power of our intelligence we can grasp and understand as obliging and binding us. In fact, God has bound us up with it through our whole being. So the natural function of conscience is to make us partakers of the eternal law of God through the created nature around us and through our own rational nature. Our bond with the natural moral law is an exalted participation in the eternal law of God manifested by our conscience whose natural function it is to reveal our likeness to God.

The supernatural revelation in Christ and the guidance of the Holy Spirit give conscience a supernatural task and power beyond its natural moral function just described. In the light of supernatural revelation, conscience fixes its attention on the word and the example of Christ and under the influence of the Holy Spirit admonishes us to be docile toward His inspirations. However, as we cautioned above regarding direct intervention by God in the individual judgments of conscience, so here also we must stress that at least as a rule the Holy Spirit does not speak by direct revelation to the particular soul. But by means of His gifts He confers on conscience a delicacy of perception and a tenderness of tact so that in the light of divine revelation projected on all the circumstances in which one is involved in particular instances one readily discerns the divine will.

The fact that God operates through second causes does not diminish the grandeur of His works or weaken their binding force. Even though medieval theologians thought that God moved celestial bodies through the activity of His angels, He was Himself no less the Mover. Similarly, even though we know today the natural laws through which God governs the world, we do not consider Him any less immanent for all that. This knowledge does not render Him any more remote from us than if we knew nothing about such laws. Accordingly, if we do not recognize in the decision of conscience the direct voice of God, we still are entirely within the realm of truth and sound reason when we speak of conscience as the voice of God. It is the voice of God, but in the sense that we must contribute something of our own in the formation of the decision of our conscience which is right in God's sight. Error is possible in our decision, but we are able to trace it to its source. The power of conscience which impels us to act according to our rational insight is always the voice of God. In a certain sense it is infallible. But in so far as it deviates from the correct norm, in so far as it ceases to be rational, it is no longer the voice of God, but is our own (evil) work.

4. *Conscience and Authority*

a. Mutual Interplay of Conscience and Authority

Conscience is not an oracle which can draw the truth from its own obscure depths or even create it. It is the proper task of conscience to move the will in accordance with the truth of which it is aware and to search for the truth prior to its decision. Accordingly, conscience and objective truth, and ultimately also conscience and the authority of God teaching us, essentially belong together. By its very nature conscience seeks illumination and guidance, which it finds naturally in the order and harmony of creation, in the supernatural order with wonderful fulness in Christ, and through Christ and the Holy Spirit in the teaching Church.

But on its part genuine authority—such is its nature—also postulates conscience. Without conscience it would not have the character of moral authority, nor be able to exercise authority over human persons. We can have moral authority over men, guiding, directing them only if authority appeals to conscience. For each individual man his own conscience is the norm of moral conduct. We call it the ultimate subjective norm, but it is always dependent, a norm which must conform to a higher norm, an objective norm! This it must always seek in the objective world of truth in order to be correct and valid.

God, the ultimate norm, the truth to which every conscience must conform, is free to determine in what way and to what degree He will teach the human conscience. But He always instructs conscience in accordance with its nature: the natural conscience through the order of nature, the conscience endowed with the supernatural grace of faith through supernatural revelation. Just as it is not alien to natural conscience to draw from the natural revelation expressed in creation and to learn from the natural communities which correspond to it, so it is also "according to nature" for the believing conscience elevated by grace and steeped in humility to harken to the word of revelation communicated to us in the Church, even though, of course, the "old man" shrinks from the ordeal of obscurity and obedience demanded of him by faith.

b. Conscience and Authority of the Church

Only one with a totally perverted concept of the real nature and function of conscience could repudiate the infallible *magisterium* of the Church in the name of conscience. Only a conscience which itself enjoys creative plenitude of infallibility in its own native right could *a priori* reject as contradictory every intervention of objective authority. The dogma of the infallibility of the Church and of the Pope in no wise breaches the integrity of conscience, but on the contrary safeguards it in the ultimate and decisive questions through the surest orientation toward truth. Through infallibility there is a clear delineation of the area in which the conscience is given an absolute certain guidance, as distinguished from the area in which under some circumstances there might arise a conflict between conscience and the lawful non-infallible ecclesiastical ruling authority. Precisely because the ecclesiastical authority is conscious of the limits of its infallibility, it will not go beyond these bounds in demanding from the individual conscience a firmer assent than lies in the objective claim to acceptance of the doctrine itself. This may vary considerably.[50]

In matters of discipline, conflict can readily arise between the attitude or decision of ecclesiastical authority and the conscience of the individual. Authority may fail in some instances to arrive at the most just and prudent decision. And the subject is far from infallible in his judgment of conscience. Nevertheless, for the very reason that the limits of certitude are clearly recognized on both sides, the conflict should not result in harshness or bitterness. But the presumption is in favor of authority. We presume that ecclesiastical authority has truth and justice on its side, provided that the one in authority is in lawful possession of his office and discharges its duties with a spirit of moral and religious responsibility. Only the most convincing reasons to the contrary can overthrow this presumption of right in favor of the superior and justify opposition to his decision. If, however, a subject forms such a firm judgment of conscience after thorough inquiry and self-examination, he may not obey the superior in opposition to this judgment of conscience. But if the subject seriously questions the legitimacy of authority or the moral probity of the precept or command, the problem and its solution belong to the controversial area of the "moral systems." The matter is treated in the section dealing with the risk or venture of conscience and also in the pages concerned with doubtful judgments of conscience.

c. Conscience and Civil Authority

Conscience is linked with authority in a twofold manner: first to the state, which derives from nature itself and receives its authorization from the natural law, an authorization which is corroborated by divine revelation. Secondly, to community, for in countless ways conscience depends for help on community and social authority in order to be rightly informed in its judgment. But when secular authority, as is often the case today, claims native and original jurisdiction in all matters of right and does not recognize any prior right to its own in point of legislation (legal positivism), its laws and commands must meet with much misgiving and frequently be examined with a very critical eye by the individual conscience. Only if authority itself recognizes the bond of conscience can the subject in conscience concede to it the presumption of right, of which we have just spoken. Laws and commands oblige only when they are in agreement with the norm of morals. It is not civil authority, but conscience in conformity with the norm of morals, which is the ultimate instance to which man appeals in rendering moral decisions.

d. Conscience: Obedience and Freedom

There can be no absolute freedom of conscience for the simple reason that conscience does not free one from the law. On the contrary, it is conscience alone which actually binds one to the law of the good. Everyone, of course, must ultimately follow his conscience; this means he must do right as he sees the right with sincere desire and effort to find and to do what is good. But there are certain moral principles which no one can fail to recognize. No one may set himself above these fundamental principles and invoke the right of conscience as justification of his act. In instances of inculpable ignorance or error, one has the right and duty to follow one's conscience, although it may be necessary occasionally for society to intervene and interfere with certain acts in order to prevent evil consequences. Tragic conflicts can readily arise in such instances.

But when conscience is in error culpably, the right of a free conscience may not be invoked. In such instances it is within the province of higher authority to correct the error and safeguard the community from the ravages of pernicious principles. It is one of the greatest evils of our day that so few generally recognized moral principles still prevail among the masses of men. Consequently and consistently men will give an entirely free rein to the erroneous conscience, culpably lax or actually malicious. To cite an example, the state does not uphold a correct conception of conscience when it appeals to freedom of conscience in permitting and legally safeguarding the spread and sale of vile literature, means of contraception, and even abortion. The state has the duty to guarantee the liberty of sane and sound conscience, but not the license of evil and perverted conscience. Failure to do so can have only one result, the inevitable violent dominance of the evil over the good.

5. *Formation and Perversion of Conscience*

a. The Conscientious Act

A distinction must be drawn between the formation of conscience as a faculty or power and the formation of particular decisions or judgments of conscience. Zeal for truth and diligent cultivation of knowledge in law and value are indispensable conditions for any training of conscience. To cultivate moral knowledge as such demands in every concrete situation zeal and vigilance in the attempt to reach the right verdict of conscience. Moreover, there must be a readiness on the part of man, limited as he is, to accept instruction and counsel. Even more important are the correct attitude toward the Church's teaching and governing *magisterium* and ultimately docility toward the Holy Spirit.

b. Conservation and Formation of Dispositions of Conscience

The excitation of conscience is a kind of challenge on the part of the objective power to love directed to the subjective readiness to love. If the readiness or willingness to love fails constantly, then eventually the objective power to love is progressively hampered and crippled. The "spark of the soul" must constantly be kept aglow through the constant will to love. And the intellect in turn must be continuously enkindled anew in its knowledge of values through the glow of love in the will. The life of values in intellect and will draws its nourishment from the rich depths of the soul. But by their own moral activity intellect and will must also enrich and deepen this permanent power to love within the recesses of the soul. Habitual refusal to love engenders hardness of heart and impossibility of loving. It is evil when conscience errs in judgment. But incomparably more tragic is the blunting and crippling of moral conscience itself. This is a hardening of heart which assumes a variety of basic types.

First, unity and harmony of personality and with it the dynamic of conscience are particularly jeopardized in the case of that flaccid type of man who quite admires the good abstractly and in theory, though he holds himself aloof from the practice of it. In a manner the intellect with its knowledge of values fails to spark the will so that warmth is lacking in the will's grasp of them. Proper cultivation of integrity of conscience includes the study of the commandments and even of the good, not only under the aspect of their intrinsic value, but also in the light of the challenge they offer us. In this connection we should note the importance of cultivating a well-ordered emotional life, since the emotions in some way or other are essential for the sparking of intellect with the drive of the will. (The impulse to mysticism is ordinarily given by affective prayer.)

Second, the greatest menace to conscience is habitual deliberate disobedience of the will when confronted with clear realization of value. This is multiplication of fault without contrition. The reaction of conscience will vary according to the diversity of personality: a) in some instances, wilful pride and egotism obscure the mind to such a degree that even incipient appreciation of value is lacking in the judgment of the conscience, though the will in the main is still ready to accept such values and accomplish the good they suggest. This is the usual reaction of strong characters who are basically sound, though the original dynamic effort of conscience to restore moral harmony and unity through conversion has failed. It is the frightful counteraction of the conscience seeking for unity and harmony. Obviously, a harmony of sorts in knowing and willing has been established, but it is a darksome, miserable bond of union. The gap is no longer in the person himself, no longer between intellect and will. The soul is no longer disturbed in its depths from this source. The stirrings of conscience are gradually blunted. But now a deep chasm yawns between the soul and the realm of values, between the soul and the basic source from which it draws all its moral riches. Unity is now established, but it is Satanic unity in the soul, and with it comes Satanic darkening: the devil is the father of lies (cf. JN 8:44). The lie has become ingrained. The good can no longer summon to fear. b) In weaker individuals blunting of conscience results in a species of "split" in the soul, with a permanent sundering of intellect and will, but in such a manner that the soul is completely dulled against the pain of such a gaping wound. In the mind there is still the light of the good. But the knowledge of the good does not stir the will and arouse it to true appreciation of the good for which it is made. It does not set the soul aglow to its very depths nor fill it with warmth. There is little depth of soul. The depth which was the basis of harmony seems to lack vitality, the depth in which knowledge should be aflame with love and love enlightened with knowledge! The person is sick to his very heart. The personality is "split."

c. Humility: Indispensable Remedy

The Christian's knowledge of values in the supernatural order based on the richness of revelation and even his knowledge in the natural order arising from the nature of man as mobile being, nearly always are far in advance of his will in choosing those same values. To a degree we must bear the blame ourselves, although our heritage of impotence of will must share the responsibility if our actions fall short of our moral knowledge. This antithesis between knowledge and realization or accomplishment may prove to be the source of a weakened and blunted conscience, although such a result cannot be considered inevitable. But if this natural antithesis creates a deep gap because of the indolence of the will, it must follow that intellect and will adjust themselves by acceptance of this separation or the gap be closed by evil will through a darkening of the mind.[51]

This danger is met only when humility closes the gaping wound in the personality, a wound which only humility can heal. Humility with sorrow and purpose of amendment is the grand natural fountain of health for the conscience of man. But the ultimate remedy for this deep wound which penetrates to the very depth of the soul is divine grace. It is the light piercing the darkness of the abyss which separates us from the kingdom of the good (God). This light dispelling the darkness, this ultimate remedy of our wounds, this gift of divine grace we must beg of God through humble prayer. One of the greatest miracles of grace given to the converted sinner is the restoration of the clear vision of good and evil and especially the renewal of vitality in a deadened conscience. *Cor mundum crea in me, Deus!* "Create a clean heart in me, O God!" (Ps 50:12).

6. *Authority of an Erroneous Conscience*

Conscience itself as faculty or power cannot be erroneous, but its decisions may be in error. Conscience as vital power can be dulled, but it cannot err. With unerring certainty it calls out that the will and intellect of man must conform in action, as they are rooted together in being. This imperative written in the soul continues in possession of infallible truth even with a background of defective moral knowledge, indeed, despite a background of a fully erroneous judgment of conscience. If the error is in no wise due to the guilt of free will, there is nothing in the faculty of conscience itself which would murmur against the execution of the erroneous judgment of conscience. Sustaining it is the whole sound dynamic of conscience. An inculpably erroneous dictate of conscience obliges the same as a correct conscience, just as a servant feels obliged to carry out the order of his master as he has understood it if he listened attentively even though the command was actually different. His master actually spoke to him, but the servant misunderstood. The condition is the same in the instance of the erroneous decision of conscience: supporting it always is the Lord whom we ultimately feel is speaking in conscience. But His voice is misunderstood. Therefore Cardinal Newman is correct in his statement: "I have always contended that obedience even to an erring conscience was the way to gain light. . . ."[52]

But in all this we assume absolutely that the error of conscience is inculpable. Frequently there is simply an error consequent to human limitations. Often too it is rooted in former sins. If there has been sincere repentance for these former faults, then the erroneous judgment of conscience arising from them can be judged as inculpable in relation to the present act. On the other hand, if error derives from a deliberately fixed and perverted attitude of mind, conscience as faculty will in some way protest against this very attitude. Only from a superficial point of view not based on a grasp of the whole situation might one be convinced that his conscience actually does command him to follow the dictate arising from that disturbed source.

The verdict of conscience, erroneous and culpable, as one element in the entire mental activity is always bound up with a warning proceeding from conscience as faculty or power, demanding that one immediately probe into the error or dam up its evil source; this implies an altering of the whole false attitude of mind.

One sins in following a culpably erroneous dictate of conscience and also in acting contrary to it. But the sin is more immediate and heinous if one acts contrary to the erroneous conscience, even should he in this manner actually do what is objectively right. For if he looks upon something as preceptive—even though he is in error—and yet acts contrariwise, he has the will, as far as it lies in him, to violate the commandment of God. Although such an erroneous verdict of conscience can be rectified, still, so long as it persists, it is actually binding.[53] And yet, according to Thomas, it would not be correct to say that the man with a culpably erroneous conscience necessarily commits sin. For not only is the choice open to him between obedience and disobedience contrary to the erroneous dictate of conscience but it is entirely within his power to correct the verdict of conscience by means of a purging of the sources of error in their very depths.[54]

Saint Thomas illustrated these principles by an example which is cited in certain current discussions. Is one obliged, we are asked, to leave the Church or deny Christ, if his conscience, or rather his erroneous conviction demands?[55] Thomas absolutely excludes the possibility that any one may arrive at such a false attitude without incurring guilt. In the atmosphere of the Middle Ages, entirely Catholic as it was, such a point could hardly be a real problem, a true *Quaestio!*

The problem actually is concerned with the conscience culpably in error. His answer is classic, since on the one hand it manifests the greatest reverence for conscience, and on the other takes a position of the sternest opposition to the overemphasis of the actual and concrete verdict of conscience. The Angelic Doctor says plainly: if anyone confesses faith in Christ or the Church, although he has formed the conviction that it is evil to do so, he sins against his conscience.[56] But from this it does not follow, in the mind of Thomas, that he must deny Christ or the Church in order not to sin. He must rather settle his disturbed conscience to arrive at a true inculpable verdict of conscience. One may appeal to conscience only if he has been loyal to his conscience throughout the process of the formation of his convictions. Viewed correctly, the culpably erroneous judgment is not really a verdict of conscience at all. The true judgment is not the superficial and confused voice of the misled man, but that deeper protest of true reason, which in this instance rather warns and exhorts: "Cleanse your conscience! Free yourself of the guilt of a darkened and confused conscience!"

7. The Perplexed Conscience

The disturbed or perplexed conscience is a particular type of erroneous conscience which arises from a transitory but violent disturbance of the capacity to form a judgment. Faced with the necessity of making a decision, there is no apparent choice that is free from sin. In such instances, if the decision can be delayed, one must first postpone the solution of the difficulty in order to deliberate upon it. But if the decision cannot be delayed the conscientious person will choose what he thinks the "lesser sin" and thus manifest his morally correct attitude. In fact, there is no question of sin in this matter; for sin is not merely a matter of intellectual judgment, but also of freedom of will, which here is lacking.

To cite an example, if one who is seriously sick thinks that he is necessarily guilty of sin either by violation of the law of the Church or by violation of the fifth commandment of God, he is nonetheless not actually guilty if he misses Mass on a Sunday or holy day of obligation because he cannot attend or because his common sense keeps him at home in bed. But he does sin if his wrongly formed conscience tells him he must attend the Sunday Mass even at grave risk of health (note that in this instance only one possibility of sin is presented to his conscience) and he acts to the contrary, assuming that his physical condition does not deprive him of the actual exercise of freedom.

If in such instances the faithful confess to having missed Mass on a Sunday or holy day because of illness, it is altogether probable that they have neither committed sin nor acted in a state of perplexity. The accusation may be no more than a formal manner of recounting their sins or a manifestation of a desire for express assurance that their conduct was correct.

8. Lax Conscience

Lax conscience means permanent moral dullness, gradual hardening of conscience. It also implies a frivolity that has become habitual and created an indifference to correction of a conscience culpably in error. The lax conscience does not face up to its grave moral obligations. It is usually the result of grave lukewarmness in the service of God, as depicted in the Apocalypse 3:16–20. The same passages indicate the remedies for lukewarmness: repentance, zeal in the study of the good, probing of conscience ("eye salve"), zeal in the doing of good works ("be clothed in white garments"). God Himself sends His visitations as remedy (Ap 3:19). The antithesis to lax conscience is the "tender conscience," the "delicate conscience." One with a tender conscience preserves himself intact with clear and vigilant discernment of the good.

9. The Scrupulous Conscience (*)

a. The Phenomenology of the Scrupulous Conscience

"The ultimate basis of man is the sense of responsibility."[1]* If we take the term *being responsible* in a comprehensive and above all in a personal sense, it means the capacity manifested in the conscience by which we are able to harken and to respond. According to the teaching of Catholic moral theology, it is not primarily or in the first instance that one must be *responsible* for something or "answer" for something. It is rather that one remains open and becomes increasingly open to the word of love which calls for response in love. Ultimate in man is his "word-response-relation" to God and to the fellowship of God's children. Conscience attains its true religious depth, its metaphysical soundness only after all things are clearly viewed in the light of divine love. On this level we must study the reality of scrupulosity in its many forms and variations.

The psychotherapist will be most concerned with the psychic reactions. He will analyze the psychic deviations which underlie or accompany scrupulosity. Far from neglecting these psychological realities, the priest and director of souls will study them and give them serious consideration. It is his special task as a moral theologian, however, to study the forms

(*) These pages on scrupulosity are from the author's ms. made in preparation for the sixth edition of his work.

(1*) V. Frankl, *Die Psychotherapie in der aerztliche Praxis.* 6 aufl. Wien 1947, 116.

of scrupulosity which do not have their source in psychic illness but in a religious-moral state. It is entirely within his province to study the form and content of religious deviation even in those forms which are accompanied by psychic defects (take, for example, the abnormal depressive states or the obsessive-compulsive tendency). He must particularly investigate the causal relation between religious instruction and guidance and the manifestations of scrupulosity, but he may not ignore the effect of psychic conditions. In the case of neurosis it is precisely the psychotherapist who suggests this religious and moral approach.

(1) *Scrupulosity Partially Due to Terror of Conscience*

The psychiatrist or psychotherapist is inclined to look upon scrupulosity as an exclusively psychic illness arising predominantly from psychic or more specifically from psychosomatic causes. But there is a type of scrupulosity which is primarily or even exclusively religious. Conditioned by religious attitudes it is more or less normal or at least rather common in the religious-moral development of the personality. In fact it often marks a critical stage in this religious growth.

We do not have in mind merely a tender conscience as distinguished from a conscience steeped in sloth and spiritual torpor. Here we are dealing with an acute disturbance of spiritual balance through shock and terror of conscience. Already in his time Cardinal Gerson, great theologian of the Council of Constance, explicitly stressed the potential spiritual value of a passing phase of scrupulosity. Such a spiritual test might prove particularly profitable at the inception of a truly religious life or at the beginning of life in religion, which the ancient tradition viewed as a continuous and ever deepening religious conversion. A man who is entirely superficial in matters of conscience may be overwhelmed by a profound realization of God as grace moves him to conversion, with the result that his previous superficial and naive sense of spiritual security—in fact, all sense of spiritual safety—is temporarily lost.

The crisis may assume aspects which would lead one to believe that the disturbance is also psychic and has created an imbalance which primarily demands medical or psychotherapeutic care. In fact, this form of temporary scrupulosity (with its anxiety and insecurity) will prove to be a fruitful stage of development, provided a correct grasp of its nature and a sense of loyalty to divine grace give one control of the situation. However, should the religious instruction and guidance be unsound, various forms of obstinate and morbid scrupulosity may develop as a result of this disturbance of conscience, particularly if the psychic dispositions are unfavorable. We shall have more to say on this point later.

It is unavoidable that the spiritually superficial man begins to fear for his salvation once he is awakened from a spirituality which is unsound, naive, and shallow. He must begin to entertain such a fear of the depth and extent of his religious and moral responsibility that he is shaken to the depths of his conscience by the violent disturbance of emotional balance. This new depth of conscience is a charge and challenge to the direction of souls. Above all it imposes upon the director the specific task of discerning the meaning of this phase of terrified conscience and of preparing the way for a salutary depth of conscience.

What we have said is quite in harmony with sound treatment of neurosis from the therapeutic standpoint: insight into the nature and cause of the neurosis and search for the subconscious motivation. However, this type of scrupulosity is quite obviously different from every neurotic form of scruple, for the deep motivation is not due to suppressed desires masking their expression in the conscious experience. Quite the contrary, the terrified conscience is altogether open to the call from God. But like Samuel in the Old Testament, who heard the voice of the Lord in the temple, the terrified conscience is in a state of confusion without a clear realization of the divine call.

(2) Scrupulous Conscience due to Neurotic Fixation

Morbid scrupulosity occurs most commonly in the instances of fear and compulsion neurosis. Usually the two forms appear together in some manner, but in such wise that in the one case anxiety (particularly if the fear is universal and not restricted to one area or object) and in the other case the psychic compulsion dominates. Although hybrid forms are not excluded, the scrupulosity marked by dread and compulsiveness must be sharply distinguished from hysteria, which ultimately seeks to create an impression in the confession through a thousand scruples.

It is not at all sufficient to take into consideration only the bad psychic condition or the proneness to depressive or neurotic states. We must inquire also into the basic reason and significance: why does the neurosis manifest itself specifically in this particular area and in this guise? The individual who is unsuited for real life because of agoraphobia or compulsion to count or repeat is indeed very ill in a profound and human sense. His illness is far worse than that which disturbs the scrupulant whose neurosis derives its whole force and meaning from the persistent fear of his obligations and responsibilities in the sight of God. The neurotic scrupulant has not lost his sense of responsibility. In the last analysis he has gone astray regarding the true nature and aspect of responsibility, whether it be because of a psychic defect, or because of wrong guidance or permanent moral indecision in decisive matters.

In the attempt we now make to classify according to type the various forms of morbid scrupulosity, we may not ignore the psychic elements. But we must at the same time give due consideration to the character of the religious deviation which lies at the root of the scrupulosity or manifests itself in it.

(a) Anxiety Neurosis

i. *General Anxiety Neurosis not Limited in Area*

This is a manifestation of a one-sided *religion of fear:* God's claim on us is viewed as a threat affecting our actual response to God; every moral effort or engagement is looked upon as a risk to our salvation. The dread of God and morbid anxiety over the assurance of salvation are centered especially on the confession of sin in the sacrament of penance and lead to the endless repetition of confessions and grotesque exaggerations in the regular reception of the sacrament.

The causes of this condition are (apart from marked psychic predisposition toward emotional anxiety) the experience of a hyper-rigorous, arbitrary, and autocratic father, a stern mother or one who is always worried, a religious instructor constantly chiding and punishing, the overemphasis of the motive of fear in sermons! Under such religious conditions there is no preparation in actual life for the experience of God's love in the soul. The divine virtue of hope and childlike trust in God lacks all affective basis. On the other hand, even a balanced preaching and instruction on the eternal truths and a moderate discipline of correction on the part of parents can already produce fear in one disposed to a reaction of phobia or depression, can release the disposition toward an anxiety neurosis or augment it.

ii. *Anxiety Neurosis Concerned with Fixation in One Area*

Some pathological anxiety fixes all attention on one area (e.g., truthfulness or chastity) and in a specific manner seeks its release. This fear of a definite or concrete object is less baffling than undefined anxiety. But it may also happen in the case of a normal psychic condition that an extreme emphasis of one commandment or duty or virtue may have a baneful effect, so that the one-sided experience gradually becomes fixed. Thus there are scrupulants who constantly accuse themselves in confession of neglect of their duty toward the salvation of others or of sins against chastity despite the contrary assurance of their confessor. They fancy themselves cooperators in every conceivable sin which others commit or they are tormented by every conceivable temptation. They hold themselves sinfully responsible for giving occasion to impure thoughts and feelings (indirectly voluntary), although such so-called occasions are in a totally different area and have no relation to chastity at all. The underlying reason is the presence of a real dread of failure in the exercise of a virtue which they look upon as extremely important. Or it may be considered as the only important virtue. Excessive emphasis placed on one duty or one virtue may obliquely have a morbid effect on the emotions, produce anxious forebodings regarding the future and disturb the whole emotional life. Endless introspection before the reception of the sacraments merely makes matters worse. Obviously at the bottom of this weakness there lurks a love for the virtue concerned, although of course it is not a well-ordered love integrated into the whole spiritual life. It can be accompanied by a partial blindness to value in other areas. Nevertheless we do not class it as an actual compensation scrupulosity, since no basic or central obligation is consciously and culpably neglected.

(b) Compulsive Neurotic Scrupulosity

i. *Compulsive Neurosis Concerned with Anxious Legalistic Quibbling*

The spirit of creativeness and initiative in the moral order is cramped by a one-sided fixation on legal prescriptions of greater or lesser significance or of no significance at all. These are viewed as taboos of a kind. Whereas those afflicted with such scrupulosity are usually normal in the practical affairs of life, they are ridiculously impractical in some spiritual matters. To cite just one example, they may be abnormally anxious in observing the Eucharistic fast. It is of more common occurrence that such scrupulants become confused regarding the positive law which requires that all mortal sins be confessed together with their number and species. Ceaselessly they are impelled to probe their memories for some forgotten detail or flaw in their confession of sins. Eventually the sacrament of penance is looked upon primarily as a legalistic, magical ritual performance which is to furnish the sinner assurance against the wrath of God. Or at least such is the emotional approach of these tortured minds. We should not underrate the value of their willingness to submit to the most painful self-humiliation—for the procedure is a veritable torture, provided it is not a manifestation of a combination of hysteria—as morally meritorious effort. Nor should we exaggerate its worth, since the penitent is under a form of compulsion and driven on by fear.

If the moral-religious life as a whole remains intact, despite this disturbance—even though the individual always suffers a loss of vital spiritual force through this legalistic cramping of effort—we must conclude that the fault is due to defect in spiritual guidance. The evil does not lie so much in a psychic defect as in lack of sound direction and moral-religious instruction. Consequently a change on these points should result in a correction of the condition and spiritual improvement.

ii. *The Neurotic Compulsion Toward Self-Assurance and the One Hundred Percenters*

What is lacking here is the practical recognition of man's actual mode of existence on earth, which is constantly a state of becoming. The forced anthropocentric-minded ethic of self-perfection corresponds to a neurotic experience of human impotence. Whereas the sound and healthy man (who does not focus his total attention on himself in the neurotic manner just referred to) is satisfied with simple moral certainty (for the natural instinct of conscience demands no more), this type of scrupulant demands the sense of absolute certainty and security. Therefore he is willing to assume the burden of an excessive legalism with its countless points of law, not well-founded indeed, in preference to the courage of the moral venture in accord with the situation itself. The extraordinary combination of a predominantly fear-slanted religion, of an ethic of self-perfection focused in the individual himself, of a juridically conceived relation to God with a taboo setting up an absolute of purely positive legalities, all this can involve even the individual who is not afflicted with a phobia or compulsion in neurotic scrupulosity.

A careful study of the entire background in the history of the moral systems from the psychological standpoint might justify the hypothesis that the attitude of a whole group of tutiorists and hyper-rigorous probabiliorists in the acrid controversy over the correct "moral system" was on the level of mass neurosis. It is at least a tenable hypothesis that on this level of mass neurosis the symptoms are the same as those which characterize individual scrupulosity with its fixation of legalistic quibbling and helpless compulsive drive for spiritual security and certainty. Indeed, the sum total of controversy in moral theology about the use of probable opinion could be explained as an epochal compulsive neurosis. Perhaps the only actual explanation of the probabilistic quarrel with its narrow focus of attention on purely positive prescriptions of the pettiest kind which are scarcely comprehensible for Christianity and for us today is that it was due to epochal mass neurosis. Of course a serious concern for a truly scientific solution of moral problems was never lacking. And one of the decisive factors in the effort of the representatives of probabilism and equiprobabilism was their concern for true Christian freedom in the spirit of St. Paul. However, in effect, the concentration of all forces for defence of doubtful laws was tantamount to a legalistic fixation of compulsive neurosis in scrupulosity: it meant damming up the more profound moral and religious energies by legalistic restraints. In the background was the Father image of God as a thoroughly absolutistic and arbitrary ruler. Such a conception of God obviously influenced Jansenistic rigorism far more profoundly than the system of probabilism which the Jansenists so heartily hated. Surely the probabilists were amply concerned with the legalistic position in placing the problem, but precisely because of their express mildness in this area there was still place in their system for trust in God. (2*)

The "legalistic" form of scrupulosity is generally very sharply distinguished from the exaggerated anxiety of certain souls regarding the duties and responsibilities which they may share with others. The legalistically restrained scrupulant (above all, the one whom we shall discuss in the next paragraph) does not enjoy direct access to the call of the hour, whereas the one whose difficulties lie in the area of concern for responsibility (regarding fraternal correction, obligation to engage in the apostolate, duty to help others in bodily need, etc.) and who is neurotically restricted does have a conscience thoroughly alerted to the situation. The anxiety of the latter may be characterized as an altogether special form of

(2*) J. Regnier goes a step further. He maintains that "it can be historically established when the phenomenon of scrupulosity actually first appeared. It developed in relatively modern times from the juristic attitudes of thought of the Latin moralists. St. Thomas and the eastern churches are not even aware of the concept." (*Der moderne Mensch und die Suende. Wuerzburg*, 1959, 31.) (The original title is: *Le sens du péché*. Paris.: Lethielleux, 1954, 33.)

misconception of human imperfection, whereas the endeavor in the other instance is caught in the meshes of mere legality. It is the effort to attain a one hundred percent legal security and safety.

iii. *Compulsive Neurotic Scrupulosity of Compensation*

This type of scrupulosity is of frequent occurrence. In the last analysis it arises from protracted neglect on the part of deeply religious natures in the most fundamental areas of religious and moral life. A cramped and restrictive effort to comply with the pettiest detail of law conceals an apathy and laxity in fundamental moral matters, particularly in love of neighbor and the cultivation of a life of prayer. There are several reasons why deep-seated neglect leads to this form of legalistic scrupulosity: not only the lack of a wholesome humility but also of that ultimate pride which for others in a similar situation leads to universal hostility or obtuseness to value or even to infidelity. (Moreover, there is a species of infidelity which in a similar way intrenches itself behind a precise decorum or the works of fraternal charity against the call of one's deepest conscience or any external summons to conversion.) Exaggerated anxiety regarding works of zeal and scrupulosity in confession restricted to the area of legal prescriptions are to be explained only in the light of depth psychology. They are escape from true responsibility, escape from the accusations arising from the depths of a conscience which has not yet been silenced.

Only a study of the whole personality in all its phases and its spiritual background, a truly sympathetic and perceptive study, will enable the director to judge the case correctly and determine its true character: is the case one of compensatory scrupulosity such as we have just described or is it basically and essentially a compulsive neurosis? The way to correction of the compensatory scrupulosity must lead to deep conversion of mind and heart, a complete and utter turning to God. But such a conversion is not at all possible without a clear grasp of the nature of the summons to conversion. Surely there is hope for success only if the call to penance proceeds from the loving conviction that it is directed not only to the sinner whose failure is due to suppressed desires, but also to the patient whose freedom is cramped and who suffers in his subconscious self from his impotence. To some extent the condition is also the consequence of unsound training, a condition for which others must bear a degree of responsibility.

b. Pastoral and Medical Care

We have already stated that the sense of responsibility lies at the root and center of the human person and likewise that this very center is endangered in the case of the scrupulant. It follows that every effort, be it in the direction and care of souls or medical and psychical, must help the individual to regain his sense of responsibility corresponding to his call from God. Above all the scrupulant must be shown the way to basic responsibility, to a living and effective realization of the word-response relation to God as a basis for every responsibility in individual instances.

To be responsble means above all to participate in the dialogue of love with God and one's neighbor. One of the principal causes of scrupulosity is the fact that some men never come to a living contact of love for God or neighbor or have lost it. Instead they fancy that they have to face a God of threat (anxiety neurosis) or a thousand stark legalities (compulsion neurosis).

Walter Nigg in his work *Grosse Heilige* writes "Tersteegen was penetrated with the conviction that contemplation of self merely made men ill and that health was restored through the contemplation of God. At any rate he was certainly on a safer path than those directors of souls who have their penitents occupied with themselves at all times." Obviously one must aid the scrupulant to come to himself in the sense that "he seeks in the present moment the preoccupation in which he finds God and His will."(3*) But he must above all break the shackles of anxiety or compulsion which imprison him in the enclosure of self. Even the self-analysis which the method of depth psychology may suggest must have as its clear and well defined goal a readiness on the part of the patient to harken to the divine summons and respond with love for God, an openness for the concerns of the kingdom of God and the needs of our fellow-men. Once we have overcome the restraints of the scrupulant, once we have granted him access to the dialogue of love *open to the thou,* the way is clear for him to grasp his true moral responsibility and esteem it. Beyond this first and most important task, which must form within the patient a new concept and image of God and neighbor, there are the following particular tasks:

(3*) W. Nigg, *Grosse Heilige*. Zuerich 1949, 334. This work is translated into English under the title *Great Saints* by William Stirling, Regnery, Hinsdale, Illinois, 1948. The reference, somewhat differently translated, is on page 219.

1) Above all the scrupulant must strive to rid himself of his false sense of responsibility and guilt. The spiritual director or (if it comes to the worst) the psychotherapist will find the patient most willing to cooperate with his efforts, most sympathetic and responsive, if the true objective is clear to him from the very beginning. The sole purpose of the director or psychologist is to help the patient come to a truer sense of responsibility. It is to help him grasp more clearly the call of his real inner self, which ultimately is God's own summons. Even in his neurotic illness he must learn to harken to this call with a more correct sense of responsibility.

As far as individual legal prescriptions are concerned, the scrupulant must be expressly advised never to indulge voluntarily in brooding analysis of past faults. At least regarding the area which is affected by his compulsive neurosis he may confess only those sins which he knows with certainty, so that without the slightest hesitation or fear and without any lengthy reflection he could swear to it—that he actually committed them with interior freedom of will and deliberation and has never confessed them. He must gradually learn to realize that he is choosing the way which is truly the most secure, if he does not refrain from receiving Holy Communion despite his doubts about being in the state of grace. For a time frequency of confession is to be kept within strict limits, repetition of past confessions is to be strictly forbidden.

A frank and confidential discussion outside the sacrament of penance regarding the points affected by scrupulosity may under certain circumstances prove beneficial by removing restraints. A wise director may stress the need for such discussion for the simple reason that the penitent's anxiety regarding his salvation and his hidden compulsions are heightened in the act of sacramental confession.

2) We must all learn to realize more clearly not only that the individual act of the neurotic scrupulant poses the problem of responsibility, but also that his very scrupulosity is often in great measure due to others. The patient himself must realize with increasing clearness that his scrupulosity is a trial and a task, for which he must here and now assume his measure of responsibility. This responsibility does not consist in bootless reflection and analysis of the past, but rather in grasping the possibilities which his illness opens up before him. We note particularly:

He should say yes to the trial and suffering which lurk in his neurosis and in the painful failure and impotence flowing from it. In so far as his scrupulosity is due to his own fault (compensatory scrupulosity) he must humbly and with confidence in God's mercy bear the burden of pain and suffering it imposes upon him. Insofar as the suffering is caused by the failure of others—and this is always the case to a considerable extent—he should accept his impotence with all its pain as expiation for the fault of others. And finally the patient must arrive at an ever greater calmness in accepting that which cannot be cured in his illness.

The scrupulant must be brought to realize that his illness may prove a barrier to the full development of his moral-religious life and his engagement for the kingdom of God. Consequently in the measure and degree in which he is still at all responsible for his acts, he must be held accountable for his subsequent defective conduct, should he culpably refuse to follow the sound and practical directives which are necessary for his mental and spiritual recovery. In this connection we should not fail to note that each case of neurosis has its own unique background and in connection with such background there is a distinct spiritual summons for each afflicted individual. Consequently each individual with the help of a prudent director must attempt to understand the special demand made of him for his own essential betterment.

3) As we have noted above scrupulosity may have its source in a psychical defect (of a depressive, phobic or compulsive structure) and in consequence it may be impossible to remove it or at least to remove it entirely. In such instances the director must not merely help the patient to accept with resignation to the will of God what he cannot cure, but he must assist him to rise from his weakened position in order to lead a spiritually meaningful life. The director must point out the moral and religious tasks which are still within his power despite his illness. He may not be permitted to fritter away his life in futile struggles. New possibility of responsibility in the area in which he is swayed by his illness will open up to him in great part only after he concentrates all his efforts in the area in which he is still the free master of his acts.

4) Since scrupulosity is bound up with a false image of God or has its basis in such an image, it is necessary to remind him constantly of the love, patience and long-suffering of God. St. Alphonse offers a loving instruction to the scrupulant in the form of the following prayer: "O my God, anxious souls deal with you as with a tyrant, who demands nothing of his subjects except anxiety and restraint. Therefore they stand in dread of every careless word they utter and every thought which passes through their minds. They think that the Lord God is stirred to wrath thereby and is ready to cast them into hell. No, no, no: God deprives us of grace only if we scorn Him and turn our backs to Him, with our eyes open and

our wills fully yielding to evil." (4*) Nevertheless the psychological disposition and preparation necessary to experience the love of God is often absent in the scrupulant. Hence there is a basic need for scrupulants to love their fellow men. First of all they need the patient untiring love of others, and secondly they must love in return. With the forces still at their own disposal they must make an effort to show loving kindness to others in little acts of friendship.

5) The neurotic scrupulant has need of a moral-religious renewal in his education. But this presupposes, as in the case of minor and immature children, the need for obedience. But obedience will fulfill its purpose only if it is not imposed purely externally or with a kind of violence as blind obedience. Rather it must be based on the relation of loving trust. The patient must sense that he is understood and trusted. Even though he is not to be allowed to repeat his confessions, still he should not be denied sufficient time to explain his position. It is wise to permit him, insofar as this is possible, to gain an insight into the source, the meaning, the course of his illness. One must seek to lead him to a capacity for self-decision and awaken in him the hope for progress: He must be made to realize that despite the manifold restrictions of his personality he is still a potentially worthy personality. In many instances one can surely maintain that the scrupulant is a noble person.

The directives of the spiritual director must always be clear and definite. They may never have even the slightest appearance of contradiction, for the very suspicion of confusion and contradiction in admonition or command would destroy the confidence of the penitent. The whole success of direction in these matters rests on the penitent's confidence. A priest who is an extremely neurotic scrupulant, to cite an example, is to be absolutely forbidden to recite the breviary. But he must be encouraged at the same time to strive for the spirit of prayer. The director must encourage him constantly to seek to pray interiorly with a truly personal spirit of devotion. Such direction is clear and avoids all confusion.

6) It is exceedingly important for the neurotic scrupulant to make a systematic effort to avoid feelings of anxiety and dread and to dismiss from his mind the compulsive impulses. He must systematically cultivate the basic capacity of distinguishing between genuine judgment of conscience and scruples in so far as he still has this power. Unto this end the

---

(4*) St. Alphonsus de Liguori, *The Way of Salvation and of Perfection* (Complete Ascetical Works of St. Alphonsus de Liguori, 2), edited by Rev. E. Grimm. Brooklyn: Redemptorist Fathers, 1926, 482 f.

attempt to hold aloof from or "objectivize" his scruples should be profitable: the patient should endeavor to view them as something alien, as a foreign body. Unto this end relaxation of mind and a sense of humor are essential. The Christian can readily laugh at anything that is not sinful. Much is already accomplished if the patient can be brought to the point at which he can laugh heartily at his own scruples. The good fight is half won!

10. Security and Risk in Matters of Conscience: Serious Effort to Avoid Risk in Prudent Decision

a. The Problem

The primary moral principles are immediately and absolutely evident. Divine revelation, above all the word and example of Christ, provides us with absolute assurance in numerous moral problems of the natural and supernatural order. The Church, noble guide of mankind and infallible teacher of truth, by her instruction and law interprets for us the word and will of Christ and applies it to the great questions of the times. In consequence we Christians are much better equipped to face the moral hazards of life than mere "natural" man left to his own resources. And yet in the multitudinous situations of real life the Christian is constantly confronted with new uncertainty and unanticipated moral risk. To suffer from uncertainty, doubt, and hazard of decision in itself indicates a degree of moral awareness or alertness. For the conceited man does not readily doubt, no more than does the man with blunted conscience reflect seriously on the dubious nature of his moral opinions.

(1) Basis of Uncertainty

A common source of error and uncertainty is ignorance, more or less culpable, in moral and religious matters. Furthermore, every incorrect attitude or defective moral orientation dulls the acumen somewhat and consequently also imperils the safety of the moral judgment. Extreme inconstancy in moral approach and conscientious effort readily leads to inconstancy in moral appraisal of the concrete situation and in the verdict of conscience, not to mention excessive anxiety and scrupulosity at all. One of the primary and universal sources of uncertainty and doubt affecting the whole moral life is man's limited earthly vision.

And a degree of uncertainty also arises from the very nature of moral duty itself. For moral obligations are concerned not only with eternal immutable truths and principles, but also with their recognition and realization in the varied concrete contingencies of life. The decision regarding the correctness of an action surely does not depend solely on the universal moral principles. It depends also on the correct and sound understanding of the unique and concrete in particular instances to which the principles must be applied. And often numberless factors enter into the situation, and these may be quite obscure in our present dark and fallen state. Only a profound knowledge of life and great prudence can rightly appraise these circumstances in all their variations and adjudge their relative importance. A trustworthy moral judgment presupposes that we discern the eternal values reflected clearly in contingent reality and render a balanced judgment of the values as to their relative merits and urgency.

(2) Degrees of Certainty or Uncertainty

We usually make the following distinctions in the degrees of certainty. First, there is the certainty of faith regarding the revealed moral truths. This certainty is absolute, not only in itself, but also subjectively or in us through the virtue of faith. Since this is a supernatural gift, no man has a right or claim to it and therefore he owes God a debt of gratitude for bestowing it upon him. Secondly, there is metaphysical certainty, which is based on clear insight into necessary truths. Thirdly, there is physical certainty, which rests on the knowledge of the laws of nature. These laws are immutable once they have been established, though one must allow for their inefficacy or suspension by way of exception through miracles. Finally, there is moral certainty in the strict sense of the word, which excludes all reasonable doubt; and moral certainty in the broader sense of the word, which excludes all practical doubt of any consequence; in the broadest sense of the word, which is the certainty of a well founded opinion with no positive argument weighing against it (*opinio probabilis, id est opinio, quae satis probari potest*). This last is adequate for practical assent of the mind, but does not exclude every prudent or reasonable fear of error.[57]

As to doubt or uncertainty of judgment, the following distinctions are pertinent: in positive doubt there is weighty reason both for and against a position, so that the arguments for neither point of view can prevail and move the mind to assent. The weight of the arguments, pro and con, may vary somewhat, but not sufficiently to make either side entirely convincing.

In the case of negative doubt there are no discernible valid arguments contrary to a position which has good positive arguments in its favor, though these latter are not entirely conclusive. (But there is always the possibility that arguments against the position may arise, though at present they are not discernible.) Hesitation arising from doubt is not so deep-seated in the instance of negative doubt as in the case of positive doubt. For the absence of tangible counter-arguments in this instance adds much to the weight of the positive arguments, even though the latter are not in themselves conclusive. Hence if earnest study does not reveal any serious counter-arguments, the negative doubt can be resolved into practical moral certainty. (But this is moral certainty in the wider sense of the term.) We should note, however, that at times we define negative doubt as lack of any discernible evidence of a serious nature for either side.[58]

There is also a distinction to be made between speculative and practical doubt in moral matters. The former is concerned with theoretical truth of an ethical or moral thesis or doctrine; the latter deals with the lawfulness of present conduct, of the act here and now.

Basic Principle regarding Doubt: practical doubt is equivalent to a verdict of conscience forbidding the act until the doubt has been cleared up practically. This principle, with its profound insight into truth, is held and taught by all teachers in the Church. It is expressed with particular emphasis by Saint Paul in his letter to the Romans when he explains the obligations regarding the obsolete dietary laws of the Jews. The "strong" must bear the "weak" in mind; they may not ignore those who look upon the laws proscribing certain foods as still binding, and who, induced by the example of the "strong," hesitate as to their own conduct. And yet despite this hesitation and practical doubt about the lawfulness of eating the foods, they violate the Old Testament prohibition and partake of the forbidden food. Says the Apostle, "He who hesitates (*diakrinó-menos*),[59] if he eats, is condemned, because it is not from faith (from conscience); for all that is not from faith is sin" (ROM 14:23).

One who performs an act despite the state of practical doubt regarding its lawfulness, incurs the same guilt of sin as to species, though not in the same degree, as he would incur through a transgression with clear and certain knowledge. We say, "incurs the same guilt of sin as to species," for one offends against the same virtue in either instance, whether by clear and deliberate transgression or only through a probable and practical violation of the law with the readiness of ignoring it. But we add, "not in the same degree," for at least in a general way there is evidence of greater alertness of mind and malice of will if one does an act which is certainly evil in the judgment of his conscience than if he only risks sinning when his conscience warns that virtue will possibly or probably be violated because of his doubt.

The effort one is obliged to make in order to acquire certainty is to be measured by the importance of the action itself and the consequences which are anticipated. Whenever the question of moral value arises, there is the demand for an attitude of zealous prudence, that is, for the earnest effort to acquire the necessary practical certainty of the correctness of our conduct. We must seek true certitude. Nevertheless, in consequence of our limited mental capacity and the extent and complexity of our moral obligations, prudence forbids us to devote excessive attention and research to trivial matters because this would rob us of the spirit of joy in doing good and, most of all, because it would greatly hamper the fulfillment of more urgent and more important duties. "It is characteristic of the disciplined man to be content in every instance with the degree of certainty which is possible in the matter before us."[60]

Speculative certainty may be beyond our reach, but practical certainty is absolutely necessary. We must arrive at this practical certainty of conscience both for action and abstention from action. The problem of acquiring such practical certainty despite theoretic doubt is taken up in the so-called "moral systems." They are concerned precisely with this point: how shall one in the state of theoretical doubt resolve the doubt—not by venturing a leap into the dark, but through the use of general "reflex principles,"—and arrive at a practical certainty of conscience?[61]

(3) *The Area of Certainty and Risk*

Doubt can be concerned even with some of the moral principles. In the realm of revealed truth, many of the derived or subordinated moral principles are in some manner obscure to us. It is surely true that, if we have in mind not so much number as significance, the area of principles resting in the certainty of faith or at least occupying an unambiguous position in the whole of Christian life is more significant. The docile disciples of the one Master (cf. Jn 6:45), who are at home "in the house of God," that is, in "the Church of the living God, the pillar and mainstay of the truth" (1 Tm 3:15), may not fall under the spell of a sceptical world's attitude which looks upon nothing as certain or absolute, the attitude of the "total doubt," which implies "total risk."

The thesis of present day existentialistic philosophy ("situation ethics") regarding insecurity, abandonment (*Geworfenheit*), and risk corresponds to the existential sentiment of man who has wandered away from the "house of truth" and been thrown back on himself. To this extent the existentialistic analyses always contain a modicum of reality. The pronouncements of a Christian "existentialism" and a Christian situation ethics, however, must assume an essentially different attitude. The Christian possesses a mystery and certainty in faith, and is also aware of a sinister abyss of sin, which are entirely unknown to non-Christian existentialism.

An earnest effort to acquire certainty is above all necessary in the application and illustration of the fundamental certainties. It has always been the special assignment of moral theology to apply these certain principles to current needs and conditions in every age. Each generation must study its own great problem in the light of these principles. Today, for example, the tremendous progress of technique, industry, and modern medicine presents a host of new problems (note particularly the problems of modern war, humanization of mass production, participation of labor in management and ownership, profit sharing, psychoanalysis, psychosurgery). In all this, moral theology can only lay the groundwork or prepare the way for the application of the fundamental principles to the concrete and individual case with all its circumstances in each particular situation. But it is the task of prudence in each individual, with the help, let us say, of sound advice of others, to make the actual decision, applying principle to particular instance.

The effort to come to certainty may prove acutely distressing in the conflict between two (apparently) contradictory obligations (a conflict of duties). The objection that there can be no genuine conflict of duties at all, since the realm of moral good is well ordered as a whole under one Lord and Lawgiver who cannot contradict Himself, is valid as far as objective law is concerned, but does not relieve the distress of the individual who is wrestling with doubts of conscience regarding such a conflict. Basis of conflict is the limitation of created being and, above all, the incurable disorder of the sinful world, which often deprives the individual decision of the very possibility of attaining the perfection of the ideal order. Precisely in this area of conflict of duties situations occur in which moral decision involves a risk, a "prudent" risk, it may well be, provided one's decision is a result of earnest reflection on the validity of one's motives and prayerful trust in the guidance of the "Spirit of truth." However, even though such guidance by the Holy Spirit is considered of capital importance[62] in moral theology, the matter does not rest there. Moral theology provides us with general practical norms leading to right discernment and prudence in the risks of decision.

In the event of conflict between a positive and a natural law, the latter enjoys the preference. Therefore should one seriously doubt whether or not attending Mass on Sunday harms his health, the obligation to care for health takes precedence. But another principle is also applicable in the same case. The goods of salvation take precedence over bodily goods in the event of conflict. If, therefore, one has good reason to fear that habitual absence from holy Mass, in itself justifiable because of reasonable concern for health, would lead to great moral laxity and even loss of faith, one would be obliged to risk the hurt to health rather than endanger salvation, provided that both cannot be safeguarded.

It is an indication of a truly Christian spirit to hesitate and seek to decide safely in choosing between an act falling under a positive law and a more perfect act transcending the limited bounds of law. In such instances prudence must be guided by the virtue of obedience and *epiky* as well. When there is a choice of several good acts within the law and one doubts and hesitates to decide, prudence, guided by a fine sense of the realities in the particular situation, must judge which good is to be preferred. The morally mature Christian will not automatically follow the path of least resistance or choose what is most pleasant. As grace moves him inwardly and the external reality of the "situation" challenges and invites him, he will turn with love to the bold and arduous, deciding valiantly for the kingdom of God.

Uncertainty and at times poignant heartache are the lot of the Christian who must choose between the intrinsically and evidently more perfect and that which is better for him in his own situation, that which is more suitable for him individually. Surely the disciple of Christ is always and unconditionally obliged to strive for perfection. But this does not mean that in every instance he must or even can do what is absolutely in itself the more perfect. He is much rather obliged to do that which in each instance corresponds with his degree of perfection and matches the growth of his spiritual powers and the urgency of the inner invitation of grace. If one sincerely wills the goal of perfect love, he must also will the necessary steps and means which lead him to it. However, in regard to these very means there is the widest scope and the most genuine variety of true possibilities.

There is an obligation in conscience to choose one specific object from among a number of possible ones only if the opposite (its omission or another positive act) would be sinful for the individual concerned.[63] But in our opinion, if any individual should form the judgment, clearly and prudently, that one specific choice or course of action is manifestly better for him, that it is here and now the wiser and more suitable, he would be obliged to follow this one course of action or choose this one specific good. He could not without some violation of conscience make a choice less suitable or worthy, because then he would be deliberately imprudent.[64] To act prudently is equivalent to acting according to conscience.

The objective of the so-called "moral systems" (rules of prudence) essentially centers in this hesitation of conscience when a choice is to be made between a good act which is not prescribed and another act which may be commanded, an act which to a degree of probability is prescribed by some law. Doubt as to whether there is a legal obligation to perform a specific act may be either a doubt of law or a doubt of fact. We have a doubt of law if there is question about the existence of a law or about its extension or application to certain specific cases. A doubt of fact refers to the existence or non-existence of certain facts from which an obligation would arise because of a precept or command which is certain and binding. Let us take, for example, a doubt about the commission of a certain grave sin. Did one actually commit a certain sin, was the sin actually committed a mortal sin, did one already confess a mortal sin committed? In consequence of the doubt of fact, there arises a doubt about the obligation to confess such a sin in this concrete instance, although there is no doubt at all about the law (obliging one to confess all mortal sin) itself which is pertinent in the case.

It is not surprising that precisely this question has been a matter of much concern in moral theology, for we are here dealing with the right grasp of fundamental problems of Christian morality, which are intimately bound up with profound and meaningful relations between law and the "freedom of the children of God."

(4) *Rational Basis of the "Moral Systems"*

Some of our more recent writers reproach the moralists of previous generations for busying themselves with this problem. According to their thinking, these older theologians should have spared themselves the drudgery and monotony of all such labor by simply devoting themselves entirely to the principle of the unrestricted imitation of Christ. What an illusion! For this is precisely the question. What is more in accord with the imitation of Christ: in every single instance and even under the burden of utterly disproportionate toil and peril to bind oneself by doubtful imposition of law or, where there is such doubt, to strive for the good in the prudent venture of one's own free decision? Nor should it be overlooked, and particularly not in the imitation of Christ, that the teacher of moral doctrine and likewise every Christian conscience must face the problem: how shall I take law and obedience seriously without excessively taxing human liberty or unduly narrowing the scope of personal initiative through a multiplicity of doubtful laws and obligations?

The earnest champions of probabilism and equi-probabilism, such was their insight, realized that the scope of freedom and initiative necessary for the development of dynamic moral life is too narrowly restricted if every doubtful regulation of law must be looked upon as binding in conscience. After these writers with great erudition defend the rights of free decision over the doubtful law, they often counsel very impressively that one freely, without any sense of compulsion, undertake the obligation of the doubtful precept wherever it appears as the more perfect at the time.

No serious moralist maintains that a mere craving for ease on the part of an ill-regulated or indolent mind can justify a disregard for a doubtful obligation. All teach clearly and unequivocally the necessity of a good intention in the fulfillment and also for the non-fulfillment of a doubtful precept. In many instances, this adequate motive is present in the very desire to safeguard our freedom with the full scope of its movement and its true spirit of initiative, in the preservation of oneself from sterile anxiety, and, most of all, in the spirit of responsibility toward the kingdom of God as we are called by divine grace in every crisis.

The controversies about the "moral systems," that is to say, regarding the limitations of truly "probable" opinion and the validity of the rules of prudence (reflex principles), are based partly on reasons dictated by conditions of the times and partly on reasons of permanent significance. That this problem of systems assumed proportions of such importance in the theology of the period is due to the preponderance of casuistry and its procedures in moral theology. Casuistic theology was primarily concerned with the duty of the confessor who, as judge in the tribunal of penance, "passed sentence" according to universal moral norms. The confessor is in a unique manner a custodian of the divine law and the divine will. At the same time, there was a very clear and general realization that one must always respect the individual in his uniqueness and vital reality and his limitations and special tasks and duties. In consequence, there was need, not solely for occasional acts of prudence, but for profound study of the fundamental problem of reconciling justice to the individuality of the penitent with respect for the rights of the law. The sacrament of mercy demands a clear distinction between the certain and the doubtful law, which in no wise may be made the basis for condemnation.

The clear distinction between absolute obligation to seek the perfect imitation of Christ and the obligation to attempt the most perfect fulfill-ment of all, and, if possible, even all strictly doubtful human laws, was not always kept in mind, above all not by the rigorists and tutiorists. But there was an underlying assumption, usually implicit or unexpressed, according to which the good is possible only in so far as it is defined by universal legal enactment. This meant that everything had to be legally formulated with all possible strictness and clarity to determine what was good. In consequence, the case, the *casus conscientiae* found as exercise in theology became the type, which readily was set up as the ultimate pattern and ideal for all moral decisions.

There never was any denial of the necessity or importance of the good intention, though the point was not always duly stressed. Likewise in the antithesis between freedom and law attention was not focused sufficiently on the ideal of freedom; and it may have seemed as though one were simply defending the formal freedom from restraint of law as such rather than the freedom of decision regarding the good. Hence the impression prevailed at times, though it was a false impression, that the probabilists wanted to safeguard the liberty to escape the law of the good as far as this was possible, not only to the prejudice of doubtful laws, but also to the detriment of zeal for the good as such.

The "party of liberty" was confronted by an attitude which in part greatly exaggerated the importance of the positive law to the detriment of fundamental moral insights into value and individual initiative. At a time when legal enactments of positive human legislation were getting the upper hand—and in the period of absolutism many such impositions of law were very arbitrary—it was reasonable to lessen the restrictions and limitations of freedom and grant greater scope to the imperiled spirit of responsibility wherever the obligation of law was patently doubtful. On the other hand, in a period in which incipient dissolution of the existing traditional order was menacingly evident, authority, law, and obedience durst not be minimized.

The study of the problem and debate about it were intensified by the frequent failure to draw a clear distinction between the varied applications of the rules of prudence (the reflex principles), first, in the area of commutative justice and the consequent legal procedures in the courts of justice; secondly, in the sphere of positive human legislation; and thirdly, in the domain of the purely positive divine laws and the laws of nature. Basically the problem was never altogether obscured, for it was created by an unwise transfer of the native principle of law and right to the moral virtue of justice and finally even to the area of divine law. Only after protracted discussion and debate were theologians finally able to determine and clearly propose the principle: the rules of prudence derived from the exercise of juridical practice can be applied only where the legal obligation as such is in question, but not where there is question of the Kingdom of God, the salvation of souls, and the valid administration of the holy sacraments.

b. The Risk of Conscience Based on Rules of Prudence

(1) *Rules of Prudence (Reflex Principles) and their Applicability*

(a) Rules of Right in the Domain of Commutative Justice

Roman Law and likewise all modern legislation recognizes in all litigation regarding property the principle of the presumption of right (*praesumptio*), especially in the point of prescription. The essential note of presumption of right and prescription is the claim of the possessor. Until the contrary is proved, it is rightly assumed that the present possessor of a thing or of the right to its use has possession by right (principle of possession, *principium possessionis*). If the right of possession of the present occupant is contested, he is not obliged to defend himself, but the entire burden of proof rests on the plaintiff. The principle is reasonable, is consistent in practice, and in most cases is in accord with truth. Most legal enactments make a restriction regarding prescription, namely, that occupancy or possession must have begun with a good conscience or in good faith (*bona fide*). This holds unconditionally in moral teaching. In fact, good faith (*bona fides*) must be continuous, which is to say that the possessor must have at least apparent reasons for the justice of his claim throughout the entire period of his possession.

Since the legal principle, *in dubio melior est conditio possidentis,* "in case of doubt the presumption of law favors the possessor," is reasonable and just, the individual conscience is therefore permitted to follow it. Nevertheless, in case of really serious doubt for or against the claim, it would be more in accord with justice to propose and accept some sort of compromise, possibly a "splitting of the difference."

(b) Transfer of the Principle to the Domain of Human Law

i. *Presumption and Possession in Doubt of Law*

Every purely positive law restricts the individual rights of subjects in favor of the common welfare. (Obviously this does not hold for laws which reaffirm and more clearly specify obligations arising from natural law. These laws may in no wise be looked upon as limitations or restrictions of liberty.) Every subject is in full possession of his moral rights of freedom over the law and the lawgivers, but not in such wise that, when the legislators enact laws, they are obliged in each instance to present proof to their subjects for the necessity of the law. But the conscience of the legislator may not ignore or lack such evidence.

Once a law has been enacted, however, the presumption of right is in favor of law. But if the promulgation of the law or its extension to this or that matter is doubtful, then the subject's right freely to decide his own moral conduct prevails. Perhaps it is difficult to demonstrate this point by a rigorous syllogistic argument. Nor do we claim for it a metaphysical insight. Here we are dealing with a general prudential judgment, a rule of prudence demanding a fine sense of moral realities. And there are cogent and satisfactory reasons for such a rule resting in the moral life itself. Obviously enough, this rule in its application provides for a more humane and prudent life than its opposite. If all doubts about the existence of human laws were to be resolved in favor of the law, which is to say, if all doubtful human laws were to be considered as certainly binding, the result would be an excessive weight and burden of authority and a corresponding loss of freedom of the individual. The free rights of the individual would be too narrowly limited and restricted. For the code of canon law this prudential norm enjoys the force of right and law. *Leges in dubio juris non urgent,* "laws do not bind in doubt of law" (C.I.C., can. 15). This holds also for those laws whose fulfillment is necessary for the legal validity of an act.

The consequent reverse of the above contained in the "presumption of right in favor of the possessor" is expressed in canon 23: *In dubio revocatio legis praeexistentis non praesumitur.* (In case of doubt the revocation of an existing law is not presumed.) This means that, if a law was truly and justly enacted, then it is binding until we have morally certain (in the broad sense of the word) proofs of its abrogation or cessation. This principle can also be validly applied to the reasons which excuse one from the obligation of a certainly existent law. If, for example, a priest is in doubt whether he is excused from the recitation of the breviary, he still must recite it. But he may surely make a request for a dispensation. The principle laid down in canon 23 obviously applies directly only to the relation of the code of Church law to prior laws. Wherefore, one may still hold today, prescinding from the relation to the pre-code laws, the contrary principle of simple probabilism, which sweepingly denies the binding force of the doubtful law as such. We wish to make this point altogether clear, even though we ourselves are convinced of the correctness of our own position in favor of equi-probabilism.

ii. *Presumption of Right in Doubt of Fact*

The first rule of prudence is *factum non praesumitur, sed probari debet,* a fact, an act or action, may not legally be "presumed" to exist or have taken place, but must be demonstrated. Therefore, before the law the accused has the right to acquittal until he is legally proved guilty and convicted of crime. There are three consequences flowing from this primary principle. First, in doubt regarding an act which entails an obligation of law, freedom prevails. For example, one who doubts whether or not he has committed a mortal sin, is not under the obligation of positive law requiring confession of all mortal sins. Secondly, in doubt regarding a fact upon which the cessation of a law (and its obligation) depends, the obligation must be considered as still existing. For example, one doubts whether or not he has recited one of the canonical hours to which he is obliged; the prayer must still be said. If, however, there is danger of anxiety on such a point, which could destroy the joy of prayer, one could consider oneself free from obligation solely because of reasonable doubt. In doubt whether or not one has discharged a debt which was certainly contracted, one is obliged to discharge it or seek condonation or some form of compromise.[65] Thirdly, when there is doubt about a factual conflict of two laws or rights, the more important of the laws is to be preferred. For example, in case of serious doubt whether fasting seriously damages one's health, the right (and the duty) to preserve one's health is in "possession."

The second rule of prudence is *in dubio omne factum praesumitur recte factum,* if an act has been performed it is prudently "presumed" that it was correctly and validly performed. For example, if it is certain that a marriage rite has been performed, the marriage is presumed to be valid before the law unless the contrary is proved. If one has committed a crime, he is looked upon as responsible until the absence of responsibility or imputability (innocence, lack of freedom, ignorance) is proved.

The third rule of prudence is *ex communiter contingentibus prudens fit praesumptio,* what takes place ordinarily or as a rule may be presumed to have taken place in the dubious particular instance. For example, the law of the Church "presumes" that children at the age of seven have the use of reason and therefore are bound by some of her laws. Wherefore, only if, in an individual instance, the use of reason is clearly and evidently absent, is the child not obliged by the Church laws just referred to, but in case of doubt the child is under the obligation.

(c) The Rules Applied to the Entire Moral Domain

If the rules of prudence (presumption, possession) can be shown to apply in matters of commutative justice and of positive human (civil and ecclesiastical) law, it readily follows that we should transfer them analogously to the positive divine law and finally also to the law of nature which lies in the very essence of created order and also to the economy of Redemption and grace, whenever there is a similar pattern of uncertainty and doubt.

In each liberty is confronted by law. We assign to them the roles of two parties contending for their rights. Liberty is first of all in possession as compared with the law. It has the "presumption of right." This means that human liberty is indeed entirely bound to God; it has its meaning, its goal, and its surety only in its attachment to God's will. But it is not predetermined in all points regarding the particular lawful manner in which man must render service to God. There remains an area of free choice which is restricted or "narrowed" only by the protective "barrier" of the natural and positive law of God. From this it is apparent that human freedom and the will of God are not at all in antithesis. For human freedom surely thrives on the good, which is summed up in the will of God. We find the antithesis rather, and it is indeed a fruitful one, in human freedom firmly established in a universal law and human freedom discerning the concrete will of God in a particular moment of time and place in the plan of salvation (the *kairos* or situation). In any instance, the freedom of the children of God is safeguarded only by the complete and loving accord with the will of God as it manifests itself, either in a universal law or providentially in the abundant favor of grace on a particular occasion.

Perhaps the various "moral systems" can be most accurately, though, of course, only summarily, characterized by a demonstration of the position they occupy in relation to the will of God, whether this be expressed in enactment of law or outside the law.

Rigorism, tutiorism, and in a measure even the old time probabiliorism viewed the entire will of God as though it were contained exclusively or predominantly in the universal law of revelation. So biased was this attitude that the advocates of these systems looked upon the "very probably" or "more probably" "not binding law" as in all instances indicating the more perfect way, the more perfect fulfillment of the divine will. This "doubtful" law was to be preferred to the seeking of the will of God under the impulse of grace given in and for the practical spiritual needs of the providential occasion, provided there was no means of determining through any imposition of law what must be the response to the call of grace.

According to equi-probabilism, whose most noted representative was Saint Alphonse Liguori, we may say that the children of God in their freedom hold the revelation of the will of God equally dear, whether it is manifested in the form of law or extra-legally, so that in each instance they prefer that which is favored by the better reasons.

According to probabilism (based on the merely probable) freedom is obviously bound up with complete attachment to the will of God. But it is entirely in "possession" as opposed to the legal obligation. Consistent with this view the obligation must be looked upon as something limiting, as "restriction" of freedom. And in consequence freedom would seem to be better safeguarded by doing the good not prescribed by the law.

Finally, in laxism there is concern for a species of human freedom without a realization that freedom is entirely and essentially attached to the will of God and safeguarded by it.

Surely there were many representatives of the various "moral systems" who themselves were scarcely aware of the ultimate underlying reasons and the logical consequences of their own positions.

But all the "moral systems" tolerated in the Church (equi-probabilism, probabilism, probabiliorism) agree that the area of application of the rules of prudence has definite limits. It may not be extended so far beyond the sphere of legal obligation as to jeopardize any good essential for salvation. In all cases of doubt, if no other good is at stake beyond the rectitude of conscience (*honestas agentis*) the rules of prudence may be applied. But if a good transcending the subjective correctness of conscience is placed in jeopardy, a good which we must safeguard, or there is menace of an evil which we must shun, the safer way is to be followed in all doubtful cases. The reason is evident. Moral conduct is not to be considered solely in the light of its inner rectitude, but also in its bearing and influence on the order of existence. Because the effects of an act quite frequently do not depend exclusively on the sincere conviction of the agent, it follows that in many cases the safe view (*sententia tutior,* not *sententia certior*) must be followed, even though the opposite position is more probable. This holds good for all in the following instances: if there is question of the valid administration of the sacraments; if one's own salvation is at stake; if the following of a merely probable opinion might result in temporal or spiritual damage to one's neighbor, which we are obliged to avoid.

i. *Valid Administration of the Sacraments*

The greatest certainty is demanded for the validity of baptism and Orders (of all the sacraments), since invalidity would have appalling consequences. We know that validity does not depend on the good faith or sincere convictions and moral life of the minister. It derives from the intention and the sacramental sign, which are called the matter and form, as required by Christ. Therefore it is never lawful in the administration of a sacrament to use matter or form which in any way would endanger the validity of the sacrament (naturally there is question only of truly reasonable doubt), assuming that under the given circumstances a certainly valid administration is at all possible.

In case of necessity, however, rather than deprive anyone of a sacrament surely necessary for salvation, we are to risk administering the sacrament even though the validity is doubtful. For the "sacraments are instituted for men," and *in extremis extrema tentanda sunt,* in desperate cases desperate measures are to be used. Let us take the example of Extreme Unction. If in administering this sacrament to a dying man we cannot in due time obtain matter that is certainly valid, we may use matter that is "doubtfully valid." Similarly, the sacrament must be administered to one who is apparently, but not yet certainly dead, always with the condition, "if you still live . . ." The same holds true of the use of matter. If the matter used is not certainly valid, the sacrament must be administered conditionally.

Where the Church can supply the deficiency and chooses to do so, as, for example, in instances of doubt regarding jurisdiction for the sacrament of penance, the validity of the sacrament is not endangered and therefore one is not obliged to follow the "safer way." Despite the doubt, we have practical certainty of validity through the *suppletio ecclesiae* (the Church supplies). Likewise the strict demand for the "absolutely safe" way does not hold regarding the judgment of the dispositions of the recipient and of his positive obligations in the sacrament, e.g., the obligation to confess certain sins. For example, a penitent who is anxious and disturbed has been advised by his director not to confess sins about whose gravity he is in doubt. He follows the advice in an instance of serious doubt and does not confess the "doubtful" sin, not because of indolence or indifference, but for the sake of obedience and in order to overcome his scrupulosity. Now even were the sin actually a grave offense in God's sight, the penitent still would suffer no harm for his conduct. If he is otherwise well disposed, the sacrament is received validly, lawfully, fruitfully. He acted correctly.

ii. *Endangering Salvation*

No one can content himself with a simple prudential norm in the great question of his soul's salvation. Is he on the right path to eternal salvation? Rather he must do all that is humanly possible to conserve the life of grace, to live and die securely in this holy state. No one may dispense himself from earnest striving and searching for the truth and the way to salvation. Anyone who is not in certain possession of the truths of faith may not rest content with his state and abstain from further inquiry by invoking a simple rule of probability in this matter.[66] Nor is one permitted, except in urgent necessity, to place himself in imminent peril of mortal sin on the mere probable assumption that perchance he may not succumb to temptation.

There are, to cite one example, various opinions regarding the sixth commandment which are perhaps probable speculatively, but to put them into practice would constitute an imminent danger of mortal sin for many individuals, as their own experience proves. Therefore to base their conduct on such positions, speculatively perhaps probable, but practically very dangerous, is not permitted.

iii. *Great Damage to Neighbor or the Community*

Scandal must be shunned with all one's power. But nevertheless not every petty occasion of scandal must be avoided at great probable personal loss or cost. Quite frequently in this matter one is obliged to obey a law which, apart from the danger of scandal, would probably (or even certainly) not be binding. "Therefore, if food scandalizes my brother, I will eat flesh no more forever, lest I scandalize my brother" (1 Cor 8:13; cf. Rom 14).

If the life of our neighbor is liable to be imperiled by actions of ours, we must choose the safest course of action so as to avoid this evil effect. The physician, for example, is obliged to make use of the safest remedies possible. He is not permitted to resort to remedies or medicines which will probably effect a cure but only at the risk of the patient's life or bodily or other harm. The physician is not permitted to experiment on the patient in this fashion unless according to all calculations the case is entirely forlorn and such hazardous effort offers the only hope.[67] War with its dire consequences may never be waged on the ground of probable right.

A judge in civil cases may not arbitrarily base his decisions on mere probable or even less than probable opinion,[68] if by such decision there is a real risk of injustice to the other party. He must render his decision on the basis of manifestly weightier reasons. The verdict must favor the party with the obviously superior arguments. In the case of good reasons on both sides, he must seek a compromise based on these very arguments and the degree of probability in favor of each party. (Note that we are not here dealing with the case of a possessor in good faith, for he surely has the presumption of right in his favor.)

(2) *Degree of Probability Required for Use of Norms*

(a) The Concept of Probable Opinion: Résumé

In the foregoing, we established certain essential limitations in the use and application of the prudential norms (reflex principles) from the point of view of their object. But important limitations must also be laid down regarding the measure or degree of probability of opinion. For not every probability is sufficient to create the "presumption" or the "possession" of which we already spoke. This is evident from the decision of Innocent XI who condemned the following proposition for its laxity: "In general, whenever we act with confidence in intrinsic or extrinsic probability, however slight it may be, we always act prudently, provided the limits of probability are not exceeded."[69] But conversely, it is equally true that not every contrary position, no matter how slight the probability in its favor, vitiates the right to adhere to a really probable opinion in favor of freedom. This flows from the condemnation of the following rigoristic proposition held by the Jansenists and condemned by Alexander VIII. "It is not lawful to follow a probable opinion, even if it is the most probable among probable opinions."[70]

Proponents of probabiliorism contend that any opinion which favors the law and is in any way more probable makes the contrary probable opinion unlawful under all circumstances. According to what is often simply called probabilism, any and every authentic probability is sufficient to form and found a rule of prudence (*qui probabiliter agit, prudenter agit;* who acts according to probable opinion, acts prudently), even though the opinion is manifestly less probable than the contrary position. (From this we have the use of the term *minusprobabilismus.*)

Saint Alphonse (equi-probabilism) teaches that the rules of prudence can be applied only where opposing positions maintain a kind of balance of probability. If a position really has significantly weightier reasons in its favor, the preponderance is also apparent. An insignificant difference cannot be determined with certainty in moral matters. If the preponderance of probability is not plain and clear (*certe*), it cannot be viewed as considerable (*opinio longe probabilior*).

According to the great Doctor, the actual sphere with which the rules of prudence are concerned is that of diversity of balanced opinions. This is the area of opinions which are equal or about equal in their reasonableness. The essential ground of his contention is the following norm or principle: Once we exclude the area in which we must seek the greatest possible certainty (regarding validity of sacraments, concern for one's salvation, obligation to avoid serious damage to others), a plain preponderance of reason is itself adequate, even without the rules of prudence, for prudent conduct, whether it be in favor of law or in favor of liberty. Therefore the contrary must be recognized as imprudent and contrary to the love of truth. "If the opinion in favor of the law certainly and unquestionably is more probable, then . . . it is morally certain or in some manner morally certain; at least it can no longer be considered strictly doubtful. Then the will can no longer prudently and without fault follow the less certain view (*parti minus tutae*)."[71] "To act lawfully we must in doubtful matters search for the truth and follow it. Where it is impossible to find the clear truth, we are at least obliged to accept the opinion which comes closest to truth. And this is surely the more probable."[72] (The words mean what is manifestly, plainly, the more probable opinion.)

This last statement particularly reveals very important aspects of our problem. We must be concerned for the truth always. A profound love for the truth must concern us far more than any position we assume in the spirit of partisanship regarding freedom of choice or the law. We may and must often content ourselves with approximation to certainty in moral matters. It is our duty always to search for the truth itself. This means we must first try to solve our doubt directly before we resort to the rules of prudence. And these rules should serve to bring us as close as possible to the truth.

Résumé: there is a moral area in which one may not be satisfied with the probable or even with the more probable opinion, in which one must follow the safe and certain path: one must follow the opinion which best safeguards the validity of the sacraments, the salvation of one's soul, the integrity of one's neighbor's rights, even though this safer opinion is less probable than the position favoring liberty. In all other questions moral certainty in the widest sense is sufficient. This includes the solitary probable opinion in the case of negative doubt, the most probable and the manifestly and certainly more probable opinion. Where probabilities of conflicting opinion are evenly balanced, or approximately evenly balanced, the safe practical judgment is possible only through recourse to reflex auxiliary principles or rules of prudence. But before one resorts to the general principles of prudence, one is obliged to make a careful effort commensurate with the seriousness of the matter concerned to settle the doubt by a direct insight into the problem, and eventually by recourse to sage counsel and instruction on the part of others.

If an opinion is clearly and plainly (and therefore notably) less probable, it can no longer be considered truly probable in relation to the more probable opinion. Since there is question of a relative probability of one opinion in opposition to another, the rules of prudence may not be invoked in favor of the evidently less probable. (With this we reject mere probabilism or "minusprobabilism.") In the tribunal of penance the confessor is never permitted to refuse absolution to any penitent who holds and follows an opinion proposed by prudent and learned moralists, even though the confessor himself looks upon it as false. If he deems that the attitude of his penitent involves peril to salvation, he must instruct him, but not under threat of denial of absolution. If a doctrine once held as truly probable is no longer so, its former acceptance by serious moralists no longer has any validity. Nor is one allowed to continue holding or following it. The confessor may never propose an opinion for acceptance if he considers it false or only slightly probable.

(b) Discernment of True Probability

One who is sufficiently acquainted with the problem and possessed of the necessary prudence must strive to grapple with the intrinsic arguments for the probability of an opinion in so far as this is possible. Not the authors, but their arguments make an opinion probable. Saint Alphonse followed this principle: the weight of authorities is as great as their arguments. "All teach that the authority of the learned has no great weight where the intrinsic reasons appear certain and convincing."[73] But if noted authors hold a doctrine, the presumption is always that they have cogent intrinsic reasons for their opinion.[74] It is therefore imprudent and unreasonable to reject their position without a study of the reasons they give for holding it.

One who does not have the necessary knowledge of the problem (or the time to study it) in order to form an opinion himself must seek the information from authoritative authors. For the faithful in general, who are not equipped sufficiently to probe into the problem in this manner, the decision of a pious, conscientious, prudent priest is sufficient, as long as they do not have justifiable reason to question the solution he gives.

"Authors are not to be counted, but weighed."[75] The authority of a single outstanding Doctor of the Church in moral matters (e.g., Saint Thomas, Saint Alphonse) may outweigh the authority of a considerable number of lesser writers. The learned authors who take up a problem only incidentally do not have, everything else being equal, the same weight of authority as an author who has made a special research into the problem and studied it from all angles. The fact that one or the other more recent author defends a certain position which the Holy See has not condemned as improbable, does not make the opinion defended truly probable.[76] Hence more is required for support of a cherished opinion of ours than the mere citation of some obscure writer who happens to hold it. We surely do not have ample authority to support an opinion if we can cite only one excessively mild author in its favor.

An ecclesiastical writer may not be invoked as authority for the solution of a problem or a case which involves circumstances and conditions totally different from those with which he dealt in his work. Since the conditions must be similar, we may not automatically and without qualification cite the opinions of older writers for the solution of current problems.

In the matter of authority, Saint Alphonse certainly ranks highest among the moralists of the last several centuries.[77] He was elevated to the dignity of Doctor of the Church primarily because of his merit in moral theology. Not only his study of specific problems or his doctrine in certain areas, but above all his "moral system" merited the approval of the highest authority in the Church, for "he found a secure way (*tutam viam*) between the extremes of too lenient and too strict theological opinions."[78] Equi-probabilism is the sound mean between rigorism and laxism, in accordance with the principle of Saint Alphonse: "It is an outrage to explain the observance of the commandments of God more loosely than is correct. But it is no less an evil to make the divine yoke more burden-some than is necessary. Severity that is altogether excessive blocks the path of salvation."[79]

But nonetheless a moderate probabilism or probabiliorism may not be set down as unecclesiastical. These systems have outstanding theologians to propose and defend them. Practically the differences between one system and the other do not loom so large today.

IV. ACT AND ACTION AS SUBJECT OF MORAL VALUE

1. *Distinction between Act and Action*

When we refer to acts as the subject of moral value, it is obvious that we are not referring to those more or less instinctive acts which are not at all on the specific level of the mental and personal activity of man (*actus hominis,* acts of man), but to the properly human acts which have their root in the spiritual center of the person, in insight and freedom (*actus humani,* human acts). If we exclude, as we probably should, many acts of mystical experience, all human acts in some way have a reference to the "organism" of the mind-body relation (nerves, brain, inner sense, psychic automatism).

But there is still an essential distinction between the act which takes place entirely in the inner realm of man and is turned inward, though not without the cooperation of the psychosomatic activity (*actus internus*), and the action which takes place in the organs of the body (hand, organs of speech, countenance) and is extended in its efficacy into the outer world. Only in this latter case do we speak properly of action (action, external act). The essential distinction between the act (inner) and the action does not derive from the degree, lesser or greater, of activity of organs. The essential characteristic of action is the intervention in objective reality, the subjective hold or grasp of the objective world. But not every human act is accompanied by an action, for not every act has the tendency of prolongation into action. In other words, the projection into the real or the effecting of the real in the cosmos of objective actuality is not the sole scope of the human act or of human freedom. On the other hand, the whole domain of objective reality is not essentially free activity. For action is human action only when the external activity is accompanied and sustained by an inner act of insight and freedom. Then we rightly employ the term *human action*.

2. Human Act as Subject of Moral Value

"The act is the person in his own mental self-assertion" (Steinbuechel). In the act one reveals the integral moral value or defect of value of the person. Obviously, only rarely does the person rise to such heights as to employ the full capacity for value within him. Such activation and ennobling of our powers is not common among men. As value or non-value is rooted in the person as habitual bearer or subject, so the act itself is the direct and active subject of the person's moral value. For the act is not a thing divorced from person; it is the person in act. But since the person does not consist simply of his individual acts, does not exhaust self in the mere series of single acts, the value of the act is always distinct from the worth of the person as such and as a whole. The value or lack of value of the individual act enters into the value of the person, augmenting it or diminishing it.

That which actually and directly sustains the value in the act is the response to value. More precisely, it is the decision of the will responding to value or putting value into actuality in the light of true insight into moral values or at least with some habitual appreciation of the value of law. The so-called real or objective values (this means the worth of the object itself, the value inherent in the situation) to which the act is directed are not immediately and intrinsically moral values. For only values related to the person can be called moral in the strict acceptation of the term. But objective values are morally meaningful. They are moral determinants. We might designate them as "indirect bearers" of the moral value in so far as they enter into the psychic reality as determining factors. This means that only those aspects of value (or defect of it) in the object which the response of will embraces, influence the moral value of the action.[80] This same thought is expressed in the old scholastic dictum: the act is specified by the object (*actus specificatur ab objecto*), the type of value (category, level of value, determinant of individual value) of the act is determined by the type of value found and sought in the object, or, in other words, the objective value determines the value of the act directed to it.

The doctrine on the intention should prevent any misconception of this scholastic dictum. For though the objective value indeed determines what virtue is practiced or violated, the intensity, the concentration of attention, the dimensional depth of the act also influence and determine value, and these do not depend on the objective value.

3. *The Action*

a. Dual Value Realized in Action

Action is not merely the prolongation of the interior act through the bodily organs, but also and primarily its projection into and grasp of extra-mental reality, with a bettering or worsening of its world of good. As every act, so every action derives its determination and its objective from some real and objective value. But the goal of the action is not a circumstance as it really is, but as it is to be realized. (For example, the inducement to action could be the challenging value of a human soul; the goal is the soul's salvation, which is not yet realized, but which must be attained.)

The normal intent of the "indeliberate" or "non-reflective" (in the sense of not reflectively directed to the agent himself) action is toward the realization of the extra-mental world of goods. The effect of the action is the "projection into the world which confronts our scope of experience" (Hildebrand), for example, the creation of values of pleasure, profit, or art, of arrangements or facts, which are calculated to promote the moral betterment of one's neighbor or of oneself. But even though the intention is not directed through reflection toward the actual good of one's own person, the real moral value is brought to fruition in some measure "astride the action" (Scheler) in the person himself, who does the act, the moral value as such always being a personal value.

Wherefore the morally good action enriches the world in two distinct values, and the unworthy action renders it poorer by two values. The higher of the values is not the objective, but the moral personal value, although the normal healthy mind with sound perspectives does not fix this in its consciousness as the primary goal of value. If one should fail to accept the objective value for itself, but make of it exclusively a means of increasing one's own worth, it no longer bears the power of enriching values.

Still it would be an error to subscribe to the notion of Scheler that one is never permitted to preoccupy oneself with personal values in one's actions. Surely they may never occupy the mind exclusively in all that one does, above all not in the acts or actions of supreme value; for example, in giving glory and love to God and in the love of neighbor one may not selfishly persist in an exclusive consideration of one's own moral worth and seek to realize it through this activity. But we may and should rejoice in humility and gratitude before God over the secondary effects of such acts. One should rejoice that the good work enriches the soul and ennobles it in the sight of God; one can and should possess singular esteem for one's own personal value in many spheres of exterior activity so as to shun compromise of personal values in the total realization of the true value in good things. Finally, one must at times be directly concerned with himself and his own acts through self-vigilance and stern discipline of will.

The most lofty personal values are the rich fruit of divine bounty, the return gift for the love of God and neighbor which forgets self in the thought of God. The ultimate intention of the disciple of Christ, arising from the depths of the heart and motivated by love, must be directed in all things to the loving glory and supremacy of God. This is the sole guaranty that the objective value of our effort and our own personal value are the true object of sincere and earnest love and are always well ordered.

b. Significance of the External Act

The pronouncement that true moral value is exclusively personal may not be construed, in the sense of a false ethic of "pure inwardness," to mean that only the inner disposition of man has any worth, and that it is of no moment at all how everything else, including the world about us, may fare. The Christian is aware of his duty arising from the order of creation to seek the right order of things in the world. He knows that he has the mission from Christ to cooperate responsibly in the kingdom of God, a mandate which is not entirely "inward."

Every sort of quietism which fears that the value of the inner disposition will be diminished and its purity sullied by active engagement in the world is alien to Christianity. In this life we are ever in the state of responsibility to the world.[81] Although the inner spirit is the heart of morality and its very light, its most evident proof and effective safeguard is action. And finally it is really of supreme importance that the world we construct reflect the eternal law of God and not the false designs of Satan. Good example, works of mercy, effective engagement in the service of the kingdom of God are positive forces which have a value distinct from the simple good intention of our heart. Even though we cannot directly establish moral values outside ourselves, we can still contribute indirectly through the objective value of our actions to the creation of a moral disposition in others and within ourselves.

If external action does not flow spontaneously from the heart of a man, we may be sure that he will soon prove inwardly false and shallow. The very absence of such action is rather clear evidence of a defect of inner genuineness and depth from the very beginning. Moreover, external activity directly influences the interior acts very profoundly and is in direct proportion to their inner depth. Through union of heart and hand (action) the appeal to the interior act, the dedication to value, reach the very depth of the soul. And neglect of opportunity offered, disregard of the occasion for the inner act to express itself externally in action and safeguard itself through external deeds, invariably leads to spiritual stagnation. Deprived of its external manifestation, the interior spirit of good is doomed to die. Of course, when there is no occasion to externalize inner sentiment and disposition or to put the inner resolution into execution, the interior act can be thoroughly genuine and deep. But ordinarily it will lack something of the vigilance and forthrightness of will which we find in the externally manifested good act. Nor may we ever overlook the fact that the effects of the action are not divorced from the inner act in man. They are bound up with it. They give it vitality, be it for weal or woe. They alert it constantly, renew it constantly. In a sense the entire interior life depends on expression in the form of external action.

c. Moral Import of External Success

Dietrich von Hildebrand says: "External success as such has no moral significance."[82] Let us suppose that someone plunges into a stream to rescue a drowning man. His action is equally lofty, whether he succeeds in the attempt at rescue or drowns in a futile effort. Accordingly, we reject every extreme of the pragmatic of success. (By teaching that external success was a sign of predestination John Calvin paved the way for the pernicious ethic of success in the world.) The very example just cited shows that the external failure of the heroic act of self-sacrifice in the attempt to rescue a drowning man, depending entirely on an external circumstance for its success, lacked nothing in personal moral value. Nevertheless, apart from other evil consequences, it would mean that such an act would be bereft of all moral value, if it were an entirely indifferent matter whether the drowning man were to be rescued or not. Because of the failure, the world is poorer for the loss of a human life, a precious value which we can scarcely appraise properly.

Success or failure in the light of serious reflection does not at all determine the moral value of the action. But the determined orientation of the action through motive and intention, earnest striving for success, the actual will to realize the objective, are very essential to the moral value of the person in the action. The spirit of indifference (which should not be confused with holy resignation) toward the universe of good and therewith toward external success of our work robs the action of its very heart of value, not to speak of the danger of crippling our whole effort for good, if such indifference deprives us of the essential energy for forthright action. Disinterestedness toward external success in good work is a species of quietism, which is not fired with true zeal for the coming of the kingdom of God.

4. *Correct Concept of Action; Problem of Morally Indifferent Acts*

If we conceive of action simply as activity in a real and objective world, as conscious and voluntary attempt at external realization, we are confronted by the question: is such activity possible without some degree of moral awareness influencing or accompanying the action? And this is simply the equivalent of the question: can there be morally indifferent actions in the real and concrete order of things? Note that we now refer to actions.

(This question regarding actions should not be confused with a similar problem which it suggests: Can there be, objectively speaking, attitudes of mind and will which have no moral value, as well when viewed from the standpoint of the action as from that of circumstance and meaningful intention. More on this point later.) We favor the opinion that there are men who in their own way produce things of value or make the world poorer in goods of value with a certain grasp of meaning, but without a moral consciousness, actually or virtually (awareness of value, consciousness of obligation). But we prefer not to designate such conduct (for example, mere "shrewd" business calculation), which lacks moral consciousness as truly "human action" in the full sense of that term. We likewise prefer to leave the question open regarding the prior responsibility. Does this defect of moral consciousness, the indifference of the "action," if it be indifferent, have its root in a previous decision which was morally evil? At present we are primarily concerned with those men—of whom there may be many—who despite a very primitive mental and spiritual outlook do have some mental capacity for material or economic matters. But meaningful moral conduct definitely demands a much higher spiritual capacity.

According to modern phenomenology there are three essential elements necessary for action: first, the awareness of a real object in itself and for me (the question is, can one be conscious of the economic meaning exclusively, realize that it is agreeable, without perceiving the meaning "in itself," the moral meaning?); secondly, the attitude assumed toward this real object; thirdly, the objective realization of it.[83] In any instance an action is "moral," which means that it can be judged to be morally good or morally bad, only if: 1) an awareness of moral value or a consciousness of obligation (even though this is only a sense of duty to examine the matter) is present; 2) there is a free response of the will to the value or to the "must," in other words, a voluntary decision; 3) the objective realization through these two elements is effected.

V. SPIRIT AND DISPOSITION

1. *Morality Not Confined to Action*

The tremendous import of "action" is evident from any study of man's duty as expressed in the order of creation and directed to the entire world of reality; it is clearly manifested in the mission command of the Saviour to the Apostles pointing to our duties toward our fellow men; it is shown

by the very existence of the kingdom of God. But only the grossest misconception of morality and the kingdom of God would restrict the **moral
good** to exterior action, to the external "fulfillment," and the whole
potentiality of external realization in the objective world about us.

The acts of faith, hope, and love do not actually and directly thrive on
"realization" through the external action. They come into existence without action and prior to action, only of course to express themselves in
action. In eternity this objective realization in action ceases, but the inner
act attains fulfillment in the utter perfection of love. Moreover, the domain
of moral activity, the sphere of the good, is much more extensive than
the area of external action. Prior to action and parallel to it there are above
all the interior disposition and spirit. Disposition and spirit of man must
sustain his action in order to impart value and depth to it. But again **we**
must note that only a misconception of what is moral sees in the **inner**
man only the foundation and root of the action, somewhat after **the**
manner of the Kantian equation of disposition and "sense of duty."

For us the inner spirit of morality goes far beyond consciousness **of**
duty, if we conceive of duty merely as the obligation to action. Surely **no**
one can deny that the notion of duty has an intimate affinity with **inner**
disposition, for one is obliged to cultivate good intentions, to shun **evil**
attitudes and purposes. But the thought of duty connotes obligation. It
suggests a "must." And surely this does not constitute the very heart **of**
inner disposition. Nor is it uppermost in the interior moral awareness.
Most essential is the interior penetration of the value inherent in the good,
or, if disposition should be evil, the corruption and corrosion by defect
of value. Mere awareness of duty, set exclusively on the "must" and the
"must not" of obligation, is the very antithesis of inner disposition **and**
right intention, which as such are grounded on consciousness of **true**
value. A lofty sense of duty thrives on the inner moral spirit. Consciousness of duty which does not spring from a deep and spiritual openness **to**
value remains purely formal. It is blind to its own principle of value,
which ultimately is the foundation of all duty.

2. *Phenomenology of the Emotions* (*Gesinnung*)

a. Emotions and the Inner Act

The interior moral disposition of man is not simply to be equated with
the interior free act in contradistinction to the action which is external.
Not every interior act is the same as the inner moral disposition to act as

such. We must also make a distinction between the emotional excitations and the deep interior disposition which is fulfilled and manifested only in the free act. The emotions arise in some manner within the psychic depths of self from the hidden psychic powers. Not through their degree of intensity, clarity, or awareness do the emotions reach the level of true human acts, which are to be judged as morally good or evil, but only through the attitude assumed by the person. It is the I at the very center of man's being which makes them such. Freedom must first be alerted, and it must assert itself in the area of the feelings. It must take them in its hold and control them and direct them, or freely submit to them (to permit the emotions to remain uncontrolled is actually such a "submission" to them) before we have free human sentiments, that is, deliberate and responsible acts of the inner emotional man.

It is quite apparent that emotions tend to manifest themselves when occasion offers and to "unburden" themselves. Such manifestation usually, though not invariably or necessarily, deepens and enriches the interior man. But the manifestation of overwrought or falsely exaggerated sentiments often results in their own exhaustion and impoverishment. However, we should not fail to note that the expression of sentiment or emotion is not of the essence, nor does exteriorization occupy an essential place in the psychological structure of the emotional disposition of man. Essential is the interior act.

b. Psychological Structure of the Emotions

How are the psychic powers affected by the emotions? Do the emotions consist in thoughts, in acts of will, or in affections and feelings?

Emotion is not arid conceptual thought, aloof from reality, though dealing with it from afar, grasping it in its essential traits and relations. Even intensely labored thinking as such is not emotion as we view it here. And yet the inner emotional life in no wise excludes intellect or the thought processes. It is rather something of the heart, a thinking of the heart (*cogitationes cordis*). Just as truly as abstract thought is not emotion, so truly also is it that a core of thought lies at the base of every emotional act which is really human and free, and this basic thought corresponds to the object and character of the emotion. It is the characteristic of emotion that all thoughts and memories arising within us are filled with and enveloped by the "stuff of emotion," with lofty sentiment and feeling.

The feelings which we might call the "affective elements" rooted in the body-soul composite of man can recede somewhat. But if the nobler element, the higher sentiment or emotion, recedes, the inevitable consequence is disruption, dissolution of the whole inner spirit of a man. The heart has gone out of him. In the loftier feelings the soul participates to its profoundest depths; in these it manifests itself. Affections concerned with nobler things, with spiritual exaltation, are not to be confused with mere moods and emotions which have nothing to do with man's spirit. The heart of man and his inner disposition itself, as also the "spiritual emotion" and sense of value which characterize and manifest them, are purposive ("intentional"). This means they are specified and their natures are determined by the objects to which they are consciously directed. On this point they agree with the intentionality of mere knowing and willing. Primarily characteristic and distinctive of emotion is the special intimate relation or tendency of the heart. The objective is immediately experienced as value or non-value.

In contradistinction to mere knowing and thinking and above all to mere willing, which is primarily busy with striving or effecting, we can therefore say of every species of emotion that it is a re-echoing response to a value or non-value centering in the subject which is the very depths of the human soul. It is quite apparent that the emotions are often accompanied by seeking and yearning, or that they release the urge to seek and yearn. And yet seeking and yearning are not of the essence of the emotions. "Sometimes love, affection, friendliness are entirely quiescent. Fully satisfied, they rest in their object without any seeking or yearning."[84] When we speak of a response re-echoing in the subject, we do not at all mean that the emotions tend to lock themselves up in the psychic enclosure of man. On the contrary, precisely because they are response, and not directly purposive, the emotions by their very tendency are attached to their object. This is singularly true even of those emotions or sentiments of man which are not accompanied by any desire or yearning. Our dispositions can place us in a much more intimate relation with an object, with a person, than the most intensive thinking or willing. For in the disposition one strikes the most intimate chord in the heart of man. As in the case of the intimate experience of conscience, the whole soul participates. The response of man's heart to value re-echoes within the object itself, and all the forces of man's soul are in some measure affected.

The inward orientation toward objective value is so complete and perfect that the emotions and sentiments are like spiritual outpourings or impulses moving toward their object. However, we do not have in mind the typically repressive and convulsive dispositions which progressively hamper and impede man's orientation toward value. They gradually lessen his power to move toward the world of values confronting him.

The contention is plausible that certain highly sensitive and susceptible individuals can be affected by the emotional attitudes of others even without any manifestation of them and without any external actions expressing them.

The psychological and moral aspects of the inner life of man are expressed positively by the affections of love, kindness, humility, reverence, justice, and purity. These have a vitalizing, purifying, enriching effect. Here we have psychic energies which in some manner precede every decision and influence it. They are an intimate approval of their object, a "purposeless" confirmation of their worth. The negative dispositions tend toward disdain and denial (as though to blot out the very existence of the object of hatred, disdain, envy), repudiation, disruption. But it is possible that the objective goal (perhaps a person) of these dispositions is totally unaffected by them. Again, they may be brushed aside or overcome. Nevertheless, in every instance, by a kind of inner compulsion, they exert a direct and immediate influence on the subject himself. The tendency is ever present to promote, to vitalize, or, if the effect be baneful, to scorn and isolate. And it is also true that in every instance the effect on the subject himself is greater. More surely and more vehemently is the subject of emotions affected than the object to which they are directed. Emotions make up the very heart of man, from which come both good and evil.

c. Object of the Emotions

The object of an emotion is ordinarily a person: God, our neighbor, a community of persons, even oneself. Material objects or possessions, plants and animals, cannot be the object of the emotions in the same profound sense as persons, nor can they be the object of emotion at all unless there is some reference or relation to persons.

Value or defect of value is not only the immediate object of emotions, but also the means by which they are aroused. But we must draw a very sharp distinction between the emotions directed primarily toward value or defect of value and the emotions directed immediately toward the person who is the subject of the value or the defect. Emotion is far more immediate and far more vital if it is directed toward the person than if it is focused on one of his virtues. Thus, for example, love for a man or

woman is much more vital than a mere love or admiration for one of his
noble traits. The faults of a person are a defect of value and therefore
deserve and demand repudiation (*odium abominationis*), but they do not
justify hatred of the person himself (*odium personae*). How deep and
painful is the abhorrence for sin, how genuine our hatred for it, if we
deplore the sin in one we love, if we truly love the person and hate the
sin!

One who is firmly fixed in his love of God sees in his neighbor, even
though he has sinned, the image of God, always worthy of his love. He
looks upon him as a true brother in Christ, capable of cooperating with
divine grace and saving his soul. From the fault and defect of worth,
which is sin, he recoils in horror, only to leave the way open for a real
and true love for the actual worth of the person.

On the other hand, one who has not at all discovered the personal
values at their truest and profoundest will readily be immersed in superficial values or in non-values. Only too readily will his emotions be caught
up in what is light or trivial, whether it be value or its defect. Obviously,
he lacks all depth of feeling in his heart. To be totally absorbed in the
thrills of sports or fascinated by the attractions of the fashions and modes
means to be utterly infatuated by a hero of the gridiron or by a movie
star. The personal values, which could release the most tremendous positive emotions, are nowhere in evidence.

Only one who is truly free spiritually, who really discerns values, is
not overwhelmed by particular values or by lack of them. Such a man,
spiritually free, always keeps his heart open to those noble moral sentiments which are owing to men and women as persons, as sympathy, pity,
reverence, and the like. He is attracted rather to the noblest values and
chooses carefully among the wealth of particular values offered him in the
world.

d. Emotions, Intention (*finis operantis*), Motive

The concepts of inner disposition of heart and intention must be kept
distinct. The inner disposition is surely the basic source of the intention, of
the purpose which directs a task or an action to its goal. But the dispositions are not constructed so as to build or form the intention (*finis
operantis*) of one's actions. A series of dispositions is surely not to be
understood as purposive, as striving for a goal in the same sense as the
intention or motive of an action. Nevertheless, the goal of intention can

still be a manifestation or intensification of the disposition, and it can also be the control of one's impulses and emotions. From this it is evident that in many ways one's dispositions are intimately bound up with one's intentions and motives.

The basic orientation of a man (this means the total potential orientation of man, prior to any particular decision) is characterized by the predominant instinctive emotions and impulses of his temperament. The basic intention is the deliberate "pre-decision" with its source in knowledge and the depth of freedom. It relates to a whole category of value, so that, as far as purpose is concerned, a decision has been rendered regarding all actions in the category. In the most comprehensive sense a basic intention is the final and intrinsically irrevocable decision of the will choosing the good—"the good intention"—which is the choice of the ultimate end, of the supreme value. A basic intention directed to evil, a total decision choosing any "value" serving lust or pride, is entirely different in its destructiveness from the momentary decision of a single and particular act. Likewise the "good intention" in its full meaning has the power to uplift and ennoble. Through the basic intention above all the inner structure of disposition and temperament is essentially determined and in turn itself determines the pattern of action. The basic good intention, if truly comprehensive and universal, affects all the particular inordinate impulses of the temperament. In advance they are disarmed and robbed of their inner offensive power. Though frequently it is not possible to prevent them entirely because they are a consequence of imperious automatism or association, still they are forestalled before every particular decision and thus their power for evil is broken.

They are bereft of their full moral significance as long as the prior free decision, or good intention, has removed their poisonous fangs. And this prior intention retains its force and validity until a new decision of the will has revoked it altogether or at least as to one or other particular instance.

A basic intention is transformed into a fundamental attitude when the entire inner man with all his instinctive sentiments and emotions, his impulses and actions, is thoroughly animated with it. When this intention dominates his whole life as its truly basic orientation, then it is a fundamental attitude and disposition with all its depth and efficacy.

The emotions are vaster in scope and more profound than any particular motive (intention) concerned with individual actions. But the basic intention and especially the fundamental attitude are more comprehensive than any isolated emotion or sentiment with its object. The decision affecting the character and the depth of the basic intention and its transformation into fundamental attitude does not take place in a vacuum, but in the dynamic area of the dominant passions.

It is evident that education, through proper discipline and cultivation of emotional life (in which we include the cultivation of the values of character and disposition), is in many ways more significant than the tense straining of will power. Of course there is no effective way of nurturing the emotional life without the dynamic force of the will, which takes up and controls the good impulses and tendencies and restrains the unruly ones. Without the harnessing of the dynamic power of will to definite purpose (*intendere*) through the intention and the resolution in the decision of action itself, there can be no true education of the emotional life.

The concepts *intention* and *motive* are almost equivalent. But intention looks to goal or end and the advantage it offers, whereas motive is concerned with motivation or the reason why one acts. However, the most basic motivation is the good viewed as end or goal (not merely as purpose).

The purpose (intention) of deliberate resolve and of action itself (the end of the agent, *finis operantis*) can remain inwardly alien (unknown) to the object acted upon. But the purpose of truly genuine sentiment or emotion (strictly speaking, the expression "purposive emotions" is something of a misnomer, for it really means the absence of authentic fundamental emotions) is not accessory to emotion, but is its very own central import. The motive of disposition or emotion is nothing else but its own object as value or non-value. The reason is that the emotion cannot be purposive or calculating as is the will in its resolve. The emotion cannot resolve, as can the will, to do something. The value invites: emotion essentially responds.

e. The Nature of the Emotions

An emotion can be more or less central, or, as the case may be, peripheral. Many emotional impulses to which one submits or which one rejects do not penetrate to the actual center of conscious life. Others press to the foreground of consciousness and occupy a broad zone of thought and conduct. A feeling of hostility, for example, which has taken deep hold of a man's heart wields a much more devastating effect and is morally more decisive than it would be if it occupied only a tiny sector of the spiritual life. From this it follows that there is some significance in the mere fact that one makes an effort to abstain altogether from thinking of the object of hatred. It is of tremendous importance to allow free scope to the sentiment of love for God and one's neighbor.

Another quality of the inner disposition is its dimensional depth. From the objective standpoint, the decisive question is how elevated is the value and how profoundly is it grasped. Is only the actual depth of value grasped and expressed, or also its most profound source, which is God? The supernatural disposition of love of neighbor "in God and for God's sake" is essentially deeper than a mere humane love of one's fellows. Not only the loftiness of the value known, but also the depth of the soul's grasp of it is decisive. This latter is most intimately bound up with the manner of the comprehension of values, that is, whether there is question of a cold and aloof intellectual knowledge of values, a vital and affective sense of value, or an intimate and conatural grasp of value. In this connection we note that the purely humane love of a noble man can be warmer and more vigorous than the religious love of neighbor of a superficial person.

There is a very important distinction to be drawn between genuine and fraudulent emotions. By this we do not mean illusory or fictitious emotion, which would be neither authentic nor unauthentic, but simply non-existent. Nor should we identify genuineness of emotion with vigor or vehemence of feeling. There is even a singular kind of counterfeit senti-ment or emotion which exaggerates feeling far beyond the conscious sense of value. At times emotion is artificially keyed up beyond the bounds of sincerity and reason. (We have an example in the "moral" outrage ex-pressed by many educators over infractions of virtues which they them-selves violate or at least fail to take seriously in their own lives outside the lecture hall.) A similar counterfeit of true sentiment is particularly charac-teristic of the snobbish enthusiasm for art displayed by many amateur "art lovers" who have no real appreciation for artistic values at all. But, of course, in such matters the individuals may not in any way be aware that their feelings are not genuine.

Not every display of feeling mars the genuineness of emotion. In fact, emotion cannot be permanently sustained without warmth of feeling, since emotion in great part has its seat in the temperament, which has the vitalizing power to evoke the feelings within us. On the other hand, holding firm to the true spirit of piety even when feeling is lacking (in this connection the doctrine on spiritual "dryness" or "aridity" is particularly significant) may be a sign of the genuine character of our inner dispositions. Firmness and tenacity of will must sustain us during the periods in which disposition and temperament are lagging. Psychosomatic feeling which depends largely on organic vigor or debility may in no wise be made the test of the true depth and genuineness of dispositions or emotions.

f. Emotions: Positive and Negative

There are both positive and negative tendencies in our emotions and dispositions. Positive emotions are characterized by affirmation and union, and they center in love. The extreme negative tendency is manifested by hatred. Hate implies an attitude of negation, aloofness, division regarding its object. However, we must note with a degree of caution that these concepts are studied from the purely psychological point of view. The moral categories of "negative" and "positive" are often the very contrary. Hatred, for example, or any other attitude which is psychologically negative must be judged as morally positive if it is the response to be given to negation or defect of value, according to the true hierarchy of values. It is morally good to detest evil. Conversely, the psychologically "positive" attitude of love is to be condemned as morally negative, if it violates the right order of values (the order of love), as, for example, if one were to love a creature more than God.

No emotion or sentiment can be totally negative. The negation always presupposes a positive basis. If one should, to cite an example, hate another for his talent and virtue, he surely manifests a psychologically and morally negative disposition. But the actual basis for this evil attitude in the heart is the psychologically positive (to be condemned as morally negative) disposition of disordered self-love. Even though the dispositions are morally positive and therefore good, to give them a motivation which is primarily negative psychologically is spiritually unsound. Such is the case if zeal for the good assumes the form of righteous indignation against evil. If one forms such an attitude toward zeal, primarily negative, it may lead to a souring of the whole moral personality.

3. *The Ruling Passion*

We can study the dominant tendency (passion, emotion, sentiment) under the most diverse aspects or points of view. From the psychological aspect, a negative tendency can predominate, e.g., in hatred or indignation.

Or morally evil attitudes can prevail, i.e., the tendency to violate the order of values through the feelings and emotions. It is very important for the psychology and ethics of emotion and disposition to determine what sphere of values occupies the principal place in a man's emotions and sentiments. Edward Spranger treats the principal "value types" (*Lebensformen*), each with its dominant value corresponding to its *ethos* or dispositional orientation. He lists the following value types:

I. The economic: this has as predominant value the economic, utility, profit. As positive *ethos,* it has devotion to work, to one's calling, to one's profession.

II. The aesthetic; its predominant value is in the beautiful and in the noble enjoyment of the beautiful. The positive *ethos* is devotion to cultural activity and to the nurture of harmonious and balanced personality.

III. The political: predominant value is force or power, racial supremacy, heroism. The positive *ethos* is the rule of power, the cult of courage and self-mastery.

IV. The theoretical: predominant value is science. The *ethos* is devotion to search for truth, truthfulness, objectivity.

V. The social: the predominant value is the good of community. The *ethos* is devotion to the "Thou," to community, to the cult of altruism.

VI. The religious: the predominant value is God, union with God, salvation of one's soul. The *ethos* is devotion to God, detachment from earthly things.

It is quite apparent that each of these value types contains positive sentiments and emotions, an *ethos* rich in values. But every type which gives free rein to sentiments of secondary value is always in danger of betraying the higher values even in the ultimate decisions and purposes. Apart from the fact that there are no types existing in a pure and unmixed state, for they are only more or less predominant tendencies and inclinations, it should be evident that they are not as such mutually exclusive. For example, the knowledge and recognition of religious values as supreme is at least theoretically reconcilable with the economic or aesthetic value type. Finally, if religious value does not occupy a place of importance in the heart and is not truly central, it must eventually follow that also in the practical decisions there will be a sharp cleavage between the "predominant" and the religious, and a false hierarchy of values will be established.

The greatest danger of all, bound up with the imbalance in the value types as inner dispositions and tendencies, lies in the orientation of all higher values toward the predominant value. There is the tendency to look upon the highest and noblest values as no more than means or instruments to serve the predominant value. We have a clear example in the business man or political leader who attends church or receives the sacraments for the sake of "public relations": the business man to impress his customers, the politician to beguile the voters. In some instances religion has been used as a trump card in the game of power politics.

Similar to these "value types" of Spranger are the "four *stadia* on the way of life," found in Kierkegaard. They are the character or disposition types in relation to predominant value: 1. the aesthetic, 2. the ethical, 3. the anthropocentric-religious, 4. the theocentric-religious. Kierkegaard does not look upon these as fixed or static types, but rather as stages of development, with the tendency, of course, toward stabilization. The economic value type, which in its capitalistic extreme and even more so in Marxism tends to destroy the moral world order, has no place in the "life *stadia*," because it does not constitute a stage of perfection of the person. It rather constitutes a supreme peril to personal value even where it possesses a positive *ethos* or has a positive moral orientation.

4. *Christian Morality of the "Heart"*

Catholic moral teaching does not approve of any ethics of the heart which stresses interiority exclusively. Christian morality is not a morality of mere interior purity of intention or spirit to the exclusion of action manifesting the right disposition and a true sense of responsibility for earthly realities and a genuine apostolic zeal for the kingdom of God. But the Catholic instruction in moral doctrine must appeal to the heart as the noble source of every good act. And in this constant appeal to the heart it has its source in the Divine Master Himself. Together with the service rendered to God with joy in every effort, there must be the cultivation of the inner disposition of spirit. Instruction and education must go beyond the ideal of mere conformity through the practice of simple obedience. They must rather awaken a genuine spirit of obedience which thrives on loving insight into the meaning of right order, into the dignity and worth of authority whose right to command rests ultimately on God, and, in so far as this is possible, into the intrinsic value of the precept or command itself.

The most essential point in this education of the heart is to awaken true love in the very depths of man's being and never to be content with factual instruction alone. In one brief statement we can sum up the essence of the morality of the heart: the great commandment is the law of love. Love is the center, the very heart of all religious and moral good. The inner spirit of love is the most intimate principle of every virtuous sentiment, decision, deed, for one who possesses it is truly moved by the love of God. No one denies, of course, that an action can possess a formal ethical correctness without the impulse of love, but the perfection of good in the religious sense can be formed only in the thought and action which are in some measure sustained and ennobled by the divine power of love. The greater the spirit of love, the purer the inner disposition of love which sustains and forms the moral act, the more profound and meritorious it is.

Genuine love, in turn, must prove itself by the test of action in patient and courageous bearing of the cross and actual obedience to the law of God. The spirit does not contradict the law. But without uprightness of heart fulfillment of the law has no moral value. The inner spirit must be the very soul of the fulfillment of the law. But it cannot stop short at this. Love is creative. It constantly discovers new avenues leading to particular good. But it is no less zealous in the study of the universal law and the divine will binding us all in all things (cf. Ps 118). Truly, love and only love helps us to discern the real meaning of the law and to recognize the special call of God. The good disposition furnishes the clear insight into the divine will and the alert attention to the divine call. This is the sense of the profound thought of Saint Augustine, constantly verified, "*Dilige, et quod vis fac.*" "Love, and do what you will!"[85] This does not at all mean that it is a matter of indifference what kind of actions a man performs (let us say, even perverted actions), as long as he possesses love. Much rather we should say it means: "Be sure that true love is the basis of your moral life, for it can produce only good." The true spirit of love imparts a marvelous sureness of right in all things, adding the splendor and value of love to the true and correct, no matter how unpretentious it may be.

It must never be forgotten, however, that inner sentiment, love above all, is more than the inner surety and safeguard of obedience. It also has its own intrinsic value. God wants not only our external deeds. Most of all He wants our hearts. "My son, give me thy heart." "*Praebe, fili mi, cor tuum mihi!*" (Prv 23:26) The fact that God really asks for our love and accepts it is one of the most salutary truths of our holy faith. We can love God truly, mightily and effectively with Christ and in Christ. If we are bound up with Christ through grace and love, then our whole inner self is sustained and enriched by His love for His Father and for men, which is far more than any mere external imitation or conformity with Him.

5. The "Heart" in Scripture and Tradition

Already in the Old Testament the inspired writers incessantly stress the truth that God does not look so much to our exterior actions, the prayer of the lips, and sacrifice. Much more does He look to the "heart," to the genuine sentiment of love, of obedience, penance. Jahweh does not complain so much about the peryerted actions of the Israelites as about their "hardened heart," about their adulterous, perverse dispositions (Is 6:9f.; 29:13; cf. Mk 6:52; 8:17; 16:14; Jn 12:39f.). The summit of the great Messianic prophecies is reached in God's promise to wash away the sins of His people, give to them a "new heart," and instill fear of Him and love for Him into their hearts (Jer 32:40; 31:33; Is 51:7; Ez 36:26). "And I will give them one heart, and will put a new spirit in their bowels: and I will take away the stony heart out of their flesh, and will give them a heart of flesh" (Ez 11:19). God does not desire the rending of garments, but the inner sentiment of penance. "Rend your hearts, and not your garments" (Jl 2:13).

Christ continues and fulfills the teaching of the Old Testament and in the sharpest contrast to the legalistic externalism of the Pharisees lays the greatest stress on the importance of the interior disposition, especially in His Sermon on the Mount (Mt 5f.). It is not primarily the external deeds which offend God, but the very thoughts and desires, the inner sentiments and dispositions. On the contrary, "blessed are the pure of heart" (Mt 5:8). The heart is the seat of disposition, above all the seat of love. Not merely our actions must be well ordered, but first of all the seat, the organ of love. The heart must be "pure," that is, it may not be filled with false love and defiled through perverse dispositions. Of its inmost nature the heart that is pure will turn to the true objects of its inner sentiments. Here in this life already it will look lovingly to God and in eternity will behold Him face to face.

Whereas the Pharisees severely condemned the external infraction of petty human prescriptions, the Lord castigated the "evil heart," the base disposition, from which, as from a polluted spring, all evil flows (Mt 15:18; Mk 7:20ff.). Without good disposition every action of ours, even sacrifice and prayer, is worthless before God. Christ complains, as did the prophet (Is 29:13), about the cult which was mere lip service because it lacked the interior disposition and good will (Mt 15:8). The most bitter reproach is St. Peter's accusation of Simon Magus: "Thy heart [disposition] is not right before God" (Acts 8:21).

Stephen hurls the charge against the Jews that they are "uncircumcised in heart," a fact which accounts for their disbelief, their resistance to the Holy Spirit (Acts 7:51). Conversion and acceptance of the faith presupposes change of disposition (Mk 1:15: "Repent and believe in the gospel." *Metanoeîn,* the Greek word for *repent,* means an inner change of thinking, an utter interior reorientation). As Stephen, so Paul also demands, instead of external circumcision, "the circumcised heart," the inner disposition of penance and change of life (Rom 2:5, 29). A "pure conscience" and pure disposition are as inseparable as the two sides of a coin (1 Tm 1:5). The very essence of imitation of Christ is to assume the inner spirit of Christ. "Have this mind in you which was also in Christ Jesus" (Phil 2:5). The new inner spirit of the Christian is made possible, not merely through conformity with the example of Christ, but also and much more through the indwelling of Christ in us (Rom 8:10; Eph 4:17-24). Christ dwelling in us is the actual source of power for this renewal within us. This grace of Christ renewing our hearts from the depths is a challenge which we dare not ignore. Because we "have put on Christ" (Gal 3:27) through a renewal of our whole inner selves, we are commanded in every action and above all in our inner sentiment "to put on the Lord Jesus Christ" (Rom 13:14; Eph 4:24; Col 3:10) with true effectiveness. The thought underlying the entire Gospel of John and his letters is that we are renewed in being, are "in love," and therefore we must take care that we "abide in love" (Jn 15:9f.; 1 Jn 2:17; 4:16), that the gift of love bestowed on us descend ever deeper and deeper into our hearts.

The doctrine on the fundamental meaning of right dispositions was always clearly taught by the Fathers and theologians. According to Augustine, "it is not the exterior accomplishment, but the moral disposition which plays the decisive role."[86] "Change your disposition and the change in your actions will follow!"[87] "If you have mercy in your heart, God will accept your alms, even if you have nothing to offer with your hand."[88] External violence cannot rob the virgin of the splendor of virginity, if only she remain pure in her resolution, in her disposition. Patient endurance even exalts the glory of virginity.[89] The disposition makes the will good or bad. "The right will is good love; perverted will is an evil love."[90]

Scholastic theology places the primary stress on the clear explanation of the intention (*finis operantis*). Not the external action, but the inner intention plays the most important and decisive role. Similarly in scholastic teaching the infused virtues are more than the impulse toward external works. They are the most intimate dispositions. They are active powers of the heart. Medieval moral theology devotes special attention to the movements of the senses and the emotional or sensual impulses which are not deliberate movements of the will (*motus primo primi et secundo primi*). The opinion prevalent until the time of Saint Thomas that these sudden impulses were to be looked upon as sinful, even though they were not deliberate (either because of original sin or, according to the more common opinion, because of previous failure to discipline and restrain the inner dispositions), shows what importance was attached to those inner dispositions. And the very fact that since the time of Saint Thomas the teaching has prevailed that these impulses are sinful only in so far as the will freely is responsible for them, merely serves to emphasize the importance of the free will in the deliberate cultivation of the good emotional impulses and the whole emotional structure.[91]

The great medieval teachers of mystical doctrine place even greater emphasis than do the other theologians on the significance of disposition and inner attitude as opposed to mere external activity. And this is not quietism, not even in the case of Meister Eckhart. Theirs is a Biblical and Augustinian optimism. The "renewed heart," the "good tree," will manifest itself in good fruits, in sustaining the good effort through action and, above all, in steadfast endurance of trial and suffering. Scotus and his school stress interiority and all that relates to inner attitudes even more strongly than does Thomas. As one would expect, the Franciscan school with its doctrine of the primacy of love or will over intellect, places singular emphasis on the doctrine of interior disposition and spirit. As was Max Scheler in our time, so medieval mysticism and scholasticism in the Middle Ages were probing the depths of the most profound mystery of Christian morality of interiority when they described true love as "co-willing and co-loving with God." The child of God does not love merely because God loves and what God loves, but he loves with a divine love, with God's own love, by force of a love bestowed and infused by God. He dwells in the heart of God.

Whereas in scholastic moral theology, despite a sound appraisal of interior disposition, the orientation was toward law (the eternal law, the law of the Gospel, and the law of nature) and the ideal of right order, the *devotio moderna* (the main representatives were Gerson and Thomas à Kempis) was slanted even excessively toward the moral disposition or inner spirit. But there was a deep theological basis for the devotion in the interior dispositions of Christ as model of our own. This moral teaching bore rich fruit, in the practical order, in the inner reform of countless monasteries. However, in such devotion there is always the hazard of overemphasis of the inner disposition and inner spirit. Only too readily the ardent zeal for the kingdom of God and the right order in the world based on the divine law gives way to a very narrow concern for mere correctness of personal attitude or exclusive interest in one's own salvation.

6. *Moral Disposition in Luther's Doctrine and in Modern Philosophy*

There is the sharpest contrast between the optimistic spirit of the Middle Ages and its noble striving for the fulfillment of a divine order in the universe and the pessimistic outlook of Luther with its denial of a well-ordered world and its condemnation of the aspirations of the human heart. His is a withdrawal from world responsibility (from the alleged "justice of works") into a "pure interiority" of the spirit where irresistible grace rules over the "totally depraved" heart of man. Such was the attitude of Luther in his quarrel with the Church that he considered obedience to her authority above all diametrically opposed to the genuine Christian attitude, as though true obedience to the Church is irreconcilable with the purest and loftiest dispositions and does not ultimately in its inner spirit turn to God (cf. Mt 18:17f.). That all good conduct must be sustained by faith and be carried out with freedom and joy is simply the ancient Catholic traditional doctrine which Luther repeats according to his own concepts.

Kant's ethic is surely also an ethic of interiority, though his sense of value is no more than a shriveled and barren conscience of obligation. It is true that we agree with Kant in making the moral decision a free and deliberate act of will. But his moral world is still too threadbare for our taste. It has nothing of value but the "good will alone." Utterly arid and dour, this ethic of Kant derives primarily from his conception of God. For him every attitude toward God is meaningless since God cannot receive anything from us.

Ethic of interiority was dealt a severe blow by Hegel, who placed the summit of morality in the state and in consequence demanded of the individual as the greatest "interior achievement" complete submission to the ethic of the state. Though it is true that he did not theoretically reject human freedom and personal responsibility, in the last analysis such freedom is completely stifled by the world spirit (universal reason) incorporated in the state. If things came to such a pass in Germany that the individual gladly acquiesced in the moral decisions of the state in every conceivable problem of life, Hegel ultimately must share the responsibility. The state and submission to its decrees supplant the personal moral sense. Absolute submission is the only worthy "interior attitude." This is the legal docility toward the state, which has little in common, surely, with the inspired concept of the sacred pages. Little remains of the profoundly personal and truly interior.

Contemporary philosophical and sociological literature[92] deals with an ethic of interiority (*Gessinungs-ethik*), but gives it a meaning quite different from the traditional concept derived from the Biblical teaching about the "heart of man." The Biblically orientated ethic of interiority stresses the primacy of love as an inward acquiescence in the love of the Creator and Redeemer, whereas the idealistic ethic of interiority is largely a reflection of a defective grasp of the real order of things. Such an ethic must in great part be ascribed to an unsuspecting aloofness from the sociological or psychological realities, which consciously responsible conduct cannot neglect or ignore. Rightly does the sociologist Max Weber[93] combat that false ethic of interiority which says: "The Christian does what is right and leaves the outcome to God," thus placing the responsibility for the evil consequences of "conduct flowing from pure dispositions" on the world, on the stupidity of others, or on the will of God who created them. Surely one must clearly realize that such a position is not in accord with the true and genuine Christian ethic of interiority. Christian ethics of the heart are indeed the very antithesis of the heartless and even unprincipled ethics of success, but they are in no wise irreconcilable with an ethic of responsibility. It is the very basic disposition, the love and loving acquiescence in that which is dear to the Divine Heart, which demands that we take the ordering of creation seriously, that we be concerned about the power of sin and the triumph of Christ to be revealed in the historic order. The history of Christian ethics of interiority, especially if we include in it also the Lutheran teaching on "utter inwardness," at least warns against the danger which it harbors. In some way interiority can degenerate into a flight from the responsibility for the Kingdom of God, just as the ethic of responsibility, because of the narrowness and limitations of man, can deteriorate into an external ethic of success.

BIBLIOGRAPHY

ADAM, A. *Tugend der Freiheit*. Nuernberg, 1947.

A.F.G. *Folie lucide? Le scrupule religieux vu par un médecin chrétien*. Lyon-Paris, 1947.

ANDERSEN, L. F. *Die Seele und das Gewissen*. Leipzig, 1929.

AUER, A. "Gesetz und Freiheit im Verhaeltnis von Gott und Mensch bei F. X. Linsenmann," *Der Mensch vor Gott* (Duesseldorf, 1948), 246–263.

AUER, J. *Die menschliche Willensfreiheit im Lehrsystem des Thomas von Aquin und des Duns Skotus*. Muenchen, 1938.

BAHHYA, IBN PAQUDA. *Introduction aux devoirs des coeurs*. Paris, 1950.

BARBEL, J., C.SS.R. *Quellen des Heils. Die Sakramente der katholischen Kirche*. Luxemburg, 1947.

BAUHOFER, O. *Maske und Ebenbild. Die christliche Lehre vom Menschen*. Luzern, 1950.

BAUMGAERTEL AND BEHN. "kardía," *ThW*, III, 609–616.

BERDIAEV, N. *The Divine and the Human*. London: Bles, 1949.

———. *Solitude and Society*. London, Bles, 1938.

———. *The Meaning of History*. New York: Scribner, 1936.

BERGMANN, W. *Die Seelenleiden der Nervoesen*. 3 Auflage. Freiburg, 1929.

———. *Religion und Seelenleiden*. 5 Bde. Duesseldorf, 1926–1930.

BERNHART, J. *Der Sinn der Geschichte*. Freiburg, 1931.

BEUMER, J., S.J. "Die persoenliche Suende in sozialtheologischer Sicht," *ThGl*, 43 (1953), 81–102.

BIOT, R. *Le corps et l'âme*. Paris, 1939.

BIRNBAUM, K. *Die krankhafte Willensschwaeche und ihre Erscheinungsformen*. Wiesbaden, 1911.

BISER, E. *Das Christusgeheimnis der Sakramente*. Heidelberg, 1950.

BISMARCK, E., C.S.Sp. *Die Freiheit des Christen nach Paulus und die Freiheit des Weisen nach der juengeren Stoa*. Knechtsteden, 1921.

BLESS, H. *Pastoralpsychiatrie*. Roermond-Maaseik, 1945.

BOPP, L. *Liturgical Education* (Marquette monographs on education). Milwaukee: Bruce, 1937.

BOREL, J. *Le déséquilibre, ses psychoses, sa morale*. Paris, 1947.

BORGOLTE, A., O.F.M. "Die Geschichtlichkeit der sittlichen Ordnung," *WissWeish*, 16 (1953), 20–33.

BOTTERWECK, C. J. "Gott erkennen" im Sprachgebrauch des Alten Testaments. Bonner Biblische Beitraege 2. Bonn, 1951.

BOVET, TH. *Die Person, ihre Krankheiten und Wandlungen*. Tuebingen, 1948.

BRAEUNING, K. *Willensfreiheit und Naturgesetz*. Muenchen-Basel, 1952.

BREMI, W. *Was ist das Gewissen? Seine Beschreibung, seine metaphysische und religioese Deutung, seine Geschichte*. Zuerich-Leipzig, 1934.

BRISBOIS, E. "Pour le probabilisme," *EphThLov*, 13 (1936), 74–97.

*BRUNNER, E. *Man in Revolt*. A Christian Anthology. New York: Scribner, 1939.

*BUBER, M. *I and Thou*. New York: Scribner, 1937.

BUSENBENDER, W. *Der Christ im Anruf der Zeit*. Frankfurt, 1954.

*BUTTERFIELD, H. *Christianity and History*. London: Bell, 1949.

BUYTENDIJK, F. J. *Gezondheid en vrijheid*. Utrecht, 1951.

CAIGNY, J. DE. *De genuino morali systemate S. Alfonsi; de genuino probabilismo*. Brugge, 1901.

CALVERAS, J. *La afectividad y el corazón según Santo Tomás en relación con los conocimientos actuales*. Barcelona, 1951.

CARPENTIER, R. "Conscience," *DSp.*, II (Paris, 1950), 1459–1575.

CARUSO, I. "Le problème de la mauvaise conscience," *Psyché* (1951), 539–551.

CASEY, D. *The Nature and Treatment of Scruples*. Dublin, 1948.

CHRISTIANSEN, B. *Willensfreiheit*. Stuttgart, 1945.

CLOSTERMANN, G. *Das Weibliche Gewissen. Seine mannigfaltigen Erscheinungsweisen nach Formen, Wertinhalten und individueller Reifung*. Muenster, 1953.

CONGAR, Y. "Culpabilité, responsabilité et sanctions collectives," *VieInt*, 18 (1950), 259–284, 387–407.

CONRAD-MARTIUS, HEDWIG. "Seele und Leib," *Ho*, 42 (1949/50), 53–68.

*CULLMANN, O. *Christ and Time*. The primitive Christian conception of time and history. Philadelphia: Westminster Press, 1950.

DANIÉLOU, J., S.J. *The Lord of History*. Reflections on the inner meaning of history. Chicago: Regnery, 1958.

DELERUE, F., C.SS.R. *Le Système moral de S. Alphonse de L. Étude historique et philosophique*. S. Etienne, 1929.

DELESALLE, J. *Liberté et valeur*. Louvain, 1950.

DELHAYE, PH. "La conscience morale dans la doctrine de S. Bernard" *Saint Bernard théologien, Analecta S. O. Cist. 9* (1953), fasc. 3–4.

DELLING. "kairós, in Kittels," *TW*, III, 456–465.

DELP, A. "Weltgeschichte und Heilsgeschichte," *StimmZeit*, 138 (1940–41), 245–254.

DEMAL, W. *Pastoral Psychology in Practice*. New York: Kenedy, 1955.

DEMAN, TH. "Probabilisme," *DTC*, XIII, 417–619.

DESSAUER, PH. *Der Anfang und das Ende. Eine theologische und religioese Betrachtung zur Heilsgeschichte*. Leipzig, 1939.

DIRKS, W. "Der geschichtliche Raum," *Frankfurter Hefte*, 5 (1950), 585–589.

DOMS, H. "Gewissen und Gnadenleben," *Anima*, 12 (1957), 101–120.

DRIESCH, H. *Das Ganze und die Summe*. Leipzig, 1931.

———. *Leib und Seele*. 2. Aufl. Leipzig, 1922.

DURST, B., O.S.B. *Dreifaches Priestertum*. 2 Aufl. Abtei Neresheim, 1947.

EBELING, H. "Die Bedeutung des Seelenfuenkleins in der Spekulation Eckharts und in der Scholastik," *Meister Eckharts Mystik* (Stuttgart, 1941).

EBERLE, A. "Die Beichtstuhlskrupulanten. Ein Erklaerungsversuch nach moderner Pathocharakterologie," *ThPrQschr*, 89 (1936), 68–85.

———. *Ist der Dillinger Moralprofessor Chr. Rassler der Begruender des Aequiprobabilismus?* Freiburg, 1951.

———. "Das 'probabile' bei Thyrsus Gonzales als Grundlage seines Moralsystems," *ThQschr*, 127 (1947), 295–331.

EBNER, F. *Das Wort und die geistigen Realitaeten*. Innsbruck, 1921.

———. *Wort und Liebe*. Regensburg, 1935.

———. *Das Wort ist der Weg*. Wien, 1949.

EGENTER, R. *Von der Freiheit der Kinder Gottes*. 2. Auflage. Freiburg, 1947.

———. *Wagnis in Christo. Maria Ward und die Idee der christlichen Selbstaendigkeit*. Regensburg, 1936.

———. "Gemeinschuld oder Strafhaftung," *ThZ*, I (1947), 114–136. Cf. *WW*, 4 (1949), 137ff.

ENDRES, J. "Die Bedeutung des neuzeitlichen Menschenbildes fuer den Gewissensentscheid," *NO*, 8 (1954), 6–21.

ENRIQUE DEL SAGRADO CORAZÓN. "Conocimiento por connaturalidad y experiencia mística," *RevEspir* (1952), 208–221.

ERMECKE, G. "Das christliche Gewissen und christliche Gewissensbildung in Moraltheologie und Moralverkuendigung," *ThQschr,* 131 (1951), 385–413.

FEUERER, G. *Adam und Christus als Gestaltkraefte und ihre Vermachtnis an die Menschheit.* Freiburg i. Br., 1939.

FEULING, D. *Das Leben der Seele.* Salzburg-Leipzig, 1940.

FLECKENSTEIN, H. *Persoenlichkeit und Organminderwertigkeiten.* Freiburg, 1938.

FOULQUIE, P. *La volonté.* Paris, 1949.

FRINS, V. *De actibus humanis.* Freiburg, 1897.

FROESCHELS, E. *Die Angst.* Basel, 1950.

GAITH, J. *La conception de la liberté chez Grégoire de Nysse.* Paris, 1953.

GAUDÉ, L., C.SS.R. *De morali systemate S. Alphonsi.* Roma, 1894.

GILEN, L., S.J. *Das Gewissen bei Jugendlichen.* Goettingen, 1956.

GRABER, R. *Frohbotschaft vom sakramentalen Leben.* Wuerzburg, 1940.

——. *Aus der Kraft des Glaubens.* Cf. Chapter: Das Ethos der Sakramente. Wuerzburg, 1950, 76–93.

GRENTE, G. *The Power of the Sacraments.* New York: Kenedy, 1951.

——. *Les sept sacrements.* Paris, 1952.

GRONER, J. F. "Geistesgeschichtliche Wuerdigung der thomistischen Gewissenslehre," *DivThom (F),* 31 (1953), 129–156, 299–314.

GRUEHN, W. *Das Werterlebnis.* Leipzig, 1924.

——. *Religionspsychologie.* Breslau, 1920.

——. *Die Froemmigkeit der Gegenwart, Grundtatsachen der empirischen Psychologie* Muenster, 1956.

GUARDINI, R. *Unterscheidung des Christlichen.* Mainz, 1935, 56ff., 151ff.

——. *Conscience.* New York: Sheed and Ward, 1932.

——. *Das Gute, Das Gewissen und die Sammlung.* Mainz, 1929.

——. *Welt und Person.* Wuerzburg, 1939.

——. "Die Begegnung. Ein Beitrag zur Struktur des Daseins," *Ho,* 47 (1955), 224–234.

——. *Freedom, Grace and Destiny.* New York: Pantheon, 1960.

GUILLAUME, P. *La formation des habitudes.* Paris, 1947.

GUTBROD, W. *Die paulinische Anthropologie.* Stuttgart-Berlin, 1934.

GUTWENGER, E., S.J. *Wertphilosophie mit besonderer Beruecksichtigung des ethischen Wertes.* Innsbruck, 1952.

HAECKER, TH. *Der Christ und die Geschichte.* Leipzig, 1935.

——. *Was ist der Mensch?* Leipzig, 1933.

HÄRING, B. *Das Heilige und das Gute.* Krailling vor Muenchen, 1950, 59ff., 74–93, 256–261.

——. "Freiheit oder Gehorsam?" *GeistLeben,* 21 (1948), 108–121.

——. "Skrupulositaet, Gewissen und Verantwortung," *Anima,* 11 (1956), 40–50. (The entire paper deals with scrupulosity.)

HESSEN, J. *Wertphilosophie.* Paderborn, 1937.

HILDEBRAND, D. VON. *Liturgy and Personality.* New York: Longmans, 1943.

——. "Sittlichkeit und ethische Werterkenntnis," *JPpF,* V (Halle, 1921), 463–602.

——. *JPpF,* III (1916), 125–251; V (1921), 463–602.

——. "Die Idee der sittlichen Handlung," *JPpF,* III (Halle, 1916), 125–251.

HIRSCHMANN, J. B., S.J. "Die Freiheit in der Kirche," *StimmZeit,* 161 (1957/58), 81–92.

HIRSCHMANN, H., S.J. *Gewissen und Gewissensbildung. Ein Werkbuch fuer religioese Gemeinschaftsarbeit.* Koeln, 1940.

HOFFMANN, H. *Die Schichttheorie.* Stuttgart, 1935.

HOFMAN, R. "Moraltheologie und christliches Gessingungsethos," *MThZ*, Heft 1 (1950), 53–63.

HOFMANN, R. *Die Gewissenslehre des Walter von Bruegge und die Entwicklung der Gewissenslehre in der Hochscholastik.* Beitraege zur Philosophie und Theologie des Mittelalters (Baeumker-Grabmann) XXXVI, Heft 5–6 (Muenster, 1941).

HOLLENBACH, J. M. *Sein und Gewissen. Ueber den Ursprung der Gewissensregung. Eine Begegnung zwischen Martin Heidegger und thomistischer Philosophie.* Baden-Baden, 1954.

———. "Gewissensbildung des Kindes," *StimmZeit*, 155 (1954/55), 118–127.

———. "Schuld und Neurose," *StimmZeit*, 161 (1957/58), 112–127.

HOMMES, J. *Die innere Stimme. Scham und Gewissen.* Freiburg, 1948.

HORNSTEIN, F. X. v. "Psychische Stoerungen und Verantwortlichkeit," *Anima*, 10 (1955), 2–14.

HUERLIMANN, K. "Person und Wert. Eine Untersuchung ueber den Sinn von M. Schelers Doppeldevise: 'materiale Wertethik' und 'ethischer Personalismus,' *DivThom* (*F*), 30 (1952), 273–298.

JAKOB, GUENTER. *Der Gewissensbegriff in der Theologie Luthers.* Tuebingen, 1929.

JANKÉLÉVITSCH, V. *La mauvaise conscience.* Paris: Presses Universitaires, 1951.

JANSEN, J. L., C.SS.R. *Geschichte und Kritik im Dienste der "Minus probabilis."* Paderborn, 1906.

JANSSEN, P. "Das Beziehungsgefuege der menschlichen Handlung und das Problem der Freiheit," *PhJahrb*, 62 (1951), 446–472.

JASPERS, K. *Psychologie der Weltanschauungen.* Berlin, 1919.

*———. *Origin and Goal of History.* New Haven: Yale University Press, 1953.

———. *Vom Ursprung und Ziel der Geschichte.* Muenchen, 1950.

JENTGENS, G. *Die Gewohnheitshandlung.* Essen, 1940.

JEROME, J. *Le scrupule.* Paris, 1950.

KLENK, F., S.J. "Geschichte als Anruf und Antwort der Freiheit, Gedanken zu Toynbee 'Studien zur Weltgeschichte,' " *StimmZeit*, 145 (1950), 376–384.

———. "Antikes und christliches Geschichtdenken," *StimmZeit*, 153 (1952/53), 274–287.

KLUG, I. *Die Tiefen der Seele.* 11. Auflage. Paderborn, 1949.

KRETSCHMER, E. *Koerperbau und Charakter.* 20. Aufl. Berlin, 1951.

KURZ, E. *Individuum und Gemeinschaft beim hl. Thomas.* Muenchen, 1932.

LABURU, J. A., S.J. *Los sentimientos. Su influjo en la conducta del hombre.* Montevideo, 1946.

LACROIX, J. *Les sentiments et la vie morale.* Paris, 1952.

LAPORTE, J. *La conscience de la liberté.* Paris, 1947.

LAROS, M. "Autoritaet und Gewissen," *Ho*, 36 (1938), 265–280.

LE BACHELET, X., S.J. *La question liguorienne. Probabilisme et équiprobabilisme.* Paris, 1899.

LECLERCQ, G. *La conscience du Chrétien. Essai de théologie morale.* Paris, 1947.

LEHMKUHL, A., S.J. *Probabilismus vindicatus.* Freiburg, 1906.

LEO XIII, *Libertas.* Encyclical Letter, June 20, 1888. *ASS*, 20: 593–613, 1888. English translation in Wynne, *The Great Encyclical Letters of Pope Leo XIII.* New York: Benziger, 1903; also in Husslein, J. *Social Wellsprings.* Vol. I. Milwaukee: Bruce, 1940.

LERSCH, PH. "Die wissenschaftliche Bestimmung des Charakters durch die moderne Psychologie," *Univ*, 29 (1954), 29–38.

———. *Der Aufbau der Person.* Muenchen, 1951.

LHERMITE, PR. *L'Image de notre corps.* Paris, 1939.

LIENER, J. "Bekaempfung oder Laeuterung der Leidenschaften," *Seelsorger*, 20 (1949/50), 162–167.

LIERZ, R. *Harmonien und Disharmonien des menschlichen Trieb- und Geistesleben.* Muenchen, 1925.

LINDWORSKY, J., S.J. *Psychology of Asceticism.* London: H. Edwards, 1936.

———. *Experimental Psychology.* New York: Macmillan, 1931.

LINHARDT, R. *Die Sozialprinzipien des hl. Thomas von Aquin.* Freiburg, 1932.

LITT, TH. *Individuum und Gemeinschaft.* 3. Aufl. Berlin-Leipzig, 1924.

LOPEZ-IBOR, J. "Zwang, Phobie und Skrupel," *JPP*, 4 (1956), 92–101.

LOPEZ, U., S.J. "Thesis probabilismi ex S. Thoma demonstrata," *PRM*, 35 (1936), 38–50, 119–127 (1937); 17–33, 157–170.

LOTTIN, O., O.S.B. *Psychologie et morale aux XIIe et XIIIe siècles.* Vol. I: *Problèmes de psychologie.* Louvain-Gembloux, 1942.

———. *La théorie du libre arbitre depuis Saint Anselm jusqu'à Saint Thomas d'Aquin.* Louvain, 1929.

———. *Psychologie et morale aux XIIe et XIIIe siècles.* Louvain-Gembloux, 1948, II, 101–417.

———. *Psychologie et Morale aux XIIe et XIIIe siècles.* Tome IV. Gembloux, 1954, 307–486.

———. "La psychologie de l'acte humain chez Jean Damascène et les théologiens du XIIe siècle," *RevThom,* 36 (1931), 631–661.

LOTZ, J., S.J. "Der Mensch das Thema heute," *StimmZeit,* 144 (1949/50), 81ff.

MARCEL, G. *Homo Viator.* Introduction to a metaphysic of hope. Chicago: Regnery, 1951.

MASUR, G. *Rankes Begriff der Weltgeschichte.* Muenchen-Berlin, 1926.

MATTAI, G., S.D.B. *Antonio Rosmini e il probabilismo.* Torino, 1951.

MERCIER, M. *Conscience.* Paris, 1936.

MESS, H. D. "Chance, Free Will and Social Sciences," *Philosophy,* (1943), 231–239.

MESSER, A. *Das Problem der Willensfreiheit.* Goettingen, 1911.

MICHEL, A. "Volontaire," *DTC*, XV, 3300–3309.

MOUROUX, J. *The Meaning of Man.* New York: Sheed and Ward, 1948.

MUCKERMANN, H. *Von den sieben Sakramenten. Grundsaetzliches zu den religioesen Fragen der Gegenwart.* Freiburg, 1930.

MUELLER, M., O F.M. *Die Begegnung im Ewigen. Zur Theologie der christlich-Gemeinschaft.* Freiburg, 1954.

MUENCKER, TH. *Die psychologischen Grundlagen der katholischen Sittenlehre.* 4. Auflage. Duesseldorf, 1953

———. *Der psychische Zwang und seine Beziehungen zu Moral und Pastoral.* Duesseldorf, 1922.

———. *Die psychologischen Grundlagen der katholischen Sittenlehre.* 3. Auflage. Duesseldorf, 1949.

MUENSTER, CL. *Mengen, Masse Kollektiv.* Muenchen, 1952.

MUSZYNSKI, F. *Unsere Leidenschaften.* Paderborn (no date).

NACHMANSSOHN, M. *Wesen und Formen des Gewissens.* Wien, 1937.

*NIEBUHR, R. *Faith and History.* New York: Scribner, 1949.

———. *Essays on the Christian Interpretation of History.* New York, 1937.

———. *Human Destiny.* New York, 1943.

———. *Faith and History.* New York: Scribner, 1949.

NIEDERMEYER, A. *Handbuch der speziellen Pastoralmedizin.* Band V, *Seelenleiden und Seelenheilung.* Wien, 1952 (Excellent bibliography, 267–290).

NOBLE, H. D., O.P. *De l'éducation des passions.* Paris, 1919.

PASCHER, J. *Inwendiges Leben in der Werkgefahr.* 2. Auflage. Freiburg, 1952.

PEINADOR, A. *De judicio conscientiae rectae.* Madrid, 1941.

PFAENDER, A. *Die Seele der Menschen*. Halle, 1933.

―――. "Zur Psychologie der Gesinnungen" *JPpF*, I (1913), 1–80; III (1916), 1–124.

PFAHLER, G. *Der Mensch und seine Vergangenheit*. 3. Auflage. Stuttgart, 1954.

―――. *Der Mensch und sein Lebenswerkzeug*. Stuttgart, 1954.

―――. *Vererbung als Schicksal*. Leipzig, 1932.

―――. *Der Mensch und sein Lebenswerkzeug. Erbcharakterologie*. Stuttgart, 1954.

PICARD, M. "Ist Freiheit ueberhaupt moeglich?" *Neues Abendland*, 9 (1954), 83–92.

PIAGET, J. *Das moralische Urteil beim Kinde*. Zuerich, 1954.

―――. *Moral Judgment of the Child*. Chicago: Free Press, 1948.

PIERCE, C. A. *Conscience in the New Testament. A Study of Syneidesis in the New Testament*. Chicago, 1955.

PIUS XII. CF. AAS, 45 (1953), 730–744. Address on International right of punishment.

POELL, W. *Die Suggestion. Wesen und Grundformen*. Muenchen, 1951.

POSCHMANN, B. *Die katholische Froemmigkeit*. Wuerzburg, 1949, 196ff.: Sakramentale Froemmigkeit.

PRETI, G. "Libertá e responsibilitá," *Studi Filosofici*, 9 (1949), n. 2.

PRIBILLA, M., S.J. "Oradour," *StimmZeit*, 152 (1953), 60–65.

PROT, M., CRISTOFF, D., et alii. *La liberté*. Actes du IVe Congrès de philosophie Neuchâtel, 13–16 Sept., 1949.

PRZYWARA, E. *Humanitas. Der Mensch gestern und morgen*. Nuernberg, 1952.

RAHNER, K., S.J. "Prinzipien und Imperative. Einige Unterscheidungen zur Situation der Katholiken in der Gegenwart," *WW*, 12 (1957), 325–339.

REIWALD, P. *Vom Geist der Massen, Handbuch der Massenpsychologie*. Zuerich, 1945.

REST, W. *Heimkehr zum Menschen: Studien ueber Grund und Wesen von Mensch und Mitmensch*. Warendorf in W., 1946.

REVERS, W. J. *Persoenlichkeit und Vermassung. Eine psychologische und kulturanthropologische Studie*. Wuerzburg, 1947.

RICHARD, T., O.P. *La conscience morale et l'expérience morale*. Paris, 1937.

―――. *Étude de théologie morale (De la probabilité à la certitude morale)*. Paris, 1933.

RICOEUR, P. *Philosophie de la volonté*. Paris, 1950.

RIDEAU, E. *Consécration. Le christianisme et l'activité humaine*. Paris, 1945.

RIMAUD, J. "Les psychologues contre la morale," *Études*, 263 (1949), 3–12.

RODRIGO, L., S.J. *Tractus de conscientia morali. Theoria generalis de conscientia*. Santander, 1954. Tomus III: *Praelectiones theologico-morales*.

―――. "De historicis exordiis et vicibus probabilismi moralis relectio critica," *MiscCom*, 19 (1953), 53–120.

―――. *Tractatus de conscientia morali: De conscientia morali reflexa*. Santander, 1956. Tomus IV: *Praelectiones theol.-morales*.

ROTHACKER, E. *Schichten der Persoenlichkeit*. Leipzig, 1938.

ROUSSELOT, P., S.J. *Quaestiones de conscientia*. Paris, 1937.

SAWICKI, FR. *Individualitaet und Persoenlichkeit*, Paderborn, 1913.

―――. *Das Ideal der Persoenlichkeit*. 3. Aufl. Paderborn, 1925.

SCHAUF, W. *Der Begriff "Fleisch" beim Apostel Paulus*. Muenster, 1924.

SCHELER, M. *Der Formalismus in der Ethik*, 120ff.

―――. *Der Mensch im Kosmos*. Darmstadt, 1930.

―――. *Der Formalismus in der Ethik und die materiale Wertethik*. 3. Aufl. Halle, 1927.

―――. *Schriften aus dem Nachlass*. Band I: *Zur Ethik und Erkenntnislehre*. Berlin, 1933.

SCHIERSE, F. J., S.J. "Der Herr is nahe," *StimmZeit*, 153 (1953/54), 161–170.

SCHILLING, O. "Ueber Kollektivschuld," *ThQschr*, 127 (1947), 209–215.

SCHLATTER, A. "Herz und Gehirn im ersten Jahrhundert," *Studien zur systematischen Theologie* (Festschrift f. Th. Haering), 1918, 86ff.

SCHMAUS, M. "Das Eschatologische im Christentum," *Aus der Theologie der Zeit* (published by G. Soehngen, 1948), I, 56–84.

SCHMIDT, H. *Freiheit des menschlichen Willens und seine Motivation durch das Erkennen.* Muenster, 1927.

SCHMIEDER, K. "Die Synderesis und die ethischen Werte," *PhJahrb,* 47 (1938), 145–153, 297–307.

SCHMITT, A., S.J. *Zur Geschichte des Probabilismus.* Innsbruck, 1904.

SCHNEIDER, K. *Die psychopathischen Persoenlichkeiten.* 2. Auflage. Leipzig, 1929.

SCHNEIDER, TH. "Der paulinische Begriff des Gewissens (Syneidesis)," *BoZ,* 6 (1929), 193–211; 7 (1930), 97–112.

SCHOELLGEN, W. *Schuld und Verantwortung.* Duesseldorf, 1947.

———. "Vom Kollektiverhaengnis zur kollektiven Schuld," *Aktuelle Moralprobleme* (Duesseldorf, 1955), 252–256.

———. *The Basic Problem of Education in Morals.* Dusseldorf, Patmos, 1956.

———. "Das Gewissen als Bundesgenosse des Seelsorgers," *LebS,* 9 (1958), 45–49. Theme of the entire paper is the formation of conscience.

———. "Der gute Wille und der rechte Weg," *Ho,* 48 (1956), 100–111.

———. "Die Leib-Seele-Ganzheit Mensch in heutiger Psychologie." *Ibid.,* 160–173.

SCHOELLGEN, W., AND DOBBELSTEIN, H. *Grundfragen der Psychiatrie fuer Aerzte, Erzieher und Seelsorger.* Freiburg, 1956.

SCHUELER, A. *Verantwortung.* Kraillung vor Muenchen, 1948.

SCHUETZ, A. *Gott in der Geschichte.* Salzburg-Leipzig, 1936.

SCHULTE, CH., O.F.M.Cap. *Nervous Mental Diseases; Their Pastoral Treatment.* London: Caldwell, 1939.

SCHUSTER, G. "Kollektiveschuld," *StimmZeit,* 139 (1946/47), 101–117.

SEELHAMMER, N. "Gewissen und Verantwortlichkeit," *TrThZ,* 56 (1947), 200–211, 288–301.

———. "Ueber die Erziehung zur Gewissenhaftigkeit," *TrThZ,* 67 (1958), 28–41.

———. "Zur Frage der Kollektivschuld," *TrThZ,* 59 (1949), 38ff.

SEESEMANN, H. *Der Begriff 'koinonia' im Neuen Testament.* Giessen, 1933.

SEMERIA, G. *La conscienza.* Firenze, 1937.

SIEBECK, R. "Wissen und Glauben in der Medizin," *Univ,* 5 (1950) 37–45.

SIEWERTH, G. "Von der Bildung des Gewissens" (from a noteworthy lecture), *Herderkorrespondenz,* 5 (1951), 187–191.

———. "Grundsaetzliches zur Frage nach der Bildung des Gewissens," *LebS,* 9 (1958), 55–60.

———. *Thomas von Aquin. Die menschliche Freiheit.* Duesseldorf, 1954.

SIMAR, TH. H. *Gewissen und Gewissensfreiheit.* 2. Auflage. Freiburg, 1902.

SIMON, P. "Gibt es eine Kollektivschuld?" *Ho,* 34 (1937), 295–305.

SIMON, Y. *Traité du libre arbitre.* Liège, 1951.

SIRKS, M. J. *Verantwoordelijkheid op grond van erfelijke aanleg.* Groningen, 1951.

SNOECK, A. "La pastorale du scrupule," *NRTh,* 79 (1957), 371–387.

———. *De Psychologie van het schuldbewustzijn.* Utrecht, 1948. Cf. *Schol,* 25 (1950), 260f.

SOIRON, TH. *Der sakramentale Mensch.* Freiburg, 1949.

SOUKUP, L. *Grundzuege einer Ethik der Persoenlichkeit.* Graz, 1951.

SPICQ, C. "La conscience dans le Nouveau Testament," *Rb,* 47 (1938), 50–80.

SPRANGER, E. *Types of Men; the Psychology and Ethics of Personality.* New York: Hafner, 1928.

———. *Zur Psychologie des Jugendalters.* 23. Auflage. Heidelberg, 1953.

———. *Lebensformen, Geisteswissenschaftliche Psychologie und Ethik der Persoenlichkeit.* 7. Auflage. Halle, 1930.

———. "Geist und Seele," *Blaetter fuer Deutsche Philosophie,* 10 (1937), 358–383.

STAEHLIN, W. *Vom Sinn des Leibes.* Stuttgart, 1930.

STEIN, E. "Beitraege zur philosophischen Begruendung der Psychologie und der Geisteswissenschaften, 2. Teil: Individuum und Gemeinschaft," *JPpF,* V (1922), 116–283.

STEINBERG, W. *Der Einzelne und die Gemeinschaft. Eine Einfuehrung in die Sozialpsychologie und die Gemeinschaftsethik.* Muenchen, 1951.

STEINBUECHEL, TH. *Philosophische Grundlegung.* 4. Auflage.

———. *Umbruch des Denkens.* Regensburg, 1936.

———. *Religion und Moral im Lichte christlicher Existenz.* Frankfurt, 1951, particularly pp. 153–230.

———. "Vom Sinn der christlichen Freiheit," *WissWeish,* 6 (1942), 73–91.

———. *Koerperkultur im Lichte des christlichen Gottes- und Weltgedankens.* Duesseldorf, 1929.

STEINMANN, A. *Die Bergpredigt.* Paderborn, 1926.

STELZENBERGER, J. "Ueber Syneidesis bei Klemens von Alexandrien," *MthZ,* 4 (1953), 27–33.

STOCKER, A. "Psychologie structurale de la personne et responsabilité," *Psyché,* 59 (1951), 595–604.

STOKER, G. H. *Das Gewissen. Erscheinungsformen und Theorien.* Bonn, 1925.

TER HAAR, F., C.SS.R. *De systemate morali antiquorum probabilistarum.* Paderborn, 1894.

———. "De triplici statu mentis post indagatam veritatem juxta doctrinam S. Thomae," *Ang* (1941), 3–35.

TERNUS, J., S.J. *Zur Vorgeschichte der Moralsysteme von Vitoria bis Medina.* Paderborn, 1930.

———. "Die Wiederentdeckung des Leibes in der philosophischen Anthropologie der Gegenwart," *Bildung und Erziehung* (1936), 90–101.

THADDEN-VAHNFROW, R.v. *Gott und die Geschichte.* Berlin, 1929.

THIEME, K. "Die toedliche Gefaehrdung des Menschen," *Ho,* 46 (1954), 209–221.

THILS, G., *Théologie des Réalités Terrestres.* 2 Vols. Bruges, Désclee, 1946–49.

———. *Tendances actuelles en théologie morale.* Gembloux, 1940. Pp. 3–20: Morale sacramentelle.

TIBERGHIEN, P. "Moral der Akte und Moral der Tendenzen," *Dokumente,* 10 (1954), 195–204.

*TILLICH, P. *The Protestant Era.* Chicago: University of Chicago, 1948. (Note: Kairos.)

TILLMANN, F. *Persoenlichkeit und Gemeinschaft in der Predigt Jesu.* Duesseldorf, 1919.

———. "Geschichte des Begriffs Gewissen," *Festschrift fuer S. Merkle* (Duesseldorf, 1922), 336–346.

TISCHLEDER, P. "Der Mensch in der Auffassung des hl. Thomas," *Das Bild vom Menschen, Festschrift fuer F. Tillmann* (Duesseldorf, 1934), 42–57.

TOENNIES, F. *Gemeinschaft und Gesellschaft.* 5. Aufl. 1922.

TURN, S., S.J. "Willensfreiheit," *StimmZeit,* 146 (1950), 430–436.

URDANOZ, T., O.P. "La conciencia moral en Santo Tomás y los sistemas morales," *CiTh* (1952), 529–576.

UTZ, F., O.P. "Der Personalismus. Wuerdigung und Kritik." *NO,* 8 (1954), 270–281.

VERPAALEN, A. P. *Der Begriff des Gemeinwohls bei Thomas von Aquin. Ein Beitrag zum Problem des Personalismus.* Heidelberg, 1954.

Vindiciae Alphonsianae. Cura theologorum e C.SS.R. (1873), 2. Aufl. Doornik, 1874.

WALDMANN, M. "Synteresis oder Syneidesis," *ThQschr*, 118 (1938) 332–371.

WALLIS, R. *Passions et maladies*. Paris, 1950.

WALTER, FR. *Der Leib und sein Recht im Christentum*. Donauwoerth, 1910.

WALTER, E. *Sakrament und christliches Leben*. 2. Aufl. Freiburg, 1951.

WALTHER, GERDA. "Zur Ontologie der sozialen Gemeinschaften," *JPpF*, VI (1923), 1–158.

WARNACH, V. "Sein und Freiheit. Blondels Entwurf einer normativen Ethik," *ZKathTh*, 63 (1939), 273–310, 393–427.

WELTSCH, FR. *Gnade und Freiheit. Zum Problem des schoepferischen Willens in Religion und Ethik*. Berlin, 1920.

WELTY, E. *Gemeinschaft und Einzelmensch*. 2. Aufl. Salzburg, 1935.

———. "Frei aber nicht ungebunden," *NO*, 1 (1947), 429–455.

———. "Soziale Bindungen der menschlichen Freiheit," *NO*, 1 (1947), 518–539.

WENZL, A. *Philosophie der Freiheit*. Muenchen, 1947.

WIKENHAUSER, A. *Kirche als der mystische Leib Christi nach dem Apostel Paulus*. Muenster, 1937.

WILLWOL, A. *Seele und Geist, Mensch, Welt, Gott*. Freiburg i. Br., 1938.

WILMS, H., O.P. "Das Seelenfuenklein in der deutschen Mystik," *ZAM*, 12 (1937), 157–166.

WILPERT, P. *Erziehung zur Freiheit*. Regensburg, 1948.

———. *Der Einzelne und die Gemeinschaft*. Donauwoerth, 1949.

WUERTH, C. E. *Die psychologischen Grundlagen der Gewissensbildung nach der Lehre des hl. Thomas von Aquin*. Olten, 1929.

ZIERMANN, B., C.SS.R. *Nervoese Seelenleiden und ihre seelsorgliche Behandlung bei Alfons von Liguori*. Heidelberg, 1947.

———. "Die Bedeutung der Gefuehle fuer das sittliche Leben," *NO*, 4 (1950), 318–324.

———. *Ringen um Sicherheit im sittlichen Denken*. Koeln, 1940.

Additional Works in English

ARNOLD, M. AND GASSON, J., S.J. *The Human Person*. An approach to an integral theory of personality. New York: Ronald, 1954.

BIER, W., S.J. "Psychological Aspects of Pastoral Work," *Proceedings of the Archdiocesan Institute of Ecclesiastical Studies*. St. Joseph's Seminary, Dunwoodie, New York, 1957. Cf. pp. 45–68.

BRUNO DE JESUS-MARIE, O.C.D. (ed.). *Conflict and Light*. Studies in psychological disturbance and readjustment. New York: Sheed and Ward, 1952. Cf. pp. 83–106.

CAMMACK, J., S.J. *Moral Problems of Mental Defect*. New York: Benzinger, 1939.

CAVANAGH, J., M.D., AND McGOLDRICK, J., S.J. *Fundamental Psychiatry*. Milwaukee: Bruce, 1953.

DUHAMEL, J., S.J., AND HAYDEN, J., O.S.B. "Theological and Psychiatric Aspects of Habitual Sin," *Proceedings, 11th Annual Convention of the Catholic Theological Society of America* (1956), pp. 130–163.

FLOOD, DOM P., O.S.B., (ed.). *New Problems in Medical Ethics*. Vol 3. Westminster, Md.; Newman, 1956. Cf. Psychoanalysis and Moral Conscience, pp. 79–142.

FORD, J., S.J. *Depth Psychology, Morality and Alcoholism*. Weston, Mass: Weston College, 1951.

HILDEBRAND, D. VON. *True Morality and its Counterfeits*. New York: McKay, 1955.

———. *Christian Ethics*. New York: McKay, 1953.

KELLY, G., S.J., AND FORD, J., S.J. *Contemporary Moral Theology*. Vol. 1: *Questions in Fundamental Moral Theology*. Westminster, Md.: Newman, 1958. Cf. Chaps. 10–13, pp. 174–312.

Man and His Happiness (Theology Library, Vol. 3). Chicago: Fides, 1956. Cf. pp. 25–175.

Moore, T. V. *The Driving Forces of Human Nature and Their Adjustment.* New York: Grune and Stratton, 1948.

——. *The Nature and Treatment of Mental Disorders.* New York: Grune and Stratton, 1943.

Nuttin, J. *Psychoanalysis and Personality.* New York: Sheed and Ward, 1953.

O'Brien, V. *Emotions and Morals.* New York: Grune and Stratton, 1950.

Ringel, E., and Van Lun, W. *The Priest and the Unconscious.* Cork (Ireland): Mercier, 1954.

Snoeck, A., S.J. *Mental Hygiene and Christian Principles.* Cork (Ireland): Mercier, 1954.

Stern, K. *The Third Revolution.* New York: Harcourt, 1954.

Terruwe, A. *Psychopathic Personality and Neurosis.* New York: Kenedy, 1958.

Vanderveldt, J., O.F.M., and Odenwald, R., M.D. *Psychiatry and Catholicism.* New York: McGraw-Hill, 1957 (2d ed.).

Periodical Literature in English

Following bibliography refers primarily to periodical literature written in English. Because of its relation to Conscience which is treated in this chapter we include here the periodical literature on Situation Ethics as well.

Allers, R., "Abnormality: A Chapter in Moral Psychology. Moral Responsibility of the Neurotic," *HPR,* 42 (1942), 727–733.

——. "Irresistible Impulses: A Question of Moral Psychology," *AER,* 100 (March, 1939), 208–219.

Bonnar, A., O.F.M. "Criminal Responsibility," *CMQ,* 9 (July, 1956), 67–73.

Carr, A. M. "The Morality of Situation Ethics," *Proceedings, Cath. Theol. Society of America* (1957), 75–102.

Cavanagh, J. R. "Criminal Responsibility and Free Will," *BGCP* 3 (Dec., 1955), 24–33.

Crowe, M. B. "The Term Synderesis and the Scholastics," *ITQ,* 23 (April, July, 1956), 151–64, 228–45.

Ford, J. C., S.J. "Criminal Responsibility in Canon Law and Catholic Thought," *BGCP,* 3 (Dec., 1955), 3–22.

Fuchs, J., S.J. "Situation Ethics and Theology," *ThD,* 2 (Winter, 1954), 25–30.

Gleason, R. W. "Situation Morality," *Thought,* 32 (Winter, 1957), 532–58.

Huerth, F., S.J. "Hodierna conscientiae problemata metaphysica, psychologica, theologica," *PRM,* 42 (Dec., 1953), 238–45.

——. *Conscientia Christiana atque de* "Morali Nova" (Booklet). Roma: Pont. Univ. Greg., 1955 (2 ed.).

——. "Adnotationes ad Instructionem S. Officii 'de Ethica Situationis'" *PRM,* 45 (June, 1956), 140–204.

Newman, J. "Ethics of Existentialism," *IER,* 77 (May–June, 1952), 321–32, 421–31.

O'Connell, D. A., O.P. "Christian Liberty" (part 2), *Thom,* 15 (July, 1952), 404–93.

Pegis, A. "Necessity and Liberty," *NewSchol,* 15 (Jan., 1941), 18–45.

Phelan, G. B. "Person and Liberty," *NewSchol,* 15 (Jan., 1941), 46–62.

Pius XII, "Moral Law and the New Morality." Allocution, April 18, 1952, *AAS,* 44 (May 20, 1952), 413–19. Engl. Trans., *IER,* 78 (Aug., 1952), 137–42.

Poppi, A. "Background of Situation Ethics," *PhT,* 1 (Winter, 1957), 266–77.

Smith, G., S.J. "Intelligence and Liberty," *NewSchol,* 15 (Jan., 1941), 1–17.

——. "Nature and Uses of Liberty," *NewSchol,* 26 (July, 1952), 305–26.

Stabb, G., O.F.M.Cap. "Some Moral Aspects of Drug Addiction," *AER,* 130 (April, 1954), 238–49.

TURNER, V. "Situation in Moral Philosophy," *DubRev*, 224 (Fall, 1950), 31–48.

WALZ, H. "Man's Freedom in Existentialism and Christianity," *CrossC*, 2 (Fall, 1951), 56–67.

WOCK, D. J., O.S.B. "Moral Consciousness and Conscience," *ABR*, 5 (Winter, 1954), 311–25.

YZERMANS, V. "Pope Pius XII and Theological Novelty," *HPR*, 56 (Feb., 1956), 381–387.

Part Three:

THE MORAL DUTY OF THE DISCIPLE OF CHRIST

O<small>UR</small> second part dealt with man in his vocation as disciple of Christ. We undertook the study of his nature, his essential characteristics, and particularly his moral potentialities (his freedom, his capacity for knowledge of the good, his conscience) and their actuation (inner disposition and action). It remains for us to explain his moral duty. This is determined by his actual existing nature and being to which in the present order the endowments of grace also belong—and by everything with which his activity can be concerned! This is the object or goal of his inner attitudes and his actions: God, neighbor, community, self, the world.

The moral norms which are the design or rule governing our moral relation with things spring from this bond of subject or agent with the object. The basic factor determining the moral import of a "must" demanded of us, which is to say the moral determinant of any act, is the object of the act—not, of course, the object as such without any qualification. It is the object as possessed of value and placed in a total order of values, in concrete relation with its surrounding world and, above all, with the man himself (in his particular situation) who acts. The ultimate determinant by which we judge the morality of an act, however, is the object plus the particular situation and the third factor, namely, the inner intervention of the agent through his act of will. This is the intention or motive by which man determines for himself the value of the object in relation to his own mind and action. It follows, therefore, that object, situation (external circumstances and interior susceptibilities of the agent) and the motive constitute the total moral object of the moral act.

We first take up the norms of morality together with the particular standards under their legal aspect of norm and law. Next we study the object of moral decision in itself and also concretely in the situation. Then follows the discussion of the moral motive. Finally, after a coordination of the foregoing, there is a discussion on indifferent acts and the presentation of a solution for the problem of the possibility of the indifferent act.

CHAPTER FIVE

NORM AND LAW

I. THE NORM OF MORALITY

1. *Norm and Value*

THE formulation of a norm is either negative (Forbidden: "thou shalt not lie!") or positive (Commanded: "Always be truthful!"). In both formulations the norm refers to the value, which is itself much richer than the norm set forth in words (above all in the negative formulation) is ever able to express. And yet the richest fulfillment of values still falls under the norm, e.g., in the saint who lives in the full light of truth and would rather die than be remiss to the slightest degree in uprightness. Value dictates norm. It is the actually significant object of the moral act. Mirrored in the objective value itself and its relation to man attracted by value, is the rule set up for man as the unalterable standard (norm) of his behavior.

A norm of morals is not arbitrary restraint interfering with liberty, but the summons and invitation to the exercise of liberty arising from the value in the object, an invitation to man to preserve and nurture value in freedom. A norm which is not founded in a value and which does not present a duty through relation to value has no moral force binding the will. Likewise commands or precepts which do not command anything intrinsically good or forbid anything intrinsically bad (purely positive precepts) must still be essentially concerned with some value. If there is no value appeal to the will, no value to preserve or cultivate, there is no true precept or command. Example: when God forbids our first parents to eat of the tree of knowledge and demands of Abraham the sacrifice of his son, the value that must be preserved is the acknowledgment of the divine sovereignty and the manifestation of created dependence. Divine dominion and created dependence are evident to those who must obey, even though the immediate significance and profound endowment of value in what is commanded is not apparent.

2. *Philosophical and Theological Approach to the Norm*

Philosophical inquiry can have as its point of departure the "must" (content or object of moral norm). Probing deeper, it can then pose the question regarding the ultimate basis of the "must" (according to norm as duty or law). Yet no philosophy could exclude (at least not practically) the scholastic axiom: "the ought rests on being"; "action follows being" (*agere sequitur esse*). In the order of knowledge the principle reads: "Knowledge of the ought corresponds to knowledge of being." Thus every philosophy arrives at the universal axiom (moral norm): man must or should act according to his being (nature). In all non-rational being the activity is determined by being, that is, by the proper nature of a thing and its relations to the world about it. It is a necessitating norm or rule. It is true also that being is an inviolably reasonable and valid (perceptible by reason) norm for man, but it is a norm directed to his freedom. Man is not bound to the norm of his own being by a necessity such as that which determines irrational creatures. Man can recognize it or "ignore" it; he can freely comply with the norm he recognizes or deliberately overstep it.

As far as the content of the moral norm is concerned, man can learn this from his own nature and its relation to the nature of the things around him. Hence this norm is the actual law of his own being and, in a manner of speaking, it is autonomous. Man is a "law unto himself" in a true sense of the word. However, if such is the case, one may object immediately: What is to prevent man from placing his own arbitrary preference—and this is also a "possibility" of his own nature—above the essential norm of his being? For the moment we answer the objection by pointing out that man descends beneath the true capacity of his own nature, that he is untrue to his nature by arbitrary violation of the essential norms of his being.

But what we have said thus far merely demonstrates the serviceableness and utility of the norm of morality. It becomes binding as a law only in so far as it derives from a legislator who has the power to bind the will of man absolutely. If we inquire into the ultimate basis of obligation in the norm of morals, all self-rule or autonomy of man ceases, that is, "it merges into the divine law" (in theonomy). Likewise the content of the norm of morality reveals its full depth and breadth only in the light of man's relation to God. Only in the full realization of what man's nature really is in relation to God and the consequent essential capacity of his freedom in God's sight, can man understand the true grandeur of the moral norm.

The theological approach in the determination of the norm of morals is basically different from the philosophical. Philosophy recognizes as the final subjective norm only reason (conscience guided by reason), whose own object (also in determining the norm of morality) is simply created being, even in its orientation toward God. Theology has as the ultimate subjective norm of morals not mere reason, but the virtue of faith, reason enlightened by faith. But the first object of faith is not man and the created order, but God. So the highest objective rule of morality is the will of God alone. Before the believer knows the content of his obligation in particular instances, he already knows through his faith that the supreme norm of obligation for him is the will of God.

God made His will known to us through Christ, who established the Catholic Church as custodian and interpreter of His revelation. Hence the immediate or proximate norm of morality for us is the will of God revealed in Christ, as it is presented by the Catholic Church (objective norm), and as it is understood by human reason submissive to supernatural revelation and inwardly enlightened by the Holy Spirit (subjective norm).

The acceptance of the Church's doctrine by faith does not prevent us from inquiry, as theologians, into the norms which the Church follows in her teaching. And similarly we may inquire reverently about the norms according to which God lays down the moral precepts for men. But one thing we must shun at all costs: ever in the remotest way to conceive of a norm outside God. We also reject every species of arbitrariness in God Himself. For this reason we radically repudiate Nominalism (juridical positivism in moral theology) with its false axiom, "God does not command anything because it is good, but it is good because God commands it."[1] On the contrary it is surely correct from our point of view to maintain that not only after we recognize something as good in accordance with its intrinsic nature is it good for us, but the fact that God commands it is a surer guaranty of its goodness than all the arguments of our reason commending it. Such is the import of our faith that we may confidently accept what God commands in the conviction that it is intrinsically and entirely good, and not merely arbitrarily decreed as good by God.

God Himself is the essential basis of all good. The commandments are imposed on us as decrees of the divine will, but in no wise as arbitrary dictates: they are decrees of wisdom, flowing from His all-holy essence, from the "eternal law" founded in His essence. "To say that justice is exclusively determination of will, is tantamount to holding that the divine will does not proceed from the order of wisdom. And this is blasphemy."[2] Therefore, we may not look upon the commandments and laws of God as a vast heterogeneous mass of individual precepts. They are a total in God's all-holy nature and will, in His wisdom, in the Holy Spirit. Therefore it is not an offense against the sovereignty of the divine will, but a mark of faith in God's wisdom to study the commandments of God with reliance on divine grace and the desire to understand them, and to view them all from one central point of vantage and in one comprehensive "norm."

However, we must carefully guard against the erroneous notion that we can deduce from one concept (such as the imitation of Christ) all particular obligations. If in the mere study of philosophy it is the task of unaided reason to remain open and receptive to the entire realm of reality, instead of seeking to deduce the whole of truth from one concept, then surely faith and the science of faith must harken submissively to the whole fulness of the divine revelation.

Only if it is based on faith is the task of understanding possible (*fides quaerens intellectum*). In the light of faith human reason has such insight that it may seek a comprehensive and systematic grasp of all individual revealed truths or precepts in the divine revelation.

3. *Philosophical Approaches in Formulation of Moral Norms*

The current philosophy of value makes a valiant attempt to formulate a comprehensive norm of morality. However, the perennial philosophy recognizes only that philosophy of value which correlates values with being, and the order of value with the order of being. In the philosophy of being the supreme objective norm may be expressed in the following proposition: the order of action must correspond to the order of being. In the language of the philosophy of value this may be formulated in the following terms: that action is good which holds fast to the order of values. Hence the norm of morality is the norm of the proper preference. In every instance one must prefer the higher to the lower value. Evil is the egotistic setting up of a "false law of preference" in inner attitude and external conduct.

Right preference must nevertheless take into consideration, not only the grandeur of value, but also its urgency. Now since in the world order and the order of reality the lower values likewise have their place, allowance must be made for them also in action. However, even though in actual life, situations may arise in which cultivation and realization of the lower value becomes more urgent and pressing than cultivation of the loftier values, still one must be ever ready to sacrifice the baser value rather than jeopardize the higher.

EXAMPLE: Prayer is loftier in the scale of values than culture and earning a livelihood, and yet the latter is often more pressing. But in the mind's appraisal of values prayer must always rank higher, so that one is prepared to forego the opportunity for culture or gain if the price be a lower esteem for prayer (disavowal of the duty to pray, loss of the will to pray). The lesser values (the useful, pleasant, cultural) are to be cultivated in the measure in which they leave room for and furnish a basis for moral values. (Therefore the higher scientific or cultural attainments can never justify an educational system which perverts youth morally and religiously.)

The obligation to preserve the order of things in the world is at once apparent from the very nature of total reality as order. Whenever a genuine value is violated, all the others in the entire order in some measure protest. But the full and integral "character of law" in the order of things is revealed only upon the discernment of the ultimate value. The very summit of values rising above and far transcending the entire order is the living Lord of values, the holy and supreme personal value which is God.

There is another significant philosophical approach. This attempt to establish a comprehensive norm of values does not, as does the value ethic just discussed, have its point of departure in the object of the moral act (object of value), but in the acting subject itself, man. It is expressed in the proposition: act as a man! The supreme standard is a balanced and harmonious activity and development of all the human powers and resources. To make man himself the point of departure is not *a priori* false. Only if man ignores the moral experience which he has of the order in which he exists and which embraces and obliges him, or if he makes this reality subservient to man as though it were secondary, or if he forms a false notion of man himself, does this procedure place the true norm of morality in jeopardy.

In the theory which places the norm in the right rule of preference, the decisive point is the "table of values." But what is the right "table of values"? Equally fundamental in the theory beginning with man is the question: what is man? Christian and Marxist agree: conduct yourself as a man. Hence both recognize the same moral norm "formally." But they disagree radically in their answer to the question regarding the nature of man. What man is can be recognized only through insight into his position in relation to the totality of reality.

We must recognize man as he really is in his true nature, in his essential relations, and principally in his orientation toward God. Man is not only directed toward God: he is subordinated to God. Once we have discerned and realized all this, then we can recognize the clear import of the norm of morality. What is demanded of us is plain. Since man does not bear within himself his ultimate meaning and import, but can be understood only in relation to God and to his divinely appointed place in the order of creation, it follows that in his actions he may not merely (or even primarily) look to himself. Above all he must look to God and to his place in relation to the rest of creation.

The norm of morality founded on ethics of value is an essential embodiment of submission and service in conformity with existing value. The formulation of the moral norm based on man as acting subject is in great part under the perspective of the ideal of personality (morality as self-development). Still, if we have the correct conception of human nature, this formulation is as much on the level of service conforming with right order as is the ethic of value. However, it is best to attempt a synthesis of the two methods, for only a fruitful meeting of subject and object can beget an adequate understanding of morality at all and particularly of the norm of morality. The norm of morality can be embodied in a proposition such as the following: in spirit and action man must attain to full correctness of being! Man is not under constraint of his own being so that he is naturally fixed or determined to pursue one course of action, but he must make an effort through the intervention of his intellect and his free will to conform rightly to all being which confronts him and to his own nature.

The norm of morality learned from philosophy is not rejected by faith, but rather broadened and deepened. Above all, the content becomes clearer and more certain in its details.

4. *The Norm as Found in Theology*

As we noted in discussing the philosophical approach to the problem of moral norms, so in our theological study the point of stress may be either the object or the subject of moral activity. If we stress the object, the norm may be stated in the following terms: the universal moral task of the Christian is to cultivate all the natural and supernatural values and use them in rendering homage to God. The principal content of the order of preference is evident. First come God and the supernatural, and only then the natural values! To press and prefer the natural over the supernatural is to fail essentially, for "what does it profit a man, if he gain the whole world, but suffer the loss of his own soul?" (Mt 16:26).

If we stress the moral subject in our study of the norm of morality, the rule of morals can be stated thus: the Christian in spirit and action must develop all his natural and supernatural powers for good and by means of the good overcome all the evil potentialities rooted within him! In this light the Christian himself is his own norm of morality as subject of moral capacities, as a body-soul entity, as individual being and member of community, as member of the Mystical Body, as creature dedicated to the divine cult, in fine, therefore, as created and restored for the glory of God through love. The concept of man as formed by Christian anthropology thus contains and reflects the Christian norm of morality rich and fruitful in content.

But if this explanation of the norm of morality based on the concept of man as subject of morality is to be accepted, it is necessary to recognize man's essential orientation toward the world of objective values (toward the kingdom of God) and his place in an order of things in which he himself is only a member. Cultivation and exercise of his lower and higher powers must proceed with balance and harmony, and this is possible only if man is centered, not in himself, but in God whose generous love invites and summons him. In other words, subjective and objective aspect of the norm of morality must complement each other.

Since neither man as such nor created being is the ultimate standard and absolute norm of conduct, it follows that we cannot stop short in our scientific investigation before we reach the absolute standard which is subjected to no other norm, the rule which is not subjected to higher rule (*regula non regulata*). This is God from whom created being derives all its being and all its validity as norm of conduct. God is the normative norm, for He is the ultimate pattern or exemplary cause of all things. All created being is patterned on His being; all bear the divine stamp. Man is made in His image and likeness, and the baptized are His children. The created order is made the norm of freedom through the Godlike capacity of man, formed in the image and likeness of God, to discern the inner meaning of all being and say yes to it. All being as bearing God's image becomes the norm of freedom for the free child of God in so far as it is seen with the eyes of the child of faith, which in all things recognize the revelation of the will of the Father in heaven, and with the child's sense of love, which discerns in every fulfillment of God's will the human response to divine love.

Therefore, the subordinate norm is man in his likeness to God. Ultimate norm (unmeasured norm or unregulated norm) is God as ultimate pattern of being. God makes the norm of His own nature, which is the ultimate pattern of being, the law. This He does by freely and creatively choosing from among the infinite fulness of possibilities in the eternal pattern of His own being a specific order of beings stamped with His likeness, and in this He necessarily sanctions their created nature as the binding norm for their activity.

When we refer to the ultimate pattern of being (*causa exemplaris*) in God, we have in mind the consubstantial image of the Father, the Word. The Word is the infinitely real image of the Father. In this "Word" of God all things are patterned and created. Since the ultimate pattern and image of all is in the Word of the Father, in the final analysis the theological explanation of the norm of morality may not neglect the reference to the second divine person. And this second person, let us note, is not merely the eternal Idea, the Logos or Word, in God Himself on which all being and all creation is ultimately patterned. The Word also became man, and in the infinite condescension of the Incarnation deigns to become the primary source and manifest embodiment of the supernatural norm of morality.

Through the new creation in Him Christ has given us new capacities and therewith also a new norm of action. Christ gave us the most perfect fulfillment and embodiment of the supernatural norm of morality in His own Person. His Person, His example, His teaching are the ultimate pattern and model of supernatural morality. He is our Lawgiver and our Law, Giver of our norm and our Norm itself. Scientific theological reflection on the norm of morality leads us to Christ! But He Himself is the concrete practical standard of our moral life. The way to Christ, manifest model and norm of our moral life, the perfect and unhampered way, is the imitation of Christ in loving faith, the way which constantly discloses newer and more precious treasures in the Life which is our model.

Christ is our norm, not in the sense of a pattern which is to be simply copied, for many of His deeds are quite inimitable, whereas others can be imitated only imperfectly and analogously. Only if we are incorporated in Him as living members of His Mystical Body can we imitate Him and discover in Him the hidden treasures of all that is good. Such imitation implies true discipleship. And the true disciple is in the state of divine friendship through possession of sanctifying grace. He is steeped in the mind and heart of Christ through the infused virtues. Discipleship means docility inspired by the Holy Spirit. It means readiness to obey Christ living continuously in His Church and teaching through her. The Church hands down the words of Christ through the Holy Spirit, who bestows upon us the spirit of docility to the divine truth. He is the Spirit of Christ.

This point is particularly stressed in order to show that the entire fulness of grace and truth is established and revealed in Christ. Above all, in Him and in His Church and through His Holy Spirit we have our supernatural being, for we are "in Christ Jesus." All this is to be borne in mind when we reflect on Christ as the norm of morality. Christ the consubstantial image of the Father and the supreme ideal for all who are called to sonship visibly embodies and manifests for us to see and hear the will of God His Father as model and rule of our life. He is both the truth and the life. He is evidence for the scientific explanation of the norm of moral life and its perfect concrete embodiment. On the exalted level of the divine likeness in man and the imitation of Christ, which are fundamentally only two aspects of one reality, the whole of moral theology and with it the comprehensive norm of morality meet.

5. Universal Norm and Particular Norms

Just as the totality of being embodies and reflects the general or universal norm, so do the lesser particular spheres of being embody and express particular norms for their own domain. The great danger in connection with norms is that they may be divorced from the domain of values which they purpose to manifest and safeguard and degenerate into mere formalities or sterile formulas. EXAMPLE: When one is faced with the obligation expressed in the commandment: "Thou shalt not bear false witness [lie]," one may satisfy himself with the clarification of the nature of a lie, with determining what is not quite a lie, and shape his conduct accordingly. He may pattern his actions on what has been formally established without any direct discernment of the value of truth embodied in the norm. One who is exclusively concerned with the normative formula without being taken up by the value which is its foundation and source will inevitably descend to a moribund legalistic morality. He will be convinced that through the formal fulfillment of the most general norms (which, because of their universality, are usually expressed in negative terms), he has attained the perfection of the moral law.

In reality the values reflected in the norms are always infinitely deeper and richer than the most correct and perfect formulation could suggest. Norms must be formulated in every sphere of value. They derive from the very manner of man's thinking, which is in general concepts and corresponds to his nature. They lead to the domain of value, reveal its outermost limits and boundaries. But one may not be satisfied with simple norms. One must discern the values which the norms embody and express.

The norms may never be violated. One must always conform to them. But values must also be realized. The particular wealth of being, the value, which transcends the general or universal must also be captured. For not merely being as universal, but likewise being in its uniqueness and particularity and its concrete individual worth bears the shape and form of normative value for our action. Our safeguard against an extremely rigid concept of all norms of conduct is vital contact with reality! In the last analysis, it is the vital contact with Christ in imitation of Him! This is truly ultimate!

II. THE LAW

1. *Concept of Law*

The concept of law is broader than that of norm. Law includes norm and connotes the intervention of the competent authority which imposes and promulgates it as binding. Saint Thomas defines law as follows: "Law is nothing else than an ordinance of reason for the common good, promulgated by him who has the care of the community."[3] This definition contains several points deserving of special comment.

1) The expression "ordinance of reason" (*"rationis ordinatio"*) in this definition of Saint Thomas refers to the foundation of law in value. This means the law must be based on the insight of reason into value. It must be reasonable. 2) It is an order or command, not a mere counsel. 3) It must have as its goal the value lying in the good of the community upon which it is imposed. 4) Only those ordinances have the force of law which are imposed by competent or legitimate authority. For Saint Thomas authority means "having the care of the community." 5) The law must be made known or promulgated.

Law is distinguished from precept or individual injunction in so far as it is imposed not solely for one particular instance, for it has a certain universal validity. It affects not merely one individual, but a community of persons. Not every superior, we should add, has the right to pass laws, even though he has the right to impose commands.

2. *The Eternal Law*

According to Saint Thomas the eternal law is "nothing else than the design (*exemplar*) of the divine wisdom, as directing all actions and movements."[4] The eternal law of God is ultimately patterned on the nature of God, on the Word which is the very essence of God. It is put into effect or becomes actual law through the free decision of the divine will to effect or actualize an entirely determined or specific order of being with its activity and, in consequence, also with the obligations binding the free creatures. The promulgation is on God's part an eternal act, even though the passive effect of this promulgation (recognition on the part of the creature) takes place in time.

The eternal law is necessary in so far as the norm of being necessarily entails and determines the norm of action. It is free as to the promulgation, which is as free as the act by which a specific world or order of things is created. No law whatsoever has the force of law except in so far as it is a reflection or expression of the eternal law, or has its sanction, its basis of obligation in it.

On the basis of "promulgation" of eternal law, we make the following distinctions of law: 1) The physical law of nature: this is consequent on the mere existence of things as necessary law of their being (without the intervention of rational acceptance and freedom). The term *law* is taken here in the broader sense, e.g., we speak of the laws of nature. 2) The natural moral law: this is given to man together with his rational nature as law of liberty, not of course in the form of innate moral ideas, but as the rational capacity and as the norm of free acts discernible through insight into the nature of man and the world by reason itself. 3) The positive divine law, promulgated by the direct revelation of the divine message to mankind. Regarding the positive revelation of God, we distinguish: a) The primitive law, which God gave in Paradise and after the fall to our first parents and through them to their descendants. b) The Mosaic law (the law of the Old Testament often called simply the Old Law), which God gave through Moses and the prophets. c) The law of the New Testament or the law of Christ, which God revealed through Christ and as the "law of the Spirit of the life in Christ Jesus" (ROM 8:2) imprinted in the hearts of Christians. 4) The positive human law.

As to the positive revealed law of God, it is concerned with the natural order of creation and the supernatural order of grace. The laws of the natural order are promulgated, not merely by positive revelation of the laws as such, but also through created being itself. And similarly and most particularly the laws of the order of grace are not proclaimed merely through the direct message of divine revelation enunciating the law as such. It is especially through the "grace of the Holy Spirit"[5] and through the message of revealed truths ,which embody the basis (the value) of obligation in the supernatural realities that the divine laws are promulgated. Thus, for example, through the revelation of the truth that Christ is really present in the Eucharist, the command to honor the Eucharist with cult is also sufficiently made known, even without express mention of the command in the sources of revelation.

A positive revelation of the law of God a) is opportune regarding that which belongs to the natural order because of the frailty and insecurity of human reason in fallen man, b) is necessary regarding the order of grace because this order is essentially supernatural and totally transcends the power of unaided reason, c) was actually granted to mankind as a (necessary or free) further determination or more precise specification of that which was not adequately determined or precisely specified in the realities of the order of creation and of grace and which God did not choose to leave to the free choice of mankind.

As to positive human law, it derives from God (from his promulgation) a) in so far as it defines more precisely the laws revealed by God or enforces their observance to the extent that this is deemed necessary for the common good, and b) in so far as human authority (ecclesiastical or civil) is empowered through natural or positive revelation to lay down more specific and precise enactments of that which is found in the order of creation or the order of grace, though less specifically and precisely.

3. Natural Moral Law and Natural Right

a. Distinction between Moral Law and Right

Natural right is a segment or an aspect of the natural moral law. The moral law embraces all that is good (morality in general); natural right (right as such) is concerned with that which is just (justice), the juridical order between man and man, between group and individual, between community and community.

Morality (the good) cannot be produced by force because it is rooted essentially in man's inner disposition. The spirit is not subject to force. But right can be enforced. However, the performance under such constraint is surely imperfect unless it is animated by the spirit of good will. EXAMPLE: Children may be made to support their needy parents, for parents in need have an enforceable right to such material help under certain conditions, but the proper spiritual attitude of children toward parents (filial piety) is not enforceable.

The object of right is the common welfare. But the common welfare includes also a very extensive domain which is concerned with the protection and nurture of individual welfare. And this includes above all the creation of an external moral climate which makes it possible for the individual and the group to attain the moral religious ideal. Right must therefore serve not only naked justice, but morality as such, though always with a view toward justice.

We said that natural right is a portion of the natural moral law. This statement rests on the presumption that right and morality belong together. For duties correspond to rights. Where there is no duty, there is no genuine right. But duty (morality) is more extensive than right, because, as we noted above, right is only one aspect of moral obligation.

b. Historical Survey

The natural moral law is found among all peoples as a reality of experience, and not least of all among the primitive tribes, though, of course, not in a theoretic philosophical form explaining the moral law or natural rights. For almost universally, and principally among the primitive peoples, the natural moral law is not based so much on the nature of man as upon religious traditions through which God made known His will (often through the "patriarch").[6] Only in periods in which the unreflecting religious consciousness is in a state of decline or decadence does the need appear for philosophical explanation of the content and authority of the moral law (let us say through the rational nature). Here we naturally make no point of denying that rational nature itself, through the order of creation, enlightens the individual with a knowledge of the fundamental demands of morality. But in the primitive peoples all things were seen immediately in the light of religion on the level of the person.

The problems of natural moral law particularly in its bearing on natural right were much discussed among the Greeks. Undoubtedly Aristotle and Plato overemphasize the authority of the state in its positive legislation by contrast with the rights of nature. Nor is the latter clearly grasped by these thinkers as a mere portion of the more comprehensive natural moral law. Of course they do recognize the existence of good and bad laws. Yet they do not acknowledge the right of the citizen to invoke natural right in opposition to the positive law (as the ancient Sophists did). But they clearly teach that there is a natural moral law which binds man even where there is no state legislation. Aristotle seeks the norms of the good in the being of things (above all, in the nature of man). Good is for him that which conforms to the order of being, but it is also that which is reasonable, since the good can lay claim to validity and oblige man only through the medium of reason. In conformity with his theory of knowledge, Plato propounds the doctrine of innate moral ideas. He finds the good not in real being, but in the "pure" region of ideas. The two principal orientations in Christian philosophy even in the conception of the natural moral law, as found in Augustine and Thomas, derive in great part from these two Greek philosophers.

The Augustinian-Platonic conception views the natural moral law more under the aspect of reason through its participation in the eternal law of God by means of divine illumination of ideas. The more mature Thomas and the whole Aristotelian tendency rather stress the order of creation and its knowability in relation to their claim on our conscience. In both Greek philosophies and still more clearly in the corresponding Christian orientations the natural moral law is held to express itself, not merely through the intellect, but also through man's inclination toward the good.

In classical Greek philosophy the theory of the natural moral law and natural right was impoverished through the notion of the total subordination of the individual to the state, which was viewed as the ultimate source of all valid laws. To obey the state was held as invariably good. By way of opposition the Sophists applied their critique to point out the contradiction and variability in the state laws themselves. Such criticism of the laws as they actually were, contributed toward a concept of world-wide natural right. The Stoa substituted a supra state with world-wide natural right for the right of each petty state. It finds in human dignity (even in that of slaves) an element common to all places and all peoples. It bases the universal validity and immutability of moral duties on the world order (cosmos), on the rational world soul, and on the rational nature of man, who is capable of recognizing the laws of the world-order through participation in world reason.

Among the Romans the notion of the rights of nature was a result of the comparison of the rights of the Roman citizens (*jus civile*) with the common rights of all the vanquished people (*jus gentium*). There was only a short step from a knowledge of this common right of peoples, gleaned through such comparisons and constantly applied, to the realization that in the nature of man and of peoples there is an existing natural basis for the positive right, namely, the natural right (*jus naturale*). The doctrine of natural right not only plays an important role in the Roman philosophy of right, but also in the Roman jurisprudence. In difficult cases, if the written law was not adequate or was deemed inapplicable, the Roman judge was permitted to apply the principles of the teaching on natural law.

The doctrine of natural right (prior to every civil right) and of the natural moral law (also abstracting from every positive revelation of God and certainly without respect to human law) is a very definite part of the Christian tradition. Only with the growth of Nominalism and the arbitrary rule of the absolute monarchs in the late Middle Ages was this clear tradition somewhat obscured. Because of his Nominalistic bias in philosophy and theology, Luther had no true concept of the natural law, though there is much dispute about his actual position. His doctrine of total depravity of fallen man and his concept of "reason the harlot" leave no room for any concept of revelation except a purely positivistic one. In the climate of Lutheranism, once faith declined, absolutistic juridical positivism had few obstacles to prevent its rise and spread.

With the rapid and progressive deterioration of faith in revealed morality at the dawn of the modern age, Catholics and Protestants (Calvinists) immediately began an earnest search for a common ground in the natural moral law and in natural right. The freethinkers of the period also manifested a serious interest. Among the most noted scholars in the field of natural right are Grotius (died in 1645) and Pufendorf (died in 1694), both of whom were influenced by Vitoria and Suarez.

In this period the doctrine of natural right was avidly embraced by the advocates of Rationalism, who with sceptical optimism relied on human reason alone for the certain knowledge of all that is good. With genuine naïveté the rationalists argued from the general principles of natural right and deduced the most specific obligations, with the result that every teacher of natural right in the declining eighteenth century was able to produce a perfect code of laws based on the doctrine of pure natural right. Variations due to conditions of place and time were scarcely noticed. Moreover, as expounded in non-Catholic circles, the doctrine of natural right revealed strong individualistic tendencies down to the beginning of the current century. All rights of the state were held to derive from the rights of the individual. There was no recognition of the community as autonomous subject or bearer of rights.

In reaction against this rationalistic attitude Romanticism subjected the egalitarianism of rationalism to a sharp critique. The criticism of the enervated "natural right" of rationalism with its disregard of the manifold diversity of peoples, was frequently perverted into an attack on natural right itself in non-Catholic circles. On the contrary, the Catholic thinkers were able to penetrate more profoundly into the doctrine of human conduct, both from the standpoint of historic development and background and from philosophic analysis of nature itself.

The climax is reached in the juridical positivism of the nineteenth century, which derives all right from the absolute and all-powerful will of the state. "There is no right unless it is granted through enactment of law." The ultimate consequence of this position is the dictum: "What the Leader commands is always right." Of what avail is recourse to his individual conscience conceded to the subject by many juridical positivists in instances in which the positive right of legislation leads to egregious injustice? In fact, the positivists have no fixed norm of right and duty binding every conscience uniformly and universally. Such is the result of the Lutheran despair of reason once the safeguards of faith have been forfeited.

Abstracting altogether from the Lutheran lack of esteem for natural right, there is an inner necessity in the very development of events in the last three centuries. When he forsook his ancestral Christian home, the "freethinker" brought with him a rich Christian heritage of religious and moral truth. Even after the light of faith had been extinguished, he still cherished the treasure of truths which were the Christian inheritance, though in the vanity of his egotistical reason, of course, he vaunted them as an exclusive possession of his own mind. Even after God was rejected, or, more specifically, after the arguments for His existence were repudiated, the basic moral principles which are deduced from the existence of God became obscured in his mind only gradually. Now, after the entire heritage of the Christian past has been squandered, only one alternative remains. Either the prodigal must return to the Father's house or he must eke out a miserable existence on the husks of scepticism and moral juridical positivism.

From this situation Protestants conclude in part that in our dialogue with the contemporary mind we should not attempt to withdraw to the common ground of natural law and right—and we might note that such a procedure has a very hazardous foundation in their principles—but that as Christians we should always and everywhere proclaim the uncompromising challenge of obedience to faith. Indeed we Catholics will proclaim the need for obedience to the faith of the Gospel and demand it of all the world without qualification or quibble. But is there any reason for us to abandon beforehand what reason teaches us about the rights and duties of all men, a common meeting ground of naturally knowable duties and rights which we share with many non-Catholic Christians? How can we preach the divine truth of the Church and expect of men obedience of faith toward the Gospel, if we cannot have confidence in their natural knowledge of the most fundamental moral duties and rights?

Of course, we may not carry optimism so far as to expect from non-Christians or even from atheists the knowledge and recognition of all naturally knowable duties and rights. For the apostasy from faith in Christ and the denial of belief in God carried with it an ever-increasing weakness of the intellect of fallen man in his natural understanding of morality and right.

Since the Church has been obliged to co-exist in an organized unbelieving world, in a milieu of unbelieving states, her doctrine on the natural moral law and natural right has taken on still greater practical significance. Leo XIII is one of the most important Catholic teachers of natural right in his encyclicals on the social order and the state. His work was continued particularly by Pius XI and Pius XII. They were keenly aware that only through the exposition of the naturally knowable moral laws and principles of right could they gain a hearing also in the non-Christian world, and in this way cooperate with all men of good will. Moreover, the enunciation of the doctrine on natural rights belongs to the exercise of the Church's pastoral magisterium over all mankind and flows from her responsibility toward the order of earthly realities. In part her very mission rests upon her proclamation of the natural law. And it forms a significant part of her message to all peoples. She is fully aware, when she is confronted by errors in the natural religious order of truth, that she herself enjoys infallible certainty in this domain of truth only in virtue of divine revelation and guidance.

The horror aroused over the arrogant assumption of "rights" by certain modern states in defiance of every moral ideal seems to favor the Catholic doctrine on natural rights. The proclamation and sanctioning of universal human rights by the United Nations surely points in this direction, even though it may well be that many representatives of the signatory powers were convinced that their resolutions were creating new rights rather than enforcing already existing ones. For a long time celebrated political theorists with a socialistic and liberalistic bias proved utterly intransigent regarding the authority of states in the matter of the rights of parents in the education of their children, if we may cite just one example of disdain for individual human rights. Any such rights of parents, they claimed, had their origin and basis in the legislation of the state. And therefore they maintained that they could also be restricted at will by the same authority. This attitude is less prevalent today.

c. The Scriptures and the Natural Moral Law

The words of Deuteronomy, "This commandment, that I command thee this day is not above thee . . . but the word is very nigh unto thee, in thy mouth and in thy heart, that thou mayest do it" (30:11, 14), are probably an indication that the law conforms to reason and is naturally knowable. In any case, the content of the second table of the decalog does not transcend the law of nature. More profound reflection on the knowability of the good also on the part of the Gentiles is found in the sapiential books. When Christ asks, "Why even of yourselves do you not judge what is right?" (Lk 12:57), He points to moral knowledge and power of judgment. Very clearly Saint Paul (Rom 2:14f. and 1:32) teaches that the law of nature is revelation of the Creator, which is written in the rational nature, in the heart even of the Gentiles, and which accuses man of his evil conduct in his conscience and deprives him of any excuse for it. In his preaching to the Christians the natural revelation in the created world and the rational nature of man are always presupposed. But the fulness and perfection of revealed truth and grace is Christ. The actual basis and motivation for the law according to Paul is this fulness of truth and grace.

d. Certainty and Error regarding Natural Law

The fundamental principles of the natural law can be known with certainty by every normal man in possession of his reason. They are in fact self-evident. Following is the most universal principle of the natural law: the known good must be done (*bonum est faciendum:* Thomas); the good must be loved (*de bono est complacendum:* Scotus). Likewise the following principles are evident to all peoples and have been actually recognized by all men: "What you do not wish others to do to you, do not do to them!" (cf. To 4:16); "Leave to every one or give to every one what is his!" The laws of nature evident to all men include at least the general precept to honor God and the essentials of the second table of the decalog.

Ignorance of the most immediate conclusions and applications of these laws of nature cannot very readily be excused. Such ignorance can hardly be inculpable. On the other hand, anyone who is living in morally debased surroundings, especially if he does not enjoy the enlightenment and guidance of faith, can readily be led astray regarding the more remote conclusions of the law of nature, though the conclusions in themselves are entirely within the reach of unaided reason. In a general way the cause must be put down as the disorder of original sin, but more particularly it is the influence of the surroundings and the limitations of talent and moral sensitivity of the individual.

One cannot be ignorant of the duties which immediately spring from the state of life one has himself chosen (for example, in married life there is the obligation to care for and educate one's children) or from one's vocation (for example, a superior by virtue of his office must care for his subjects) without the onus of guilt. But one may fail to have a clear understanding of the manner and means of the fulfillment of such duties, or of the more remote consequences of the essentials involved in the state of life or vocation (for example, the obligation on the part of parents to bequeath a suitable inheritance to their children) without incurring guilt.

e. Immutability of the Natural Law

As such, the moral law of nature is immutably valid. But its application is variable according to the changeableness of conditions. For example, it is an immutable principle of natural right that every man has the right to his dignity as man and to the development of his personal capacities. He has these rights also in regard to his work. From this applied principle we may draw the further conclusion that actual slavery is unlawful at any time. Saint Paul implies as much in his prescription regarding the treatment of the slave "as a brother" (PHLM 16). But an immediate emancipation of the slaves and a subversion of the whole social structure would have placed the human dignity of the emancipated slaves in even greater jeopardy. Similarly, from the principle of the dignity of man we deduce certain conclusions regarding the inalienable rights of the serf or vassal in relation to his feudal lord in the feudal system, though we can in no wise prove his total independence, because this would have made defense and administration, the duty of the feudal lord, impossible of fulfillment. In consequence the emancipated serf could not have enjoyed that peaceful existence and opportunity to work to which he had the right.

From this same title of natural right to human dignity we conclude to a conditioned right of co-management for the worker in present-day industry because it offers to the working class in this age of propertyless masses and mass production in industry the only assurance of preserving industrial peace and the dignity and integrity of personality of the workman. The problem has not yet fully crystallized and requires much more study and research. However, the assumption of an absolute right of co-management for every laborer is untenable, for this would practically make the wage contract immoral. It is entirely untenable to assume that the right to co-management is based on natural right itself for labor as a whole, on the hypothesis of an essential claim based on man's nature as such and valid for all times and all circumstances. We can surely conceive of an eventual social reform so comprehensive that extensive participation in ownership by the working classes would vitiate all the arguments advanced for co-management today. The very discussion regarding right of co-management may have already contributed much to the current clearer realization of the importance of the historical context in the application of immutable principles.

Today we see clearly that the eternally valid propositions of natural right also include the duty of acting in accord with historic exigencies and situations. Man must act rightly in the historic context, though it cannot be rigidly and statistically determined for all times what is historically correct and right. Only the knowledge of the immutably valid essential laws of natural right and of the historic situation makes it possible to form a judgment in every individual instance as to what is "historically right" and therefore also, in the full sense, "right according to nature."

In the application of the law of nature there can be no epiky in the true sense, provided epiky is construed as a meaningful fulfillment of law or an application of law which transcends the mere letter. For the moral law of nature and natural right is not at all a "law of the letter," but an unformulated law and right resting in and ever to be read anew from nature itself in its permanence and changing historical conditions. Obviously, the most universal formulations are always correct in formulation also, though a knowledge of the variable conditions is necessary. To cite an example based on the principle "to each one his own," only from a knowledge of conditions can one determine what "his own" means for the individual. The application of a universal principle of natural right demands the virtue of equity (*aequitas*), the just and at the same time prudent "sense of the situation," as a basis and premise for a naturally just and historically right action and particular conclusion.

As objections to the doctrine of the immutability of natural right certain facts are adduced from the Old Testament which apparently contradict the principle: the sacrifice of Isaac (Gn 22:1ff.), the command to extirpate the Canaanites (Dt 7:2),[7] the spoliation of the Egyptians by the Israelites in their flight (Ex 12:35f.). This latter can very readily be explained as justifiable compensation for unpaid forced labor. The other two facts are not in violation of the fifth commandment (natural law) which forbids the taking of the life of an innocent person on one's own authority. The meaning of the commandment is that not man, but God alone, is the absolute master over life and death. Therefore, as God acts through the forces of nature, so also can He act through the human instruments He chooses in the exercise of His exclusive right. He can and may set the term of an innocent man's life, which may be the greatest of graces rather than an evil. God could demand the sacrifice of Isaac as a victim through an authentic revelation. As a matter of fact, Isaac was not sacrificed, though the obedient journey of sacrifice made of Abraham and Isaac types of Christ's dolorous way to the sacrifice of Calvary. Such was the design, such the grace of God. The primitive inhabitants of Canaan had forfeited their right to national existence because of their vices and their polytheism. Their idolatry proved a constant source of temptation to the Israelites.

A closer study of the matter from the standpoint of Scriptural exegesis shows that God entered into the covenant with the Israelites as they actually were historically, with their national virtues and faults as influenced by their environment. Only the customs, laws, and defects which were absolutely incompatible with their position as people of the covenant and with its providential mission would God have to eliminate. The imperfect national institutions prevalent up to the time of the covenant became "religious" institutions upon entry into the covenant with God, that is, divinely sanctioned institutions of the Chosen People, by means of which the divine pedagogy only gradually purified its crude concepts and morals.

As regards the legislation of Israel, we are not to think of all its prescriptions as emanating immediately from God. As to content and substance, the civil laws of Israel were not immediately revealed to Moses, but were taken into the orbit of revelation through the enactment of the covenant. The Israelites who fell away from the people (the theocracy) by gross transgressions of the tribal law, by the same token apostatized from the covenant. Much of the evil conduct of the patriarchs (lies, deceit, impurity) is merely reported without comment and hence is not at all approved by the sacred writer. In fact, the absolutely unfathomable mystery of predestination to grace and the divine governance through grace is discerned more clearly when thrown against a background which is frequently dismal and sombre.

f. Is Dispensation from Natural Law Possible?

In the true sense of the word there is no dispensation from the natural moral law, nor can there be.[8] But in its application a law or right of our nature can be robbed of its binding force through a change of nature (hence, not through mere variation of external circumstances!). We know from revelation that original sin had a most dire effect on all mankind. Because of this sin and its evil effects throughout the history of mankind, human nature by comparison with the "nature" of original justice, and probably also by comparison with "pure nature," has deteriorated. In consequence, with the forces at his disposal and without the grace of Redemption, fallen man could not observe all the precepts according to the lofty moral standard which man in his primitive integrity was able to keep. This fact sheds some light on the toleration of polygamy and the bill of divorce in the Old Testament and in some measure explains what seems a toleration of evil. But it must not be thought that unrestricted polygamy, as practiced by Solomon, for example (cf. Dr 17:17), or the callous and unjust issuance of a bill of divorce, is reported by the inspired writer as free from guilt or even as ideal.

In the study and discussion of the Old Testament law and morality we must attempt to distinguish more sharply than we usually do between the norms of law (juridical law) and moral ideals. Divorce is never approved as a moral ideal in the Old Testament. There is a simple command (Dt 24:1ff.) not to dismiss the wife without a bill of divorce and not to resume married life with her after her dismissal and remarriage. This was plainly a restriction placed on free and easy divorce. The bill of divorcement is regulated as a legal form, but divorce itself is not inculcated as something morally irreproachable. "Moses, by reason of the hardness of your heart, permitted you to put away your wives" (Mt 19:8). This is to say that, assuming the moral immaturity of his subjects, the lawgiver could tolerate many moral imperfections, in fact, even moral abuses and place legal checks on them in order to avoid greater moral evil. Saint Thomas is of the opinion that the objective of the juridical regulation of the bill of divorce by Moses was to save the lives of many wives who might have been exposed to great peril had there been no such legal restrictions. Succinctly he states his conclusions regarding the problem of Old Testament law on divorce in the lapidary pronouncement: "Therefore the lesser evil was tolerated to avoid a greater evil."[9]

However, it should not be overlooked that so great an authority as Pope Innocent III,[10] and with him many other theological writers, hold that there was a direct divine revelation which "permitted the patriarchs to have more wives than one." But the Pope says nothing regarding the form and manner of the revealed message. Nor is his teaching an infallible doctrinal decision nor even so much as an authoritative pronouncement on this point specifically. It is rather an incidental statement in a letter of the pontiff dealing with the marriage of pagans and the Pauline privilege.

Any solution of this problem of divorce and polygamy which is based on the assumption of divine authorization of the practices as an actual moral regulation of Jewish conduct must stress the distinction between the primary and secondary principles of natural law. That part of the natural law can be considered secondary and within the area of divine dispensation which is most suitable indeed to fallen and unredeemed nature, but not as such obviously and unconditionally binding and within the reach of man's power. In consequence, an exemption from it is not altogether excluded in view of the abject condition of fallen man. An inclusive or indirect toleration, or even a direct toleration of what this portion of the law forbids, may be granted because of fallen man's "hardness of heart." But only God through his instruments of revelation can grant such a direct "permission" or toleration.

There is another solution which approaches the problem from the standpoint of mere juridical toleration through judicial norms. But this explanation also must have recourse in some manner to a divine revelation, since the legal system of Israel attained the status of "divine right" through revelation. Essential to both attempts to solve the perplexing problem is the reference to the disturbance of the original order of the Creator through the hardened heart of man. This fallen condition of man is the basic reason for permitting a norm less exalted than the perfection of the law of nature would impose.

In this connection it is well to note that at all times students of moral right have had to face the thorny problem of toleration of evil. Is legal toleration and "regulation" of moral abuses permitted? Is it perhaps even more prudent than absolute prohibition which might result in even greater evils because of the malice of many individuals? Thus, since the days of Augustine, many learned theologians have held that a legal regulation and with it also a species of public "toleration" of "legalized" prostitution under certain circumstances is lawful, provided it does not imply formal approval of this degrading vice and result in a multiplication of sins. Similarly Christian politicians and jurists may cooperate in a legal regulation of civil divorce. But it is permitted only on condition that the circumstances do not favor a more rapid spread of the evil of divorce and the legal cooperation clearly does not imply moral approval of an evil which these leaders believe they cannot prevent by legislative action. Legal toleration or more accurately the hedging in of moral abuses, viewed in its totality, must serve and promote better morals.

4. *The Positive Divine Law*

a. Law of the Old Testament

The Old Testament forms a coherent unit of three diverse kinds of law: 1) the cultal law, 2) the judiciary law, 3) the moral law. It is of the very essence of the Old Testament theocracy that religion (cult), morality, and law be bound together in the greatest possible intimacy.

The law of cult or ceremonial regulates the divine worship established by God. The cult of the Old Testament is the perpetual memorial of the covenant of election and at the same time the most vital announcement of its fulfillment in Christ. Just as the entire cult of the Old Testament had value in God's sight only because of its reference to Christ from whom it derived its force, so too the noblest function of the many meaningful liturgical prescriptions was to keep awake the yearning for Christ and excite a sense of sin and of need for redemption in relation to Christ. With the coming of Christ and His perfect cult, the Old Testament ceremonial law was abolished. In the event of any further observance, it would now be a "death-dealing law" because in the deepest dimension of its meaning it assumes that the Saviour has not yet appeared.[11]

The "judicial" law (civil law) had as its task, as did the cultal law, to unify the Chosen People and to segregate them from the Gentiles. Because the covenant meant God's sovereignty over the people who as a whole were the bearer of the covenant of election, the transgression of the law of the covenant, in so far as it lay within the power of the transgressor, meant the frustration of the divine designs in the covenant and apostasy from it.

With the founding of the universal Church, the spiritual norms of her law replaced the juridical norms, temporal and spiritual, of the Israelitic theocracy. Had the entire Chosen People entered the Church in a mass, she would have had to abolish all the legal norms which related to segregation. Such was their love and missionary zeal in their call to the Jewish mission, however, that the Apostles in the beginning observed the judicial law, including the dietary prescriptions and the requirements of legal purity, in order not to sever themselves prematurely from the people whom they converted.

But still they could not observe the law in their mission among the Gentiles for fear of alienating these converts (cf. GAL 2:11ff.). Out of love for the Jewish Christians some few things were required of the Gentile converts by the Apostolic Council, in conformity with the advice of Saint James, but no more than the co-existence of Jew and Gentile in the current situation demanded (ACTS 15:19ff.). Since the time of Christ the judicial law is a "dead law."[12]

The moral law of the Old Testament as the clear revelation of the natural law is without doubt more specific and precise in its determinations and enjoys a loftier sanction because of the loving alliance between God and His people. The moral norms of the Old Testament are summed up in the decalog and in the great commandment. Their binding force as natural law rested on the rational nature of man, who can grasp them by use of his natural endowment of reason, and on the positive declaration of the divine will in the revealed message of the covenant. They derived their special obligation and sanction as well as their greater precision from the covenant as such.

As to their formulation, the Old Testament precepts are in great part negative (prohibitive); this makes them readily comprehensible, for a prohibition is very easy to understand. Although there is a natural tendency to formulate universal concepts by establishing limits negatively (whereby what has been set within bounds still has a positive value), the negative in the covenant has another reason, a special reason. It is not the positive fulfillment of the commandments, but the free divine choice which gives the Israelite his share in the covenant of election. He does not first have to merit the covenant, but he can deserve to lose it. Clearly the negative commandment warns against transgression, for this is apostasy and loss of the great gift of the alliance.

As to their substance, the moral laws of the Old Testament preserve their binding force also in the New Testament, both in virtue of the natural law and in virtue of the positive specification of this law through the revelation of the Old Testament. The Old Testament revelation surely preserves its character as revelation also in the New Testament. However, its binding force, interpretation, and sanction no longer derives from the Old Testament, but from the New.

b. Law of the New Testament: Law of Christ

(1) *Law of Christ Compared with Old Testament Law*

(a) Jesus and the Law

Jesus rejects the "precepts of men" and the "traditions of men" (MK 7:7f.) which make the scribes equal to the law. Instead of the interpretation of the law which the synagogue often corrupted, Jesus Himself comes forward as the only authentic interpreter of the law (Sermon on the Mount!). Above all He attacks the false legalistic spirit which takes refuge in the literal interpretation and fulfillment of the law and neglects the necessary submission to God's holy will (MT 23:23).

Jesus does not simply abolish the law taken as a whole, for it is the gracious revelation of the will of His Father, but He brings it to perfection. He is indeed the "ultimate Word of the Father," the perfect and final revelation and fulfillment of His immutable will (MT 5:17). He restores the perfection of law with all the original imperative of the law of nature (MT 19:5ff.).

Jesus supplants the law (the Mosaic law as covenant and institution) through His mediatorship. He Himself is the only Mediator between God and all the redeemed. But the supplanting of law through mediatorship does not at all mean the abolition of the imperatives of the law. The very notion of forgiveness of sin and the fact of forgiveness show very clearly that the claims of the law and the judgment of the law were correct. The "keeping of the commandments" is still the condition for entry into life. But obedience to the commandments of the law attains its fulfillment only in the imitation of Christ (cf. MK 10:17ff.: the rich young man) and in acceptance of the special invitation of grace transcending the law.

The transgressor of the law (the prodigal son, the sinful woman, the good thief) can be saved, not by a simple change of attitude toward the law, but through the favor of Christ's grace. Above the verdict of the law is the Saviour's power to forgive sin. But with the pardon of sin there is bound up the demand of fulfillment of the law in the future ("Thy sins are forgiven thee" [MT 9:2], but "sin no more!" [JN 5:14; 8:11]). Truly the "imperatives of the law" made by Christ are not lighter. They are rather sterner and more far-reaching than those of the Old Testament (cf. MT 5:43ff.).

The transgression of the law of Christ (without sorrow and re-infusion of grace) means forfeiting of salvation. "Lawlessness (*anomía*)" and sin are the same (MT 24:12); where lawlessness reigns, love grows cold. This is surely true of the love of the lawless. But the first meaning of the axiom is that love grows cold universally with the increasingly general disregard of the law.

(b) Paul and the Law

Saint Paul views the law of Christ primarily under the aspect of the cross of Christ. The great concern of Saint Paul is not simply the emphasis of the interior disposition in contradistinction to mere external observance of the law, for interior disposition in the religious thought of the Jews of the Old Testament and among the Jewish Christian converts had the same univocal meaning. For Saint Paul the great contrast is between obedience to the law on the part of man limited to his own resources on the one hand, and adherence to Christ the Saviour and the fulfillment of the perfect law of Christ through the power of His death on the cross on the other hand. Fundamental for Paul is not the fulfillment of the law, but union with the cross of the Lord.

Only from the cross of Christ does Paul say no to the law though it is not rejection of obedience to the law as such, but to the law as the way of salvation in which man places his whole trust in the law alone. If the law alone can lead to salvation, "then Christ died in vain" (GAL 2:21).

One who after the death of Christ seeks to impose upon the Gentiles the Old Testament law with all its legal norms and cultal prescriptions, which in the profoundest depth of their meaning referred to Christ who was to come, shows that he holds the law itself (without its intimate bond with Christ) in higher esteem than redemption through the cross of Christ. It is to be noted, however, that Paul does not have in mind solely the obsolete prescriptions of the Old Testament law. In the most generic sense he speaks "of the law" in so far as one endeavors to make it an economy of salvation, an actual master and saviour.

The cross is the authentic fulfillment of the law. The end of the law which is perfect obedience to God and perfect love for one's neighbor (ROM 8:34; PHIL 2:5ff.) is attained through Christ's loving obedience on the cross. In this act all honor was rendered to God the Father. In this act the disciples (in the Holy Spirit) were given the power and the example of perfect "obedience to the law." Only through faith in Christ and in the power of His cross do we attain to new obedience (compare ROM 6:11) in the spirit of love. It is, therefore, a sin against the law and even more so against the cross of Christ if one seeks to attain the end of the law without confidence in the grace of salvation.

The cross of Christ says yes to the judgment of the law (GAL 2:19; 3:13; 2 COR 5:21). The verdict of condemnation for sin in the law was confirmed on the cross in an incomparable manner (ROM 5:6ff.). The malediction of the law was upon each and every transgressor. Of itself the curse of the law must fall upon them all irrevocably. But it is radically averted through the cross of Christ, since He took upon Himself the judgment of condemnation even to save the offender, if only he turn to the Saviour in repentance.

The law is good in itself (1 TM 1:8). "The law indeed is holy and the commandment holy and just and good" (ROM 7:12, 14). For ultimately the law is nothing else than the good and holy will of God. Among the rabbis the emphasis was placed on the human accomplishments in accordance with the requirements of the law. But Paul and all the sacred writers of Old and New Testaments see first of all the living will of God manifesting His mercy and grace in the law. Consequently, when Paul speaks of the law, he does not mean merely the Pentateuch which is the great code of the law for the chosen people (many passages have this meaning), but above all the imperative will of God as such. It is the will of God with its challenge and imperative as set down in the Holy Scripture, as written in the hearts of the Gentiles, as announced in its perfection in Christ.

For Paul the law (the imperative divine will) is always bound up with the beneficent will of God. Rightly understood, the law is a diverse manifestation of divine grace and love. Precisely for this reason does Paul attack the misconception of law, the "order" of law in which the legalistic achievements of man are placed above the order of salvation (the beneficent love of God).

The law must be observed and fulfilled. To refuse to submit to the law means to be "hostile to God" (ROM 8:7). Evidently this was also valid for the Old Testament cultal and judicial law, but obviously only so long as it remained in effect. In contrast to the intellectual pride of the Pharisees, who were "knowers of the law," Paul teaches that the fulfillment of the will of God as revealed in the law is of decisive importance rather than the abstract study of the Scriptures or the theoretic recognition of the law (cf. ROM 2:13). But despite all earnestness in the execution of the imperatives of the law, one must always bear in mind that the ultimate source of salvation is not the law and its fulfillment, but the cross of Christ.

The law purposes through its prohibitions to prevent sin (ROM 7:12ff.). At the same time the law also reveals the true nature of sin as rebellion against the manifest will of God (ROM 7). The clear and positive revelation of God's will as a loving will shows in all its horror the singular heinousness of the moral revolt (ROM 3:20) and its consequent unique imputability (ROM 4:15; 5, 13f.). The sin of Adam and the sins of the people under the law merit an entirely different measure of punishment than the sins of men who had no positive revelation of the will of God (though, of course, they had the "law" written in their hearts). So the law, which should have prevented sin, multiplied it still more because of the malice of men and augmented the number of transgressions (ROM 5:20; 7, 5ff.).

This multiplication of sins was not an essential consequence of the "good law" as such. The law is weak because of the sinful, "carnal" state of man, *dià tês sarkós* (ROM 8:3; cf. 7:5f.; 7:25). Thus the law brings death to the unredeemed man (1 COR 15:56). The law without grace has the force of death. (It is evident that the new law which as such is a manifestation of grace cannot in any way be "deadly.")

Even though the multiplication of transgressions was not the inner purpose of the law, still God chose to lead man through the conflict and crisis in his sinful condition provoked by the law to a realization of his need for redemption. Since the sinful frailty of man is such that no man can observe the entire law in its integrity, this wholesome result must be universal and affect all men. In radical opposition to the Pharisees, Paul looks upon the law as necessarily a whole. One cannot cancel out a transgression of one precept through fulfillment of another. There is no balancing of fulfillment and violation; the whole law must be fulfilled. Even though only a single precept is broken, the transgressor has in principle violated the law that is God's imperative will (GAL 3:10). But this very fact excludes the hope of salvation through the law. With the law alone, without the grace of God (without the cross of Christ), therefore, everyone would be lost, for the very reason that with his "carnal" powers he could not fulfill the law in its entirety. This judgment is all the more true for one who has the cross before him and still reverts entirely to the law (GAL 3:12).

Thus God through the law "shut up all things under sin" (GAL 3:22; ROM 3:9), so that the hope of salvation would spring from the cross alone. Since man by a single transgression of the law is exposed as a sinner—and all other observance of the law cannot revoke this judgment—it follows that precisely the law itself prevents the sinner from anticipating salvation from the law alone. Wherefore the law, even in this dreadful feature which unmasks the sinner with all his frailty, also points to Christ. "Therefore the law has been our tutor in Christ" (GAL 3:24).

Since the whole Old Testament law (which includes the cultal, judicial, and moral precepts, and also the covenant) before Christ was orientated toward the grace of Christ (ROM 10:4), who is to come, so after His coming the law must be viewed entirely in relation to Him. It must be seen in the light of Christ and measured by His death on the cross. For this reason the Christian must acknowledge gratefully that as a man redeemed he is no longer under the dominion of mere law, since he is in the economy of salvation and grace (ROM 6:14). In the light of the love and grace of Christ the disciple of Christ must discern what portion of the obsolete Old Testament law may still be observed. If only he holds himself aloof from any false trust in an "abolished law" (in this instance, the cultal and judicial law), the result will be a profound awareness of the dominion of Christ's grace. And in this realization of the dominion of grace he will be ready in the spirit of Paul to bear the burden of law (which means the external observance of customs which derive from the law) precisely in those instances which serve to "gain the Jews" for Christ (1 Cor 9:20). But the only law which imposes this obligation is the "law" of the love of Christ, the "law of the spirit," which demands of us that in love we "bring forth fruit unto God" (Rom 7:4).

(2) The Essence of the "New Law"

To present the specific characteristics and the content of the New Testament law is the task of moral theology as a whole. Some of the characteristically Christian elements have already been treated in the section on the norms of morality. Here we must present the most striking features as they are indicated in the Biblical texts. It is the "law of Christ" (Gal 6:2). Christ, even before the Incarnation, is the center toward which the Old Testament law tends (Rom 10:4; Gal 3:24) as He, the personal Word of the Father, is also the Teacher of the Gentiles in the natural law. Christ in His redemptive passion, His resurrection, and above all in His sending of the Holy Spirit, is the true Lawgiver of the New Covenant. Christ also promulgated His "new law" externally in words of supreme and final authority and through the glorious deeds of His redemptive love, which as new and ultimate standard forms the new in His law (Jn 13:12ff.; 15:12ff.). He confirmed the imperative of the Ten Commandments (as remaining in force, determining what is forbidden, the *"prohibita,"* setting up a limit or "deadline" of transgression).

Especially in the Sermon on the Mount (Mt 5:ff), in the high-priestly prayer, and in the farewell discourse to His apostles (Jn 13:31–17:26), He expressed in words charged with all the majesty of His divine authority the inner compulsion of the "law of the spirit." This new law of its inmost essence is far more than a bar or hedge shutting out sin, more than an extrinsic imposition of will laying down a minimum requirement. It is rather the grace of the Holy Spirit knocking at the door of man's heart. It is the high goal of perfection inviting and summoning (the law setting a goal to be striven for: *Zielgebot*). Though His law is all this, Christ is not for such a reason less a lawgiver than Moses. In fact, in a much more real sense is He "Legislator."[13] In His divine-human kingdom He is equally herald of the Father's will bestowing grace and the loving object to whom we direct our obedience.

Our whole relation to the law must be studied in the light of Christ. Most essential for the disciple of Christ is its inwardness. His Master does not merely impose His obligation upon the disciple from without, as a human lawgiver is wont to do and as the law of Moses in so far as it was law "of the letter" (2 Cor 3:6f.) did, but from within and above all from within through living incorporation in Him. Thus the Christian living in grace is furthest removed from lawlessness. He is not lawless (*ánomos*), although he is not "under the law" (*hypò nómon*). He is not under the ancient law of Moses and even less under any mere law of external force. He is one who "lives in the law of Christ" (*énnomos Xristoû*); this means he has his law from within through incorporation in Christ. Christ Himself is law to him in that he has been taken into Christ through the Holy Spirit (1 Cor 9:20f., compare Rom 6:14).

One point must be stressed most emphatically. The essence or core of the imitation does not consist in external conformity and surely not in a mere external relation with Christ ("confronting" Christ). The imitation is above all life in Christ, the life flowing from the most intimate union of grace with Christ.

The laws are written "into their mind, and upon their hearts" (Heb 8:10; Jer 31:33). Most essential in this "new law" is the renewal of disposition and of the inmost heart of man through the grace of the Holy Spirit. "The Old Testament was written in a book with the sprinkling of blood (Heb 9). Thus the Old Testament law is a covenant in the letter. The New Testament, on the contrary, is a covenant in the Holy Spirit, through whom love is poured forth into our hearts (Rom 5). And so the Holy Spirit in so far as He effects (*facit*) love in us, which is the fulfillment of the law, is the New Testament."[14] "The New Testament consists in the pouring forth of the Holy Spirit who teaches us from within. . . . Therefore it says in the scriptures: 'I will put my laws into their mind' (Heb 8:10). The plural form 'laws' is used because there are many commands and counsels. He also prepares the heart for good deeds. Therefore it says: 'Upon their hearts I will write (*superscribam*) them' (Heb 8:10), which means that upon knowledge I shall inscribe love. 'The charity of God is poured forth in our hearts by the Holy Spirit'" (Rom 5:5).[15]

The law is "the law of the Spirit of the life in Christ Jesus" (Rom 8:2). As faithful interpreter of Paul, Thomas says that the "new law" only "secondarily" consists in that "which is proposed to the Christian, whether it be in word or writing, whether it be for faith or for action." "What is most characteristic in the law of the new covenant and what gives it its entire efficacy is the grace of the Holy Spirit which is given through faith in Christ. And so the new law is fundamentally (*principaliter*) the grace of the Holy Spirit Himself." Beyond this, the word and letter of the law "pertain to the preparation for the grace of the Holy Spirit and to the right use of this grace."[16] "What else are the laws of God, which are written by God Himself in our hearts, but the grace of the Holy Spirit, through whose presence love, which is the fulness of the law, is poured forth in our hearts?"[17]

Because basically the Holy Spirit Himself is the new law, it is essentially a "law of life," a life-giving law. The Old Testament law was dead in so far as it was expressed in letters and without the force of the Holy Spirit, who was not bestowed in such abundance in the Old Testament and not at all except in reference to the new law. Hence it could develop into a "deadly law" in consequence of the deadly power of sin (*hamartía, sárx*) and in accordance with its predominantly negative character (as expression of the threat of punishment of death). The new law, on the contrary, is essentially law of life, inner impulse and élan of an ever expanding new life.

It is a law "in Christ Jesus." For the Holy Spirit is for us the gift of Christ exalted in glory and signifies vital incorporation into Christ. "The law of the spirit of the life in Christ Jesus has delivered me [us] from the law of sin and death" (ROM 8:2). For through the redemptive death of Christ, who bore for us the verdict of condemnation for sin, the external law lost its perilous character and its impotence, for as fruits of the Redemption we have received the Holy Spirit. He it is who has broken within us the inner corrupt propensity to sin (*sárx*) through our incorporation into Christ (ROM 8:3f.). Thus, through the infusion of the Holy Spirit, we are no longer under the dominion of sin, no longer under the regime of the law, which was given to man because of his sinfulness, but under the gentle rule of grace (ROM 6:14). We have passed from the dominion of law to the dominion of the grace of Christ, "who has risen from the dead, in order that we may bring forth fruit unto God" (ROM 7:4).

But since the baneful influence of the past aeon of sin and dominion of law constantly persists in its endeavor to enslave us, we are never secure. We are always liable to fall back again under the dominion of sin and the law. One who does not really harken to the inner voice with the heart of a child does not follow the light and the impulse of the Holy Spirit; one who carries out the law only as a serf under constraint "is still under the rule of sin, whereby the will of man begins to choose what is opposed to the law. Through grace this dominion is broken, so that man fulfills the law not as though he is under the law, but free. 'Therefore . . . we are not children of a slave-girl, but of the free woman . . . in virtue of the freedom wherewith Christ has made us free' (GAL 4:31)."[18]

Through the grace of the New Testament sacraments the Christian is no longer radically under the dominion of sin and the purely external law, though the carnal man and the spiritual man remain in conflict with each other (GAL 5:17). Therefore the Gospel, which proclaims the freedom of the children of God from the domination of the law, is the sharpest warning to flee from the works of the "flesh" (*sárx*). Only "if you are led by the Spirit, you are not under the law" (GAL 5:18). For the "fruit of the Spirit is: charity, joy, peace, patience, kindness, goodness, faith, modesty, continency. Against such things there is no law" (GAL 5:22f.). Against the lust which ruled the old man, the carnal man, the prohibitive law fulminated its threats and interdictions. "The fruits of the Spirit," however, which are the signs of the genuine freedom of the children of God, do not flow from mere orientation toward the prohibitive universal law, but from the childlike docility toward the Holy Spirit.

Therefore the Christian who endeavors to regulate his moral life exclusively "according to law" is incurring a dreadful hazard. Christian morality, which is life according to the "law of grace," is gravely endangered by exclusive orientation "according to law," if this is taken in the sense of external prohibitive universal law. The danger is only increased if one goes so far as to claim "freedom" in opposition to the inner guidance of grace, that is, if he should attempt to defend his position on the ground that he violated no universal law. Such defense could be based only on the "carnal principle" which governs the "old sinful man." The richness of a life according to the "law of grace" violates no prohibition of law because this life indeed lies within the confines of law. It is loftier than the lowest restriction of law, but is infinitely grander and richer than the parched and barren spiritual life based on mere external law. "Mere concern with the law which is pure legalism results in minimalism . . . progressively increasing legalization of the religious and secular life . . . it concentrates the moral forces on the defensive negative limits of the law . . . But in this manner the actual verdict of conscience, the meaningful 'fulfillment' of the law through the guidance of love cannot at all be achieved. . . . The 'appeal to love' must have the final decisive word!"[19]

The new law as a "law of grace" forbids us to give to the ethical, that is, to our "must," the primacy of position and reduce grace to the level of aid and means in the fulfillment of the law. In the order of values the sequence is not "law and grace," but "grace and law." First comes the "centering in Christ in grace" through the Holy Spirit. The movement of grace to the corresponding supernaturally good act then follows. Our duty and our free cooperation with grace is only third. Grace is more than the law and the summons. But the law of the Christian is expression and summons of grace. Those who are "in Christ" see in the imperative will of God, first of all, the loving purposes of God, both in the form of external law and in the inner impulses of grace. In the "task" they see first and always the "gift."

In the true Christian all this must manifest itself consciously and through a constant progress in virtue. The consequence will not be a weakening of spiritual life, but its progressive deepening in the spirit of joy. If the love and grace of God are truly foremost in the mind of the Christian, then the task of inner grace and its external expression through the word of love (external law) is all the more compelling. And in the process the domain of morals will be progressively removed from the restrictive hedge of minimum requirement, from the external limitations through prohibitive commandments. It will be elevated to the lofty heights of the Sermon on the Mount, the heights of the purposive precepts directing man toward ideals and goals (*Zielgebote*). The genuine scope of Christian morality is the formation of Christ in us. "The ten commandments protect the outer periphery of the realm in which Christ will be formed in us."[20]

The new law is "the perfect law of liberty" (Jas 1:25; 2:12). The new law is the "perfect law" because it is the law of the grace of the Holy Spirit, because it is given by Christ, the perfect revelation of the Father to us, and because in substance and content it is so exalted as to be incapable of further perfection. Only gradually, of course, can the individual come to a realization of this perfection as he progresses in his total submission to the "royal law" (Jas 2:8). He can enter into this perfect law with deeper understanding and appreciation only through submission in faith to the teaching and guidance of holy Church, the Bride of the Holy Spirit. Divorcement from the Church means severance from the "law of faith" (Rom 3:27), from the font of grace which is faith, from the bond of charity which is the goal of faith.

If, as the apostle James says, the "law of Christ" is the "perfect law," then we must logically hold that least characteristic of it is one of the very essential features of all human law, namely, its purely external restrictiveness. Essential to all human law are the clear and definite limits indicating the minimum requirements which all must and can meet, and in addition the imposition of obligation from without! The "perfect law" of the New Covenant is not without its minimum universal requirement. Clearly there are limits and bounds set by the commandments (the prohibitions of the decalog). But it does not consist in these. It is a law of perfection, which in its very essence must embody the highest ideals of the "royal command," the goal of perfect love. This all-embracing law contains a rebuke for those who deliberately fall short of its ideals (Jas 2:9). There can be no doubt about its external promulgation through Christ's own word and His deeds of love. But what is truly its unique characteristic is its promulgation through the grace of the Holy Spirit.

The law of Christ is a "law of liberty" (Jas 2:12) because it is the "law of love" (cf. Gal 6:2), because as the "law of faith" it is essentially the gift of the divine love and the dynamic embodiment of love (Gal 5:6). But where love is rendered for love through the inner force of love, there dwells the highest interior freedom. Grace and love in the Holy Spirit unite the human will totally with the will of Christ. The words of Saint Thérèse of Lisieux expressing this law of liberty have become its classic formulation. She said, "I always do my will," simply because the true disciple in the "law of liberty" completely conforms his will with that of Christ.

In the new law even the external directives are not a restriction, but a hedge and safeguard of inner freedom. From the mere natural standpoint it is true to say of the moral law: "The ultimate basis of the law and the source of its necessity is the freedom of the will of man himself, in so far, namely, as the harmony between our will and right reason should be assured. Utterly absurd therefore is the assumption that man, because he is free, must be without law; for this can only mean that freedom must be irrational."[21] Thus the inner law of faith and grace also embraces the external directive in the form of a prohibitive precept with a minimum requirement and the maximum imperative of the "royal law" (Jas 2:8) of love, expressed in the Sermon on the Mount.

In actuality the real source of the freedom of the children of God is the Holy Spirit with His graces and gifts. It is preserved by docility and adaptibility toward our sole Teacher and Master, Christ, who simultaneously teaches exteriorly through His word, through His example, through His Church, and from within through the Spirit of truth.

Any other attitude except a sense of restlessness and impatience regarding the duty of submission to the inner guidance of grace would be incompatible with this perfect law of liberty. This law of grace cannot be reconciled with rigid adherence, in the spirit of the former slavish submission, to the mere external letter of the precept with its minimum requirements and defensive insulation against the inner summons of grace and the call of the hour.

Hence, that which makes the new law a law of liberty is not the mere reduction of the countless particular prescriptions of the old law to comparatively few precepts in the New Covenant. But it is true, of course, that useless universal laws and general precepts needlessly multiplied do imperil the spirit of genuine freedom. This spirit should manifest itself in an integral fulfillment of the whole new law with that essentially free effort which is in accord with the needs of the hour. Great and holy men who in the spirit of Christian freedom undertook to observe a strict religious rule and carried it out most faithfully earnestly caution against the imposition of a multiplicity of prescriptive regulations.[22] The new law demands of the individual, indeed, as Thomas remarks in the passage already noted, a much higher perfection than the Old Testament. But for its proper exercise and development this very spirit of freedom seeking not only the good, but what in each instance is best, has a claim in prudence on the human lawmaker. In wisdom unto sobriety he should restrict his legislation to what is really necessary and suitable for the needs of the time.

Were all Christians to live in accordance with the "perfect law of liberty," many positive restrictions and sanctions of law would be superfluous. A great part of the ecclesiastical and civil law is necessary only "because of sin," because of the lawlessness of the "old man." But it does not shackle the free child of God, who is totally dedicated to the law of love.

Only he can rightly speak of the freedom of the children of God, with all that it implies, who has declared total war on the "works of the flesh," who really is ready to live "from the spirit" (cf. GAL 5:13; 1 PT 2:16). But with the "spirit" is given this freedom as new being. And the gift of freedom implies duty and responsibility.

(3) *The Role of External Law in the Protestant Ethic*

Since the Reformation there has been much discussion and divergence of opinion in Protestant theological circles regarding the nature and rôle of external law. However, nowhere in all Protestant thought do we find the clear and simple notion of external law which characterizes Catholic theology and according to which the law is primarily the guide to the correct perception of the inner law of freedom and love. In the mind of the Reformers the primary role of the law is that of "accuser." "The law is always the accuser" (*lex est semper accusans*). The first purpose of God in the law and, accordingly, the first function of the law itself (often called the theological use) is to drive us to despair or move us to total and trustful abandonment to Christ in faith (fiducial faith). Thus, as regards man and his own power and person, the law has the purpose to bring him to shipwreck in order that he may cleave entirely to Christ. The majority of Protestant theologians apply this doctrine, not merely to the Old Testament law and the negative precepts, but also and very specifically to the Sermon on the Mount, which accuses us more inexorably than the decalog itself.

It may help us to understand this attitude of the Protestants if we bear in mind that they are very much concerned with the sense of man's sinfulness and need for Redemption. They fear the danger of external legalism and seem to be haunted by the thought of false legalistic justification as found among the Jews and condemned by Saint Paul. Though the Catholic theologian shares such concern and stresses the need to avoid mere externalism, and also looks upon the law as accuser (thus he gives law a theological function), he follows a totally different approach in explaining the nature and rôle of the law.

According to the common teaching of Catholic theologians, the proper and primary rôle of law is to direct us to the right understanding of the divine will in its loving summons to us. According to the first purpose of God, the external law in essential context with the inner law of life is intended for the guidance of man. We may concede to the Protestants that in so far as man is "carnal," the law accuses and condemns him; it "betrays" him into a false sense of security, of purely legalistic justification or as occasion of the multiplication of his transgressions, exposes his sinfulness. In so far as the law tends to make man conscious of his sinfulness and need for redemption, it has a "theological function," according to Catholic teaching. "The law is given in order that grace may be sought after; the grace is given in order that the law may be fulfilled."[23] For the sinner to whom the understanding of God's loving mercy is alien, the imperative menace of the law is first of all accusation, humiliation, shame.

Because he cannot flee from the imperative will of God which pursues him in the law, he will not readily turn from the grace of God and close his heart to the divine mercy offered to him in Christ. So it is that external law according to the mind of God's mercy is always our tutor in Christ.

But since the tendency to evil and the lure of the "old man" still persist even after justification, the law is also a constant summons to humility for the justified. In fact, even the very law of perfection formulated in the Sermon on the Mount makes it increasingly plain that he still has before him a long journey toward the integral fulfillment of the "perfect law of liberty." Therefore the law constantly summons him to pray humbly for the assistance of divine grace, so that he may persevere in the law of grace and liberty.

If the Protestant attitude toward the law stresses the anxiety regarding the law, this is consistent with the emphasis on man as a sinner. Here too we note a marked difference between the Catholic and Protestant approach. Since Catholic theology sees the baptized essentially and primarily in the light of the operation of grace, it cannot look upon the justified man as still a sinner in the Protestant sense of "sinner and at the same time just" (*peccator simul et justus*). The justified man is not on the level with the unregenerated sinner. Surely it is true that the great saints protested that they were sinners. And every Christian must be aware of the danger of sin lurking within him. But even though we gladly concede this point and do speak of the justified man as still a "sinner," the term does not have the same penetrating meaning in Catholic thought, does not pierce to the very depth of the reality which is man converted by grace, as does the simple statement that man once a sinner is now truly transformed inwardly by the infusion of grace which makes him inwardly and objectively a child of God.

From all this it follows that the first aspect under which we should study the function of the external law for the child of God is directive, the guidance to the right use of interior grace.[24] According to the Catholic teaching—and the difference between the Catholic concept and that of the Protestant thinkers is very marked—the sequence or order of the function of law is from within outward. Quite consistently it sees the exterior law from within, from the interior law of the merciful love of God. Thus our theology is preserved from the peril of perverting the revealed law into stark legalism and is at the same time able to furnish law with a more positive orientation toward the accomplishment of the Christian tasks.

The Protestant teaching with its undue stress on the law as "accuser" and on man as sinner and its claim to utter interiority in submission to Christ in the liberty of the children of God is involved in the very evils it dreads. On the one hand, the Protestant teaching places the Christian man entirely under the interior "law of complete liberty" without the direct guidance of any revealed external precepts. On the other hand, it imposes upon him the obligations of human statutes with a degree of harshness that is tantamount to the starkest legalism. Here we have the political use of the law to which Protestant ethics very generally leads (the second function of law).

Not only is the clear conception and appreciation of the law of nature lacking, which would permit valid objections to be raised against certain human statutes on the basis of the natural law, but the interior law of nature and grace is bereft of its bond with the manifestation of law in the revealed word of God. In consequence there is the pure interior law of God on the one hand, and, completely isolated from it, a "political-civil function" of the revealed word. Having no way to interiorize the external revealed law as direct expression of the inner law of grace, Protestant theology accepts this political use of the law. Thus external revealed law is reduced by the civil-political power to a proportionately stronger "legalistic" and secularized role.

It is an important function of Catholic moral theology to explain the true meaning of human law in the light of the natural and supernatural essential law. Either everything is animated by the new law of grace in the Holy Spirit, by the inner law of the children of God, or morality will become "legalistic" and externalistic through an extreme orientation toward law and right.

The fundamental distinction between the Catholic and Protestant conception of the law revealed in the Word consists in this: the Catholic doctrine attributes to the divinely revealed law, as the expression of the natural and supernatural order of being, an absolute universal validity which allows no exception; to the statute law, to the purely positive law, on the contrary, a great flexibility and suppleness as the immutable essential law and the situation may demand. Protestant ethic, however, as a rule rejects the absolute universal validity of laws, even of the ten commandments. All the more rigid and inflexible is the positive statute of human law, from which there is no legal appeal by recourse to a court of higher instance.

5. *Human Law*

a. Human Law and the Following of Christ

When Saint James says, "There is one lawgiver" (JAS 4:12), he does not thereby reject human law as superfluous, but on the contrary indicates its supreme source, the source of all right and law, God. Similarly our moral life in the domain of right must not be reduced to human subjection and human law, but must always in its inmost depths remain centered in the following of Christ. But if Christ directs us to the Church and her law and, in the secular sphere, to the civil laws, it follows that obedience to them is obedience to Christ Himself. The following of Christ, however, must also furnish us with the measure and the limits of our obedience to human laws.

Christ Himself in His own life gives us the example of obedience to the norms of law and the cultal precepts of His own people, as also of the perfect fulfillment of the moral law as such. He pays the tax for Himself and Peter; He makes the pilgrimage to the temple at the prescribed liturgical times. He observes the Sabbath (though, of course, not according to the barren formalism of the Pharisaical interpretation). He lives in the midst of a human family, choosing to practice obedience. He carries obedience to secular authority to the extreme of unresisting submission to its iniquitous verdict of death, victim of the most heinous legal murder ever perpetrated in human history. It is true that He did pronounce a stern condemnation of this injustice against Pilate and even more against the Sanhedrin. More than once he castigated the narrow legalistic and even sinful interpretation of law enunciated by the Pharisees. And still He did not withdraw from the oppressive obedience to human authority whenever obedience was not contrary to the will of the Heavenly Father.

Jesus "himself knew what was in man" (JN 2:25). Through painful experience He knew the deficiencies of the secular and religious authority and the craven weakness of His own apostles, and yet He placed them and their successors over His Church with legislative authority. "He who hears you, hears me" (LK 10:16). "As the Father has sent me, I also send you" (JN 20:21; compare MT 16:19; 18:18).

Only too frequently secular authority proves sinful and unbelieving. Obedience to such authority, and for that matter even obedience to ecclesiastical authority established by Christ, cannot be practiced for long without painful realization of the frailty and imperfection of the bearers of that authority. It also must be borne in mind that the laws imposed by men do not possess either the clarity or the certainty of the divine laws regarding the absolute good. But since man has a social nature, he is simply under the necessity of human law. He stands in need of authority and its law for his moral development. But most of all it is the community which has need of law in order to create the climate for the individual person to move within a realm of order in the service of the community, and to enrich the soil for moral growth and development of community itself. Doubly necessary because of original sin is the penal regulation through law. Were there no legal restraints checking the abuse of freedom by evil men, the enticement and violence on the part of the evil would rob the good of their freedom to act virtuously. (Here we see the great error in the Western-Democratic "concept of freedom.") The law with its sanctions is an indispensable means of education for men in their frailty and a shield against human malice (ROM 13:3ff.).

The imperfection of human laws and the consequent burdens often weighing so heavily upon men are a part of the cross of Christ which we must share with Him. The cross which He Himself bore He cannot lift from the shoulders of His disciples. In the cross of Christ the problem and crisis of human authority was revealed in all its poignancy and horror. By patiently suffering a death inflicted in the name of the law, legal murder through mockery of justice, Christ redeemed our subjection to human legislation, which often imposes an almost intolerable burden upon us. Bearing the weight of the woeful inadequacy of human laws has become far more than a mere matter of expediency. Now there lies before us the sanctified way of obedience to the will of God our Father, consecrated by the footprints of Christ who followed this way obediently to the death of the cross (PHIL 2:8).

But human law is not merely a cross; in its inner sense it is the way to justice, a support of weakness, a fulfillment of the order of the divine wisdom, a work of love through community and for community. Above all, we must note that even the laws of the Church are clothed in the vesture of earthly imperfection and therefore cannot escape the problem and crisis of all that is human. But in their inner depth there is a heavenly security. Does the Church not possess in her task of guidance through law the assistance of the Holy Spirit, so that she cannot command anything sinful and, at least in essentials, anything false? Likewise through the Church the burden of the problem of civil law is greatly lightened, since she as the infallible guardian of the morality of her children can caution them against morally dangerous and sinful laws.

The persistent problem of submission to imperfect human laws has not merely a negative phase. There is also a positive phase. Obedience to law constantly directs our attention, with ever increasing emphasis, to what lies beyond the legally regulated, to the actual basic sources of the good, though human law can do little more than give us a hint of it. Precisely through the painful experience of the limits of human legislation the Christian is constrained to look into the mirror of the perfect law of love, to adhere to the spirit of Christ.

There is a certain advantage in this very imperfection of legislative enactment. It serves to remind us that law and fulfillment of law are only a portion of the moral perfection. "Even though no society can live without law, neither the family, nor the state, still they do not live through law, but in the law. Marriage, family live through love."[25] This is singularly true of the Mystical Body of Christ, of the Church, and of our relation to her. She too lives in the law; that is, she has a legal domain which is essential to her life, but she does not live through law. Law is not the source of her life, for she lives through the love of Christ and the grace of the Holy Spirit and through the fulness of grace and love of her members, which, of course, also implies obedience to her laws. The legislative activity belongs to the pastoral care of the Church, which is a function of love.

Subjection to legislative authority of men produces the spirit of humility in man. Submission is a constant reminder of our created nature. Man is not a god. In prayer indeed we can directly approach God and speak to Him. However, only if we join in community and obey its laws to the best of our ability, only if we do the works of love in the reign of law will our obedience and our love be acceptable to God.

The constant necessity of applying to human law the test of the eternal law of God and the law of the imitation of Christ through divine grace does not in the slightest diminish the value of obedience to men. The value is in fact enhanced, since obedience is anchored more firmly than ever in its foundation of eternal values. These basic principles enable the Christian to act wisely despite the imperfections of human law. The virtue of epiky permits him to look beyond the letter of the code of human law, necessarily only imperfect and often entirely inadequate, to the actual meaning of the law opened up to him through his vital union with Christ. In fact, the very inadequacy of human law will prove beneficial if it prevents the Christian from holding too fast to the mere letter of the law and its external observance or from exhausting all his efforts in the service of men.

b. Obligation to Observe Human Law

The obligation in conscience to observe the laws of the Church is clear from the establishment of ecclesiastical authority by Christ. Obligation in conscience to obey civil law can be shown through natural reasoning from the social nature of man. Sacred Scripture clearly teaches that human authority is derived from the divine: "By me kings reign, and lawgivers decree just things" (Prov 8:15). "Admonish them to be subject to princes and authorities, obeying commands, ready for every good work" (Ti 3:1). "Let every one be subject to the higher authorities, for there exists no authority except from God, and those who exist have been appointed by God. Therefore he who resists the authority resists the ordinance of God. . . . For it is God's minister to thee for good. . . . Wherefore you must needs be subject, not only because of the wrath, but also for conscience sake. . . . Render to all men whatever is their due; tribute to whom tribute is due; taxes to whom taxes are due; fear to whom fear is due; honor to whom honor is due" (Rom 13:1-7). Very terse is the evangelist's rendering of the injunction of Jesus: "Render, therefore, to Caesar the things that are Caesar's" (Mt 22:21; compare 1 Pt 2:13ff.).

These texts clearly prove the principle that there is an obligation in conscience to obey human laws. But there is still the problem regarding the extent of this obligation. Do all laws oblige in conscience? This problem merits special investigation.

(1) *All Just Laws Bind in Conscience*

Just laws bind in conscience by reason of their intrinsic legal justice, which means their agreement with the law of God. Likewise anyone who deliberately and culpably violates a just law is in conscience bound to submit to just punishment. We look upon a punishment as just if it measures up to the importance and intent of the law in relation to the common welfare and as far as is possible takes into account the degree of personal guilt and the corrective value of the chastisement.

In the light of this principle we attempt to solve the problem regarding the existence of purely penal laws. There is a widely held theory that many laws, entirely just and proper in themselves, do not oblige one in conscience to fulfill the work prescribed (or to abstain from some action), but merely to submit to the penalty imposed for violation.

In criticism of this position we hold that to say a law itself does not bind in conscience is tantamount to saying that it does not bind at all. Moral obligation and obligation in conscience and likewise "in conscience" and "under pain of sin" have the same meaning. Apart from genuine law, which implies the concept of "will to oblige," there are directives, suggestions of the lawgivers (*regulae directivae, non praeceptivae*), which do not actually seek to bind the subject unconditionally. But they do point to a goal of the law, which the subject is to strive for either in accordance with the suggestion of law or in some other way corresponding to the purpose of the law. There are many rubrics in the Church's liturgy and, for that matter, also religious constitutions of such a character. But one is not altogether free from fault morally if he carelessly disregards these suggestions of the lawgiver or if he simply casts them aside frivolously and without any good reason or motive. However, we are concerned here only with true laws as such.

According to the theory which defends the existence of purely penal laws, the subject of the law has a species of free choice. He may either fulfill the precept itself or accept the penalty for violating the law. He may choose either alternative without any sin. This theory I look upon as entirely false. It makes no provision for a truly just punishment at all. For if there is no obligation to perform a task, the refusal to perform it cannot be sinful; and where there is no sin or guilt, punishment is meaningless or simply unjust. At best the punishment might be viewed as a "disciplinary" measure for purposes of education, but not strictly as punishment for violation of a law. But we may ask, why should there be such a stern effort to educate in the doing of things which one does not choose to make obligatory at all? (The imposition of exercises of humility and penance by the religious rule is an entirely different matter. Such exercises are not at all punishments for violations of law.)

Moreover, it is foolish to hold that the legislator has no desire to affect the conscience simply because he tries to attain his purpose by penalties regardless of the conscience of the individual. The obligation of law does not flow from the attitude of the lawgiver or the summons he may direct to the conscience, but from the agreement of the law itself with justice and right. Finally, it is a universally valid proposition that when the legislator fixes a sanction to a law, he is particularly intent on the observance of the law and looks upon the violator as deserving of punishment.

(2) *The Impossible Law*

A law which cannot be observed because of moral or physical impossibility does not oblige. However, if any essential portion of the law is just and morally possible, this part must be kept. EXAMPLE: If payment of one's assessed taxes is absolutely impossible, that part of the amount which is just and which one is able to pay must be paid. If one should not be able to attend the entire Mass on a day of obligation, he still is obliged to attend the essential part or parts if he is able to do so. However, the obligation ceases altogether if only a non-essential portion of the law can be kept.

(3) *The Unjust Law*

Unjust laws in themselves do not oblige in conscience, for they are not truly laws, since they lack the inner source of obligation, legal justice. Laws and commands which prescribe anything intrinsically immoral may never be obeyed (compare ACTS 5:29). More specifically, if the law goes beyond an exactment which is not just and demands that something intrinsically sinful or evil be performed, the subject has the duty to resist passively and refuse to perform the act. He is not permitted to observe the law, must refuse obedience. But active resistance or uprising, revolt against the law or against authority, is not permitted. From this it is evident that not every law which is opposed to the moral law justifies active resistance to the lawgiver. Only when the authority itself is unlawful or when its activity in some measure tends to undermine the moral law, the moral order of society, is active resistance in place, provided that resistance does not worsen the evil conditions and there is good reason to hope for the correction of the abuses and the restoration of right order.

(4) *Submission for Sake of the Common Welfare*

Should the law, though unjust, not prescribe anything immoral, but only what is morally good or indifferent in itself, the law as such, taken objectively, is not binding in conscience. But it does bind the conscience in so far as the general order, the avoidance of scandal, right-ordered self-love, the avoidance of greater internal disturbance or unrest or of serious external punishment may demand. Accordingly, under certain conditions even the violation of a law that makes unjust (not immoral) demands can be gravely sinful if disobedience results in an unduly great harm to the common welfare or to an innocent third party. Conceivably one might also commit sin by obeying such an unjust law, if circumstances were such that obedience to its unjust behests would conflict with duty toward others. To cite an example, the payment of excessively unjust taxes could inflict great harm upon one's family.

In the violation of an unjust law, the penalty imposed is binding in conscience only when one has incurred guilt in the transgression, for otherwise the penalty would be unjust. Still, in view of the fact that refusal to submit to the penalty much more readily subverts public order and causes scandal than does a mere tranquil ignoring of the law, the Christian may in many cases be obliged in conscience to submit to the penalty even though there was no guilt at all, or only a so-called "juridical" and not any "theological" guilt. In my opinion this is the only justifiable acceptation of the term "purely penal laws" in moral theology.

(5) Obedience to Evil Authorities

The obligation to obey authority does not derive from the moral integrity of the legislator or superior, but from the legitimate authority of the one who issues the command and from the justice of that which he commands. The Church has condemned the proposition of Wyclif and Huss that there is no civil power or ecclesiastical power possessed by any one in mortal sin.[26] It is quite evident that notoriously malicious legislators do not create an unquestioned *a priori* presumption of right in favor of the justice of their legislative acts. Such cases must be judged by the subject himself in a personal decision regarding the justice of the law. If need be, he must seek the aid and counsel of responsible and prudent men who are acquainted with the facts and the moral principles involved. On the contrary, if the superior or lawmaker is truly good and just, the subject may presume that a law is just and right; in fact, he must assume that it is just unless the contrary is obviously more probable. Such is our teaching.

c. Manner and Degree of Obligation

There is a grave obligation to observe a law if by intent and purpose or special circumstances it is of considerable importance for the common welfare or for the protection of the welfare of the individual. The mind and intent of the legislator may be gleaned from the tenor of the language employed in the formulation of the law or from the severity of the sanctions annexed to it. In contemporary canon law it is generally conceded that the threat of severe sanctions annexed to a law implies also a grave obligation in conscience to obey the law. The sanction itself is not the basis for the grave obligation in conscience, but a true sign of the serious obligation.

Moralists teach (almost) universally that legislators cannot forbid under penalty of mortal sin something that is in every sense of slight importance, for even the divine law itself imposes only slight obligations in matters of little moment. In fact, a serious obligation binding the conscience in petty things would prove to be only a snare for men on the path of salvation, and therefore would conflict with their true and genuine welfare which alone is just reason for law. But we may not overlook the point that a thing in itself insignificant can readily become important and significant because of a particularly serious purpose or altogether singular circumstance, and therefore can become a matter of grave obligation. This holds, for example, in regard to the obligation of silence. In some instances a slight indiscretion in speech, an imprudent word, might frustrate projects of tremendous moment, not to speak of the silence imposed by the seal of the sacrament of penance. Since authority usually has a better over-all view of such matters, we must form our judgment in measuring grave or slight obligation on the basis of a study of the terms in which the command or law is couched.

The purely positive human law, ecclesiastical law included (in contradistinction to the inculcation and specification of a natural moral law through human law), does not as a rule bind under an unduly great burden (*cum damno relative gravi*), hence, usually not at the risk of life, great loss to one's honor and good name, grave damage to health or property. (Obviously the inconvenience or burden intrinsically and essentially bound up with the observance of the law cannot in any way exempt one from the obligation of keeping the law, even though the inconvenience or burden be very great.) Only a disadvantage which, when placed in the balance, outweighs the good intended by the law can free one from the obligation of the law.

In special circumstances, the common welfare, the life or salvation of one's neighbor may be at stake (this holds, to cite an example, in regard to the tasks soldiers or priests may be called on to perform in the line of duty) or violation of the law may be the source of great scandal or cause greater evil for the violator than observance of the law. In such instances, human law likewise can bind, even though health and life itself be placed in jeopardy, because the common weal takes precedence over private welfare. But it is quite obvious that, strictly speaking, such an obligation does not arise from the human law as such, but through the intervention of a higher natural or divine law.

The legal obligation arising from a human law is directly concerned with the external act and only indirectly with the right interior attitude toward fulfillment. But it would be an error to assert that the law merely commands the external performance and has nothing to do with interior disposition. This would be tantamount to a complete divorcement of law from morality. Law and right are in the context of morals, with an intrinsic reference not only to the external welfare of the community— this surely in the first instance—but also to the morality of the subject. This holds even though the legislator in actual fact places all the stress on exterior performance and manifests no concern for dispositions, because we certainly must take into consideration, not merely the factual intent of the lawmaker, but the ultimate inner purpose and meaning of the law itself.

It is particularly false to look upon the laws of the Church as demanding no more than mere external performance of a work in the fulfillment of one's duty according to law. If the universal order of law and morality forms a harmonious whole, then *a fortiori* there is perfect harmony between the "Church of law" and the community of grace in the Mystical Body of Christ. The Church's code of law serves the order of grace! The external obligation of human law may never be sundered from the law of grace of Christ, which always invites the sentiments of man's heart.

By way of further clarification of this point, we must note that, if the interior disposition was lacking when the external act was performed, there is no obligation to perform the act again unless the very validity depended on the disposition itself (this is true in the case of an oath, of certain contracts, specifically of the marriage contract). There is always the obligation before God (human legislators have no such claim) to repent of one's neglect and to assume the proper interior attitude which was absent when the act was performed. But it is evident that the obligation of human law does not demand the utmost perfection of virtue in the interior disposition with which the law is observed. Even the divine law does not lay claim to such interiority as to demand that every act spring from the depths of a soul steeped in virtue, but only that one avoid violation of the virtue and in general strive to attain it in its perfection.

d. The Object of Human Legislation

The sole object of an imperative of law is an act which is in itself morally good or at least indifferent. The object of the law may not transcend moral possibility. It must be morally possible to fulfill and not extraordinarily difficult. Because law has a universal validity, it may not impose obligations exceeding the capacity of the average subject of the law; hence, it may not require heroic acts. Of course, it is true that great public emergencies, such as war, may demand extreme sacrifices of the masses; and experience proves that under such conditions the most arduous achievements are possible. But since these extraordinary deeds are performed by the generality of men only under the pressure of exceptional circumstances, they lose much of their heroic character. Heroism is not an affair of the masses.

The law as such may also forbid good or indifferent acts in so far as they may prove hurtful to the common welfare under certain conditions or circumstances. Conversely, the prohibitive positive law does not have to outlaw all evil actions or impose punishments upon those who commit them. For the function of law is not the exact equivalent of that of morality. Civil law may tolerate many evils in order to prevent even greater evils (for example, the prevention of an enslavement of conscience by a Puritanical police regime), but it may never declare them licit. In fact, even the appearance of moral approbation of evil must be scrupulously shunned. Men are altogether too prone to look upon that which is legally tolerated as morally permissible.

The objective end of the law is in the first instance the common welfare. Civil society is entrusted with the common welfare in economic and cultural matters, especially with the tranquillity of order in the group life and group effort to attain these goods. But since earthly possessions by their inner purpose are subordinated to religion and morality, civil legislation must so foster them that the public order in these goods facilitates the attainment of salvation for each individual or at least does not render it more arduous.

Civil authority has the moral obligation to restrict and combat moral evil by legislation if this is necessary to safeguard the moral culture of the community, its interior peace and security, social justice, or the inalienable rights of the individual. One of the basic rights which the state must secure, to cite an example, is the protection of youth against manifest moral contagion and seduction (through laws restricting the production and distribution of pornography). In consequence, evil is to be attacked by the state whenever it threatens to become an overt force which unjustly handicaps the freedom to do good.

The state is not just a servant of the Church in its exercise of legislative authority. But the state is a servant of God, and is obliged to consider itself such in its own domain, as the Church is in hers. The state must discharge its functions in such a manner as to further the mission of the Church rather than obstruct it.

The object of the law must be just; that is, the law must be necessary or at least useful for the furtherance of the best interests of all. It is unreasonable and unjust to impose unnecessary burdens! Justice requires first of all that advantages and disadvantages be equitably distributed. This means that the weak and dispossessed enjoy the right to special protection and the socially powerful the duty to bear the greater burdens; those who have merited most are entitled to greater honor. Such is the sense of distributive justice (*justitia distributiva*). Moreover, if the legislators overstep the bounds of their competence, the law is unjust. Unilateral regulation of spiritual functions by the state, to give an instance, is unjust even though identical legislation, as a matter of fact, might be enacted by the Church. (Likewise, commands of a religious superior which lie totally outside the framework of the rule would be unjust.)

Secular lawmakers are not competent to prescribe purely interior acts. These do not belong to the attainment of the legislative goal. An enactment prescribing internal acts can neither be enforced nor adjudicated. In the words of the Roman canon of jurisprudence (which is in conformity with the law of nature), *"de internis non judicat praetor."* Nor has civil authority any right to judge the sentiments of the heart. One who is accused and questioned in a matter of this kind may justly refrain from answering the charge. Even though the right disposition is required for the fulfillment of the law (see above), the subject is nevertheless not obliged in any instance to answer for it to secular authority.

The Church by virtue of an internal forum entrusted to her by God has the power to command purely internal acts. The internal forum (*forum internum*) is concerned with the internal care and guidance of souls, above all, in the sacrament of penance, and beyond this through the internal extra-sacramental forum with the spiritual or internal guidance of souls outside the sacrament. In some measure the Church can judge and even "constrain" by sanctions, obviously with the spiritual means at her disposal, in spiritual internal matters through the judicial tribunal of penance. It is a moot point whether the Church can directly prescribe purely interior acts through her legislation. As a matter of fact the Church as lawmaker does not command any purely interior acts except in so far as she interprets and clarifies the divine law. But if she imposes external works, by her very nature as mediatress of salvation she demands not merely external performance, but also the sentiment of the heart in so far as this belongs to the moral and religious significance of the act.

It is one of the distinctions to be made between civil and ecclesiastical legislation that the state is concerned most of all with the external legal performance and with the interior act primarily only in so far as the exterior act cannot exist without it (thus a valid oath presumes the intention of invoking God as witness). The Church, on the contrary, in her legislation looks first of all to the salvation of souls and, therefore, also demands external actions as well, but always in reference to the increase of grace in the Kingdom of God. It is true of the Church law also that the direct object of the legal obligation is the external action, whereas the inner disposition is only the indirect object. But still where the interior act is demanded for validity or for the meaningful performance of the act, it binds as directly and immediately as the external act (for example, the intention of hearing Mass on Sunday as prescribed for the faithful, the intention of offering the Mass for the people of the parish on the prescribed days, and the good dispositions for the prescribed Paschal confession and Communion). In these instances, if the interior act has been neglected, the obligation of the law has not been satisfied. The act in its entirety, if it is possible, must be repeated.

e. The Subject of the Law

All the subjects of the lawgiver who are morally responsible for their free acts are bound by human laws in so far as the intent of the law concerns them. It is generally assumed according to canon law that all children who have reached the age of seven are capable of the use of reason, so that they are bound to observe the laws of the Church unless the contrary is stated. As regards penalties of law which are *"latae sententiae,"* (taking effect by the very fact that the law has been violated), the Church looks upon those who have reached the age of puberty as sufficiently capable of reason and responsible for their acts so as to fall under these penalties.

Not all laws are universal. The lawmaker can narrow the circle or category of subjects of his law, although it is evident that he is not permitted to do so in an arbitrary fashion. The legislators themselves (most particularly when there is question of a legislative assembly or other law-making bodies) are bound by their own universal law, by particular laws only if they belong to the group bound by the law. The laws of the state first of all bind all the "citizens" of the state. (The term is used to include subjects who may not be citizens or have the rights of citizenship.) Institutions within the state with the right to make laws can legislate only for their own membership. "Strangers" who are subjects of other states are bound by the laws of the region in which they reside in so far as these laws are enacted for the public order and security or determine the legal formalities of juridical acts. Strangers remain under the laws governing their domicile or their state in the matter of civilian rights and duties, property and offices, which they may possess there.

According to international law rulers and their ambassadors in foreign lands enjoy the privilege of extra-territoriality. This means that they are not bound by the laws of the country even in regard to the "legal formalities" (except in instances in which the second party in a contract may be so bound). In a sense they carry with them their domicile and its laws.

In point of right itself, the laws of the Church bind all who are baptized, even schismatics, heretics, excommunicates, except in so far as the law expressly exempts them, for by the very fact of baptism one acquires the rights and duties of citizenship in the Church.[27]

Clerics, by right, are free from those civil laws which as such are in conflict with their status as clerics.

f. Interpretation of Law

Even the most brilliant legislator can scarcely hope to formulate laws and coordinate them with such clarity as to remove all possibility of doubt and perplexity regarding their meaning and application, particularly when there is a great diversity of conditions to which the laws apply. As a result there is need for interpretation of the laws.

The most certain way to dispel such doubts is through authentic interpretation by the lawgiver himself and by his lawful successor or representative. If there is question of the interpretation of a really doubtful law or of an interpretation which widens or narrows the scope and application of the law, then the interpretation becomes binding only upon its promulgation. A rescript or a decision made for an individual case would not of itself unqualifiedly be an authentic interpretation of a law. If the case in point is a typical one, however, one can conclude with considerable assurance to the intent of the legislator.

Usually the interpretation of law is made by jurists versed in the science of jurisprudence, whose interpretation is not "authentic," but "doctrinal." Their study is concerned with the tenor of the words in the text of the law itself, with the context, with parallel passages in the law, the purpose or intent of the law, the circumstances and motive of the legislation, the nature of the law itself (*ratio legis*).[28] The value of doctrinal interpretation is gauged by the weight of arguments presented and the authority of the jurists. Moral unanimity among the interpreters on a point of law is tantamount to moral certainty of the correctness or validity in law of their view, for the simple reason that the lawmaker could not pass over such an agreement in silence if he did not himself acquiesce in it.

In certain democratic countries interpretation and application of the law are entirely distinct from the legislative and executive power. These functions are properly within the competence of the courts. Not only the laws, but also the constitutions of the States and the Federal constitution are subject to the interpretations of the courts, which have no legislative authority.

In a right-ordered and law-abiding community custom constitutes an excellent interpretation of the law. The force of custom is such that it can introduce new laws and make existing laws obsolete. In order that custom enjoy the force of law, introduce new laws, or change existing laws, the custom must be reasonable, that is, no sound objection may be raised against it, and it must be calculated to further the common good. It must remain in possession for a proportionately long time. (The CIC, cn. 25ff., determines how long the time must be to establish customs "according to law," "beyond the course of the law," "contrary to the law.") It may not be repudiated by the legislator. It is correct to say that in effect the consent of the lawmaker confers on custom the force of law and that he really permits existing law to be modified or become obsolete through silent approval of the custom. It follows that any law resting on custom loses the force of law through contrary authoritative legal enactments, in so far as these latter contradict the custom. But in general it is not to be assumed that the promulgation of a universal law is sufficient to invalidate a juridically sound particular custom to the contrary if this point is not expressly stated in the law.[29]

Since custom is a source of sound understanding and faithful observance of law, too frequent changes in legislation may prove very harmful. On the other hand, a false conservatism and unduly protracted delay in introducing changes in laws which altered conditions of time and place make imperative may easily result in great injustice in the laws themselves.

Epiky is the interpretation of the law in the particular situation, an interpretation not according to its letter but according to its spirit. Because of this spirit of the law, one assumes that in his equity and wisdom the legislator had no desire to include certain extraordinary instances in the general norms. According to Saint Thomas, epiky is a virtue, the daughter of prudence and equity. It is a virtue and not, according to a conception rather current, but totally false, a species of self-dispensation from the law or an indolent shifting of its burdens. According to the true conception, epiky as readily inclines one to accept burden and strain beyond the letter of the law if its intent and purpose and the common good demand it, as to hold oneself free from the onus, when one must assume in all fairness that the lawgiver does not will to impose such a burden in altogether singular circumstances—or at least not in the specific manner prescribed by the letter of law. The use of epiky by the subject assumes, therefore, the existence of the virtue of epiky in the legislator. From all this it is apparent that epiky is not evasion of law, but a nobler fulfillment than the letter prescribes. It flows from the spirit of true freedom which delivers us from the serfdom of the mere letter of law and from the craven ease of self-seeking.

Authorities agree that it is not permissible to make use of epiky in cases of doubt regarding a law which is both reasonable and observable. Especially is this the case if one can readily approach the lawmaker or his representatives for a solution of one's problem. However, this does not at all imply that a constant readiness to place any and every petty perplexity before one's superiors is advisable. Obviously, the use of epiky is futile and unlawful if the subject must honestly concede that he does not have a true insight into the intent and bearing of the law. As daughter of prudence, epiky presupposes a clear decision, presumes that one will act more perfectly under this particular set of circumstances if he does not fulfill the law or fulfills it in a different way than that prescribed. If the matter is doubtful, one must obey the law or seek guidance regarding one's duty and under certain conditions request a dispensation.

The virtue of epiky in the concept of Aristotle and Thomas[30] coincides in great part with certain elements explained in the so-called "moral systems" (application of the rules of prudence). Perhaps we can retain much of the permanent value hidden in the controversies in moral theology over the application of the rules of prudence by viewing them in the history of theology as development of the Thomistic teaching on epiky. Theology would have been spared many a false start if this point of departure had been consciously kept in mind and followed.

g. Freedom from the Law

(1) *Freedom by Withdrawal from the Law*

One who withdraws from the jurisdiction of the legislator or leaves the territory where the law prevails is free from the law. For example, one may leave a diocese in which there is an obligatory day of fast and enter a diocese where no such obligation exists. Whatever be his reason for leaving, there is no obligation at all as far as the positive law is concerned. And his conduct is in no way objectionable morally if he has a worthy motive for his action.

If the time required by the law as an essential part of its fulfillment has expired, the subject who has failed to do what the law required, whether culpably or inculpably, is free from the legal obligation (for example, from the recitation of the breviary on any particular day after midnight of that day). If, however, the time fixed legally is only to urge one to perform an act in itself independent of the prescribed time (for example, the annual confession of sin), the obligation still remains in force after the time prescribed has expired. In fact, the obligation is doubly urgent.

(2) *Freedom from Law through Excusing Causes*

Physical or moral impossibility to fulfill the law simply frees one in conscience from observing the law. Should one foresee, however, that deferring fulfillment will render it impossible later on, one is obliged to satisfy the law at an earlier period if the law should oblige at this time. For example, a priest knows that he will be too busy to recite the breviary in the evening. He must recite it earlier in the day! However, he is not obliged to "anticipate" the recitation on the previous day, even though he knows that he will be prevented from saying it the next day.

Invincible ignorance frees one from the law and ordinarily from the penalty annexed to the law. Nevertheless at times "punishments" are inflicted where there is only a "juridical guilt." However, such procedure is admissible only if exaction of the penalty is necessary for the common welfare. The penalty in question, in matter of fact, is not true punishment. It rather has the nature of a required work necessary for the correction of a legal breach to safeguard the common welfare. Ordinarily such a penalty for mere juridical guilt is justified only on the presumption of law or fiction of law that there has been some degree of moral guilt in the ignorance of the law. We might ask very pointedly whether such a fiction of law still has any valid basis in view of the incredible number of laws on the statute books of the modern state.

Vincible (culpable) ignorance does not excuse one from guilt and in general also not from punishment for violation of the law. Still canon law imposes many penalties, especially those of serious nature, only if the transgressor is aware at least in a general way of the full gravity of the law and also of the sanction annexed. In any instance the malicious will to be ignorant (*ignorantia affectata*) does not free the offender from the guilt or from the punishment.

Laws which prescribe certain legal formalities (*leges irritantes*) under penalty of invalidity of the legal acts concerned usually make no allowance for the excuse of inculpable ignorance. The purpose of such laws is to maintain the proper exercise of authority over the legal nature and consequences of these acts.

(3) *Abrogation of Legal Obligation*

The clearest and most obvious form of cessation of law is its complete or partial abrogation by a competent legislator. Subsequent legislation abolishes previous laws in so far as they are incompatible with the more recent enactments. After total reorganization of an entire domain of law, all relevant laws in this area cease to oblige. In case of doubt the abolition of a prior law is not to be presumed, and the recent enactment is to be interpreted in a sense conformable to the previous legislation in so far as this is possible.

Apart from the express abrogation of laws through legislative authority, laws may automatically cease to bind if they lose all intent and purpose. If the law no longer has any meaning for the community or even has become baneful, or if the purpose which the lawgiver had in mind in enacting the law is in no manner of means attainable any longer, the law ceases or at least ceases to bind for the duration of the untoward conditions. If one of the purposes of the law is still in effect, then the corresponding obligation likewise remains.

Should the law be based on some universal assumption (of a danger threatening the common welfare or the welfare of the individual), it is binding upon the individual even in instances in which he would not be affected. The reason lies in the hazard that the decision of one individual in his own favor, that the law does not bind him, would readily become general. Only too readily many others would form the same judgment, with his case in mind, with the result that soon the whole purpose of the law would be frustrated. An example is the law forbidding the reading of certain books.

(4) Privilege

The privilege is an exemption from law. Through this "prerogative" or "special right" of the privileged, persons (also moral persons) or places can be exempted from general laws.[31] The standard to be set up both in granting and in using privileges must be the general welfare.

(5) Dispensation

Dispensation exempts from the immediate obligation of law in certain cases.[32] In contradistinction to privilege, dispensation is not a permanent plenipotentiary power or an objective special right. Since laws which are of profit to the entire community may be less suitable for certain persons or cases, the lawgiver has the right, at times even the duty, to dispense from them. Still it would prove very detrimental to the laws to leave to the individual every decision regarding exemption from grave laws, even in instances of doubt. The legislator surely cannot assume that each individual has the perfect possession of the virtue of epiky, which for that matter does not actually refer to strictly doubtful cases. Therefore a regulated provision for dispensation is a necessity of law. Especially in the instance of burdensome laws (for example, the law on forbidden books) and for the instance in which there is no clear judgment on exemption through excusing causes or epiky, there is no practical way open except that of appeal to the lawgiver or one having full authority for a dispensation in such matters.

The superior lower in rank than the legislator can dispense only when the full authority is granted to him. If dispensation is given without reason, the superior who grants it is guilty of sin; and in the event that he is not himself the actual lawmaker but subordinate to him, the dispensation is likewise invalid. In cases of doubt the dispensation is both valid and licit. A dispensation obtained by offering false reasons or motives is invalid. Should the reason for the lawful dispensation cease to exist entirely, the dispensation also ceases to exist. If the immediate basis for right is withdrawn, the right ceases.

CHAPTER SIX

THE MORAL OBJECT IN ITSELF AND IN THE SITUATION

I. OBJECTIVE VALUE AS BASIC DETERMINANT OF VALUE

THE objective value (*objectum materiale*) of the action is the primary consideration in forming a judgment of its morality. To form a comprehensive judgment on the moral quality of the act, however, the objective value is not to be considered in itself alone, but in the situation with its determinants. And finally, not the existing objective value in its world of reality, but the value to which one holds by inner disposition is the basic determinant for the moral character of the act. EXAMPLE: The objective value of almsgiving lies in the relief it offers to a needy fellow man. From this is derived its essential moral character. But the alms is actually given in a concrete instance to a particular and altogether concrete individual with all the concrete circumstances in which he exists and for an altogether specific motive on the part of the donor. If the latter, for example, manifests no concern at all for the plight of his fellow man and is concerned, let us say, only with some futile motive of self-exaltation or makes of the alms a bribe, then the objective value with which the act of generosity is related is not relief of human misery.

Even though in effect there is actual relief of another's distress, the act is not specified by this object, but by the objective actually intended—to satisfy one's vanity or to gain advantage from bribery, for example. Should the recipient of the alms be an unworthy individual who exploits the sympathy of others to obtain the wherewithal for indolent living or even for vile and sinful purposes, the donor cannot ignore such circumstances on the plea that his motive was to relieve human misery. By the very nature of the case the evil attitude of the recipient vitiates the act of generosity if and when the donor becomes aware of it.

Intrinsically, the objective "value" can be morally good, indifferent, or bad. The value which is in itself morally indifferent can be made morally good or bad through some law commanding it, the situation, or the inner disposition (the intention). An object morally good in itself can become a morally prohibited object here and now because of the situation in which the act is performed. Note this example: the divine cult surely has an exalted value; but when her child is seriously sick and without care at home, a mother may not attend the divine service in Church without neglect of her duty.

Since all created values are situation-centered (this means that they are relative, conditioned by changing circumstances), the acts related to them are not good under any and all circumstances. God alone is absolute, unconditioned, independent of all circumstances. Therefore the acts of the theological virtues in so far as their object is the Uncreated Value, are of themselves under all circumstances intrinsically and unconditionally good. Of course even acts of the theological virtues are human acts and time-structured and may interfere with other acts made necessary by the situation. Hence even such acts directed immediately to the absolute value of God depend on the situation of the one who performs them.

To foster the values of convenience or profit, life, or culture, can be called indifferent or good, as one may look upon them. They are indifferent since they are not universally commanded; they become good through the correct inner spirit with which they are fostered and rightly ordered. It is more correct, however, to say that their cultivation is in itself good. They are values created by God, indeed, and entrusted to man. Therefore, to nurture them is good, assuming that the right order of values and the right stress of values are maintained both in inner spirit and exterior conduct.

Since no material thing is essentially evil, there are strictly no intrinsically evil actions from the standpoint of material values. But material things by their very nature can have only a relative value. It is morally evil to make an absolute of them, to make them ultimate ends. All relative values must be properly subordinated and coordinated in a correct hierarchy of values. To pervert this order is evil.

From the standpoint of the objective of an action, there are evil actions, some of which are intrinsically and unconditionally evil. If an action violates an eternal value which must be preserved under all circumstances, such an action is essentially evil. Note this example: a lie is an essential violation of the value of truth; adultery, an essential violation of the good of fidelity, justice, holiness of the sacramental bond; both are always evil. Killing of a man is not an unconditionally evil action because the bodily life of one's neighbor is not a value which must be preserved under all circumstances. Only the unjustified attack on the life of one's neighbor is always evil.

II. THE UNIVERSAL AND THE INDIVIDUAL

Morality does not flow solely from the universal and essential determinants of the object, but from all the general and particular value characteristics and not least from those relations to total value which are the basis of value, and from the position the object holds in the order of values. The values which are to be fostered or to be realized by our acts are always individual or concrete values, though, of course, they cannot exist without a universal determinant of value. This means that the cultivation of individual values may never conflict with the absolutely and universally valid standard of value.

The universal, man, exists abstractly only in the mind, not in the real order. Only the individual exists in time-space realization of the universal human nature in concrete individual richness. Similarly with our acts. We must cultivate not only the common human value of man as such. The value of the individual must also be fostered and brought to its full perfection. The most general principles of moral theology are inferred from immutable essential properties of man and his essential relation to the totality of being. These general principles must be held as inviolable always and under all circumstances. But only a false notion would lead us to believe that they determine fully and exhaustively the rule and ideal for every action. Universal definitions and essential principles can, of course, determine the frontiers, but they cannot exhaust the unique riches of each individual person. Just as God calls each individual man by his own proper name, so must each individual in his moral activity look upon himself as both bearer and object of unique and incommunicable missions, duties, rights. *"Agere sequitur esse,"* "action follows being." By being we mean the whole of being, the universal essence and the total concrete structure of its individuation. The existent being in itself and in its situation—all this is the measure and standard of action.

III. CIRCUMSTANCES OF ACTION AS DETERMINANTS

OF MORALITY

The principal circumstances which modify the value of action are enumerated in the classic mnemonic verse: *quis, quid, ubi, quibus auxiliis, cur, quomodo, quando.* This means that the kind and degree of moral value of the action depends upon the countless possible characteristics and associations of the person who acts (who, *quis*), of the object (what, *quid*), of the place (where, *ubi*), and the time (when, *quando*), of the ways, means, directives, collaborators, (with what helps, *quibus auxiliis*). The kind and degree of value also depend on the instigations from within and without (*cur,* why) as well as on the manner or mode of the action (*quomodo,* how). Every one of these variable circumstances is a determining factor in the moral structure of the action. Not only is each variable circumstance an influencing factor in itself, but there is also a characteristic coincidence of each with all the others in a common context modifying the moral framework of the action.

The circumstance can augment the moral value or goodness of the act or aggravate its defect of value, its malice, on the same level and thus not change its nature. But it can also be the primary determinant of value or non-value and thus modify the very moral nature of the act. It can transform the act inwardly or merely concomitantly serve to lessen or augment its value.

Especially important are the circumstances which change the species of the moral act, for according to the Council of Trent all mortal sins of which one is conscious must be confessed together with the circumstances which modify the moral species.[33] The reason for this obligation is evident, for the circumstances which change the species of the sin in reality are nothing else than additional sins (in other terms, the violation of another virtue). Should one, to cite a very simple example, confess that he has committed an act of impurity with others, he confesses the sin against the virtue of purity (including cooperation in the sin of others and the scandal), but not the sin against justice and the sacrament which is contained in the sin of adultery.

The aggravating circumstances, which change the "theological" nature of the sin, that is, make of a venial sin a mortal sin, are of the greatest importance (also to be confessed in the sacrament of penance). We have an example in the act of stealing or embezzlement. To steal a great sum of money even from a rich man or a petty sum from a man in great need would be a grave sin, whereas depriving a rich man or even a man of moderate means of a slight sum would not be grave sin. (There are many circumstances which in some way change the sin without changing the moral or theological categories. Surely they are significant in moral theology, but there is no obligation to mention them in confession.)

A brief explanation of the most important kinds of circumstances follows.

Quis (who): not only is the individuality of the agent who acts significant (his character, temperament, talent, sex), but also the degree of perfection he has already attained, his vocation and state (is he a priest, a physician, father of a family?).

Quis quid (who and what): this means the relation of the agent himself to the object of his own act.

Quid (what): this does not really mean a circumstance, but rather the very object of the action. But since a highly diversified and variable relationship exists above all between object and agent, the *"quid"* (what) can also be listed among the circumstances under a certain aspect. Thus if one looks upon the moral value concerned as the object of the action and does not consider the object merely the sensible or perceptible object in its materiality, then this latter may be placed among the circumstances. An example of the object of the action in acts of chastity or acts in violation of chastity would be the virtue itself or the violation. But we should then make a distinction between object and circumstance in relation to this object. There is a distinction of circumstance between the violation of the same virtue through sinning with an innocent child and sinning with one already perverted by such sins.

Ubi (where): the place in which the action occurs can be important for the value or non-value of the action. A contract of sale in itself good may be made in a church, in the market place, or in a place which an honorable man may not enter. A murder committed in a church or consecrated place takes on the character of sacrilege.

Quando (when): the time in which the action takes place can be important. To work on a Sunday or holy day of obligation without sufficient reason is sinful. To devote time to prayer when others have need for our help may be sinful rather than virtuous.

Quibus auxiliis (auxiliary helps): the words refer to the means used in the performance of the act or the cooperators in the act. (In the pejorative sense we use the term of those who are accessory to the sins of others. They are not free from guilt.) Even the good end or purpose can in no wise justify the use of evil means (cf. ROM 3:8). In this instance, not only the employment of sinful means would be sinful, but the intended result itself would partake of the malice of the means used. Not only is the malice of means not mitigated by the moral loftiness of the end sought, but the very wickedness of the means may be aggravated. If, for example, one were tempted to further the kingdom of God through lies and deception, he should be made to realize that such base procedure is more pernicious than to further secular projects by the same vile methods. However, it must also be borne in mind that error and lack of reflection can mitigate the guilt.

The incessant accusation that "Jesuitical morality" upholds the false doctrine that the good end justifies any means, rests on malicious calumny or misconception of facts. The Jesuit moralist Busenbaum did indeed defend the proposition, *"cum finis est licitus, etiam media sunt licita,"*[34] if the end is lawful also the means are lawful, in his *Medulla theologica moralis.* But this simply means that in the entire context, if the end is good, the means which naturally correspond to the end are also good and worthy. And this doctrine is correct. If eternal salvation is the end to which man is destined, it follows that all the means necessary for his eternal salvation must also be good and commanded. Similarly, if one is obliged to safeguard one's health, then the natural means of preserving health are also lawful.

Cur (why): the urge from without (enticement, threat, coercion) must be taken into consideration in the appraisal of responsibility. The mode or manner of the action is also to be noted (*quomodo,* in what manner). It is a particularly important circumstance if we include under it, as some authors do (see *La Loi du Christ,* I, 422f.) the effect of an action which is not intended, though it is foreseen or should be foreseen. This is called the indirect voluntary. Unforeseen effects of the act increase neither merit nor culpability except when absence of such foresight is due to culpable neglect. However, if evil results from the action as such, and hence not solely from an unhappy chain of circumstances and the faults of others, this effect, if it should be foreseen, cannot be characterized as involuntary or unintentional. And the reason is apparent. One who intends the cause intends and wills also the effect which is intrinsically bound up with the cause.

Often an evil effect is not the result of the act itself as such, though it is foreseen as practically certain to follow under a given set of circumstances. We have an example in the case of a woman who knows that her husband is readily aroused by her acts of piety. He will resort to vile and profane language if she attends Mass or religious service. A more significant example is that of material cooperation. One's own act is not evil and has no intrinsically evil effect, but one knows that under the concrete circumstances concerned one's fellow man will misuse it, making it the means for evil purpose. (By contrast, in formal cooperation one's action of itself is to be characterized as an influence, as partial cause of an evil effect which must be avoided. Wherefore it is evil, although the agent himself may deplore the evil effect.)

The following principles establish a rule of conduct in this matter of cooperation:

FIRST PRINCIPLE: It is never permitted, directly or indirectly, to cooperate in an act which is in itself evil, even though one anticipates the very greatest good as result of the act.

SECOND PRINCIPLE: There is no universal obligation to omit a good or indifferent act because of the evil effects which it may also have because of the hazard of circumstance or the malice of others. But there must be a proportionate (this means in relation to the evil effects which are feared) reason for performing such an action. If such were not the case, the agent would show that he does not sufficiently abhor the evil result and therefore would have to be held responsible as though he intended the evil.

THIRD PRINCIPLE: If no relatively higher good (one's own salvation or that of others, justice toward a third party) is at stake, ordinarily love of neighbor, zeal for the kingdom of God, and frequently justice itself command us to omit actions which will have foreseen but unintended evil effects.

FOURTH PRINCIPLE: The obligation to prevent or avoid the unintended evil effects of our actions is all the more urgent, 1) the more baneful the effect can be, 2) the more directly and immediately it flows from our action, 3) the more the duties of our state of life or of our vocation command us to prevent such evil effects.

EXAMPLES: The physician is not guilty of any sin if in the performance of his duty he examines a woman patient, though he is aware that he will experience sexual excitement, assuming of course that he neither intends to have such experience nor consents to it, and also that he exercises the necessary precaution to avoid yielding to it. Similarly a priest is not guilty of sin in administering the Holy Eucharist to a penitent to whom he denied absolution in the sacrament of penance if refusal to give Holy Communion would be a violation of the sacramental seal of secrecy. It is not a sin to kill an insane man in order to ward off an attack on one's life or on the life of another, provided that the direct purpose of the killing is no more than a justifiable defense of one's own life or that of the third party, not the killing of the fanatical attacker, and that the defensive action does not exceed the actual requirements of self-defense.

Killing a man through careless driving is culpable if the driver can reasonably foresee the possibility of the misfortune and still neglects to take the necessary precautions against it. However, a hunter would not be guilty of sin if, despite all the customary rules of prudent caution, he shot a human being whom he mistook for an animal, because he did not foresee the evil result of his act.

A pregnant woman is guilty of sin if in illness not constituting a danger of death she makes use of remedies which are capable of restoring her health but at the same time of endangering the life of the child through miscarriage (third principle). Doubly guilty, of course, would be the direct effort to produce the miscarriage for the purpose of freeing the cruel mother of the burden of caring for the infant (first principle).

The evil effect can be permitted, however, if in extreme danger of death for the mother a remedy is applied or an operation is performed to save her, which directly and immediately combats the disease and only mediately or indirectly creates a risk of miscarriage for the infant (second principle). On the contrary, even in the most extreme danger to the life of the mother, it is never allowed directly to cause or to intend a miscarriage (first principle).

IV. ESSENTIALISTIC ETHIC, CASUISTRY, SITUATION ETHIC

Actualistic philosophy,[35] which is an offshoot of existentialism, dissolves the permanent essence or substance into a series of individual discontinuous acts not linked with any substratum of essence. This system accentuates the singularity and incommunicability of the individual person, of the individual act, and, above all, of the individual situation. For that matter a theistic morality must also stress such singularity, for it looks upon each individual person as addressed by the ineffably holy God and called by his own personal name. But this latter kind of individuality is consistent with the continuity of the individual in his acts and also with his participation in all being. It in no way severs his bond with all other things, especially not with those having the same nature.

All the modern philosophical trends exercise a profound influence on contemporary moral teaching, at least in the mode of presentation and the manner of emphasis. In part, modern situation ethics represents in effect a reaction against an all too rigidly rationalistic ethic of essences, an ethic which was not able, in its knowledge of the essence identical in all and in the fixed and permanent bond of obligation, to recognize that which lies beyond, namely, that which is irreplaceable and non-transferable in the individual and in the situation. Such biased perspective ill served the good and sound moral system based on the study of essences (morality of fundamental principles). In consequence of such bias, stability and solidity paid the price of impoverishment, inflexibility, and aloofness from reality. Nevertheless, a general ethic of essences is indispensable. Even outside the Church today, such an ethic is not without honor and is found in the form of material value ethic: there are values, fixed, constantly exigent, substantial; and as a result there are also fixed objective laws, because there are constant and permanent essences. At this center of universal validity the scholastic ethic of essence, the contemporary value ethic, and the ethic of constant law all meet, no matter how utterly diverse their points of departure.

In its entire history Catholic moral doctrine never confined itself exclusively to the study of the permanent nature of man and the goods, values, and laws which have a claim on him. The multiplicity of morally significant circumstances was also taken into account, with the result that the need for casuistry was clearly recognized. It is the specific and characteristic concern of casuistry to study all these circumstances, their meaning, their mutual relation, their relative importance for a proper appreciation of the moral act. There is, of course, the hazard that on the one hand casuistry might overemphasize the circumstances and thus neglect or seriously slight objective values and principles. On the other hand, the casuistic method might create the impression in the minds of some that casuistic analysis of the various circumstantial determinants is final and ultimate in the individual concrete instance. In reality, casuistry belongs altogether to essentialistic ethics which it enlarges and expands through a wealth of incidentals, diverse but constantly recurring.

Casuistry is part of the ethic of essences, for even the circumstances which are accidents are presented with the same essential and universal validity as the substance. At best, casuistry features the typical among the many, for even in practice it can have an insight only into what is typical in particular cases. But beyond lies the irreducible (which is therefore not to be judged by inference from anything else) of each individual situation, the meeting of a unique individual man in the special context of given circumstances.

Catholic moral teaching has never failed in the clarity of its insights into the practical moral situations with their wealth of meaning and constant challenge to analysis and research. This has been spelt out in the treatment of the virtue of prudence. True insight, full understanding of the individual situation is possible only through the supernatural tact of conscience and the influence of the infused gifts of the Holy Spirit. But from the scientific point of view morality based on principles and casuistry must prepare the way for the judgment of prudence in the particular situation. Thus a study of nature itself, which is constant and universal, and the typical or characteristic circumstance form a sound basis for the judgment of prudence which is never permitted to conflict with universally valid principles and the constant type in practice, but still in some manner expresses something going beyond them.

An extreme form of situation ethics is proposed by the Protestant Eberhard Griesbach.[36] He rejects every species of permanence of nature, but unconsciously and somewhat deviously he at least comes to an essential relation, which is to be the basis of the so-called irreducible conduct: to an I-Thou relation. And thus finally he also establishes a permanent principle valid in all cases: to be open to the dialogue with the Thou and thus oppose the malice of the I, which threatens to develop its tendencies contrary to the law.[37]

With perfect candor Karl Rahner traces similar trends in the framework of Catholic thought. Though he recognizes the basis for the claims of situation ethics, with true discernment he rejects the false claims of such an ethic and its hostility toward the ethic of essences: "Since it is true, and in so far as it is true, that the individual is not merely an instance of the universal human nature (which he also is), but is likewise a unique and incommunicable individual, therefore and to such an extent he also has a task and a summons. Since this cannot be submitted to him univocally through universal norms and commands, it is made known uniquely through an individual function of conscience. For the simple reason that each of us exists as an individual concretely, there is an ethic of the singular and a corresponding function of conscience. But since the singular and unique in each man does not remove that which is common in man, but rather centers in the universal human, there is an individual ethic only within the framework of a common normative ethic (this is surely also real, a point which is only too often overlooked).

"It is a normal thing that the Christian conscience attain maturity in the individual, also in the layman. That is as should be. . . . But this maturity of the Christian conscience does not consist in an emancipation. It is not shuffling off the universal norm proclaimed by the gospel and the Church through an appeal to a unique situation and the rights of one's own conscience. Spiritual maturity is an autonomous capacity to apply these norms to one's own concrete situation . . . a capacity to discern one's Christian duties and tasks even in trying situations. Because of their abstract and universal nature, even the custodians of the norms in the Church's pastoral office may find it difficult or even impossible to point out how they are to be applied practically and concretely here and now. Spiritual maturity should make the Christian individual himself capable of applying the universally enunciated norms personally even in such perplexing situations."[38]

V. SITUATION, CONSCIENCE, PRUDENCE, GIFTS OF THE HOLY SPIRIT

We are next confronted with the question: how, through what faculty or in virtue of what gift, does the Christian recognize the claim of the unique situation? The situation is unfolded before us through our recognition of the essential exigencies of being and the eternally valid moral principles. Thus the knowledge of the Christian moral doctrine clearly presents the framework in which the situation is to be studied. Excluded is any insight which would radically conflict with the spirit of Christ.

But the insight into the situation does not merely stop short of contradiction of the spirit of Christ; it must positively penetrate into and claim the full reality and respond to all the claims and demands of the moment. Only the virtue of prudence is equal to this demand of the situation, for prudence is nothing else than the profound and vital approach to the concrete reality and its claim upon us. Therefore, the virtue of prudence presupposes a deep and conscious intimacy with real life. But such insight is not possible without an idea of the great laws of the real order and their moral exigency. But only that man is truly prudent (grown to full stature of reality) who possesses also an intimacy with the good, who conaturally harkens to its call from the heart of the real.

The shrewd man has the capacity to view reality in the light of his own plans and purposes. The prudent man is just as alert, but he discerns in the course of terrestrial events how to place all things in the service of the good, ultimately in the service of God. The virtue of prudence reaches perfection only with the aid of the gifts of the Holy Spirit, which impart

sensitivity for the inner impulses of divine grace and at the same time
bestow alertness for the challenge of the hour of decision. Only through
the gifts of the Holy Spirit does prudence penetrate to the very heart of
reality: then the soul hears the loving voice of God in all things and
accepts the invitation to the childlike service of love. Only the gifts of the
Holy Spirit make our knowledge Christ-formed so that we, through
profound intimacy with Him, in some measure penetrate reality and its
demand on us with the eyes of Christ.

Because of the power of the gifts of the Holy Spirit we do not face
reality as something devoid of life. We face the living God who speaks
to us both exteriorly through created things and interiorly through His
gifts. Therefore, the gifts of the Holy Spirit do not in any way make us
neglect the voice of reality (and, in consequence, of prudence) as though
we directly and without the test of reality submitted interiorly to the voice
of the Holy Spirit. This can be a rare and singular mode of operation
of the Holy Spirit. But ordinarily the gifts (above all wisdom and counsel)
follow a continuous and progressive procedure and are based on the virtue
of prudence.

The gifts of the Holy Spirit complete and perfect prudence particularly
in regard to right knowledge of self, to "the testing of spirits," affecting
us through profound movements and impulses. We arrive at perfect
prudence only through docility to the guidance of grace by the Holy
Spirit, and through such prudence we become foresighted and discerning
in the face of the manifold corrupt insinuations of our fallen nature and
the evil spirit.

Another question arises. What function does conscience assume in
regard to the situation, especially the perplexing and extraordinary situation seriously concerned with salvation? In the tract on conscience we
already rejected the notion that the individual conscience is a kind of
oracle. Now we see that the voice of conscience, if it be correct and
perfect, is in reality a judgment of prudence or, as the case may be, a
result of the guidance of the Holy Spirit. Of course not every judgment
of conscience flows from perfect prudence (still less from the gift of the
Spirit). The conscientious man is called upon to inform himself regarding
the limits of his own prudence, and not rely exclusively on his own judgment or be stubborn and intransigent if his own prudence fails him in
individual instances or is not equal to his moral needs. The truly prudent
man will not scorn the advice of more prudent and competent men. He

will not depend altogether on his own natural awareness, but will rather pray for the assistance of the Holy Spirit and neglect no source of counsel.

Of course if one should have exhausted every resource of prudence, it can happen that the subjectively binding judgment of conscience fails to measure up to the demand of reality (and hence to the perfection of prudence). The voice of prudence is therefore always the voice of conscience (in so far as there is a question of duty), yet the voice of conscience unfortunately is not always the voice of perfect prudence. Where prudence fails to be effective, there is no judgment of conscience, but pure illusion and self-deception.

VI. SITUATION AND PLANNING THE FUTURE

Since man is rational by nature and possessed of a fixed and determined end, he must also live according to a plan. In so far as he directs his whole life to a fixed end (the acquisition of eternal salvation, progress in love), he must estimate the means which are available and with plan in mind set himself to his purposes and tasks (cf. Lk 14:28ff.). If he does not proceed in this manner, he cannot be regarded either as prudent or as constant and reliable. But planning with the forces at hand in each instance always exposes man to the danger of inflexibility and self-importance. Ever and anon God must strike down, as far as the means and methods are concerned, our most cherished plans for the future in order that we may learn, not to seek our own will, but to realize that perfection consists in the readiness to accept what God wills.

Loyalty to self, firm adherence to principle, constancy of mind must unite with an ever-ready openness of attitude toward the unforeseen and varying demands of the moment. What is demanded of us today for personal perfection and promotion of the kingdom of God may prove a real obstacle under different circumstances and eventually may have to be abandoned (for example, many ascetical practices). What we learn from the current situation as the will of God must be done indeed; what appears as the will of God for tomorrow must be planned beforehand and under certain conditions prepared for, but always with the willingness to look for new dispositions and directives from God. Any other kind of planning for the future is not in accordance with the lesson of the situation as the hour of grace given by God, and only serves illusive vain glory (cf. Jas 4:13ff.). In our plans for the future a constant openness to the varying demands of the situation is nothing less than the right attitude toward God's providence. It is constant conformity of our human planning with the divine design in the order of nature and grace.

VII. COMMAND AND COUNSEL, COMMAND AND VOCATION

The diversity and individuality of men and situations are responsible for a uniqueness of duty and obligation for different individuals and diverse situations. This individualization gives rise, not merely to counsel which should be followed, but frequently also to strict duty and obligation which can be as binding as a universal command. Human society, especially the Church, such is its essential organic character, must fall back on individual distribution of services. "For as the body is one and has many members, and all the members of the body, many as they are, form one body, so also is it with Christ . . . God has set the members, each of them, in the body as he willed. Now if they were all one member, where would the body be?" (1 Cor 12:12ff.)

The universal command or law, by its very essence, is directed to community or universality, binding all. Counsel would no longer be counsel if it would oblige the entire community or universality. The "evangelical counsels" and all that is recommended in divine revelation without being actually commanded (either to be carried out in accordance with a strict precept or to be used as a means to attain an end which we are obliged to strive for) are proposed to all Christians as matters which in themselves are counseled.

The question remains for the individual in every instance: is all this really of counsel for him in his concrete situation? Indeed, in view of his powers and his special duties in life, the counsel can prove an obstacle and morally hazardous, and therefore not at all to be counseled. Rather one might be advised to pursue a contrary course. If, for example, one possesses no aptitude for a life of virginity or perfect chastity, it would be not merely inadvisable, but even sinful, under such circumstances to oblige oneself on one's own initiative to this exalted state of life. On the other hand, one may clearly see that precisely the call to priesthood or religion or some other special state offers the opportunity to carry out an important task or assignment for the Kingdom of God and that God has equipped him precisely for such activity. Or he may prudently judge that only through following the evangelical counsels can he save himself from grave danger to his soul's salvation. If the grace of God has led one to such insight, it seems reasonable to hold that the word of the Lord applies strictly: "Let him accept it who can" (Mt 19:12).

"Those to whom it has been given" (Mt 19:11) refers to those whom God has granted the special gift of grace, unique individual endowments, and the clear realization of a vocation. Such are strictly obliged to co-operate faithfully and gratefully with the grace of God. (It goes without saying that we do not assume without qualification that failure to follow the call is always a mortal sin.)

Great is the Church's concern to preserve and protect the freedom of choice in the vocation to sacerdotal or religious life. But it is not at all her mind that the clearly recognized call of grace can be ignored as though it imposes no obligation at all, on the pretext that surely there is "no law" in this matter, as though the guidance and directive of grace were not the most actual of laws for the genuine disciple of Christ. Precisely on this point does the pure "legal" morality part ways with the morality of grace.

In his encyclical letter on the Catholic priesthood, Pius XI says: "A long and painful experience teaches that a betrayed vocation (let no one consider the term too harsh!) is a source of tears."[39] Above all we must declare that the disposition, the motive, which turns one away from a clearly recognized vocation cannot be good. "Anyone who fails to harken to the divine call because of laziness will not be found guiltless on the day of judgment."[40] After he has explained the usual motives which can lead to a rejection of a clearly discerned call from God, Saint Bernard says: "This is the wisdom of the flesh and the devil, hostility to salvation, the throttling of life, the mother of laxity, which awakens the divine wrath. Guard yourself! Great is that which is offered to you. The more joyfully and eagerly is it to be grasped."[41]

The true disciple of Christ fashions his life not merely according to the commandments with their inviolable obligation affecting him as they do every other man. He is also guided by the counsels. In consequence, he will harken to the call of the hour. He will show concern for the needs of the kingdom of God and the needs of his fellow men. And with intimate and tender susceptibility to the inner guidance of grace and the stern test of his own powers for good he will always choose that which God has specially preferred for him. It is love, precisely love, and the personal relation to Christ, which grants us such alertness to the voice of God. If the Christian, after serious examination of his powers and motives and after humble prayer for guidance, does not recognize a clear call to a particular vocation, whatever it may be, there can be no question of any obligation.

The traditional teaching persistently inculcated since the patristic age on the subject of the obligation of the clearly recognized "vocation" to a life of the evangelical counsels also holds (for the same reasons) for the whole domain of the counsels and individual gifts of grace and duties. Each individual must use all his gifts according to the powers given him (compare Mt 25:14ff.). He must cooperate with every grace, follow the path laid out for him by the very nature and condition of things. "Each man has before him the picture of that which he should be. As long as he is not this, he does not possess the fulness of peace" (Friedrich Rueckert). What is admirable in a particular saint is not to be counseled universally for every other man if it is not his vocation.

This concept of things, as we have explained it, not only does not contradict the spirit of freedom. It is the very expression of the exigence of the true freedom of the children of God, for whom deeds of love and the guidance of grace through the special divine providence are actually the law. Of course it must be stressed all the more emphatically that the whole domain of counsel and the sphere of the individual is not to be reduced to legal restrictions, but rather excludes all coercion and judgment from without.

The term "works of supererogation" (*opera supererogatoria*) nevertheless has a profound meaning by comparison with that which is demanded by the universal prescriptive commandments and in the light of the plenitude of grace which brings forth these works and gives them the promise of "superabundant" merit. The Christian who cooperates with complete loyalty with divine grace and uses all his natural and supernatural gifts in the service of God will always look upon himself with increasing humility as an "unworthy servant." He will never feel that he has offered God anything of "supererogation," never anything beyond what he owes (cf. Lk 17:7–10).

As to the controversy on the point of obligation concerning the following of the "evangelical counsels" or a special vocation, which is not the object of a universal law and demanded of all men, it is asked whether the counsel or special vocation can become an obligation in conscience for any individual. But the very question presented in this way insinuates the legalistic manner of presentation of moral questions. For the mere legal-minded man who has not at all placed himself under the regime of the

Holy Spirit the question of the obligation of a counsel is a species of false problem, which is answered before it is really presented. On the contrary, one who really has made the actual law of the New Testament, the inner law of grace, his own law does not approach the problem in any legalistic sense at all. The problem is not posited under the bare aspect of a legalistic form: is there an obligation under pain of sin or not?

Just as we cannot speak truly of the freedom of the children of God regarding those whose whole activity is under the constraint and threat of law, so also the question regarding the obligation of following the counsels is actually a question only after a certain level of the truly spiritual life has been attained. If irreplaceable vocations are frequently lost for the kingdom of God, the cause is not ordinarily a brusk rejection of the divine call, a direct sin against the vocation, but a longer series of failures in the spirit of docility toward all the impulses of divine grace.

The clear recognition of vocation ordinarily presupposes a filial attitude toward the guidance of divine grace. If the budding vocation never comes to flower, if there is no clear awareness of the call, then the question of obligation never properly arises to confront the conscience. In consequence, there can be no direct sin against one's "vocation." The failure is rather of a more general nature. If a vocation manifests itself through the movement of special grace, then the knowledge of it presupposes the existence of a docility and adaptability toward the guidance of this very grace. But this also means essentially that the question regarding an obligation in such a conception of things arises from the spirit of the freedom of the children of God, and not from fear.

However, once the vocation has been discerned and accepted, the question regarding the obligation to follow a counsel or, more particularly, the divine call may arise in the form of a temptation. If the individual has already bound himself by a sacred pledge or promise, then the question of vocation presents itself from the standpoint of the law of loyalty, of reverence to God. If he has not bound himself, there is still the question of fidelity to an earnest resolution by which he has once given his inner yes to grace. But should one who has recognized the call have descended to the mere legal level of moral life, so that he permits himself to be driven more through fear and law, then from this standpoint there is no longer reason to think either of a real vocation or of an obligation under sin to follow what is only counseled, although there may be question of a legally definable obligation on the basis of a vow, or of an office one has assumed, or of a serious peril to one's salvation.

Abstracting from any legal obligation, the imperative based on a vocation once recognized and then become burdensome because of lukewarmness does not, properly speaking, consist of a legal obligation to follow that which is merely counseled as such. There is rather an obligation to assume the attitude toward God of adopting the directives of grace as the actual law of the spiritual life. The lapse from the heights of spiritual freedom of the children of God in which there was the loving discernment of the special call and mission of grace to the level of the legalistic attitude in the spirit of the carnal man cannot occur without disloyalty to God's grace, and this means it involves the commission of sin. Wherefore we may well say that the story of lost vocation is always the tale of many spiritual faults, lesser or greater sins, which can be clearly shown to violate the norms of the universal commandments.

The obligation to heed the special call is not to be placed in the class of purely legal prescriptions—this is quite evident—nor should the question be studied abstractly as an isolated problem. What is truly obligatory for the child of God is openness to the special needs of one's fellows in every instance, openness to the great concerns of the Kingdom of God, and above all docility to the inner guidance of grace, which alerts us to a realization of the gracious will of God for us in the whole ensemble of the interior and exterior situation. Once this general attitude is present, then the power of clearly discerning the particular vocation will not fail us. Then, too, one will see in clear perspective the long chain of rich graces which led up to this condition and knowledge. The true child of God does not heedlessly pass by or ignore the special love of God.

The individual is also directly confronted by what is counseled. But if he should recognize clearly in what is counsel for men in general the way prescribed for him by the loving providence of God, then he must make the final decision in the face of the alternative: shall he abandon himself with the fullest trust to the divine guidance or have recourse to the general law in opposition to the call of special grace?

"As soon as one clearly realizes that God has called him for a particular mission, let it be called what it will, that which is in itself only a counsel becomes for him an inescapable duty."[42] "There is no mere counsel in the individual concrete instance, that is, after consideration of all the special circumstances in each instance. And hence the one called by a special vocation, the one invited by such grace, may be guilty of sin, not because he does those lawful acts which run counter to the counsels, but because of non-compliance with the counsel itself, since he is called to compliance with it, invited to it. Many a one, however, is guiltless because of special conditions and circumstances which are such that he would sin against other duties if he should follow the evangelical counsels."[43]

There are ecclesiastical writers, however, who maintain that the counsel contains no obligation, either for the generality of men or for the particular individual to whom the grace is offered: "No one is obliged to practice the evangelical counsels, but every one is obliged to love and to honor these counsels."[44] And yet practically all these authors stress the point that "on the other hand, however, there is no counsel which could not under certain circumstances become a duty for the individual. I realize, for example, that I cannot save my soul in the world outside of a religious order and I am bound to enter a religious order. But still, even in such a case it is not the counsel as such which is binding."[45]

Characteristic of this attitude which views the counsel as not obligatory even for the individual to whom the special grace is offered but only "on account of accessory circumstances" is the explanation of O. Zimmermann.[46] This writer offers so many plausible instances in which the counsel can become obligatory because of special circumstances that we can hardly find anything further to add to them. Over and above all this he holds, and many others agree with him, that the rejection of a counsel by the one specially called is in itself an "imperfection." "Imperfection means the omission of the fulfillment of counsel . . . and usually it is the act by which one transgresses a divine counsel."[47] "Although the imperfections are not sins, they still are opposed to the true will of God and to the divine good pleasure . . . the saints repent of them as of sins. God punishes the saints severely for these faults. He reproaches them sternly in His mystical converse with them."[48]

For our part we mean the same when we term this disobedience "venial sin." The distinction is largely theoretical. The opinion just referred to attaches great importance to the point that sin is limited to opposition to some universal law, whereas the teaching we defend sees the essence of sin not merely in such opposition to universal law. It is found, above all, in opposition to the new law of the "Spirit of the life in Christ Jesus" (Rom 8:2) as rendering the inner grace fruitless and sterile. But this view must also take into account the external circumstances and, above all, also the inner energies and needs of the individual who is called. For God's inner guidance forms a whole with His external providence. On the other hand, even the proponents of the opinion that the divine vocation to that which is only counseled does not oblige in itself, concede that the divine call can transcend the external conditions and circumstances and that God can directly present a counsel to an individual with all the force of command.[49]

This entire problem of the relation between command and counsel reaches the stage of full clarification only in the light of the problem of the choice of the more perfect: is the Christian always obliged to the choice of the more perfect good?

Every Christian, regardless of his state of life, is obliged to strive for perfection. Inwardly through the life in Christ every Christian is directed toward an increasingly more profound and radical imitation of the Master. For every Christian the great commandment of love is imposed as a strictly obligatory end and ideal to be striven for. The new law of love demands from everyone that he at all times avoid doing anything contrary to Christian love, or transgressing any of the universal precepts. The new law of grace which is formulated in the commandment of love further demands that no one cease striving for its perfect fulfillment.

Yet despite all this, there is no universal obligation in conscience to do that which is most perfect in itself, always and in every individual instance. "The law of the Spirit of the life in Christ Jesus" (Rom 8:2) is a law of progress. It would even be presumptuous for the novice in the Christian life to attempt that which is always the most perfect without a special and clear indication of God's will and the special challenge of the circumstances as a divine sign. For truly that which is in itself the most perfect only One could never fail to accomplish and fulfill: Christ.

Every Christian, however, is bound to do that which he himself, with the aid of God's grace, realizes to be most conformable to his state and his powers. Should anyone with the help of divine grace arrive at the prudential judgment that a particular action or choice of vocation is, according to all evidence, the most suitable for him, he is not truly prudent or truly submissive and docile toward the interior Teacher, the Holy Spirit, if he still chooses what is obviously less suitable for him. This holds good whether the object be the more perfect or the less perfect. Quite frequently, however, there is question not merely of one particular act or choice, but of a veritable multitude of possibilities with very little to differentiate them. Where no clear and express differentiation can be made, only personal initiative can be responsible for a decision without fear of disobedience to God's guidance.

Should nagging anxiety to choose the more perfect always and in every instance create in an individual a hazard to the spirit of interior freedom, he would have to choose for a time, with full awareness and of set purpose, that which is in itself the less perfect (though never anything in itself evil) in order to safeguard his spiritual life against anxiety and scrupulosity. In such an instance, the less perfect becomes for him the most perfect, so long as his will remains fixed in the determination never to be deflected from striving for the perfect love of God.

The spirit of the freedom of the children of God is totally alien both to caprice and to anxiety. It blossoms most richly where the Christian nourishes only one passion, namely, in all things to discern and accomplish the loving purposes of God with childlike trust and without a trace of craven fear.

To lag behind the Christian ideal consciously and deliberately, to neglect consciously and deliberately actions which one clearly recognizes as most conformable to one's spiritual condition, is more appropriately termed, not a mere "imperfection," but "sin."[50] To resolve, as a matter of principle, not to strive for perfection in the love of God and neighbor constitutes an absolute peril to our salvation. The conscious omission of what is concretely the more perfect in the individual instance for the one concerned is in itself and as such only a venial sin. This is true if we view the matter in a general way, but where a general precept binding in conscience is involved or where the special circumstances give rise to a common obligation, there is mortal sin.

There remains the vast area of mere "imperfections."[51] Mere imperfection is defect in striving for the ideal of the Gospel in our dispositions and actions without any deliberate fault on our part. Above all, imperfections are the many perverted acts contrary to the commands of God, in so far as the defect in them is not due to any guilty act, but rather to an outcropping of a general state of imperfection. The many petty and ill-regulated and secondary motives which insinuate themselves somewhat obliquely into our best acts, even though we are not aware of them, are imperfections, but not sins. They are sins at worst in their root, in so far as the divine appeal to us for a more profound interior conversion of our hearts was previously neglected or delayed.

God does not punish mere imperfections as such, for punishment implies actual guilt. He purges His children of their imperfections in loving mercy through crosses and sufferings. On the contrary, as the saints testify, He punishes the conscious rejection of the movement of His special graces. Truly His punishment is in turn in the ultimate instance a grace, a purifying visitation of the beloved soul.

Though the particular act viewed subjectively is in no way a sin, but only an imperfection, it still may be traced to our sins. Often it has its roots in some way in an actual previous culpable defect or in the guilt of another, and is for this reason displeasing to God. Subsequent recognition of this type of imperfection is always a divine summons to reflection and humility.

CHAPTER SEVEN

THE MORAL MOTIVE

I. SIGNIFICANCE OF THE MOTIVE FOR
MORAL VALUE OF ACTION

As we have already explained, that which first determines the moral value of an action is the object. This means that one must first of all act in conformity with reality. Action is entirely good morally only if it is in conformity with value given or value realized. It is evil if it does not tend to be in harmony with the object. We have likewise made clear that it is not the objective value or content of the object simply in its own being-in-itself which determines the value of the act, but only in so far as it is discerned or should be discerned. Objective value or non-value of the action passes over to the human act only when it is really discerned in the act and also in some way sought as the end of the act, or, in other words, only when the motive corresponds to the objective value or the content of the object. Object, therefore, demands the corresponding motive.

If one were to inquire which exerts the greater influence on the value of the action, the object or the motive, we should answer that the object is the matter, the motive is the form or soul animating the matter. But it must not be forgotten that the object (objective content) of the action itself must possess a value or be value-formed prior to the act. Accordingly, the value structure in the object itself safeguards the motive against failure to conform with reality and assures its objective soundness. In this sense we should say that the object is primary. But what is ultimately decisive beyond the value of the act is precisely the objective rectitude of the motive.

The correlated concepts, disposition and motive, belong together, though they cannot be absolutely equated. Disposition becomes motive in so far as it is directed to the reason or purpose of the action. Disposition is broader than motive, for according to its concept the motive is directed entirely to the action, whereas the disposition is not exhausted in setting the action into motion and in "motivating" it.

Our Christian teaching on dispositions has shown that it is not the materiality of the external act, but strictly the "heart" or disposition which is the source of good as well as of evil. Similarly it is true that the motive imparts the ultimate form for the moral value of the action, although of course we should not overlook the fact that the objective correctness of motive is to be judged by the object of the action.

The world of values already exists with its appeal to the good before the action. But it is the motive which is charged with the basic meaning and is the effective motive power turning to the good in each instance in so far as it is freely chosen as the moving cause of the action. Since the motive ultimately determines both external choice and inner value of the action, vigilant concern regarding our motives is a basic task of our moral life.

Motives are awakened within us through our encounter with the values in the world about us, although our desires and instincts also exert an influence. In the motives arising within us our profound attitudes and intimate aspirations, consciously or unconsciously, are expressed. New motives due to effort and tension are less numerous than the spontaneous forces arising from the hidden depths of our heart. Especially as long as good and bad sentiments are in sharp conflict with one another, one must persist in the conscious vigilance over one's motives and constantly submit them to test and proof. Lasting success in this matter is possible only if one keeps before one's eyes the eternally valid standard of values: only one who walks before God, who constantly stands in the light of faith, will recognize in their full clear meaning his own motives and their moral value. Since undisciplined evil tendencies always engender the blindness of self-deception, one must always resort to the spirit of self-abnegation as the best of aids in the probing of one's motives.

II. ON THE PSYCHOLOGY OF MOTIVE

To impart energy and rectitude to the will in the spiritual life, the possession of a dominant motive is truly decisive. The force and drive of particular motives is sustained in great part through attachment to the motivation as a whole. There is more involved than a fundamental and ultimate decision for good or evil. There is question also of the special form which the ideal assumes, of the *leitmotif*. The example of the saints offers a vast wealth of such ideal goals: one sees everything in the light of the divine glory (the motivating ideal: "all to the honor and glory of God"); another thinks only of the Kingdom of God; another lives only for the imitation of the crucified Christ or the salvation of souls; some saints—such was their temperament and their past experience—fixed their eyes on the abyss of horrors which is hell, with the dread possibility in mind that they might be estranged from the love of God; conversely, there were saints who constantly looked forward, serenely and jubilantly, with expectation of the heavenly bliss; some were consumed with the thought of self-oblation as victims for the conversion of sinners or with the fire of zeal in furthering the kingdom of God.

The dominant ideal or the ideal of life coordinates all the particular ideals or motives, imprints upon them the stamp of its own character, imparts its own particular color, its force, its depth, its spiritual rhythm. A concern for this point is significant in the education of one's self spiritually as well as in the education of others in the spiritual life. For the effective existence and adaptability of the particular motive in relation to particular virtues is assured only if the motive is embedded in the more fundamental ideal of life, in the *leitmotif*.

In all this, however, one must caution against the formation of a rigid system excluding all the motive forces which cannot be made to fit in with it. But a system, a totality, an organic coordination of all the particular motives in the grand basic ideal of spiritual life is a goal which must absolutely be sought. The entire wealth of motivation in the spiritual life is measured and sustained throughout by its coordination with a consistent and rightly ordered ideal as one's goal.

The unique form of the ideal of spiritual life or basic motivation is essentially keyed to the age, sex, temperament, character, and position in life. The educator may do no more than suggest to his disciple an ideal which has an appeal for him and which in the light of his individuality and particular situation is in conformity with God's special call to him. Point of departure must be the existing potentialities for good in the disciple, the already existing effective motives animating him in so far as they are capable of moral elevation. But it should be noted that the most perfect motive is not the most effective in every instance and in every situation.

It is very important to realize how the motive is grasped so that it may be placed before the individual properly. Some are easily influenced by appeals to sentiment; others, by intellectual arguments. But the emotional values should not be underestimated in the matter of motivation, particularly not when great obstacles stand in our way. Only great enthusiasm enables us to marshal all our forces and set them to work for the good. Nevertheless, if the hard core of reason, the meaningful content of motive is not clearly in evidence, so that the mind can be impressed and the reason readily assimilated, the enthusiasm engendered by emotion and vivid imagination is like a brilliant flare suddenly lighting up the darkness and as suddenly dying down again.

The motive must be vividly impressed on mind and memory in the form of an idea or at least of an image rich in sense. The motive most safely abides in memory, available for practical application, if it is rightly enveloped in the totality of motivation with a clear perception, as far as this is possible, of the practical opportunities for application to good. This can be effected most readily in meditation or instruction by reference to the opportunities which one can prudently foresee will arise in the future.[52]

It would be a grave error in the education of youth to neglect entirely the many secondary motives, whether it be because of our concern for the basic motive itself or for the sake of the lofty ideal of purity and moral unity in the spiritual life.

Obviously, the morally baser motives must be uprooted from the soul, but not the more lowly and ordinary motives, such as respect, social concern, honor, utility properly understood. One should not renounce such motives as long as they are in themselves sound. In fact, one cannot really give them up, especially not in the first stages of the spiritual life, without a serious crippling of the potential energy of the will. "E. Kretschmer points out that in most spiritual decisions not merely one sole motive is operative, but rather an entire bundle of motives participate in the action. Even where the highest moral motives are strongest in evidence in our consciousness, there are more egotistic motives on the lower level of consciousness, which place their impulsive force with its intrinsic powerful dynamism at the service of the realization of the moral ideal. The result is the fusion into one unique impulse of the elementary instinctive urges with the ethically superior motives. The fusion is the more readily successful the more the instinctive though dynamically dominant forces remain active only at the margin of consciousness, whereas the ethical urges are perceptibly dominant, as they must be in all truly moral conduct. With this in evidence we must consider it our duty to favor and foster the conscious predominance of the ethical without losing sight of the more elementary and instinctive impulses."[53]

The harnessing of the elementary "instinctive forces" for moral motivation is of the greatest importance. There is no reason to fear that the loftiest moral motives will be muddied by the admixture of the elementary instincts and motives if these latter are really controlled and constantly animated by the former. The important point therefore is to breathe a new spirit into these common and lowly motives. Obviously one must be on guard constantly against the danger that they become independent or even predominant.

The stronger the purest and loftiest motives become, the more the elementary auxiliary forces may recede. They need not in reality disappear entirely, but may permit themselves to be more and more animated by the higher motives. Weight and influence of the various loftier motives must be proportionate to the degree of the religious-moral progress. During the first stages of conversion, legitimate love of self, reasonable self-interest, and especially a fear of hell, and the dread of the meaninglessness and futility of all our effort and sacrifice will be the most effective influences. Still *a priori* the hierarchy of motives must be preserved with an absolute validity. Hence, though one may appeal forcefully and vividly to the humbler motives in the inferior order, still all these must be subordinated to the fundamental and principal motive of love of God and neighbor, the ideal which may never be disregarded.

Since in the course of time even the intensive acts of motivation must lose something of their fervor or suffer defeat by counterforces, their frequent renewal is of the greatest importance. Especially is this true of the basic and fundamental motive. This is also called the renewal of the "good intention." But the important point is not the number of "good intentions," but rather their inwardness, depth, and sincerity, and their effective extension to all our activity. Just as the good intention in relation to all our activity in general, so likewise the special motive or intention in reference to an area of particular duty must always be kept fresh and vital.

It would be false to hold that, in reality, absolutely all our activity flows from motives we once adopted in full consciousness and constantly renewed. Depth psychology reveals the existence of the totally or partially unconscious motivation in our lives. It is important to raise these obscure and unwilled motives to the clear light of consciousness in order to invigorate them or render them impotent. The examination of conscience which looks only to the individual acts of virtue or to particular faults does not penetrate by far so deeply as the investigation into the motives and underlying dispositions which influence us.

But there can also be excess in the reflection on motives. The force of the motive can be enervated by persistent and untimely self-observation. Total submission of self to a value is not always commensurate with actual self-reflection. Conscious motivation and ceaseless reflex consciousness of that motivation are not the same thing. There is a time for everything. And everything must be in due proportion. One who walks in the presence of God can be assured that the magnetic needle of motivation will never deflect from the steadfast pole of the love of God. Love will warn him always. Hence, keeping one's eye on God is more efficacious in the moral life than any direct reflective self-observation without reference to God.

III. BASIC MOTIVE AND VIRTUE

Adoption of a dominant motive could be misconstrued as renunciation of the wealth of motivation. There can be no doubt that the theological virtue of love must unite and coordinate all other virtues. Love must be the ultimate and most comprehensive motive. But for all this we may not slight the motive lying just before us, the value at hand. Love and obedience are not the only virtues. And they themselves are perfect only when accompanied by all the other individual virtues in their train.

Each virtue lays claim to its own proper motive. If one were to practice a virtue only because of a motive that is alien to the virtue, not at all for the proper motive, he would not formally practice the virtue at all. If, for example, one is chaste merely in order to shun disease, he practices moderation or exercises care for his health, but does not practice the virtue of chastity. One who is chaste only because he dreads damnation has indeed a wholesome fear of hell, but he does not possess chastity as a virtue. Only he possesses chastity as a virtue who is aware of its proper worth and beauty and elects to practice it for these proper values as such.

The immediate motive corresponds to the object of the virtuous action (*finis operis*) in each instance. Our own motive for action (*finis operantis*) is good if it corresponds with this object. However, not every divergence between the motive of the agent and the internal essential finality of the action is by the very nature of the case sinful, but only if it be a motive in contradiction to a morally significant objective value. Thus, for example, one is not guilty of a sin against chastity if his strongest personal motive is the maintenance of health or fear of hell, if only he does not positively exclude the value proper to chastity.

Since every action is centered in a multiplicity of relations, a whole series of good motives is possible, which may be viewed as distinct, each in itself, or as forming a context in a recognized hierarchy of values. To cite an example, one may make a donation for a diocesan housing project principally because he wants to further the social prestige of the Church. He has a thoroughly good motive, even though he is not at the same time moved by the economic and moral misery of homeless human beings as the ideal of perfection demands. His action is not one of ardent love for those who desperately need shelter and his bounty.

Since it is scarcely possible to exhaust the wealth of the value-relations by adopting all the corresponding motives of our acts, man is free to cultivate above all those motives which appeal to him, the motives corresponding to his ideal of the good life. For example, it is quite possible to do all one's good works for a love of immortal souls, let us say by offering up all we do for the conversion of sinners. Of course it is to be assumed that the good work is performed because it is good (hence, in some way because of a motive that directly corresponds to it). Then one may add other still nobler motives. In a manner of speaking, all these works can be offered to God as a kind of prayer of petition, of propitiation, of thanksgiving. A worthy and potent motive for all can be the thought that one's thought and action have an influence for eternity on the Mystical Body of Christ.

IV. DISCIPLINE OF WILL AND SPIRITUAL FORMATION

In his work on the training of the will Lindworsky (cf. note 52) pointed out the danger of overestimating the pure technique of exercising oneself in will power. Such discipline without deeper motivation is not much more than mere "training." Even though he overshot his mark, this noted psychologist directed our attention to the need for a more profound cultivation of motive. Man as a body-soul unity absolutely stands in need of the technique which comes from training and exercise. Exercise is essential for mastery over stubbornness and native resistance to good; it imparts a certain external proficiency. But it does not have the value of virtue except through the virtuous motive which animates it. One must concede the point to Lindworsky that in times of spiritual crises it is not the external exercises and the habitual repetition of acts which enable the soul to stand firm. This is possible only through motivation profoundly rooted in conscience, although motivation is much more easily sustained if the action has become familiar through exercise than if it is new and untried.

A single act flowing from an intense and vital experience of love for God (that is, a profoundly motivated act) can lead to greater progress on the way of virtue than a thousand merely formal acts of the presence of

God. A solitary sublime act of sacrificial renunciation arising from the inmost love for one's neighbor leads one more deeply into the realm of the virtue of fraternal charity than a thousand external exercises or gestures without vital realization and experience of the real value of service to others, that is, of the real value of one's neighbor whom one must serve.

Usually one single act does not open the way to the depth of value. Precisely planned coordination and tenacious effort make it possible for man to penetrate ever more deeply into a moral motive. Not merely meditation on motive leads us into the inner realm of virtue, but motive pondered and likewise put into action (for we are not pure spirits). Moreover, precisely the zeal manifested in this exercise is usually evidence of the high esteem for virtue. It shows that we are taken up with the motive of virtue.

One of Lindworsky's insights must absolutely be accepted as genuine: in education of self and of others it is not sufficient to insist merely on the performance of the external act. The motive must ever be kept in mind and presented with all its vital significance. Only in this way can we really arrive at virtue, not merely through exercise or "training." Perhaps secular lawmakers may be altogether satisfied if they constrain men to a mere external or mechanical compliance with their laws. But the educator must place everything in the light of the value of virtue, always indeed in the light of the highest loving value which is God. Similarly, as far as the practice of virtue is concerned, we must ever be on the alert against the danger of pursuing a futile course, a course of mere mechanical acts of virtue. The danger can be met and overcome only through constant revitalization of our motive, the very point Lindworsky wishes to stress and which makes very plain that the importance of the role played by meditation in the spiritual life can scarcely be exaggerated.

V. FUNDAMENTAL MOTIVES IN RELIGIOUS-MORAL LIFE

1. *Love of God, Supreme and Fundamental Motive*

Over and above the motive proper to each particular virtue there must be operative in all our activity, if it is to be perfectly good and supernaturally meritorious, the comprehensive motive of love embracing all the others. But it does not follow at all that the motive must explicitly intervene in every single action, but that it must be vitally operative. Of course, it does mean that the motive of divine love must be renewed with sufficient frequency that it is in some degree effective, influencing and animating the individual act. But we cannot at all fix a minimum period of universal validity, after which the motive would cease to be effective without further explicit or implicit renewal. But it is clear that as long as divine love remains in the heart of man and his motives are still virtuous, it must follow that the motive in some way exerts its ennobling influence, no matter how faintly. Evidently, however, Christian perfection demands that the Christian see to it that this divine and basic motive impel and animate all his activity, not merely in some fainthearted manner, but with all possible force and interior penetration.

The central motive of Christian morality is love, love in so far as it is obedient. Man's relation to God is the relation of filial love, with its call to eternal participation in God's own love. Still, His love amidst the trials of our earthly pilgrimage is not the love of an equal whom God loves as His like, but the love which is to be proved, the love of a creature for his Lord and Creator. It must manifest itself in acts of religion in which love always adores and in acts of the moral virtues where love is stamped with obedience, where love always obeys (cf. HEB 10:5–9). Accordingly we may also look upon obedience through love as the fundamental motive. Or if we turn to the basic objective value and basic motive of obedience, we can say: the basic motive must be the will of God, loving and loved.

And since the love of God and His paternal will were revealed to us and given to us to share in Christ, the fundamental motive must ultimately be God's loving will for us in Christ, who brings to us the love and message of His Father. Ultimately the fundamental motive of the Christian merges into the ideal of the following of Christ. The pilot light, the fundamental motive, the ideal of life for the Christian must in some form or other be reducible to obedience and love, as God has taught them to us through Christ and through Him demanded them of us, and as we offer them in return to God in Christ and through Christ.

2. *Reward and Punishment: the Motives of Hope and Fear*

The Protestant ethic vaunts its superiority over Catholic morality in that it entirely represses the motive of reward and punishment. Rather than superiority, this is impoverishment and falsification of reality. The motive of reward and punishment can, of course, imply great imperfection, a) if it is considered the central and ultimate motive, b) if it flows from the mere egotistic urge, from self-interest or personal profit.

The motive of reward and punishment is not the loftiest and may not be the central motive of the Christian. But it should not be overlooked that at the beginning of conversion to God (before and at the time of the conversion), it is often the stronger (the more dynamic) motive which first awakens love. Preaching and spiritual direction, nevertheless, must awaken this motive and appeal to it in such a way that it merely serves to aid and complement the motive of loving obedience.

Reward and punishment, if they are to awaken morally lofty motives and constantly influence all stages of perfection, may not be considered purely from the standpoint of the human subject. It is true that reward means the enrichment of self, and punishment means menace and impoverishment of self. But reward must above all be viewed as flowing from the just and loving bounty of God. Punishment must be viewed from the angle of the malice which deserves punishment, from the holiness and justice of God who cannot admit to the society of His love one who has given himself over to evil. Under this aspect the motive of reward and punishment belongs inseparably to the perfection of the motive of love. It is an essential and glorious consequence of the divine love that it truly beatifies man. But it is also an essential consequence, glorious but terrible, of that divine love that it truly accepts as "no" the "no" spoken to love and ultimately abandons the one who rejects God's love to the desolation of his refusal. Whoever fails to take this consequence of the divine love seriously, and hence does not permit it to influence him as a motive for his spiritual life, not only diminishes the force of the motive of love, but also falsifies it.

Rightly viewed, the motive of reward and punishment is nothing other than the theological virtue of hope, in so far as it is for us the fundamental impulse toward the good. In heaven fear and hope cease to be. But to exclude them here below is to ignore the fact that we are still pilgrims and sojourners. Even in heaven there is something which corresponds to the motive of reward: we shall not merely love the God of love and glory in Himself, but also in the beatitude He bestows on those He loves.

Just as love does not exclude justice in social life but, on the contrary, includes it, so the perfect motive of obedient love necessarily includes the motive of reward and punishment resting on the divine justice. And if kept within the bounds of the right and moderate, the motive of reward and punishment may include the terrestrial recompense, the temporal punishment, in so far as God promises the one and threatens the other.

It depends on the divine generosity whether the good is requited a hundredfold already in this life or a still greater reward for it is prepared in heaven through cross and suffering. Should not the Christian, in so far as he is still a sinner, fear already in this life the wrath of God, the curse of sin? Surely sin itself is pregnant with the works of evil and must bring forth its fruit, since it divorces man from the source of all joy and all blessing.

Such was His wisdom in instructing and guiding His people in the Old Testament that God stressed more sharply than in the New Testament the motive of earthly rewards and earthly chastisements (sanction of reward and punishment), first of all for the Chosen People as a whole, and then for the pious individual. He had not yet pointed out the way of love in the cross of Christ. But we see how He gradually introduces mankind through Moses and the prophets to the motive of love. The people are urged to serve Him, not merely for sake of reward, but also because of the covenant of love between them and God. Reward and punishment were above all to be considered as signs of His love to the people of the covenant and as a manifestation of His jealous zeal in safeguarding the bond of loyalty to the covenant against transgression. The lament of the just in the Old Testament when misfortune befell him can be rightly understood only if we realize that the pious Jew sought earthly blessing less as a reward than as a pledge of the divine favor.

Even in the Old Testament, sin was looked upon as more than a juridical transgression with punishment as its consequence. 1) In regard to God, sin is really a matter of guilt deserving of punishment. It is a crime against God, holy and faithful, a breach of loyalty to the alliance of love. 2) As regards man, sin does more than make one liable to external punishment; it is rather an interior disorder, spiritual death (GEN 3), separation from the source of life. Superior to the juridical principle by which sin was to be punished, which men had to acknowledge throughout, there was, already in the Old Testament, evidence of the divine mercy which pointed to the coming Redeemer. In consequence the motive of fear is not the sinner's anguish of despair, but invitation to conversion.

In the New Testament the example of the cross of Christ shows the more glorious way. As disciple of the Crucified, the Christian has the strength to bear the cross and endure suffering in the service of God without regard for temporal reward. But even today there is constantly in evidence the principle of earthly sanction for good or evil in the education of peoples to Christ. Already in this world the good is the fertile seed of peace and order; evil, the seed of destruction. It would not be wrong for the Christian to find a place in his moral motivation for the influence of this truth also.

The Lord Himself promised His apostles who took up the cross and followed Him in the way of self-renunciation a hundredfold reward for this life (Mk 10:29f.; compare the beatitudes Mt 5:3ff.). This is surely not in any way the wage of a servant in the bright shining coin of earthly mintage, but the beginning, the earnest money attesting to His beatifying love. The Christian does not sigh for the wages of a servant or for earthly rewards, but for salvation. He seeks repose only in God (the Augustinian enjoying, the *frui*); all the rest he awaits in order to use it (*uti*) as means to the eternal blessedness of love.

Love in the state of our earthly sojourn with its trials and tests must always be accompanied with hope, and hope with wholesome fear. The motive of fear wrested from the context of Christian motivation would be a dreadful demoniacal fear. But wholesome fear bears in its wake the fear of reverence. Reverential fear is only the pole of true love. Hence it is true that "The fear of the Lord is the beginning of wisdom" (Prv 9:10). Saint Augustine in particular often points out in his incisive manner the connection between the Christian motive of love and fear: "To love with chaste fear and to fear with chaste love."[54] The motive of recompense and chastisement in the Christian sense, therefore, is not a diminution of love, but a path to love, a shield and guard of the correct love, a portion, an overflow of love. *"Pietas timore inchoatur, caritate perficitur!"*[55]

3. *The Social Motive*

a. The Power of Custom and Public Opinion

One of the principal forces of motivation in the conduct of the morally immature is the importance attached to custom, the concern for the opinions and reactions of the people around them. "One does not do that!" Or, "It's customary to do it this way!" Bergson calls this social motivation one of the two sources of morality, the other being the recognition of value. But we must clearly realize that custom taken in itself is not moral, but rather disposes to morality; it is rather pre-moral or infra-moral in motivation. Nevertheless, embedded in actual motivation of value, the power of morally correct custom and public opinion constitutes a strong subsidiary motive which can be thoroughly filled with a moral spirit through genuine docility and loving concern for the sentiments of one's fellows.

Even for the morally mature and noble, being torn from the soil of surrounding and tradition constitutes a dreadful peril, precisely because a strong support for formation of motive and effective exercise of motivation is lost if the unfortunate individual thus uprooted is not accepted into a new community with all its values. Such is the lot of servicemen and even more so of refugees. True concern in such matters is also of the greatest importance for the worker in the field of the foreign missions. If the recent convert is not accepted socially with love and tenderness in his new surroundings, his uprooting from the inherited moral tradition may prove fatal, especially in the period of development before the new and lofty Christian motives have been absorbed and made a part of his spiritual life.

Even the morally mature Christian must cling to the moral attitudes and customs of his surroundings as "rules of procedure," at the risk of losing the rôle he plays in life with its social standing and influence. With a sharp critical eye to their inadequacy, he must keep a firm hold on these rules of procedure with a profound sense of responsibility, for his whole conduct will react on the general level of morals in the community for good or evil. The result will be that he will elevate or lower the moral level of his surroundings. It clearly follows that attention to the moral reactions of the surroundings in their moral context must be a motive of conduct, for in no other way can one exert an effective moral influence upon them.

b. The Motive of Honor

For many men the most effective motive is preservation of their good name and reputation, their concern for personal honor. This motive also can be pre-moral, infra-moral, as well as morally good and noble in accordance with the reasons one may have in striving for it: glorification of self or responsible relation to the value of honor founded in its intrinsic worth. To safeguard one's own honor is very important in resisting temptation. Sense of honor is above all an important prerequisite for effective work for the good of the community. For the Christian and especially for the priest the motive of honor becomes a genuine motive of love if he looks upon himself in all things as a member of the Church and an apostle of Christ. But there are limits to seeking honor, the stern limits of the cross of Christ.

c. The Motive of Love of Neighbor

Every social motive must ultimately be founded in the love for others. And this love of our fellows must flow from the love of God and through our good intention return to Him. The spirit of responsibility for our fellowmen, zeal for the Kingdom of God, must be the fundamental motive influencing all our conduct, because really in effect all our activity has a repercussion on others and on the whole Mystical Body of Christ.

CHAPTER EIGHT

THE PROBLEM OF INDIFFERENT ACTIONS.
COORDINATION OF OBJECT, CIRCUMSTANCES,
AND MOTIVE

THE external action is determined in its moral value by its object, by the external situation, and the intention of the agent. But there are instances in which neither the object nor any of the countless circumstances so rigidly determines the moral significance of the action that one would have to hold that it is essentially good or essentially bad, so much so indeed that it could be done only with a good intention, or oppositely, only with a bad intention. In other words: the ultimate determination of the good or bad belongs to many actions because of their object itself or because of one or other circumstance, whereas in the case of other actions only the motive of the agent is decisive in making the act good or bad. For an act to be morally good, all three elements (object, circumstances, motive) must be right. This is expressed in the scholastic axiom: *bonum ex integra causa, malum ex quolibet defectu,* that is, moral good depends on the integrity of all factors in an act; evil, on any defect in it.

Obviously we should note that mere incidental circumstances or motives that are only incidentally awry, which do not affect the essence of the action, do not in every instance vitiate the entire action. They rather diminish its value or simply constitute an incidentally imperfect or bad act. In fact, a particular action can be made up of a number of acts. A number of internal acts can be merged with one action in such a way that one single imperfect or venially sinful act would not deprive the whole of its moral value and worth.

The study of these morally significant factors (object, circumstances, motive) suggests above all the following inquiry: all these moral factors being taken into account, are there morally indifferent actions? Is there beyond the domain of the good and the domain of the bad also a domain of the morally "insufficient," the morally indifferent? We inquire most particularly: is there beyond the morally good and morally bad motive also a motive which is "insufficient" or indifferent? (Can it ever be morally "insufficient" or indifferent, if one in his conduct does not heed the moral significance of his conduct?)

I. HISTORY OF THE PROBLEM

The ancient Cynics and Stoics admitted the existence of a domain between the good and bad, namely, an *adiáphoron,* the area of the morally inadequate or indifferent. Many of the Fathers of the Church and the Franciscan School follow this threefold division. But the majority of theologians, particularly the Thomists, reject absolutely and in principle the possibility of purely indifferent acts. Passions were aroused in Protestant theology regarding this point in the so-called Adiaphoristic controversy.

II. ANALYSIS OF THE PROBLEM

There is no value-free being, but only value-centered or value-related being, and alongside this the non-value in the defect of being (*privatio*). Nevertheless, not all being in itself has moral value or important moral value. Surely there are also other values; there is the pleasant, the useful, the beautiful, the value of the noble life. Man can freely purpose the good in any object under any aspect of value (of the useful, the pleasant). Must we conclude that the moral aspect of value can be lost in this regard for the other values? Not at all! The moral point of view is not one point of view among many, nor is it a mere coordination of the other aspects of value. The moral point of view is always present with a basic priority, whether the position assumed by the will toward a value object is in harmony with it or not. In every free action there is a value at stake, for when there is no question of value of any kind whatever, every participation of the free will would be meaningless. But the action may not merely be aligned with one value alone (this point is morally significant since every value is created by God), but must be so adjusted to it that no higher value is violated in the process. Here we have the moral signification of action!

Every moral action presupposes an awareness of value, for the will can turn only to a value which it recognizes. Granted that every value in concrete reality has also a moral significance for man, it follows that the decisive question is whether every action presupposes an awareness of moral value. Is it not conceivable that a merchant, to cite an example, would be preoccupied entirely with the question of profit in his transaction, without the slightest notion that other values were also at stake, such as justice, love, preservation of higher personal values? The notion that his transaction will be of profit for him does not unqualifiedly include an awareness of moral value.

The problem confronting us is concerned first with a fact, then with a principle.

It seems probable to me that someone on a very inferior level of development of personality may be capable of an awareness of such values as lie in profit or utility, or even of the beauty of a thing without having reached the stage of awareness of moral significance. Still, granted that neither in the clear awareness of the foreground of consciousness nor in the dim obscurity of the background there emerged the moral significance of the activity, the question still would arise whether such a purely purposive action without awareness of moral value would be a human action in the full sense of the term, and how it should be judged by the standard of values.

A purposive action without moral awareness is, from the standpoint of values, always imperfect, beneath the dignity of man, whether we assume an undeveloped personality or a degenerate one. We look upon this judgment as valid, whether we view it from the standpoint of the nature of man or from the nature of the moral object itself.

Man as a spiritual being must necessarily assume a position toward the surrounding world in accordance with his higher spiritual nature controlling and directing all his powers. If he acts spiritually, it must be with a unified approach. He cannot detach one of his faculties (for example, the capacity for use or profit) from the total ensemble of his powers with such exclusiveness as to deprive the higher powers of their participation. He cannot avoid that they be drawn into the effort with a "sympathetic" cooperation. Clearly the values of use and profit, of convenience and pleasure, and the like never exist in isolation: profit and use are always to be controlled and regulated so that they are just profit and right use, as being of advantage to the person as a whole or as disadvantageous. The normal adult is capable of grasping this relationship at least implicitly and aloofly and of conforming to it. If he fails to do so, his action cannot be characterized as merely inadequate or indifferent morally, for it lacks an essential perfection in the moral order.

The following consideration seems of primary importance according to the author's way of thinking: in order that the action be moral in character, it is not essential that the agent be directly and explicitly aware of its moral import in each individual instance, and still less that he possess a conceptual moral grasp of its importance. Sufficient would be an implicit awareness which, on occasion, would become explicit. The agent would probably think of the moral meaning of the action explicitly only when disorder emerges and makes itself felt, and the encounter forces the latent and implicit awareness of the moral values to the foreground of consciousness. Once the moral sentiment is fully awakened in man, it is effective, if not explicitly, then implicitly, and in the background of every conscious and free action. The example of the balance scale comes to mind. Perfect balance requires the greatest precision, and the precision of the scale indicates what is out of balance; and even should the scale be out of balance, it would still plainly indicate the need for balance and precision.

Were a psychologist to demonstrate that in a certain act there is no expression of moral sentiment effective at all, I would not hesitate to reply that in such an instance there is no morally indifferent action, but one which lacks the essential perfection of the truly human act. But I would not wish to make the unqualified assertion that the act is culpable or sinful (except when the defect is the result of deliberate fault), but should hold that it is a humanly defective action. Such actions which do not reach the rational level of human maturity we can find in children and in the mentally ill, who indeed are capable of acting with "purposive reason" or "reasonably," but not strictly morally. Such acts might perhaps be found among men who have largely deadened their conscience, their sense of moral values, so that in many instances it is not even subconsciously active any longer. On the contrary, it seems reasonable to hold that among men who have a normal conscience and normal mental power the consciousness of moral values attains the level of true spiritual or psychic activity and efficacy in every act.

No matter how the question of indifferent acts is answered, it is not at all possible in any case to establish legitimately and reasonably a morally "inadequate" or morally indifferent zone, in which conscious and free man may lay claim to a lawful title of escape from the morally significant or from the domain of the moral. As man develops morally, he becomes more and more conscious of this.

Perhaps one could call the external actions which admit of a good as well as an evil motive morally indifferent. But in this instance it must be clearly borne in mind that we are speaking only of the action abstractly and generically or, in the instance of a concrete action, are abstracting from an entirely essential factor, namely the motive, which most of all determines the inner act and mediately also the external action. Beyond this, we may not at all characterize as unqualifiedly indifferent the external actions which admit of a good as well as a bad motive. In fact, such action is not really indifferent in itself, that is, indifferent in relation to motive, for in the right order of things it of its own character calls out for the right motive and opposes an evil motive. Only the good motive is objectively correct and appropriate for a good action. Obviously it cannot exclude an evil motive, but it must condemn as alien and repugnant any motive except the good. And surely if the external action is in itself repugnant in any way whatever to the right order of things, then it is even less indifferent to the motive of the inner act. Of itself such external action demands that it be omitted, and indeed because of a good and worthy motive. It could admit of a good motive only in so far as the agent was not aware inwardly of the contradiction to the right order.

Against the position which maintains the possibility of perfectly human but indifferent acts there is the argument based on the universality of the holy and the good. Anyone who believes in God, Creator of all being, cannot assume that man made in His image has a domain of conscious and free action which is without moral importance in its relation to God, for which he would not be responsible to God. And just as little can he assume that he could have motives of action which neither conform to the laws of God nor contravene them. The only possible domain that can be admitted between the good and the bad as a third area, neither good nor bad, is that which is not penetrated by the clear insight of the moral conscience or leavened by its influence, not fully taken up with the spirit of moral responsibility, not yet placed fully in submission to the vigilance of true moral freedom. But such a domain is not what is usually meant by the indifferent realm, lying between the morally good and the morally bad.

The solution presented here, in my opinion, should in great measure satisfy the proponents of both positions in this controversy over morally indifferent acts. As to the principles involved, that is, from the standpoint of value and claim to value, there is no median area between good and bad (the position of the Thomists); but psychologically, that is, as far as facts and actualities are concerned, there may be many acts, at least in morally undeveloped or immature persons, which suggest that the moral conscience is not as comprehensively developed as the psychological conscience. In such instances of a moral lag there may be many deliberate acts which are not in the area of strictly moral human acts at all (an approach toward the attitude of the Franciscans).

III. THE TEACHING OF SACRED SCRIPTURE

The teaching of the Sacred Scripture is clear and obvious: God exempts no area of human life, no free act whatever, from the claim of the love of God, from the demand that it be centered in God. "Whether you eat or drink, or do anything else, do all for the glory of God" (1 Cor 10:31). "Whatever you do in word or in work, do all in the name of the Lord Jesus, giving thanks to God the Father through him" (Col 3:17). The Lord Himself teaches that "of every idle word men speak, they shall give account on the day of judgment" (Mt 12:36).

According to the Scriptures there are certain things which are permitted (neither prescribed nor forbidden). However, whatever one's decision may be regarding these things, the motive for the decision must be the love of God. In many passages Saint Paul shows that the attitude expressed in such phrases as "surely it is nothing evil in itself" cannot be decisive for the Christian. Against the possible objection that "all things are lawful" (in the sense of not evil in themselves) he warns that "not all things edify" (1 Cor 10:23). One is not permitted to do things which are in themselves lawful, if one is "enslaved" thereby. Even the body and all its needs must be made to serve God (loc cit.). The excuse that the action is indifferent is invalid if slight and neglect of the true welfare of one's fellow man are involved (1 Cor 8:9; 10:23ff.; Rom 14:15ff.). Clearly Paul points out, regarding the attitude toward the Old Testament prescriptions of law, how something in itself indifferent (which at another time was legally prescribed) becomes evil when through false conceptions it is placed in contradiction to a truth of Christian revelation (Gal 2:5) or when it is demanded of others through selfish motives (Gal 6:12). On the other hand, the same indifferent acts can have the loftiest moral value, if they are done through zeal for souls, through tender concern for the weakness of one's neighbor (1 Cor 9:19ff.).

BIBLIOGRAPHY

ALTHAUS, P. *Gebot und Gesetz. Zum Thema "Gesetz und Evangelium."* Guetersloh, 1952.
AMBROSETTI, G. *Il diritto naturale della riforma cattolica.* Milano, 1951.
ARNOLD, F. X. *Zur Frage des Naturrechts bei Luther.* Muenchen, 1937.

AUER, A. *Der Mensch hat Recht. Naturrecht auf dem Hintergrund des Heute.* Graz-Wien-Koeln, 1956.

———. "Gesetz und Freiheit im Verhaeltnis von Mensch und Gott bei F. X. Linsenmann," *Festschrift fuer Th. Steinbuechel* (Dusseldorf, 1948), 246–263.

AUXENTIUS A ROTTERDAM. "De obligatione canonica religiosorum tendendi ad perfectionem," *ComR,* 31 (1952), 250–275.

BALCUNIAS, V. *La vocation universelle à la perfection chrétienne selon saint François de Sales.* Annécy: Académie Salesienne, 1952.

*BARTH, K. *Theological Existence Today.* London: Hodder, 1933.

BATTAGLIA, F. *Il problema morale nel existenzialismo.* Bologna, 1949.

BAUER, C. "Die Naturrechtsvorstellungen des juengeren Melanchthon," *Festschrift fuer Ritter* (Tuebingen, 1950).

BEHN, S. *Philosophie der Werte.* Muenchen, 1930.

BELGION, M. *Victor's Justice.* Hinsdale, Illinois, 1949.

BINDER, J. *La fondazione della filosofia del diritto.* Torino, 1945.

BLAESER, P., M.S.C. "Das Gesetz bei Paulus," *Neutestamentliche Abhandlungen,* XIX (Muenster, 1941), 1–2.

———. "Glaube und Sittlichkeit bei Paulus," *Festschrift fuer Meinertz* (Muenster, 1951), 114–121.

BOBBIO, N. *Il diritto naturale nel secolo XVIII.* Torino, 1947.

BOISMARD, M. E. "La Loi de l'Esprit," *LumVie,* 21 (1955), 65–82.

BRANDT, W. *Freiheit im Neuen Testament.* Muenchen, 1932.

BRISROIS, E., S.J. "Le Sartrisme et le problème Moral," *NRTh,* 74 (1952), 30–48, 124–145.

*BRUNNER, E. *Man in Revolt.* Philadelphia: Westminster Press, 1947.

———. *Divine Imperative.* Philadelphia: Westminster Press, 1947.

———. *Gerechtigkeit.* Zuerich, 1943.

BUGGE, CHR. "Das Gesetz und Christus nach der Anschauung der aeltesten Christengemeinde," *ZntWiss,* 4 (1903), 89–110.

———. *Das Gesetz und Christus im Evangelium. Zur Revision der kirchlichen Lehre "de evangelio et lege."* Christiania, 1903.

CARRO, V. *Vitoria y los derechos del hombre.* Madrid, 1947.

CATHREIN, V., S.J. *Die Einheit des sittlichen Bewusstseins* (Three Volumes). Freiburg im Br., 1914.

———. *Recht, Naturrecht und positives Recht.* 2. Auflage. Freiburg, 1909.

CERFAUX, L. "La théologie de la grâce selon saint Paul," *VieSpir,* 83 (1950), 5–19.

CHRISTMANN, H. M., O P. "Vom Geheimnis des Einzelen," *Die Kirche in der Welt,* 4 (1951), 359–364.

CHROUST, A. H. "The Philosophy of Law from S. Augustine to S. Thomas," *NewSchol* (1946), 26–71.

CONRAD, H. "Recht und Naturrecht bei Thomas von Aquin," *Die Kirche in der Welt,* 2 (1949), 265–270, 443–448.

CONWAY, W. "The Act of Two Effects," *ITQ,* 18 (1951), 125–137.

CREVE, A., O.P. "De epikeia volgens Thomas van Aquino en Suarez," *MisMor* (Leuven, 1948), 255–280.

CROWE, M., C.SS.R. *The Moral Obligation of Paying Just Taxes.* Catholic University of America Press: Washington, 1944.

DANIÉLOU, J. "Les conseils évangéliques," *VieSpir,* 58 (1948), 660–674.

DAVITT, TH., S.J. *The Nature of Law.* St. Louis and London, 1951.

DENNING, A. *Freedom under the Law.* London, 1949.

DIEL, P. *Psychologie de la motivation.* Paris, 1948.

DIETZE, H. *Das Naturrecht in der Gegenwart.* Bonn, 1936.

DI MONDA, A. M. *La legge nuova della libertà secondo S. Tommaso.* Napoli, 1954.

DIRKS, W. "Wie erkenne ich, was Gott von mir will?" *Frankfurter Hefte,* 6 (1951), 229–244.

DODD, C. K. *Gospel and Law. The Relation of Faith and Ethics in Early Christianity.* New York: Columbia University Press, 1951.

DOMBOIS, H. *Naturrecht und christliche Existenz.* Kassel, 1952.

EGENTER, R. *Von der Freiheit der Kinder Gottes.* 2 Auflage. Freiburg, 1949.

———. *Das Wagnis in Christo.* Regensburg, 1936.

———. "Ueber die Bedeutung der Epikie," *Philos. Jahrbuch der Goerresg.,* 53 (1940), 115–127.

———. "Kasuistik als christliche Situationsethik," *MThZ,* 1 (1950), 54–65.

ELERT, W. *Das christliche Ethos,* 89ff., 387ff.

ELLUL, J. *Die theologische Begruendung des Rechtes* (translated by O. Weber). Muenchen, 1948.

ELTER, E., S.J. "Sitne in doctrina morali S. Thomae locus pro imperfectionibus positivis non peccaminosis," *Greg,* 10 (1929), 21–29.

ENDRES, J., C.SS.R. "Situation und Entscheidung," *NO,* 6 (1952), 27–36.

ERMECKE, G. *Die natuerlichen Seinsgrundlagen der christlichen Ethik.* Paderborn, 1941.

———. "Moraltheologische Grundsaetze zur Zoll-Gesetzgebung," *ThG,* 42 (1952), 81–96.

FASSBENDER, M. *Wollen eine koenigliche Kunst.* Freiburg, 1923.

FLUECKIGER, F. *Geschichte des Naturrechts.* I. Band: *Altertum und Fruehmittelalter.* Zollikon-Zuerich, 1954.

FUCHS, E. *Die Freiheit des Glaubens. Roemer 5–8 ausgelegt.* Muenchen, 1949.

FUCHS, J., S.J. *Situation und Entscheidung.* Frankfurt, 1952, 53–65.

———. "Situationsethik in theologischer Sicht," *Schol,* 27 (1952), 161–183.

———. "Ethique objective et ethique de situation. A propos de l'Instruction du Saint Office du 2 fevrier 1956," *NRTh,* 78 (1956), 798–818.

———. "Lex naturae." *Zur Theologie des Naturrechts* (Duesseldorf, 1955).

FUNK, J. *Primat des Naturrechtes* (St-Gabrieler Studien 13). Moedling, 1952.

GEPPERT, W. "Zur gegenwaertigen Diskussion ueber das Problem des *tertius usus legis,*" *Evangelische Kirchenzeitung,* 9 (1955), 387–393.

GHOOS, J. "L'acte à double effet, étude de théologie positive," *EphThLov,* 27 (1951), 30–52.

GOGUEL, M. "Le paulinisme, théologie de la liberté," *RThP,* 3e sér. 31 (1951), 157–180.

GRIESBACH, E. *Gegenwart. Eine kritische Ethik.* Halle, 1928. (Opposes ethics of law and favors situation ethics.)

GUTBROD AND KLEINKNECHT. "Nómos," *ThW,* IV, 1016–1084.

HADROSSEK, P. *Die Bedeutung des Systemgedankens in der Moraltheologie.* Muenchen, 1950, 262–281. (Regarding the obligation to follow the counsel in the concrete individual instance.)

HÄRING, B. "Faule Situationsethik oder toter Legalismus?" *Klerusblatt,* 36 (1956), 356–359.

———. "Die Stellung des Gesetzes in der Moraltheologie," *Moralprobleme im Umbruch der Zeit* (Muenchen, 1957), 133–152.

———. *Der Christ und die Obrigkeit.* Augsburg, 1956.

HAMEL, E. "Loi naturelle et Loi du Christ," *ScEccl,* 10 (1958), 49–76.

HAMM, F. *Geschichte der Steuermoral in der Kirche.* Trier, 1907.

HÄRING, J. "Recht und Gesetz nach katholischer Auffassung," *Katholische Rechtsphilosophie.* Vol. XVI of Kohler's *Archiv fuer Rechts- und Wirtschaftsphilosophie* (1923).

HARTMANN, N., O.F.M. "Das Individuationproblem," *Die Kirche in der Welt,* 4 (1951), 353–358.

HASLER, V. *Gesetz und Evangelium in der alten Kirche bis Origines.* Zuerich, 1953.

HEUFELDER, E. M., O.S.B. *Die evangelischen Raete. Die biblisch-theologischen Grundlagen des Ordenslebens im Blick auf seine Erneuerung in unserer Zeit.* Wien, 1954.

HILDEBRAND, D. VON. "Ueber die Idee des himmlischen Lohnes," *Zeitliches im Lichte des Ewigen* (Regensburg, 1932), 23–46.

——. *Wahre Sittlichkeit und Situationsethik.* Duesseldorf, 1957.

HIRSCHMANN, H., S.J. "Situationsethik und Erfuellung des Willens Gottes," *GeistLeben,* 24 (1951), 300–304.

HORST, F. "Naturrecht und Altes Testament," *Evangelische Theologie* (1950/51), 253–273.

JANSSEN, A. "De lege mere poenali," *JP,* 4 (1924), 119–127, 187–201; 5 (1925), 24–32.

JEANSON, F. *Le problème moral et la pensée de Sartre.* Paris, 1947. (This work is inimical to the ethics of law and favors situation ethics.)

JOEST, W. *Gesetz und Freiheit. Das Problem des tertius usus legis bei Luther und die neutestamentliche Parainese.* Goettingen, 1951.

JUNG, C. C. *Psychologie und Erziehung.* Basel, 1945.

KOCH, A. "Zur Lehre von den sogenannten Poenalgesetzen," *ThQschr,* 82 (1900), 204–281; 84 (1902), 574–620; 86 (1904), 400–424.

KOLNAI, A. *Der ethische Wert und die Wirklichkeit.* Freiburg im Br., 1927.

KOPF, J. "La loi indispensable pédagogue," *VieSpirSupp,* 4 (1951), 185–200.

KRAMER, H. G. *The Indirect Voluntary or Voluntarium in Cause.* Washington, 1935.

KUECKENHOFF, G. *Naturrecht und Christentum.* Duesseldorf, 1948.

KUSS, OTTO. "Die Heiden und die Werken des Gesetzes (according to ROM 2:14–16), *MThZ,* 5 (1954), 77–98.

LACHANGE, L. *Le concept de droit selon Aristote et saint Thomas.* Ottawa-Montréal, 1948.

LACKMANN, M. *Vom Geheimnis der Schoepfung. Die Geschichte der Exegese von ROM 1:18–23, 2:14–16 und ACTA 14:15–17; 17:22–29 vom 2. Jahrhundert bis zum Beginn der Orthodoxie* (Stuttgart, 1952).

LACOULINE, P. *Imperfection ou péché veniel.* Québec; Université Laval, 1945.

LECLERCQ, J. *Essais de morale catholique.* I (Paris, 1946), 85–100; IV (1947), 97–105.

LEGAS-LACAMBRA, L. "La fundamentación del derecho de gentes in Suárez," *Rev. Españ. de Derecho Intern.,* I. (1948), 11–44.

LE SENNE, R. *Obstacle et valeur.* Paris, 1934.

LINDWORSKY, J., S.J. *Erfolgreiche Erziehung.* Freiburg, 1933.

——. *The Training of the Will.* Milwaukee: Bruce, 1929.

LINSENMANN, F. X. *Lehrbuch der Moraltheologie,* 126f. (regarding the obligation to follow the concrete and particular counsel in each individual instance).

——. "Untersuchungen ueber die Lehre von Gesetz und Freiheit," *ThQschr,* 53 (1871), 64–114, 221–277; 54 (1872), 3–49, 193–245.

LOTTIN, O. *Psychologie et morale aux XIIe et XIIIe siècles.* II (Gembloux, 1948), 469–489.

——. *Psychologie et morale aux XIIe et XIIIe siècles.* II (Louvain-Gembloux, 1948), 9–100.

——. *Le droit naturel chez Saint Thomas d'Aquin et ses prédécesseurs.* Bruges, 1931.

——. *Loi morale naturelle et loi positive d'après S. Thomas.* Louvain, 1920.

LOTZ, J. B., S.J. "Sein und Wert. Das Grundproblem der Wertphilosophie," *ZKathTh,* 57 (1933), 557–613.

LYONNET, ST., S.J. *Liberté chrétienne et loi de l'Esprit.* Rome, 1954.

McGARRIGLE, F. J., S.J. "It's All Right If You Can Get Away With It," *AER* 127 (1952), 431–449.

MANARICUA, A. E. "La obligatoriedad de la ley penal en Alfonse de Castro," *REsDc,* 4 (1949), 35ff.

MANSER, G. *Das Naturgesetz in thomistischer Beleuchtung.* Fribourg, 1944.

————. *Angewandtes Naturrecht.* Fribourg, 1946.

MARCHELLO, G. *Il problema critico del diritto naturale.* Torino, 1936.

MARINO, A. DI., S.J. "L'epikeia cristiana," *DivThom* (P), 55 (1952), 396–424.

MARITAIN, J. *The Rights of Man and Natural Law.* New York: Scribner, 1943.

————. *Neuf leçons sur les notions première de la philosophie morale.* Paris, 1950.

MARTENS, H. L., S.J. "Kierkegaard und die Situationsethik," *Schol,* 26 (1951), 556–564.

MATTHES, H. "Theologische Ethik als Geistesethik. Die Dynamik des Hl. Geistes zur Ueberwindung des *Impossibile legis,*" *ZSysTh,* 16 (1939), 68–131.

MAUSBACH, J. "Ethik und Recht," *Katholische Rechtsphilosophie.* Vol. XVI of Kohler's *Archiv fuer Rechts- und Wirtschaftsphilosophie* (1923).

————. *Naturrecht und Voelkerrecht.* Freiburg, 1918.

MEERSEMAN, G. "La loi purement pénal d'après les statuts des confréries médiévales," *Mélanges J. de Ghellinck,* 2 (1951), 975ff.

MENNESSIER, A. I. "Conseils évangéliques," *DSp* (de Viller), fasc. XIII (Paris, 1950), 1592–1609.

MENTHON, FR. DE. *Gerechtigkeit im Namen der Menscheit.* Neustadt, 1946.

MESSNER, J. *Das Naturrecht. Handbuch der Gesellschaftsethik.* 2. Auflage. Innsbruck-Wien, 1950 (extensive bibliography).

MICHEL, E. The works of this author: *Partner Gottes, Renovatio, Ehe, Glaeubige Existenz* all bear the stamp of the existentialistic opposition to the ethics of law.

MITTEIS, H. *Ueber das Naturrecht.* Berlin, 1948.

MORTA-FIGULS, A. "Suárez y las leyes meremente penales," *REsDc,* 5 (1950), 503–599.

MOTTE, A., O.P. "L'obligation de suivre la vocation," *Le discernement des vocations religieuses* (Paris, 1950), 27–44.

MUCKERMANN, H. *Das Ethos der Existentialphilosophie.* Berlin, 1950.

MUELLER-ERZBACH, R. *Die Rechtswissenschaft im Umbau.* Muenchen, 1950.

MUELLER, M. "Der hl. Albertus Magnus und die Lehre von der Epikie," *DivThom,* 12 (1934), 165–182.

NEWMAN, J. "Existentialism and Ethics," *IER, fifth series* 77 (1952), 333–342, 421–431.

NIEDER, L., C.SS.R. *Die Motive der religioes-sittlichen Paraenese in den paulinischen Gemeindebriefen. Ein Beitrag zur paulinischen Ethik.* Muenchen, 1956.

NOLDIN, H. "Zur Erklaerung des Poenalgesetzes," *ZKathTh,* 33 (1909), 126ff.

OSBOURN, J. C., O.P. "The Morality of Imperfections," *Thomist* (1942), 388–430, 669–691.

OTTENWAELDER, P. *Die Naturrechtslehre des Hugo Grotius.* Tuebingen, 1950.

OZEN, H. VON. "Biblische Gerechtigkeit und weltliches Recht," *ThZschr,* 7 (1950), 270–292.

PASSERIN-D'ENTRÈVES, A. *Natural Law.* London, 1951.

PAYOT, J. *Education de la volonté.* Paris, 1941.

PESCH, W., C.SS.R. *Der Lohngedanke in der Lehre Jesu, verglichen mit der religioesen Lohnlehre des Spaetjudentums.* Muenchen, 1954.

PIUS XII. "Address on Conscience and Situation Ethics," March 23, 1952, and April 19, 1952, in *AAS.*

PRADELLE, A. DE LA. *Maîtres et doctrines du droit des gens.* 2. éd. Paris, 1950.

QUERVAIN, A. DE. *Gesetz und Freiheit.* Stuttgart, 1930.

RAHNER, K. "Ueber die gute Meinung," *GeistLeben* 28 (1955), 281–298.

————. "Situationsethik und Suendenmystik," *StimmZeit,* 145 (1949/50), 330–342.

————. "Der einzelne in der Kirche," *StimmZeit,* 139 (1946/47), 260–276.

REDING, M. "Bedeutung des Vorbilds nach Aristoteles und Thomas von Aquin," *ThQschr,* 131 (1951), 53–60.

REINACH, A. *Zur Phaenomenologie des Rechtes.* Muenchen, 1953.

RENARD, G. *La valeur de la loi.* Paris, 1928.

RENARD, V. D. *La théorie des leges mere poenales.* Paris, 1929.

RICHARD, T., O.P. *Étude de théologie morale. Le plus parfait.* Paris, 1933.

RINTELEN, F. J. VON. *Der Wertgedanke in der europaeischen Geistesenwicklung.* Halle, 1932.

RIQUET, M. *Sa Majesté la Loi.* Paris, 1924.

ROMMEN, H. *The Natural Law.* A study in legal and social history and philosophy. St. Louis: Herder, 1947.

ROTH, P. "Naturrecht und Menschenrechte," *StimmZeit,* 146 (1950), 412–422.

RUIZ-GIMENEZ, J. *Introducción elemental a la filosofía jurídica cristiana.* Madrid, 1945. Cf. T. Urdanoz, Ciencia Tomista, 70 (1946), 336–348.

SACCHETTI, G. B. *Imperfezione e colpa.* Roma: Gregoriana, 1945.

S. Congreg. S. Officii. Decretum de "Ethica Situationis," *AAS,* 48 (1956), 144f. English translation, *AER,* 135 (July, 1956), 64–6.

SALET, G. "La loi dans nos coeurs," *NRTh,* 79 (1957), 449–462, 561–578.

SALSMANS. *Droit et Morale.* Bruges, 1925.

SCHELER, M. *Der Formalismus in der Ethik und die materiale Wertethik.*

SCHILLING, O. "Die Rechtsphilosophie bei den Kirchenvaetern," *Katholische Rechtsphilosophie.* Vol. XVI of Kohler's *Archiv fuer Rechts- und Wirtschaftsphilosophie* (1923).

———. *Christliche Sozial- und Rechtsphilosophie.* Muenchen, 1950.

———. *Naturrecht und Staat nach der Lehre der alten Kirche.* 1914.

SCHLIER, H. *Der Galaterbrief.* 11 Auflage. Goettingen, 1951.

SCHLINK, E. *Gesetz und Evangelium.* Muenchen, 1937.

SCHNEIDER, J. "Die Verpflichtung des menschlichen Gesetzes nach Johannes Gerson," *ZKathTh,* 75 (1953), 1–54.

SCHREY, H. H. "Die Wiedergeburt des Naturrechts," *Theologische Rundschau,* 19 (1951), 21–75, 154–186, 193–221.

SCHUELER, A. *Verantwortung.* Krailling vor Muenchen, 1948, 157–172.

SCHWANE, J. *De operibus supererogatoriis et consiliis evangelicis in genere.* Muenster, 1869.

SEELHAMMER, N. "Situationsethik und Christliches Gewissen," *TrThZ,* 62 (1953), 80–90.

SODEN, C. "Das Naturrecht in der Situation," *Ho,* 32 (1935), 488–500.

SOEHNGEN, G. *Gesetz und Evangelium.* Freiburg-Muenchen, 1957.

STADTMUELLER, G. *Das Naturrecht im Lichte der geschichtlichen Erfahrung.* Recklinghausen, 1949.

STAFFELBACH, G. *Die Vereinigung mit Christus als Prinzip der Moral bei Paulus.* Freiburg, 1932.

STEINBUECHEL, TH. *Die philosophische Grundlegung der kath. Sittenlehre.* 4. Auflage. I (1951), 237–257.

———. "Existentialismus und christliches Ethos," *ThQschr,* 128 (1948), 1–27.

———. *Christliche Lebenshaltungen in der Krisis der Zeit und des Menschen.* Frankfurt, 1949. Cf. "Zur Frage der Situationsethik," *Herderkorr,* 4 (1949/50), 456–459.

"Steuer und Steuerhinterziehung," *Herderkorr,* 3 (1949), 293f., 350. Significantly, the hierarchy of Holland support the position that the tax laws are essentially binding in conscience.

STONE, J. *The Province and Function of Law.* Harvard University Press, 1950.

STRATENWERTH, G. *Die Naturrechtslehre des Duns Skotus.* Goettingen, 1951.

SUESTERHENN, A. *Die naturrechtlichen Grundlagen der internationalen Zusammenarbeit.* Wiesbaden, 1952.

THIELICKE, H. *Theologische Ethik.* I, 154–238.

THOMAS AQUINAS. I-II, q. 18 a.8 and 9.

TILLMANN, F. "Um eine katholische Sittenlehre," *Menschenkunde im Dienste der Seelsorge* (Festschrift F. Th. Muencker). Trier, 1948.

———. *Handbuch der kath. Sittenlehre.* 3. Auflage. III 198ff.

TRAPP, G. "Selbstbestimmung und Motivbezogenheit im Akt des freien Willens," *Schol,* 28 (1953), 526–542.

TROMBERTA. *Utrum ecclesia habeat potestatem praecipiendi actus mere internos?* Surrenti, 1920.

UTZ, A. F., O.P. "Krise im modernen Naturrechtsdenken," *NO,* 5 (1951), 201–219.

VANGHELUWE, V. "De lege mere poenali," *EphThLov,* 16 (1939), 383–429.

VECCHIO, DEL, G. *Philosophy of Law.* Washington: Catholic University, 1953.

VERDROSS, A. "Was ist Recht? Die Krise des Rechtspositivismus und das Naturrecht," *WW,* 8 (1953), 587ff.

WAGNER, K. *Die sittlichen Grundsaetze bezuelich der Steuerpflicht.* Regensburg, 1906.

WARNACH, V. "Sein und Freiheit, Blondels Entwurf einer normativen Ethik," *ZKathTh,* 63 (1939), 273–310, 393–427.

WELTY, E., O.P. "Wie denkt die katholische Soziallehre ueber die Grundrechte des Menschen?" *NO,* 3 (1948), 5–26.

WELZEL, H. *Naturrecht und materiale Gerechtigkeit.* Goettingen, 1951.

WENDLAND, H. D. "Das Wirken des Hl. Geistes in den Glaeubigen," *ThLitZtg,* 77 (1952), 457–470.

WILMSEN, A. "Zum Problem der sittlichen Sanktion," *Festschrift fuer A. Wenzel.* (Muenchen-Pasing, 1950), 160–174.

WIMMER, A. *Die Menschenrechte in christlicher Sicht.* Freiburg, 1953.

WOHLHAUPTER, E. *Aequitas canonica.* Paderborn, 1936.

WUENSCHEL, E., C.SS.R. "De obligatione sequendi vocationem religiosam," *Acta et documenta congressus de statibus perfectionis* (Roma, 1950). Editiones Paulinae, II (1952), 647–671.

———. "L'obligo di corrispondere alla vocazione religiosa secondo S. Alfonso," *Vita Cristiana,* 20 (1951), 227–240.

WUST, P. *Ungewissheit und Wagnis.* Salzburg-Leipzig, 1937.

ZEIGER, I., S J. "Naturrecht und Natur des Rechtes," *StimmZeit,* 149 (1951/52), 468–472.

Additional Works in English

BERTKE, S. *The Possibility of Invincible Ignorance of the Natural Law.* Washington: Catholic University of America, 1941.

DOOLAN, A. *Order and Law.* Westminster, Md.: Newman, 1954.

HERRON, M., T.O.R. *The Binding Force of Civil Laws.* St. Anthony Guild Press, Paterson, N.J., 1958.

KELLY, G., S.J. AND FORD, J., S.J. *Contemporary Moral Theology.* Vol. 1, *Questions in Fundamental Moral Theology.* Westminster, Md.: Newman, 1958. Cf. Ch. 1–3, pp. 3–41; Ch. 7–8, pp. 104–140.

———. *Man and His Happiness* (Theology Library, Vol. 3). Chicago: Fides, 1956. Cf. pp. 271–336.

WU, C. *Fountain of Justice.* New York: Sheed and Ward, 1955.

Periodical Literature in English

CONNERY, J., S.J. "Shall We Scrap the Purely Penal Law?" *AER,* 129 (O., 1953) 244–53.

CROWE, M. B. "Natural Law Before St. Thomas" (bibl.), *IER,* 76 (Sept., 1951), 193–204.

———. "St. Thomas and the Natural Law," *IER,* 76 (Oct , 1951), 293–305.

DE KONINCK, C. "General Standards and Particular Situations in Relation to the Natural Law," *Proceedings, Am. Cath. Phil. Association,* 24 (1950), 28–32.

DOHENY, W. "Eternal Law Background of Natural Law," Vol. 1, *Proceedings, Natural Law Institute*. Notre Dame, Ind., 1947.

FARRELL, P. M. "Sources of St. Thomas' Concept of the Natural Law," *Thomist*, 20 (Jl., 1957), 237–83.

HART, C. A. "Metaphysical Foundation of the Natural Law," *Proceedings, Am. Cath. Phil. Association*, 24, 18–28.

KILZER, E. "Natural Law and Natural Rights," *Proceedings, American Cath. Phil. Association*, 24 (1950), 156–60.

LOTTIN, O., O.S.B. "Natural Law and Right Reason," PhT, 3 (Sp. 1959), 10–18.

McANIFF, J. E. "Natural Law, its Nature, Scope, and Sanction," *FLR*, 22 (D., 1953), 246–53.

McKINNON, H. "Natural Law and Positive Law," Vol. 1, *Proceedings, Natural Law Institute*. Notre Dame, Ind., 1947.

O'DONOGHUE, D. "The Thomist Concept of Natural Law," *ITQ*, 22 (Ap., 1955), 89–109.

PIUS XII. "The Church and Natural Law," *HPR*, 55 (Ap., 1955), 592–94.

STRAUSS, L. "Natural Right and the Historical Approach," *RPol*, 12 (O., 1950), 422–42.

WU, J. C. "Natural Law and Our Common Law," *FLR*, 23 (Mr., 1954), 13–48.

———. "Christianity, the Natural Law and the Common Law," *ABR*, 6 (Summer, 1955), 133–47.

Part Four:

THE FOLLOWING OF CHRIST
PLACED IN JEOPARDY

CHAPTER NINE

NATURE AND CONSEQUENCES OF SIN

I. CHRIST REDEEMS MAN FROM SIN

THE Incarnation, the life, the passion, and exaltation of Christ cannot be understood without relation and reference to sin (ROM 8:3; HEB 2:17). The Incarnation is the first step made by God, gravely offended by sin, toward the reconciliation of man the sinner. Sin alienates man from God. But the sinner who is far off from God is brought nigh to Him again by the coming of Emmanuel, the "God-with-us" who restores us to the love of the Father. The life and passion of Christ is the combat of the Divine Hero against sin and the power of evil centering in the devil. The obedience of the Servant of Yahweh triumphs over the pride from which sin and all evil flows (PHIL 2:7f.). As the supreme act of obedience and love the death of Christ on the cross expiates the disobedience of our first parents. The resurrection of Christ is the sign of His victory over sin and the consequences of sin (suffering and death).

Already John the Baptist calls Christ "the lamb of God, who takes away the sin of the world!" (JN 1:29; cf. Is 53:7). Jesus was entirely penetrated with a realization of the fearful actuality of sin (note the prodigal son, the unjust steward, the parable of the vineyard, of the evil spirit who departs only to return with seven others worse than himself; His frequent admonition: "Sin no more"). He reveals Himself as the Saviour of sinners, as Conqueror of sin ("The Son of Man came to save what was lost" MT 18:11; LK 15; "I have come to call sinners, not the just" MT 9:13; LK 19:10). The inestimable boon for salvation which Jesus brings to us is the pardon of sin. To pardon sin is His supreme power and right in the work of salvation ("But that you may know that the Son of Man has power on earth to forgive sins . . ." MT 9:6; LK 5:24; Jesus in the house of Simon the Pharisee and the sinful woman, LK 7:49). Jesus refers to His death as a salutary sacrifice for the forgiveness of sins ("This is my blood of the new covenant, which is being shed for many unto the forgiveness of sins" MT 26:28; He institutes baptism "for the forgiveness of . . . sins" ACTS 2:38). He grants power to His Church to forgive sins in His name (JN 20:23).

After His death, the apostles and the community of disciples did not look upon Christ as one sent to build a terrestrial realm in which suffering was banned, but as the messenger who was to inaugurate the era of salvation through conquest of sin (1 Jn 1:7; 2:2; 3:5; Rom 6; 8:3; 2 Cor 5:21).

Christ is the judgment of sin. He is the *Crisis* on which turns spiritual life or spiritual death. In the tribunal of Christ sin is unmasked, with all its hideousness revealed. If the law in its time according to the teaching of Paul revealed sin in its true light as enmity, as revolt against God, as provocation of God (Rom 5:13; 7; 8:7), the same holds true, though in a different, far profounder sense, of Christ. When sin is viewed in the light of the personal enunciation of God's will, its incredible effrontery assumes an aspect quite different from that which is seen only in the light of reason and the natural order. Still more audacious and perverse is it when seen in the light of the love of God, who sent His only-begotten Son to announce His loving will through Christ Himself. "If I had not come and spoken to them, they would have no sin. But now they have no excuse for their sin. He who hates me hates my Father also. If I had not done among them works such as no one else has done, they would have no sin. But now they have seen, and have hated both me and my Father" (Jn 15:22–24). Sin shows its true face in the light of such manifest proofs of God's love in Christ: it is hatred of the loving will of God. In the parable of the vine dressers, Christ shows plainly the degrees of sin, from non-payment of tribute, to the murder of the prophets, to the murder of the only-begotten Son of God (Mt 21:33ff.).

Christ confronts man with a decision. This decision means the crisis between life and death in the spiritual order. Christ is the cornerstone, the stone of "contradiction," of destruction or construction. He "is destined for the fall and for the rise of many" (Lk 2:34). Since the coming of Christ man can rise to incomparable heights of grace. But his possible fall is also much deeper. The depth now is abysmal. Before the coming of Christ mankind was not at all capable of the malice which His rejection inaugurated. In the Holy Spirit Christ now continues this work of separating the evil from the good. He convicts the world of its sin because it does not believe in Him. Through the word of Christ and the work of the Holy Spirit the world is convicted of the gravest of sins (Jn 16:8), since it envelopes itself in its darkness shutting out the light.

II. THE FOLLOWING OF CHRIST AND SIN

Man's redemption through Christ is the great turning point of all history. The power of evil was struck in the heart. Christ appeared as the Victor over sin and death. Now is the hour of decision for each individual.

In union with Christ through baptism and the obedience of faith he participates in the conquest of sin through Christ (Rom 6). All the sacraments, even the sacraments of the living, point to the power of the cross of Christ and its victory over sin. They are also a living imperative to the Christian to engage in the ruthless struggle with sin. The Christian must fight against sin, resist "unto blood" (Heb 12:1–4). He must be profoundly convinced that it is an utter contradiction to be in Christ and to continue to live in sin (I Jn 3:6, 9; Rom 6).

The Christian has died to sin once and for all (Rom 6:2; 6:10ff.). He is freed from sin. It can no longer reign over him; this means he no longer stands powerless, bereft of strength under the mere law. Now he stands in grace, in the power of Christ who has overcome sin (Rom 6:14, 18, 22). But he may never for a moment forget that he has this power which triumphs over sin not from himself, but only through the closest vital union with Christ. One who does not cling to Christ remains in sin, is the slave of sin, totally chained by the force of sin (Rom 7; Eph 2:1). Conversely, anyone who remains bound to sin shows thereby that he has not truly united himself to Christ, has not truly "known" Christ, and does not follow Him in living faith (1 Jn 2:4; 3:6). Thus there remains for the Christian the sole alternative, either to cling to Christ or to die in sin.

Even though he has entered the ranks of the disciples of the Master, the Christian must ever remain aware of the dread earnestness of the struggle against sin. The sign of victory is the cross. The disciple is not exempt from the painful struggle against the devil and the flesh, against sin in the world and the evil tendencies in his own heart. Notwithstanding these forces of evil, the Christian may not hesitate so much as a single moment: he is baptized unto the cross of Christ, unto combat, but also in the resurrection, in the triumphant power of Christ (Rom 6). John and Paul, who cast such a powerful light on the triumph of the grace of Christ over sin, also are aware of the sharp antithesis between the holiness of baptism and the actuality of sin in the Christian community. Indeed the Christians would be liars if they should maintain that they committed no sin (1 Jn 1:8). But their sins may not be "sin unto death" (1 Jn 5:16), which would sever them from Christ, the source of their life.

External profession of faith in Christ does not of itself guarantee that we really live in Him. He that hates his brother abides in darkness and in the power of sin (1 Jn 2:11; 3:11ff.). For the Christian who has sinned, Christ, our advocate with the Father, is the only consolation (1 Jn 2:1ff.). If one has separated himself from Christ after he has been enlightened by faith, has closed his heart to Christ, although he has recognized Him in the Holy Spirit as the Son of God, his sin is unpardonable (Mt 12:31f.; Heb 6:5ff.; 10:26ff.; cf. 1 Jn 5:16ff.). The most heinous of sins, therefore, is to close one's heart to the impulse of the spirit of Christ, to alienate one-self entirely from Christ through infidelity (Jn 8:24; 16:9). But this sin is not, as the Reformers assumed, the only sin which excludes one from the kingdom of God, from the life of grace in Christ. Above all, the sins against love of neighbor (Mt 25:41ff.), the sins against justice, chastity, truth (cf. the "catalog of vices," Gal 5:20f.; Eph 5:3ff.; Col 3:5; 1 Cor 6:9f.; Rom 1:28ff.) exclude one from the union of grace with Christ.[1] But nevertheless, if faith and hope in Christ still remain, the door to the heart is still not completely closed, at least not to the work of the Holy Spirit, so that the path of return to Christ is not shut off and conversion may still be hoped for.

III. THE BIBLICAL DELINEATION OF SIN

The true nature of sin in all its malice can be understood only in the light of the sanctity of God, the majesty of His love, and His will to save mankind, only in the light of the history of salvation. New Testament and Old Testament reveal the dreadful character of sin in a number of concepts which must be studied in their totality if we are to grasp the meaning of sin in all its characteristics and consequences. In his emphasis on the relation of the three primary characteristics of sin, Saint John (1 Jn 3:4; 5:17) reveals the principal distinguishing features which manifest themselves more or less in every sin: sin is, first, the loss of salvation, loss of God (*hamartía*); secondly, it is opposition to the divine will expressed in the law (*anomía*); and thirdly, it is violation of the justice owing to God, guilt (*adikía*).

1. *Sin Is Perdition, Loss of God (hamartía)*

Hamartía, sin in the Biblical sense, is, first, the individual evil act, the transgression (the more common use of the term). Very often, however, the term refers also to the state which results from sin and which in turn is the fertile soil of further sin.[2] Sin is not something impersonal, an impersonal principle or power for which the individual is not responsible, something which excuses the sinner and frees him from guilt and blame. The experience of sin and the seeming incapacity to liberate oneself from its power have given rise to numberless systems of explanation and liberation (Manichaeism, astrology, various psychological explanations, such as psychoanalysis) which make of sin a mere principle of pure malady afflicting man. The sad experience of Augustine, and his profound wisdom, gave him an insight into this error which is equivalent to flight from conversion.[3]

The state of sin is an essential result of the act of sin and also a punishment flowing from the act. Underlying assumption and presupposition for sin is the basic freedom of man to do good. Nevertheless, the sinner vaunts his freedom to do evil. With unrestrained self-exaltation he seeks to prove his freedom by turning to evil and loses thereby the power for good, to the extent that God does not graciously keep him from falling. Such is the thought of Saint Paul who says in his letter to the Romans that God punishes sin through further fall into sin (cf. ROM 1:18–32). When God abandons the sinner to the very law of his own sinfulness, he falls irrevocably into the serfdom of sin. "Everyone who commits a sin is a slave of sin" (JN 8:34).

Sin as deliberate renunciation of God tears man away from God, the source of his freedom, the font of all good, the Giver of salvation. As a result, from the act of sin flows the state of perdition, loss of salvation, loss of God. The sinner seeks self, makes of self a god (GN 3), and by this fact makes of himself his own enemy. By sin he places himself in contradiction to himself and to the world God has created (GN 3:17ff.). He strikes out on his own path and, like the prodigal son in the Gospel parable, deserts the house of his Father for the land and house of strangers. The result is loss of salvation, for the alien land is the domain of Satan, God's enemy, into whose hands sin has committed him (JN 8:34; 9:31; 1 JN 3:8).

"On the one hand the sinner is responsible for the sins he has committed. Through his own fault he wanders in the darkness. On the other hand, once he has fallen, he continues to sin by a kind of necessity because he cannot do otherwise except to continue to stray in this darkness and slavery to the devil. . . . But he can break the chains of this fatal enslavement, though only through faith in the divine revelation in Jesus (JN 8:31ff.)."[4]

To sin is to refuse God the honor due Him (ROM 1:21), to refuse the worship which belongs to God and substitute a human cult for the divine (AP 17:4ff.). Therefore sin necessarily involves loss of glory and beatitude, to which all revelation of the majesty of the Lord is directed (Cf. AP 21:27; 22:11, 15). It is particularly the sins against the divine cult, the sins against religion (AP 13:1, 4, 15; 14:11; 16:9; 17:3ff.; 18:7; 21:8) which most sharply and clearly manifest this formal characteristic of sin as attack upon the divine honor and glory with the consequent apostasy from the beatifying splendor of the divine majesty.

One who has been baptized into the life of Christ is radically freed from the enslaving power of sin. He is no longer bound by the chains of Satan and the evil constraint of the unredeemed *"sárx"* (the carnal old man). The optimism of salvation belongs essentially to the apostolic glad tidings.[5] It is the good news of sin vanquished by the victorious power of Christ and of the Christian participation in the triumph. "The Christian is in a state of antithesis between the two realities: radically he is freed from sin, redeemed, reconciled, sinless, but in point of fact he is in conflict with sin which threatens him, attacks him, oppresses him. He must be summoned to *hagiasmos*"[6] (holiness), to a life which is nourished by a state of sanctity, which leads to sanctification, to the glory of God, and to perseverance unto death. Precisely because he is sanctified and lives in the plenitude of salvation does his sin show its true malice. Only in the light of this sanctity does grave sin fully manifest itself as perdition, loss of one's soul, apostasy from salvation.

Not only does sin mean perdition, loss of one's own salvation, or the hazard of loss of one's soul, but also, even though in varying degrees, an attack on the salvation of one's neighbor, diminution of the plenitude of salvation of the Mystical Body of Christ, of the kingdom of God. This very aspect of sin, the antisocial aspect, is particularly significant. The loss to others is not easy to restore. Moreover, it constantly begets further evils. Surely the thought of it must make everyone who knows something of the mystery of salvation shrink in terror from the slightest sin.

2. Sin Opposes the Revealed Will of God (anomía)

According to Saint Augustine, sin is "a thought, word, or deed against the eternal law." Sin is not solely objective contravention of the eternal law of divine wisdom, but it is also a deliberate attitude of subjective opposition to the law. In this matter it is very important to determine the form and manner and also the clarity with which the holy will of God was revealed in the law.

The Gentiles had no law. They did not possess the law of the Jewish Dispensation. But they were not by this fact excused from guilt of their sin, for when "the Gentiles who have no law do by nature what the Law prescribes, those having no law are a law unto themselves. They show the work of the Law written in their hearts. Their conscience bears witness to them" (ROM 2:14f.). Even the sins of the pagans are not mere opposition to a norm immanent in the world. They are not merely unreasonable acts, but acts in oposition to the will of the Creator manifested in the created order of nature. For this reason Alexander VIII condemned the distinction between theological and mere "philosophical" sin. The notion found in many religions of an inferior type that "sin" consists predominantly or even exclusively in a ritualistic-cultal offense and not at all in culpable violation of the order of creation is shocking evidence of the apostasy from the living faith in the Lord of creation, the Founder of every order and every just law.

Still more sharply is sin exposed as opposition not solely to a norm, but also to God Himself, to His gracious revelation of the law, by Moses and the prophets. The alliance of love with Israel makes of sin a refusal of this gracious law of the covenant, defection from fidelity to the alliance of divine love (Is 1:2–4), adultery (JER 3:20). The melancholy fact that man makes of the clear manifestation of the loving will of God in the gracious law an occasion to multiply his transgressions, his sinful deeds (ROM 5:13; 7:8, 13; GAL 3:19), and to harden himself still more in sin, reveals the true condition of the sinner—a condition already existing before the positive revelation—as "hostile to God" (ROM 8:7). "This thought of hostility became the constitutive element of the Pauline concept of sin"[7] (cf. ROM 3:9ff.; 5:10; COL 1:21; EPH 2:14).

In its encounter with the law revealed in the covenant of love, sin is the haughty animosity of self-assertion against the supreme dominion of God and His loving solicitude for man. In the light of revelation sin is the flight into self-deception (HEB 3:13), into the lie (JAS 3:14; JN 8:44ff.; ROM 1:25), into the darkness which dreads the light and is hostile to God (cf. JN 1:5ff.). But the full brutal force of opposition and hostility toward God is manifested in the light of the revelation of the new law, in the bright light of the unbounded love in Christ (cf. JN 15:22ff.).

In the New Testament the grace and love of God in the Holy Spirit is revealed as the essence of the new law. Wherefore the vilest of sins, the most heinous in its malice, is the sin against the Holy Spirit (MT 12:31; HEB 6:4ff.). Specifically the sin against the Holy Spirit (we might call it the final and ultimate sin against the Holy Spirit) is apostasy from Christ whom the testimony of the Spirit has accredited in the voice from heaven, in the miracles of Christ, in His Holy Church, and in man's heart and conscience. Every resistance of the heart to the new law of grace, to the inner guidance of the Holy Spirit, has some affinity to this sin. There lurks the danger that we will eventually succumb, for we have made the first step toward this last and desperate sin.

Precisely because we are in the light of the "law of liberty" (Jas 1:25), every sin bears the mark of lawlessness, not solely in the sense of external transgression of the bounds of law, but in the refusal of the invitation of grace, which is really the law of the children of God. Such is the imperfection of man and so superficial are many of his acts that there must be a vast variation and gradation in the development of this virulent character of sin with its hostility to God.

3. Sin as Supreme Injustice and Guilt (adikía)

Every form of injustice, even the violation of the just claims of fellow men, and above all the violation of the divine rights, is sin (1 Jn 5:17). What is actually the real malice in every sin is not the injustice between man and man, but the denial of obedience owing to God, who is our Lord and Master. Because God lays claim to His sovereignty over us in the revelation of the dominion of love, in the saving love of His only-begotten Son, and in the mission of the Spirit of love, the refusal of filial love is the most outrageous injustice against God. Thus the coming of Christ showed how sin was manifestly hatred of God (Jn 15:22ff.). Now sin means to prefer the "polluted world," condemned on the cross, to the infinite love of Christ (2 Pt 2:20), to exchange the loving service which the child owes to God for the once discarded slavery of Satan. Since God lays claim to His right as a right of His love and not merely as right of power, all refusal of love, all violation of the great commandment of love, falls under the actual (Biblical) concept of injustice.

Injustice flows from impiety (the asebéia of Rom 1:18ff.), which refuses to adore and glorify God; for it is the first right of God that His rational creatures turn all things toward Him. If the man who has been justified commits sin, his act is in contradiction to the justice of God he has received; it is a rejection of the life based on the heavenly justice bestowed through grace. The grave sin of the Christian viewed in its fulness of malice means that one has "trodden under foot the Son of God," has "regarded as unclean the blood of the covenant" (Heb 10:26ff.), has presumed, despite the inspirations of the Holy Spirit, to curse Christ (cf. Mt 12:31). But even more than all this, the injustice of sin bears the mark of ingratitude, immense ingratitude against the incomparable infinite love, for life flowing from the love of God must be a constant thanksgiving (a continuous *"Eucharistia"*). Injustice manifests itself not only in the act itself, but the act bares the melancholy state of injustice, the loss of salvation, the state of guilt (1 Jn 1:9).

The consequence of injustice is the guilt corresponding to the deep impiety of his act, the state of sin and guilt. By his act the sinner does his evil best to make himself forever unworthy of the imitation of Christ, unworthy to live the life of grace in Christ. He can never again follow Christ without a new summons of grace. And the call of grace cannot be rightly understood and followed unless the sinner recognizes his sin, and not merely as injustice and as guilt which only the mercy and power of God can efface! God demands of him also the way of penance and atonement, the perpetual sense of his guilt and of the justice and mercy of God.

In the light of the true impiety of sin, we may well ask: when man sins and continues to live in sin, is he actually conscious of its dreadful character, of the loss of salvation, of the lawlessness of his acts and state, of the hostility toward God? There is a sin of malice, often called the sin of the "hand upraised" against God. It is the Satanic sin, the "sin against the Holy Spirit," in which the awful depths of malice are fully apparent. But there are also mortal sins in which the sinner progressively obscures his insight into the horror of his offenses, which he removes by a lie to himself: "he lies them away." Finally there are venial sins in which the actual malice of sin, the aversion from God, is not present, though the tendency to this aversion and the menace of it are not at all absent.

Ordinarily the sinner, even though he offends God gravely, does not have as his immediate purpose or his first express intention the direct turning away from God, the aversion from God (*aversio a Deo*), but rather a specious or fallacious love for a created good (*conversio ad creaturam*), which is ultimately a false self-love to which he is lured by the mirage of his own pride and concupiscence. Nevertheless, in every mortal sin man's conscience is in some measure aware that perverted seeking of created good is incompatible with the permanent union with God, with the following of Christ. It follows that, when one consciously turns to the "world" in opposition to God, implicit in his act is his renunciation of the following of Christ.

When compared to the indirect rejection of Christ implicit in every disobedience in serious matters, the direct renunciation of Christ (in the sin of hatred of God and positive infidelity) represents in its intrinsic malice of will and finality only an aggravation, albeit a tremendous one, of the refusal of obedience inherent in every mortal sin. Yet on the other hand there is an immense chasm between the "sin of malice" and the grave "sin of weakness," even though the latter does deprive us of sanctifying grace. The former is a final definitive, we might call it a total, rejection of Christ, whereas the mere sin of weakness is indeed a grave abuse of freedom, a preference for self (for one's pride, for one's concupiscence), and an actual withdrawal from the imitation of Christ, but surely not by direct rejection or with definitive and total finality.

If the sinner who has fallen through human frailty still clings to faith and hope, then he will see in his very sin his own injustice against himself. He confesses, not, of course, by the act itself, but in his faith, to which he still clings, Christ as his lawful Lord and Master and, through his hope, Christ as his Saviour. In this manner he still preserves for himself the plank of safety by which he can return to Christ.

IV. TEMPTATION TO SIN

The possibility of sin is based on the imperfection of human freedom. Sin flows from the free will. But free will is tempted by pride, by concupiscence, by the evil world, and the devil. The devil is "the Tempter" (1 THES 3:5; MT 4:3). In some manner or other, every temptation which endangers our salvation is connected with the one who wages incessant war against God principally by seeking to lead men into sin (GN 3:1ff.; EPH 6:12; 1 COR 7:5; MT 4:7; MK 1:13; LK 4:2). Wherefore we must beg God to be delivered from temptation; for if we are reduced to our own resources, we cannot resist the devil (MK 14:38; MT 6:13; 26:41; LK 22:40, 46). To expose oneself to temptation means to deliver oneself over to the dominion of the powers of darkness.

The devil does not himself always tempt us directly, but he usually employs his satellites, especially the evil world, which, like the devil, clothes itself in a vesture of light, veils its evil purposes and its evil spirit. Only the man who is docile toward the guidance of the Spirit of God is able to judge rightly regarding the deceitful spirit of the world, whereas carnal man is not able to know clearly what is the work of the spirit of God and what the work of the spirit of lies (1 COR 2:15ff.).

Neither the devil nor the evil deceitful world can force man to sin. Should one simply be constrained by external force or coercion without actual freedom, that which one is forced to do is not sin. One has merely endured or suffered violence passively. Temptation which proceeds from without is dangerous because of the inner pride and concupiscence of the "flesh," of the "old man" to which it appeals. What actually lures and "decoys" the frail will of man is the tendency to evil in man himself, which through the external lure in some measure "conceives" and "brings forth" evil (cf. Jas 1:15). Therefore, as to what may be an actual temptation to sin for the individual, and consequently what he must earnestly avoid with all his might depends essentially on his inner firmness or, more specifically, on his inner susceptibility to the external temptation. If up to the present a particular external situation has constituted a danger which cannot be shunned, one's first duty is to guard vigilantly the movements of the "carnal man" and to pray fervently to the Holy Spirit for His grace. Only with the aid of this grace can man break the evil spell of temptation at all times (Lk 22:40, 46).

Even though one should feel strong and confident regarding a particular external temptation and not in the slightest degree susceptible, he still may not contribute by his action toward the temptation of his fellow man, but he must do everything possible by word and deed to make his fellow man aware of the true nature of temptation, in order that he himself may not also be tempted (Gal 6:1).

The temptations which are said to come from God are entirely different. When God tempts us, it is to test and try our virtue and alert us to danger. He does not lead us into evil. "God is no tempter to evil, and he himself tempts no one" (Jas 1:13). The world and the devil make every effort to allure "carnal" man to evil. Similarly God offers His grace to the free will of man in order to lead him to good in the hour of trial. The temptation which man himself culpably seeks out or the occasion which his sloth in prayer and vigilance turns into a danger for salvation does not come from God, though it is not without the divine permission. From God comes the test, the providential tribulation in the form of external visitation and abundant inner grace (at least the rich grace of prayer). This providential trial is in the mind of the Apostle when he says: "Esteem it all joy, my brethren, when you fall into various trials (*peirasmoi*), knowing that the trying of your faith begets patience" (Jas 1:2f.; cf. Jas 1:12; 1 Pt 4:12). God puts man to the test with a trial which but for the loving guidance of grace would really be a temptation, for the purpose of purging the dross and leaving the pure gold of virtue (Sir 27:6). In this manner He tried Abraham, Job, Tobias. "Because thou wast acceptable to God, it was necessary that temptation should prove thee" (Tb 12:13). "The Lord your God trieth you, that it may appear whether you love him with all your heart, and with all your soul, or not" (Dт 13:3).

If we do not seek the temptation ourselves, having perhaps already partially yielded to it, if it comes, not from us, but from God, then God will be faithful and bountiful with His grace (1 Cor 10:13). For God does not seek our defection, but our perseverance in trial, for which He has promised the palm of victory (Apoc 3:5).

The most effective helps in overcoming or escaping from temptation are reception of the sacraments, prayer, meditation which gives us insight into the allurements of sin in the light of the wisdom of the cross, vigilance over all disordered thoughts and feelings, mortification, and above all flight from all wilful occasions of sin. In the actual moment of temptation our only recourse must be firmness of resolution, rejection of seductive thoughts and images, flight from the external occasion (place or person) if this is possible, and an orientation of mind toward indifferent objects which hold our attention readily, and most of all giving our heart to God.

V. MORTAL SIN AND VENIAL SIN

1. "Grave Sin" and "Mortal Sin"

The term *grave* is used in contrast to the smaller, lesser sins. As far as the object itself is concerned, the transition from the one to the other may be continuous, with the consequence that the distinction is only "gradual." Thus, for example, in transgressions against the property of others, the passing from the tiniest amount to the greatest is gradual or continuous. And yet it is evident that at some point the sin becomes a grave offense.

Subjectively viewed, there is an essential distinction between grave sin (mortal sin) and lesser sin (venial sin). There is a certain absoluteness in the distinction between the two. The term *mortal sin* is used to indicate the death which it bears with it to the spiritual supernatural life of the soul in the state of grace. If this life is present in the soul, mortal sin by its very nature will destroy it.

What is objectively a grave sin is not by that very fact always a mortal sin subjectively, but it is true that what is subjectively a grave sin is always subjectively a mortal sin. For this reason the distinction between mortal sin and grave sin in the same order (objectively or subjectively) is not to be construed in such a way as though something could be gravely sinful without at the same time being mortally sinful.

In the Church's ancient penitential discipline the distinction was made between *"crimina"* or sins which excluded the offender from the ecclesiastical communion (apostasy, adultery, homicide) and the other sins which did not involve such excommunication and were not subjected to the public penitential discipline. But the fact that other grave sins were not subjected to this discipline is not at all a proof that they were not looked upon as mortal sins.

Hermann Schell maintained that the so-called sins of weakness, which were due to man's concupiscence and passion for the world and self, were grave sins, but not mortal sins. For Schell mortal sin was only the sin of direct revolt against God, spiteful resistance to God with the "hand upraised" against God. A thousand passages of the inspired pages can be cited in refutation of this doctrine of Schell, particularly those which contain the catalog of vices given by Saint Paul, in which the principal sins are those of weakness. And of these Paul makes the comment that they who commit them "will not attain the kingdom of God." This is specifically the case regarding those who commit sins against purity, typical sins of weakness. Those who commit them will not attain the kingdom of God (GAL 5:19ff.).

If the sin of weakness is subjectively a grave sin, if it is committed with full awareness that a grave law is being violated and with that degree of freedom which is essential for grave sin, then it is in every instance also a mortal sin.

The distinction made by Linsenmann[8] between sins of weakness and sins of malice is misleading. "There is a malice of the will," says this noted author, "and that which flows from it is mortal sin; and there is a weakness of will . . . and that which flows from it is venial sin, and of this it is correct to say, 'to err is human.'" This is correct only if by weakness we mean the inherent frailty and impotence of will which makes it impossible to avoid all sins, even the slightest. To lead a life of such perfection indeed is practically impossible without altogether singular help from God.

Erroneously the Reformers held that the only mortal sin was the sin against faith. In condemning this error, the Council of Trent lists certain sins of weakness (with reference to the catalog of sins found in 1 COR 6:9ff.) which exclude "from the kingdom of God not only those without faith, but also those with faith," since they can be avoided with the help of God's grace. Even though these sins do not entail the loss of faith, they nevertheless separate men from the grace of Christ.[9] The sins of unbelief, however, are far more desperate, for they destroy the very foundation of the supernatural life.

There is a certain malice also in the sins of weakness, the malice of disobedience and defect of love which cannot be divorced from any sin which is subjectively a grave offense.

2. Mortal Sin and Venial Sin

a. The Essential Difference between Mortal and Venial Sin

There is a "theological" distinction between mortal and venial sin which is concerned with their whole essence. Mortal sin extinguishes the supernatural life of sanctifying grace in the soul. Venial sin in some manner is opposed to this same life of grace, but not so directly as to destroy it. Three elements must be present in every mortal sin: first, an object strictly commanded, or strictly prohibited, in actuality or at least in the estimation of the agent. This is often called "grave or serious matter"; secondly, clear awareness of conscience regarding the command, the seriousness of the law, often called full advertence; thirdly, the free decision of the will, often called full consent of the will. Should any of these three elements be missing entirely or substantially, there is no mortal sin committed; at most the offense is venial.

As to the first point, were anyone to look upon an unimportant command as weighty and serious, or consider something insignificant or secondary as really significant and essential, and despite this attitude of mind, violate the command or neglect what was considered important, then that person would be guilty of mortal sin. In such a case the gravity of one's sin arises, not from the importance of the object, but from the evil decision of the will to violate an important commandment of God (or commandments regarding serious matter). But should an over-anxious conscience create the notion in one's mind that a little sin of surprise in a very petty matter (for example, a slight lack of candor in response to a question) is a mortal sin, as a rule such a fault would not be a mortal sin at all. The reason is that such an act is not completely and entirely free. In cases in which a pathological anxiety makes a mortal sin of every petty disorder, it is altogether certain that there is no grave guilt, for the simple reason that we do not have full liberty and capacity to avoid all such petty acts. Persons thus afflicted surely do not scorn the divine law at all. It must be also noted that we may attach no importance to the judgment of conscience which makes a mortal sin of these acts after the fact. It is the moral judgment which precedes the act and accompanies it which is the decisive factor.

As to the second point: the degree of knowledge and advertence necessary (for mortal sin) must be such that one can see clearly that the act is gravely sinful or at least that there is a serious obligation to inquire about the gravity.

As to the third point: if the knowledge of the importance of the act or the degree of actual advertence to its gravity is essentially lessened, the freedom of the act itself is correspondingly diminished, for the freedom of the act does not go beyond the bounds of the moral consciousness. However, it may happen that the freedom of the act may not be total and complete, even though there is clear knowledge and full advertence of the mind. An absolute and certain control over the degree of freedom is not possible. Nevertheless, ordinarily the judgment of one's own prudent conscience is valid when the question arises: did I act with full freedom? Have I used all the powers of my free will? However, it should ordinarily be looked upon as a rule of prudence that an act which is based on full knowledge and advertence is truly under the control of the free will and is entirely a responsible free act.

Venial sin does not essentially contravene the divine law. It is not an actual contradiction to our orientation to God, our ultimate end. Consequently, venial sin never destroys the supernatural habit of love.

A sin is venial either because of its nature or object (*ex genere suo*) which is actually unimportant or presumed to be of little importance (smallness of matter), or because of the imperfection of the act (*ex imperfectione actus*), which is due to some lack of knowledge or advertence or lack of freedom.

There is an essential distinction—we might call it an infinite distinction—between mortal and venial sin. In fact, the term *sin,* when applied to venial sin, is used analogously,[10] for in its full and proper sense the term *sin* means only mortal sin. Likewise, in the full and proper sense of the term, *disobedience* to God applies only to mortal sin, whereas by comparison venial sin is only imperfect obedience. Subjectively, mortal sin is the total orientation to created good as ultimate end: it contradicts supernatural love and destroys it. Venial sin by its nature can co-exist with the soul's fundamental orientation to God, does not involve actual opposition to the habit of divine love, but fails transiently to realize or actualize it.

Though we must warn against the danger of self-deception on this point, there must be some realization or conscious awareness of this infinite chasm between grave sin and venial sin. Surely there is a total difference between the spiritual life of one who is ready to forfeit the divine friendship rather than his own perverted will, and the spiritual status of another who realizes his own tardiness or incapacity in submitting his whole self even in little things to the guidance of divine love, though holding fast to essentials with basic good will.

b. Teaching of the Church

The Council of Carthage, approved by Pope Zosimus (418), expressly taught that even the just man, the "saint," correctly and rightly must pray for himself: "forgive us our trespasses!" But if one who is in the state of grace commits sin, without ceasing to be just or holy, then such sins must be venial. Therefore, there are lesser sins which "burden" grace, but do not destroy it.[11] The Council of Trent explicitly teaches that there are sins which do not destroy the state of grace;[12] in fact, the Council teaches that, without a special privilege of grace, it is not possible even for the saint to avoid each and every venial sin (the sum total of venial sins);[13] but it condemned as no less an error the teaching that even the saints commit sins in their every act, at least venial sins.[14] Pius V condemned the rigorous doctrine of Baius that venial sins by their nature deserve eternal punishment.[15] From all this it should be evident that venial sin is such by its very nature (or perhaps it is better to say, as we shall note later on, through the imperfection and frailty of man's nature). Surely it is not to be derived from the arbitrary decree of God.

Venial sins can be removed in a variety of ways,[16] though it is always commendable and advisable to confess them contritely.[17] However, venial sin is not simply dismissed and forgiven by God. Pardon for all sin, venial and mortal, comes through the redemptive merits of Christ alone. Venial sin cannot be pardoned unless one is sincerely detached from it.

c. The Words of Scripture

Though the terms *mortal* and *venial* sin are not found in Sacred Scripture, the concept and distinction are very evident in Biblical thought.

There are many references to the "death" connected with sin. In his letter to the Colossians Saint Paul says that the Christians "were dead" before their conversion because of their transgressions. After their conversion they are brought to life (2:13). The texts in which the Apostle refers to physical death as punishment for sin should not be cited as simply referring to mortal sin, for the concept of mortal sin in the first instance includes the notion of loss of the life of grace (ROM 6:23) rather than physical death. Saint John in his first letter speaks of a sin which is "in death": "he who does not love abides in death" (3:14). In the same letter (5:16) he refers to the "sin unto death." The term probably does not refer simply to mortal sin as such, but to the sin of impenitence, which surely leads to eternal death. For our purpose all those passages are significant which speak of a sin which excludes from the "love of God," from "the kingdom of God" (cf. GAL 5:19ff.; 1 COR 6:9), from eternal beatitude, of a sin which will be eternally punished.

The immense difference between mortal and venial sin is indicated in the Scriptural symbol of speck and beam (MT 7:3). Obviously the Lord, in speaking of "specks," does not refer to sins or faults which exclude one from the kingdom of heaven. Nor does He, when He teaches His disciples to pray for forgiveness, "forgive us our trespasses," mean to imply that these are faults which exclude them from the ranks of His followers. Such a supposition would mean that they should have to pray daily for pardon from grave sins, surely an absurdity. The same point is evident from the first letter of Saint John (1:8) and the letter of Saint James (3:2): the words clearly show that there are sins of which one may be guilty without ceasing to be numbered among the just. The passage in PRV 24:16, "A just man shall fall seven times and shall rise again," refers to external misfortunes, and cannot be adduced as Scriptural proof for the distinction between venial and mortal sin. The just man falls into misfortune and rises from his misery through the divine help. (It should be noted that the passage does not say the just man falls seven times a day.)

d. Tradition

The Fathers of the Church unanimously testify to the conviction of the Church that slight faults do not entail the loss of grace. The controversy over the rigorous Stoic position according to which all sins were equal in guilt offered the occasion to the early ecclesiastical writers to stress the doctrine that it is irreconcilable with divine mercy to punish every sin, even the slightest, with eternal death.[18] Saint Augustine contributed much to the precision and clarification of the doctrine of the essential distinction between mortal sin and lesser sins. It is interesting to note that he considers it impossible to distinguish clearly in every instance between mortal and venial offense, but he says that God expressly chose to leave these boundaries somewhat obscure in order to caution us against a frivolous and heedless attitude toward venial sin.[19] However, he does not deny that usually there is a basis for a sound moral judgment giving us practical certainty in these matters.

Since the problem of venial sin poses great theoretical difficulties, it is not surprising that theological study did not offer a ready solution. Only after a considerable period of time did speculative theology manifest some mastery of the question. As one might expect, scholastic theologians, without ever denying the distinction between mortal and venial sins, offered a great diversity of speculative solutions. Only with the teaching of Aquinas and the theology of Trent (in opposition to the errors of Luther) does the discussion reach a conclusive stage, though the problem still remains a thorny one.

e. The Problem

The basic question to be answered is concerned with the reason for the immense distance between mortal and venial sin. What is to account for this total essential diversity? Is not the malice of transgression essentially the same, whether the commandment violated be great or small? Does it not consist essentially in disobedience, in contradiction, in resistance to the will of God? Might not one readily assume that the mere difference of a degree, one degree more or less, in the disturbance of the order of creation could not account for the loss of grace in one instance if it were not lost in the other? Such is the basic question.

The German theologian Artur Landgraf (died in 1958) says that after Saint Bernard's time, "probably no scholastic dared to question the axiom: that which is contrary to God's command is grave sin."[20] Many writers drew the conclusion, "that venial sin is not forbidden by God and hence not contrary to His will."[21] For this same reason, Scotus holds that venial sin does not contravene an actual commandment, but is rather the neglect of a counsel. (Any such position is untenable.) As indicative of the obscurity which still clouded the study, the scholastics as a rule, when discussing venial sin, concerned themselves only with the so-called *motus primi,* the first movements of emotion which are only imperfectly controlled by our free will (hence, they dealt with the imperfect acts in the strict sense of the term).

The isolated attempts (later on the same approach was followed by Baius) to base the distinction of venial and mortal sin and the compatibility of venial sin with the state of grace on a positive decree of God as such, were unanimously and energetically rejected by the scholastic writers. By the very nature and essence of venial sin it does not destroy the state of grace. Hence, it cannot simply and as such contradict the divine will. It is not opposed to the law in the sense of the *contra legem,* but is rather beyond the law (*praeter legem*). It does not imply a radical re-orientation away from the last end of man, but only a slackening of pace or a momentary cessation in the permanent orientation toward the last end.[22]

Already in his time William of Auxerre offered a solution which Saint Thomas later perfected. Venial sin does not destroy the habit of divine love in us, even though it is not actually animated by the basic dynamic of the permanent orientation of love. It does not have the intent, nor does it have the force, to alter this radical orientation of love toward God. But it does arrest the pace of love. And let us note, the permanent orientation toward God through love corresponds to the great commandment. Consequently venial sin, by its very nature and in its totality, is not a breaking of the law, not an attempt to remove or efface it, is not simply contrary to the law. And yet, no one can deny that it does weaken the zeal or ardor, the force or vigor of love and does breach the ramparts of defense dangerously.[23]

According to the conception of Saint Thomas as found in his later works, every morally good and correct act of one in the state of grace is in some manner under the influence of charity. For this influence of charity, the renewal of the so-called good intention is not essential, as long as one remains free from mortal sin. From this point of view Thomas sees in venial sin a disordered act, which indeed does not alter the fundamental orientation of love, though in its imperfection it fails to open itself to the animating force of habitual love. In venial sin there is nothing of the vigor of love. But there is likewise nothing which is directed against the principle of permanent orientation toward God. We might say that venial sin has neither the power nor the will, neither the force nor intent, to reverse this orientation.[24]

The commonly accepted teaching that pure spirits, and the same is very probably true of Adam before the fall, cannot commit venial sin, should shed some light on the present problem. Basically we reason in this manner: since the angels do not reason discursively, as we do, but grasp in one immediate concept both principle and its application, end and means, it is immediately evident to them that the transgression even of the slightest commandment is really against God's will, is a contradiction of the divine will, and therefore is grave sin. Somewhat similar was the case with Adam: before the fall there was no concupiscence reigning in his members; his spiritual powers worked together in full vigor and complete harmony. For him infraction, even the slightest, or regarding the pettiest object, was not possible without the responsibility of the clearest consciousness and the fullest freedom. His unimpaired intellect had a clear insight, quite different from that of his fallen children, into the whole texture of end and means. Nor could it fail to discern also how the slightest thing is under the dominion of God. Therefore, for the angels and also for our first parents there was only the one alternative, perfect obedience or full disobedience. Excluded was any imperfect obedience, and with it any venial sin.

If we bear these points clearly in mind and do not overlook the fact that the scholastics treated venial sin under the exclusive or at least under the primary aspect of the first indeliberate motions (*motus primi*) of the will, it becomes clear that the scholastics looked at venial sin as imperfect in act. Ultimately they based the slightness of venial sin (its essential difference from mortal sin) not on the basic diversity of the degree of gravity of the commandment or of the point prescribed, but on the imperfection of the act. Caution is to be observed in the use of the term "imperfection of the act." We surely may not conclude (also not according to the view of the scholastics) that there are no venial sins as to species, that there is no "smallness" of matter which makes the venial sin such objectively (the objective disorder of the act itself). But even the venial sin which is such objectively is in some way due to the imperfection of man's act in the present state.

In conclusion, the right solution of our problem seems to me to lie in the imperfection of fallen man, who cannot make a final decision (no "perfect act") normally regarding a slight object. Surely there can be a final decision regarding an object of little value, but not for its own sake as such. In fallen man we do not have a pure state or position of complete good or utter evil. The man who has turned to God through his basic intention and resolve is not yet free from other basic tendencies. Evil still lurks within him. Alongside the conscious, fully deliberate orientation of his fundamental intention toward the good, these other tendencies and urges, even though they have been revoked or recalled in principle, still retain something of their evil power. Similarly the basic, naturally good tendencies are constantly cropping up in the man who has turned to sin. Obviously one must predominate, for two basic complete principles of equal force, two fundamental orientations, cannot co-exist in man. Whenever a fully clear and deliberate decision has been made for good or bad, the other basic orientation ceases to be ultimate and free. From this it follows that venial sins are acts of secondary orientation. They are not acts of complete departure, sweeping aside the prior fundamental orientation to God, as it were casting it into discard. In this sense they simply do not attain the fulness of the act of human orientation.

It clearly follows that venial sin committed by one in the state of sin is different in kind from the venial sin committed by one in the state of grace. The former is sustained by the perverted fundamental attitude of one who is turned away from his last end and partakes of that attitude fundamentally, though without sinking to its full depth of malice. The latter, viewed in the light of one's last end, is slight or insignificant deviation from the central purpose and direction. It is not from the very core or center of final personal decision, but rather from the movements of evil concupiscence, movements which remain in fallen man even after his conversion to God, but which may be called external or peripheral. As long as man retains his basic orientation to God, as long as he clings to the state of grace, these movements are not able to press forward to the heart of final personal decision.

One of the consequences of this position is apparent (on this point we have the universal agreement of moral theologians): whenever a clear and basic personal decision, such as we have described, enters into the transgression of a commandment which is of little importance, whose object is slight (that is to say, whenever there is the total engagement of the person in opposition to the will of God, even though it be relative to a matter in itself unimportant), there is mortal sin. For this total engagement, this basic orientation of self, is tantamount to actual scorn of the lawgiver and a manifestation that one is turning from his last end which is God, that he places his final end in his own self-will.

When F. Zimmermann makes the point that "objectively venial sin is and continues to be only venial even if it is committed in full and conscious deliberateness,"[25] his statement is admissible in the sense that deliberate venial sin is possible. It is true that semi-deliberate sins are not the only venial sins. No one denies this point. But all this is correct only if we admit also that the human will even in the full consciousness of the slightness of the act of evil (abstracting from the basic evil orientation, the disdain for the law) does not normally engage the total power of decision for evil in man. Otherwise the act would be a mortal sin. Hence one might well question the blank statement that "a sin which is venial by its very species or nature (*ex genere suo*) can never become a mortal sin through the perfection of the act (*ex perfectione actus*)."[26] There can also be an act which we rightly call "perfect" in the sense of definitive and ultimate, concerned with the basic orientation of man in his whole depth, even though it be concerned with an insignificant object or be occasioned by something in itself quite petty. This from the viewpoint of awareness of value makes the act a "perfect" act and a mortal sin. Here ultimate values are concerned.

Zimmermann cannot justly cite the text of Thomas[27] from the *De Veritate* in favor of his position. Note the words: "But, when one consents to a venial sin after any deliberation, no matter how much, he does not have contempt of God, unless, perhaps, he would judge that the sin is contrary to a divine commandment."

The deliberation to which Saint Thomas refers when he speaks of these cases is not of the kind to which we have been referring. He does not have in mind the profound reflection on the very nature of moral disorder in its opposition to God. Thomas never for a moment denies that there are sins which in their species or nature are venial. But it is quite obvious that the examples of venial sins which he suggests as a rule (immoderate laughter, useless words, jocose lies[28]) are so insignificant that we should rather reckon them among the imperfections. Imperfections of this kind are venial sins, if they are conscious and deliberate despite a clear awareness that they are not in accord with right order. We often speak of them as "deordinations." If they are inadvertent and indeliberate, they are imperfections only.

A sin which is only venial by the nature of its object is no longer to be considered merely venial if the one who commits it clearly perceives that his transgression constitutes a serious danger to the salvation of his neighbor. If this act of his readily leads another to commit a sin which is objectively a grave offense against God, then there is a serious obligation to avoid the "venial" sin. To do otherwise would be to disregard the danger to the salvation of our neighbor and plainly show that one's own self-will in this insignificant matter is of greater importance than one's neighbor's loss of his final end, God.

Where slight matter "coalesces" into grave matter (a case in point is the multiplication of petty amounts which taken singly are petty thefts, but which together may inflict great damage on another, or the multiplication of petty acts of defamation which in their totality seriously harm the good repute of our neighbor), a multiplication of many venial sins does not constitute a mortal sin—this is never in itself possible—but the one mortal sin is committed at the moment the offender is disposed to permit the accumulation of amounts of the ensemble of acts to become a serious and important matter.

Much discussed is the question: is the resolution to avoid all mortal sin, but only mortal sin and not venial sin, in itself a grave sin? One must not overlook the fact that by the very terms of the resolution, mortal sin is expressly excluded. Accordingly one would say that the individual's conscience does not judge such a resolution as "gravely culpable." And yet this manner of reasoning is not altogether convincing. We must rather distinguish between the mere theoretical and "conceptual" exclusion of mortal sin and the real exclusion. Surely logically the proposition excluding all mortal sins is a universal proposition. But practically and concretely the mere exclusion of mortal sin by an abstract proposition does not necessarily and in every instance involve an exclusion of actual mortal sin. The "conceptual" notion can be false, for the moral sense may still be aware that something is seriously in disorder, that one is not actually resolving to avoid all mortal sin.

I do not think that it is possible to give a categorical reply to the question. There is need for a greater precision in our distinctions. Were one to take it upon himself basically and in principle not to make anything of venial sin at all, his attitude doubtlessly would be a kind of disdain, the equivalent of that scorn for the law of God which all authors condemn as seriously culpable. But if one is determined to avoid every mortal sin under all circumstances, even though human weakness does dampen his courage so that he does not resolve sternly to combat certain habitual venial faults, he surely does not bear contempt and scorn for God's law. The disdain and disregard for God's law as a matter of principle is absent, and surely there is no grave sin committed in such instances.

Were one of set and conscious purpose determined to commit one or the other venial sin occasionally (for example, refuse to forgo a bit of tomfoolery and unkind needling of an unsympathetic fellow man, without seriously offending him), this would not be evidence of deep contempt of the divine law in principle. One is not completely set upon ignoring all venial sins as though they were mere trifles, but merely neglects to resist the evil inclinations in lesser matters because of moral imperfection and frailty.

Every free and basic decision which contravenes a commandment is mortal sin. By free and basic decision we mean a human decision with full knowledge and liberty flowing from the very core and center of free responsibility for that which is final and ultimate in man. When the frail will of man is beset by the urge and drive of evil concupiscence, by the influence of passion, the free acts bear the malice of mortal sin only if the free and responsible individual in the very depths of his being has a moral realization that his decision is of final and ultimate consequence.

I do not consider it beyond the realm of possibility that on a very exalted level of religious-moral perfection, the transgression of a commandment in a matter in itself slight (for example, an ordinary but fully conscious lie)[29] could be viewed as so diametrically opposed to the divine law and so sharply adverse to the resistance of the alerted conscience, that the conviction would be justified that God is gravely offended by such a transgression. In this case one would not have to explain the strict attitude toward venial sin as arising merely from an erroneous conscience.

If our conception of the distinction between mortal and venial sin, soundly based as it is on the teaching of Augustine and the scholastic writers, has ultimately its sole foundation in the imperfection of the act, it follows that the distinction between mortal and venial sin "as to species" is not entirely inflexible. It is somewhat fluctuating. Therefore the proposition, "Some things are only venial sins by their very nature," is not a metaphysical proposition, but must be understood morally. And this means that such is the miserable moral condition of ordinary man factually and concretely since the fall that certain commands, certain petty objects ordinarily will not be the matter for a final decision called forth from the depth of freedom or penetrating to the very depth of freedom. Therefore, the judgment that something is only venially sinful "as to species" constitutes a rule of prudence for ordinary judgment, but does not give us any assurance that one can simply dismiss without hazard to salvation any and every command that is not in itself important with the excuse that it is "only a venial sin." Concern with the solution of the speculative problem as we have stressed it so sharply in these pages, significantly enough, persistently plagues all theologians. Every school or shade of teaching in moral theology is preoccupied with it, and it is central to the study of ascetic theology.

If we wish to look back on our past and determine with all possible certainty the culpability of our acts, to discover what was mortal and what was venial sin, we must take into account the importance of the act and its object, but still more our deeper dispositions and intentions. If one in his heart is resolved to pursue a course of action which involves only petty things objectively, but with the determination to proceed, whether the acts be mortal or venial sin, he acts with an evil disposition. He acts from the inner depth of an evil heart and commits a grave sin.

This sharp emphasis of the importance of the inner attitude is very uncomfortable if one seeks to form a judgment about his condition of soul on the basis of external rules. Nevertheless, as to the special obligations which govern the reception of the sacraments, these are in no wise more onerous or rigorous than the rules which apply in the simple determining of what is venial sin as to species. Every speculative attempt in theology must ultimately observe as its rule and as its test in application the defined doctrine of the Church and also the universal ecclesiastical practice. Hence, as long as there is doubt whether the culpability of the inner disposition and decision is grave or only slight, we should follow the eminently practical rule of prudence universally proposed: if the object of the act was slight, then it is presumed that one was not guilty of any grave sin. This rule should be followed with all tranquillity of conscience, even in approaching the Holy Eucharist.

Ordinarily it is very difficult to form a clear and certain judgment regarding the gravity of one's own past offenses, for one cannot easily avoid the pitfalls of self-deception. The danger is all the greater the more one is inclined, because of one's self-love, to minimize the seriousness of the commandments.

Another practical norm should be kept in mind: it is much more important and with the aid of grace also much easier to orientate oneself to God as one's last end, once we have turned from sin, than to rack one's conscience over past guilt. Little can be gained by grubbing over such points as to whether my sin was mortal or venial. The more earnest our will is to follow God's commandments in all things, the greater is also the subjective certainty regarding the state of grace. As far as past sins are concerned, we need never fear that the grief over our sins will ever be too intense, our sentiment of penance ever too severe, or our gratitude for the divine pardon ever too great. The saints were not guilty of **excess** when they repented of venial sins more earnestly than others do of their grave offenses, for even venial sin, though never comparable in malice to mortal sin, is a far greater misfortune than any earthly misfortune. It is, indeed, in some greater or lesser degree, placing **in hazard** the imitation of Christ.[30]

CHAPTER TEN

DISTINCTION OF SINS

I. SPECIFIC AND NUMERIC DIVERSITY

U<small>P TO</small> this point we have explained the nature of sin in so far as it is common to all sin as an offense against the holiness of God. The root is always the one same evil disposition of aversion from God, but it admits of very diverse degrees of malice and culpability. Man surely does not commit his offense directly against God, but rather in opposition to the order revealed by God in nature and grace by evil acquiescence in the created order. Sin, therefore, not only offends the infinite value of God's holiness under many aspects, but also the manifold created values. Accordingly, the diversity of the domains of value violated create a diversity of kinds of sin, or diverse species of sin.

Man is not like the pure spirits. He does not exploit the totality of his power of decision once and for all in one tremendous act. Like his reason, which is discursive, so his decisions are successive and diverse. He may decide and repeat his decision or repent of it. Previous acts can be repeated and reconfirmed or recalled. From such repetition flows the series of numerically diverse sins when man offends God. Both the distinction as to species and the distinction as to number must be explained with all possible clarity, for the very important reason that all mortal sins, according to the Council of Trent, must be confessed together with the species and number.[31]

1. *Specific Diversity of Sins*

Diversity in the kind of sin committed, which is called the specific difference or species of sin, may be determined 1) by the diversity of the value which is violated by sin, or, in other words, by the virtue which is opposed by sin; or 2) by the essential duties or obligations which a value creates or which a virtue imposes; or 3) by the manner in which sins offend against the right balance or measure of virtue through defect or excess.

As to the first point, we stress the scholastic axiom: "the act is specified by the nature of its object" (*actus specificantur ab objecto*); this also holds for the determination of the species of sins. And since there are diverse moral values corresponding to the various kinds of virtues, we can apply the same principle by noting the relation to the virtues: the nature of a sin is specified or determined according to the virtue which the sin violates.

EXAMPLES: Infidelity and doubt against faith are sins against the virtue of faith. These sins offend against the value of the veracity of God making Himself known to us in His supernatural revelation. Despair sins against the virtue of hope. Hatred of God is a sin against the theological virtue of love. It directly offends against the value of divine love. Superstition is a sin against the virtue of religion. It offends against the justice due to the absolute supremacy of God over us. Scandal offends against the virtue of love of neighbor, particularly against the eternal value of his soul's salvation.

One single act very often violates several virtues. Thus if one were to steal a chalice belonging to a church, one would violate both justice and religion.

As to the second point, regarding the diversity of species of sin based on the diverse duties or obligations imposed by one and the same virtue (or based on the diverse aspects of value in the same virtue), the following examples illustrate the point. The virtue of religion demands of us that we adore God and Him alone. Disregard of this virtue by adoring false gods is idolatry. But the same virtue also demands that God be honored in a manner worthy of His supreme dignity. To offend on this point is superstition or superstitious cult. By the same virtue we are forbidden to use the powers hostile to God to unveil mysteries or to seek occult knowledge. On this point the sin of divination violates the virtue of religion. Astrology belongs in part to divination, in part to idolatry, for man accepts the norm of conduct not from the commandments of God, but from the occult design sought in the secrets of the heavenly bodies. Religion commands respect for the divine name. Opposed to this respect is the whole gamut of abuse of the divine name, from profane language to blasphemy. Blasphemy adds a new species, because it violates not only the reverence for the holy name of God, but also directly offends against the love of God.

To transgress against a positive law or command violates the virtue of obedience. Usually transgression of the law of the Church includes violation of the virtue which the law purports to safeguard, for the precepts of the Church are always imposed for the protection or furtherance of some particular virtue. If a positive command or precept is concerned only with obedience, if no other virtue is demanded by the command, then what is commanded may be considered indifferent as far as species of sin is concerned. There is no additional species of sin over and above the sin of disobedience. Accordingly, one may confess the sin without mentioning the nature of the command with the simple statement, "I was disobedient to my parents" or the equivalent. (However, if one has violated a commandment of the Church, he must mention the nature of the command, e.g., "I ate meat on Friday.") However, the delicate and alert conscience usually is concerned with the value safeguarded by positive laws or commands, for example, the value of life safeguarded by the traffic and speed laws. The earnest Christian cannot fail to realize that sins against human life, his own and others, can be committed in the violation of such positive laws.

As to both points just discussed: the virtue of love of our fellow man, or the value of our neighbor, embraces an entire series of distinct and diverse values, each of which imposes different duties. To the good of one's neighbor belong, to mention only the more important, the value of eternal salvation, the value of the immortal soul, the value of mental health, bodily life, honor and good repute, property, and the right to property and respect. Some of these values can be violated by one and the same sinful act. To cite just one example, one who seduces his neighbor to sins against purity (the producers of pornographic literature and contraceptives expressly strive for such ends) himself sins against chastity and also against love of neighbor in a variety of ways: he robs him of grace (value of eternal salvation), especially of the virtue of chastity (possibly of virginity), and in certain instances and under certain circumstances also of his honor and good name, health, opportunity of a worthy marriage or a suitable occupation.

As to the third point, certain virtues are centered in the mean between two extremes, between too much and too little. For example, one can be too much concerned about material goods and be guilty of avarice, or one can be too little concerned and be guilty of wastefulness or prodigality. The two are distinct species of sin. Similarly, one may violate the virtue of generosity or liberality. In this case the situation is reversed: the prodigal man gives too much; the avaricious gives too little.

Regarding these distinct species of sins, we must caution that the individual is not to be considered subjectively guilty of them except to the extent that he was at least in a general way aware of the values or commandments at the time he offended against them. Moreover, the obligation to confess one's sins according to the species and number binds only those who are subjectively guilty of these diverse kinds of sin.

Accordingly, in the confession of his sin the penitent's own recital in the sacrament is not to be measured rigidly by the pattern of difficult distinctions made by learned theologians, but rather by his own individual capacity of discernment and the judgment of his conscience at the time when the sin was committed. If he was ignorant or unaware of an objectively specific distinction of sins, that is, if he did not recognize the added serious disorder in his sinful act, he is not obliged, nor is the confessor permitted to oblige him, to complete the confession through such a scientific distinction. But it would be far from correct to conclude that these distinctions themselves are futile. Each individual conscience should progressively develop an awareness of the many diverse values which protest against the multiple sins which violate them.

2. *The Numeric Distinction of Sins*

If a single sinful act offends against many virtues, it follows that one numerically same sin contains many species of malice. Though these are many specifically different sins, we usually do not speak of them as numerically many sins. But if one single sinful act contravenes only one virtue or offends against one sole obligation in such a manner that only one species of sin is involved, we may have a numerical distinction or multiplication of sin. Such would be the case if there were many objects (persons or goods, many possessors of the value) concerned. This is the common teaching of authors.[32]

EXAMPLE: If one should in one single act summarily defame a whole group of people, let us say seven, he has committed seven sins of detraction in the sense of seven sins numerically. If a married man sins against chastity with a married woman, he commits two sins of adultery numerically, because he offends in justice against two marriage contracts. Obviously, there is a great difference between calumniating one person and seven persons, between violating one marriage or two. But I cannot agree with the authors in holding that one same external act, a single act, can include numerically many sins of the very same species. But this is not to deny what seems quite evident, namely, that one single sinful act can contain the malice of diverse specific offenses.

A number of external actions physically distinct can form a unit (one sin) taken as a whole, in so far as they flow from one single interior decision of the will and externally constitute a unit in the moral sense of the word. This holds at least for the penitent's recital of sins in confession. We can cite an example: the vile resolution to seduce a virtuous maiden imparts a kind of evil unity to all the particular words, proposals, deeds which finally culminate in the one infamous completed action. We should call all this one sin. If, however, the seducer employs means which offend against other virtues (theft, violence) and are not by their nature constitutive elements of his one evil project, he is guilty of further sins in species and number. But though the external actions are viewed as one external sin, this sinner commits interior sin as often as he renews his evil resolve deliberately and decides anew to reject the divine grace and continue in his infamous design.

Should one plan a theft and avail himself of all the devious devices to further his plan, he commits one sinful action numerically. Should he, however, purpose to commit many acts of thievery, diverse in themselves, he includes in one single interior resolve a great diversity of sinful actions and in the execution of the plan also commits a number of numerically distinct sins. These actions, despite the one interior evil resolve, do not form a unit, morally speaking.

It is correct to say that there are numerically as many interior sins as there are new sinful acts of decision in the will, as many external sins as there are sinful actions constituting a unity. In the purely internal sins of evil disposition and sentiment or intention, the permanent evil disposition is the actual sin. One who has such an evil disposition commits sins inwardly as often as he renews his evil attitude or wilfully approves of it in his mind. One who is living in hatred and enmity is guilty primarily because of the persistence of the hostility. But the number of interior hateful acts against his neighbor is far from being a matter of indifference.

The penitent in perplexity regarding the number of sins he has committed is well advised if he confesses his evil disposition and states whether the internal acts of enmity were only occasional or frequent. Ordinarily the confessor is not obliged to question the penitent on the frequency of such interior acts, if the penitent himself does not refer to them. He should not harass the penitent regarding merely interior acts where there has been a persistent evil disposition, or probe into the exact number. Exact computation is impossible, and as far as the judicial verdict in the sacramental tribunal is concerned quite frequently it is futile.

In the matter of evil resolve and intention, the number of sins is also to be reckoned as equal to the number of deliberate interior acts; this is to say that they occur as frequently as the renewal of the evil intent or the approval of it in the mind. We must note that the protracted and persistent adherence to evil is much more wicked and therefore more important in the study of sin than the mere enumeration of the acts of sin. Exclusive stress on the counting and adding of the individual acts might convey the impression that one who struggles constantly against sin and temptation, though he may often succumb, has committed a greater number of actual sins and is therefore a much greater sinner than one who simply continues in his evil ways without any effort to rise. On the contrary, the condition of the latter is far worse spiritually. His salvation is in far greater jeopardy.

II. DIVERSITY IN THE GRAVITY OF SINS

We have already dealt with the distinction between venial and mortal sins, but there is also a diversity of gravity and malice in mortal sins themselves. Sin is greater in malice the more exalted the value against which it directly offends and the more important the dimension in breadth and depth of the violation of this value. A sin may be opposed to a lesser value, however, and yet be objectively and subjectively a graver sin than another sin which violates a higher value, for the simple reason that other values may also be involved. Thus, to cite one example, the solitary sin of impurity (pollution) from one point of view is more serious than a sin of impurity with another, because the solitary sin is unnatural. Nevertheless, the sin with another is far more evil if viewed in the whole context, because sins with others also offend against the salvation of one's neighbor and may readily involve many other values. Moreover, they ordinarily presuppose a more positive determination of the free agent who commits the sin than does the solitary sin.

Most heinous are the sins which directly attack God, and all the more grave the more they offend the divine honor and love. The height of malice lies in the sins of hatred of God, blasphemy, and infidelity. Next in malice are the sins against the humanity of Christ. Then follow the sins against the sacraments, which contain the sacred humanity or are bound up with it most intimately. We place last the sins which offend against purely created values.[33]

Seduction and scandal offend against a value which in itself is more exalted (the soul's salvation) than the bodily life destroyed by the crime of murder. But since seduction and scandal cannot directly destroy grace and the soul's salvation, but do so only through free cooperation of the other party, and murder itself is the entire and complete cause of the destruction of bodily life, it follows that, from this aspect, murder is more malicious.[34] Murder of the unborn infant, however, has an altogether special malice, for it not only destroys the bodily life, but makes baptism impossible and robs the infant of eternal glory.

The gravity of guilt, however, depends on the degree of liberty with which the offense was committed. Deliberate malice increases, weakness lessens, guilt. Sin committed with clear knowledge and full attention or advertence is subjectively a greater offense than sin committed in a state of ignorance and inadvertence. In general, sins of malice are more heinous than sins of weakness. For this reason, to cite an example, an unworthy Communion is subjectively not as grave as the sin of murder, because as a rule the sin of unworthy Communion, grave as it is, is due to fearful respect for human opinion and frailty (sinful thoughtlessness).

To arrive at a thoroughly sound estimate of the gravity of sins, one must take into consideration not merely the importance or seriousness of the sin in itself, but also the gravity of the consequences which flow from the sin. This important point seems to have been overlooked in the work of August Adam, *The Primacy of Love* (English translation: Newman Press, Westminster, Maryland, 1958).

In a praiseworthy effort to place the sin of impurity in the correct category of sin in relation to other sins, he fails to focus sufficient attention on the ruinous effects of this sin in the whole context of the religious-moral life, especially the consequences of the frequent and habitual sin of impurity. Such is the dreadful power of evil concupiscence that sins of impurity readily tend to place man's whole moral freedom in danger. Permanently enslaved by this sin, he loses all zeal for the things of God.

Classification of sin according to gravity may be carried to excess. One should not exaggerate the importance of the categories of malice. Man is a unit, a composite whole, and human good is also indivisible. One who fails to subordinate passions and emotions to the spirit, fails to animate them with the spirit and keep them in right order, cannot claim a right-ordered relation with God. Often the lowliest things are quite basic (the foundation) for the higher things; and it may be a very grave injustice to accuse the spiritual director or pastor of neglecting the beauty of the tower of the spiritual edifice, if he concerns himself with a much needed reparation of the foundation. It would be blameworthy on his part to neglect the more basic spiritual task, which should not and cannot be delayed without imperiling the whole structure.

We repeat that sins of malice, "sins of the spirit," which are rooted in pride, are much more serious than the sins of frailty, rooted as they are in concupiscence. These latter ordinarily are not the result of premeditation, nor does the decision of weakness so profoundly affect the entire personality as the decision of malice. For this reason the sins of malice are more difficult to efface by true sorrow.

III. SINS OF OMISSION AND COMMISSION

Perhaps the sins which consist in the commission of evil do not constitute as grave a peril for the kingdom of God as the more numerous sins of neglect of the good which must be done. Neglect of our obligations is readily disregarded or shrugged off with slight excuses. For this reason it is of primary importance for us not to focus our attention only on the things we may not do, on that which we must avoid. Emphasis of the negative is not sufficient. We must point out what one must do, what one can and should do with the aid of divine grace. We must stress the positive. For that matter, however, we may never lose sight of the fact that ultimately the sin of omission is not merely negative. Sins of omission are actions, for they are really culpable only in so far as one by a free act neglects the good which he knows he must do.

The external occasion of neglect of duty may be something in itself good; it may be a licit act, which becomes evil and is morally forbidden because it involves the omission of something obligatory. In such an instance the malice of the act is not distinct from the neglect of the good. Hence only the sin of omission need be mentioned in confession.

The sin of omission is committed at the moment when one actually places the cause of the omission or neglect. EXAMPLE: One might in some manner foresee that he would miss holy Mass on Sunday morning if he drank to excess and was intoxicated on Saturday evening. If in spite of this knowledge he got drunk on Saturday night, he would be guilty both of the sin of drunkenness and the sin of omission by neglecting to attend holy Mass on Sunday. This latter sin of omission is committed when the guilty man knowingly indulges to excess or resolves to do so, not on Sunday morning. In fact, he is guilty of the sin of missing Mass even though, for some unforeseen reason, the Mass is not actually celebrated as was anticipated. A major cleric who postpones the recitation of his office without reason until late in the day, even though he realizes that urgent and pressing duties will make the later recitation impossible, commits the sin of omission when he makes the resolution to postpone the prescribed prayer.

IV. SINS OF THE HEART AND SINS OF ACTION

Every sin is first committed "in the heart" of man. It arises in the evil disposition and intention (whether there is question of a habitual disposition of evil or one single interior evil act). There are certain sins which are entirely interior, sins of the heart. The principal ones are these:

1. Interior complacence in evil, especially mental approval of former sins or inward regret that one has not committed a sin.

2. Mental complacence in pictures of the imagination, in concepts and thoughts about evil things (*delectatio morosa*).

3. Evil desire, the will directed toward evil which is not within the power of accomplishment. In this instance one does not actually want to do the evil thing, simply because it is not possible. This is called "inefficacious desire" for evil.

4. The evil intention, the actual will or resolve to do evil. This is called the "efficacious desire" for evil. The intention is present and one is guilty even though some external circumstance may prevent it and the desire may never be carried out.

All these four interior kinds of sin, as to species, bear the same malice as the external act to which they refer, but they do not always have the same degree of malice as the external act (Mt 5:28). It follows that the penitent must accuse himself in the confessional of the violation of the virtues against which these interior acts have been directed. Authors hold that it may be possible for morally immature and subnormal persons to fail to recognize the malice of purely "interior acts" (those indicated by 1, 2, 3, above). But surely a normal man cannot fail to perceive the malice of an evil resolution or intention, if he realizes that the action he plans to carry out is sinful.

As to point 1: it is intrinsically lawful to rejoice over the good resulting from an evil action, provided that the rejoicing over the result does not include pleasure in the evil action itself. Should an unwedded mother say she is happy over her infant or that she rejoices to have it, we cannot conclude that she is happy over her sin.

As to point 2: obviously it is morally irreproachable for one to enjoy insight into the nature and essence of an evil act. Similarly, it is not sinful to reflect on evil actions or sins or to speak of them, provided all this be done with prudence and to a good purpose. Reflection on sin is immoral (*delectatio morosa*) only if what is in the mind in a somewhat abstract manner is taken up by the will with joy and approval. The evil enjoyment then arises from evil approval of the thoughts and ideas, from interior inclination to evil.

We do not condemn one who laughs in amusement over the comic and ingenious elements in a sinful action or over the ridiculous phases of a sinful conversation, so long as there is no manifestation of approval of the sin itself or danger of scandal. Married folk do not sin through the pleasure taken in thinking of the marital life, for they may enjoy that which God has designed. They rejoice in something which is good. Under certain circumstances, however, such thoughts may prove profitless and even hazardous, as far as good morals are concerned.

V. SOURCES OF SIN: THE CAPITAL SINS

The capital sin which is uniquely the source of all sins is original sin, through which disorder entered into our human nature as the root of the entire brood of evil inclinations and tendencies. The so-called formal element of original sin is derived from the original rupture of man's friendship with God, from the revolt of man's spirit against God. A material element is the rebellion of the flesh against the spirit as punishment for the revolt of the spirit against God. Even after baptism a proneness to revolt against submission to God remains in man and a propensity of the flesh to tear itself away from the guidance of the spirit. Thus the two most profound disorders reaching down into the deepest roots in man are pride and concupiscence of the flesh against the designs of God and the order of the spirit.

Saint John sums up these perilous tendencies in man as threefold: "All that is in the world is the lust of the flesh, and the lust of the eyes, and the pride of life" (1 Jn 2:16). The term *lust of the flesh* means the inordinate craving for the pleasures of the senses. It is the disorder in the natural and intrinsically good instinct for self-preservation by means of food and drink and enjoyment, as well as through the instinct for preservation of the species through the union of the sexes. From this flows impurity, intemperance in food and drink and enjoyment, indolence. The "lust of the eyes" is the disorder in the natural urge for possessions (riches, elegance in dress, munificence, external splendor). From this flows avarice and prodigality or wastefulness. Lust of the eyes and lust of the flesh are the fountainhead of spiritual indolence (*acedia*), which may fluctuate feverishly in its enthusiasm for work and likewise in seeking ease and pleasure. The "pride of life" is the perversion of the divinely designed spiritual tendency toward preservation of one's own dignity and honor. It is disorder in the natural desire for that which is grand and noble, but difficult to attain. Here lies the root of haughtiness, vainglory, envy, unjust anger.

Whereas Saint John mentions three capital sins, theology for ages (from the time of Evagrius Ponticus, about 400) listed eight. Later the number was reduced to seven capital sins (principal sins, root sins): vainglory, envy, anger, avarice, lust, intemperance, spiritual sloth.

Since the time of Gregory the Great, pride is no longer considered as one of the capital sins. Hence we now enumerate only seven. More correctly we might speak of a twofold pride. One we enumerate as vainglory or haughtiness and list first among the seven capital sins. The other is the pride which profoundly characterizes every sin, which lies at its very root. In reality it characterizes not only the direct revolt against God, but also the so-called sins of frailty in their very own—though often veiled—malice. The ultimate and most basic root of all sin is simply the refusal of the will to obey God, the craving for self-mastery.

1. *Vainglory (Pride)*

Man is clothed with an incomparable dignity particularly through baptism. Ever conscious of this admirable gift of God, he should always submit humbly to the divine will. He should remain upright and sincerely highminded, disdaining with just pride all that threatens to debase and degrade, with a pride that is truly holy because it never fails to recognize God's supreme grandeur, never fails in childlike gratitude toward God from whom all human dignity flows. But if man is so preoccupied with his own dignity as to have no regard for God, if he seeks his own dignity before men without increase of his true worth before God and without regard for God, then he is guilty of pride, vainglory, self-exaltation. This vainglory deserves to be called vanity, in so far as it relies on pretense, on petty and ridiculous claims to superiority. Or should there be real merit, it strives for undue honor from mere men and neglects the true and noble honor of the children of God. This is vanity indeed.

From the evil root of pride springs overweening ambition, craving for honor, ostentation, and presumption. The proud and vain man in his ostentation flaunts his own superiority for all the world to see, and in his presumption he assumes positions and undertakes tasks which are far beyond his true capacities. Often, too, envy springs from a disordered ambition and love of honor which cannot bear to have others honored more than ourselves. The remedy for pride and vainglory is meditation on the transcendent majesty of God, on the humiliations and suffering of Christ borne in the most profound humility of the God-man, and finally on the dreadful consequences and dire punishment of the sin.

2. *Envy*

Envy is a perversion of the natural instinct to emulate the excellence of others. Envy begrudges one's neighbor the good he possesses because it seems an obstacle to one's own excellence and glory. Therefore it differs from hate, which begrudges one's neighbor all that is good. But the two often intermingle. The daughters of envy are tale-bearing, detraction, calumny, rejoicing over the misfortune of others, bitterness, and finally hatred.

The malice of envy is all the greater (abstracting from the subjective elements of knowledge and advertence) the more noble the good which is the object of envy. Frightful is the sin "against the Holy Spirit" which begrudges another the very love and grace of God. Of course it cannot be sinful to be displeased over the temporal success of another which proves to be a source of great damage to his salvation and the kingdom of God, assuming that this is the true reason for one's displeasure. Nor is it the sin of rejoicing over the misfortune of another if one is glad that the proud enemies of God are crushed and humiliated, or that the suffering of a fellow man has led him back to God.

The danger of the sin of envy is best met by meditation on the loving generosity of God toward all men, by the practice of humility and love of one's fellows, by childlike submission of self to the all-wise dispositions of divine providence.

3. *Anger*

The passion of anger, often called temper, is the instinctive urge to suppress and repel whatever is hostile to us. Well-ordered temper or anger is a tremendous force at man's disposal in the struggle against the obstacles to the good. It is a weapon which can assure victory in the combat against the enemies of virtue, in the struggle for the lofty objectives and ideals which are difficult to attain. Anyone who is incapable of anger cannot be dynamic in his love. For if we love the good with all the dynamic force of body and soul, we will oppose evil with equal dynamic force. The Christian ideal is not indolent lassitude, nonchalant resignation in the face of evil, but energetic intervention against it with all available force, including that of anger. The Sacred Scripture extols the flaming anger of Phineas against the enemies of the divine honor (Nm 25). The Lord Himself is a striking example of manly, holy wrath (Mt 21:12; 23:13ff.).

Anger becomes sinful anger when it exceeds the just bounds of prudent moderation. To be stirred to greater wrath over the mistakes and faults of others than over our own which are no less serious, is an example of sinful anger. Another example is anger over petty trifles (the whole purpose of anger is to overcome the difficult and arduous in the path of the good and virtuous). It is also sinful to fly into such a rage as to destroy the tranquillity essential for the sound use of reason. And anger inspired by evil motives is surely also sinful. Anger as a capital sin consists primarily in the disordered desire for punitive repression of all that does not correspond to our own desires, in the disordered desire for revenge, damage, destruction. We must distinguish in anger (and in every other passion) between the emotional agitation stirring within us, no matter how violent it may be, and the conscious consent to it.

It is no more than venial sin to exceed the bounds of just moderation in one's anger. But danger lurks in uncontrolled temper. There is the risk of committing mortal sin in such instances, if one knows in advance that anger will destroy self-control and all power of free deliberation. Unjust wrath is by its nature a mortal sin since it offends against justice and love.

The daughters of wrath are impatience, indignation, insult and abuse, quarrels and blows, cursing. The remedies against wrath: meditation on the mercy and mildness of Christ, thoughtfulness and circumspection which does not yield to the first impulse of anger, a wholesome sense of humor which enables us to see what a ridiculous thing angry excitement can be in ourselves and in others.

4. *Avarice*

Avarice is inordinate pursuit of material values. The avaricious man attempts to acquire wealth, to increase it constantly, and to cling to it passionately. The highest degree of avarice sees earthly goods as the final end of existence. It is "service of Mammon," abandonment of the heart to the attachment to the perishable and ephemeral (Mt 6:21ff.). The Apostle calls it "idolatry" (Eph 5:5). Greed ranks next to pleasure-seeking as principal cause of the current flight from childbearing: men esteem the promotion of business and the conservation of inheritance more highly than the value of the person as found in the begetting of children. Joy of material possession has become greater than the delight in giving life to man.

Avarice usually leads to hardness of heart against one's fellows, to lust for power, to injustice and loss of all scruple in the choice of methods to attain one's aims, to insensibility in all things of the spirit (spiritual indolence). Remedies against this sin are profound contemplation of the vanity of all earthly things, meditation on the grandeur of the things of eternity, and finally sincere walking in the footsteps of the Master carrying His painful cross.

5. *Lust*

The natural craving for bodily gratification which accompanies and arouses the response of the love union of man and woman is a fruitful force for the propagation of the human race. Sexual pleasure, which is the expression and manifestation also in the flesh of genuine love-giving, is designed by the Creator of our nature to counteract the natural repugnance to the burdens of parenthood, and to vitalize the love-attraction (*eros*) of the spouses. The entire natural relationship of man and wife is made holy through the sacrament of matrimony, and the sexual urge and desire are not excluded from this sanctifying effect. The sex instinct, whenever it is animated by the spiritual love of person, and ultimately by the supernatural love of charity, is good and worthy of man. But such spiritual vitalization is possible only where the sentiments of the heart and the inner attitude toward the domain of sex are regulated by the laws of God.

Sought for its own sake, however, or indulged in without discipline or restraint, sexual pleasure becomes the source of unspeakable corruption, suffering and sin, profanation of the mystery of love and of life, loss of true love, injustice toward one's fellows and relatives, scandal and seduction, insane egotism, incapacity for the true love which brings felicity to men, insensibility for things spiritual. The remedies for this evil: self-discipline and mortification, joy in spiritual and specifically in religious things, the fervor of divine love.

6. *Intemperance*

The instinct for food and drink and for rest and recreation comes from God. This enjoyment is good, granted that it is reasonable. It is disordered, unreasonable, sinful if one takes greater pleasure in food and drink than in the higher things, if one's mind is entirely occupied with food and drink and enjoyment.

a. Intemperance in Eating, Gluttony

Intemperance in eating, gluttony (*gula*) is lack of restraint in the enjoyment of food and drink. The glutton seeks inordinately for the delights of the palate, is excessive in his desire for good food. Fastidiousness despises plain and wholesome foods. By their nature gluttony and fastidiousness are surely only venial sins, unless they prove a dangerous temptation to other sins, to grave sins (neglect of duties of one's state of life, callousness toward the hungry, grave damage to one's health). The glutton or gourmand who reaches the extreme of which it can be said that "their god is the belly" (PHIL 3:19) surely cannot be excused from the guilt of mortal sin; for he makes of food and drink a ridiculous and debased final end of man.

Gluttony conflicts above all with the imitation of Christ crucified. Consequently it is most effectively overcome through contemplation of the cross, through mindfulness of the duty of penance and mortification. Important also is the stern realization of the divine punishments, meditation on the pains of purgatory and of hell.

b. Intemperance in Drink, Drunkenness

In view of the fact that alcoholic beverages are not generally an indispensable factor in the preservation of health, the misuse or abuse of them usually constitutes a greater sin than intemperance in food and nonintoxicating drink. The reason is that danger of abuse in essential things cannot so readily be avoided as abuse in superfluous things. This applies also to the use of other means of enjoyment and indulgence and the danger of intemperate use of them, for example, tobacco and morphine.

Excess of drink which reaches the point of complete drunkenness depriving one of the use of reason and moral freedom is a grave sin. "Drunkards" . . . will not "possess the kingdom of God" (1 Cor 6:10; cf. Is 5:11). Drunkenness is a grave sin not precisely because of excess of drinking as such, for this of itself and by its nature is only a venial sin, but because it degrades and debases human dignity. The gravity of the sin also arises from the dire consequences of the excessive use and misuse of alcohol. There is the danger to health and morals, the destruction of love for one's relatives and friends, and even the hazard to the health of offspring, for excessive indulgence in alcohol is a source of familial degeneracy.

Drunkenness is a mortal sin by its nature. However, should one be overcome one or the other time because he did not realize the potency of the drink served him or overrated his own capacity to resist its effects, he cannot readily be accused of mortal sin. In such instances there are usually a lack of premeditation and full deliberation which are essential for mortal sin. But once an individual knows his own weakness and is aware of the danger of overindulgence, should he still continue to indulge, he cannot be excused on the score that he did not have the intent to get drunk. Graver still is the sin of direct and premeditated drunkenness. Bartenders or tavern keepers who for love of gain serve the overindulgent drinker or the confirmed alcoholic in such a manner that he deliberately becomes intoxicated commit a grave sin against love of neighbor (through cooperation in his sin). They are also guilty by intent of a sin against temperance.

c. Immoderate Use of Tobacco and Drugs

Moderate smoking or use of tobacco in other forms can be morally unobjectionable and good, if the use is for purposes of recreation, fostering of sociability or reasonable social entertainment, better enjoyment of one's work, alertness and attention, or some other reasonable motive. But it cannot be denied that weak-willed individuals often fail to be moderate in the use of tobacco, whereas complete abstention lies within their capacity. The abuse, especially in the case of adolescents, may seriously damage the power of will, the capacity for work, interior freedom. The matter has been much discussed in recent years, but there can be no doubt that in many instances smoking constitutes a very grave danger to health. It may be the occasion for egotism and extreme self-indulgence and theft. Far more dangerous than the use of tobacco is the use of other narcotics (opium, morphine, heroin). To combat drug addiction and cure the addicted, and likewise to prevent the vicious production and sale of drugs especially to adolescents, in view of the widespread character of the evil, is a most urgent social duty. The "addicted" (this is true also of alcoholics) are morally obliged to abstain from the use altogether. This must be unconditionally demanded of them. Ordinarily there is no other cure.

Except for such obligation, the total abstention from alcohol and tobacco cannot be imposed as binding in conscience. But the good example of total abstinence may be an act of great love of neighbor, particularly on the part of priests and religious working among non-Catholics who readily take offense in such matters. Total abstention as a work of atonement for the great evils of drug addiction is one of the noblest forms of mortification and love of one's fellows. Anyone who realizes that his attachment to food, drink, tobacco is a major obstacle to his progress in perfection, is obliged to free himself from such attachment through mortification.[35] Finally, we may never forget that the Christian views and judges sense pleasure and enjoyment in earthly things in a manner quite different from that of the good pagan. For the Christian the highest wisdom is Christ, Christ crucified (cf. 1 Cor 2:2; Gal 6:14).

7. Spiritual Sloth (Acedia)

In traditional theology the seventh capital sin, called sloth, is not repugnance to work, or disordered desire for repose and enjoyment (the term for this vice is *pigritia,* laziness), but the lack of zeal for things spiritual. It is feebleness and lack of spirit in opposing the heavy pull and pressure of earthly things and rising to the level of the divine. Spiritual torpor is frequently manifested by undue concern for external affairs and worldly things. Since sloth is the very antithesis to love of God and to joy in God and all that refers to God, the slothful man is pained and grieved that he is called to the following of Christ, to friendship with God with the serious obligation of renouncement and great spiritual effort they entail. This kind of sloth is grave sin. It is not surprising that sloth in spiritual things should lead to indulgence and pleasure-seeking, and even to extreme material activism.

The spiritual sloth which is no more than a certain laxness or feebleness in the service of God due to a degree of repugnance in fulfilling the commandments is in its nature a venial sin. We note in this instance that the slothful individual still does keep the commandments. In fact, we might say that it is often a proof of loyalty to keep the commandments in spite of a general lassitude and a serious temptation to slackness in the divine service. To fulfill one's serious obligations conscientiously under such conditions and without the sense of joy and consolation which usually accompanies the fulfillment of God's law may be taken as proof of basic earnestness and loyalty to God.

The fruits of sloth are: discouragement and pusillanimity, neglect of the burdensome precepts, such as attending Mass on days of obligation and abstaining and fasting according to the law of the Church, inconstancy, loquacity, indolence or the other extreme of external activism, aversion for good admonition, finally hatred of the good altogether.

Since sloth arises from a heart steeped in the worldly and carnal and from low esteem of the divine things, the best antidote to sloth is the spirit of mortification and frequent contemplation of the love of God and His promises. Earnest and soul-stirring eloquence setting forth the eternal truths regarding the "last things" should above all arouse men from their spiritual torpor.

BIBLIOGRAPHY

BACHT, H. "Die Welt von heute und das Gespuer fuer die Suende," *GeistLeben* 31 (1958), 7–16.

BARTMANN, B. *Die Erloesung, Suende und Suehne.* Paderborn, 1933.

BEUMER, J., S.J. "Die persoenliche Suende in sozialtheologischer Sicht," *ThG*, 43 (1953), 81–101.

BROUILLARD, R. "Tentation," *DTC*, XV, 116–127.

*BUBER, M. *Good and Evil: Two Interpretations.* New York: Scribner, 1953.

CATHREIN, V., S.J. *Die laessliche Suende.* Freiburg, 1926.

———. "Unvollkommenheit und laessliche Suende," *ZAM*, 3 (1928), 115–137, 221–239.

CREUSEN, J. "Imperfection ou péché véniel?" *NRTh*, 58 (1931), 21–34. Cf. also the bibliography in the previous part dealing with imperfection and venial sin.

DANIÉLOU, J. "Adamo, etc. Discussion sur péché," *Dieu Vivant*, n. 4, pp. 83–136.

DE LA NOË, F. *Der Mensch in der Versuchung.* Zuerich-Paderborn, 1955.

DURKIN, C. F. *The Theological Distinction of Sins in the Writings of St. Augustine.* Mundelein, 1952.

EBERLE, A. "Ueber die Versuchung," *ThQschr*, 94 (1941), 95–116, 208–232.

ELLER, E. "Die Versuchung in wertphilosophischer Sicht," *StimmZeit*, 137 (1939/40), 26–34.

GALTIER, P., S.J. "Le sense du péché à entretenir," *RevAsM*, 28 (1952), 289–304.

GERIGK, H. *Wesen und Voraussetzung der Todsuende.* Breslau, 1903.

GILLON, L. B. *La théorie des oppositions et la Théologie du péché.* Paris, 1937.

GUTBROD, "anomía," *ThW*, IV, 1077–1080.

HAAS, J. *Die Stellung Jesu zu Suende und Suender nach den vier Evangelien.* Studia Friburgensia NF, Heft 7. Fribourg, 1954.

HAUSHERR, I. "L'origine de la théorie orientale des huit péchés capitaux," *OrCh*, 33, 3 (1933), 164–175.

HEINEN, W. *Fehlformen des Liebesstrebens in moralpsychologischer Deutung und moraltheologischer Wuerdigung.* Freiburg, 1954, 95–151, 323–332, 334–341, 414ff., 447–470.

HENSE, F. *Die Versuchungen und ihre Gegenmittel.* 3 Auflage. Freiburg, 1902.

HORVÁTH, A. M., O.P. *Heiligkeit und Suende im Lichte der thomistischen Theologie.* Fribourg, 1943.

JIMÉNEZ-FAJARDO, J. *La esencia del pecado venial en la segunda edad de oro de la teología escolástica.* Granada, 1944.

KIRCHGAESSNER, A. *Erloesung und Suende im Neuen Testament.* Freiburg, 1950.

KOEBERLE, J. *Suende und Gnade im religioesen Leben des Volkes Israel bis auf Christum.* Muenchen, 1905.

KORN, H. J. *Peirasmos. Die Versuchder Glaeubigen in der griechischen Bibel.* Stuttgart, 1937.

KRAUTWIG, N. "Bewaeltigt der moderne Mensch die Suende?" *GeistLeben*, 26 (1953), 20–31.

LANDGRAF, A. *Das Wesen der laesslichen Suende in der Scholastik bis Thomas von Aquin.* Bomberg-Muenchen, 1923.

———. *Dogmengeschichte der Fruehscholastik.* Vierter Teil: *Die Lehre von der Suende und ihre Folgen.* Regensburg, 1956.

———. "Die Stellungnahme der Fruehscholastik zur Frage 'utrum veniale peccatum possit fieri mortale,'" *AAcST, Nova Series*, I (1941), 78–126.

———. "Die Bestrafung laesslicher Suenden in der Hoelle nach dem Urteil der Fruehscholastik," *Greg*, 22 (1941), 80–119, 380–407.

———. *Dogmengeschichte der Fruehscholastik.* Band II. Regensburg, 1953.

LETTER, P. DE "Venial Sin and its Final Goal," *Thomist*, 16 (1953), 32–70.

LOTTIN, O., O.S.B. *Principes de morale.* Louvain, 1946. II, 251ff.

LYONNET, ST., S.J. *De peccato et redemptione.* Romae, 1957.

———. *Monde moderne et sens du péché* (Semaine des Intellectuels Catholiques 1956). Paris, 1957.

MONTANARI, F. *Il peccato.* Roma Studium, 1946.

MONTY, V. "Péchés graves et légers d'après le vocabulaire hebreu," *ScEccl*, 2 (1949), 129–168.

MOTALE, E. *Le occasioni.* Torino, 1939.

NOBLE, H. D., O.P. *De l'éducation des passions.* Paris, 1919.

OLEŠA JURIJ, K. *L'invidia.* Roma, 1952.

QUELL, BERTRAM, STAEHLIN, GRUNDMANN, RENGSTORF, "hamartía," *ThW*, I, 267–339.

RABLOW, P. *Die Therapie des Zornes.* Leipzig, 1914.

RÉGNIER, J. *Le sens du péché.* Paris, 1954.

RONDET, H., S.J. *Notes Sur La Théologie du Péché.* Paris, Lethielleux, 1957.

SCHAUF, W. *Sárx. Der Begriff "Fleisch" beim Apostel Paulus* (NtAb, XI, H. 1 and 2). Muenster, 1924.

SCHOELLGEN, W. "Suende als isolierte Tat und als Symptom einer inneren Entwicklung," *Anima*, 7 (1952), 143–148. Cf. *Anima* (1952), note Part 1 throughout.

SCHRENK, "adikía," *ThW*, I, 150–163.

SÉJOURNÉ, P. "Les trois aspects du péché dans le 'Cur Deus homo,'" *RevSR*, 24 (1950), 5–27.

THOMAS, A. "L'orgueil et les psychoses," *EtCar*, 19 (1934), 87–111.

TILLMANN, F. *Handbuch der kath. Sittenlehre.* 3. Auflage. III, 250ff.

VILLER, M., S.J. "Colère," *DSp*, II (1950), 107–113.

VOEGTLE, A. "Woher stammt das Schema der Hauptsuenden?" *ThQschr*, 122 (1941), 217–237.

VOLK, H. *Emil Brunners Lehre vom Suender*. Muenster, 1950.

WROE, J. P., AND TRETHOWAN, I. "Mortal Sin and the Moral Order," *DR*, 70 (1952), 37–52.

ZIERMANN, B. *De definitione peccati actualis secundum mentem divi Thomae Aquinatis*. Bonn, 1935.

ZIMMERMANN, F. *Laessliche Suende und Andachtsbeichte*. Innsbruck, 1935.

———. "Das Wesen der laesslichen Suende," *DivThom* (F), 12 (1934), 408ff.

ZUERICHER, J. "Satan und die Versuchung zur Suende," *Anima*, 4 (1949), 145–149.

Additional Works in English

BRUNO DE JESUS-MARIE, O.C.D. (ed.). *Conflict and Light*. New York: Sheed and Ward, 1953. Cf. Darkness and Sin, pp. 3–106.

GALTIER, P., S.J. *Sin and Penance*. London: Sands, 1932.

HILDEBRAND, D. VON. *True Morality and Its Counterfeits*. New York: McKay, 1955. *Man and His Happiness* (Theological Library, Vol. 3). Chicago: Fides, 1956. Cf. pp. 229–270.

Periodical Literature in English

AUMANN, J. "Theology of Venial Sins," *Proceedings Cath. Theol. Society of Amer.* (1955), pp. 74–94. "Venial Sins and Christian Perfection," *CrossCr* 9, (Sept., 1957), 262–70.

LETTER, P. DE. "Venial Sins," *RevR*, 9 (Sept. 15, 1950), 225–33.

———. "Venial Sin and its Final Goal," *Thomist*, 16 (Ja., 1953), 32–70.

———. "Venial Sin: Paradox and Illogicality," *ITQ*, 22 (Jl., 1955), 258–64.

———. "Offense Against God," *IER*, 87 (My., 1957), 329–42.

———. "Meaning of Sin," *Clergy Monthly* 23 (Mr., 1959), 49–61.

OSBOURN, J. C., O.P. "The Morality of Imperfections," *Thomist*, 4 (July–Oct., 1942), 388–430, 649–691.

PONTIFEX DOM M., O.S.B. "Sin and Imperfection," *DR*, 42 (Ap., 1944), 95–101.

ROBERTS, J., O.S.B. "Injustice of Sin," *DR*, 71 (Summer, 1953), 233–42.

RONDET, H. "Towards a Theology of Sin," *ThD*, 4 (Autumn, 1956), 171–76.

TRETHOWAN, DOM. "What is Mortal Sin?" *DR*, 69 (Summer, 1951), 289–300.

WROE, J. P. "Mortal Sin and the Moral Order: Reply to Dom Trethowan, with rejoinder," *DR*, 70 (Winter, 1951), 37–52.

Part Five:

CONVERSION

CHAPTER ELEVEN

INVITATION AND RESPONSE TO THE
IMITATION OF CHRIST

I. THE NECESSITY OF CONVERSION

MORTAL sin plunges man into the abyss of perdition. He has lost salvation, and is hopelessly estranged from God. In this desperate situation man receives the earnest yet joyous invitation of the grace of Christ: "Repent, for the kingdom of heaven is at hand" (MT 4:17; MK 1:15). The call to repentance which comes from Christ is essentially the glad tidings to the sinner; for if he has a sense of the misery of his sinfulness and is prepared to accept the offer of salvation, the invitation of grace is the "good news" of salvation.

Precisely because the invitation to conversion is the glad tidings of the kingdom of God breaking in upon sinful mankind, because it is an incomparable imperative of grace, it is pressing and urgent. The sinner is offered the possibility of return to the home of the Father. The salvation of God appears in the form of His only-begotten Son. To refuse to turn from sin, to fail to return home, means to scorn the kingdom of God, to scorn Christ, the only-begotten of the Father.

The situation in which the glad tidings of the coming of the kingdom resounded over the human race was one of universal guilt: the whole race was in the fallen state through sin. "For we have argued that Jews and Greeks are all under sin" (ROM 3:9ff.). "But the Scripture shut up all things under sin, that by the faith of Jesus Christ the promise might be given to those who believe" (GAL 3:22). Because the salvation offered to those who believe, the kingdom of God proclaimed in Christ, is the absolute antithesis to sin, therefore the glad tidings inherently constitute an urgent demand for conversion, for a turning away from every sin.

Clearly the imperative of grace inviting to conversion does not make the same appeal to the Jew as to the pagan, to the "just" Pharisee as to the religiously neglectful masses and the morally debased publican. But common to all, the way to Christ is only through *metánoia,* through conversion that arises from the very depth of the human heart. Christ Himself is the messenger of the glad tidings. He Himself proclaims that conversion is possible and invites men to turn from sin.

Everyone who reads the Gospel attentively is struck with the vehemence with which the Lord proclaims the necessity of conversion, particularly for those who are "just" according to the law. The point of stress in the conversion, however, is not the mere work of man, but the "heart," the interior conversion to Christ, to the kingdom of God, something altogether different from anything found in the mere thought and design of man, even the man who presumes to be just. Only the humble of heart with deep realization of their emptiness and misery and need for help (Mt 5:3), only those who are penetrated with a consciousness of their need for a total conversion, a truly "revolutionary" conversion (note the words of our Lord on true penance and punishment, addressed to the Pharisees and Scribes, especially in Jn 7ff.), are ready for the kingdom of God and able to accept it. The public sinners are closer to the kingdom of God because they are fully aware of their need for profound conversion of heart, than the "just," who presume upon their zeal for the law and its rigid observance and reject conversion and refuse the invitation to the kingdom (cf. Mt 9:11ff.; 21:28-32; Lk 14:16-24—parable of a great supper; Lk 15:11-32—parable of the prodigal son).

We note the particular insistence of Paul on the universal necessity for conversion. Salvation is possible only through humble confession of this need for redemption, need for Christ the Redeemer of all men. According to Paul, men must turn from the proud and arrogant self-sufficiency relying on the letter of the law to the inner justice of the heart given only in and through grace (letters to the Romans and Galatians). Men must turn from the false wisdom of the spirit of the world to the cross which is the wisdom of God (Corinthians). They must turn from every vice, for those who live in sin can have no "participation in the kingdom of God" (note Paul's catalogue of sins).

There is an obvious difference between the sermons of repentance which the apostles preach to the pagans not yet baptized and the words addressed to the Christian community. Even though the glad tidings of the kingdom of God are first of all a penitential sermon demanding conversion of heart (this is particularly evident in the Acts of the Apostles), still the baptized is one reborn, one already basically converted, who obviously is to lead a life free from mortal sin. Such is the tremendous power of grace.[1]

Therefore the summons to repentance and conversion directed to the Christian who has grown lax and fallen into sin has an element of extreme rigor, even of menace in it (cf. Ap 2-3; 1 Cor 5:1; 2 Pt 2:20ff.; 1

J<small>N</small> 3:9f.; 5:16f.; H<small>EB</small> 6:4ff.). The marvelous work of salvation wrought by God at the first conversion, still in the memory of the Christian who has sinned, is a mighty call to penance if he should have fallen into a sin which "excludes from the kingdom of God": "And such were some of you, but you have been washed, you have been sanctified, you have been justified in the name of our Lord Jesus Christ, and in the spirit of our God" (1 C<small>OR</small> 6:11). The Christian, having been reborn in baptism, having tasted the gifts of God in the Eucharist, must fear that a total spiritual collapse leaves no way open to him for conversion except an unexpected miracle from God (H<small>EB</small> 6:4ff.; 1 J<small>N</small> 5:16ff.).

If it is true that the Christian who has squandered the grace of the first conversion must now manifest great earnestness for its renewal, it is likewise true that the persevering Christian must also harken to the call for conversion. Though the summons is in a different manner altogether, it is still an exhortation to conversion: that which began in conversion must attain a new dimension in depth, the depth of a "second conversion." This invitation to a more interior and intimate, a more profound renewal of conversion, is an especially mighty "imperative of grace," a message from the kingdom of God: you are children of light: therefore walk as children of light! You are placed in the kingdom of His beloved Son: walk therefore worthily of such a call! You are dead to sin: therefore mortify in yourselves all the works of sin! You are risen with Christ: walk therefore in the power of the resurrected Christ! (Cf. R<small>OM</small> 6; 12:2; 1 C<small>OR</small> 5:7ff.; E<small>PH</small> 2:1ff.; 4:20ff.; 5:8; C<small>OL</small> 1:21ff.; 2:20ff.; 3:1ff.) These "summons to conversion" refer to every one baptized. Every Christian must harken, for we all stand in need of constant conversion. The example of the saints should convince us, for none who has taken the call seriously has ever been convinced that he no longer stood in need of conversion.

II. THE NATURE AND CHARACTERISTICS OF CONVERSION

1. Negative Phase: Renouncement of Sin

a. Religious conversion is a breaking away from the state of perdition and loss of salvation, a giving up of the state of sin (*hamartía*).[2] The biblical *hamartía* is not merely the single sinful act, but also the evil condition resulting from it, the state or condition of perdition, the evil disposition and attitude which is estrangement from God.[3] What is dreadful is not merely the sin as an act, but the poisoned root, the evil disposition from which further individual sins (of course, through free consent of the will) grow. Conversion means conquest of the old man of sin, held captive by sin (this is the carnal existence, the existence through the flesh, the *sárx*), in order to attain a new and spiritual (*pneumatic*) form of life created and guided by the spirit of God.

The convert must renounce every sin, not merely any and every individual sinful act, and every habitual sinful action, but first and foremost the whole mode of his existence. His heart must be changed. He must be entirely transformed in disposition and inner attitude. Obviously man is not equal to this task if he relies on his own resources: one who is estranged from God, far off from Him, can be brought back to God only if God Himself comes to him with His grace. Hence, to turn from perdition, from the loss of God and loss of salvation which are inherent in the state of sin, one must unreservedly accept the dominion of God which comes to man in Christ through the Spirit of God.

The first thing that man can contribute toward his conversion is the acknowledgement that he has not merely done evil deeds, committed sins, but that he himself is evil, that he stands in need of redemption and complete spiritual transformation. Therefore, the Lord's sermon on the kingdom of God (the work of conversion) has an entirely different aspect when directed to the poor sinners who recognize and confess that they are really sinners, than when addressed to the proud and self-satisfied "just" who vaunt their own observance of the law. Proud observers of law, indeed, who mask their evil heart, the inward perversion from themselves and their fellowmen through individual legalistic observances! Christ certainly does not criticize their zeal for the law, but His saving love impels Him to bring these "whitened sepulchres" (Mt 23:27) to the necessary realization that the external façade is useless if the heart does not sincerely turn to God and to one's fellow men.

b. Religious conversion necessarily means turning away from every violation of law. The convert turns from all lawlessness (*anomía*) and submits entirely to God's law. John particularly stresses the truth that every infraction of law, every resistance to law (*anomía*) is sin in its loss of salvation and estrangement from God (*hamartía*) (1 Jn 3:4). One who resists the law shows thereby that he is hostile to God, since the law is the express manifestation of God's love and His sovereign right. Even though every individual voluntary transgression of the law does not necessarily manifest the fully conscious and open hostility against the divine legisla-

tor, still it always is a sign that man is living in a state of alienation from
God.

Paul shows (above all in Rom 7) how the loving will of God expressed in the law becomes an occasion for the sinner to offend against
the law. If "the law indeed is holy and the commandment holy and just
and good" (Rom 7:12) and it nevertheless multiplies the number of transgressions and leads to works of death, then it is quite plain how hopeless
the state of sin is, how hopeless the corruption of heart (Rom 7:13). To
turn from this opposition to the law requires a complete renewal of heart.

c. Conversion turns from the injustice against God (*adikia*: cf.
1 Jn 1:9; 5:17) which is manifested in every sin. Sin is iniquity, injustice
(1 Jn 5:17), the refusal to give God the honor due Him (cf. Jn 7:18),
refusal of filial love, filial obedience, which is owing to God by a
thousand titles of love and justice. Hence, we repeat, conversion demands
total renewal of the heart. It demands a new justice which leads all things
back to God, offers all to Him in honor and obedience from a heart profoundly loving Him. Only in this way do the inner justice in men's hearts
and interior justice in the world attain their full value from conversion
to God. Let no one flatter himself that this new justice comes from himself. Only if God extends His pardon of injustice to man and places
him in a new relationship to Himself, is it possible. Hence, it is obvious
that the call to conversion, invitation to pardon, addressed to us by Christ
is truly glad tidings, the imperative summons of grace.

d. Conversion is aversion from the lie (in the sense of Saint John:
1 Jn 1:6; 2:4, 8; Jn 3:20f.; Ap 22:15). Sin is the stark antithesis to "being
in the truth," to "deeds of truth" (Jn 3:21; 1 Jn 1:6; Eph 4:15). Sin is a
lie (Rom 3:7), conformity with the spirit of this world (Rom 12:2), with
the diabolical spirit of lies, the "Father of lies" (Jn 8:44). Conversion,
therefore, demands a complete change of heart, indeed a fully "new
spirit," the "spirit of truth" (cf. Rom 12:2).

Because the divine truth condemns the sinner, pronounces him guilty,
brings him to a realization that he has in some way fallen into the
clutches of the devil and his wiles, therefore conversion is possible only if
he follows the painful path of perseverance in this accusing truth which
alone can set men free. At every level of its progress conversion is a "yes"
to this truth of God, regardless of what it may say of us and demand of
us.

This utter renewal of our thinking with the renouncement of all false wisdom of men is absolutely demanded by the imperative of the divine wisdom (which is "folly" for the "old man," the "carnal" man) of the cross (cf. 1 COR 1:23f.; 2:1ff.).

2. Positive Phase of Conversion: Return to God

What is proper and essential to the movement of conversion can be grasped only in the light of its ultimate orientation. Since the Lord announced the glad tidings with the appeal for conversion, it is important for right understanding not only of conversion, but also of the imitation of Christ, to penetrate to the very heart of the meaning of the call.

The Lord's call to *metánoia* (*metanoeîte*, MT 4:17) is totally misunderstood if we see in it first of all a demand for works of penance (the call: do penance). Nor do we reach the full depth of its meaning through a simple philological analysis of the term itself, "change your mind," come to a different way of thinking! Surely conversion does demand a total change of thinking and ultimately also a spirit of penance (and works of penance). But the very core of the call, "*metanoeîte*," is pure glad tidings: "Return home, for the kingdom of heaven has come to you!" The word itself is already found in the Greek Septuagint, where "*metánoia*" is used to translate the Hebrew "*schub*," which above all promises the return home from the Exile, and is very often connected with the term *epistréphesthai* or replaced by it (return, turn around, return home; cf. ACTS 3:19; 5:31; 17:30; 26:20; 1 PT 2:25).[4] Thus the call to conversion is filled with yearning, with the nostalgic yearning for return to the temple with the glory of the Lord, for the restoration of the perfect friendship with God in the alliance of love. The appeal should re-echo in the very depths of the pious hearts of the Israelites. Likewise in the great parable of the prodigal son, the central New Testament text on conversion, are clear echoes of the cry of the prophets urging the people to return home to the first love of the covenant with God, indeed to an even more intimate friendship with God (cf. JER 3:14).

Therefore conversion is in every way the most utterly personal movement, the restoration of the bonds of personal intimacy with God, a recovery and reacceptance of the most personal and holy rights, the rights of the child, which had been lost until now: "I will get up and go to my father" (LK 15:18). New ideas and thoughts can have a profound transforming effect on man, but infinitely deeper is the effect of personal intimacy, the relation of friendship in human life. Conversion is not simply personal friendship, but the unique friendship of the child with its heavenly Father. It is the total giving, the perfect submission to God, who has created us for Himself, who is Love which alone can take total possession of our hearts, Love which is our whole beatitude (cf. 1 Pt 2:21-25).

The word which expresses the central theme of conversion in the Bible corresponds to the characterization of conversion found in current phenomenological psychology of religion: "conversion is personal relationship to the Supreme Being established or re-established in a crisis."[5]

The so-called "mere moral conversion" is incomparably inferior to the true religious conversion of which we speak. The moral conversion is a mere renunciation of some species of non-value or defect of value for a new relation toward moral values. The sinner sincerely turning to God may be in a most miserable moral condition (in his knowledge of values and his determination of will), but still he is on a level entirely different from that of the strenuous moral-minded individual who with all his moral irreproachability looks only to himself and not to God, who does not deign to acknowledge the majesty of God with His rights over men as their Lord and Father. It may well be that the religious convert will nurse his wound for a long long time. It may be he will bear the scars of his moral defeats for the rest of his days. But his inner submission to God is a hymn of praise to the sovereignty of God and, above all, to the divine mercy, and his moral effort, humble as it is, re-echoes this hymn of praise. It is rooted in good soil. "There will be joy in heaven over one sinner who repents, more than over ninety-nine just who have no need of penance" (Lk 15:7), who make of their moral integrity a pretext for self-seeking, for turning to self and not to God.[6]

3. Conversion and the Kingdom

Already in the Old Testament the theme of conversion as found in the prophets was bound up with the Kingdom of God. Conversion is intimately united with the restoration of the divine sovereignty,[7] with its grace and the alliance of love. And the bond of dominion in turn comes through the conversion of the sinner to God. The sermon of repentance as found in the New Testament, both in the preaching of John the Baptist and of Christ Himself, has as its theme the coming of the kingdom. The basis for conversion, the joy and urgency of its entire motive which impelled the sinner to make his great decision is expressed in the call: "Repent, for the kingdom of heaven is at hand" (Mt 3:2; 4:17; Mk 1:15). True conversion means to "seek first the kingdom of God" (Mt 6:33), "enter into the kingdom of God," "accept the kingdom of God" in simplicity and humility as a child accepts the gifts of its parents (Mt 18:3; Mk 10:15). The kingdom of heaven means conflict, sword and shield against the kingdom of this world; therefore, no one can share in the kingdom of God (consider himself converted) who seeks a corrupt peace with the spirit of the world (Mt 10:35). The kingdom of God suffers violence (Mt 11:12; Lk 16:16).

Even though externally it is trial and struggle and suffering of persecution, within (i.e., according to its real nature) it is a "kingdom of peace," a kingdom of grace, of justice, of incipient revelation of the loving sovereignty of God. No one "shall enter the kingdom of heaven" with hollow assurances or empty formulas, but only through the firm determination to conform to the will of the Father in heaven (Mt 7:21). Into the kingdom of heaven "there shall not enter . . . anything defiled, nor he who practices abomination and falsehood" (Ap 21:27; 22:15). "Or do you not know that the unjust will not possess the kingdom of God?" (1 Cor 6:9f.; Eph 5:5; Gal 5:21; catalogue of sins). Insistently the kingdom of God turns particularly to those who groan under their sins (cf. 1 Cor 6:11). And with insistence must it be stressed that persistence in sin excludes the sinner from the kingdom of God, for by its very nature sin and the kingdom are irreconcilable. Sin obstructs the path to the kingdom. Sin corrupts and destroys the kingdom within us.

Since conversion corresponds to the coming of the kingdom of God, no one can sincerely pray the Our Father with its petition, "thy kingdom come," if he does not have the will to convert, or if he is "converted," refuses to deepen his first conversion. It also follows that if one should pray the Our Father sincerely, he must logically seek true conversion. For this reason conversion necessarily and from its very inception is something apostolic; it bears an apostolic note, if it is entirely genuine. And the conversion will be all the more steadfast, the more the new convert is convinced from the very beginning that he must become a living active member of the kingdom of God, that the call to conversion is also the summons: "Be you yourselves as living stones, built thereon into a spiritual house, a holy priesthood" (1 Pt 2:5).

All conversion, all prayer and all effort to promote the coming of the kingdom of God looks back to the first coming and forward to the second coming. The first coming of the kingdom of God is redemptive. It begins with the Incarnation and is effective through the passion and resurrection of Christ. The second coming is the advent of the kingdom in glory by the Parousia of the Lord in the Judgment. Conversion is made possible through the coming of the kingdom in the work of Incarnation and redemption, through the promise of the second coming. The motive of conversion receives its force, its attraction, its urgency, its power to bless and make us happy from the coming of the kingdom of God.

Precisely because the kingdom of God bears with it the imperative of conversion, repentance and return to God partake of the inexorable gravity of the final judgment. The imperative of conversion is based on the eschatological urgency of the kingdom of God. The period of the divine reign in the kingdom is the urgent hour of decision for men. In the full prophetic perspective of John the Baptist the coming of the kingdom of God includes both salvation and judgment, final salvation or final loss in the judgment, according to the position taken in relation to the coming of the kingdom, according to the response to its call for conversion.

Christ also in his invitation to repentance refers, not only to His first coming in grace, but also to the second coming. Again and again He refers to the uncertain hour of His second coming for judgment and the final salvation and reward (cf. Mt 11:20ff.; 12:41f.; 26:24; Lk 13:3ff.; 19:40ff.; 23:28ff.; Jn 15:6; 17:12). Whoever refuses to convert, despite the incomparable graces of the kingdom of God directly coming into our midst, his condemnation will be more dreadful than that which befell Sodom and Gomorrha (Lk 10:11ff.).

Our time of salvation is the "last hour" (1 Jn 2:18), the hour of crisis, of decision and separation. The time between the first coming and the second is the hour of grace coming from the patience of God who wills to grant all the time to convert. For this reason the punishment of those who have squandered this time of grace will be all the more terrible (cf. Rom 2:4ff.; 2 Pt 2f.). "How shall we escape if we neglect so great a salvation? For it was first announced by the Lord" (Heb 2:3).

Through the reception of the glad tidings and baptism "our salvation is nearer." In view of the uncertainty of the last hour, the obligation is all the more pressing; we must "rise from sleep . . . and lay aside the works of darkness" (Rom 13:11ff.). The deceptive forces of darkness can be withstood successfully only by one who unmasks and combats them both in his own heart, and in his surroundings, with the "armor of light" (ROM 13:12).

Because *metánoia* (conversion, return, return home) is gift and duty, invitation and summons of the kingdom of God which comes to us through grace, gift of the glorified Christ through His Holy Spirit (cf. ACTS 5:31), it consists essentially of tension and trial. But it is also the jubilant nostalgic expectation of the final revelation of the kingdom of heavenly glory. The sermon on repentance re-echoes with jubilation: with exultation and the joy of triumph it tells of the coming of Christ in grace, of His glorious victory, of His death and resurrection. But there is also the note of invitation and warning, the announcement and the threat of the final coming of Christ "in his kingdom" in "power and majesty" (MT 16:28; 24:30; 26:64). The exhortations to conversion based on references to death and the particular judgment must be studied in this same eschatological perspective (cf. ACTS 3:19ff.; 17:30f.; AP 2:5,16; 3:3, 19ff.).

4. *Conversion and the Effects of Divine Grace*

We cannot rightly grasp the nature of conversion and the profound character of progress in the Christian life from the mere standpoint of human conduct or the fixed norms of law governing it. Only through the divine action of grace are external law and the human mind itself raised to such a level of greatness, to the gentle and forceful imperative of conversion and re-conversion.

In the Old Testament penitential appeals of the prophets there is a constant undertone of joyous expectancy, of glad tidings. God Himself will save His people, the "remnant," through judgment (cf. HB 3; OS 14:1-6). God overwhelms His people with gifts; He visits them through judgment. In His law He offers them guidance, goads them on, accuses them of sin, for the purpose of saving them and leading them on to an ever more sincere and intimate union of love. The way that is pointed out to the people of Israel is through earnest and sincere conversion of heart. Only those who convert will be saved (ZA 1:3ff.). There is clearly a direct appeal to human freedom which we may not ignore, but it is equally evident from the preaching of the prophets that not only the visitation, but also the inner conversion in the depths of the heart is the working of divine grace. It is God's work.

At the very inception of conversion God "will pour out upon the house of David, and upon the inhabitants of Jerusalem, the spirit of grace, and of prayers" (ZA 12:10–14). By force of this spirit they will acknowledge their misery with contrite hearts. And they will see "whom they have pierced" (ZA 12:10). In sorrowful prayer for conversion and return home the sinner realizes that all depends on God, but just as truly he realizes that he must cooperate with the grace of God: "Convert us, O Lord, to thee, and we shall be converted" (LAM 5:21; JER 31:18; Ps 79:4, 8, 20). The prophetic message very clearly asserts that the Messianic conversion does not consist merely of the offering of new and better works to God, but of a profound renewal of the heart of man, the source of his love. And this is the good news: God Himself will cleanse the soiled heart with pure water (ZA 13:1; cf. Ps 50:9). He will pour forth His spirit and remove the "stony heart" and create in man a "new heart," a "heart of flesh" (Ez 11:19; 36:25–29; 39:29; Is 4:4f.). The law which resounds in our ears will lead to conversion only because of the law which God Himself writes in our hearts (JER 31:33ff.). The conclusion is inexorable, inescapable: man must renew his heart; he must live from a newness of heart (Ez 18:31).

The New Testament fulfillment of the prophetic promise expresses even more clearly the imperative of salvation, the duty of conversion. With constant newness of summons the imperative of salvation and conversion comes to every human being through the influence of the Holy Spirit effective in the operation of grace and the new creation. The fulness of the era of salvation and the new law of the eschatological age burst upon each of us with this tremendous imperative of repentance.

a. Conversion and Operative Grace

The call to conversion is not merely the appeal of the Gospel and the commandments made to all mankind. God calls to each individual in particular. The invitation to conversion is a personal gift to each human being. And the gift of conversion is strictly personal (cf. ACTS 3:26; 5:31f.; 11, 17f.; JN 6:44; AP 2:21). It is a basic Christian dogma[8] that the very first step toward conversion and every subsequent step on the way of conversion is preceded by grace beckoning and calling from within. God calls each one of us by name. He calls each one individually, not merely externally through the Gospel, but also through interior grace. But the call is not compelling, and the actual conversion is not wrought without the free consent and cooperation of the individual.

Saint Augustine elaborated the Biblical teaching on the rôle of divine grace in conversion very accurately. His *Confessions* are far more than a humble confession of his faults in the sight of God. They are a magnificent chant of praise and thanksgiving for the divine assistance through the whole history of his conversion. Augustine extols the admirable mingling of the external dispositions of the divine providence and the interior enlightenment and movement of divine grace. "My good deeds are thy dispositions and gifts; the evil in me my transgressions and thy judgment upon them."[9] "The Lord it is who calls the dead from the grave: He Himself moves the heart. . . ."[10] "God effects that you confess, in that He calls with a loud voice, that is, with great grace."[11]

Moral theology draws a very important conclusion from this. If conversion is not to be viewed solely from the standpoint of external law—even though we view it in the general context of God's providence as "external grace"—but in the light of special intervention of Divine Providence and the inner illumination and impulse of grace, there arises the question of the delay of conversion. The classic question of the later moralists is very pertinent: how long can a sinner postpone conversion without committing new sin? One cannot brush aside the question with the assertion of the "principle," "there is no law" which sets a limit to the time for conversion. The great law of the kingdom of God and of conversion is grace: "Today if you shall hear his voice, harden not your hearts" (Ps 94:8). In the rejection of grace there lies, not only a great danger to salvation, but also a special defect of love and gratitude, a sin.

A difficulty arises regarding the obligation of confessing all one's sins, as well as regarding the judgment the confessor is to make and the penance he is to impose for sin in accordance with the guilt of the penitent. However, we are not to assume that the penitent is obliged to confess every refusal of the grace of conversion, unless the penitent is aware of specific and palpable instances of such rejection of grace. Much of this would already be evident to the confessor from the general nature of the confession and the extent of time in which repentance is delayed. As to the integrity of the confession, we deal with a generally applicable external norm. Here we have in mind the inner rule of grace governing one's life, not merely the law of integral confession.

Nevertheless, one of the clearest and most telling means of judging the state of the sinner is the promptness of his rise after sin: does he immediately or at least shortly after his fall into any sin respond to the impulse of grace; does he reflect inwardly and awaken acts of sorrow, or does he resist the grace which cries out aloud to him to convert? Or is the habit of resistance to grace so inveterate that he scarcely can hear it knocking at his heart?

The great danger of postponement of conversion arises from the very role which grace plays in the work of conversion; because grace is God's gift, and not man's own property of which he can dispose as he chooses, the sinner must fear in each instance that the grace rejected may be the last. He must fear that God will offer no further grace of conversion, that He will withdraw from him, will not enlighten him so clearly, will not knock again at his heart so loudly and perceptibly. Especially great is the danger of neglecting the great hours of grace, the popular mission or retreat, the contact with an extraordinarily holy man or a notable confessor, earthly trials such as sickness, all of which offer occasion for reflection. Since interior freedom necessary for conversion can come to us only through grace, every hour of grace squandered means a hazard to freedom, diminution of freedom, aggravating the inclination to resist the loving invitation and design of God.

b. Conversion and "Justification" (Infusion of Sanctifying Grace)

The first impulse toward conversion comes from God. And every subsequent step on the way to complete conversion is under the influence of divine grace. Even the very core and center of conversion itself, that which is its inner actuality, the welcome home extended to the one who is converted, can be nothing other than the work of divine grace, an act of incomparable divine generosity. From this unique operation of divine grace, namely, from the divine readiness to forgive and the divine promise of pardon, two basic imperatives flow: first is the command to "be reconciled to God" (2 COR 5:20: *"katallágete tô theô"*: "God, as it were, appealing through us" . . . that we "be reconciled"). Since "justification" of adults demands the free cooperation with prevenient grace, the offer of grace implies the command or imperative of grace: we must follow the path of sorrow and pain, which is also the path of hope and joy. Even more comprehensive is the second imperative of the grace of justification: "Be now in reality what you are!" live in accordance with the new creation which God has wrought within you. On this basis Christian moral theology must study the working of God's grace in conversion.

1. According to Saint John the very culmination and crown of conversion, that which makes up its very essence, is the "rebirth from God." The return home and the welcome in the Father's house are not external things, but interior phenomena which transform man inwardly. They are truly a rebirth from God (Jn 1:11–13), a birth from above, "of the spirit" (Jn 3:5). Hence conversion is infinitely more than merely giving up sin; in fact, it is more than the pardon of sin: it is the gift of a new life; it is being conceived and being born from the seed of God (1 Jn 2:29; 3:9; 4:7; 5:1, 4, 18). Not only the sins of the past are wiped away by the divine pardon, but the bonds with sin and the slavery of the world are broken from within: "We know that no one who is born of God commits sin; but the Begotten of God preserves him and the evil one does not touch him" (1 Jn 5:18). "Because all that is born of God overcomes the world" (1 Jn 5:4). The rebirth from God means the implanting of a "new heart." Therefore, it can and must express itself and preserve itself through a union of love with God, an entirely new relation of love toward God and all who are born of God (Jn 14:12ff.; 15:2, 8ff.; 1 Jn 5:1f.).

The antithesis between this grace of rebirth and every sin, particularly mortal sin, is so sharp that Saint John employs the boldest terms to impress this imperative of grace upon us: "Whoever is born of God does not commit sin; because his seed abides in him and he cannot sin, because he is born of God" (1 Jn 3:9). The Apostle is well aware that the newly reborn Christian can actually commit sin again and thus lose the gift of new birth. But this appears to him utterly unheard-of, utterly unthinkable, because grave sin is not only a contradiction of the external law of God, but also of the inner principle of divine life and all its vital spiritual forces. The Christian should abhor mortal sin as something unthinkable.

2. No less forceful are the concepts and figures used by Saint Paul to express the work of divine grace in the return of the sinner to the Father's house: on God's part, conversion is inner renewal, a "new creature" (kainè ktísis, 2 Cor 5:17); it is a work which can be compared only to the creation of the world, to the "let there be light."[12] Through God's action the convert becomes "a new creature" according to the Spirit. Through the Spirit of the Lord the old man, the "carnal" man, is destroyed. "If then any man is in Christ, he is a new creature: the former things have passed away; behold, they are made new!" (2 Cor 5:17; cf. 2 Cor 3:16ff.; Eph 4:22ff.; Gal 6:8.)

3. The new convert, now a new creature, receives through the Spirit

of the Lord the Spirit of adoption as son and with it the new "freedom" of the children of God (cf. ROM 8:10–17; 2 COR 3:16ff.; EPH 5:8; GAL 4:4f.). And also he receives a new and radically different rapport with the law: he is no longer to be driven like a galley slave from without under menace of the law. He is no longer under a law made impotent by his sinful state and yet powerful in its accusation of sin against him. It is the law of freedom, of grace, which from within teaches him to discern the voice of the Father, the invitation of love, in the external law. For him the real law is the law of love; the bond of love between a child and its heavenly Father governs him entirely.

4. God's acceptance of the convert is a "justification through grace." It is not a mere legal "declaration" of justice based on works which perchance will be performed according to the external law (ROM, GAL). Nor does God establish a mere human justice, a just relation between man and man. An incomprehensible "justice of God" lays hold of man through grace. Therefore, the truly just attitude of man converted is not to glory in the law or vaunt the works of the law. And just as little is it a moralistic shopping about for spiritual bargains or falling back on minimum requirements or duties of the external law. The man justified by grace must be possessed of the deep conviction that he is bound by obedience, the ceaseless obedience, the obedience without limits, and bound as well by love without limits, the obedience and love of a child. Through obedience and love he is bound to bring forth the "true fruits of justice."

5. The work of the Spirit of God in the soul makes of conversion a passage from darkness to "light in the Lord" (EPH 5:8), with the corresponding obligation to "have no fellowship with the unfruitful works of darkness" (EPH 5:11ff.), but to reject them utterly and to bring forth the mature "fruit of light" (EPH 5:8ff.).

6. Through baptism our return to Christ becomes, in efficacious figure and sign and in incomprehensible mysterious reality, death and resurrection with Him, a passage from death to a new life, a transfer and welcome to the heavenly home in Christ's eternal kingdom (ROM 6; EPH 2:1ff.; COL 2:13,20; 3:1ff.; cf. JN 5:24).

In the thought of Saint Paul the conclusion is entirely evident: there is the most compelling imperative to mortify the dead works of darkness, the works of the old man, the "carnal" man (ROM 6), to shun every resemblance to the world with its obscurity (ROM 12:2), by force of and in accordance with the marvelous Paschal renewal. We must "purge out the old leaven" (1 Cor 5:7f.). To live "in Christ Jesus," to possess "the Spirit of the life in Christ," exacts of us with all insistence a mode of life patterned on the life of Christ and complete docility to the Holy Spirit. "He who says that he abides in him, ought himself also to walk just as he walked" (1 Jn 2:6; cf. 1 Jn 1:6; 1 Cor 3:3; Gal 5:16, 25; Col 2:8; Rom 8:1; principally Rom 6).

c. The Law of Rebirth in the Light of Divine Grace

The norm of the Christian life and the whole impulse toward Christian living are the effects of divine grace working upon us and within us: this is an existence truly Christian lived in and through the Holy Spirit! The incomparable imperative of grace exacting Christian conduct after conversion (this is the continuous conversion, the *conversio continua* or *conversatio,* in the terms of the vow in the Benedictine Rule) has nothing of the automatic about it, nor is it something spontaneous, as the urge to grow in a plant. It is an imperative addressed to the free will of man. The old natural freedom, of course, has made way for the new freedom of the child of God. And still, as long as we sojourn in this time and tide of earthly trial, we must constantly face up to the responsibility of preserving this liberty and enriching it amid the ever-present peril of our own free rejection of grace.

In many passages the inspired writer urges the one who is reborn to become also in his conduct and his thought entirely that which he is really and radically through the divine action. He must become that which God has really wrought within him, and which he has basically already embraced. But there is a vast background of conviction in this body of Scriptural thought that the world itself still has a hold on man himself. On that residue or remainder of carnal existence after conversion the world still has a dangerous grip. The work of conversion is not completed until the reborn Christian permits himself to be guided entirely and utterly by the Spirit of God.

The moral warnings suggested by the new life of the convert (cf. the catalogue of sins found in Paul and John) very clearly show that the negative precepts of the law (the *prohibita*) are not without meaning for him. However, he does not stand under the law any longer, in the sense of being subjected unwillingly to its burdens and accusations. Surely he must definitely heed the warning against transgression. He must be entirely in the clear of the dread frontiers of death indicated by the prohibitions of the law. But he may not make of them the complete program of his new moral life. Their restrictions must be a matter of course to him. But the guidance which is unique and proper to the Christian reborn does not flow from the external law, set down in written statutes, but from the Spirit of Christ. It is the inner guidance of grace. In all this the "spiritual" man does not presume to place himself in opposition to the externally established law: on the contrary, the law is now written in his heart; it has become something deep and intimate to the new convert. Now with the eyes of a child, he sees in the law of God the wise dispositions of the heavenly Father. In this sense he is not under the old law and still is not without the law. He is *énnomos Christû* (1 COR 9:21); this means that the new existence in Christ, the new life in Christ, is the law which has laid hold of him. The divine life (*zoé*) itself is now the actual norm of his life. He feels bound from within to live up "to the mature measure of the fulness of Christ" (cf. EPH 4:7, 13).

The man spiritually reborn through conversion would indeed become a "transgressor of his law" in a true sense of the term if, despite the clear and conscious inner guidance of divine grace and the personal imperatives of the interior law of the supernatural life, he should excuse himself from following the promptings of grace, on the plea that he need do no more than the minimum required by the prohibitions of the law. The inner law never contradicts what is prohibited by the external divine law, but it does oppose the servile attitude of self-excuse: "there is no universal law to the contrary; therefore I am free to follow the course I choose. I am not obliged to follow the promptings of grace, the impulses toward progress in grace." To set one's sights on the minimum requirement of law in order to escape from the call of grace and the law of grace is to fall from the "law of grace."

The negative precepts of the decalog, the two tables of the law, are not a perfect and adequate expression of the inner law written in the heart through our assimilation to Christ. This is manifested rather by the Sermon on the Mount, the new law of the kingdom of God promulgated by Christ, the law of disinterested and unbounded love, humility, and love of the cross. The prohibitive precepts (contained essentially in the decalog) lay down the minimum requirements. They fix the boundaries which all must respect (prescriptive precepts). The Sermon on the Mount determines the ideals and goals toward which we must strive (purposive precepts). Unlike the prescriptive precepts of the external law, these purposive precepts emerge and clearly reveal their obligatory boundaries only as one progresses interiorly in the new life. The movement toward the goal, toward the full realization of the law of Christ, is a strict duty arising from the new existence, the life in Christ. The approach, the progress toward fulfillment, must be an expression of the interior growth and the inner guidance of the Holy Spirit.

Altogether essential to the law of the disciple of Christ is spiritual growth and progress, the deepening of the first conversion, the continuous "second conversion." It is not like the growth of a plant, spontaneous but not free. It is the growth of the image of God in the freedom of the child of God; hence, second conversion demands constant effort, the energetic impulse which summons all the forces of the soul. There will be times of quiet unobtrusive growth, times also of tremendous defensive efforts, moments of extraordinary grace, which account for the breakthrough to new depths and heights.

Moral progress in the "second conversion" in many ways may be compared to the scaling of the peaks by the Alpinist. Persistently he climbs, with his eye fixed on the goal. He may slip occasionally, fall back a step or two, but he holds on steadily and, particularly in the time of hazard and peril, he is most determined in his assault of the peaks, until finally against overwhelming odds he has attained to new heights.

Interior progress may be characterized as gradual passage from simple observance of the commandments with their burdens and difficulties to the keen alertness for the directives of the Spirit of God, communicated to us through inspiration from within and the situation without, in an ever clearer appreciation of what is essential, the love and glory of God and the effort to promote His kingdom.

5. The Sacramental Dimension of Conversion

In the actual economy of salvation, conversion enters into an essential relation to the holy sacraments, particularly to baptism, penance, and the Holy Eucharist. Since the sacraments are not merely arbitrary or accidental accessories in the work of man's redemption, but the divinely instituted revelation and development of the way of salvation itself, a sacramental dimension enters essentially into every salutary conversion, even though the convert does not actually receive any sacrament. In the traditional language of theology this means that no non-Christian can attain justification without at least the "baptism of desire" (*baptisma flaminis*) or baptism of blood, in the event that sacramental baptism is not possible. Similarly the conversion of the baptized sinner from the state of mortal sin to the state of grace is not effected without at least an implicit readiness to receive the sacrament of penance.[13] Saint Thomas says that the acts of conversion belonging to the virtue of penance lead to the infusion of sanctifying grace only "in so far as these acts have a relation to the Church's power of the keys, and hence it is clear that the pardon of sins is the work of the virtue of penance, but more essentially of the sacrament of penance."[14] Every salutary conversion is, indeed, "through faith and the relation to the power of the keys of the Church directed to the passion of Christ, and thus it effects in a twofold way (that is through the virtue of penance and the sacrament of penance) the pardon of sin through the suffering of Christ."[15]

Every salutary conversion—it does not matter at all whether one has received a sacrament of conversion or not—derives its efficacy from the one sole proto-sacrament, in which all sacraments center and from which all derive their grace, the sacrament of Christ in the mystery of His death and resurrection. Conversely, every salutary reception of a sacrament, particularly the sacraments of baptism and penance,[16] which are sacraments of conversion, presupposes the spirit of conversion, of *metánoia,* active interior conversion. Putting the matter more precisely, we should say that the sacraments through the divine operation which is proper to them excite in us the efforts we make to convert and return to the Father's house. The sacraments bring forth these efforts, perfect them, sanctify them.

The structure of the sacraments of conversion clearly indicates the essential features of conversion. There are three steps or stages to be noted. a. Conversion is the personal encounter with Christ through faith and the trustful anticipation of full assimilation to Him in love. b. Approaching the sacraments of the Church and the return to God through these sacraments of the Church is the foundation and source of an intimate relation to the kingdom of God and its visible manifestation, the Church of God. c. The return of the sinner effected through the actual reception of the sacraments makes him a participant in the sacred cult of the Church with the sacred obligation of divine worship in which he is entered through the sacraments.

a. Conversion as Sacramental Encounter with Christ

In their structure the sacraments of conversion clearly show that personal encounter with Christ is the actual import and purpose of conversion. Conversion is essentially Christo-centric.

(1) *Encounter with Christ in the Sacrament of Faith*

The sacraments as the grand signs of faith are sacred admonitions directing us to be one with Christ in faith. Their administration, even when they are entirely and exclusively borne by the Church herself subjectively, as in the case of infant baptism, is always a mighty incentive to conversion. "If we study the accounts of the conversion of peoples of ancient and modern times, it strikes us that the religious influence on which the conversion depends proceeded primarily from sacred worship."[17] The recently published *Directory of the French Bishops for the Pastoral Administration of the Sacraments* is particularly significant in this connection. According to the introductory statement of Msgr. Guerry, it bases its whole purpose on this same principle, the purpose being "a grand movement of sacramental evangelization by means of the sacraments and flowing from the sacraments."[18] "Evangelization and sacramental life cannot be viewed as contradictories."[19] The fruitful administration and reception of the sacraments by virtuous priests and laity imbued with profound faith is of primary importance for the work of conversion among believers and non-believers. On this point considerable importance is to be attached to the language employed. Every effort should be made to have the faithful understand the meaning of the sacred words and actions (cf. 1 Cor 14:1–24).

The whole work of repentance and conversion can and must be viewed in the perspective of the holy sacraments and be directed toward them, because the sacraments are *par excellence* the "signs of faith." In these visible and perceptible signs, which deal with things we can see and hear, there is the assurance of our faith that we encounter Christ in a manner suited to our human nature, composed as it is of body and soul.

Since conversion is through personal encounter with Christ, it must begin with trustful faith in Him. The sinner must be assured that God is inviting and calling him to repentance. He must be convinced that God calls him by name to save him from eternal perdition. The sacraments of conversion which he is invited and urged to receive are heavenly pledges to the individual sinner that Christ died and arose from the dead, not merely for all men universally, but for him specifically. Accordingly, faith[20] which awakens hope in the sinner's heart is the first step toward conversion (cf. Heb 6:1; 11:6ff.; Acts 20:21; 26:18). In faith Christ Himself is our light. This light reveals to the sinner the seriousness of his condition and points the way of hope, the way which is Christ, the way which is offered to all earthly pilgrims in the holy sacraments.

But faith without the fruit of charity, even if it rise to the heights of the most ardent trust in redemption through Christ (the mere fiducial faith of Luther), is not perfect faith. Without love faith is not complete and authentic conversion. Christ desires to take over man in his entirety through the sacrament, his intellect, his heart, his will. This He does when faith blossoms forth in the fulness of hope and love.

A clear and penetrating analysis of all the stages of conversion is found in the *Confessions of Saint Augustine*. The great Doctor studies all the psychological steps of conversion, all the tremendous impulses to which grace moves the sinner, from the faith which enlightens the mind to the hope which raises the heart, from the first steps of faith to the final conquest of the will and the firm decision of the will through the grace of the Holy Spirit.[21]

Genuine encounter with Christ in the sacraments demands faith, hope, and a submissive will. On the part of the sinner there must be a readiness to obey and at least an openness toward the movement of grace by which divine love is infused into the soul. This Christ Himself gives either through the sacrament of conversion or at least because of the sacrament (this we call the desire to receive the sacrament, which may be explicit or implicit, the *votum sacramenti*).

In the sacrament the salutary action of Christ and our own encounter with Him (in the event that our own cooperation is not lacking) are wedded in a marvelous experience of faith, for the sacraments are "signs of faith" through which we approach Christ and He comes to us with His grace. The fruit of the union of conversion with the sacrament of conversion is a sacred pledge from heaven that Christ Himself encourages, sanctifies, and perfects our own frail effort to convert and return to the Father's house. It is Christ's work in us "because he continues forever, has an everlasting priesthood. Therefore he is able at all times to save those who come to God through him, since he lives always to make intercession for them" (HEB 7:24f.; cf. 1 JN 2:1f.).

Our conversion looks to pardon of sin (cf. LK 3:3; 24:47; ACTS 3:19), has as its goal and hope the pardon of our sins which Christ in the sacrament (or with reference to the sacrament) holds out to us as the grace earned in His passion and resurrection. Thus it is correct to say that conversion takes place in reference to the sacrament where Christ awaits us in the visible signs of faith. Through the invitation of the sacrament the crippling fear of our incapacity is transformed into humble trust in the infinite mercy of God in Christ. Particularly is this true of baptism, penance, and the Holy Eucharist. Conversion bears a very special visible relation to these three sacraments, for in them the true character of conversion as encounter with Christ is revealed with singular clearness and force.

(2) *Assimilation to Christ in Baptism*

Baptism is the fundamental sacrament of repentance and return to God (cf. Acts 2:38). Already in the preaching of John the Baptist the penitential appeal and the baptism of penitence were one, evidently a prophetic image of the future baptism of the Holy Spirit which actually sealed the conversion of the sinner (Mk 1:4; Lk 3:3,16; Acts 13:24; 19:4ff.). According to the pregnant phrase of Justin the Apologete,[22] baptism is "the bath of conversion (*lutròn tês metanoías*) which can purify only those who themselves convert (those who return home, *metanoésantes*)."

Forgiveness of sin and the sinner's return to the Father's house in the love of God take place in baptism "in the name of Jesus"; this is to say, through the fulness of power and the action of Jesus, through the efficacy of His presence, through the invocation of His Name, through the bond of His ineffable love.[23] All this places in the sharpest relief what we have already said about the nature of conversion as encounter with Christ. Sinner and Master meet: the sinner with his confidence, Jesus with the power of His passion and resurrection and the great promise of final salvation on the day of Parousia.

In baptism Christ Himself awaits the sinner to welcome him home to the Father's house, to give him a share in the fruits of the redemption. His presence and power give to all the steps of the convert leading to baptism their force and security. By baptism the sinner turns to Christ in his repentance, and Christ turns to the sinner to welcome and accept him. But preparation for conversion must be such that this acceptance by Christ meets no obstacle placed by the sinner. Baptism as efficacious sign clearly symbolizes the goal of conversion: assimilation to Christ in His suffering and His resurrection, an assimilation which already bears within it the seed and the pledge of the ultimate community with Christ in the kingdom of glory (cf. Rom 6; Col 3:1ff.; 1 Pt 2:21-25).

Because baptism can be received only once—such is its nature as the fundamental sacrament of conversion—and because it is on Christ's part the most profound and irrevocable possession and commitment, it never ceases to demand conversion and reconversion of the sinner. By its inmost nature baptism demands of us a constant deepening and maturing of our first conversion, of our return to Christ, of *metánoia*. This imperative affects even those who were baptized as infants. For those fallen into sin it is a perpetual warning to seek again the way of penance, the return to the first conversion.

(3) *Sorrowful Encounter with Christ in Penance*

The second sacrament of conversion, the sacrament of penance, places the sinner anew before the mercy of Christ, if he has again turned his back to His Saviour and Father after having received the grace of pardon and assimilation to Christ. This sacrament has often been called "the second plank of safety after the shipwreck of sin."[24] It is the bitter remedy of salvation which the Christian should not require after he has received the fulness of salvation in baptism.[25] The baptismal consecration to Christ and the intimate union with Him in the Holy Eucharist (to which baptism is essentially directed) are in themselves and as such simply irrevocable (1 Jn 3:9; 5:18). Therefore complete apostasy from Christ, after the reception of baptism and the illumination of the other sacraments of initiation (confirmation and Eucharist), is also irreparable (cf. 2 Pt 2:20ff.; Heb 6:4ff.), at least without a miracle of God's mercy in the moral order. The institution of the sacrament of second mercy and the invitation extended to the sinner to make use of it are unique manifestations of the divine loyalty of Christ (1 Jn 1:9), who, faithful to His work of grace once begun, brings back even the unfaithful and disloyal to loyalty.[26]

The great Fathers of the ancient Church defended the consoling doctrine that the fallen Christian could be reconciled again to God. With all the ardor of Christian sympathy they defended this teaching against the callous severity of the early rigorists.[27] During the early controversies regarding penance the tenderness and sympathy of Mother Church were manifested time and again. Basically her attitude and her action were defense of the incomprehensibly great fidelity of Christ and grateful praise of the infinite mercy of God. But this very same ancient Church which had at heart the true defense and salutary administration of this sacrament, also taught through a very stern and palpable penitential discipline the essential difference between the first sacrament of conversion and the reconversion through the second sacrament, the "toilsome baptism."[28]

Baptism is the unique welcome extended to the sinner returning to the Father's house. It can be granted only once. One who commits mortal sin after baptism offends against the incomparable love of Christ and His Church. To obtain mercy after this fall, he must submit to the judgment of her tribunal. With "bitter tears and strenuous penitential effort," he must approach the grace-giving tribunal of Christ and the Church and accept humbly the penance which is imposed. Through these means he must be made aware of the inconceivably immense bounty of second reconciliation. Despite all his efforts the penitent may not be restored to his full baptismal innocence, but in this tribunal of grace he may celebrate a true home-coming. Even the toils and pains of contrition, of humble confession, and the wholesome acceptance of the imposed penance are all signs of love for him, signs of the saving power of the passion of Christ.[29] They too invite the sinner to gratitude and renewal of loyalty.

Sorrow is indispensable for conversion in the sacrament of penance, as it was for the conversion in baptism. But to this sorrow of penance belong the necessary steps of confession of sin and satisfaction (at least the desire to make satisfaction)[30] as well. Since these steps on the way to conversion, sorrow, confession, and satisfaction (the willingness) as a part of the "sacramental sign" (the quasi-matter)[31] enter into the very intimate constitution of the efficacious sacramental matter and form,[32] they possess a unique sacramental dignity and value and reveal the true intimacy of our personal encounter with Christ in the sacrament. Christ Himself comes to the sinner through His Holy Spirit and leads him to ever more intimate union.

The sinner's encounter with Christ in the sacrament of second conversion must be viewed in the bright light of the assimilation to Christ in the baptismal conversion. Once the life of grace is lost through mortal sin, the baptismal character remains, forever accusing and condemning the baptized, until grace is restored. But grace is given in accordance with the spiritual disposition of the penitent, who "is made like to Christ in His passion, through the pains of his atonement."[33] And the penitent in this second conversion must submit to the judgment of a tribunal, a tribunal of grace and mercy which is to be viewed in the light of the final judgment. Thus the encounter with Christ in the sacrament of penance must be related to the encounter with Christ in His second coming to judge all men: the sinner for whom the truth of the second coming of Christ in judgment implies a dreadful menace, a terrifying warning to do penance, may now participate in the ardent yearning of Mother Church for the merciful and gracious judgment of Christ. "In the dim light of the confessional there is already some glimmer of the glory of Christ, in which He is to come to judge the living and the dead. Cross and penance are judgment of sin. They are anticipation of the future general judgment and therefore refer to the coming of the divine dominion where sin and the power of sin ultimately will be vanquished."[34] From all this it should be evident to everyone how great must be the earnest disposition and sacred assurance of victory with which we encounter Christ in the sacrament of second conversion.

The other sacraments, since they are "sacraments of the living," are not sacraments of "first conversion," but have as their purpose to give further growth and perfection to the grace and friendship with God already in the soul. But since all the sacraments (each in a diverse manner) have as their purpose the maturity of the first conversion, they have also secondarily (*per accidens*) the capacity and function to complete and perfect the first conversion which is still somewhat immature. Such is the common and safe teaching of theologians. No more is required of the recipient who may be in the state of mortal sin than an entirely sincere inner detachment from mortal sin through true sorrow (at least imperfect contrition or attrition is required) and reception of the sacrament with a good conscience (often called good faith).

Thus primarily the Most Holy Sacrament of the Eucharist, *par excellence* symbol and pledge of love, to which the sacraments of conversion and all other sacraments turn most intimately, confers sanctifying grace on everyone, "even though he be in mortal sin, provided his conscience does not reproach him with the guilt of it, because he is not aware of it and is not attached to it."[35]

"Even though his previous sorrow does not attain to the measure or height of love, he still obtains, provided only that he approaches the sacrament with reverence, the grace of divine love, which perfects his sorrow, and also the pardon of his sin."[36]

Anyone who possesses genuine sorrow for his sins, though it be imperfect, is truly on the way to Christ; and when he approaches a sacrament of the living in good faith, he has the will to approach Christ. Wherefore we may apply to him the words of Christ spoken in His first instruction on the sacrament of His love: "Him who comes to me I will

not cast out" (Jn 6:37). This truth, which is most consoling particularly
for souls distressed by anxiety of spirit, holds not only for reception of the
Eucharist, but for the reception of all the other sacraments,[37] and is of
primary significance and importance in the case of Extreme Unction.[38]

The important practical difference between the Eucharist and the
other "sacraments of the living" is this: for the reception of the other
sacraments as such, according to divine and ecclesiastical law, the earnest
endeavor to excite and elicit perfect contrition with the resolution to confess the mortal sin in due time is sufficient. For fruitful reception of the
Holy Eucharist, however, sacramental confession of all mortal sins of
which one is conscious is required, unless there are most urgent reasons
for reception of Holy Communion and there is no opportunity for confession.[39] Anyone who has neglected to confess a mortal sin without any
serious fault of his own (for example, because he has forgotten) in his
previous sacramental confession, may nevertheless receive the Holy
Eucharist and any other sacrament of the living without prior confession
of this forgotten sin. It is sufficient if he has the good will to confess the
sin in the next confession (at least no later than his next paschal
confession).

b. Conversion in the Sacramental Community of the Kingdom of God

There is an essential relation of conversion to that great reality which
is the kingdom of God. To understand this relation, we must study in
detail the holy sacraments not merely as instruments of salvation, used
by the individual, but under their social-ecclesial aspect as well.[40] The
entire work of conversion and salvation is not a matter of mere individual
relation between man and God; it possesses a dimension of community;
it is a matter of the kingdom of God. The kingdom of God approaches
us visibly through Christ living in the Church throughout all time. It is
precisely the sacraments (and the teaching and pastoral office) which
form the fundamental elements of the Church in her visible and invisible
reality as the kingdom of God. In their visible structure as operative signs
they point commemoratively to the intervention of the kingdom of
God in the Incarnation, in the passion and resurrection of Christ and in
the descent of the Holy Spirit. And prophetically they point to the final
revelation of the eternal kingdom of glory. Their efficacy is "in the power
of God" (*ex opere operato*), for they are immediately operative signs of

Christ coming to us in grace, signs of the Holy Spirit newly moulding and transforming the soul from within. Wherefore they manifest essential aspects of the kingdom of God descending from heaven and of the eternal dominion of God taking hold of the soul within. Signs of divine grace, they "signify and effect our incorporation in the Church. As signs of the Church herself, the sacraments are gifts of grace in the community (of God) and in reference to the community, which it is their function to build up and deepen."[41]

When we analyze the intimate bond between conversion and sacrament, we come to realize that conversion is at its very depths a gift, for the form or the words of the sacrament clearly indicate that conversion is an effect of the fulness of grace and of the apostolic spirit of the Church. It necessarily implies a grace-giving incorporation into the Church with the perpetual obligation of gratitude to her. Of its very nature it forms the basis of the relation of solidarity with the Church and of the obligation to be concerned with her needs. As incorporation in Christ, conversion means that we form one body with all who belong to Christ, with all members of the Church. Therefore conversion is under a law of life, life with a sanction. This is the law: conversion is authentic and firm, rich in the depth of insight and outlook, in proportion to the earnest endeavor the convert makes to become a living member of the kingdom of God, and thereby of the Church,[42] with a sense of solidarity which makes him active in cooperating and working with the other members. One who is not ready to live in the Church, with it and for it, with a deep sense of all its meaning, willing to fight, suffer for the Church, is not really altogether converted, has not altogether entered into the "kingdom of God." This law is a true imperative of the kingdom of God.

It is an imperative of all the sacraments, but particularly of the sacraments of conversion.

Through the reception of baptism one becomes a member of the Body of Christ and thereby a "personal member of the Church of Christ with all the rights and duties of a Christian."[43] In consequence, baptism requires of the new Christian the spirit of a child in relation to its father, the familial spirit in relation to the Christian community, and the joyous participation in the familial celebration of worship (cult) in the Church. Confirmation perfects the work which God wrought in the soul through baptism. Similarly, the fruit of confirmation must be a constantly progressive conversion,[44] which demands of us by its very nature an ever bolder effort for the Church as the kingdom of God, with a profound consciousness of our responsibility.

All the sacraments, particularly the two sacraments of conversion, are directed to the Holy Eucharist, which is the efficacious sign of the unity and love of Christ in the Church. It clearly follows that conversion also, by its most intimate nature, must have as its goal love of unity with the Church and all her members, a love which grows increasingly vigorous day by day. Eucharist means unity flowing from sacrificial love. Accordingly conversion, which is directed to the Eucharist, by its essence demands a spirit of sacrifice, increasing constantly. It demands the spirit of self-oblation for the Church. And this spirit must grow increasingly ardent day by day.

Recent research in the history of dogma has shed considerable light on the ecclesial character of the sacrament of penance with its social dimension in relation to salvation.[45] The point is brought out very strikingly in the explanation of this phase of the sacrament of penance by the medieval scholastics, who hold that the most proper and the first effect (*res sacramenti*) of penance—as is the case with the Holy Eucharist— is the unity of the Church.[46] By excluding the sinner from the Sacred Banquet until he repents and does penance (receives the sacrament of penance), the Church wishes to bring him to a fruitful realization of the dread fact that mortal sin by its nature excludes the Christian from the full participation in the community of love of Christ and His brethren in the Church.

"We exclude certain individuals from the community of the altar, in order that they may find through penitential conversion reconciliation with Him, whom they have despised when they committed sin."[47] "One who commits a mortal sin is excluded (*excommunicatus*) from the community by the judgment of God."[48] For every genuine Christian who realizes that the Eucharist must be the means of faith and life for the true disciple of Christ, exclusion from the Sacred Table is a terrifying "grace unto conversion and penance,"[49] a warning to convert anew and with a greater earnestness to the community of love, which is the Church.

It might be well to refer in passing to a melancholy inadequacy found now and again in the preaching on penance. Our exhortations to repentance and to reception of this sacrament should be based on its relation to the Eucharist. To deal with the Holy Eucharist merely under the aspect of "one of our duties" which must be properly performed and "one of the means of grace" always available is very one-sided and superficial. Such procedure in preaching fails completely to explain the profound inner relation of the two sacraments to each other and to the whole sacramental kingdom of God, the Church.

That sin is socially pernicious and conversion socially constructive is very clearly expressed in the various penitential rites of the Church, particularly in the rite of the sacrament itself; the contrite sinner confesses not only before God, the source and goal of the entire sacred community, but also before the Church militant and triumphant and, above all, in the presence of the priest, visible representative of God and the Church. For sin has offended the Church, marred her harmony and unity; and conversion must lead the sinner back again to the community of love and life in the Church. Conversion—such is the clear meaning of the rites of the Church—is not the result of personal effort, but grace and gift from the sacred community of the kingdom of God, with which the sinner by his own free endeavor must cooperate toward reacceptance.

The satisfaction imposed in the sacrament of penance (we see this most clearly in the ancient public penitential discipline of the Church) places in clear relief the right of the community to reparation for the scandal and the inner disorder of sin. But this painful penance also reveals the tremendous power of grace contained in the imperative of conversion: the sacred community intervenes to reconcile the sinner. It imposes the penance which he merits as punishment for his sin. But through this intervention of the sacred community, the penance becomes a gift in a communion of suffering with the redemptive suffering of Christ and a most effective means of penance and expiation in the entire Mystical Body of Christ for the reconciliation of the sinner. The new convert is again admitted into the ranks, an honored living member of the Mystical Body. Now again he can share in the spiritual work of building the living temple which is the kingdom of God.

An eloquent testimony to the social nature of conversion and its culmination in the *agape* of the Eucharistic Banquet is found in the ancient solemn rite of public penance which is still retained in the present *Pontificale Romanum.*[50] After the Church in the ceremony of public expulsion has made the sinner conscious of the antisocial and disruptive character of his sin and with loving kindness has led him through all the stages of penance, she offers the prayer of reconciliation: "Admit them again, O Lord, into the bosom of thy Church. . . . May thy Son purify them of all their misdeeds and graciously grant them access to the most sacred Banquet. . . . Grant to them, O Lord, that after the remission of their sins, they may without harm be restored to thy Church, from whose unbroken community they have strayed away through their sins . . . in order that thy Church will not be made desolate in a portion of her body, so that thy flock suffer no harm . . . and replace the redeemed member with the others in the unity of the body of the Church . . . so that, having put on again the nuptial garment, they may deserve to approach again the royal feast from which they were cast out!" (cf. 1 Cor 5:4f.,11).

This rite manifests very forcefully how conversion is pointed to the sacred fraternal banquet, to the most Holy Eucharist. It clearly shows that by its very nature conversion to Christ cannot and may not be divorced from conversion to the assembly of the saints, which is the Church, the Bride of Christ. Wherever outside the visible circle of the Catholic Church a true and salutary conversion takes place, it is granted by Christ with reference to His Church. And it must be accredited to the attitude of the sinner only in so far as in desire he is seeking the holy community and is turned toward this community in his return to his heavenly Father. Quite pertinently can the words of the liturgy, *"ubi caritas et amor, Christus ibi est,"* be paraphrased: when one returns home to Christ, there is the beginning of the kingdom of the sacred, loving community!

The faithful should be correctly instructed on the relation between conversion and the kingdom of God. Correct appreciation of the inseparable bond between them, between the sacramental structure of the kingdom of God and conversion, should create in the mind of every Christian the firm conviction that the sacrament of penance means far more than a "command to confess one's sins with sorrow." It is rather the bountiful offering of divine grace from the kingdom of God. It rests on the sacred rights of the community of love, which is the Church, to which the sinner must return. It is Christ's welcome offered only in the community of love, which is His Bride, the Church. In this sacrament the penitent again says yes to atonement from the very depth of his heart: with profound sentiment he unites himself again to the community of the kingdom of God in the spirit of atonement and gratitude.

Exclusive or even one-sided stress on individual salvation in teaching or preaching the doctrine of grace and sacraments, of sin and conversion may prove a hindrance psychologically in the approach of the faithful to the sacramental ecclesial way of conversion. Wrong concepts arising from such a method of instruction may bar the way to conversion or at least rob it of much of its fundamental social fruitfulness. Individual salvation, individual encounter with Christ, in every instance depends altogether on union with the community of the kingdom of God, on conversion to the community of the Body of Christ. Individual and community are not in antithesis. They form one indivisible totality. Individual and community are connected in mutual enrichment and unity. We cannot sever the Church and her members from Christ, nor Christ from the Church.

c. Conversion as Cultal Orientation and Obligation

The sinner in refusing God the honor due to Him centers his life in himself; he seeks his own glory (cf. Jn 5:44; 7:18). Accordingly, conversion must result in a new orientation of the sinner's entire life toward the glory of God. And this fundamental orientation of conversion is also clearly manifested in its efficacy and urgency through the sacraments of conversion. Even in the Old Testament the "sacraments" of the Old Law were essentially pointed toward cult, toward the worship of the divine majesty. The sacraments of the New Law, however, confer far more than mere external or cultal purity. They produce inner dispositions for the perfect worship of God in Jesus Christ.

The first and fundamental sacrament of conversion, holy baptism, frees the sinner from sin specifically through a "consecration." The character of this sacrament is a profound interior assimilation to the priesthood of Christ. In an incomprehensibly marvelous manner this consecration lays hold on the soul and sets it apart for the cult of the New Testament, a cult which is bound up most intimately with Christ, the Priest, through the most profound and sacred dedication of the whole heart and soul to Him. Therefore our dogmatic teaching holds that the baptismal character in so far as it is consecration to cult calls for the virtue of divine love and sanctifying grace. According to the Scripture, "consecration" means a sharing of the divine sovereignty in order to give glory to the divine majesty.

All the sacraments, but most particularly the three which imprint a character, baptism, confirmation, and Holy Orders, are "signs of cult and elements of cult." "The sacraments are actions of Christ, who exercises through the ministry of the Church His priesthood which has as its purpose to give honor to God as well as to effect the salvation of men."[51] Conversion through its basic sacrament, namely baptism, is essentially directed to the Eucharist, the heart and summit of all divine worship: the consecration received in baptism as fruit of the sacrifice of Christ confers on the recipient of the sacrament the fulness of power and the mission to participate in the sacrifice of Christ and the Church. The principle of conversion as well as its end and purpose resides in sacrifice, which gives glory to God. Conversion as the gift of sacrifice of Christ essentially engages one in cult. "For if the blood of goats and bulls and the sprinkled ashes of a heifer sanctify the unclean unto the cleansing of the flesh, how much more will the blood of Christ, who through the Holy Spirit offered himself unblemished unto God, cleanse your conscience from dead works to serve the living God?" (HEB 9:13f.) "We have confidence to enter the Holies in virtue of the blood of Christ . . . we have a high priest over the house of God, let us draw near with a true heart in fulness of faith, having our hearts cleansed from an evil conscience by sprinkling, and the body washed with clean water" (HEB 10:19ff.).

To return to Christ and His Church through baptism, sacrament of the divine home-coming, implies, therefore, the honor, the right, the duty to orientate our whole life toward the glory of God in holy priestly cult and constantly renew it through the liturgical realities.

Mortal sin cannot efface this orientation to priestly cult stamped on the soul by the indelible mark of baptism and confirmation; but it does make the sinner unworthy and incapable of praise agreeable to God (above all, incapable of total participation in the Eucharistic celebration through reception of Holy Communion and of a life which has the full value of divine worship). The sacrament of reconversion (penance) restores this dignity and worth for which the sacramental character clamors, or in the words of the penitential ritual of the *Pontificale Romanum:* the sacrament of reconciliation restores the sinner to "the holy altars."

From all this it is quite evident that the sacrament of penance and, with it, conversion wrought through it cannot be too intimately bound up with the Eucharist. It is of great practical importance that the instruction of the sacraments make this clear to the faithful. The sermon on the sacrament of penance and the ministry of the sacrament itself through the priesthood of the Church center in the sacrifice of Christ and have their goal in the sacrifice of Christ for the glory of God. Men must be brought to a keen realization of the truth that the Christian deprived of habitual grace neither shares fully in the celebration of the Holy Eucharist nor forms his life to an "adoration in spirit and truth." This thought must be more vigorously brought home to all the faithful by the preacher and director of souls than such considerations as, if we may cite just one example, how great a part of the Sunday Mass may be omitted without committing a mortal sin.

The full power of the priesthood of the Church to reconcile sinners is in a measure implied in her priestly power to offer the sacrifice of Christ. As Mystical Body of the high priest Jesus Christ, the Church which has the mission to co-celebrate with all her members the cult of her Head, must also—as a consequence, we may say—have the full power to efface sin, the great obstacle to worthy celebration of the most Holy Eucharist and to a truly cultal life.[52]

Through the intervention of Christ and His Church the very initial steps of the spiritual home-coming of the sinner have a cultal significance: humble contrite recital of our sins is to praise the mercy of God. Satisfaction imposed in the sacrament and in union with it the entire dolorous way of conversion and atonement have the value of real cult, not, of course, in themselves, but united with the sufferings of Christ.[53] The final perfect fruit of conversion and reconciliation is glory (*doxa*), the light of heavenly glory in which we see and give glory to God forever. This is eternal cult. "Grace and glory are of the same nature, because grace in us is nothing else but the inception of glory."[54] So our transformation through the light of glory and the glory we give to the majesty of the Father and Christ are nothing less than the full revelation of the basic entelechy of that which we receive in embryo through the sacraments, namely, grace.

Through this valence of the sacramental character and the cultal orientation of the sacrament of penance and the very nature of grace itself there are clearly defined the tendency and obligatory finality of every meritorious conversion. The source of every authentic religious conversion consists simply in this: man ceases to makes himself the center, the standard, and the goal of his thinking and acting, and begins to direct all things to God, all Highest, all Holy.

The radical orientation of one's entire life after conversion (and already in conversion itself) toward the glory of God in unity with the high priest Jesus Christ is a mighty, an absolute imperative of grace, for the action of God through Christ and the Church upon the sinner is directed to this goal. And conversion itself, the "working out of salvation with fear and trembling," in order to be genuine and solid, must be sacerdotal: it must be pointed to the glory of God and the salvation of the brethren; for there is no salvation except through the high priest, Christ, and in union with Him. In the progress of conversion, in the growth of the Christian life, this "priestly finality" (entelechy) must manifest itself with increasing clearness.[55]

CHAPTER TWELVE

THE CONVERT'S SHARE IN CONVERSION

Accokding to the Council of Trent sorrow, confession, and satisfaction are three essential parts of the sacrament of penance which are acts of the penitent.[56] We treat them here in relation to the sacrament, and likewise as the dispositions and acts which properly are elements of every genuine religious conversion as such.

I. CONTRITION

1. Humble Self-knowledge, Preparation, and Fruit of Sorrow

Without basic humility and a humble recognition of his own lowly condition on the part of the sinner himself, contrition is impossible. On the other hand, only through contrition can the sinner come to humility itself, that humility which is truly necessary for profound self-knowledge and self-improvement. Fundamentally in its deepest roots every sin springs from pride and at the same time increases dangerously the dreadful evil of pride. Nevertheless, through the bitterness of its effects on our mind and heart, through the sense of humiliation with which it affects us, sin offers us a remedy for its evil, an antidote, the call to humility. As long as the sinner is not totally enslaved by pride, sin immediately affects him with a sense of degradation, with a humiliating inward distress of soul. The natural reaction of his sinful disposition is to suppress this sense of humiliation in order to permit pride to gain an even more profound control of the soul.

In this conflict contrition is the great force of the free counterimpulse of humility. "Contrition removes the natural suppressive force of the pride of our nature. It crushes the barrier of pride which permits only that to rise up from our past which tends to appease and justify pride itself."[57]

Contrition should not be confused with the mere natural sense of pain arising from the sting of sin itself in the soul, or with the sense of shame and guilt which results from natural remorse. It is a free movement, a counterimpulse reacting against the grip of guilt on the soul, against the progressive tendency of sin to suppress, blind, harden. The very first steps of contrition are the effort of humility, insofar as it still can arise from the healthy regions of the sinful soul. Sustained by the humiliating influence of the consequences of sin, humility in its beginning is also the beginning of sorrow. It is the acknowledgment, perfected in freedom, of one's own sinfulness and consequent misery. And the more profoundly the sinner is moved by contrition, the deeper will be the descent of humility into the abyss of his own sinfulness through a purified vision and appreciation of all that is holy and good.

Saint Augustine, the great psychologist among the Fathers of the Church, says very trenchantly that the first step toward liberation from the slavery of sin, the first step on the way of truth, is "humility, and the second step is humility again, and the third step is humility; and as often as you may ask, I would give the same answer, humility."[58] Augustine is speaking from the experience of his own conversion. He knows what obstacles pride places in one's path and how the humble contrite prayer before God brought him light and strength.

No less true is the experience of men since the days of Augustine. Sad experience has repeatedly confirmed the conviction that precisely the greatest sinners fail to realize the depth of their abasement and, therefore, do not feel the need of ecclesiastical penance.[59] "Precisely this is one of the most dismal effects of guilt, that it conceals itself in its very growth and deadens the sense of its own existence."[60] "The punishment of pride is the incapacity of a true conversion."[61]

The scholastic term for contrition, *"attritio, contritio"* (attrition, rubbing, friction, gnawing) expresses very strikingly the basic element of humility underlying sorrow. "A contrite and humbled heart, O God, thou wilt not despise," *"Cor contritum et humiliatum, Deus non despicies"* (Ps 50:19). The Latin terms *attritus* (rubbed small through friction) and *contritus* (rubbed exceedingly small through friction) express the essential distinction of sorrow according to the lower or higher theological motive. The first, attrition, is often called imperfect contrition and has as its motive fear with a beginning of love; the latter is based on mature and perfect love. The beatitude, "blessed are the poor in spirit (*ptochoì tô pneúmati*)" (Mt 5:3), is most probably to be interpreted in such a way as to imply the humility of the contrite heart: blessed are they who, having been made humble through the spirit of God (or bowed down in spirit), stand before God in the acknowledgment and admission that only God can help them in their poverty (cf. Is 61:1; Lk 4:18). The next words in Mt 5:3, "for theirs is the kingdom of heaven," in stressing the relation between the "kingdom of God" and conversion, offer a new proof that the *ptochoì* are those who bow down in humility and not simply those who are victims of earthly poverty. Of course, the state of earthly poverty does have a special relation to the "kingdom of heaven," since the rich and avaricious only too readily shut out humility and sorrow from their hearts.

The typical examples of conversion found in the Bible teach the same lesson of the importance of humility for true repentance. Thus in Lk 18:9ff., we have the contrast between the proud Pharisee vaunting his virtues and the publican who was pardoned, and of whom the Lord says: "Every one who exalts himself shall be humbled, and he who humbles himself shall be exalted." The same evangelist (7:37ff.) gives the account of the woman who was known as a sinner. She is pardoned as she washes the feet of the Lord with her tears and exposes herself to open contempt and sarcasm at the house of the Pharisee. Most typical of all is the prodigal son who has been brought to the depth of utter degradation through his sins. With a profound humility equal to his offense he cast himself before his forgiving father with the words: "I am no longer worthy to be called thy son" (Lk 15:11ff.).

In the Protestant "revivals" the most abject consciousness of one's sin plays a capital role. Rightly so! But even humble recognition of one's own sinfulness is only one of the elements of repentance; it is not integral conversion. The Council of Trent condemned the teaching according to which the entire conversion consists "in the acknowledgment of one's own sin through a terrified conscience and in the firm and trusting conviction that one has obtained remission of his sins through Christ."[62]

2. *The Comfortable Fallacy of Psychoanalysis*

True contrition viewed as a remedy of psychic illness has something in common with psychotherapy, which also aims at psychic healing of the mental disturbance, disruption of spirit, and morbid sense of guilt in tortured human beings. Sorrow seeks the way to health in the deepest levels of the soul, in its oneness with God, through the painful and humble way of total recognition and admission of one's own sinfulness. Obviously there is a world of difference between this approach to mental health and that of naturalistic psychoanalysis, which totally excludes the deepest source of psychic illness, sin or deliberate moral guilt, offense against the eternal spiritual values, offense against the Lord of love, and with all this the great salutary remedy of true repentance through contrition. To the psychoanalyst who is imbued with the principles of Freud and cannot deny the coincidence of sense of guilt and psychic illness, "religion and sense of guilt" are "archaic remnants," "neurotic fictions."[63] "The consciousness of guilt which confronts him in his clinical experience appears to him as an obstacle to emotional balance and social adjustment."[64] We do not have to deny the truth of this observation, but we cannot accept the principles which explain it, nor their application to mental therapy.

Externally the remedial procedures of the psychoanalyst have a great deal in common with the stages of contrition: he follows a method which probes into the deepest folds and levels of the soul, just as contrition penetrates the ultimate basis and motive of guilt. Yet the goal of the psychoanalyst is in direct contradiction to that of true sorrow. He assumes from the very beginning that at the root of the sense of guilt and the mental illness, there can be no real guilt, and he exerts himself to the utmost to create the same conviction in the consciousness of his patient. Instead of real guilt he sees some kind of complex, a primitive sexual experience, a repression which has nothing to do with guilt at all. In his mind only "erroneous" notions of guilt, not real guilt or sin, are responsible for this pathological condition of the mentally ill.

The psychoanalytical treatment may have "success" in freeing the patient from his neurosis. The neurotic who had been tortured by a sense of guilt and a guilt complex may now be made to "see through" the mocking role played by the unconscious and the pressures and the "deadening influences of exaggerated notions of guilt." After his treatment he may have attained to a "liberating" awareness which removed his "false guilt complex" and with it the neurosis. But is the patient really cured of his ills? Is he really in good health? Conceivably he is cured in a mere animal sense. But man is not a mere animal. Such a patient is not sound in his spiritual depth, in true awareness of his freedom, his responsibility. He does not have a true and sound realization of his call by the living God. Nor is he correct and sound in his attitude toward the possibility of defection from his own true dignity. He simply ignores this dreadful possibility altogether. The awareness of himself as a person which is the focus of all his being, the center and source of all his power, has been "flicked away" together with the sense of guilt. Spiritually he is not restored to good health.

The fallacy underlying Freudian psychotherapy goes beyond its exaggerated emphasis of the role of the libido, sexual or genital. The capital error is its failure to recognize the spiritual factors of personality, which are real and objective factors. In consequence, there can be no discernment of the difference between the phenomena produced by the instinctive psychical impulses and the phenomena which are basically spiritual. As a result, the psychoanalyst also fails to make a distinction between genuine sense of guilt with the morally "culpable" depression arising from it, and the false sense of guilt with the psychical depression which is not at all morally culpable. The former are basically responsible; the latter, indeliberate psychical complexes. Secondly, he fails to distinguish between the natural spiritual distress of conscience which penetrates the whole soul and the true cause of the distress, the moral guilt or sin. Thirdly, he fails to distinguish between natural remorse or sense of guilt and that pain and grief of soul which is true sorrow (particularly supernatural sorrow) arising from the noblest freedom of spirit (a developed or deliberate and willed pain of conscience based on noble motives).[65]

Obviously the psychoanalyst cannot correctly gauge the true nature of the deliberate guilt which runs counter to the movements of conscience, "the suppression of conscience," which is largely responsible for the psychic trauma and neurosis. In fact, psychoanalysis must be condemned as a kind of neurosis. Just as neurosis is often a sinister endeavor of the psychic nature to solve a profound problem or discharge a grave responsibility through escape to an easier and superficial level (which is false), so is this psychoanalysis an attempt to find psychic health, in the manner of the neurotic, on a false and shallow level, on a false basis, because the true profound basis of the problem is ignored and disregarded.

And still there are points to be learned from psychoanalysis, of value to our moral theologian and pastor of souls. First of all he must beware of falling into the very error he criticizes: the error of unilateral approach. He must avoid the error of reducing all things to a free and responsible spiritual source, just as the psychoanalyst in accordance with his naturalistic and materialistic bias reduces all to the subconscious. It is simply not true that the only sense of guilt is due to moral guilt or sin which produces a culpable moral depressiveness to be removed only by means of true contrition. There is also a false guilt complex, a point which has been proved by the study of depth psychology. It is a consequence of indeliberate psychosomatic experiences, bad surroundings, or false education. To stress contrition as the sole remedy in such instances can only worsen the evil condition of the patient. By the very nature of contrition as the way to salvation there must be a clear and rigorous distinction between real guilt with genuine consciousness of sin and all false sense of guilt. To correct the latter, genuine psychotherapy is frequently indicated. But it must be altogether free of the false assumptions of the Freudian school, even though it use the procedures and methods developed by Freud, Adler, and Jung.

There are points of contact between genuine psychotherapy and the way of contrition. The remedy of contrition opens the hidden depths of the soul in seeking the very roots of moral guilt. Similarly psychotherapy is often confronted with actual moral guilt which both estranged man from God and produced an illness of soul in the sinner, because he preferred to seek refuge in the unknown instead of following the salutary way of sorrow. The psychically ill should be offered the boon of all necessary medical therapy in such a manner that the way to God, with conscious freedom and responsibility, and if need be, the way to sorrow, are not closed, but rather made easily accessible.

Above all, moral theology and care of souls must take to heart an experience of depth psychology. This experience proves that many neurotics are sick and wounded by harsh contact with the moral law, because a false and biased concept of law was taught them. Obviously it would be far from correct to draw the conclusion that the concept of law is to be altogether eliminated, to be replaced by rules of hygiene.[66] Only the false concept of law is to be eliminated, and with it the false concept of guilt. The inexorable validity of the moral law must remain inviolate, for it is the manifestation of the wisdom and love of God.

3. Mere Ethical Regret and Religious Sorrow

The sharpest distinction to be made regarding the nature of sorrow is based on the truths of faith: one who in his sense of guilt experiences only a sense of regret over infractions of the standards of hygiene which safeguard psychic health is not following the painful way of humility and does not attain to moral health. Any one who sees no more in sin than a hazard to his own self-perfection or a conflict with some legal norm (a dead law) or at best only an impersonal value, has only a "monological" repentance; that is, he is thrown back on himself in his sorrow and left to his own resources. The principle which holds him guilty can condemn, but it cannot heal the wounds of sin.

To experience sorrow because of infraction of law, because of the violation of legislation passed by a lawmaker (without the support and assurance of the love and grace of God manifested in the legislation), will never reach the height of true repentance. The result of such regret will be only morbidity and, above all, a sense of impotence which readily leads to violent repression of all that opposes the law or at best the making of many resolutions. And all this without the deep dimension of true sorrow will never produce a true transformation of the sinner.

True sorrow is essentially religious. It presupposes supernatural faith in a God who lovingly calls us by name. "There is a deep and essential intimacy between the feeling for God (*sens de Dieu*) and the sense of sin."[67] Contrition is a central act of the virtue of religion, because God is holy and we are sinners, because religion means personal encounter between God and man. To repent of sin is the right response of sinful man to God, all-holy, whose sanctity means consuming zeal of anger against sin, but also consuming zeal of love for the poor sinner.

In religious sorrow the sinner is shaken to the very marrow of his bones at the thought of the malice of his offense against the majesty of God: "Depart from me, for I am a sinful man, O Lord" (Lk 5:8). But at the very same moment the misery of his own sinfulness hurls him into the arms of the infinite mercy of God: "Lord, to whom shall we go? Thou hast the words of everlasting life" (Jn 6:69). Religious repentance afflicts the sinner to the depths of his soul, not merely because sin is disobedience to the legislator, but also disdain for the incomparable grace and love of the heavenly Father. Man holds fast to his sorrow and is healed by it precisely because he realizes how unfathomable is the mercy of God who has revealed Himself to us as love.

In the light of the Christian faith, sorrow for sin assumes the form of a "sacramental encounter" with Christ. Just as the Christian beholds his offenses in the light of the dreadful divine judgment which Christ took upon Himself on the cross, so he views his repentance and sorrow for sin in the light of the infinite redemptive love of Christ. He knows that in the incipient stages of contrition the mercy of Christ has already approached him and pressed into his heart the assurance and pledge of His readiness to forgive him and reconcile him to God. He realizes that his sorrow foreshadows the encounter with Christ, which will take place with all effectiveness in the sacramental tribunal of grace, the sacrament of penance.

Religious repentance and contrition are expressions of the vital forces of the virtues of faith and hope, which remain as infused habits even after the commission of mortal sin: one who has committed a mortal sin that is not opposed to faith is brought to a realization of the fearful character of his sin only through the light of faith, and through the glad tidings of the divine mercy invited to salutary contrition. In the heart of the believer who has fallen into mortal sin there still remains, provided the sin has not been directed against faith and hope, the judgment of faith over his sin and the summons of hope to repentance. In the very midst of his sin he still concedes through the force of the virtue of faith which he still possesses, that he is in the wrong and God is right.

He has not gone to the extreme in his sin of uttering an ultimate and absolute no to the mercy and love of God. Even though his sin was grave and destroyed the life of grace, his state is still infinitely less evil than that of the positive unbeliever, whose sin is simply "a sin unto death" (cf. 1 Jn 5:16), because such a sin totally destroys all that could move the sinner to salutary contrition. For the sinner who has not lost the virtue of faith, contrition reinvigorates and fructifies faith and hope after the sterilizing action of sin. In the incipient sorrow and repentance, the faith which the sinner still possesses sheds light on the dreadful nature of sin in its opposition to the holiness of God. Hope still sustains him so that he will not despair as he hovers over the fearful abyss of final perdition, but will flee to the boundless mercy of God.

We must conclude that every effort to convert the believing sinner must direct its appeal above all to his Christian faith and hope. Even though his faith is "dead" by reason of his sinful works, it is still a firm bond which binds him to the word of God, a supernatural reality, a point of departure from which every effort toward conversion must proceed. And hope awaits the glad tidings of forgiveness and spiritual return to the Father's house.

4. *Repentance: Revolution by Free Decision, Rebirth through Grace*

"Contrition is the most revolutionary force in the moral world."[68] The first re-direction of life is not through the good resolution, but through contrition. Through profound sorrow the whole life of man receives a new orientation. If we are to understand how sorrow is possible at all and learn something of its intimate modalities, we must surely study the spiritual resources and forces which remain in the soul even after man has fallen into mortal sin. We have already referred to the virtues of faith and hope which are not destroyed by every mortal sin. But even with these infused habits, contrition is utterly impossible without new impulses of supernatural grace, for it is a new movement in the soul, a new beginning, with a new freedom as its point of departure. In contrition, particularly in the profound and comprehensive sorrow which affects his whole being, the sinner overcomes his evil past, leaves behind him, not only the sins of the past, but also his whole sinful self. Now he begins anew with a new freedom. A truly profound sorrow reaches into the very depths of the soul, affecting it with pain as it cauterizes the wounds of sin. But sorrow also reveals new treasures as it opens up whole new regions of spiritual freedom.

Not without reason did traditional theology look upon contrition as a moral miracle. Nevertheless, sorrow for sin is not totally inexplicable from the point of view of human liberty. There is an essential difference between the freedom of man and that of the angel. The mode of actuation of man's freedom, and this is particularly true of fallen man, is entirely different from the actuation of the angel's freedom: for the fallen angel contrition is not possible without a miracle (it seems impossible to us as far as the ordinary power of God and the providence of His divine wisdom are concerned, though it seems within the sphere of His absolute power). The angel is a pure spirit, has no matter-and-form, but only pure form. Consequently, the totality of his freedom is exerted and exhausted in one sole decision, one single sinful act.[69] This means that with one fell stroke his freedom for the good, his freedom for sorrow, which is the sole avenue of return to good, is utterly lost. Man, however, does not cast away the whole treasure of liberty with a single deed (apart from the sin "against the Holy Spirit," or the "sin unto death," 1 Jn 5:16f.; cf. Heb 6:4ff.; 10:26f.), does not squander all his freedom through one single act of evil, nor does he for that matter fully develop his freedom for good except through a long series of good acts. Consequently there remains even after mortal sin something of freedom for good, though, of course, this is diminished with every subsequent evil act. This "something" of good remaining after mortal sin is gathered up in contrition under the influence of divine grace for the counteroffensive against evil. Through repeated attacks the lost bastions of true liberty can be regained and even new areas of spiritual freedom won in the noble conquest.

This new growth of freedom in the warm light of divine grace is not like the growth of plants. We prefer to employ the military metaphor. The new freedom and the new growth are counterattacks against the predominant sin. It is breaching the enemy's lines in fighting for the good. Or shall we call it a revolution which overthrows the entrenched tyranny of sin. The final and decisive breakthrough to perfect contrition (which justifies the sinner) should not be classed with ethical growth or revolutionary attack (counteroffensive) against the entrenchment of evil forces, but rather as a new birth. In the deep dimension of human spiritual transformation, it is rebirth wrought by God through divine grace. At this lofty level the noblest summoning and harnessing of freedom for good which are possible to man are wedded to the richest of divine grace. In the perfect contrition which brings justification to the sinner the restoration of the supernatural image of God in the soul bears with it the new freedom, the "freedom of the children of God." This is a divine gift already exerting itself in the very act of loving sorrow. As sorrow deepens through love and divine grace, "the freedom of the children of God" also grows stronger and richer and constantly asserts itself vigorously in opposition to the "freedom" to evil. And this it recognizes only as a menace to the soul. Thus contrition gives birth to the glorious freedom which constantly and ceaselessly aims at union with obedience and love in response to the divine will and the impulse of divine grace.

5. Definition of Contrition

According to the definition given by the Council of Trent, contrition is grief of soul, abhorrence for sin committed together with detestation of the past evil life and the resolution to avoid sin in the future.[70]

a. "Grief of Soul"

The grief which is an essential element of salutary contrition is not merely the suffering of remorse passively (not "the terror of conscience"[71] because of sin). It is a free act. It is the active and voluntary acceptance of grief of conscience through a supernatural motive. In the beginning one's own loss and the risk of eternal perdition occupy the first place in this grief of soul. But as sorrow deepens and is purified, it turns to grief over the offense given to the divine Lord and Father. Salutary grief of soul is assimilated to the pain of Christ and united with the passion of the Saviour. The sinner realizes how Christ suffered pain and agony over his sin and loss and over the offense to God His Father. Only through pain can man die to sin. But the grief and pain can give life only because they are united with the pain and death and resurrection of Christ.

Contrition is a grief of soul, a distress of spirit of the will and heart arising from a new encounter with value. In so far as this grief of spirit is a free act of the will in response to the judgment of faith, "it must surpass every other grief or pain"[72] because, in the light of faith, sin is the greatest evil.

"The other sorrow is in the sensitive part, and is caused by the former sorrow, either from natural necessity, in so far as the lower powers follow the movements of the higher, or from choice, in so far as a penitent excites in himself this sorrow in order to attain a (higher and purer) sorrow for his sins. In neither of these ways is such sorrow necessarily the greatest, because the lower powers are more deeply moved by their own objects than through redundance from the higher powers. . . . Neither is the sorrow which is assumed voluntarily greater than other sorrows . . . because the lower does not obey the higher appetite infallibly . . . and because the passions are employed by reason, in acts of virtue, according to a certain measure."[73]

Because of the spiritual unity of man, it is quite suited to man that genuine sorrow be emotional. In some way it reacts on the whole attitude of man and may be reflected in his countenance. But the degree and manner of the emotional reaction aroused by our sorrow is very much a matter of individual psychological temperament and even of temporary psychical conditions or states. To those who place the primary stress on emotional experience in their lives, we must point out that the one decisive factor in true contrition is the spiritual grief elicited by the free will of the sinner. However, it is basically wrong to tear totalities asunder or even set them in opposition to one another. To seek an isolated "arid" grief of the will to the total exclusion of every impulse of feeling or emotion is to thwart the spontaneous and normal development of true grief of soul. Meditation on the corporeal and mental sufferings of Christ, beginning with a vivid picture of the agonizing Saviour in our imagination, and on the second coming of Christ to judge the living and the dead, and similar mysteries is particularly calculated to arouse "integral" and, consequently, more effective grief of soul over our sins.

In the early Church the monks of the East, though otherwise somewhat suspect for Hellenistic spiritualism, did not at all disdain the bodily influence in their grief of soul for sin. In fact, they prayed humbly for the "gift of tears" and even assiduously fostered and encouraged it[74] through the manner of their meditation, through their life of poverty, solitude, and self-denial. However, they were not at all oblivious of the rule of prudence which Thomas so correctly emphasizes, namely, that perceptible grief may not exceed the just limits of prudence, for excess could readily lead to nervous irritation and mental imbalance.[75]

In the Scriptural instances of contrition for sin, the grief of soul affects the entire man: the penitent woman "began to bathe his feet with her tears" (Lk 7:38) and Peter "went out and wept bitterly" (Mt 26:75). Paul, in his misery, "could not see, and he neither ate nor drank" (Acts 9:9). In numberless passages in the Old Testament the prayer of contrition is shown to be bound up with tears and other manifestations of grief.

From all this we must conclude that the profound grief of soul which marks the true conversion is not an arid act of the will alone, but a grief or distress of the "heart," the seat of love in man. Not merely terror and anxiety, but above all the pain of love affects the whole man.

b. Detestation of Sin Committed

Contrition is the verdict of condemnation directed against each individual sin committed and the entire life of sin, a verdict of condemnation which the contrite sinner sustains with Christ and through the grace of Christ. The penitent, with the aid of grace and by his own free decision, makes his own that verdict of the heavenly Father which Christ took upon Himself on the wood of the cross. Sorrow is a terrified yes to the dreadful judgment which Christ will pronounce on the unrepentant in the last judgment. It is a yes filled with hope, a grateful yes to the merciful judgment of the cross, in the blessed shadow of which the tribunal of penance stands. Contrition looks hopefully to the merciful judgment of the cross after the dreadful earnestness of the final judgment (Lk 23:31: "if in the case of green wood they do these things, what is to happen in the case of the dry?") has shaken the soul to its depths. "For all of us must be made manifest before the tribunal of Christ" (2 Cor 5:10), realizing that "if we judged ourselves" through the judgment of condemnation in sorrow for sin, in the judgment of Christ, then we would "not be condemned with this world" (1 Cor 11:31f.). Contrition is a salutary "hatred of our ancient manner of life."[76]

Detestation of sin is a verdict passed upon oneself and one's sins in the presence of the kingdom of God against which one has offended, and therefore in the presence of the Church, which demands of us in the tribunal of penance (using her power of the keys) a true eschatological earnestness. And she holds out to us the salvation of the kingdom of God. Christian contrition, in its causes, motives, and essential direction, is "sacramental." This means it is orientated in hope toward the sacramental tribunal of mercy and carries with it the obligation to submit oneself in the sacrament of penance to the judgment of Christ and the Church.

c. Firm Purpose of Amendment, Element and Result of Contrition

(1) *Purpose of Amendment Is Sterile without Contrition*

The Council of Trent teaches very emphatically that contrition does not consist in mere "cessation of sin with the resolution to lead a different life,"[77] but entirely and essentially in positive opposition to the sins of the past which are deserving of detestation.

There is a psychological aspect of this truth which Max Scheler analyzes in a masterly fashion.[78] "The genial masters," says Scheler, "tell us: don't be sorry, but make good resolutions and change the life that lies before you! But these same gentle masters do not tell us where the source of power lies with which we are to make the firm resolutions, and more important where the source of power lies to put the resolutions into practice, if the person has not been freed beforehand by contrition from the determinative grasp of the past."[79] "The more you are borne along 'progressively' in the stream of life—Prometheus and never Epimetheus—the more dependent and enslaved you are through the press of a guilty past. You are merely fleeing from your own guilt when you resolve to scale the peaks of life. Your pretended assault is a flight in disguise. The more you close your eyes to that which you should repent of, the more unbreakable are the chains which drag you down when you seek to move your feet."[80] "The way to utter self-contempt almost always is paved with the good resolutions that were never carried out, and that were not the fruit of real contrition."[81] "Note how paradoxical this is: even if it were true that the sole value of contrition consisted in its power of producing future betterment in will and action—though the supposition is not true—still the immanent sense of the act of sorrow could refer solely and alone to the evil past, excluding any purposive intention referring to the future and future betterment."[82]

Contrition is essentially more than a means of arriving at a good resolution. By force of its own import and through a kind of inner necessity, it is a renewed response to value which has been violated, a humble prayer of the sin-laden heart to God offended by sin.

It is evident psychologically and theologically that one cannot start anew by simply passing from a state of guilt to a different mode of life without the purging flame of contrition. Guilt and sin in a portion of our past life are not simply a thing of the past. By force of their innermost tendency, they continue to exert themselves in many ways as sinister influences. "Such is the curse of an evil deed that constant evil it must bear" (Schiller).

Only a perverted attitude could account for an appraisal of this basic primitive experience on the basis of mere external conditions caused by sin in the world, which man is powerless to change or control. We are concerned with much more than the external conditions and facts, with something in man himself. This truth is much more valid and unexceptionable when applied to the inner fatal fecundity of the guilt which contrition has not effaced. Every sin, even every sin in thought, leaves its mark on the psychic structure of the human soul. Every unrepented sin has a sinister obscuring effect, a cramping effect on true liberty. The less man dares to face his past sin, the more freely and effectively does it continue to exert its influence within him "unawares." It enters into all future acts as loss of value and as deadening burden. Only "contrition deadens the life nerve of guilt through which it continues its influence. It expels motive and action, the action with its root, from the life center of the person, and thereby makes possible the free spontaneous beginning, the virginal beginning of a new manner of life. Hence contrition effects moral rejuvenation."[83]

"The Christian knows that every resolution which is not born in the pain of sorrow for sin remains stale and sterile, because it did not arise from the ultimate depths and above all did not come from God, was not conceived in God. Only sorrow softens the hardness of our nature so that a permanent 'new orientation of will' toward God founded on that which is ultimate can be impressed upon us."[84] These words point to the important truth that the psychological basis is rooted in the theological: every mortal sin implies offense against God, indeed entry into a state of guilt and hostility toward God. A new beginning, a religious beginning confirmed with a religious determination and purpose, and the purpose can only be the resolve to lead the life of a child of God and friend of God again, is futile without contrition. A religious beginning has no meaning and cannot be put into effect without the renewal of hope that one will be accepted as a child of God through the generous bounty of the divine pardon of our guilt, and this in turn is not possible unless the sinner tears himself away from sin inwardly through contrition. The resolution, "I will renew my life as God's friend," without the grief of sorrow and the humble prayer admitting guilt, "Father, I have sinned against heaven and before thee. I am no longer worthy to be called thy son" (Lk 15:18f.), would be terrifying insolence and hideous self-deception. Only a man psychically unbalanced would approach his creditor with such an attitude: "Don't worry! I will not incur any further debt!" He should pay what he owes first of all, or beg that the debt be canceled!

(2) *Purpose of Amendment Essential for True Contrition*

Just as the firm purpose of amendment derives its force from the grief of contrition, so the sincerity and depth of sorrow are revealed in the purpose of amendment.[85] "For there is no sorrow which does not at least implicitly bear the basic design of a 'new heart' from its very inception. Contrition kills only to bestow life. It destroys only to build up. Indeed, contrition builds secretly where it appears to annihilate."[86]

For the purpose of amendment to be fashioned firm and strong, contrition must mature and ripen; and reciprocally the sinner may not be remiss regarding the firm purpose to sin no more, in order that the ardor of contrition may not diminish before the will to improve is firmly set. Grief of soul will not abide long in the heart of the sinner (without being dissipated in work or pleasure or laxness of spirit) unless in due time the resolution is formed to live as a child of God. With the hope of being accepted again as a child through God's generous and loving bounty, the sinner resolves and longs in his heart to live as God's child, henceforth and always, with the aid of divine grace. Thus fortified by divine hope, the most potent motive force of incipient contrition, the will must decide on a new life. It must make the decision in due time to undertake this new life in the spirit of the liberty of God's children to which it aspires.

If he understands the psychology of conversion, the spiritual director will bear two important points in mind: he will not attempt to harvest the ripe fruit of good resolution before the seed of contrition has sprung up; nor will he permit the anguish of contrition and the grief of conscience to grow overripe, but will garner the harvest of good resolves which have ripened under the glow of contrition and the warmth of hope.

If a resolution fails to mature, no other recourse is possible except prayer for the divine help and the profoundest descent into the living source of contrition, meditation on the motives for sorrow. Purpose of amendment can progress only so far as contrition, the heavenly "eye salve" (Ap 3:18), has restored the clear sight of heavenly vision.

(3) *Qualities of Purpose of Amendment*

The good resolution must flow from contrition in its entirety and exhaust all its potentialities. Accordingly, it must have the same qualities: it must be universal and comprehensive. For conversion to God demands not merely a modification of our life to the extent of shunning one single evil act or of performing one particular good act. There must be a new orientation and a new formation of the whole spiritual life in Christ. The firm purpose of amendment is the utter abandonment of the will to the will of God, the generous submission to all the imperatives of grace which flow from the remission of sin and the renewal in Christ. In the resolution to amend his life, the sinner should summon all the forces of his being through the dynamism of active contrition. With all his powers he should "aspire to the loftiest heights of ideal being" and, as he climbs the heights, repudiate and cast off the old self.[87]

The destruction and "reconstruction of the ultimate material intentions"[88] must include very clearly defined specific and particular resolutions. The explicit particular resolutions and purposes must above all be directed to those objects and zones of danger which up to the present caused postponement of conversion and always proved occasions of special sins. The purpose of amendment must also be serious and decisive. It must reach the very root and heart of the evil. It is not enough, to cite just one example, for an adulterer to resolve never to commit the sin of adultery again, if he is not prepared to banish the evil desire for his accomplice in sin from his mind and heart. Seriously lacking in earnestness is the resolution of the sinner who has offended God habitually by sins against purity, if he does no more than resolve to shun every gravely impure deed, but does not specifically include the will to shun flirtations and immodest conduct also.[89] I do not assume, of course, that such a resolution, which in its superficiality scarcely reaches the root of the evil, is under no circumstances sufficient for justification in the sacrament of penance. Contrition and purpose of amendment can be sincere, even though they are sadly lacking in depth.

As long as contrition fails to penetrate into the profoundest depths, casting light into the remotest shadows, consuming the dross with its ardor, there usually remains, as consequence of the past sins, a partial blindness to value. This interferes with the direct insight into the truth that the sincerity of the resolution to avoid a sin demands necessarily and unconditionally the corresponding resolve to uproot all affective attachment to the sin. In the first stages of conversion a moral obscurity creates a kind of practical dullness in application of our purpose, which fails to perceive that this particular action or particular abstention of action is demanded by the explicit resolution. What we have expressly resolved in our firm purpose of amendment absolutely and unconditionally includes far more than we have clearly realized. Then suddenly we see the full implication. But it may be only after further spiritual development and maturity, and often because of the shock of painful lapses into sin. Then comes the clear insight. Many things we have been doing are simply irreconcilable with the purpose of amendment which we have made and constantly renewed. This is the moment of grace! But if the grace is disregarded, it will prove the occasion of grave relapse into sin. Disregarding the warning may prove spiritually disastrous!

It is the task of pastoral prudence to choose the most propitious moment to direct the penitent to a higher moral plane and thus confront him with a more thoroughgoing decision. In some instances, of course, a more specifically defined resolution is in order. Thus, for example, the confessor may not be satisfied with a mere "universal resolution" to avoid mortal sin, if he has reason to assume that a penitent who is confessing many mortal sins for the first time is not altogether sincere and his contrition not altogether genuine and efficacious. The director or confessor must make use of every opportunity to induce the penitent to form resolutions which are as clear and specific, as pointed and particular, as his spiritual status at the moment may demand.

Surely it would be most imprudent to confront the newly converted penitent, particularly if his antecedents, background, surroundings are quite irreligious, with a multitude of particular decisions and resolutions at the very outset of his repentance. This is especially true of those points which are not immediately necessary to lead the penitent to the next essential step in the path of conversion from sin. It is particularly important for the confessor to observe such caution if it is clear to him that the penitent, in his present spiritual weakness and his incipient contrition, is not altogether equal to the task.

The "law of progress" is a fundamental norm of life. Even the life of grace is a law of progressive conversion. Therefore it must also be a basic norm of all our efforts in the pastoral care of our fellow man.

The purpose of amendment must be prudent. Conversion itself demands—note how emphatically we stressed this point—an effort to attain the pinnacle of perfection, the life totally influenced by divine grace. But this same imperative to strive for ideals and goals demands that in each instance we move forward step by step toward the goal. And if grace invites and urges that we go forward by leaps and bounds, and make notable progress, then prudence demands great generosity of us both in resolution and in execution.

Every resolution on the path of conversion must be humble. One's own sad personal experience and even more so the experience of the guidance through divine grace caution us to transform every resolution into prayer, since God alone grants that we both will and accomplish. Humility requires us to recognize the true nature of all our actions and resolutions. Not only our actions, but also our resolutions, are all imperfect and fragmentary. Therefore we must pray for more light, for deeper spirit of sorrow and more generous purposes of amendment. And from our humility must spring clear, specific resolutions to shun in the future all proximate occasions to mortal sin with all our might.

6. Perfect and Imperfect Contrition

(Contrition of Love and Contrition of Fear)

Not only are there various stages of depth and efficacy in the contrition which turns the sinner to God, but there is also a diversity of motivation. There are higher and lower planes of sorrow for sin. It would not be psychologically sound to deny all validity to sorrow which is not motivated by the most exalted ideals, or to demand the most perfect motivation in the very first stage of conversion from sin. This surely would be contrary to any sound "psychology of conversion" (which really is nothing more than a method of studying the ordinary manner of Divine Providence in leading men to salvation). Just as the law of progress[90] governs the whole moral life in general, so does it set the norm for the process of repentance, and this includes, as we have stressed more than once, the dynamic spiritual breakthrough from the enslavement of sin.

"Psychological" motives may have a place in salutary conversion and contrition. This is to say that, in the providence of God, conversion and contrition may be occasioned and conditioned by temporal and natural motives, such as profound disillusionment in secular and material things, bitter distress because of the natural consequences of sin, deep realization of the despicable and hateful character of sin. In itself grief aroused by such natural motives in the soul has no salutary value. But in the divine guidance of the sinner through grace it can play a rôle of considerable importance in the course of events leading to the contrition which brings justification. The same is true of a simple "servile" fear and sorrow, which falls short of the pure distress and pain over the loss of the divine friend-ship and has not reached the stage of abhorrence for the actual malice of sin. It is no more than a dread of temporal scourges or perhaps of the eternal pain of sense in hell. Though these acts in themselves have no direct value for eternity, they are of inestimable worth if they pave the way to true sorrow.

The sinner is restored to the divine friendship, is again made just in God's sight, either through perfect contrition, which is effective even prior to the reception of the sacraments of conversion, or through the worthy and fruitful reception of the sacrament with imperfect sorrow (attrition).

a. Perfect Sorrow (Contrition)

We can come to an understanding of perfect sorrow only if we view it as a mystery of loving dialogue between God and the sinner on whom God bestows grace: the merciful love of God so touches the heart of the sinner that he responds with repentant love. Such is the force of that love and the newly bestowed freedom of the child of God that the sinner responds with loving repentance for his sin. If we view this from the human perspective, we say that through this sorrow the sinner abhors his sin as it behooves a contrite child of the heavenly Father, namely, through love, so that he is again welcomed by God to the state of friendship and grace. Perfect contrition is the return home. The prodigal son returns to the house of the Father with all its warmth of love which contains and includes the Father's welcome and the pledge of His acceptance. It is the sorrow which the child of God makes habitual, for he constantly deplores his past sins because of the love for God, even after he has returned home.

Perfect contrition does not center its motive in man and in his deci-sion, but in God, whose holiness and love he has offended by his sin. But this does not at all imply that perfect sorrow excludes the distress of soul over the bitter consequences of sin in man. But the insight into one's own sin and misery revealed the deep hideous nature of our offense, made known to us how ungrateful, how disobedient, how hateful we were toward the all-holy and all-good God. None of the other supernatural motives founded on fear and hope are expelled when the motive of love enters. Rather they are purified, invigorated, and elevated to the dignity and value of the sorrow whose motive is love.

From this it follows that in content (*materialiter*) imperfect contrition is implicitly included in perfect contrition. All that is really "servile" in fear and hope is eliminated ("perfect love casts out fear, because fear brings punishment," 1 Jn 4:18), in order that the fear and hope which are holy, pure, and childlike may grow strong, for without them man's love could not be a response to the love of the All-Holy (of the *Mysterium tremendum-fascinosum*).

b. Imperfect Contrition (*Attritio*)

Imperfect contrition, often called attrition, stops short of the lofty motive of divine love. Its own proper motives can be on various levels. There is a true sorrow which is supernatural and efficacious, even though it springs from fear and does not reach the exalted plane of motivation through love; it still "disposes" man for reception of grace.[91] However, it is still an open question: how does this sorrow dispose one for grace, immediately and directly or only more or less indirectly and remotely? Theologians still are engaged in discussion regarding the motive of fear as the basis of sorrow: does such fear as the sole motive for contrition, even though it efficaciously keeps one from committing sin, furnish the penitent with the required disposition for justification through the sacrament? One point is altogether certain: the disposition of fear which shuns mortal sin only in the negative sense—"if there were no eternal tortures of hell, I would not avoid mortal sin"—is not adequate. Such a frame of mind is entirely incompatible with the true sorrow required for fruitful reception of any sacrament of conversion.[92]

It is the predominant teaching of present-day theologians, in agreement with the doctrine of Saint Thomas and the greater number of theologians at the Council of Trent,[93] that the sorrow essential for fruitful reception of the sacraments must in some measure include the kernel or beginning of love. However, the Council of Trent did not choose to decide the question.[94] And Alexander VII forbade theologians who discussed and debated the matter to accuse their opponents of heresy.[95] The extreme view that perfect contrition is demanded for fruitful reception of penance has not been condemned by the Church, but is no longer defended by any theologian.

In practice, not only should the confessor seriously heed the admonition of the Church and lead the penitent, as far as this is possible, to perfect contrition,[96] but the penitent himself should consider himself bound to strive for sorrow through love. He should not be satisfied with anything less than the beginning of love of God in the motive of his contrition. In matters on which eternal salvation itself depends, the "safer way" must always be chosen.

If the grand truths of faith regarding the nature of our eternal salvation, as beatifying love, and of hell as the utter exclusion from the divine friendship, are explained and preached according to their true nature, it is hardly possible, psychologically, that those who approach the sacrament of penance with genuine "sorrow of fear" (the fear of hell) are not also somewhat motivated by love. Their sorrow based on fear will not lack the "beginning" of love. We may justly blame faulty instruction if this sorrow on the part of many Christians does not go beyond the mere dread of the tortures of hell, often called the pain of sense, and the devil. But obviously this does not at all imply that the forceful explanation of the secondary horrors incurred by loss of eternal salvation should be ignored in Christian instruction. The thought of such punishment for sin can play an indispensable role in the conversion of sinners in the awakening and stirring of the conscience through wholesome fear.

As to the essence of conversion (*metánoia*, return to the Father), it is perfectly clear that imperfect contrition is indeed a beginning, but also no more than a beginning of conversion. The completion, the return to the Father's house, is achieved in the instance of imperfect contrition through the divine action in grace. Through the efficacy of His grace in the holy sacraments, God raises imperfect contrition—such is its immanent potentiality—to the level and degree of perfect contrition. The attrition in the sacrament becomes contrition (according to the Scholastic axiom: *"ex attrito per justificationem fit contritus"*). If God bestows the habit of perfect contrition (*habitus*), this cries out to the repentant soul for the sorrow based on love. Now the repentant sinner is faced with the compulsive imperative to make an act of perfect contrition, the act of sorrow based on love. Since the sacraments, even the sacraments of conversion, entirely and essentially tend toward love, the minimum that must be demanded of the recipient is a serious effort to love, specifically to repent of his sins through love. This effort is sufficient even though the penitent does not succeed in arousing sentiments of perfect contrition.

In the light of the evidence of theology and practical experience that conversion is not perfected and is not permanent if it is not anchored in love, Saint Alphonse in his method of popular mission for his Congregation set aside the second half of the mission for the *vita devota,* for the exercise of charity.[97] In my opinion, it is an unpardonable violation of the theological principles of conversion for parish priests and missionaries to close the mission immediately after the terrifying preaching on the "eternal truths." After the faithful are so profoundly shaken by such preaching, there should follow the constructive and fruitful period, the "week" of gratitude, joy, love, to close the exercises.

7. The Object of Sorrow

Contrition must be kept aloof from every trace of a false sense of guilt. The object of repentance, in the strict sense of the word, is only one's own personal sin, and only to the measure and degree of personal responsibility. Contrition is detestation, by the sinner, for all his sins in general and for each sin in particular, also to the measure and extent of his consciousness of the sin. In itself sorrow extending to all sins in general is sufficient. The positive divine command obliges us to confess contritely all mortal sins. But we are also under the necessity of combatting the hidden psychological forces which have been deposited without assimilation and control in our subconscious by past sin and which lead to future sin. In consequence, there is the obligation to make an earnest effort to be sorry for each sin in particular. However, practically, this objective is implied and realized in the sorrowful confession of all mortal sins and in the soulful examination of conscience.

Truly profound sorrow is not limited to grief of soul over particular sinful acts and their motives. To one who is profoundly repentant, they indicate the accumulation of malice and the pressure of massive guilt and create in him a sense of horror and humility. One who is really contrite does not merely admit that he has committed a sin: "I have committed such and such a sin!" Rather he exclaims in grief, "Woe is me, that I have sunk so deeply into sin!" Each and every sin manifests (according to its gravity) the vile fecundity of previous sin and, above all, the insufficiency of previous contrition and penance. Contrition reaching to the depths of the soul, contrition utterly without reserve, would have seared the very roots of evil and the breeding places of "unfruitful works."

"Guilt itself creates within the soul the hidden forces which nourish particular evil tendencies. Contrition must penetrate into this realm of the soul's deepest recesses, into the secret kingdom of her guilt. And descending into these sinister depths it must awaken a true awareness of that obscure and clandestine realm in the mind and heart of the sinner."[98]

From the standpoint of strict obligation regarding confession of sins and reception of Holy Communion, one may readily excuse an occasional fault of the kind referred to on the ground of absence of knowledge and free decision. But the matter assumes a different aspect when the penitent considers the obligation to amend his life. He is obliged through the spirit of contrition to strive earnestly for self-improvement. With this obligation in mind he should feel impelled to admit with all his heart: "Such evil has grown up within me through lack of deep and genuine sorrow. So blinded am I in my sinfulness that even without clear and conscious intent or awareness, I have been so lacking in caution that I could (for example) calumniate my fellow man, scandalize him!" In this very way, precisely those sins regarding whose subjective seriousness I might correctly have misgivings cry out to us and demand of us a deeper distress and grief of soul over our own sinful state.

Though in the sincerest sorrow we may have recalled and disavowed our past sins and evil habits, though we may have honestly and firmly resolved to shun all future sins, still, when we are not on our guard, there may be a recurrence of the evil habit, a semi-deliberate breaking out of the evil. Surely this cannot be held against us as gravely sinful. But the frequent or constant recurrence of the habit in the form of bad dispositions and attitudes and semi-deliberate acts should be a warning to us at all times to deepen our spirit of sorrow for sin, to repent anew and with all our heart for our sins, to admit humbly and prayerfully that we are guilty: "God be merciful to me a miserable sinner, for all this weakness truly shows how truly I am a sinner in God's sight!"

We may not overlook the serious aspect of the evil inheritance of man: many defects are due neither to actual nor to past personal fault, but are the evil fruit of original sin, the sins of our forefathers, and the oppressive burden of evil surroundings. Such deficiencies cannot excite us to true sorrow in the strict sense of that term. (But we may not ignore the fact that we ourselves find it very difficult to appraise our own share of the fault because of neglect of graces in the past, which may have contributed much to the condition of those unhealed inherited moral wounds.) Hence, even after we have pondered our responsibility, we are not permitted to absolve ourselves of all blame. Much more advisable is it for us in the spirit of genuine Christian solidarity to sorrow deeply over so much offense against God and such spiritual loss to souls. This distress in our hearts is a kind of "vicarious sorrow" or grief of soul, and its genuineness is proved by the ready disposition for sacrifice of expiation and an unselfish spirit in the apostolate for souls.

We must, of course, make a clear distinction between this vicarious grief of soul based on Christian solidarity (in the language of the Fathers it is *penthos*) and contrition in the proper sense,[99] which is always concerned with one's own sins. The former is a spontaneous projection of the grief of soul for one's own sins (repentance in the proper sense) and a sure sign of its authenticity and depth. It is proof that contrition has its motive and vital center in God and in that society of salvation which is the kingdom of God. But we must never lose sight of the fact that the specific and particular task of contrition is always "the crushing and softening of the hardness" of one's own sinful condition and "in this sense there is no contrition for the sins of others."[100]

When we are confronted by the failings of our fellow men, a true spirit of contrition will not only safeguard us from thoughtless and hasty condemnation of others. It will not only pose the question: would I not perhaps have fallen still deeper into sin had I faced the same temptations? The spirit of contrition will confront us as members of the Mystical Body of Christ with the demand: how much has our own neglect of grace or our failure to cooperate fully with all graces offered to us contributed to the sins of others? How many sins might have been avoided if we personally had labored wholeheartedly for the dominion of the kingdom of Christ? This question must be pondered particularly in the light of the menace to freedom and salvation of our fellow man arising from the poisoned atmosphere of our age.

These characteristics of sorrow are particularly evident in the grief of soul (*penthos*) of the saints of the Eastern Church. Their compunction of spirit is concerned not merely with the particular conscious transgressions of the law, with deliberate sins, but most of all with the neglect of graces.[101] The holy servants of God shed tears of sorrow because they themselves and others fail to attain the degree of perfection which God plans for them, because of a neglect of the graces offered. In short, offense against God and remissness in the endeavor to attain spiritual perfection as the result of every kind of sin is the basis for constant *penthos* in their hearts.

8. *Contrition as Permanent Disposition and Frame of Mind*

The Bible, theological tradition, and, not least of all, the lives of the saints give evidence that contrition must go beyond the one simple essential act of conversion from sin. There must be a permanent disposition of sorrow. The mere act of sorrow alone, even though it is based on perfect love, does not rend open the depths of the heart hardened and knotted up by repeated sins, as the full dominion of loving repentance demands. With the growth of sorrow there is also growth and progress in love, and with the development of love there is growth in sorrow.

Since we do not ground the actual law of Christian life entirely in the restrictions of the commandments, but in the urgency of divine grace essentially, it follows that the life of grace is exacting in its demands on our love. Since this life of grace springs from the incomparable mercy of the divine welcome extended to the prodigal son loaded down with his sins, the response in love may not be that of the indifferent and faint-hearted. It must be the love of praise extolling the mercies of God with humble and contrite heart. It must be an imperishable *"eucharistía metà syntetrimménes psychês,"* to use a phrase of Mark Eremita, who best expresses the ideal of the holiness of the East.[102]

Unless it is founded in love of gratitude, the disposition of compunction cannot be in accordance with the glad tidings of the welcome of the prodigal to the Father's house (but rather with the Lutheran teaching of the *peccator simul et justus*). And it would lead rather to illusory sorrow and even despair. Without the profound accompaniment of the contrite heart, all sentiment of love would only too readily degenerate into arrogance of presumption and ungrateful self-deception.

In the measure in which our compunction deepens are the wounds of past sins healed. An antidote is furnished us against the reopening of the old wounds.[103] The penitent becomes spiritually attentive to the invitations of grace, indispensable means of progress, with the result that even the slightest disregard of the divine summons to good causes sorrow for such neglect. This deep sense of sorrow continues to grow in the soul as one progresses in holiness. Many passages of Scripture describe it very graphically. In his sorrow the psalmist exclaims, "I have labored in my groanings, every night I will wash my bed: I will water my couch with my tears" (Ps 6:7). Equally striking are the words of the prophet, "I will recount to thee all my years in the bitterness of my soul" (Is 38:15). Though he had labored under appalling hardship and peril and had succeeded in his tremendous effort to spread the kingdom of Christ beyond all the other apostles, Saint Paul confesses with earnest and humble sorrow for his past, that he is still unworthy. "I am the least of the apostles, and am not worthy to be called an apostle, because I persecuted the Church of God" (1 Cor 15:9).

Penitents with such profound and humble sorrow never think of the awakening of contrition as a duty solely for beginners.[104] Yet their sorrow is a far cry from the scrupulous anxiety of spirit which impels the penitent to make a harassed and repetitious inquiry into the nature and number of his sins, with the ceaseless haunting fear that some may not have been confessed. The true disposition of sorrow creates the ready disposition to confess one's sins humbly and suggests on special occasions of grace the renewed confession of sins already confessed (general confession), not, however, because of restless chafing of conscience, but because of the humble spirit of gratitude to God for the pardon already given him. "Through the pardon of guilt and eternal punishment God has bound us fast to Him through the bond of habitual sorrow for our sins."[105] It is a bond of gratitude.

9. "Blessed Are They Who Mourn, for They Shall Be Comforted" (Mt 5:5)

It is dreadful that we can master life only by following the darksome and painful path of sorrow, but the simple truth that there is a way for us to obtain life at all is glorious."[106] Sorrow is entry into the pain and sadness of Christ's passion. But its countenance already reflects something of the glory of resurrection. Just as the Lord does not extoll all suffering without qualification, but only that which one bears with Him and for Him, so too He blesses only that mourning and sadness which is borne in union with His agony on Olivet and mingles with His cry of dereliction on the cross. In meaning and purpose our suffering and mourning must unite with His. All the sadness which the sufferings of this life bring to us must flow back into the one great sadness over sin, offense to God, loss of our souls, peril to salvation. "For the sorrow that is according to God produces repentance that surely tends to salvation, whereas the sorrow that is according to the world produces death" (2 Cor 7:10). Sorrow in the heart according to God keeps the repentant sinner from being swept into the turbulent maelstrom of countless earthly afflictions.

One who sorrows in Christ over the offense against God in sin (the *penthikos*, as the Greeks particularly called the monk, whereas Benedictine monasticism gave him the name *conversus,* the converted) bears the trials of life with a brave and joyful heart. He purifies his heart and keeps it free from the world's vanities, so that it is open to the divine consolations which God does not withhold from the humble and from those who are purified from sin. Sorrow according to God already bears within itself the joy which the Lord exhorted His followers to seek and which He promised them as precious gift of the Holy Spirit. For its very first step is made in the hope of salvation. Sorrow according to God is an attitude which arises from the grateful heart and is itself a constant hymn of praise to the divine mercy.

The sadness of spirit which rends the heart brings in its wake countless blessings: it is the "eye salve" which heals spiritual blindness (Ap 3:18). It is the dynamic of heavenly freedom, which preserves the soul from the numbness of sterility. It is the remedy which purges the conscience and frees it from its nagging pain, the salutary power assuring us against relapse into sin, the counterweight of grateful love restraining our pride. It opens our lips for salutary confession of sin. Through it God purges the heart so that it can bring forth fruits worthy of conversion and penance (cf. Mt 3:8f.; Jn 15:2). It prepares the heart for the sacrament of pardon, which imparts to the devout soul "peace and serenity of conscience with profound consolation of spirit."[107] It creates zeal for souls, with constant readiness for sacrifice for the salvation of our fellow men. It is not easily resigned to the triumph of evil in the world around us. "Blessed are those who mourn."

II. CONFESSION OF SIN, CONFESSION OF DIVINE MERCY

1. *Confession as Element of Conversion and as "Sacramental Sign"*

One of the essential acts in every genuine conversion is the confession: "I am a sinner, who stands in need of the divine mercy." In this universal form the confession of sins is prerequisite for the fruitful reception of baptism, the basic sacrament of conversion. (We do not refer here to the baptism of infants.) It was even said of the baptism of John, that "they were baptized by him in the Jordan, confessing their sins" (Mt 3:6). Since Christian baptism is administered "for the forgiveness of . . . sins" (Acts 2:38; cf. Lk 24:47), there is implied in the very voluntary reception itself the confession that one is in need of pardon of sins. Still the Church does not demand a confession of individual sins for baptism, since it is not her mission to remit in the sacramental tribunal sins which were not committed by her members.[108]

But in the "laborious baptism," as the Fathers called the sacrament of penance,[109] the Church demands by virtue of positive divine law the confession of all mortal sins committed after baptism. As the Council of Trent teaches,[110] the fulness of power given by Christ to the Church to forgive sins or withhold forgiveness (Mt 16:19; 18:18; Jn 20:23) gives to the Church the right by divine law itself and also imposes on her the duty to demand the explicit confession of all individual mortal sins, as far as the penitent is able to recall them. The law is positive but far from arbitrary. Like all true laws, so this law also is an expression of the laws of life: the Christian, child of the Church, has sinned against her; in consequence, because of his very status, he must confess also before the Church, which turns to him again with the face of divine mercy.

It cannot be proved that the urgent exhortation of the Apostle, "Confess, therefore, your sins to one another" (Jas 5:16; 1 Jn 1:9), refers directly to sacramental confession. But in any case it clearly teaches that the disposition or readiness to confess our guilt before our brother, in the presence of the Church, is a step in the path of conversion from sin. Confession of one's sin as an element in the task of conversion was known already in the Old Testament (Lv 5:5; Prv 28:13)[111] and even in the non-Christian religions.

The sinner's acknowledgment of his sins with all their guilt in humble self-accusation before God is inseparable from conversion from sin. The disposition to confess also in the presence of the Church is a consequence of sincere self-accusation before God, because the return to God cannot be effected without turning anew in contrition to the community of the saved. Nevertheless, we must note that confession before man, even before a representative of God and His Church, cannot have the same absolute and unqualified binding force as confession in the sight of God. The minimum demanded as well as the maximum to be striven for in this matter is revealed to us by the positive divine law, by the ecclesiastical interpretation, and likewise by the dictate of the virtue of prudence in the light of the inner nature and development of conversion itself.

2. Confession: the Law and the Ideal

Willingness to confess one's sins and doing more in this regard than the minimum laid down in the law is in itself an effect and sign of a genuine spirit of repentance. And yet the moral theology of the following of Christ may not shirk the responsibility of clearly distinguishing between this minimum of duty in obeying the positive divine and ecclesiastical law and the lofty ideals set before us by the virtue of penance and inviting each individual to do far more than merely obey the law in confessing his sins. Thus every penitent under the impulse of grace in each instance is summoned to a loftier ideal than mere conformity with the minimum of the law.

The confessor, who acts as spiritual judge in the tribunal of penance, must abide by this same minimum requirement of the law in the discharge of his duty. He has no right (by threatening the penitent with refusal of absolution and questioning his sincerity of disposition) to demand more than the minimum exacted by the law. Of course, since he is the guide and physician of souls, he may urge a more profound and wholesome spirit of humility, with all the kindliness of a spiritual father. And for the penitent, the clear grasp of the bare requirements of law is important likewise. If going beyond the requirement would be imprudent and likely to interfere with other duties which are more important or with indispensable steps in conversion, then his very seriousness in following in the footsteps of the Master should restrain him from doing more than he is required.

A rigorous imposition of the obligation to confess—in the stern spirit of law—may prove damaging to souls. Should the confessor demand what is excessive (to cite an example from the confession of children, should one require of children, in contravention of all justice, that they confess all their venial sin under pain of alleged sacrilege), the result might well be a serious religious crisis or a dangerous cramping or crippling of the powers of the soul. It is obvious that more important religious and moral duties will frequently be slighted under such conditions. Let us admit that the following statement of Hirscher is correct in principle: "Everyone who seeks to palliate his fault and hedges in his self-accusation does not have a real sense of penance. His confession is vain achievement merely satisfying the norm of law, and his predominant concern is to get by as easily as possible."[112] The statement is theoretically and abstractly correct, and yet there may be instances in which it is entirely sound (for example, to remedy or forestall scrupulosity) to adhere strictly to the line of the minimum requirement of law. But in others the very realization that the demands of the general law are extremely mild would constitute a reason to go beyond the law and, in the spirit of genuine freedom and childlike docility, follow the inner guidance of the Holy Spirit.

3. Theological and Psychological Significance of Confession

The interior disposition of contrition is manifested externally by confession and elevated to the sacramental efficacy of sign. Auricular confession in the forum of the Church corresponds to the audible absolution of sin through which the merciful favor of God encounters the experience of faith. And such is the meaning of this sacred sacramental sign (which effects what it signifies) that it suggests to the penitent to endeavor with all his might to measure the holy sincerity of his self-accusation with the sacred loyalty of Christ who has given him the solemn pledge of assurance that He will graciously pardon his sin. He should endeavor with all his power to measure the depth of the sorrow he manifests with Christ's own consuming zeal for his salvation, with Christ's own wish to blot out his sins. Through the confession of his sins he should seek to give honor to the mercy of God with deep and humble piety, measuring this desire to honor God's mercy with the desire of Christ and the Church to honor the heavenly Father through the use of the sacramental power in pardoning sin.

Our self-accusation is an element of the efficacious sacramental sign and thereby partakes of the effective act of Christ the priest. For this reason our confession must be more than mere recital of our sins, even though it be contrite. It must be raised to the dignity of the divine worship by which God is praised, his justice acknowledged by our contrite self-accusation, and His mercy glorified. Therefore the sacramental accusation must be kept free from the taint of an overweening confidence in our first show of progress, no matter how desirable the evidence of our sincerity may be, no matter how plainly the first efforts in self-improvement manifest the earnestness of our resolutions. The humility of our attitude must attest that we look to the divine mercy for pardon of our sins. Through God's mercy alone do we expect pardon and the beginning of a new life in filial love springing from the liberty of the children of God.

The nature of confession as perceptible (the sign in the recital of sin corresponding to the audible words of absolution) and as cultal, praising the mercy of God, demands that it be oral, if possible. Only for a just reason may some other kind of manifestation of sin, such as accusation in the form of writing, be permitted. The question has been raised regarding sacramental confession and absolution by means of telephone. Can a penitent in case of necessity accuse himself of his sins—through generic confession—and validly receive absolution? The point has not yet been clarified. Since there is presence of a kind uniting penitent and confessor in the telephone communication—the perceptible words of absolution consequent to the audible self-accusation are obviously the most sensible element of the sacramental sign in this sacrament—the possibility that such a confession is valid would permit the use of the phone in case of necessity, for example, in the instance in which the penitent is critically ill and the usual bodily presence is impossible. However, because of the uncertainty regarding the actual validity of the act, absolution could be given only conditionally.

Contrite confession to the priest has the special merit and cultal value of satisfaction and expiation arising from the union of sacrament and redemptive passion of Christ. Frequently the sacrifice involved in the humiliation of the accusation itself is the most painful and valuable element of the satisfaction. Humble self-accusation is of inestimable worth in the essential structure of conversion.

By its very nature sin tends to hide in the darkness and shut out the light, or at least mask itself as good. "Every one who does evil hates the light, and does not come to the light, that his deeds may not be exposed. But he who does the truth comes to the light that his deeds may be manifest" (Jn 3:20f.). "As long as man clings to evil and does not confess it before God in his sorrow, so long must he desire to withdraw it from the light of God's judgment—as our first parents hid themselves from God after their sin."[113] Confession before God and to His human representative counteracts this dread of the light, the darkening power of sin, for it rips the mask of deceit from evil and casts light into the most hidden recesses of guilt. Only confession reawakens in the sinner the full realization that for God the darkness of night is as the light of day (Ps 138). Consequently, confession of sin is an important step in conversion, for conversion is passing from the darkness to the light of truth and love (cf. 1 Thes 5:5; Rom 13:11f.). "God is light, and in him is no darkness. If we say that we have fellowship with him, and walk in darkness, we lie, and are not practicing the truth" (1 Jn 1:5f.). Confession exposes the darksomeness of our guilt and thus opens our soul to the rays of truth and the love of God. "Through confession we prepare ourselves for the free and perfect transparency of the divine love which penetrates all things; the inaccessible light of God (1 Tm 6:16) becomes accessible through grace."[114]

Humble confession of sins, by which we acknowledge that the good work belongs to God, not to us, is a necessary preliminary for the incomparable honor accorded to us sinners to be admitted again into the light of the divine glory. "And have no fellowship with the unfruitful works of darkness, but rather expose them! . . . All things that are exposed are made manifest by the light: for all that is made manifest is light" (Eph 5:11ff.). The unreserved manifestation of our heart with all its recesses and depths, the song of praise of the divine mercy through confession of our sins, places us in the light of the love and glory of God. Correct self-accusation is opening the heart to the love of God. "Love is light, is accessibility; evil, on the contrary, is self-seeking, darkness, imprisonment, solitude."[115]

The love for God, "whom he does not see," is to be tested by the love the Christian has for "his brother, whom he sees" (1 Jn 4:20). Similarly God has made confession of his sins to his brother, to the visible representative of the Church, the test by which the will to confess before God is assured and proved genuine."[116]

Man has not sinned in his mind alone. His body has shared in the guilt. In some manner his sin visibly offended against the honor due to God. In grace likewise there is reference to the visible. Through grace man receives the pledge and seed of the visible glory which is to come, when he shall shine in the community of the saints. All this suggests how appropriate it is that man, at least in some small measure and from time to time, externally acknowledge his sinfulness in order to proclaim salutary union and solidarity with the Church in giving glory to God. With penetrating insight Mounier says: "The Christian is a being who accuses himself"[117] from the depth of his entire body-soul and social personality.

Contrition is the deep spring from which flows the rich religious value of confession. It is also the strength to "overcome the sense of shame which in the last moment would seal the lips of the penitent."[118] Conversely, confession before the visible Church imparts to contrition a deeper dimension in its most basic components, humility and sincerity. Frequently self-knowledge itself attains the maturity which is so essential only through confession of one's faults. What we clearly formulate and communicate in explicit terms to our fellow man is by that very fact impressed much more clearly and sharply on our own consciousness. "No mere internal formulation and accusation of our sins can breach the prison wall of self-enclosure and sin and thus set us free. Only through explicit formulation in the spoken word does our self-accusation assume visible form and emerge before us in clear and compelling light."[119]

To this value of accusation of our sins in the sacramental tribunal we must add the aid which is given the penitent by a good father confessor. On the basis of the sincere confession the confessor can contribute much toward a deepening of the penitent's self-knowledge and sorrow, abstracting altogether from the supernatural effectiveness of the words of absolution freeing him from his sins. Hence there is little room for wonder that a man who has given up the holy practice of sacramental confession should seek a substitute in psychoanalytical "confession." Of course, this is not a confession in sorrow at all, but merely an unabashed exposure of one's inner self to a physician. "Instead of going to confession, they go to the psychiatrist."[120]

Confession to a man in sight of God is like raising a shield against the forces of hypocrisy and self-deception which only too readily would attack us frail mortals because the concealment of our fault may be morally justified and even necessary to prevent scandal and the loss of honor essential to our social duty and position. Sacramental confession, however, is a powerful means of maintaining the proper attitude toward acceptance of the shame and humiliation deserved by our sins. Willingness to confess our sins implies that we have the readiness, which is morally necessary, to take upon ourselves this humiliation and shame. But the very sanctity of accusation and the inviolability of the seal give us the assurance that our neighbor will be safeguarded against scandal and our own good name preserved intact. With all this in mind it is not difficult for us to understand why self-accusation is found even outside the Church, and, among Catholics, even outside the sacramental tribunal. The reason lies in the profound religious significance and the fruitfulness of confession of sins.[121]

But it is only the confession of sins in the sacred tribunal of the sacrament which is truly profound and salutary. It is the sacramental accusation in the presence of God, all-powerful, all-bountiful with His grace of pardon, in the presence of the community of salvation, the Church. Mercy and grace are granted only in Christ and before Christ, the Incarnate Word. It is the "word of God . . . living and efficient and keener than any two-edged sword, and extending even to the division of soul and spirit, of joints also and of marrow and a discerner of the thoughts and intentions of the heart . . . there is no creature hidden from his sight . . . [but for whom] all things are naked and open to the eyes . . . to whom we have to give an account" (HEB 4:12f.), who is also our high priest with "compassion on our infirmities" (HEB 4:15). Only in Christ and before Christ can we "hold fast our confession . . . and draw near with confidence to the throne of grace, that we may obtain mercy and find grace to help in time of need" (HEB 4:14ff.).

4. *The Precept of Integral Confession*

The positive divine law obliges the Christian to confess all the mortal sins he has committed after baptism which have not been directly remitted through the Church's power of the keys. Mortal sins must be confessed according to their number and species, including all circumstances which change the nature of the sin, in so far as the penitent is conscious of them after careful examination of conscience.[122] A positive precept of the Church specifies this divine commandment, forbidding one to defer confession of serious sins beyond a year without grave reasons (specifically not beyond the next obligatory Paschal confession).[123]

Theologians distinguish between material and formal integrity of confession: material integrity is actual integral confession of all grave sins according to number and species. Formal integrity is the sincere will to make a materially integral confession, manifested or expressed in the actual confession of one's sins according to the measure of one's knowledge and power.

For validity of confession the good disposition or good will must be externalized through some perceptible sign of sorrow. According to a probable teaching it is permitted to give absolution at least conditionally to a dying man, even though he can give no sign of his sorrow, provided one can reasonably assume that he would confess if he were able. In this point we follow the sound principle that we may use extreme measures when there is extreme need.

Confession of sins is materially and formally incomplete if the penitent through grave fault omits a mortal sin. It is formally incomplete if he should consciously omit what he thinks is a mortal sin, even though it should be no more than a venial sin. In either instance the reception of the sacrament is sacrilegious. Confession is valid and the reception of the sacrament fruitful (worthy) even though the penitent forgets or neglects to mention a grave sin because of some slight carelessness or neglect. The confession is likewise valid if, despite the earnest disposition to make an integral self-accusation of sins, a mortal sin, clearly recognized as such, would be concealed because of a profound and essential restriction of freedom of action, let us say because of a pathologically excessive sense of shame. Obviously the individual penitent himself can scarcely form a sound and unclouded judgment in such a matter, to the extent that he could feel really excused from the obligation of repeating the past confessions in question (by a general confession). Much less could a penitent form such a judgment previous to the confession and hold himself excused from the obligation of integral confession on such grounds. But it is good for us to bear in mind that there is the possibility, and the occurrence may not be altogether rare, that the concealment of mortal sin in such cases does not invalidate the confession. Such an explanation sheds considerable light on the perplexing case of many souls who suffer infinite agony because of a sin concealed in confession and still lead a pious penitential life and only after protracted distress of soul finally are brought to confess the sin.

The precept to confess all mortal sins according to their number and their "lowest" species (this is to say, one must mention "all the circumstances which change the nature or the species of the sin") obliges the theologically instructed penitent to accuse himself in accordance with his theological knowledge regarding a very difficult matter. What is a circumstance changing the nature or species of a sin? And what constitutes a new sin numerically?

Surely it would not be just to expect or demand an accusation of sin in accordance with such difficult and subtle distinctions as to species and number from a penitent who is not at all versed in theology. (As to this point, it is quite true that we must instruct the faithful also in such matters, after they have received instruction on all the more important problems regarding the faith and the truly Christian life.) For the ordinary faithful the following neat and simple rule should apply: they must mention in confession everything which constitutes an entirely new kind of mortal sin and also indicate the circumstances in a given case which make of what would otherwise be only a venial sin a certainly mortal sin. Prudently and circumspectly the confessor has the obligation to help the penitent to make a "materially integral" confession. But he surely is not obliged in every case to formulate his questions in accordance with the most thoroughgoing theological studies on the subtle distinctions of species and number, but according to the degree of intelligence and the capacity for distinctions of the particular penitent before him.

There is no unconditional obligation according to law to accuse oneself of those circumstances which do not alter the species of the sin, even though they enormously aggravate the gravity of a mortal sin within the same species. However, should the father confessor reasonably interrogate the penitent (there may be proximate occasion of sin which he must be told to avoid, or an essential spiritual remedy for true repentance is to be suggested, or there may be an obligation to restitute ill-gotten goods, or there may be question of some ecclesiastical sanction), he is obliged to respond truthfully and candidly. A deliberate lie regarding an important matter would render the confession invalid and sacrilegious, though such would not be the case were the lie to escape embarrassment and the matter not serious. In fact, even were such an untruth concerned with a serious matter, taken in itself it would not necessarily be proof that the penitent incurred grave guilt or had an unworthy disposition making fruitful reception of the sacrament impossible.

The number of mortal sins is to be indicated as precisely as possible. If the penitent cannot recall the exact number at all or not without great effort (many penitents cannot recall the precise number of their sins, at least if the number is higher than ten or if a long time has elapsed since the previous confession), it is sufficient to give the proximate number (for example, if one were to say, "About a hundred times," the precise number could be ninety times or a hundred and ten times, or more or less often). And once this is done, every further effort to calculate with greater precision should be dismissed! The Christian has better use for his time than to fritter it away creating scruples and distress of soul. Should he later recall the exact number of his sins, and specifically discover that the number first confessed was certainly too low, he is not obliged to make a point of correcting the discrepancy except in the event that it was very notable, so that the confessor, with the more precise number before him, would have formed an entirely different judgment of the penitent's state of conscience and have imposed a much more severe penance. The mortal sins in excess of the number confessed were directly remitted by exercise of the power of the keys, for the very term "about" did indicate the will of the penitent to mention the possibly larger number, and both Church and confessor had the will directly to remit them.

"Also the secret sins (interior sins) which violate the last two precepts of the decalog"[124] and obviously also the shameful sins against the sixth commandment must be confessed according to number and species. On this point we say that they must be confessed as a general rule. But a caution is to be observed. If a materially integral confession in matters of the sixth commandment is not possible without exciting impure images and dangerous temptations (whether the danger concern the penitent, or, something which is less probable, the confessor himself), then the penitent is excused from the obligation of making a materially integral confession. Not only is he excused, but the stricter moral precept to avoid unnecessary dangers and temptations simply forbids him under such circumstances to attempt to confess integrally.[125] But the serious obligation still remains for the penitent to present a true picture of his spiritual condition by a humble sincere confession, so that it is possible for the confessor to form a correct judgment in the sacramental tribunal.

Thus, for example, a penitent making her confession after her conversion from a long life as a prostitute should not attempt to refresh her memory by recalling all the evil deeds of her past. It is quite sufficient to confess that for a specific period she had plied her vile trade. All the rest—that the sins confessed implied countless unchaste sins of deed, word, and thought of the most diverse kind—is sufficiently confessed. It would be highly imprudent for the confessor to press with more specific and particular questions in order to obtain material integrity through calculation of each sin, something which is simply impossible, entirely futile, and possibly damaging to his honor as a priest and confessor. There are many holy duties involved in such a confession: faith and trust, praise of the divine mercy, new respect for the soul of the penitent newly sanctified, appropriate purpose of amendment through a new life—all these are to be awakened in the heart of the repentant sinner. It would be simply appalling if penitent and confessor should expend all their energies in a concern for factual integrity, which is not in place at all and which would really prove hazardous. Much more important than rigid "enumeration" of individual sins (already implicitly confessed) is the great concern for solid fundamental conversion, though, of course, many questions on the part of the confessor may be necessary to achieve this end effectively.

Formal integrity of confession is infinitely more important than actual material completeness. Therefore, the confessor is not permitted to jeopardize the essential formal completeness of the confession made by a penitent in good faith in accordance with his disposition and capacity by rigorous and excessive stress on number and species in the self-accusation.

Prudent instruction of the faithful clearly indicating what is required and what is not required for integrity should prevent many unworthy confessions (experience proves the point) or at least greatly lessen spiritual distress. Inept instruction may lead the penitent to believe he is bound to the impossible or to what is most unseemly, and yet he is restrained in this matter because of a contrary fear of conscience. In such instances a kindly word from the confessor assuring him that his confession is adequate, that he should no longer reflect on these things, that they are not to be the object of further examination or self-accusation, is a great boon. This advice can really free the penitent from the crippling hold of anxiety and release powerful energies—till then held in the grip of unreasoning fear— for a new beginning in the spiritual life.

The precept of material integrity binds in proportion to the human powers of the penitent and in right proportion to the other essential elements of conversion. There is a spiritual hazard in applying any positive precept—even one so holy as the one we are here discussing—without regard for other precepts and circumstances.[126]

The effort required in the examination of conscience for valid confession must be judged in the light of the penitent's attitude at the time of his confession. If he did what he thought he was obliged to do under penalty of mortal sin when he prepared for the reception of the sacrament of penance, he is not obliged to repeat his confession, even though later on, as his spirit of penance deepens, he may feel that his previous examination of conscience was very imperfect. This subsequent conviction is not an adequate reason for repetition of the confession, provided that it was valid in every other regard. However, the penitent does have the obligation to confess, in his next confession, any grave sin which he is certain he overlooked or forgot in the previous reception of the sacrament of penance.

Anyone who wishes to receive the sacrament of penance, even though his conscience does not accuse him of any mortal sin not yet confessed, can and may accuse himself of a mortal sin already confessed and pardoned in the sacrament or he may confess his venial sins. From the standpoint of mere obligation, a generic confession is sufficient. Following is an example: "I have committed no mortal sin since my last confession. I accuse myself of all my venial sins." However, no particular formula of words is necessary. Obviously, pious souls who confess frequently should be urged to confess their venial sins more specifically to obtain greater fruit from such "confessions of devotion."

There is no obligation, from the strict standpoint of law, to confess any sin if there is a prudent doubt that we have actually committed it, or a doubt about its gravity. Canon 906 of the code of canon law repeats in precise terms the Tridentine doctrine (sess. 14), which mentions solely the obligation to confess mortal sins "of which one after earnest examination of conscience knows he is guilty (*conscientiam habet*)." But we cannot at all claim that one knows that he is guilty of a mortal sin if after adequate self-examination he still has a prudent doubt whether he has actually committed the sin or whether it is really a grave sin.

Quite often careful examination of conscience in the light of the practical "rules of prudence" can clear up our doubt and result in a practical certainty. For example, a Christian who is serious and earnest in his moral life as a general rule, may simply decide in his own favor and reasonably assume that he is not guilty of mortal sin, if he doubts in this one instance about his guilt. On the contrary, a penitent who "drinks in sin like water" cannot prudently decide in his own favor in the case of a similar subjective doubt. Scrupulants must decide the cases of doubt in the negative (not consider themselves guilty of mortal sin) if the doubt lies in the domain of their anxiety, at least as regards the obligation to confess the "doubtful" sin.

A penitent who has sincerely tried to make a good confession or who thought at the time of the confession that he made a good confession is presumed to have done so, even though he later begins to doubt its validity or doubts whether or not one or other mortal sin was actually confessed. In these instances there is no law or precept imposing any further obligation. We apply correctly the simple rule of prudence: "Every past act is presumed to be validly performed unless the contrary is proved." Accordingly, one is obliged to confess only those sins in the sacrament of penance which he is morally certain he has never previously confessed in any valid confession.

Should a penitent have sincerely confessed a sin as "doubtfully" grave and then later come to the conclusion that it was certainly a mortal sin, there is no obligation to repeat the accusation in the light of this new knowledge, for the power of the keys in the Church directly remitted the sin as it actually was, even though the penitent confessed it as "doubtfully" grave. For the sinner wanted to confess the sin and the priest wanted to pardon it as it really was.[127]

If one has no doubt about the gravity of the sin itself, but doubts whether he committed it before or after his last confession, he must—at least according to the rules of equi-probabilism—confess the sin. (The obligation to confess is in certain "possession" and prevails over the subsequent doubt about the fulfillment of the duty of confessing the sin.) However, according to the rules of probabilism, the penitent or confessor may make the decision in favor of freedom from obligation in every instance of prudent doubt regarding any obligation arising from a law or precept.

In this entire discussion one important point may never be left out of

sight even for a moment: we are here dealing with obligations arising
from precepts or laws regarding the confession of sins in the sacrament
of penance. Obviously, for everyone there is never a moment, least of
all when there is danger of death, in which we are not bound by the imperative of divine grace: we are always required to be and to remain in
the state of grace. If there is doubt about our possession of this state of
the love and the grace of God or doubt about the loss of grace, we must
choose the safer course.

In the event that one has committed a sin which probably is mortal, he
is obliged as soon as possible to respond to the first invitation of divine
grace and elicit an act of perfect contrition in so far as this is in his
power. One who with good reason questions his own capacity to awaken
perfect contrition is obliged to implore God earnestly for this grace,
provided he does not have the opportunity to receive the sacrament of
penance. One who has the opportunity to receive this sacrament surely
does well to sanctify and complete his own efforts of repentance through
the reception of the sacrament. Yet even in the instances in which we
have held that he is not obliged to receive the sacrament of penance, he
can attempt to elicit an act of perfect contrition and then receive a sacrament of the living (for example, Holy Communion). The result is the
certain restoration of sanctifying grace, about which he was in doubt,
provided he was genuinely sorry for his sins. In this case at least imperfect
contrition (attrition) is essential.

It is not unlikely that some will entertain doubts about being in the
state of the divine friendship, because they fear they have not been able
to be sorry for their sins because of perfect love of God (perfect contrition)
after they have committed what is probably a mortal sin. We hold that if
there should be no opportunity for them to receive the sacrament of
penance, it is more advisable for them and all who are not strictly obliged
by the law of God (or, more specifically, by the precept of the Church) to
receive the sacrament of penance previously, to approach the Eucharistic
table with the earnest desire for their salvation than to remain in danger
of losing their soul through false fear.

5. Reasons Excusing from Material Integrity of Confession

Apart from the instance already cited, in which the danger of temptation against the virtue of purity might excuse the penitent from the
necessity of integral confession or even make it unlawful, every true

impossibility of confessing integrally also excuses the penitent. Impossibility is either physical or moral.

It is sufficient for a dying man to express in some perceptible manner his interior sorrow and therewith his readiness to confess, provided he can do no more than this. One who is critically ill makes a good confession if he does as much as he can without danger of worsening his critical condition. Ignorance and forgetfulness also excuse a penitent, provided the condition is not culpable or at least not gravely culpable. Generally speaking, there is no obligation to prepare for confession through the use of written notes, even though there is good reason to fear that without such notes much will be forgotten in the accusation. Such means are extraordinary and often involve the danger of violation of secrecy and fostering scrupulosity. Nevertheless, some noted moralists demand such use of helps to the memory of the penitent in those instances when the dangers referred to are absent in particular concrete cases and weakness of memory is very great.

If the penitent cannot find a confessor who understands his language, he may request absolution and receive it, even though his accusation is limited to mere signs or gestures manifesting his sorrow and will to confess. The same principle applies in the case of the deaf-mutes who can find no confessor conversant with the sign language. No penitent is obliged to make use of an interpreter in order to make a materially complete confession of his sins, although the use of an interpreter is not forbidden if scandal is avoided and other necessary precautions against any abuse give assurance that the procedure is truly prudent.[128]

Want of time in which to recite one's sins in full completeness excuses the penitent from the obligation of making an integral confession particularly in danger of death. Soldiers at the front under attack and civilians near the battle line or in the danger zones (for example, under threat of bombardment) may be given general absolution in time of war, provided there is not sufficient time for them to make the usual detailed confession of all mortal sins. However, all who wish to receive the sacrament must give some external sign expressing their sorrow, and be sincerely disposed to submit all their mortal sins to the power of the keys by confession according to their number and species at the proper time. General absolution under the same conditions may be given when there is an extreme dearth of priests in relation to the number of the faithful, if integral confession with absolution of the individual penitent would have to be long delayed.[129]

Crowds eager to confess in the brief period of huge congresses of the faithful do not justify a curtailing or abbreviating of the confessions of penitents through a violation of material integrity.[130] The hasty confessions on such occasions were considered an abuse by Bishop J. M. Sailer who already in his time suggested that they clamored for intervention and correction by ecclesiastical authority. Still in particular instances absolution could lawfully be granted after a curtailed confession, if confessor or penitent were unavoidably pressed for time and the penitent had no other opportunity to confess his sins for some period of time, or if he had already begun his confession and there were no available time to complete it.

The danger of violation of the seal of the confession can likewise excuse a penitent from the law of material integrity. Cases in point are instances when confessions are heard in crowded hospital wards or in confessionals stationed close to pressing groups of penitents waiting to receive the sacrament. As to this point, every pastor and director of souls should make every effort to arrange for "closed" confessionals stationed at a sufficient distance from the groups of penitents, pilgrims, or other faithful, as the case may be. Such conditions are psychologically favorable to penitent and confessor for the grand and salutary work in the sacrament of penance.

Under certain circumstances the fear may be justified that the confessor himself may incur a great risk to his own salvation because he would be scandalized over the sins of his penitent (for example, a person in an important position or office). This danger could be a reason for excusing the penitent from the law of material integrity in his confession.

To me it seems that an excessive sense of shame might prove almost insurmountable in instances in which the penitent comes into daily contact with the confessor or in which there is a very special relationship between confessor and penitent. In some very special instances there may be sufficient reason to excuse the penitent from the law of material integrity of confession, if no other confessor is available, or if one may not approach another confessor without exciting considerable astonishment or comment. Such instances may be found particularly in closed communities. There is a stricter view in this matter held by many authors, but it seems that an obviously necessary condition on which the milder view is based is overlooked, namely, that the penitent must have and does actually have the good will and earnest disposition to confess the sin which excites so much shame. He is quite willing to confess the sin to any other father confessor when he finds the opportunity to do so.

The danger that the confessor might be able to conjecture the name of the accomplice in the sin confessed to him is not a sufficient reason to excuse the penitent from confessing it. However, the penitent must guard against any such revelation of the other guilty party.

For all the preceding instances two basic principles hold good and should never be lost sight of: 1) the motives which excuse the penitent from making a complete and integral confession are valid only if no other confessor can be found without excessive difficulty or effort, or if the penitent would be constrained to defer his confession for a considerable time or postpone it at the risk of losing his soul. For anyone burdened with mortal sin who feels incapable of eliciting an act of perfect contrition, remaining in this miserable state without the divine pardon given in sacramental absolution is a very serious matter. 2) The sin or sins omitted through defect of material integrity because of weighty motives must be confessed when the reasons for the exemption no longer hold. What was incomplete must then be made complete, and the defect must be supplied at the next confession. This may be the Paschal confession. But in the interval, if no new mortal sin has been committed since the last valid absolution from mortal sin (even the general absolution, as indicated above), the penitent may receive Holy Communion, without previous reception of the sacrament of penance. On this point he should tranquilly receive the Holy Eucharist and dismiss all anxiety.

6. Integrity of Confession and the Following of Christ

The explanation of the minimum requirements of the law and the corresponding exemptions from its obligation only partially answer the query of the true disciple of Christ, "How shall I confess, and what shall I confess?" No one is free to ignore the law and its minimum demands as we explained it. As to rigid requirements, we exact no more from the disciple of Christ than an absolutely demonstrable minimum. But the follower of Christ is well aware that his Master invites him to surpass these legal bounds and through His grace calls him by name to do so. For him the "sum of the law" is the divine grace which leads him on step by step in the spirit of penance, into the depths of sorrow and purification, and likewise guides him along the path of humble and profound self-accusation. And as his sorrow deepens, the spirit of self-accusation attains greater depths of self-abasement.

We noted the reasons for adhering firmly to the strict demands of the law under certain circumstances and on certain occasions, because of the need and desire to make spiritual progress in more important things. The penitent inclined to scrupulosity is often strictly obliged to conform to the prudent decision of his confessor and not exceed the demand of the law by any voluntary confession of sins. In matters of chastity, the detailed explanation must also be measured by the minimum requirement of law in so far as the honor of the sacrament is concerned, but not so far as the self-abasement of the penitent and the seeking of counsel and guidance are in question.

The penitent who has the earnest will to deepen his repentance will often feel utterly dissatisfied with the mere accusation of his sin. He will examine the secret shameful motivation[131] for his sin in order to expose it. In a spirit of deep distrust of self, he will probe into the imperfection of the good he has done to discover what evil may have resulted from it. Where special reasons account for limiting our confession to the bare requirement of the law (to cite one example, the father confessor may have lost patience for any further details), the examination of conscience itself should offer occasion for deeper and humbler self-examination. This examination of conscience must constantly be drawn into the sacrament more perfectly since it disposes us intimately for confession and absolution. It should become more intimately sacramental, in so far as it becomes conscious self-accusation before God, in the light of faith, in confidence in the mercy of God, with the most perfect disposition of heart which prepares the penitent to submit to the tribunal of the Church in the most humble and salutary self-accusation.

This readiness to confess in the spirit of obedience to grace rather than in mere obedience to law is expressed above all in the "confession of devotion" and in the general confession.

7. Confession of Devotion

Confession of devotion is the voluntary confession of venial sins or of mortal sins which have already been confessed and forgiven in the sacrament of penance. The confession of these mortal sins is called a general confession, if all or at least an entire group of sins committed throughout a considerable period of time is again submitted to the power of the keys in the sacrament.

Venial sins can be remitted in many ways, even without sacramental confession and absolution. The most excellent and effective way is the frequent, humble, fervent reception of the Most Holy Sacrament of the Altar, which is the "antidote through which we are freed from our daily faults."[132] Through loving converse with the Lord of Love in the Sacrament of Love there is driven from the soul that laxity which is the source of most of our venial sins.[133] The Holy Eucharist has been instituted above all "as the spiritual nourishment for the loving union with Christ and the members of His Body. . . . But because this unity is effected through love, whose ardor brings to us not only the remission of guilt, but also of the punishment, we receive in consequence by a certain concomitance with the principal effect of the sacrament also the remission of punishment . . . in the measure of the fervor of our piety."[134]

Fervor demands the spirit of penance. If penance is lacking, if piety is lacking, if one is attached to his venial sins, not only is the effectiveness of the Holy Eucharist lessened in the blotting out of venial sins, but the fruitfulness of all the sacraments of the living is diminished.[135] From this we can gain an insight into the need for sorrow in relation to the sacraments of the living. The Holy Eucharist and all the other sacraments of the living cry out for preparation which includes a deepening of sorrow and the spirit of penance. If Christ offers us the opportunity, it follows that we should place before Him our own effort to increase and deepen our contrition in the sacrament of penance, in which the frail human sorrow will be increased, perfected, and sanctified by the Master Himself in the unique way of sacramental efficacy.

A deep realization of this thought prompted the French hierarchy to lay down the basic principle of the *Pastoral Directory of the French Episcopate* (N. 45): "Even though confession of venial sins is not required before every reception of Holy Communion, nevertheless the frequent reception of Holy Communion suggests and invites us to a correspondingly frequent reception of the sacrament of penance, which is of particular value in the attainment of true purity of conscience."

The pretext that the present practice of confession of devotion in the Church is contrary to the ideals of the early Church as shown by studies in early ecclesiastical history is utterly absurd.[136] The early Church did far more than we are doing today to maintain a lofty penitential ideal and a living spirit of penance among the faithful. It should also be borne in mind that there is a development of the rich treasure of the faith, not merely on the level of doctrine, but also in practice and discipline. One of the most significant domains of such development is precisely in the use of the sacraments.

Not the confession of devotion as such, but the superficial and routine manner in the reception of the sacrament of penance is a bar to the tremendous earnestness that should characterize our approach to the sacrament of conversion. Only too readily the practice of confession degenerates into mere habit or routine, because of constant confession of venial sins without true sorrow. Such confession of venial sins to which one is still attached is not only mechanical and superficial, but even perilous to the spiritual life.

The minimum standard of practice in this matter of confession of devotion, which practically every right-living Catholic observes as a matter of course today, is set by the annual Paschal confession. Though the practice is almost universal in the Church, it is not strictly required by the ecclesiastical law for those who are not "conscious of any mortal sin."

Stress on confession of devotion, important as it is, should not obscure the true doctrine that the center of the whole spiritual life, and of all true piety, is not the sacrament of penance, but the Most Holy Eucharist. The practice of receiving the sacrament of penance, therefore, must be such that it serves the more devout and more frequent reception of the Eucharist, and in no wise interferes with this central ideal.

8. *Repetition of Confession and General Confession*

Confession must be repeated and mortal sins must be re-confessed if one's previous confessions have been invalid or even sacrilegious. In such instances the penitent is obliged to confess or re-confess all mortal sins which were committed since the last worthy confession. However, in the instance in which the penitent confesses to the same priest to whom he has already confessed a great portion of his sins, even though in an invalid reception of the sacrament, and the confessor is able to recall these confessions at least in a general way, it is not necessary to make a detailed confession of the sins according to number and species. It is quite sufficient to submit them to the keys in a general way with true sorrow. It may occur that an invalid confession is followed by a series of worthy receptions of the sacrament of penance, without any validation of the unworthy confession because the matter was overlooked or forgotten. In such a case the penitent is not required to repeat the confessions made in good faith, though he must confess that he made one unworthy confession and re-confess the mortal sins included in that sinful reception of the sacrament.

Repetition of a confession or confessions, or a general confession, is to be counseled if there is a prudent doubt about the validity of previous confessions. It is most salutary to make a general confession on the occasions of special grace when God grants the soul a livelier and more heartfelt sense of sorrow (spiritual exercises, missions, entry into a new state of life). Deepening of sorrow for our sins opens the profound recesses of the heart to the influence of the sacrament of penance, so that the deep wounds of former sins, not yet fully healed, may be exposed to its healing power.

"Through frequent confession to a number of priests," says Saint Thomas, "there is effected a greater remission of the penalty due to sin, both because of the humiliation in the self-accusation which is considered a penitential act, and because of the power of the keys."[137]

We must severely condemn the exaggerated statements made by some preachers regarding the frequency of unworthy confessions, despite the laudable desire to arouse in the hearts of the faithful an appreciation of the great benefits of general confession!

It is a matter of practical importance to note that the penitent who makes a general confession without being obliged to do so should not be required to confess all mortal sins according to number and circumstances. Surely material integrity is not only not required, but it may be inadvisable in many instances. It is sufficient if the penitent accuses himself of the more serious and the more typical sins committed in the period in question. In matters of purity detailed enumeration of all sins is to be strictly avoided, particularly if they be many and varied.[138] Scrupulants and penitents much inclined to anxiety of spirit should be counseled not to make general confessions, unless there is a clear and certain obligation to do so because of previous unworthy reception of the sacrament of penance.

9. Moral Theology Directed to the Whole Christian Life

We have stated very emphatically that the Christian conscience must be formed regarding confession, not merely according to the measure of the rigid demand of law, but according to the spirit of obedience to the inner guidance of grace. We must make a further distinction, a much more profound distinction which is of great importance in explaining the tasks of moral doctrine and moral instruction: there is a very marked difference between moral as a "school of life" whose purpose is the formation of all spiritual domains in the mind and heart of Christ, and a moral slanted almost exclusively toward the sacrament of penance, a species of "confessional moral," whose principal ideal is the guidance of the confessor in the correct exercise of his role as judge in the tribunal of penance, and the guidance of the penitent in the task of "integral" confession. These latter are important functions of moral theology, yet it must be remembered that while penance plays a capital role in the whole spiritual life, it is not the whole of Christian life. Such a statement, however, is in no way designed to discredit the manuals of moral theology which aim primarily at the formation of good confessors and limit their goals primarily to this function.

III. SATISFACTION AND ATONEMENT

1. *Satisfaction (Penitential Works) as Expression of Repentance*

Penitential works are a valuable means of expressing and cultivating sorrow or true conversion of heart. Genuine contrition necessarily entails the inner disposition of will to make reparation (*votum satisfactionis,* desire for satisfaction), because sorrow by its very nature signifies an acknowledgment of the offense committed against God. In fact, since sorrow is a voluntary and patient acceptance of the grief and distress over sin, it is in some measure the first stage of satisfaction.[139] Sorrow also is the seed of the will to do penance, which first expresses itself in the readiness for self-accusation in the presence of God and before the Church and then in patient submission to divine visitations and humble acceptance of the satisfaction imposed by the Church. The penitential effort initiated in sorrow and self-accusation is completed and perfected by the actual satisfaction in bearing up under penitential suffering (*satispassio*) and the performing of the penitential work itself (*satisfactio*).[140] Since the humiliation of self-accusation and the pain of satisfaction are the development of what is implicit in all sorrow, it must follow that through them contrition grows and matures, for it is the actual conversion of the heart.

Penitential efforts should not be conceived as the soul of repentance. But the sincere acceptance of the pain of sorrow, the humble self-accusation, and the performance of works of satisfaction do ripen the "fruits befitting repentance" (Lk 3:8; Mt 3:8). And should these fruits be entirely lacking, one should perforce conclude that the repentance itself is not genuine. The tree comes before the fruits. If Christ speaks of repentance "in sackcloth and ashes" (Mt 11:21), this does not imply that penitential works are the very essence of the *metánoia* proclaimed as the glad tidings of salvation, but rather its spontaneous expression flowing from it with increasing spontaneity as the repentance itself grows deeper and richer.

The primitive Church with all her insistence on penitential rigor was keenly aware that true repentance of heart with the inner disposition of penance is indispensable for the sinner in returning to the Father's house in love, but likewise that it is sufficient. For this reason she pardoned the sinner and reconciled him to God in the hour of death, even without the previous performance of penance.[141] If, on the contrary, she showed herself inexorable in exacting a strict discipline of prescribed penance, it was for the purpose of repairing the scandal caused by mortal sin. But the Church realized also that the performance of the prescribed penance had, as a result, the deepening of the penitent's sorrow and the preparing of his heart to receive sacramental reconciliation with greater efficacy.[142]

2. *Penance as Homage to God*

Penance is loving acknowledgment of the justice of God and trustful prayer begging His mercy. The sinner who does penance recognizes in the compunction of his heart the wrong he has done to God, to the utterly transcendent divine justice which both punishes and saves. In dread and terror he says yes to the holy justice of God which punishes the impenitent, and in love and gratitude he says yes to the saving justice of God which visits the contrite of heart through corrective punishment and purifying trials. Though he is repentant and contrite, the sinner fully realizes that works of penance, no matter how great, cannot give him a rightful claim to pardon. His penance turns to the divine mercy in humble submission of will to the justice of God.

The penance of the Christian is never isolated. It always stands in the shadow of the cross of Christ, who offered the great expiatory sacrifice in His blood, placating the justice of God, giving infinite praise to the Heavenly Father and begging His mercy for sinners. All confidence in works of penance is simple trust in the satisfaction wrought by Christ, who alone imparts to the fruits of penance value and dignity.[143] For this reason the penances imposed by the priest in the sacramental tribunal of grace do not in any way make of penance a "tribunal of wrath and punishment,"[144] but an act of praise of God's saving justice in Christ, with Christ, and through Christ and His infinite work of satisfaction for sinners.

From all that we have said it is quite obvious that the sacramental satisfaction, the "worthy penitential fruits of repentance," cannot be adequately explained in terms of juridical law. Here we go far beyond any juridical category, even though the Latin word *satisfactio,* our "satisfaction," is an analogous term derived from the language of Roman jurisprudence. There is reference to justice, surely, but it is not the petty or narrow commutative justice of law, but the transcendent mystery of the consuming and saving "justice of God."

3. *Penance in Its Salutary and Historic Effectiveness*

The sharp emphasis which the Western Church[145] places on penance under its juridical aspect is not specious juridicism, but an expression of the theocentric orientation which places God in the center of religion and morals. It implies the primacy of the virtue of religion by contrast with moral betterment. For it is of the very heart of religious betterment, the very essence of conversion, that man turn again to the justice and holiness of God with all earnestness. From this very earnestness a true and correct moral betterment will inevitably follow. It is for this reason that the Council of Trent[146] was greatly concerned that an overindulgent penitential discipline which failed to arouse in sinners a vivid sense of atonement due to God might readily lead to superficiality and inconstancy of conversion, if the sinner did not realize the mortal gravity of his offense.

Nevertheless, the Church does not fail to exhort the father confessor to concern himself likewise with the salutary character of penance, which should be proportioned not only to the gravity of the sin committed, but also to the needs, the physical and moral capacity of the penitent.[147] Just as the disposition of sorrow grows deeper and deeper only gradually, so it is with the penance. If sorrow has not reached the profoundest depths, we cannot look for a disposition favorable to severe or austere penance. Repentance and sense of reparation, sorrow and penance, must develop with an equal pace. So closely are they interwoven that they come into existence together and progress together to full maturity.

Abstracting from the reverence for the consuming and purifying holiness of God which it fosters, penance has a most salutary effect as antidote against the evil forces aroused in man by his sins. "Now, the movement whereby one moves away from something is contrary to the movement whereby one approaches it. . . . Consequently, the will must abandon sin by moving in a contrary direction from those movements whereby it was inclined toward sin. Now, it was inclined toward sin by appetition and enjoyment in regard to lower things. Therefore, it must move away from sin by means of certain penances whereby it suffers some injury because of the sin that it has committed. For, just as the will was drawn toward consent to the sin by means of pleasure, so is it strengthened in the detestation of sin by means of penances."[148] We may add that not only the enjoyment of lower things lures one to sin; man is drawn to sin also through the pride of self-will. And penitential acts not only afflict the senses, but they also tend to humble our self-will. Therefore the penances imposed by the confessor as well as our voluntary acts of penance and mortification should, in so far as this is possible, be chosen as direct antidotes to sin and more particularly as remedies correcting the causes of sin.

For a correct understanding of the profound salutary force and the complete religious and moral import of satisfaction, we must study it in the light of the deep "historical" dimension of the human act.[149] The hour of grace, the hour of moral decision, sustains the entire weight and burden of the past and, through the right grasp of the past, an infinite fruitfulness for all the future. The more completely the moral-religious decision captures and "elaborates" the past, the more it opens up new domains of freedom previously closed. Every decision imparts new meaning, not merely to the particular act, but also to the whole past. And the new meaning affects it in its totality. If we fail to transform the perverted past (precisely through imparting this new meaning to it) actively and positively, we must unavoidably bear up with it, sustain it passively as a crushing burden which hampers our freedom and diminishes the value of all our particular acts and attitudes. Just as the disposition of sorrow kills the life nerve of the evil sentiments and attitudes of the past, so the spirit of penance gives to the particular acts the sense of atonement, freeing and redeeming the past, the sense of prayer for pardon, the sense of the virtue of religion which looks to the past in the form of gratitude for pardon attained.

Here we have a striking parallel between our actions and their significance in the context of our past and present and the historic significance of the actions of Christ in the history of salvation. His action is the law of history and the norm for our penance. Really and effectively He entered into the very heart of the history of mankind, opening up the new era of salvation (the new aeon) through the work of redemption. Precisely in so far as and only in so far as it is work of satisfaction, redemption of the old aeon, of the universal guilt of Adam and his progeny, does it open the new era of salvation to mankind. He took upon Himself the whole burden of the past ages with all their sin and evil, by giving to all His holy acts the ·value of satisfaction, of expiatory offering. And therefore those who follow Christ can find no path of freedom for the future unless they humbly bow to this law of the satisfaction of Christ. New meaning must be imparted to our sinful past through grateful fulfillment of the power of atonement given to us in and through Christ.

4. *Following Christ through Sacramental Assimilation to Him*

Through penance we follow Christ in His passion. In the sacrament we are assimilated to Him in His passion and, bearing His cross, we follow Him. The ultimate and deepest meaning of satisfaction is expressed in the truth of our initiation and participation in the mystery of the redemption. Christian penance is more than a mere means of wiping out the penalties for sin still held against us. It is more than the healing of the weakness due to sin—as significant as all this truly is. The ineffable value, the dignity and efficacy of Christian penance derive from our interior objective assimilation to Christ through the sacraments. And this assimilation to Christ is actively and spontaneously expressed in acts of penance. Our sacramental assimilation to Christ, constantly deepened and enriched by works of penance, perfects and ennobles our entire life in the imitation of Christ.[150]

"Penance derives its force from Christ and His passion and forms us into likeness of Him."[151] "The force of the suffering of Christ brings its bounty to us through the sacraments, which make us conform to the passion of Christ."[152] Thus the imperative of grace demanding the spirit of penance calls out to us from the suffering of Christ, inviting us from within, through the sacramental likeness which is within us. "The suffering of Christ obliges us to undertake some satisfactory punishment through which we are made like to Him."[153]

To be obliged to atone means one must expiate a fault. To be permitted to atone is a grace from the passion of Christ, a bounty of grace and a task of grace through the holy sacraments. Among the most sublime forms of the imitation of Christ is expiation through love, manifesting itself in self-renunciation and willingness to suffer in union with Christ.

Whoever has "put on Christ" (GAL 3:27) in baptism, whoever has been stamped with the seal of participation in the priesthood of Christ in baptism, confirmation, and Holy Orders, whoever is united in holy Mass with Christ, the Priest who offers, the sacrificial Lamb who is offered, must in a genuine spirit of penance "put on the Lord Jesus Christ" (ROM 13:14). In union with Christ he must gratefully offer penitential fruits of conversion; putting on Christ also in action and attitude, he must be priest and sacrificial lamb in and through Christ. For the Christian all that is painful and laborious, all mortification and self-denial must have the sacramental quality of penance. They must be expiatory offerings assimilated to the suffering of Christ. With particular eagerness we must embark on the dolorous course of sorrow, of self-accusation and satisfaction imposed in the sacramental tribunal of penance, because through these the assimilation to Christ is directly realized.

The very prayer of the father confessor pronounced over the penitent immediately after the absolution shows the bond with Christ: *"Passio Domini nostri Jesu Christi, merita beatae Mariae Virginis et omnium sanctorum, quidquid boni feceris et mali sustinueris, sint tibi in remissionem peccatorum, augmentum gratiae, et praemium vitae aeternae."* (May the passion of our Lord Jesus Christ, the merits of the Blessed Virgin Mary and of all the saints, and all the good you have done and the evil you have endured, redound to the remission of your sins, the increase of grace, and the reward of eternal life.)

This prayer shows that all our actions and sufferings in some manner are joined in "sacramental" unity with the redemptive suffering of Jesus Christ and with the suffering and good works of Mary and the saints. If our expiation derives its value from this unity with Christ and centers in it, then we must make the dispositions of Christ our own (cf. PHIL 2:4f.). We must unite our sentiments with those of the saints and offer the sacrifice of our satisfactions gratefully and prayerfully, not merely for ourselves but also for all the brethren.

Cardinal Cajetan[154] explains the doctrine of the "treasury of the Church" in the following statement: all the saints as living members of the Body of Christ, united through all their sufferings and good works with the dispositions of Christ, cannot do otherwise than gain merits and offer satisfaction not only for themselves but also for the whole

Church. In former ages the public nature of the penitential discipline of the Church with its public class of penitents, which many pious souls also joined, vividly testified to the salutary sense of corporate solidarity in the work of satisfaction. Though the severity of public penitential discipline is now only a lesson of history, the solidarity in the work of expiation is no less explicitly revealed in the veneration of the Sacred Hearts of Jesus and Mary. Lacking this profound note of reparation, this cult would only too readily descend to the level of a sentimental "devotion." Devotion to the Sacred Heart, to the Holy Cross, and to the Precious Blood of our Redeemer is essentially expiatory.

We can sum up the whole sublime significance of reparation in the pregnant words of the Orthodox theologian, Svietlov: "to form in ourselves the mystical Christ, to become like to the Saviour also in the oblation of the sacrifice of expiation."[155]

5. *The Spirit of Penance: Difficulties*

It is not sufficient for us to make acts of contrition; we must also have the spirit of contrition. Similarly, it is not enough to perform acts of penance; we must also manifest the spirit of penance. The acts of penance must always be kept within bounds of right reason by the virtue of prudence, but such restriction does not excuse one from the spirit of penance. All are obliged to possess the spirit of penance, though not all are called to an explicitly austere penitential life after the manner of many saints. The readiness or disposition to do penance as such should measure up to the gravity of the sins one has committed. But in fact it corresponds to the progress and degree of sorrow and compunction, which in turn are measured by our love for God. The promptness with which one expiates for sin grows only through the growth in love for God and neighbor. To nourish the spirit of penance nothing better can be found than grateful and meditative consideration of the pardon granted us sinners through the suffering and death of Christ. The pledge of the passion and death of Christ in our souls through sanctifying grace should be redeemed in penance and reparation in the spirit of humble gratitude (cf. Lk 7:43) to God for this gift. All our acts should be permeated with this spirit of penance. The reward is exceedingly great.

Postponement of repentance or refusal of repentance because of fear of the pains and humiliations bound up with it springs from the spirit of impenitence, which is the very antithesis of the spirit of penance. If it does no worse, the lack of the true spirit of penance manifests itself in the greatest possible shirking of mortification, in straining after comfort, in entertaining the conviction that there is no need for "second conversion." Many who are far from impenitent may lack the spirit of penance because they do not realize the need for constant conversion and consider themselves repentant.[156]

6. "Fruit Befitting Repentance" (Mt 3:8; Lk 3:8; Acts 26:20)

The true fruit of penance, the fruit of genuine conversion, is the new life of the following of Christ. Nevertheless, the Council of Trent formally condemned the assertion of the Reformers that "the best penance is only the new life"[157] for various reasons: 1) Because they positively excluded penance by expressly rejecting the very works of penance which the Church imposes on the penitent or which he freely imposes on himself.[158] 2) The new life in the mind of the Reformers was a necessary and "automatic" fruit of faith. The element of true freedom of the act was absent. Nor did the Reformers admit that deep sorrow was a prerequisite for the new life. The new life in freedom is not possible without true sorrow and the readiness of penance springing from contrition. 3) The innovators also held that works of penance as such were an insult to the perfect sacrifice of Christ and totally devoid of cultal value.[159]

This false teaching, however, does not represent the universal position of Protestantism today. One noted Protestant theologian of the present period, to cite an example, has the following to say on the point: "Divine expiation renders human expiation as little superfluous as divine pardon make human punishment useless. And likewise without expiation all moral betterment is illusory. Only the one who conceives the just punishment as 'necessary,' and this means as 'expiation,' has had an insight into his injustice and can make himself a better man."[160]

In utter contrast to the errors just explained, we attribute to the new life of the imitation of Christ a truly expiatory value. This new life is truly a carrying of the cross, day by day, and is truly expiatory. Parallel to the penitential works and in many ways surpassing them is expiatory suffering, the prompt willingness to say yes to the divine visitations in the spirit of atonement.[161]

In agreement with tradition, the Council of Trent sums up the grand categories of voluntary penance as "fasting, almsgiving, prayer, and other works of piety."[162] Fasting comprises all voluntary pain, privation, or mortification for the purpose of saying no to all indolence and disordered desire in the spirit of expiation. Almsgiving says no to all egotism and craving for possession and comprises all works of effective love without which all other forms of penance would be worthless and insipid (cf. Is 58:1–7). Prayer includes first of all honor, good fortune, and salvation. In the present state of mankind, prayer is an authentic work of satisfaction if it is steadfast, conscientious, and decorous. However, it would be misleading if we were to give the impression that prayer were penance in the first instance or as such, or that it is the sole practical form of true penance.

As to the sacramental penance imposed in the tribunal of grace, one must bear in mind that the penitent may possess the requisite disposition for absolution, even though he may not yet be disposed for a really suitable penance. Often the confessor must rest content with the indispensable minimum, though he is not permitted as a rule to defer the admonition that God demands from the penitent, if not immediately, then at some later time, the worthy fruits of penance. The penitent who will not accept a relatively modest penance suitable to his capacity is unworthy of absolution. The moderate penance which measures up to the needs and capacities of the penitent is precisely the most suitable test of his dispositions of soul. It is wise to offer the habitual sinner or the relapsed sinner, about whose disposition there is grave reason to doubt, opportunity to refute the presumption which stands against him by imposing a solid wholesome penance (eventually also a "purpose-of-amendment penance"). Such a penance is dependent on the penitent's own earnestness and steadfastness and is effective both as sacramental penance[163] and as voluntary penitential exercise. Thus the confessor might suggest that if the penitent fall again into his sin he immediately receive the sacrament of penance again, if he drink to excess again, that for each instance of drunkenness he give alms to the amount of the price of the drinks, if he curse or swear or use profane language, he recite the Glory be to the Father for each vile word, if he is guilty of unjust or idle gossip about his neighbor's faults, that he recite an Our Father. . . .

The radically different circumstances in our age render any return to the ancient rigor of penitential discipline impossible, but they cannot and do not forbid us to sustain the true spirit of penance. This at least is required of all: to bear the trials and hardships of our daily life in the spirit of renunciation. If we cannot bear them joyfully, we must at least accept them with patience.

7. The Spirit of Penance, Purgatory, and Indulgences

Catholic doctrine and practice concerning purgatory and indulgences[164] constantly remind the faithful of certain important aspects of the doctrine on penance. Particularly significant is the teaching on the communion of saints and the necessity of atonement through works of satisfaction in this life. Through satisfactory works in this life we can fruitfully atone for the remaining temporal punishment due to sin after the guilt has been blotted out. What still is unatoned after this life remains until the soul is cleansed in purgatory. Through the communion of saints our satisfactory and expiatory works are fruitful also for the souls in purgatory. But the suffering in purgatory, it should be noted, adds nothing to the merit of the holy souls.

It would be very superficial, however, to view the doctrine of satisfaction too narrowly or even exclusively in the light of the "removal of temporal punishment due to sin." We should be slighting the essential relation to the following of Christ found in all works of satisfaction, not to speak of their importance in the progress of conversion and the new life, or with reference to the glory of God and the salvation of our neighbor. For this reason it is rather puerile to speak of a simple choice to be made between atoning for temporal punishment in this life or awaiting the stern punishment of purgatory. There is a like point to be stressed regarding indulgences. Rightly considered, they are far from being a dispensation from the earnest disposition of penance. They are rather a constant warning against the neglect of penance and an admonition for us to supplement our defective penitential works by a proportionately deeper spirit of penance and the constant union with the Mystical Body of Christ.

8. The Spirit of Penance and Reparation

The spirit of penance flows primarily from the penitent's perception and realization that he must make restitution for his violation of justice and love in a new spirit of gratitude to God. Consequently, the genuine spirit of penance will induce him to do everything necessary to repair the evil done to his neighbor and the community, a task which at times demands great sacrifice. Reparation must be made for the violation of love, for the scandal caused, for damage of our neighbor's honor or his property. True conversion cannot be reconciled with the will to hold fast to unjust gain or any other profit of our sin (cf. Lk 19:8).

BIBLIOGRAPHY

ACKEN, B. VAN, S.J. *Die Beichte, das Sakrament der Versoehnung, des Friedens.* Paderborn, 1938.

ALLERS, R. "Some Psychological Aspects of Confession," *Conflict and Light (EtCar)*, 51–82. New York: Sheed and Ward, 1953.

ALLIER, R. *La psychologie de la conversion chez les peuples non-civilisés.* 2 Vols. Paris, 1925.

AMANN, E., AND MICHEL, A. "Pénitence," *DTC*, XII, 722–1127.

ANCIAUX, P. *La théologie du sacrement de pénitence au XIIe siècle.* Louvain, 1949.

ANLER, L. *Comes pastoralis confessarii.* Fulda, 1947.

BAUR, B., O.S.B. *Die haeufige Beicht.* 2. Auflage. Freiburg, 1951.

―――. "Die Beicht der laesslichen Suenden. Grundsaetzliches und Praktisches," *ThG*, 35 (August, 1943), 73–82.

BEHM, WUERTHWEIN. "metánoia," *ThW*, IV, 972–1004.

BERBUIR, E. "Theologie des Bussakramentes," *WissWeish* (1952), 81–97.

BERGUER, G. *Traité de psychologie de la religion.* Lausanne, 1946, 49–132.

BEUMER, J., S.J. "Die Andachtsbeichte in der Hochscholastik," *Schol*, 14 (1939), 50–74.

―――. "Andachtsbeichte in der nachtridentinischen Theologie," *Schol*, 13 (1938), 72–86.

―――. "Laessliche Suende und Andachtsbeichte" *Schol*, 11 (1936), 243–250.

BITTER, W. *Angst und Schuld in theologischer und psychologischer Sicht.* Stuttgart, 1953.

―――. *Die Wandlung des Menschen in Seelsorge und Psychotherapie.* Goettingen, 1956.

BLIC, J. DE, S.J. "Sur l'attrition suffisante," *MelScRel*, 1 (1945), 329–366.

BONZELET, H. *The Pastoral Companion*, 11 ed. Chicago: Franciscan Herald Press, 1956.

BRETON, V. M., O.F.M. *La confession fréquent. Histoire, valeur, pratique.* Paris, 1945.

BRUNNER, A. "Aus der Finsternis zum Licht. Ueber das Bekenntnes der Suenden," *Geist-Leben*, 23 (1950), 85–94.

―――. "Reue und Vergebung," *GeistLeben*, 25 (1952), 98–106.

BUKOWSKI, A., S.J. *Die Genugtuung fuer die Suende nach der Auffassung der russischen Orthodoxie.* Paderborn, 1911.

BUYS, L., C.SS.R. "De practijk van biechten en biechthoren," *Uitgave van het Instituut tot voorlichting in die zielzorg van aartsbisdom Utrecht* (1946).

―――. "Devotiebeicht," *Nederl. Kath. Stemmen*, 38 (1938), 193–203, 234–244, 295–311.

CAPELLO, F. M., S.J. *Tractatus canonico-moralis de sacramentis.* T. II: *De poenitentia.* Torino, 1946.

CHANSON, A. *Pour mieux confesser.* 4 éd. Arras, 1951.

CHARRIÈRE, F. *Ego te absolvo. Réflexions sur le sacrement de pénitence à l'usage du clergé.* Mulhouse, 1938.

CHRÉTIEN, P. *De poenitentia.* 2 ed. Metis, 1935.

*CLARK, E. T. *The Psychology of Religious Awakening.* New York, 1929.

DIETRICH, E. K. *Die Umkehr im Alten Testament und im Judentum.* Stuttgart, 1936.

DIRKSEN, ALOYS, C.PP.S. *The New Testament Concept of Metánoia.* Washington, 1932.

DONDAINE, H., O.P. *L'attrition suffisante.* Paris, 1943.

DORONZO, E., O.M I. *De poenitentia.* 3 Vols. Milwaukee, 1951.

ENGELMANN, U. "Heilende Busse," *BM*, 26 (1950), 41–46.

FERNÁNDEZ, ALONZO J. "La disciplina penitencial en España romanovisigoda desde el punto de vista pastoral," *HS* (1951), 243–311.

GALTIER, P. "Le sens du péché à entretenir," *RAM*, 28 (1953), 289–304.

———. "Satisfaction," *DTC*, XIV, 1129–1210.

———. *De Paenitentia. Tractatus dogmatico-historicus.* Editio nova. Roma, 1950.

———. *Aux origines du sacrement de Pénitence. AnalGreg.* Roma, 1951.

GARRIGOU-LAGRANGE, R., O.P. *The Three Ways of the Spiritual Life.* London: Burns-Oates, 1938.

———. *La seconde conversion et les trois voies.* 3 ed. Paris, 1951.

———. *L'Église et le pécheur.* Coll. Cahiers de la Vie Spir. Paris, 1948.

GEWIESS, J. "Metánoia im Neuen Testament," *Die Kirche in der Welt,* 1 (1948), II, 149ff.

GOLDBRUNNER, J. "Vertrauenskrisis im Beichtstuhl," *Anima,* 5 (1950), 229–238, and *Menschenkunde im Dienste der Seelsorge* (1948), 61–70.

GRAEF, R. *Das Sakrament der goettlichen Barmherzigkeit.* Regensburg, 1949.

GROTZ, J. *Die Entwicklung des Busstufenwesen in der vornizaenischen Kirche.* Freiburg, 1955.

GRUEHN, W. *Die Froemmigkeit der Gegenwart. Grundtatsachen der empirischen Psychologie.* Muenster, 1956. Note particularly 40–106, 163–237.

GUARDINI, R. *The Conversion of Augustine.* Westminster, Md.: Newman, 1960.

HÄRING, B., C.SS.R. "Umweltseelsorge im Bussakrament," *LebS,* 6 (1955), 235–245.

———. "Grundzuege der Bekehrung," *LebS,* 7 (1956), 109–114.

———. "Seelenheil und Theozentrik in der Mission," *Paulus,* 20 (1948), Heft 3, 3–15.

———. *Frohes Beichten.* Freiburg, 1956.

HAUSHERR, I., S.J. *Penthos, la doctrine de la componction dans l'Orient chrétien.* Roma, 1944.

HEYNCK, V., O.F.M. "Contritio vera. Zur Kontroverse ueber den Begriff der contritio auf der Bologneser Tagung des Trienter Konzils," *FranzStud,* 33 (1951), 137–179.

HILDEBRAND, D. VON. *Transformation in Christ.* New York: Longmans, 1948.

HIRSCHER, J. B. *Moral,* II, 406–543. Other handbooks of moral theology, e.g. Martin and Dieckhoff, may be consulted with profit.

HOFFER, M. *Metánoia. Bekehrung und Busse im Neuen Testament.* Dissertation. Tuebingen.

HORVATH, A. M, O.P. "Suendenvergebung in sakramental Geschehen," *DivThom* (F), 17 (1939), 133–174. •

HUERTH, F., S.J. *Schuld und Suehne vom psychologischen und fuersorgerlichen Standpunkt aus.* Koeln, 1931.

*JAMES, W. *The Varieties of Religious Experience.* London, 1902.

JANINI CUESTA, J. "La penitencia medicinal desde la Didascalia Apostolorum a S. Gregorio de Nisa," *RevEspT,* 7 (1947), 337–362.

KELLY, G., S.J. *The Good Confessor.* Dublin, 1952.

KRAUTWIG, N., O.F.M. "Die Gefaehrdung und Erneuerung des Bussakraments," *GeistLeben,* 24 (1951), 18–25.

———. "Reue als Tat und Gnade," *GeistLeben,* 22 (1949), 101–110.

———. "Bewaeltigt der moderne Mensch die Suende?" *GeistLeben,* 26 (1953), 20–31.

LANDGRAF, A. "De Lehre der Fruehscholastik von der knechtliehen Furcht," *Dogmengeschichte der Fruehscholastik,* IV, 1 (Regensburg, 1955), 276–354.

———. "Der zur Nachlassung der Schuld notwendige Grad der contritio nach der Lehre der Fruehscholastik," *Dogmengeschichte der Fruehscholastik,* III, 2 (Regensburg, 1955), 244–276.

———. "Suende und Trennung von der Kirche," *Schol,* 2 (1930), 210–248.

———. "Suende und Gliedschaft am geheimnisvollen Leib," *Dogmengeschichte der Fruehscholastik,* IV, 2 (Regensburg, 1956), 48–99.

LE BLOND, J. M. *Les conversions de saint Augustin.* Paris, 1950.

———. *L'Église éducatrice des consciences par pénitence.* Congrès national de Nancy, 1952. 2 éd. Paris, 1953.

LEIST, F. *Kultus also Heilsweg.* 2 Auflage. Salzburg, 1954.

MAINAGE, P., O.P. *La Psychologie de la conversion.* 3 éd. Paris, 1923.

MICHEL, A. "Pénitence et confession aux premiers siècles," *AmCl,* 62 (1952), 708–715.

MILLER, I., S.J. "Katholische Beichte," in the Collective Works: *Medizin—Philosophie—Theologie,* Heft 7 (Innsbruck-Wien, 1946).

MOERS, M. "Zur Psychologie des Reueerlebnisses," *AGP,* 55 (1926), 298–360.

MUELLER, H. J., C.SS.R. *Die ganze Bekehrung. Das centrale Anliegen des Theologen und Seelsorgers J. M. Sailer.* Studia theologiae moralis et pastoralis edita a professoribus Academiae Alfonsianae in Urbe. Salzburg, 1956.

MUELLER, R. *Frohe Botschaft von der Busse. Busse und Beicht im Christenleben.* Stuttgart, 1952.

NÉDONCELLE, H. *J'ai rencontré le Dieu Vivant. Témoignages avec deux études sur la conversion.* Paris, 1925.

NOCK, A. D. *RACh* (Th. Klauser, 9 Lieferung, Stuttgart, 1951), 105–118.

O'BRIEN, C., O.F.M. *Perfect contrition.* Dublin, 1952.

ODDONE, A. "I fattori della conversione religiosa. Le vie di Dio nelle conversioni," *CC,* 91 (1940), 32–41, 184–196.

ORAISON, M. "Suende, Beichte und Tiefenpsychologie," *Anima,* 7 (1952), 131–143.

PENIDO, M. T. L. *La conscience religieuse. Typologie de la conversion.* Paris, 1935, 41–131.

PERINELLE, J., O.P. *L'attrition d'après le concile de Trente et d'après saint Thomas d'Aquin.* Kain, 1927.

PIGLIARU, A. *Saggio sul valore morale della pena.* Sassari, 1952.

POHLMANN, H. *Die Umkehr als Zentralbegriff der christlichen Froemmigkeit.* Leipzig, 1938.

POSCHMANN, B. *Busse und letzte Oelung. Handbuch der Dogmengeschichte.* Band 4, Fasc. 3. Freiburg, 1951.

———. "Die innere Struktur des Bussakramentes," *MThZ,* 1 (1950), Heft 3, 12–30.

———. *Paenitentia secunda. Die kirchliche Busse im aeltesten Christentum.* Bonn, 1940.

———. *Die abendlaendische Kirchenbusse im Ausgang des christlichen Altertums.* Muenchen, 1928.

———. *Die abendlaendische Kirchenbusse im fruehen Mittelalter.* Breslau, 1930.

POST, L. "Zur Kontroverse der Andachtsbeichte," *ThG,* 31 (1939), 40–52. Cf. *BullThom,* 5 (1939), 553–564.

RAHNER, K., S.J. "Vergessene Wahrheiten ueber das Bussakrament" *GeistLeben,* 26 (1953), 339–364.

———. "Schuld und Schuldvergebung als Grenzgebiet zwischen Theologie und Psychotherapie," *Schriften zur Theologie,* II (Einsiedeln, 1955), 279–297.

———. "Das Gebet der Schuld," *GeistLeben,* 22 (1949), 90–100.

———. "Vom Sinn der haeufigen Andachtsbeicht," *ZAM,* 9 (1934), 323–336.

———. "Zur Theologie der Busse bei Tertullian," *Festschrift fuer Karl Adam* (Duesseldorf, 1952), 129–167.

———. "Die Busslehre im Hirten des Hermas," *ZKathTh,* 77 (1955), 385–431.

———. "Die Busslehre des hl. Cyprian von Karthago," *ZKathTh,* 74 (1952), 257–276, 381–438.

RUS, G. N. *De munere sacramenti paenitentiae in aedificando Corpore Christi mystico ad mentem S.Thomae.* Romae, 1944.

SACHLIM, H. "Die Fruechte der Umkehr. Das moralische Fundament der Predigt Johannes des Taufers, Christi und der urspruenglichen Kirche, beleuchtet durch LK 3:10–14, *StTh,* 1 (1947), 54–68.

SAILER, J. M. *Handbuch der christlichen Moral,* I, 462–568.

SCHELER, M. "Reue und Wiedergeburt," *Vom Ewigen im Menschen.* 3 Auflage. Berlin, 1933, 5–58.

SCHELFHOUT, O. "De psychologie van bekoring en zonde, Wroeging en berow," *ColGand,* 26 (1939), 88–100, 176–189, 235–250.

SCHMAUS, M. "Reich Gottes und Bussakrament," *MThZ,* 1 (1950), Part 1, 20–37.

SCHNAKENBURG, R. "Typen der Metanoiapredigt im Neuen Testament," MThZ, 1 (1950), Part 4, 1–13.

SCHOELLGEN, W. "Psychotherapie und sakramentale Beichte," *Aktuelle Moralprobleme* (Duesseldorf, 1955), 106–118. Cf. also the same title in *Cath,* 1 (1932), 145ff.

SCHREIBMAYR, F. "Busse als Heilsvorgang," *Christliche Besinnung.* 6, 31–61. Wuerzburg (no date).

SCHURR, V., C.SS.R. "Theologie des Bussakramentes," *Paulus,* 22 (1950), 2, 102ff.

SEELHAMMER, N. "Recht und Pflicht der Frage des Beichtvaters," *TrThZ,* 61 (1952), 96–106.

SEMMELROTH, O., S.J. "Theologisches zur haeufigen Beicht," *ThG,* 40 (1950), 4–12.

SHEEN, FULTON. *Peace of Soul.* Note the Psychology of Conversion.

SIEGMUND, G. "Schuld und Entsuehnung," *StimmZeit,* 137 (1939/40), 324–332.

SPICQ, C., O.P. "La penitencia impossible (HEB 6:4–6)," *CiTh,* (1952), 358–368.

STAKEMEIER, E. "Glaube und Busse in den Trienter Rechtfertigungsverhandlungen," *RoemQschr,* 43 (1935), 157–177.

TER HAAR, C.SS.R. *De occasionariis et recidivis juxta doctrinam S. Alphonsi aliorumque probatorum auctorum.* Torino, 1939.

VIEUJEAN, J. "Echtes und falsches Schuldgefuehl," *Anima,* 9 (1954), 245–266.

VISSER, J., C.SS.R. "De excusatione a praecepto integritatis confessionis propter defectum temporis," *Euntes docete,* 3 (1950), 75–88.

VOGEL, C. *La discipline pénitentielle en Gaule, des origines à la fin du VIIe siècle.* Paris, 1952.

WALTER, E. *Das Siegel der Versoehnung. Die Ueberwindung von Schuld und Suende des Christen im Sakrament der Busse.* Freiburg, 1938.

WUNDERLE, G. "Zur Psychologie der Reue," *ARP,* II/III (1921), 39–108.

ZIMMERMANN, F. *Laessliche Suende und Andachtsbeichte.* Innsbruck, 1935.

ZOERLEIN, J. *Die oeftere Beicht. Pastoraltheologische Gedanken zur Verwaltung des Busz-sakramentes.* Stuttgart, 1947.

Additional Works in English

BOUTIN, L. *Penance: The Most Human of the Sacraments. Ottawa;* University of Ottawa Press, 1954.

GALTIER, P., S.J. *Sin and Penance.* London: Sands, 1932.

HEENAN, J. *Priest and Penitent.* New York: Sheed and Ward, 1937.

HEINISCH, P. *Theology of the Old Testament.* Collegeville, Minn.: The Liturgical Press, 1950.

LEMONNYER, A., O.P. *The Theology of the New Testament.* London: Sands, 1929.

PHILIPON, M., O.P. *The Sacraments in the Christian Life.* Westminster, Md.: Newman, 1955. Cf. 181–212.

Periodical Literature In English

CONGAR, Y. M., O.P. "Idea of Conversion," *Thought,* 33 (Spring, 1958), 5–20.

LAVARD, B. "Sin, Penance, and Compunction," *CrossCr,* 9 (Mr. 1957), 24–44.

LETTER, P. DE, S.J. "Vi Clavium ex Attrito Fit Contritus," *ThSt,* 16 (S. 1955), 424–32.

———. "Two Concepts of Attrition and Contrition," *ThSt,* 11 (March, 1950), 3–33.

WINZEN, D. "Metánoia: Penance: Virtue and Sacrament," *Orate Fratres,* 25 (Mr. 1951), 145–51.

Part Six:

GROWTH AND PERFECTION IN THE FOLLOWING OF CHRIST THE CHRISTIAN VIRTUES

CHAPTER THIRTEEN

THE VIRTUES IN GENERAL

1. *Virtue as Ideal*

IN THE past century the prevalence of bourgeois ethos created a spirit of cynical disdain for virtue. "For some, virtue was a shrewish old spinster, toothless and wrinkled";[1] for others it was mere braggadocio or futile bravado; for many it was but ineffectual mediocrity. By contrast, in classical Hellenism virtue was the shining splendor of the magnanimous spirit aspiring to the loftiest summit of moral excellence. It was the perfection of harmony and the true wealth of the noble mind utterly devoted to the good. Yet there was a fatal defect in this ancient concept of virtue; it was anthropocentric. It centered in man. For the ancients, virtue did not consist in worshiping God.

For the Christian, virtue is unique and inimitable; and yet it imposes on us the obligation to imitate the "goodness and loving-kindness" toward men, the humility and sublimity, the selfless love of Christ. Christ taught us what virtue is, above all in His own all-embracing love. What virtue is appears in the very excess of His loving sacrifice by which He offered Himself for the glory of God and the salvation of mankind. In Christ there is the most tremendous union of opposites without force or constraint. In Him is the most perfect and harmonious balance of virtue with all the haunting beauty of consummate goodness.

Virtue is steadfastness and facility in doing good springing from the very heart of man. *"Virtus est bona qualitas mentis, qua bene vivitur, qua nemo male utitur."*[2] (Virtue is a quality of inner goodness through which one lives well, through which one avoids acting badly.) One who is endowed with great gifts can use the wealth of his endowments for good as well as for evil. But virtue is that inner equipment of the forces of the soul which is turned exclusively to the good life and which cannot be misused. It transcends noble endowment and capacity. It is a permanent capacity (*habitus, héxis*) of the soul's powers assuring that constancy in good action which makes a man true to himself in the multiple hazards of decision and in the most diverse situations in life.

Virtue is much more than bravery of a sort. It is the perfect accord with the good, the most basic harmony with what is good. To be virtuous means more than to decide for the good in a general way, for the virtuous man is completely taken up with the good in the profoundest depths of his personality and to the final and ultimate external activity in the use of his freedom. Perfect virtue is the fundamental right attitude so deep-seated as to have become a kind of second nature. From this point of view, virtue is one, not diverse. To be chaste and no more, to be moderate and no more, or merely just, is not as such the same as to be virtuous simply and without qualification. To be virtuous one must be taken up with the good in its whole depth and breadth.

The Greeks looked upon prudence as the sum and summit of virtue. To be prudent in the sense understood in Hellenic intellectualism was to manifest the most comprehensive virtue. Much is to be said for this approach to virtue, for only one who is fully conversant with the good and has a truly interior and profound sense of the good can discern the good correctly in every situation and instance. Such judgment springing from deep intimacy with the good also guarantees its accomplishment in our actions. On the contrary, one who fails to pierce the very heart of the good in his practical judgment cannot be assured of any harmonious accomplishment of the good. For the Greek (Aristotle, Plato) whose philosophical orientation was toward being, merely subjective dispositions were not sufficient to constitute real virtue or prove its existence. For him virtue opens the door to reality. It is open to objective reality and truly realizes it. For him the essential element of virtue was prudence responding to the demands of being in its judgment and its command. Beyond this right response to objective reality, there still persisted in the appraisal of prudence as highest virtue a bit of the Socratic optimism, according to which virtue could be taught. To know well was assurance of doing well.

We would not raise any objection to this esteem of prudence as the comprehensive virtue, were it clearly implied that prudence had love for the good at its very heart. There is no objection if prudence is understood in the sense of the Biblical "wisdom," the goodness which "savors" (*sapere, sapientia*) only the good, which goes far beyond the purely theoretical and speculative in distinguishing good and evil and with delicate sense and tact of conscience points to love in the heart of the good.

The Christian does not presume on his own powers to acquire the prudence which is wisdom. Its source is the teaching and example of Christ, and it is a gift of His Spirit breathing it into our heart, the Spirit of wisdom and love. This wisdom, for which the cross of Christ is not at all folly, can be only a grace from above (*agápe*) flowing from God's own loving revelation of Himself in Christ. Its grand ideal is the mission of fulfilling the great commandment of love in the following of Christ.

It does not condemn the Hellenic ideal of harmony and balance in human good which is sought after in the perfection of the mean (*mesótes*, as the loftiest evaluation of prudence which determines and decides upon the just balance or right proportion, the middle way in all things), but far surpasses it. The Christian ideal of virtue is not man himself and human prudence or the mere balance and harmony of human life.

The fount of virtue, the center and measure of virtue, the goal of virtue is the love of God. For the Christian, virtue in its most comprehensive sense is love. To be virtuous means to abandon oneself to the love of God which gives itself to us. It is the imitation of the love of Christ, the heroic renouncement of self, the outburst of love for God and neighbor. Though, of course, this love is folly to the pagans, it reveals itself as "wisdom," as true prudence, to the mind of the disciple of Christ, who perceives because he loves. The task of "prudence" as a Christian virtue is above all to point the way to love. In the spirit of faith and with the help of the gifts of the Holy Spirit it opens the way for the entry of love.

Augustine in his time clearly proposed this primordial law of Christian virtue. For him the cardinal virtues of the Greeks are no longer the summit, but the way to divine love; they are instruments of divine love. Virtue in its fullest sense is that which places the life of the soul in order, for the right order in living is consequent on the right order in loving. To love rightly is to possess perfect virtue, for the order of love is the order of charity (*"ordo amoris, ordo caritatis"*). Only the love of God with the noble retinue of virtues animated by it can establish this order in the soul, so that it can rightly perceive the true hierarchy of all the values of love and respond to them. Every order of love, that is, every virtue centers in the free orientation of man to God, the supreme and most lovable good. Therefore it can have no other source than God bestowing Himself upon us with His love: from Him comes all its force and power.

There is a vast difference between this authentic concept of Christian virtue and the false notion which views virtue merely as something negative, as mere restraint of evil or avoidance of evil. That man is truly virtuous who is inwardly equipped for the fulfillment of the great commandment of love. That man is virtuous who is conscious of the source of his virtue. He realizes that he has been endowed by the love of God and does not glory in himself as though virtue derives from his own efforts.

2. The Many Virtues

All the grand ethical systems conceive of the many particular virtues as included in one fundamental or primary virtue or attitude of soul. For the Greek it is prudence or, more specifically, wisdom. For the Stoic, with his pride of virtue, it is the interior order of reason in the wise man who will not allow any passion to disturb his emotional balance and poise of mind (the *apátheia*). For Kant there is practically only one virtue, the supreme and universal sense of duty, even though there are many particular virtuous duties or tasks. For the Christian it is the abandonment to God's loving self-giving which demands the free response of our gratitude in return.

Just as there is no unanimity in the schools of moral thought in determining the primary virtue in which all others are centered and united, so there is no accord in distinguishing and classifying the many particular virtues in which the basic virtue manifests itself. There is what might be called the subjective tendency based on the teaching of Plato according to which the particular virtues are specified and grouped according to the powers and faculties of the soul, which are placed in right order by the particular virtues. Thus the four cardinal virtues especially are coordinated through their relation with the four powers of the soul: prudence corresponds to the intellectual power in its practical aspect; justice gives to the will firmness in relation to the known right; temperance restrains the affective life in its longings and desires; fortitude (courage) controls the affective life in its impulses to vehemence and anger (aggressive acts). Whoever accepts this explanation of the multiplicity of virtues must find a way of subordinating all the other particular virtues as potential parts of one or other of these four.

Aristotle holds that the virtues are specified by their object. In this sense his position is objective. The virtues viewed under this aspect are determined by the particular domain of value to which each virtue is related and directed. The Christian teaching on the virtues goes very far in the direction of Aristotle. And with special stress the modern theory which correlates virtue with values (the application to objective value) sees no other way to explain its intrinsic nature except through this relation. The unity of virtue rests in the unity of good in God. Plurality of virtue corresponds strictly to plurality of moral values.

Thomas reconciles and combines the two points of view: virtue is diversified according to the powers of the soul in so far as it opens up to them and gives to each of them the good it demands. And like the acts of the powers and virtues, so the virtues themselves are ultimately determined and specified by their object (*specificatio ab objecto*). Ultimately and in the final analysis the particular virtue is perfect only if it takes its place in the integral hierarchy of all the virtues and is rooted in the primary and basic virtue in which all are centered. Should one, for example, act justly but not chastely, it is quite evident that he does not exercise justice because of a profound love of the good. Obviously he has not pressed on to the very heart of this virtue. He is not centered in the indissoluble totality of the good summoning him to integral perfection, beyond which ultimately God, the Lord of all good, stands. There is a measure of agreement between this position and the thesis of the ancient Stoics, according to which man is good in all virtues or good in none. Possession of one virtue implies possession of all the rest.

Splendor and dignity of particular value can exist only in concert with the whole hierarchy of values. Individual virtue is truly authentic as order and beauty only if it is set in the entire order of all virtues. If we take prudence as an example, we should make the point that every particular virtue, if it is to be perfect, presupposes the existence of perfect prudence as constant and correct appreciation and judgment, both in general and in particular, regarding the good as the heart and center of all virtue. Such perfect prudence in relation to one virtue is possible only if it is perfect prudence in the most comprehensive sense, prudence simply and as such. From the Christian viewpoint, or from the standpoint of the primacy of love, the principle may be stated in the following terms: whoever possesses perfect love, must manifest love in its full integrity, love with all its necessary elements and in all its areas.

Theoretically and speculatively this position is altogether unassailable. But actual life vexes the theologian in this very area by calling for solution of many thorny problems, as we may see in the brilliant novel of Graham Greene, *The Power and the Glory*. In this brilliant piece of fiction the "whiskey priest" manifests heroic humility, unselfishness, and a spirit of sacrifice, an invincible spirit of faith and love, and yet he is a sot. With such an example in mind, we should say that the Stoic doctrine would be verified—that man has all virtues or none at all—if man were psychically perfect. But it is altogether conceivable that a man be grounded in virtue to a certain serious depth and yet, at least according to all appearance, fail partially, or even totally, in one or the other particular virtue.

The riddle is explained ultimately by the wounded condition of fallen man. In the present instance there are certain psychic defects in the constitution of an otherwise entirely responsible man, which seriously handicap him in certain points. According to his inner spirit the whiskey priest is not a toper. He abhors his "vice." But in his condition his free will is not sufficiently powerful to overcome the excessive resistance of his nature to the perfect good. Defect of a particular virtue in its exterior exercise is not always to be accounted for by an absence of fundamental dedication to the good. Fundamentally and in the depth of his character one may be devoted to the good, and the inner beauty and loftiness of virtue may be apparent to him. But the effort demanded of him is very great. Often the narrowness and prejudice of social pressures from the world around him rob him of much of his independence, or combine with his own psychic limitations to weaken his will.

The whiskey priest in Greene's novel, at any rate, is a strictly borderline case. It cannot be considered normal or usual, for the presence of such deep humility, such readiness for sacrifice and love of enemies, is ordinarily so effective in fortifying the interior freedom and healing the psychic defects of man's nature that no such striking contradiction between the grandeur of the total virtue and the flagrant lack of particular virtue is possible. "True holiness demands, effects, and really is the most exalted health of soul."[3]

From the standpoint of attachment to virtue, that is to say, from the point of view of the radical adherence to the good as such, the struggle of the poor whiskey priest for temperance is more perfect virtue than the total abstinence of an epicure who forgoes drinking entirely in order to indulge more freely in other delights of life. Obviously, the "temperance" of the whiskey priest (viewed in the light of the requirement of the perfection of virtue that it be exercised with ease, joy, constancy) is very far removed from perfection.

If it were established that his intemperate drinking was a grave and deliberate fault of his will, this very fact would prove in any instance that the unfortunate man not only lacked all real attachment to the virtue of temperance, but also to the very nature of good itself. It would be proof that even his many good qualities were not really virtues at all flowing from a deep and genuine attitude of goodness. They could be only inborn or acquired inclinations, the beautiful ruins of an edifice decayed from within, for a decisive characteristic of every virtue is its basic attachment to all good as such. In every virtue man says yes to all that is good.

3. Acquired and Infused Virtues

a. Virtue as Infused Power

The immense contrast between the Stoics' haughty concept of virtue and the Christian idea is brought into sharpest relief in the teaching on the infused virtues. This infusion of virtue means that the special equipment of the powers of the soul for the Christian life of virtue flows directly from God's generous love. God does not merely confer supernatural character and value on the various acts of virtue through the cooperation of actual grace, but He sanctifies the very root and source of these acts through the infusion of the supernatural virtues.

It is the clear teaching of the Church that with sanctifying grace the supernatural virtues of faith, hope, and love are also infused into the soul.[4] Because of this, the permanent power to make acts of faith, hope, and love, with the help of actual grace, has the express quality of a gift of divine love.

Theologians commonly hold that, in addition to the theological virtues, also the supernatural moral virtues are infused into the soul,[5] as powers or dispositions. This common teaching is based on a declaration of Innocent III[6] and the Council of Vienne.[7] "Together with the baptismal grace the noble retinue of all the virtues enters the soul."[8]

It does not follow simply from the infusion of the moral virtues that man is spared effort in the acquisition of moral perfection. According to very many theologians, the infused virtues do not in themselves impart any facility at all in the exercise of virtue. They do no more than elevate the basic powers supernaturally, informing and equipping them for the supernatural exercise of virtue. On such a basis the aid of grace makes possible a supernatural activity and eventual facility in the moral life of man.

Our doctrine on the infused moral virtues clearly reveals the source and basis and also the end and goal of Christian virtue: the foundation and source is the Holy Spirit with His transforming and renovating grace; end and goal are Christ and the Father, the imitation of the spirit of Christ through the force of His Spirit.

The life of virtue in the Christian consciousness is essentially more than performance based on law or abstract idea. It means to be transformed in the Spirit of Christ, sustained through the love and example of Christ, active imitation of the virtues of Christ, and formation of our life in them by means of the supernatural forces which attach man to Christ in bonds of grace.

Noteworthy is the explanation of the supernatural character of the Christian virtues given by Michael Sailer. "Virtue is called Christian because it is found in the disciples and friends of Christ. It is the overwhelming force of the resolution to conform to the laws of the most exalted sanctity and justice in accordance with the teaching, the example, and the spirit of Christ, and under the influence of His Holy Spirit."[9] "I will conform to the divine and eternal both interiorly and exteriorly, in order to give glory to the divine and eternal: this is the dominant sentiment which forms the very nature of virtue and its end and purpose."[10] There are three characteristic adornments of Christian virtue, according to Sailer: conformity to the divine, first as law, secondly as formal pattern, thirdly as ultimate end and purpose.[11]

The Christian virtues, and this refers not only to the theological virtues but to the moral virtues as well, are divinely given powers, are interior possession of our being by the virtue of Christ. In this, Christian virtue is most sharply distinguished from all laborious efforts at self-perfection, in which striving for virtue centers entirely in the petty human ego. Christian virtue has its source of power in Christ and tends with exalted end and aim toward Christ.

Christian virtue as directly and immediately infused by God carries with it the duty of most humble submission to God, the Giver of all virtue-powers, and to Christ, the Model of every virtue and above all of humility. Only through humility, which attributes nothing to oneself but, on the contrary, with a perfection of loyalty far transcending the demands of mere law, refers all to God, does virtue attain the noblest splendor of beauty. Nothing could obscure even the "mightiest" of virtues so much as self-complacent contemplation of one's own ego, which attributes to itself the whole achievement of virtue, whereas in all truth and reality its fundamental source is God.

b. Virtue as Acquired Facility

Man can attain moral perfections even without the infused virtues. The natural likeness of his soul to God endows him with the inclination and power to do good. But without the inner formation through the Holy Spirit, all his efforts can acquire no more than purely moral virtue. The moral-religious supernatural virtue transcends all such efforts. And the purely moral virtue is true virtue only in so far as it is, at least in tendency, orientated toward God, toward religion. Its religious supernatural value, that is, its character as virtue of the disciple of Christ, begins only with the infusion of a new power by God, a power which assimilates the soul with Christ.

As far as appearances and the external efforts to attain moral perfection are concerned, we cannot make a clear-cut distinction between the infused moral virtues on the one hand and the merely natural virtues on the other. However, the entire orientation of virtue and its interior form differ from the merely natural moral virtue if such virtue is sustained by the infused supernatural habit, if it is virtue in the school of the divine Master, if it is enlightened by faith, animated by hope and love, and in the profoundest source of its strength assimilated to the Spirit of Christ.

The scholastic notion of virtue stresses particularly the constancy, facility, and perfection of its exercise, qualities acquired in considerable part by habitual repetition of acts. However, nothing could be more false than to place the principal stress on repetition and habit, particularly on mere mechanical exercise and material habit. "Virtue is the very antithesis of mere habit."[12] Habit and exercise can never take the place of the decision, always fresh and free, for the good, based on the inner spirit with its intimate sentiment for good. If habit degenerating into mere routine or unreflecting repetition supplants the vital engagement of the person, virtue is dead. On this point Kant is correct in stating that "virtue is moral force in pursuit of its duty, which should never become a habit, but always spring from the spirit as entirely fresh and creative."[13] "Virtue is neither Stoic indifference (apáthia) nor mechanical habit, but a spiritual power of joyful achievement. Nor is it superficial virtuosity. It is the child of profound decision, even when it is a permanent disposition for the good. But it remains animated by joyful acceptance of the value which is hidden in it. This consent to value is love of value, and consequently virtue is possible only where there is true insight into value and love of value."[14] The most decisive factor in virtue is the profound hold upon us exerted by the value with which it is invested. This relation to value exalts virtue immeasurably above the mere observance of law through fear of punishment or hope of reward. Virtue thrives whether nourished by profound consciousness of value or animated by an enthusiastic love for the good.

Despite all this, we are not permitted to minimize habit and exercise of virtue. Particularly in our fallen state, the frailty of our nature is very great and the exterior obstacles to the good multitudinous. Under such adverse circumstances it is not easy to accomplish good without the facility and suppleness of habit generated by the faithful exercise of many good acts. Nevertheless, should the force of freedom resulting from insight into value and the love of value be dissipated, the habit itself will soon collapse. At best, if habit is supported by natural inclinations or by the force of perseverance, it furnishes a provisional barrier of defense against the multiple attack of sin.

c. Virtue, Striving for Virtue, Beauty of Virtue

It is a cherished thought of Max Scheler that the truly good action does not flow so much from striving for happiness as from the inner fulness of beatitude itself, and that the good man loves virtue, not so much in order to grow rich in goodness, but that he rather loves virtue because of his own inner wealth of goodness. There is an aspect of truth in both phases. We must always do the good if we are to become good at all, if we are to acquire a facility in doing good, if we are to merit increase of the infused virtue. In fact, the ultimate end of the good is not the virtuous quality of one's own self but obedience to God and love for Him. And yet it is also true that the good act presupposes goodness of being. To do good, one must also be good. There can be no genuine exercise of virtue without an interior wealth of virtue or at least a certain measure of inner virtue. This point is evident from our doctrine on actual grace, which is "helping" grace, and even more so from our teaching on the infused moral virtues. Only because we bear within us the power or faculty for good (we must note that this power is given to us and remains in us under peril of loss through our own frailty) can we do the good, developing the facility in doing good. In so far as we do good, in so far as we exploit the inner power of the virtue already existing within us, can we gain a higher degree of aptitude and through the grace of God also a higher degree of the infused power. (This is not to deny that even the sinner can do supernaturally good acts with the aid of grace.)

The virtuous man acts virtuously because of the wealth of virtue within him and by this very activity in turn grows inwardly richer in virtue. And the less he ponders his own enrichment in this process and the more he devotes himself to the good because of inner affinity to it, the more will he be enriched through the bounty of grace.

We cannot at all increase the infused virtues by any direct action on our part, in so far as these virtues are infused. By doing good, we can only merit such increase through the grace of God. But we can directly increase our facility in the acquired virtues through constant practice of them, at the very least to the extent that the new acts of virtue surpass in intensity the existing measure of the power and facility of the virtues. But if the good acts in the exercise of virtue are remiss and do not respond to this measure and lag behind the existing degree of the interior power of the virtue for a considerable time, this is always a sign of excessive weakening of the aptitude of the virtuous habit, though not necessarily of a diminution of the infused virtue itself, for its degree and growth are usually held to be proportionate to the degree and increase of sanctifying grace which is not diminished even by venial sin.

Virtue is interior riches and interior beauty, which are often reflected in our countenance and in our external work. These riches are all the more beautiful the less the man of virtue ponders it himself. The éclat of virtue is still more pleasing to God and man the more the virtuous man himself, despite his wealth of virtue, is convinced he must still strive for it ceaselessly, as though he is far from possessing it. For the greater the wealth of the power and capacity for good, the broader are the horizons revealing new tasks and realms of virtue.

The man of virtue does not do good in the first instance with his own self-improvement uppermost in mind. And in so far as he reflects on himself, he sees the potentialities for good as obligations still to be fulfilled rather than the good he already possesses. The virtuous man is inebriated with the beauty of virtue, not so much as it exists within himself or in his capacity or facility of performance. Much rather he perceives the nobility and sublimity of the values of virtue as inviting and summoning him to greater heights of goodness. Virtue is to him a mistress whose "inner nobility first of all places obligation upon him."[15]

Most beautiful in virtue is the splendor of the good in one who himself is unaware of it. It is the espousal of the seeker of virtue with the haunting beauty of the value of virtue in the nuptial chamber of human liberty. Virtue is real and vital only in man. It does not flutter in the firmament above us as virtue, but at best as an ideal inviting and summoning us. Surely the Christian does not look upon himself as confronting an idealistic demand of an abstract value or ideal. He faces the infinitely perfect Christ, in whom virtue in the profoundest sense becomes incarnate.

Human virtue here below never attains its full perfection. In fact, in this earthly vale of pilgrimage virtue is rarely without conflict. But even under assault virtue grows strong because the real source of its strength is not in man but in the grace of God. "I can do all things in him who strengthens me" (PHIL 4:13).

In Christian virtue the triumphant dawn of the new era breaks, and endless vistas open to the final goal of all things. Christian virtue is powerful in combat through the power of the passion of Christ and is the incipient revelation and realization of the victory of Christ. And in Christ it is constantly on the march to the full and perfect epiphany of the glorious kingdom of God.[16]

It does not pertain to the essence of virtue that it should eliminate all painful effort and sorrow and remove all exterior obstacles to its exercise. But still in the very assault of temptation and in the mortal conflict with evil there shines in Christian virtue the light of deliverance, the glow and thrill of holy joy. "Only vice or the lack of virtue renders the doing of good difficult and toilsome, whereas the possession of virtue imparts to every good action a certain sweetness and light, which calls to mind the blithesomeness and beauty of a lovely bird fluttering in the sunlight."[17]

The acquisition of virtue presupposes all the sweat and toil of tremendous effort. But the pain and sweat of effort do not constitute the virtue. They cannot even produce virtue, for virtue is above all else a "free gift of grace for whose joyful acceptance all effort and strain of will are only the necessary preparation."[18]

Christian virtue flows from the riches of love received and at the same time increases this very wealth which is its source. In origin and goal it is "religion": man's bond with God realized through God, and the homage rendered to God by man and God's "homage" to man. In its source, in its approach, in its end, it is beatitude, for it is the gift of God all-blessed. Fulfilled through the joyous riches of grace, it in turn prepares the way for the highest riches of eternal fulfillment. But it is apparent that the path of Christian virtue reaches to Calvary and passes under the shadow of the cross of Christ.

CHAPTER FOURTEEN

THE CARDINAL VIRTUES

IN THE *Secunda Secundae* Saint Thomas first treats the three theological virtues and then takes up the four cardinal virtues. This very arrangement in itself, and even more so the text as such, makes it clear that the actual foundations, the "hinges" (*cardines*) of the Christian life of virtue are not the four cardinal virtues, but the theological virtues. (Our arrangement is not in opposition to this order of Saint Thomas.[19] Here we take up the cardinal virtues and explain them principally only as fundamental attitudes. We treat their intrinsic tasks according to the theological virtues.) Nevertheless, in the actual presentation of the moral virtues from early patristic times, the Stoic scheme of four basic virtues, already found in Aristotle and Plato, has been followed. With rhythmic beauty the Book of Wisdom refers to the four: "What is richer than wisdom, which maketh all things? . . . And if a man love justice: her labors have great virtues; for she teacheth temperance, and prudence, and justice, and fortitude, which are such things as men can have nothing more profitable in life" (Wis 8:5-7).

Though Saint Ambrose in this tradition externally follows the scheme of four cardinal virtues in their Stoic form, in content these virtues are for him the means and the approach to the love of God, the first rays of the life of grace in moral activity. This Christian form and aspect of the cardinal virtues is particularly clear in Augustine: "Since virtue leads us to the blessed life, I maintain that virtue is nothing other than supreme love for God. For as I understand it, the fourfold virtue is no more than a diversity of the effect of one same love. Thus those four virtues (would that they would be found with the same value in the hearts as the words are on the lips of all) I define without any hesitation as follows: temperance is love bestowing itself fully and without reserve on the object loved; fortitude is love gladly enduring everything for the beloved; justice is love serving the beloved alone and therefore ruling others rightly; prudence is love wisely discerning the means leading to the beloved amid the obstacles which would bar the way. But we have already noted that the object loved is not simply any object indifferently, but God, supreme good, supreme wisdom, supreme peace. We may with a slight variation define these virtues in this way: temperance is love serving God totally and without corruption; fortitude is love gladly suffering all for God's sake; justice is love serving God alone and thus ruling all else with reason and right order; prudence is love clearly discerning what is helpful and what is hindrance on the path to God."[20]

In the area of the moral virtues the cardinal virtues rightly occupy the first place both as general attitudes and as special virtues. As general attitudes they are effective in each moral virtue at the very least as prerequisites. Prudence points the way of the good; it places practical reason in right order. Justice gives the right orientation to the will; it looses the grip of selfishness in matters of objective justice and right. Temperance maintains a balance in the appetites (concupiscible) of desire, holding to the right mean between dullness and lust. Fortitude (courage) keeps the aggressive (irascible) appetite under control, maintaining a balance between timidity and insolence. Prudence and justice order and regulate the two spiritual powers of the soul, while temperance and fortitude control sensual desire and rebellion, thus keeping the principal psychosomatic capacities in order.

Viewed as a special virtue, prudence is the art of right counsel and guidance; justice is the fulfillment of the obligation to pay what is strictly due to others to the point of equality; fortitude is the spirited engagement for the good even at the risk of life and limb; temperance is the disciplining of sensual desire, particularly through chastity.

I. PRUDENCE

The moral conscience resting in the spiritual nature of man orientates his spiritual forces to the good, to the will of God. In the dictate of conscience he hears the demand of his spiritual nature that he do good (the command of God), that he choose the concrete value present here and now (*hic et nunc*). Conscience does not merely whisper this command faintly and as from afar, but enunciates it with such force and clarity that the claim of the good is simultaneously the demand of the profoundest depths of his spiritual being itself.

How must man be equipped to discern rightly in the reality which is creation and the reality which is redemption his duty in each instance? How equipped to know what shall be done in every case, recognizing the will of God in each given moment, in the "hour of grace"? How equipped so that his decision and effort are suited to the needs of the kingdom of God? The answer is that, above all, he must be endowed with the virtue of prudence. In so far as it is the Christian virtue of prudence, it must be in the last analysis a profound docility: we see in Christian prudence the manner in which we, taught by God, are in turn docile to His inspirations.

1. *The Inspired Concepts of Prudence*

As all wisdom, so prudence must be considered a gift of God: "The Lord giveth wisdom: and out of his mouth cometh prudence and knowledge" (Prv 2:6). Eternal Wisdom itself is the teacher of prudence (cf. Wis 8:7—the noted passage which refers to the four cardinal virtues). It is only through a divine gift in Christ that we become rich "in all wisdom and prudence"; therefore, this is one of the principal objects of our prayer (Eph 1:8ff.). Eternal Wisdom itself says emphatically: "prudence is mine" (Prv 8:14; cf. 8:11; 10:23). This is so true that without wisdom as gift of the Eternal Wisdom there can be no true prudence at all. Conversely, the gift of wisdom in men would not be perfect without the aid of prudence with which it completes its work (cf. Prv 14:33; 17:24).

Even though prudence is to be considered a gift of God, man is not by that fact simply dispensed from the duty of making an effort to acquire it, to study it (Prv 1:3; 4:1; 4:7; 16:16). To acquire it implies, first of all, to pray to God for it; then also to work for it through thoughtful observance of the commandments of God (Bar 3:9), developing prudence through exercise in prudence, through attention to elders and prudent men (Ti 2:2ff.).

The Sacred Scripture places a very special stress on the works of prudence: it preserves us from the perverse and intriguing ways of sin; it protects us from the artful and seductive wiles of the deceitful Temptress (Prv 2:11ff.; 7:4ff.; 8:14ff.); without prudence it seems impossible to evade her deadly bewitchment. Prudence preserves us from all defilement (Bar 3:11ff.). Only the prudent man understands how to speak rightly and also how to remain silent at the right times (Prv 10:19; 11:12; 17:27; Sir 19:28). The steps of men must be guided by prudence (Prv 15:21). Prudence enables us to judge correctly regarding the rich and their wealth; it imparts right discernment of men (Prv 28:11; 27:19). To prudence belongs right counsel (Dt 32:28) and watchfulness (1 Pt 4:7). Prudence makes one circumspect and vigilant; the prudent man knows that the coming of the kingdom of God, the advent of the Lord, does not depend on human effort. This knowledge alerts us for the coming of the Lord and spurs us on to the supreme engagement for the kingdom of God

(Mt 25:1ff.; 24:36ff.). Above all, the "servant whom his master has set over his household" must be "faithful and prudent" (Mt 24:45f.).

The qualities of prudence must be adapted to this present age: since the Lord sends His disciples "like sheep in the midst of wolves," they must be "wise as serpents." But their prudence must be utterly different from the wolfish prudence of this world upon which they pass judgment by being as simple and "guileless as doves" (Mt 10:16f.). This prudence which makes us "wise as serpents" and "guileless as doves" is not a thing which men acquire through exclusive trust in their own intelligence and cleverness. It is something which belongs to those who submit themselves entirely to the guidance of the divine spirit (Mt 10:20). The prudence of the spirit is opposed to the prudence of the flesh (cf. Rom 8:6), to the "wisdom that is of the earth," to the prudence which the "children of Agar" serve (Bar 3:23). Just as true prudence means "life and peace" (Rom 8:6) and has the promise of eternal happiness (Mt 24:45ff.), so the prudence of this world falls under the constant reprobation of the crucified Lord (1 Cor 1:19ff.), and its recompense can only be death (Rom 8:6).

And still the Lord does not hesitate to exhort His disciples to strive for still greater prudence precisely through holding up for their emulation the "prudence of the children of this world": if these men of the world summon every effort and employ every means to the full capacity of their powers in the attainment of their miserable goals, how much more must the "children of light" devote all their earthly gifts (most of all their wealth) and all their natural and supernatural powers to the service of the kingdom of God (Lk 16:8ff.).

By word and example the Lord taught us true prudence: at His very first public appearance as a child of twelve, "all who were listening to him were amazed at his understanding and his answers" (Lk 2:47). When He confronted His enemies, His conduct and His words were always as sincere and candid as they were prudent, so that "they could not resist him." Above all is His prudence apparent in His progressive preparation of the minds of His disciples for the announcement of His imminent passion and death and the revelation of the decisive truth that He is the true Son of God. Only gradually, as their understanding of divine things developed, could they accept such tremendous truths. In opposition to the false prudence of the world, through word and even more so through the most sublime act of His life, the folly of the cross (1 Cor 1:19ff.), He establishes the new heavenly way of prudence: "He who loses his life for my sake, will find it" (Mt 10:39; 16:25).

2. *Prudence: Philosophical-Theological Analysis*

a. Prudence in the Hierarchy of Christian Virtues

The Biblical term *prudence* taken in its most comprehensive sense is practically equivalent to the notion of "wisdom." Prudence and wisdom are antithesis to the "folly of the sinner" who in his blindness fixes a goal and means adapted to it, which inevitably will lead to perdition. Wisdom is the greatest gift of God: it gives to man the light and force to seek his salvation in the love of God and to contemplate and to love all things in that light and love alone. In its Biblical sense, wisdom embraces the theological virtues and the gifts of the Holy Spirit corresponding to them, above all, the gift of wisdom. This wisdom, which is no less the glow of love than the splendor of the Spirit, is the actual source and fountain of prudence. To be prudent, one must first be wise.

It is not the task of prudence, as a virtue distinct from wisdom, to orientate man toward his supernatural end. This task befalls the theological virtues ("wisdom"). Prudence busies itself "about the means proportionate to the end," as Thomas says, following Aristotle. This means that prudence must watch over the exercise and practice of love.

Wisdom inclines man to "find savor" in God, to cling to Him. The moral virtues set the will in right order regarding the various particular areas of value in the service of God. It remains for prudence to concern itself with concrete moral acts, inspiring, counseling, judging wisely. "Moral virtue, in so far as it is the basic attitude of voluntary approval and acceptance of the good, is the foundation and necessary condition of prudence. But prudence in turn is presupposed as a condition for all concrete realization and actualization of this fundamental attitude of good will here and now. Only one who simultaneously loves the good and wills it can be truly prudent, and still only one who is already prudent can do the good."[21]

In the ultimate analysis we see in prudence the noble handmaiden of the fundamental attitude of man in matters of religion and morals. Obviously, it is effective as a Christian infused virtue only if enlightened by faith and informed in love. Though it is only a virtue in the service of this fundamental religious and moral attitude, it plays the role of directing and guiding the moral virtues. In the actualization and realization of the virtues through concrete and specific acts which measure up to the demands of the moment, prudence acts as counselor and director in setting the standard for the other virtues. In so far as the objective practice and execution of virtue in harmony with concrete circumstances belongs to every virtue, all the other virtues depend on prudence.[22] Though all virtues act by force of their own nature, they can be effective concretely only through the virtue of prudence. Only through prudence can they be brought into harmony with the exigencies of the kingdom of God in the concrete and practical order.

As such, the theological virtues are not directly influenced by prudence, for their activity is orientated directly and immediately toward God without concern for the measure and balance provided by prudence. But in so far as these same virtues must manifest themselves in acts of the virtue of religion and the other moral virtues, they also have need for the guidance of prudence. On the other hand, prudence is the noble handmaiden of the noblest mistress, wisdom. It is the role of prudence, in the light of wisdom and in the service of wisdom, to discern the true reality of the moment, perceiving in each situation the hour of grace (*kairós*) granted by God, seeing in it the divine message and mission, with practical concern for the ways and means of becoming active for love of God.

Prudence has "two faces, one turned to the objectively real, the other to the good to be made real."[23] Prudence has a twofold task: to appraise the objective concrete realities correctly, and to discern and decide on the action which the realities demand in each instance. Prudence is "orientated toward reality to perceive and accept it, and toward will and action to command them."[24] It is prudence that perceives the providential and salutary significance of every moment, which but for prudence would flow on and mingle in endless confusion of meaningless events. Through prudence the law of God explored by the disciple of Christ in the light of faith and with the savor of wisdom, becomes the law of the hour.

The Christian has an understanding of what is good in general through his knowledge of the moral law in the light of faith and with the aid of reason enlightened by faith. But in the practical situations of life, which are often obscure and complicated and at times apparently of little significance, only prudence can discern what is truly good, what is in harmony with the spirit of Christ in the particular instance, in the concrete set of circumstances which beset us.

The traditional doctrine on the virtue of prudence probably is the best evidence of this point. With the greatest clearness this Christian moral teaching insists on the particular will of God for me, in its particular relation to me in each concrete situation (the *kairós,* the hour of grace). For the prudent man, and only for the prudent man, is every hour the hour of grace, the hour of decision for the kingdom of God. In the teaching of Saint Thomas, we note likewise the particular insistence on this high esteem for the moment of grace. He holds that there is a distinctive role or function of prudence or, more specifically, a distinctive virtue which is affined to the virtue of prudence or is a potential part of the virtue. In the particular situation the *"Gnóme"* (the "sense of the situation") is concerned with numerous situations or instances which simply cannot be clearly grasped or judged in the light of universal rule or norm.[25]

This truth is brought out even more clearly in the teaching on the gifts of the Holy Spirit. Prudence is accompanied by a sense of the will of God (subjectively this is the *"Gnóme"*) in the concrete circumstances of particular instances, which is not learned *a priori* or from a simple scheme or outline on the virtues. Docile and completely responsive to the gift of counsel conferred by the Holy Spirit, this virtue of prudence does not apply a mere universal norm, but rather directly senses that the loving will of God is immediately embracing and moving it in the hour of grace. (Naturally this in no way implies any violation or neglect of the universal law.) Prudence clarifies the situation, even the most obscure situation, in such a manner as to see in it the will of God manifesting itself clearly. In the situation prudence sees and hears the will of God.

If the moral-religious life of the Christian were nothing more than a schematic or *a priori* application of the universal law, then our teaching about prudence, the *"Gnóme,"* and even the gift of counsel would be superfluous.

The virtue of prudence goes beyond the mere external or visible actualities. It is above all concerned with the supernatural realities. As infused virtue, prudence is the eye of faith focused on the needs of the moment. And in the measure of the growth of the life of grace, it is progressively submissive to the guidance of the gifts of the Holy Spirit.

Christian prudence is both infused and acquired. This means that the prudent Christian man is fundamentally inclined to believe and harken humbly (he has a fruitful capacity for silence in harkening to God's truth and for growing enlightened in faith under the guidance of the Holy Spirit) and at the same time to search zealously and intently for the message of reality.

Moreover, prudence thrives in the soil of humility and in the humble and reverential acknowledgment of the given actualities and their limited possibilities for good. Nor is it the task of prudence to be concerned with eternal values alone, for in the heart of every concrete reality the prudent man seeks to discover the will of God and to orientate his actions toward the real world. He alone is truly prudent who submits to the necessities of the historic hour, since this is the providential hour for him, in which he is placed. It is the hour which opens to him and offers to him the real, though precise and limited, possibilities for good. On this historic hour he is to impress the seal of the kingdom of God. He alone is prudent who humbly accepts the lowly conditions of life and welcomes that which God sends him in each concrete situation, even though the messenger of the divine may be the most unprepossessing. The imprudent man, on the contrary, revels in dreams of service to God in a better world, meanwhile neglecting the call and demand of the present hour. He schemes and plans and stubbornly follows the pattern of his own ideals, all the while disregarding the real order of things.

The virtue of prudence is not concerned with reality in the manner of the disinterested observer. Prudence busies itself with active engagement in reality. Hence, every species of quietism is foreign to it, and as well every false "interiority" which sees only the inward disposition and attaches no importance to the correctness of external action. The Christian practices prudence as an active citizen and soldier of the kingdom of Christ. We have said all that needs to be said regarding the essence of prudence when we say that it serves the kingdom of God in the urgency of its reality. Saint Thomas teaches that the principal function of prudence is the imperative of action.[26]

Not without reason does Thomas retain the Aristotelian notion of prudence as primarily the virtue for politics and warfare.[27] If we transpose this Aristotelian concept into the realm of the Christian, we cannot fail to recognize that also Christian prudence deals with politics and strategy in this world, though only because and in so far as it is a virtue which leads the active engagement for the kingdom of God. It is military service, but the service of the peace of Christ in the war for the good.

Saint Thomas expressly repudiates the notion that prudence is exclusively concerned with the service of self-perfection.[28] He does not hold that prudence is ultimately concerned most of all with the interior virtue or perfection of the one who acts,[29] and least with the rectitude of his external effort or good action. Since it is the task of prudence to direct the active engagement of love, it must possess the same interior orientation as love itself, which "is not self-seeking" (1 COR 13:5) but rather serves one's neighbor and especially "the common good of all."[30]

It should not surprise us that now and then Saint Thomas employs Aristotelian terms in treating prudence without expressly repudiating their origin. However, anyone who really grasps his meaning can readily see that, though the terms are identical, prudence for Thomas is an entirely different thing than for Aristotle. It is not something deployed in the service of man's own self-perfection, the furtherance of earthly happiness, or the welfare of the earthly state.

The highest goal of man, the noblest task of the divine love which inspires and rules him, is the honor of God, the manifestation of the divine glory, the recognition and hallowing of His Name in fact and deed in the world. Since it is the role of prudence to direct the active endeavor of love which proclaims the dominion of God, one may say that the Christian esteems prudence as highly as he esteems his loftiest duty: the proclamation, the increase of the divine honor and glory. Is it not true that the lack of respect for the divine name and the great damage done to the kingdom of God, though due to lukewarmness of love, is principally caused by neglect of the practice of prudence?

External works truly proclaim the honor and grandeur of God only if they are the expression of the interior splendor of grace and love which makes us members of the kingdom of God's glory. Accordingly, the perverted notion which envisages prudence as exclusively orientated toward external activity, to the prejudice of the inner life, must be repudiated. Quite the contrary is true. One of the particular tasks of prudence is to set such limits to external activity as to allow for the just demands of the inner life of intimate union with God. Accordingly, prudence regulates the repose, the gathering of new forces from within, with the ultimate end in view, of course, to direct the active endeavor of man to the good.

Just as in the kingdom of God the external act, the doing of things—no matter how important it may be—is not the highest and the ultimate, so too prudence is not the most exalted virtue. The theological virtues are higher. They are the life with God and from God. They are the orientation of our whole inner selves toward God. But still by their inmost nature they demand action. By action they are manifested and tested. Since they must be expressed and tested in action in this time of grace in the kingdom of God, they too have need for the virtue of prudence.

b. Moral Conscience and Prudence

It is the exalted task of prudence to provide that man, through his conscience, hear the voice of God, speaking in and through rightly understood reality. It is the task of prudence to provide that the voice of conscience which urges the free will to act be the right answer to the divine demand in the hour of trial. The verdict of conscience, in the degree that it is really the true and certain voice of conscience, is neither more nor less than the verdict of prudence. The false dictate of a culpably erroneous conscience does not flow from prudence, but rather from defect of prudence or from its imperfect manifestation or functioning. The inculpably erroneous dictate of conscience, on the contrary, is a real act of prudence, even though, of course, it lacks something of the perfection or facility of the virtue. Or the equipment of the virtue is in some measure lacking in perfection and facility.

Conscience throughout impregnates with its dynamism the acts of prudence or, more specifically, the acts of the potential parts of prudence, transforming the prudential verdict into the verdict of conscience. In other words, conscience guarantees that man feels the imperative force of his own prudential judgment. But the discernment of the good present here and now does not spring from the power of conscience as such, but from the activity of the virtue of prudence.

Abstracting from the inner force of obligation awakening the sense of duty based on the moral condition of man, we note that the dictate of conscience corresponds entirely to the prudential judgment. Hence, as to its content, the dictate of conscience flows from the work of prudence, though its compulsion is from the ⁄faculty of conscience. Conscience sustains and supports all with its dynamism. *"Synderesis movet prudentiam"* (conscience moves prudence).[31] Where conscience is crippled or stunted, prudence is also impotent and uncertain. A conscience that is sound, alert, forthright is the best guarantee for the correctness of the prudential acts of deliberation and judgment.

c. The Potential Parts of Prudence

According to Saint Thomas[32] the three principal acts of prudence are *consilium* or counsel (deliberation, pondering advice), judgment or *judicium* (judging the situation), command or *praecipere* (command to act, imperative, the determination of the form and manner of the execution of the action). The third act is the end and goal of the first two, whose correctness it presupposes. In this sense it is the most important; but from another point of view, of course, the act of deliberation appears the more basic: one who deliberates with complete correctness will infallibly arrive at the right decision for his action. One who averts his gaze from the majesty and beauty of the moral good at the very inception of his deliberation and fails to resist the lure of sense and pride, has already forfeited the rectitude and force of the prudent decision.

Perfect deliberation (taking counsel with oneself) is called *eubulía* (being well advised) by Aristotle. He uses the term *sýnesis* (insight in accord with the law) for that moral perfection of judgment which resolves cases by simple deduction from universal norms, and the term *gnóme* (a sense for the unique situation) for the perfection of judgment in situations in which the general regulations and laws are not clear and adequate. The virtuous attitude concerned with the insight into the unique situation (*gnóme*), in the teaching of Aristotle, corresponds to epiky. Epiky is the sympathetic discernment or insight into life on the part of the legislator, who is not held captive by rigid forms of law. It is the part of prudence, especially of *gnóme,* to see in the lawgiver a leader endowed with insight and moderation, and not lacking in epiky. In the Christian moral teaching on love, which far transcends all the norms of mere legalistic justice, the sense for the unique situation would naturally assume a far more important role than in Aristotle, for whom the supreme principle of morality is justice (a type of justice which is much more rigid than the Biblical justice, and lacking the deep rich meaning of the Biblical concept).

d. The Formation in Prudence

For the full and comprehensive exercise of its functions, nearly all the forces and faculties of the soul must contribute to the perfection of prudence, although the very rectitude of these same forces already presupposes prudence. This is to say that all virtues must in some manner be present before one can be truly prudent, and all must likewise contribute to the perfect and complete fitness of prudence. The principal powers and virtues which prudence must enlist in its service may be logically divided according to the threefold stages of activity already referred to.

A) Necessary for the perfection of deliberation and counsel: 1) a faithful memory (*memoria*),[33] which never loses sight of the universal Christian principles and commandments and, above all, of the accumulated experience which forms the moral wisdom of the past; 2) a profound understanding and insight (*intellectus*),[34] which penetrates to the central values at the very core of things and grasps unique situations in their true meaning; 3) clear reason (*ratio*),[35] which enables one to pass readily from insight and experience to new insights through rational inferences; 4) submissive docility (*docilitas*),[36] which with humble spirit recognizes one's own inadequacy and is always prepared to add to one's learning, and profit by the advice and experience of others.

B) In order that deliberation and sound counsel may lead to a secure and inerrant decision there is need for 5) readiness and accuracy (*sollertia*).[37] Should prudence lack this quality, there is danger that despite adequate insight and deliberation scrupulosity and indecision might result, so that reflection and deliberation would never reach the point of decision. The common result is delay in the very decision to act, which is the end and purpose of prudence.

Occasionally the lack of readiness and accuracy in judgment arises from the desire for too great a certainty. Some men look for more than the moral certainty prudence requires. Prudence does not demand, nor should we seek, metaphysical certainty in moral matters. But there is also the very opposite extreme which destroys true certainty altogether, when haste and lack of reflection precipitate judgment and decision to act before deliberation can study the matter thoroughly. Lack of deliberation is not in the first instance an error of execution—it merely becomes evident in the execution—but execution based on hasty and inadequate deliberation and judgment.

C) Prudence enlists the following qualities principally, though not exclusively, in forming the correct imperative of action (*praecipere*): 6) foresight (*pro-videntia,* from which the term *prudence* is derived, because it is foremost among all the parts of *prudentia, "quia est principalior inter omnes partes prudentiae."*[38] Foresight gauges the effects or consequences of action and omission for the future and acts accordingly; 7) circumspection (*circumspectio, quae respicit "omnia quae circumstant"*)[39] which looks to all the circumstances. It takes into account all the important conditions or circumstances under which our activity is exercised; 8) precaution,[40] which wisely anticipates the obstacles to our actions and prepares to surmount them. These eight qualities or perfections of prudence just enumerated are not merely natural traits or capacities, but in serving prudence they partake of the virtue itself. In their perfection they contribute to the vigor and effectiveness of the virtue of prudence.

e. Acquisition and Cultivation of Prudence

The infused virtue of prudence (the capacity or power proportioned to the supernatural end) rests on faith and hope. It is infused into the soul with love. But facility and effectiveness in exercise of the virtue are a matter of personal effort. They must be acquired "in the sweat of one's brow" through the cultivation of the eightfold auxiliary qualities, just referred to, and all the moral virtues upon whose existence and growth prudence depends.

For the cultivation and training in the virtue of prudence there is required above all: the acquisition of the indispensable moral knowledge (which is concerned rather with the contemplation of the doctrine and example of Christ than with mere theoretic or conceptual study, though clear concepts are far from superfluous) through experience and instruction, through sharpening of the prudential judgment in casuistry. It should be noted, however, that the case study in the casuistic exercise should not be set up as an infallible model or norm for all possible cases in real life. And on the other hand, the popular instruction should not slight the use of vivid illustrations in the form of examples and practical cases! Above all, the Christian must be trained to appreciate the importance of serious deliberation and counsel.

Every man must particularly cultivate that aspect or quality of prudence which most concerns him. For example, the scrupulant must exercise himself much more with the readiness and forthrightness in judgment than with the deliberation and self-reflection in the virtue of prudence. Nature has not been equally generous in bestowing the gift of prudence on various individuals. Not all are sufficiently prudent, even with the best of effort and good will and with true progress in holiness, to become directors of the spiritual life. But as Saint Thomas expressly teaches,[41] all who are in the state of grace possess sufficient prudence to acquire eternal life. And "if they stand in need of the advice of others, they are able to decide prudently at least to such an extent that they can obtain good advice from others, distinguishing between good and bad counsel."[42] From this passage of the Angelic Doctor we can see what importance he attaches to the gift of discernment of spirits or discretion. Such is the prudence of the Christian according to the traditional teaching.

The more prudent one is, the less will he be likely to spurn the counsel of others. "The secret of progress in life is to know how to add the experiences of others to one's own."[43] With such readiness to accept the advice of others the gift of discernment must grow, at least to the extent that one knows how to distinguish between trustworthy counselors and the imprudent or perverse.

Because of the intimate connection between prudence and conscience what we have said regarding education of conscience is of application also here. Since prudence in a measure is the "tact of conscience in the situation," it can be delicate and safe only where the moral conscience which supports and compels it is tender and vigorous. The virtue of prudence can flourish only in the soil of sound conscience, in a personality in harmony with self and God. Therefore the very best training of conscience and also of prudence consists in growth in the love of God. No formation in prudence is of any value unless it is animated and dominated by love. If divine love fills the heart of man, it suppresses all subversive influence of perverse inclinations which might cloud the judgment of prudence. Love alone, such is its intimate affinity with the good, is able to understand the love-language of reality expressing the will of God.

The words of Saint Augustine, so often quoted, so often misunderstood, can be understood in the light of this explanation. They really mean: "love, and do what love wills." Love does not render prudence and its qualities superfluous. But only love can rightly guide and utilize prudence.

f. Prudence Perfected through Counsel

Since prudence is rooted so deeply in celestial wisdom, it receives a powerful impulse from the gift of wisdom which gives man on earth a taste for heavenly things and a foretaste of the beatific love to be realized in eternity. Nevertheless, the gift of the Holy Spirit which corresponds directly to prudence and actually exalts and elevates it is the gift of counsel. Through counsel the Holy Spirit Himself directs the first act of prudence, deliberation, with such perfection that the subsequent acts are assured of a solid basis and their correctness is guaranteed.[44] Under the inspiration of the gift of counsel, the soul gladly submits to the divine dispositions and directives, for the gifts are divine helps which make the soul submissive to the slightest movements of the Holy Spirit.[45] Attentiveness to the voice of God becomes far more important than "being true to oneself" or adhering rigidly to one's own personal plans or designs for living. In every perfect activity of prudence, the gift of counsel is operative. It makes for suppleness and responsiveness to the slightest whisper of the divine will; it creates a capacity for that silence which is attentive to God's voice, whether it speaks directly to the heart or through external dispositions and visitations. Such is the gift of counsel as ordinarily understood.

The gift of counsel pertaining to the Christian virtue of prudence most clearly reveals the enormous difference existing between supernatural prudence and the Greek concept of the virtue. This latter, even though we abstract entirely from the fact that it serves a different end and purpose, rests on human and personal perceptiveness, on one's own imperative of prudence, whereas the Christian virtue implies humility. The Christian prudent man is active in his very submission to the divine dispositions and the inspirations of the Holy Spirit. How keenly he is aware that he is truly prudent in the spirit of the Master, if he is totally devoted to Him as pupil and disciple, and totally and utterly submissive to the Spirit of Jesus Christ!

Many moral theologians have slighted the teaching on the gifts of the Holy Spirit, and with disastrous consequences! Such neglect could only mean the loss of that Christian optimism according to which "they all shall be taught of God" (JN 6:45). If one failed to place any trust in the power of the Christian to recognize the loving will of God except through the universal norms of law applied to the particular case falling under the law, then it would follow that the great law of love must lose all value of obligation except where some law explicitly applied the norm. However, the moral theology in which the teaching on the gifts of the Holy Spirit plays the role which it assumes in Saint Thomas is, in the best sense of that term, personalistic. In such theology the Christian does not confront a frigid impersonal law, but the divine call of grace summoning him "in this very hour." The Christian who is truly prudent, entirely docile to the inner Master, the Holy Spirit, will harken to the will of God lovingly calling to him, both in the external universal law which binds him, and in the exigency of the unique situation and in the special call of divine grace.

g. The Sins against Prudence

The exposition of Saint Thomas on the faults and vices opposed to prudence is a model of psychological insight and critical discernment.[46]

The term *imprudence* may be used purely negatively to denote a simple absence of prudence. In this sense, imprudence does not directly serve an evil end, at least not basically or as a matter of principle. However, the man who simply lacks prudence fails to use means which correspond to the right end or purpose, either because he is somewhat lacking in natural endowments or has not had adequate training, or because he is remiss in the ardor of his charity. Much of this imprudence may be laid to the door of our sinful heritage due to original sin. And in many cases the fault lies in our own sinful or neglectful antecedent conduct which has not been fully corrected and repaired. Even the truly repentant man and the man who has progressed on the way of holiness are often imprudent because of human frailty. But this frailty must be accompanied by humble readiness to profit by every instance of imprudence.

Positive imprudence,[47] which is the sin of imprudence, likewise, does not imply that the end or purpose of our action is evil, but that we have been culpably neglectful in our endeavor to suit the means to the end (the kingdom of God). We have failed to choose rightly the means toward the end. Such imprudence arises from culpable ignorance, from thoughtlessness, lack of attentiveness, lack of reflection, indecisiveness.[48] According to Saint Thomas, the principal source of imprudence is abandonment to impurity and voluptuousness.[49] Nothing so obscures one's judgment or interferes with the correct perspective in appraising the particular object of the senses as enslavement in sensual desires.

In a broader sense of the term, every act contrary to the judgment of conscience, hence, contrary to the effective decision of prudence, can be called imprudence. It is an act of folly. In this sense the Sacred Scriptures speak of the "folly" of sin. Actually we are not dealing with a defect of prudence here, but with a lack of "wisdom," lack of the love for the good.

Abandonment of man's true end results in the total ruin of the virtue of prudence and the consequent vice of imprudence. The "prudence of the flesh" places experience and acquired knowledge at the service of evil ends. The sharpest reproach of the inertia of the Christians is the activity of those who are wise with the "prudence of this world." All too readily Christians excuse their "do-nothing" laxness by pleading lack of natural endowment in prudence or cleverness (cf. Lk 16:8). On the contrary, those who are prudent according to the flesh reveal that the passionate engagement in attaining a goal naturally releases immense energies in the discovery and employment of ways and means to reach it.

Carnal prudence is "hostile to God" and serves the kingdom of Satan. To dedicate oneself to it means to fall victim to death (Rom 8:6). Allied with this carnal prudence is the excessive concern for the temporal and material and for the future, which at least hinders the total and undeviating engagement of prudence for the kingdom of God.

According to Thomas, "avarice," the greed for wealth and power, is the polluted source of carnal prudence. Though it does not extinguish the judgment of reason, as does enslavement in sensuality, it has a still more dire effect. It places the judgment of reason at the service of injustice.[50] We should also note that there is likewise the carnal prudence which busies itself with petty things without turning from the last end of man. This preoccupation of prudence is venial sin.

Final enemy of prudence is astuteness (*astutia*), the slyness which "moves in crooked ways to its end."[51] The man of intrigue lacks the "simplicity of the dove," uprightness and sincerity. Astuteness, ruse, is sinful even though it is made to serve noble ideals. In fact, it is so foreign to the "kingdom of truth," which it should serve, that it has a malice all its own. Contrary to this mundane shrewdness, whose weapons are misrepresentation, deceit, and lies, are the simplicity and disinterestedness of the true Christian who remains aloof from all deviousness and even chooses the ways and means of his actions in all uprightness and truth.

II. JUSTICE

1. *Justice as Fundamental Attitude*

It is true of the virtue of justice, likewise, that in the Christian system of virtues it is more exalted than in the pagan systems. Both in its inner structure and in its position in the hierarchy of virtues, it is loftier than the justice of the pre-Christian systems. As a Christian virtue it is altogether dedicated to the service of the theological virtues, particularly love, and must be studied in the light of love.

Precisely in their concept of justice and the position it occupies in the moral system as a whole do we find one of the gravest deficiencies in the ethics of the ancients of the Western world. Even the Greeks, despite the high level of their culture, and more so the Romans, could not perceive that the first and fundamental natural virtue of the will can only be love. On the contrary the elevated moral teaching of Confucius places first among the four basic virtues, "benevolence" or "wishing well," the right attitude of soul toward one's fellow men and the community. "The portion which heaven has bestowed on the sages is the virtue of benevolence, justice, urbanity, and prudence. They all have their root in the heart. They manifest themselves in the radiance of the countenance, in the posture of man, in his whole physique."[52] These words clearly indicate an ethic of interiority rather on the Biblical level, with which the preaching of the

Christian moral teaching, especially in the Far East, should be able to come in rapport much more effectively than with the doctrine of Aristotle.

The classic Greco-Roman hierarchy of basic virtues, which grants absolute primacy to justice and reckons love among the mere passions of man, means a depersonalizing of the human ethos. For, as commonly understood, justice in the first place really and directly regulates the relation to objects, the use of material goods and the relation to one's fellows in regard to the material order and material possessions, not in regard to man's interior value in love. But it is love which unfolds the actual I to the Thou and discovers the living fountain of value in the Thou. Then only comes what is second—and no one doubts that it is also very important— justice between the I and Thou, between the I and the We of society, justice which establishes the right order regarding the goods of the individual and the community.

Nevertheless, the pre-Christian notion of the cardinal virtue of justice does at least suggest something of love. We might say that there are certain indications or perspectives which may be interpreted as pointing to love or at least in some measure allowing for such enrichment through personal love. In effect, justice is the general virtue or moral attitude of will which seeks to give to every being that which belongs to him, more specifically, to every person or community of persons. In the broadest sense of the term this is justice taken objectively. Objectively it measures up to and satisfies the true value of the object and simultaneously satisfies the demands and aspirations of the subject in relation to value. Thus understood, justice is that attitude of openness toward value which disregards every other claim on the will of moral man, but is entirely prepared to fulfill all the demands of value of one's own person seeking values and of the other person demanding values. Thus justice is readiness to respond to and to fulfill the exigency of value, of the I seeking value, of the Thou demanding value (of the whole object of justice demanding it).

Just as prudence is the comprehensively correct appraisal and understanding of value and its obligation in the particular situation, so justice is the corresponding virtue of the will which on its part alone actually enables the practical reason to judge with objective correctness, and this means to be prudent. Justice, therefore, grasps the objectively correct decision and the imperative of prudence and puts them into effect without permitting arbitrary or unobjective motives to mislead the will. Thus conceived, justice is the most elevated of the moral virtues. Its force lies in the moral love of value and of the person. Prudence depends on justice, as do fortitude and temperance, for these virtues must depend on an attitude of will completely given over to the right demands of value. As attitude of will justice is antecedent to prudence. But to realize the virtue of justice in acts of justice, obviously the right standard set up by prudence (the judgment of conscience) and the control of the passions must be prior. Temperance and fortitude are virtues only in so far as they are orientated morally by justice and love, for surely in itself the disciplining of the affective life would mean little. Only through the orientation toward the exercise of justice do fortitude and temperance assume their true and proper character as virtues.

2. *Justice and Particular Virtue*

Taken in the common or usual sense, justice as a cardinal virtue is more restricted than the justice we have just described. It does not embrace love of moral value and person. According to the current definition which is given by Saint Thomas, justice is the "firm and constant will to give to each one his due."[53] This is the same as to give each one his own or grant every one his right. Domain of right and domain of justice are equivalent.[54] By right, Thomas means that which is strictly owed to another according to equality, actually according to an equality of proportion.[55] "To give to each his own" does not at all mean to give absolutely the same to each and every one. The equality is rather an equality of proportion; that is to say, it must correspond to the dignity and power of each individual. Only in the instances in which one is exactly like another can there be a claim to equal right absolutely; in so far as one is different from another, there is a corresponding diversity also in the measure of rights and of the claim to rights. In the whole moral life of man there is the rhythm of capacity and obligation, of talent and responsibility, of rights and duties. Impressively Saint Paul pictures the corresponding diversity of gifts and tasks, of rights and duties, in his example of the human body with its various members and functions (1 Cor 12:12–26).

In the stricter sense of the term, justice is embodied in those instances where there is absolute equality. This is in the domain of commutative justice, which demands exact equality of value between what is given and what is due in return. Common to every species of justice in the strict sense is that it regulates or governs not so much the concord of minds and hearts (the task of love), but rather the measure of external performance, the order of things and possessions. But justice in the Biblical sense of the term, which thrives on the bountiful love of God freely giving Himself, always measures things by the standard of love and constantly does far more than is strictly required. But this justice is love.

3. *Classification of Justice*

Justice is classified according to the kinds of rights which it regulates, according to the subject or bearer of the rights, and the executor or the one who carries out the rights.

a. Commutative Justice

Commutative justice is particularly regulated by the private right of contract, according to the principle of equality of give and take. The subject of the right and the one responsible for executing the right is the private person (or the community as a moral person); object of the right is the private advantage or profit, the private good of the individual (physical or moral). Commutative justice commands that exchange be of equal value, and it forbids violation of the right of another or any deprivation of his right. Principal violations of commutative justice are theft, fraud, unjust damage.

b. General or Legal Justice (*justitia generalis, legalis*)

The subject of the right in this species of justice is the community. The object, end, or purpose is the common welfare. Responsible for its execution or discharge is the community through its official organs or representatives and also the individual in his relation to the community. The bearers or subjects of authority practice this type of justice by passing and furthering legislation favorable to the common welfare. The subjects or citizens exercise the virtue by faithful obedience to such laws with the realization of their importance and relation to the common good.

For Saint Thomas general or legal justice assumes the aspect of a comprehensive virtue of the will in the measure in which it directs all good action to the general good of the community as a whole.[56] Especially under this aspect the Angelic Doctor places justice first among the moral virtues, for the universal good has priority over the private or particular good.[57] In the larger theological sense we should say: the highest virtue does not consist in the explicit effort to further one's own perfection taken in itself, but in the disinterested service for the common good, that is, in the engagement for the glory of God and the kingdom of God. For this reason neither fortitude nor temperance is the summit of moral virtue, since their object is the interior order of the soul. The highest rank is reserved for justice, which orientates everything toward the highest good of one's neighbor or, more specifically, of the whole community, and ultimately to God. It is evident that virtue is all the higher the more explicitly it turns to the common good and abstracts from the person of the virtuous individual himself.

However, legal justice in its more ordinary acceptation is not so comprehensive. It is restricted to the object of legal (executive, dominative) activity exercised by those in authority and the fulfillment of laws in relation to the common good.

c. Distributive Justice (*justitia distributiva*)

Subject or bearer of the right in this form of justice is the individual in his relation to the community. End or object of the right is the private or particular good of each individual member of the community. Responsible for its fulfillment is the community exercising justice through its official organs and representatives. Distributive justice regulates the measure of privileges, aids, burdens or charges, and obligations of the individual as member of the community. The individual member has fundamental rights over against the community, rights which the community must preserve and guarantee for him. He himself practices distributive justice as a virtue by accepting uncomplainingly the just distribution of burdens and privileges without making immoderate or excessive claims against the community. Under a democratic constitution which permits each individual to press his own claim to rights and help assess his own share of duties, the virtue of distributive justice has a unique importance for the citizen himself (not merely for those in authority). It must regulate political propaganda and the duty and exercise of suffrage. The virtue is violated by sins of demagoguery and fanatical partisanship favoring individual or class in opposition to the common welfare.

Legal and distributive justice correspond to each other and must in some measure be coordinated. In the measure in which the individual devotes his powers and resources to the common welfare, the community must show its concern for his particular welfare. One who does more for the community is entitled to greater respect and advantage from the community itself. Participation in privileges, on the other hand, obliges the individual member of the community to ever greater effort to dedicate himself and his resources with a fuller sense of responsibility to the community.

But caution is to be observed in the application of this principle: one who has accumulated a great portion of the national wealth or resources, whether by just means or unjust, and in consequence must pay higher taxes, is not automatically entitled to greater honors and privileges. Only if his effort is proportioned to his resources! Only if he, with his huge share of the wealth and resources of the community, actually does much more than the less favored possessor of material goods, does he contribute what we have a right to expect from him. But if, on the contrary, he keeps his clutches on his swollen possessions to the detriment of others of the community who are hindered thereby in their efforts to seek their own rights and the common welfare, from the standpoint of proportional equality he must be considered a menace to society unless he makes an altogether extraordinary contribution to the community. Should the princes of privilege voluntarily surrender their excessive privileges and possessions which prove prejudicial to the community, they are deserving of admiration and praise. But it is just and right to constrain them to do so, should they fail to recognize the demands of the common welfare.

d. Social Justice

A fourth type of justice has been accepted in our moral teaching since the publication of the encyclical on the reconstruction of the social order (*Quadragesimo Anno*). Social justice is concerned with the common good and may be termed "justice of the common welfare" or "justice of the community." Its object is constituted less by the rights founded in law than by the natural rights of the community and its members.

Social justice presupposes commutative justice as a condition. To cite an example, in the study of the wage problem we note that the principle of equality of compensation of work and wage is first established. Social justice, then, concerns itself with problems which go far beyond such points of commutative justice. It considers employer and wage earner as members of various social groups: the worker is paid his wage as the breadwinner or as a member of a family; wages and profits are computed with an eye to the good of the enterprise and the general economy.

Social justice does not find the ultimate solution of the problem posed by the relation of capital and labor in commutative justice based on material equality, nor does it find it altogether in legal and distributive justice imposed by superior authority sanctioning and enforcing the observance of commutative justice. It looks beyond in the interest of the community, above all, to those who are economically and politically weak, who, though they have nothing to give, still have natural rights to be respected both by community and by men of property and possession.

The infant has the inalienable right to life, sustenance, and education. Every community or social group, from the family to the state, must respect this right and more particularly safeguard it. Parents owe the child what is necessary for its physical and spiritual development on the basis of social justice, that is, in virtue of their very character and position as parents which nature has given them in the community. This social duty arises from their possession of goods, from their capacity for work, and from their very quality as parents. But likewise the very quality of the child as a child makes it incumbent upon it to cooperate within the family, contributing its share to family work and enterprise as far as this is possible and assisting the parents in their declining years and in time of need, as loving return of parental care and affection. Yet such cooperation is not to be viewed in the narrow sense of a compensation to be paid in the measure of commutative justice. It is rather the response which the child, as a child, owes to its parents.

Likewise in the political order, the state (from the smallest group, the tiny village, to the nation and to the society of nations) has the obligation to safeguard for every member of the community, life, sustenance, and the opportunity of work, in so far as the individual has not himself forfeited these rights through his own fault. "Social justice imposes the obligation of assisting those in need, in so far as it may be necessary to enable them to live in a manner worthy of human beings. The right to assistance in social justice arises from the natural right to life on the part of those in need and is measured by this right. Continuation of the assistance to the needy is conditioned, however, by the need itself. As soon as the needy individual can help himself, the obligation of any further assistance ceases."[58]

Under many aspects, social justice coincides with legal and distributive justice, which, of course, it enlarges through the idea of the "social vocational order," organized from below. But it goes beyond legal and distributive justice and also beyond commutative justice in its requirement that even the individual, without waiting for law or precept, must come to the assistance of the needy. The rich must give from his superfluity, for the needy have a natural right to such help so that they can live in a manner worthy of human beings. Under this aspect social justice represents, contrary to the common conception of the last centuries, an enlargement of the obligations in justice in contradistinction to the "mere" obligations in charity.

Social justice places in sharp focus, more than the other three types of justice are wont to do, those duties of justice which flow immediately from the social nature of man and also from the social purpose of the material goods of this earth. But it coincides with the other three kinds of justice in so far as it does not actually aim at regulating the harmony of hearts in the community. Nor is its object concerned with the giving of external goods from an abundance of love, but with the order of goods themselves, with material service and material values on the basis of a right.

As Thomas holds for general justice, so too for social justice: its ultimate object is the common welfare. But the actual basis of the right is not exchange in service or goods, but the essentially social nature of man even in regard to material goods and material service.

On the rich, social justice places the obligation of renouncing even justly acquired rights and possessions, in so far as the need of the whole community or its individual members may require. Social justice is the basis of the strict right of the inculpably needy to necessary assistance from the superfluity of his neighbor, in so far as they are bound together by the bond of community solidarity.

Social justice also transcends legal justice in so far as it forms the basis of the unity and coexistence of peoples through an imperative of justice, abstracting entirely from every treaty or contract and the actual existence of a society of nations. A nation which possesses superfluity is obliged to come to the rescue of its less richly endowed neighbors and contribute from its superabundance at least to the extent that the impoverished people can live in a morally sound and humanly worthy manner. (Such means as providing outlets for congested populations through emigration to sparsely populated areas are particularly significant today.)

As presented in the *Reconstruction of the Social Order* (*Quadragesimo Anno*) the concept of social justice belongs to the juridical order and is based on the law of nature. As such, it is not strictly a supernatural concept. But such a notion of social justice could not be formed by man in his present state without the revealed concepts of God and man. In this concept humanity looks upon all its possessions as a trust from God and the human race itself as a family of many members in God's sight. In the sense of the *Reconstruction of the Social Order,* social justice far transcends the order or relation of *"do ut des"* (give and take) between individual and individual, between community and individual. It can be discerned only through the perspective of faith in God, the Giver of all earthly gifts and powers, the Father of all children of men. It is the familial justice of the children of God.

But it is not yet the familial love of the children of God, for such love has a far loftier task than the regulation of the material matters of service and possession. But this familial justice "presupposes love under a twofold aspect. First, only love can induce the giants of industry, the powerful in the economic order, to renounce their privileges and the unjust industrial order; secondly, only love can widen the horizon narrowed by the bias of social rank and possession and open up to man the splendid vision of the varied social groups, each with human rights of its own. Under this twofold aspect, love is the foundation of social justice, as its dynamic moving force, as its power of insight into that which in each particular instance, is just."[59]

e. Vindicative Justice (*justitia vindicativa*)

Vindicative justice is the temperate will to restore violated justice by means of a punishment which is in proportion to the guilt. It is primarily a virtue in the superior who, in imposing punishment and assessing the degree of punishment, should have no other purpose in mind than the furtherance of the common welfare (public order and security, universal respect for justice, confidence in authority) and, if possible, correction of the guilty. It exists also in the citizen or subject in so far as he demands punishment for violation of law, not through a spirit of revenge, but because of a genuine zeal for justice and the common good, and if the subject himself be an offender, in so far as he submits in the spirit of reparation to the punishment he deserves.

4. *Characteristics of Justice*

Three characteristic traits distinguish justice from the other moral virtues:

1) The precise and determinable character of the obligation. Whereas the obligations arising from charity allow for a considerable margin

corresponding to the capacity of the individual, the domain of justice can be objectively determined or delimited, at least as a matter of principle. The traditional norm of the "just mean," of course, refers in its strict acceptation only to commutative justice. In commutative justice the equality between the debt owed and its payment, between service rendered and service due, is established by the object itself, whereas in the cardinal virtues of fortitude and temperance the "virtuous mean" may be determined only by reference to the agent and to the situation in which he acts.

On this point we note particularly the essential difference between social justice and commutative justice. Obligation arises from the existence of a demonstrable right to which the duty of fulfillment of the right must correspond. Whereas in the case of commutative justice there is always a right acquired by one's own achievement or act, social justice is often the basis for natural rights to which a natural obligation in one's fellows or in the community corresponds.[60]

2) A real order of things: material possessions and real goods are the object of justice. In the very broad sense, we may say that all human goods or possessions fall under justice, even the right to truth, fidelity, and honor, but in the strict sense it is the right to things (material goods) which is the object.

3) Possibility of enforcement: recourse to competent authority to obtain one's rights has always been looked upon as characteristic of justice. This flows from the fact that the rights to be enforced can be definitely determined. For that matter, even social justice is justice and in so far as it is really justice, it can be enforced at least basically and in principle (an example is the obligation to give up one's superfluities in time of universal deprivation). But the limits of enforcement are set by the actual clear determination of rights and by the strict demands of the common welfare. And this latter can be disturbed and obscured, not merely through the attempt to enforce doubtful rights or through unlawful use of authority, but also through inopportune vindication of rights that are legitimate and certain.

In so far as justice is a moral virtue, it does not go further than what is enforceable in principle on the basis of a right. But it goes far beyond the bounds of force itself. As a moral virtue, its motive does not lie in mere fear of the law and its sanctions, but in one's own moral sense of right and duty. Often only a really vigilant sense of moral responsibility can gauge correctly in practice the extent of justice with all its diverse obligations. The laws cannot always present the requirements in precise detail. The

Christian concept of social justice presupposes a morally mature man, fully conscious of his responsibilities.

5. Justice and Love

Evangelical perfection presupposes the fulfillment of the demands of strict justice, but in many points surpasses it: 1) The individual should fulfill that which justice demands in a spirit of love, though this in no way implies that he should look upon his deed as a singularly exalted act of love, if he does no more than simple justice demands, even though he is motivated by the spirit of love. 2) Love does not fix its gaze constantly on the minimum required by right or law but, on the contrary, thinks only of the need of one's neighbor. It extends loving kindness even to those who have forfeited the right to it through their own fault, in imitation of the heavenly Father who "makes his sun to rise on the good and the evil" (Mt 5:45), and who bestows upon us the gifts of grace, even if we have squandered His bounty through our own neglect. 3) Love is ever ready to surrender its own rights in favor of others, assuming always that the rights are such that they can be renounced without prejudice to the community and peril to one's own salvation (cf. Mt 5:38–42).

6. Human Justice and the Virtue of Religion

To subordinate the virtue of religion to the cardinal virtue of justice is in a measure justified only if this cardinal virtue is not primarily looked upon as the justice which exists between man and man and concerned only with the order of material goods and rights. It is contrary to the sense of Sacred Scripture to look upon the virtue of religion as a mere appendage and extension of human justice.

The revealed concept of justice proceeds from the justice of God, which manifests itself as well in the verdict of wrath as in the graciousness of mercy, in punishment and in pardon. The most astonishing work of divine justice is the justification of the sinner through grace. Already the prophets of the Old Testament announce that God's judgments save and heal. The most terrifying and most salutary expression of the divine justice is the expiatory death of Christ on the cross, which enables the unjust, the sinner, to hope in the salvific justice of God, if only he accept it with all his heart.

According to the revealed concept in the Bible the sanctity and justice of God is placed first; then follows the justice bestowed on men by God (which is both gift and task); and finally the fulfillment through man's love for God, a love owing to God on countless titles of justice and love. Only thereupon and from this approach do we have human justice, which is true justice in the Biblical sense only if it is made to refer to God, only if it is performed in the loving obedience owing to God.

The honor rendered to God in religion fulfills all the requirements of justice no less than does human justice, even though there is no relation between equals nor a strict equality between God's gift to man and man's gift in return. But "justice" is fulfilled in the loftiest sense of the word, for in religion there is the most primary and basic gift and task. It is justice par excellence. This is the sense of the words of Jesus to the Baptist: "so it becomes us to fulfill all justice" (MT 3:15).

The justice of God is superabundant justice. It bestows its blessings, distributes justice. It justifies sinners through grace wherever something of good will still is present, even though it may appear utterly lost in the immensity of guilt which only merits punishment. For it is divine justice, bestowing on the most miserable and needy of creatures the most undeserved benefits with a generosity to which they do not have the slightest claim in justice or right. And yet the scales of justice are truly balanced because to our petty claim there is added the superabundant merit of Christ. This divine justice is manifested in the sacred drama of the divine-human death of the God-man in incomprehensible love on the cross.

The reverence of the creature for his Creator, of the child for God its Father, is due in the strictest sense of justice. It is payment of the most absolute debt. Man should also be conscious of this debt, conscious of his utter incapacity to attain the measure of justice for which he must constantly strive, since he can never give God the honor He really merits. He cannot glorify God according to that superabundant measure of glory which God has already revealed to His creatures and which He will reveal in all fulness in eternity.

The Christian should guard against the mistaken notion of applying to God and his relation to God the univocal concept of human justice. The concept of justice is analogous when applied to God. The concept of human justice with all its rigidity must be enriched with the thought of the divine justice. In reference to God, the true Christian will never seek the exact limits of right, nor will he fear that God will not justly reward his good deeds and his merits. The divine bounty always transcends all human effort. The Christian will rejoice in the thought that for all eternity he will pay his debt of thanksgiving to God, a debt which the most loving zeal and the most zealous gratitude, the most ardent veneration of God seems to multiply a thousandfold. In this spirit the Christian does not think of works of "supererogation." The more we are permitted to love and honor God, the less will we be convinced that we have been acquitted of even the slightest part of our debt to Him, and the deeper indeed will we have fallen into the debt of loving Him. But sin, the refusal to honor, obey, and love God, bears within itself, in the fullest sense, the defect of value which is injustice, of which all injustice among men is a mere shadow (though a dismal shadow indeed) and a projection.

III. FORTITUDE (COURAGE)

1. *Nature and Rôle of Fortitude*

The virtue of fortitude gives us the strength and readiness to endure every kind of suffering, and even death itself, for a just cause, for the kingdom of God, or our own eternal salvation. It is the role of this virtue to repress the rebellion of the emotions against suffering and death, to discipline and control all the deep sentiments of fear and terror, if they should attempt to interfere with our generous engagement for the good, even at the cost of life itself. On the other hand, the virtue of fortitude in its action must avail itself of the dynamic force of the passion of anger (the revolt against evil) when it is confronted by the menace of injustice.

The virtue does not require at all that fear and revulsion against suffering and death be completely eradicated. The courageous man continues to see in pain and death an evil which his nature must fear and fear legitimately, but his apprehension does not paralyze his supreme decision for the good. The brave man fears the loss of his soul more than he dreads suffering and death. He shrinks from sin and offense against God more than from the persecution of men. Anyone who would be entirely insensible to suffering and persecution could not possess the virtue of fortitude at all. A desperate man who can see nothing in earthly existence to live for, does not practice fortitude if he risks his life in some hazardous gamble.

The acts of this virtue may be classed as active, consisting in positive attack, and passive, consisting in resisting attack, holding firm against evil. The brave man attacks the enemies of God, the enemies of justice, in order to further the triumph of the good in the kingdom of God. He attacks with the most suitable weapons. He does not hesitate, if it is necessary, to oppose violence with violence. But he will not defend the spiritual interests of the kingdom of God with violent means, particularly not if the enemies of God have not on their part resorted to violent attack.

Fortitude does not merely defend the good cause in this struggle with weapons which are effective in such warfare. Defense is often more glorious in the confession of the faith, in the use of the weapons of the spirit opposing evil and injustice. And often injustice responds with tyrannical imposition of agonizing disabilities, suppression of rights, and open violence.

The soldier of the kingdom of God in this world often has no means to combat injustice except resistance in patience (*patientia, perseverentia*). He persists in holding firm. Since this perseverance in holding firm against evil is more repugnant to man's nature than the attack of the enemy, Saint Thomas rightly calls it the principal act of fortitude.[61]

True grandeur of soul and total mastery of the emotional life belong to constancy. The reason is quite evident: the auxiliary forces of the passion of anger which strengthen resistance are often paralyzed by long and persistent resistance to evil, while the uninterrupted endurance of suffering only serves to make one aware of its magnitude. And without special assistance of the Holy Spirit the immediate sense of holy things becomes very weak because of the pressure of the affections rising up against the will to suffer. It follows that without real greatness of soul and perfect mastery of the emotions there can be no true constancy against evil. Under present conditions, such is the state of the "malice" in the world, the principal act of virtue of the courageous fighter for the kingdom of God is constancy; for the evil man shall gloat over the triumph of violence unto the end of time, whereas the Christian in union with His crucified Saviour shall possess his soul in patience (cf. Lk 21:19) and shall inherit the kingdom through the triumph of death, in constancy against the immeasurably great violence of the world.

The most exalted act of fortitude is the suffering of martyrdom, enduring death for Christ, for the faith, or for Christian virtue. Similar to martyrdom is the heroic death of the soldier in battle, provided his motive is unselfish obedience or zeal for the triumph of justice. Readiness to endure death belongs to the perfection of the virtue of fortitude. For one who is willing to suffer merely to a certain degree or up to a point, but not to drain the chalice of suffering to the bitter dregs, who is not willing to sacrifice his life, fighting and enduring in the engagement for the good, does not possess the ultimate determination for the good. He is not brave.

2. The Relation of Fortitude to the Other Virtues

Only love for a higher good justifies the sacrifice of lesser goods. One who is prepared to suffer and die must be aware of what he is sacrificing and of the reason for his sacrifice. Only one who appreciates his soul more than bodily life, one who esteems the goods of the other life more than earthly goods, can be courageous in the true sense of the term. Fortitude must serve the love of God, if it is to be perfect virtue. "Fortitude without justice is an instrument of evil."[62] This shows the superiority of love and justice over fortitude. Love and justice are virtuous in themselves. Fortitude becomes a virtue only through serving love and justice.

The impetuousness of the athlete and the brashness of the reckless soldier, who think of nothing but awards, acclaim, or promotion, are not virtue but vice, for life is worth more than cheers, honor, or even service awards. "To accept death is in itself not praiseworthy, but only if it is directed to the good."[63]

Fortitude must also be prudent: even in the endeavor to do what is just and right, one is not allowed to take needless risks of life. Surely if one can serve justice better or equally well in another way, it is not lawful to risk one's life even for justice. One must properly and prudently evaluate the whole situation, carefully appraising the merits and importance of the cause one is to serve, the magnitude of the effort required, and also the dangers involved. On the other hand, a perfectly prudent decision is possible only if courage, habitual courage, removes the blinding force of the extremes from right and left: heedless, foolish temerity and fearful, quaking timidity.

Companion to fortitude is the virtue of magnanimity, which trusts to accomplish great things in the combat for the good cause, though always relying on the aid of divine grace. Temerity or presumption, which recklessly plunges into unnecessary dangers, is the very antithesis of true courage. Genuine fortitude combines triumphant readiness to face the hardships and pressures of life with a wholesome misgiving regarding one's own power and resources. Though ready to die, the martyrs trusted valiantly in the grace of God to win the victory over death, if God called them to die. But still they did not ordinarily expose themselves to the danger of martyrdom, for they mistrusted their own frailty.

A fine example of such courage mingled with prudence is the conduct of Saint Thomas More. Meticulous in awaiting the providential summons to martyrdom, he failed to make the slightest move to hasten it beyond fulfilling his duty of professing the truth of faith. Throughout he was animated with joyful trust that the call from God would be accompanied with the grace and strength of martyrdom.

3. *Fortitude as a Virtue and as a Gift of the Holy Spirit*

The virtue of fortitude is sustained by the gift of the fear of the Lord. The true fear of God as a gift of the Holy Spirit influences filial fear of offending God so vitally that by comparison all anxiety over suffering through human malice pales into insignificance (cf. Mr 10:28). Moreover, the gift of fear of the Lord strengthens the wholesome mistrust of one's own powers so that the courageous man places his entire trust in the power of God. The man of true courage is also a humble man of prayer.

The virtue of fortitude is perfected by the gift of fortitude. Through the strength of this gift, the courageous man has the divine assurance that with God's grace he will be able to overcome all dangers, withstand all trials and sufferings sent by God, even death itself, in the engagement for the good cause. This gift bestows on him the joyous spirit of magnanimity so that he will boldly undertake and complete lofty and perilous projects, supported by the divine help. It gives him the courage to face the hazards in the most exposed positions in the war for the kingdom of God, to go far beyond the general call of duty, specifically to take upon himself the greatest burden and pain in atonement for sin. The gift of fortitude emboldens the Christian to abandon himself entirely to the consuming love of God and to endure the fire of passive purification in the mystic way.

Fortitude as a virtue disposes one to sacrifice bodily life to attain salvation (cf. Mr 10:39). The virtue of fortitude together with the gift of fortitude dispose man to undertake arduous tasks freely, to bear painful and onerous burdens for the salvation of souls and the kingdom of God. Through the gift of fortitude the Christian receives the courage to abandon his own petty self and to sacrifice himself utterly with joyful confidence for the cause of God, realizing that he will be more safely sheltered in God's hands than in his own, despite all his cautious concern for his own safety.

IV. TEMPERANCE

1. *The Rôle of Discipline and Moderation*

"Prudence looks to all existent reality; justice to the fellow man; while the man of fortitude relinquishes, in self-forgetfulness, his own possessions and his life. Temperance, on the other hand, aims at each man himself. . . . For man there are two modes of this turning toward the self: a selfless and a selfish one. Only the former makes for self-preservation; the latter is destructive. . . . Temperance is selfless self-preservation. Intemperance is self-destruction through the selfish degradation of the powers which aim at self-preservation."[64]

The instinct for nutrition, food and drink, is motivated by the desire for conservation of the bodily life of the individual; the sex instinct is motivated by the desire for conservation of the human species. These instincts must be subordinated as means to their end and purpose. If they are made ends rather than means and are not subordinated to the pattern and design intended by God, they become forces of destruction. To this extent they wreak havoc upon the bodily life of the individual, ravish the spiritual and intellectual life and endanger the soul's salvation.

It is the purpose of the virtue of temperance to moderate these instincts of man for self-conservation and conservation of the race, not merely in themselves but also in their relation to the end of the race as a whole. In a larger sense, it is the function of temperance to keep in balance the entire emotional and spiritual life. This is to be achieved not simply through orderly conformity with the varied world of values, but through direct control of the spiritual faculties and their activity. This means through understanding of self and conscious effort at self-discipline.

Temperance is indispensable as a special virtue for man living in the disorder of original sin. "Since the first sin man has been not only capable of loving himself more than he loves God his Creator but, contrary to his own nature, inclined to do so."[65] To the degree that man loves himself more than God, he loves himself in an inordinate manner and thereby places himself in disorder. Hence, the first requisite for the acquisition of the virtue of temperance is the orientation toward God. We must turn our eyes to God and discipline ourselves, with God entirely in mind as the supreme and most lovable good. "The discipline of temperance is not attainable except through unselfish preservation of one's inner self; it cannot be attained if man is concerned with himself alone."[66]

Temperance can be practiced as a virtue by fallen man only through zealous self-knowledge, self-conquest, and mortification. But mortification is not to be a destruction of the instinct itself (the natural desire for food and drink, for self-sustenance, for knowledge and power, for recreation and games, the sex urge itself), but only of the unruly and rebellious tendencies or, more specifically, the deeper roots of disordered emotions.

Stoical insensibility and absence of desire are as contrary to the virtue of temperance with its discipline and moderation as the lack of discipline and moderation.

2. *Importance of the Virtue of Temperance*

Though temperance ranks last in the list of cardinal virtues, this is no proof that it is the least important, absolutely speaking. Precisely because the desire for food and drink, the desire to satisfy the sexual urge, are rooted in man's indestructible instinct for existence itself (self-conservation), they exceed, when they degenerate, "all other powers of mankind in destructive violence."[67] Licentiousness (incontinence and impurity) not only mars the beauty and fortune of the inner harmony between body and soul, but also directly involves the spiritual part of man in the disorder. Intemperance makes one imprudent and, in consequence, also unjust. Except for hatred and envy, no vice so clouds and obscures the judgment of prudence as does intemperance.

"Unchaste abandon and the self-surrender of the soul to the world of sensuality paralyze the primordial powers of the moral person: the ability to perceive, in silence, the call of reality, and to make, in the retreat of this silence, the decision appropriate to the concrete situation of concrete action."[68] The undisciplined and immoderate indulgence in sensual things obscures the vision for spiritual values. When the primal forces become enervated and purposeless, the power of decision in the free will is broken.

Intemperance, moreover, places obstacles in the way of love. It destroys the capacity for true love. Love seeks submission without asking for reward or compensation. Love has the aloofness of reverence. Love essentially tends to exalt and ennoble the one loved. But intemperance leads to abandonment to the selfish craving of lust (the very contrary of submission and devotion); it misuses (the opposite of reverence); it desecrates and draws others into sin (the contrary of the ennobling work of love).

The splendor of the virtue of temperance flows from the spirit of dedication, reverence, and love. This holds true equally of the virtue of temperance as practiced in marital chastity in the sacrament of marriage or in the virginity of the consecrated bride of Christ. Temperance as a virtue is always nourished on love and always lives for love. Moderation in food and drink, the well-balanced cultivation of intellectual curiosity, the firm governance of the temperament and emotions in mildness and gentleness attain the lofty splendor of perfect virtue only if they are animated by love. Curbing the craving for food with no other motive than bodily health cannot be compared with the grateful enjoyment of food in the true spirit of temperance. Far more exalted than restraint for reasons of health is the partaking of food and drink with thanksgiving to God and the sense of triumph over material things according to which one may enjoy the food and drink or abstain from them as love for God, for self, for one's neighbor may demand. In love of God we may enjoy our food and drink, our repose of spirit, but not with a selfish quest for mere pleasure. But most of all we rejoice in the love of the Giver. And we are happy that partaking of food and drink makes us capable of renewed service for God and our neighbor.

Since love of God is not possible unless it is accompanied by temperance, this virtue also partakes of the urgency and necessity of love itself. It was a particular insight of Augustine to perceive the deepest Christian sense of temperance in the service of love: the virtue of temperance "promises us the purity and incorruptibility of that love which unites us to God."[69] "Temperance is not the stream. But it is the shore, the banks, from whose solidity the stream receives the gift of straight unhindered course, of force, descent, and velocity."[70]

3. Initial Stages of Temperance and Its Perfection

Saint Thomas distinguishes between continence and self-control and the perfect virtue of temperance (*temperantia*). Pieper calls the former "tentative sketch"; the latter, "perfected realization." "The first is less perfect than the second, because by the former, the directing power of reason has only been able to mold the conscious will, but not yet the sexual urge, whereas by the latter will and urge are both stamped with 'rational order.' "[71]

Even though the merit of the act is in the free decision regulating passion, still Saint Thomas holds that the total object of the virtue of temperance goes beyond the mere effective opposition of the will to disordered craving of passion. On the contrary, he is confident that the firm and constant attitude of the will, which heals and regulates in the loftiest manner, can so influence the passions as to make them conformable to right reason. In the desires and urges, the passions themselves become reasonable.

On the point of merit, the movement of the will animated by love is the sole decisive factor. The merit is therefore the greater, the stronger the love and the greater the obstacles and difficulties challenging the decision of love. However, as to the beauty and perfection of the virtue, that virtue is highest which not only confirms the will in the contest, but which also coordinates the emotional life. That virtue which controls and "informs" the more violent or dynamic urges and instincts is loftier than the one which merely restrains and controls the weaker ones.

As the virtue of temperance is contrary to the vice of intemperance, so continence is opposed to incontinence, though the latter is rather fault and defect in disposition than actually and totally a vice. The distinction between the two is of capital importance for the director of souls in the discernment of spirits and the guiding of diverse personalities through pastoral care. There is a species of intemperance which is not merely a sin of human weakness, but rather of human malice. It is the basic attitude of intemperance or licentiousness in the man who not only fails to repent of his sin, but gloats over it. He rejoices that he can still sin, because sin has become a second nature to him.[72] The intemperate man has made of license a matter of principle to which he clings with all his evil heart. The incontinent man, however, has at least the will to restrain himself, even though he is overpowered by his disordered passions and fails in individual instances (and he is responsible for these sins). But his sin is not sin of malice; it is sin of weakness. However, even his sins of weakness may in certain instances be mortal sins.

Intemperance viewed as a fundamental moral disposition is manifested in its most virulent form in the man who not only offends, but glories in his offense (cf. Rom 1:32). To acquire the virtue of temperance or keep it intact becomes particularly difficult for many principally because of the unfavorable climate of opinion in which they live. Not only do men worship the idol of a high material standard of living and bodily enjoyment, but they even attempt to make lust and adultery appear normal and morally inoffensive. The most effective means at the disposal of the incontinent to avoid sinking into the abyss of intemperance is humble confession of his faults, bound up with the sincere and upright endeavor to create a better trend in the social circles in which he moves.

4. Species of Temperance and Cognate Virtues

We may divide the virtue of temperance on the basis of the desire for food and drink and the instinct of sex. Accordingly, we speak of moderation in matter of food and drink and the moderation which falls under the virtue of chastity. As to the point of moderation in matter of food, an important act of temperance or continence in the use of food is fasting. Temperance in drinking or sobriety is particularly significant in the use of intoxicating beverages. Chastity is safeguarded by the sense of shame. The proper cultivation of this natural sense of shame in the service of chastity is called modesty, which is a potential part of chastity. The noblest expression of chastity is virginity, which should not be confounded with a mere negative celibacy or the shunning of marriage by the misogamist who hates the opposite sex or seeks to escape the burdens of lawful marriage.

The virtue of temperance also demands moderation regarding the standard of living and material enjoyment. Mass production of consumer goods in industry and large-scale advertising leads those who have no understanding of moderation to complete absorption in the creature comfort ideal of living. Confronted by the modern technical and cultural achievements made available to the masses, the Christian should attempt to use them prudently as their master, never permit them to make him their slave (cf. 1 Cor 6:12).

Virtues related to temperance express the inner harmony and poise of temperament: clemency or mildness strikes upon the right mean in judgment, guidance, discipline. The extremes are irascibility and its contrary, easygoing indolence. In the cultural or intellectual domain the noble desire for learning or studiousness (*studiositas*) is the right mean between superficial curiosity and slothful neglect in intellectual and cultural formation. As to correct deportment and the social graces, there is the right mean of moral propriety and good manners which avoids the extreme of fastidious elegance (affectation, foppishness) on the one hand and the extreme of crudeness (slovenliness, rudeness) on the other. The delightful virtue of good humor is the happy mean between empty buffoonery or hilarity and dour moroseness. The desire for honor and recognition is kept in restraint by humility, which is the right mean between the extreme of pride and inordinate craving for acclaim and abject self-abasement. However, we prefer to stress humility and meekness as distinctly and essentially Christian, as forming a basic attitude which with reverence underlies every Christian virtue, though Saint Thomas (following Aristotle) treats them as expression and potential parts of the virtue of temperance,

5. *Perfect Temperance, Self-Denial, and Mortification*

a. Discipline and Moderation

Man in his fallen state can neither acquire nor preserve temperance without self-knowledge and self-discipline (without asceticism). The interior disorder in man is so great that the virtue of temperance demands not only the exercise of asceticism in general, i.e., methodic self-discipline, but beyond this also a methodic self-denial, renunciation of those pleasures of sense which are compatible with the virtue of temperance. To arrive at the right mean of true temperance and true self-possession, fallen man, with his tendency toward excessive indulgence in the pleasures of the senses, must "act contrary" (*agere contra*). This means he must launch a counterattack against evil by voluntarily renouncing certain legitimate enjoyment of mundane things, particularly by restriction of sense pleasure. This conscious "acting contrary" does not aim directly at the middle way, the median between extremes, but it is still an authentic act of temperance because it has the same objective as the virtue of temperance: to swing the pendulum back to center by an energetic and dynamic counterthrust against lawful enjoyment itself. Basic to this will to "act counter" is the resolute Christian determination to fail by excess in the moderation of that same activity which seeks no more than the virtuous mean rather than to endanger one's salvation. The Christian keeps in mind the words of the Saviour, "If thy eye is an occasion of sin to thee, pluck it out" (Mr 18:9).

In many particulars self-denial and mortification go beyond the virtue of temperance: self-denial is concerned with both body and soul, with the realm of the spirit and the realm of the senses.

The Christian is aware of a profound truth which the haughty Stoic did not so much as suspect, that disorder lurks, not only in the passions, but also in the spirit of man. Perhaps particularly in the spirit of man! Therefore self-denial must begin with the will, the understanding, the memory. The will must learn to renounce its pride of autonomy and independence. The grand means is obedience in things of the spirit. Understanding and memory must renounce the selfish and solitary pursuit of pleasure. In humility and true self-denial they must constantly remain open to the light of faith with its deep obscurity of revealed mystery. The obedience of humble faith is the way to fulness of true light.

The next step is mortification of the imagination, of the feelings, of the emotions, and the senses, and last, but certainly not least, the renunciation of external possessions. Self-denial is essentially the will to renounce voluntarily all things in so far as they in any way obstruct the path of perfect love for God and neighbor. The mortified man makes sacrifices even though the present enjoyment of certain things, the enjoyment here and now, would not prove an obstacle to the love of God. His motive is self-discipline in preparation for critical situations in which his virtue would be really imperiled. Self-control, which means discipline and moderation, is principally in the category of the ethical, whereas mortification, self-denial, penitential exercise, love of the cross are religious concepts, religious values. Unlike temperance, they do not look first to the inner harmony, to the self-preservation of man (though in the second instance they also do this), but immediately and directly to submission to God, to the exercise of penance and expiation before God, then to the acquisition of new love for self and all creatures. And this is love in God and from God.

Renunciation and the rejection of false love do not spring from an unreligious contempt for creation, but have as their goal a love of creation, purged and purified. And this is possible only if man prepares himself, through self-denial and renunciation, to sacrifice everything which proves an obstacle or could prove an obstacle to radical submission to God. Only one who is ready to renounce all things for God's sake and is truly capable of making such a sacrifice can rightly use these same created things. Only one who constantly makes the painful sacrifice of a portion of self and the world through love for God can truly love himself and the world in God.

Since, as a matter of fact, fallen man persistently tends to love himself and creatures, not for God's sake, but apart from God or even in opposition to God, a sacrificial, voluntary mortification and self-denial in spiritual life at all stages is indispensable. Even apart from the demands of temperance and transcending its demands, self-denial is indispensable as an element in the following of Christ.[73]

b. Mortification, Path to Joy

The greatest source of sorrow for man is his own inner disorder in his love of self and creatures and his pursuit of pleasure. Now mortification is the direct antithesis of this straining after indulgence; and a lofty and effective motive for external mortification and earnest penance can be and should be the thought of the higher joy, the joy of the spirit, the joy of raising our minds in converse with God (the *mentem elevas* of the Preface for Lent). Voluntary renunciation of the satisfaction of sense desires, even should they be legitimate, is an expression of the lofty esteem for the joys of the spirit. The voluntary acceptance of pain suppresses the domineering world of sense and makes the spirit more readily accessible to the celestial joys. The Christian, unlike the Stoic, has no illusions about the painful character of human suffering and sorrow. He has no desire to destroy the sensibilities, but only to coordinate the senses in the structure of the perfect man who is assimilated to the risen Christ.

Christian self-conquest and self-denial have no part in hatred of self or in the desire for self-destruction. The enthusiastic love of the cross which we find in the saints is not inspired by any unnatural sadism which gloats over self-torture. The cross is always hard to bear for man with his frail senses (otherwise it would not be a cross at all), and mortification is painful; but in the profoundest depths of soul a fountain of joy of an entirely different order springs up. Only this joy can impart to man the strength to endure and accept freely the pain of renunciation. The admonition of the Master that we should display joy in our countenances when we fast, that we should use the ointment of gladness (Mt 6:16ff.), has a much more positive meaning than merely concealing our penitential performance. The manifestation of joy in doing penance is entirely in conformity with the rejuvenating force of love from which the will to fast flows and to which it is directed. Through fasting and renunciation of the enjoyment of sense the inner joy should become so strong that it overflows more and more in the countenance.

Renunciation prepares the way for a joy in creatures that is deep and pure, similar to that of Francis of Assisi, even though the first purpose of all renunciation is directed to the uncreated Love, which is God. Thus fasting bears with it the savor for spiritual things. It also brings with it a capacity for the wholesome enjoyment of food and drink in the spirit of joyful thanksgiving to God, altogether apart from the fact that for the moderate and temperate man food is far more palatable and in general more wholesome than for the intemperate or glutton.

c. Interior and Exterior Mortification

In itself the inner mortification or abnegation of oneself and the rebellious will is superior to the exterior mortification of the senses. But such is the unity of man that disorder can be properly combatted and curbed only if it is attacked on all fronts at the same time. Moreover, the abnegation of the spirit has need for external mortification as its own spontaneous expression and its motive force. Just as unbridled sensuality oppresses the spirit, so exterior mortification strengthens the spiritual powers. It arises from the spirit of renunciation which is in the will and in turn fortifies and vitalizes it. Nevertheless, external mortification harbors dangers to the will and the spirit if the subjugation of the senses is not accompanied by complete and utter submission to God in holy humility, or at least by the earnest desire for it.

It is universally true that every kind of asceticism and self-denial is dangerous, if the principal foe of the religious man is not clearly recognized and combatted. This is the inner spirit of pride dominating the heart of man. But it is no less true that asceticism and self-denial are essential for interior submission. The true and humble submission of spirit under God is impossible if man does not subject his senses to the law of God through the exercise of renunciation and mortification and obedience to the law of God.

d. Voluntary Mortification and the Divine Visitations

The most profound purification of sinful man is possible only in the providential school of suffering. Though mortification, voluntarily chosen, is of great importance, the sufferings sent by God are the most precious, because in these there is the least room for self-will and the greatest possibility for exercise of obedience in the purest submission to God.

Through external suffering (passive purification of the senses) God purifies the senses and likewise the spirit (passive purification of the spirit) of man. The warmth of His gifts is accompanied by the purging and purifying pain which has the force of drawing men to Him. But our submission to this purging pain sent by God is never secure unless we train ourselves for acceptance of the divine will, prepare for it through active purification of the senses and the spirit by the voluntary imposition of renunciation and pain. The divine visitations often demand tremendous sacrifices. To rise to the heights in the spirit of acceptance is possible only if man has made himself equal to the occasion through voluntary mortification.

Self-imposed practices of penance without the suffering and trials sent by God only too readily pave the way for pride and self-will. On the other hand, restriction of mortification exclusively to the trials and sufferings imposed by God without the voluntary acceptance of renunciation and affliction readily diminishes the force of free and willing acceptance, or even seriously endangers it.

e. Mortification and the Imitation of Christ

"And he said to all, 'If any one wishes to come after me, let him deny himself, and take up his cross daily, and follow me'" (Lk 9:23). Christ has gone before us, showing us the way of self-denial, of voluntary self-abasement and acceptance of the most painful sufferings. It is true that during His public life the penances practiced by the Master were, as a rule, not extraordinarily rigorous. On this point we note the contrast between Christ and John, His precursor (Mt 11:18f.). Clearly it was the Lord's will that the precursor should be a man of great penitential rigor, with a manifest vocation for penance. Thereby He fixed the sign and seal of penance on the very portal of the New Testament.

Even though Christ did not specifically require more of His disciples than the fast prescribed by the law, to which He Himself also conformed, nevertheless He made clear to them that they would fast after He had departed (Mt 9:15), that fasting together with prayer constitutes a mighty weapon against the vilest spirits of hell (Mt 17:20). Also to be borne in mind is the utter sinlessness of Christ's nature. One of the principal reasons for bodily mortification is entirely absent: Christ did not possess a fallen nature; He had no need to discipline His will for patient and submissive acceptance of what the Father would impose upon Him. But none the less, in perfect freedom He chose as His portion poverty, homelessness, persecution, the toilsome life of a craftsman, and finally the no less arduous public ministry throughout the length and breadth of Palestine. In His forty-day fast, with its dreadful rigor, He committed to the Church an ideal and pattern for the penitential life. And finally—and this is the very central point for all understanding of Christ's penance—He offered His life in agony and pain.

The saints sought to fulfill the words of Saint Peter, "Christ also has suffered for you, leaving you an example that you may follow in his steps" (1 Pr 2:21), not merely through patient endurance of suffering and persecution, but also through voluntary exercise of severe penance. Love of the cross and bodily mortification on the part of the saints is living the mysticism of the passion (vividly portrayed with deep inner spirit in the notes of Blessed Henry Suso). Since the tenth century the practice of scourging oneself has come into vogue as a penitential exercise in memory of the Saviour's painful scourging at the pillar. Carl Feckes says: "Scarcely a canonized saint failed to practice this form of penance."[74] Nevertheless, each age has its own specific variation of bodily mortification suited to the conditions and needs of the times.

The Christian has the vocation of penance. He is called to follow Christ, who freely suffered and died for us, through the voluntary exercise of self-denial and mortification. But the penance of Christians will vary greatly, both in manner and degree, for each individual is not to perform exactly the same penitential acts as every other individual follower of Christ. However, in general, the way of self-denial and mortification, in union with Christ, is traced by the sacraments. The way of penance is the sacramental way.

Eloquently Saint Paul explains holy baptism as dying with Christ. Particularly in his letter to the Romans he carries out this striking figure. We follow the path of Christ to glory, but it is the path of suffering and dying to ourselves (ROM 6:5; 8:17). Those who are baptized must "put to death the deeds of the flesh" (i.e., the deeds of fallen man) (ROM 8:13). "They who belong to Christ have crucified their flesh with its passions and desires" (GAL 5:24). The Apostle says of himself: we are "always bearing about in our body the dying of Jesus" (2 COR 4:10). "I bear the marks of the Lord Jesus in my body" (GAL 6:17). "I chastise my body and bring it into subjection, lest perhaps after preaching to others I myself should be rejected" (1 COR 9:27). As members of the Mystical Body of Christ, we must in our own place and for our own part fulfill and complete through voluntary abnegation and mortification what Christ wrought for the whole Church. "What is lacking of the sufferings of Christ I fill up in my flesh for his body, which is the Church" (COL 1:24).

Saint Paul does not mean to deny the sufficiency of the suffering of Christ. It was truly superabundant. But it is a law of the Mystical Body of Christ that the members must follow the same path as their Head in the application of the fruits of redemption through Christ. It is the path of voluntary suffering for themselves and for one another. We are indeed baptized in one body, baptized in the death of Christ. But the death of Christ is completed and perfected in us only if we all, who form one body with Him, continue to suffer and work with Him who is the Head. By voluntary mortification we share mystically in His dying in act and spirit.

One of the important effects of the sacrament of confirmation is to strengthen the Christian so that he endures suffering with courage, so that he is prepared to engage in mortal combat for the kingdom of God fighting to his last breath. Paul uses the example of the athlete, who for the sake of some contemptible objective to be gained by the "contest abstains from all things" (1 Cor 9:25). Today it might be equally apposite to refer to the fools of fashion. We might note the excessive sacrifices they are prepared to make for a standard of elegance set up by ridiculous vanity! The Christian, on the contrary, must gird himself for the stern struggle of life with all its hazards. The power of victory does not come to him through personal effort, but the natural and supernatural endowments bestowed upon him must be constantly exercised. For the saints, fasting and every kind of mortification were initiation and exercise in the school of martyrdom. The weak, the delicate, the infirm cannot at all face up to the gruesome forms of martyrdom to which Christians are exposed in our time. The grace of confirmation, which demands promptness and readiness to give one's life for Christ, is therefore the law of grace obliging the Christian to abnegation and mortification.

By its very nature the sacrament of penance requires the exercise of acts of penance. Such was its meaning throughout the whole history of its practice in administration and reception. The convert from sin must be a penitent. In gratitude for the expiatory efficacy of the passion of Christ, he must be disposed to share in the work through voluntary exercise of penance. It is no exaggeration to say that remissness in the spirit of conversion, the failure of second conversion and profound renewal of life, among those who receive the sacrament of penance, is due to lack of penance. Only too often the penitents are not profoundly penitential.

The supreme manifestation of voluntary abnegation and suffering for the sake of God and neighbor is the sacrifice of Christ on the cross. "God so loved the world that he gave his only-begotten Son, that those who believe in him may not perish" (Jn 3:16). Just as men before Christ could find no better expression of their obedience and their love for God than sacrifice, so God Himself chose the way of sacrifice and indeed of the greatest sacrifice, the offering of the life of His own Son in the most excruciating pain, as manifestation of His love for men. "Therefore, the Christian must learn through his participation in the Eucharistic sacrifice to make of his life a consecrated sacrificial offering to God."[75] It is not a matter of mere chance that the Church from her very inception enjoined great sacrifice for the celebration of the Eucharist: the offering of gifts, the Eucharistic fast preceding Holy Communion, which involved a total fast for an entire day particularly on the vigils and station days.

According to the Apostolic Constitution *Christus Dominus*[76] of January 6, 1953, there are two basic principles governing the Eucharistic fast: 1) the Church, as always, lays great stress on fasting before reception of Holy Communion in order to foster the spirit of sacrifice befitting the sacrament and to awaken the spirit of reverence; 2) the high esteem for the Eucharistic fast still should not render the frequent, even daily reception of Holy Communion impossible for any individual who possesses the necessary dispositions for sacrifice, even though he cannot fully comply with the strict rule of the Eucharistic fast.

The *motu proprio* of Pius XII of March 19, 1957, enunciated the ecclesiastical law of Eucharistic fast in the following clear and succinct form: no matter at what time of day or night the Holy Sacrifice is offered or Holy Communion is received, the celebrant of the Mass is required to abstain from all solid food and all alcoholic drink for three hours before the beginning of Mass, and the one who receives Communion, for three hours before reception of the Sacrament. For an hour before the celebration of the Mass the celebrating priest must abstain from all other food and drink likewise. And the faithful who receive Holy Communion must do the same for an hour before reception of the Sacrament. However, the drinking of water is never forbidden, for this no longer pertains to the Eucharistic fast. The sick, even though they are not confined to bed, may partake of liquid food and drink (though not alcoholic drink) up to the time of the celebration of the Mass (for the priest celebrating the Mass) and to the time of the reception of Holy Communion (for the individual receiving Holy Communion). Under the same conditions they may also take liquid and solid medicines. It is no longer necessary to consult one's confessor on these points. Nevertheless, the *motu proprio* admonishes all who can do so without disadvantage to conform voluntarily to the former strict practice of the Eucharistic fast.

The relaxation in the practice of the Eucharistic fast, as the Apostolic Constitution expressly states, purposes to focus attention all the more clearly on those interior and far-reaching dispositions which create a spirit of atonement, a spirit of sacrifice. In the friend of Christ, the Holy Eucharist must constantly awaken an ever greater determination to share in Christ's own work of atonement for the offenses against His Father's honor and to undertake voluntarily suffering and mortification for the salvation of sinners in their misery.

The sacrament of Holy Orders imposes the task of penance in a very particular manner on the minister of the altar. He is bound by a sacred and urgent duty to make of his entire priestly life a consuming sacrifice which he offers to God in union with Christ, the Priest and Victim.

Matrimony, too, no less than the other sacraments, points to the cross of the Lord. The graces of the sacrament and the obligations it imposes necessarily relate to the cross. On the cross Christ acquired His bride the Church, and until the day of His second coming the Church will bear the burden of His cross and celebrate the triumph of the victory of the sacrifice on the cross. Wherefore, Christian marriage, which in its depth of mystery of grace possesses the lofty dignity of symbolizing this great mystery of Christ and the Church, cannot survive without sacrifice and renunciation. Marital love, which the sacrament demands and sanctifies, is fed on the selfless spirit of the mutual sacrifice of the spouses.

Extreme Unction, the anointing of the sick, sacrament of the "anointing for death," imparts the strength and vigor and imposes the sacred obligation to accept death willingly and gladly, as sacrificial death in union with the sacrificial death of Christ. Essential preparation for this sacrament and for the holy suffering and dying demanded by it is the life-long discipline in the pain of death through a constant dying to one's self by mortification.

Baptism itself is an anointing for death. In this first sacrament the Christian receives an anointing for death. The final anointing is in Extreme Unction. The significance of this "last anointing for death" in Extreme Unction was cast into very sharp relief in the Middle Ages by a rigorous practice following the reception of the sacrament. After he had been anointed in the sacrament, the recipient (if he survived) was bound to perpetual continence in marriage, to abstinence from many kinds of food, in a word, to a life of very austere penance. One who was solemnly anointed for death in the sacrament was to seek nothing further in this life than the cross of Christ. Though the practice cast a very significant light on the penitential nature of Extreme Unction and the value of penance in preparation for death, its very rigor led to neglect of the sacrament on the part of very many. In consequence, the practice was abandoned.

f. Obligation to Perform Acts of Bodily Mortification

Innocent XI, in condemning the erroneous doctrine of Molinos, clearly teaches that voluntary mortification is spiritually wholesome and fruitful and therefore is not to be abandoned.[77] The Synod of Issy made the following pronouncement in condemnation of Mme. Guyon: "Mortification pertains to every state of life and therefore acts of mortification are frequently necessary. To turn the faithful away from mortification under pretext of piety is, therefore, to condemn Saint Paul and presupposes an erroneous heretical doctrine."[78] Benedict XIV[79] speaks of the necessity of works of penance in order to sustain the spirit of Christian perfection. But he also makes a distinction between the degree or measure of bodily mortification which is universally required for Christians and the special vocation of certain saints to extraordinary austerity.

Saint Thomas Aquinas says especially of fasting that it is not required merely by positive law of the Church, but by the very law of God. In her law of fasting the Church did not merely determine more specifically a matter of supererogation, but a matter which was in a general way obligatory.[80] Francis de Sales very quaintly calls mortification "oats to quicken the donkey's pace." Of fasting he says: "The evil spirit fears us more if he knows that we are prepared to fast."[81] Moritz Meschler, S.J. (died in 1912), says: "Without suitable works of penance one can scarcely be a truly spiritual man. The neglect of bodily penance is usually due to sloth, weakness of spirit, and dominance of the senses. . . . Esteem for penance and exercise of penance is rightly looked upon as the distinguishing characteristic of the Catholic spirit as opposed to the aversion for mortification which the Reformers displayed. In fact, the sincerely repentant man is penitential almost by instinct. He has committed sin; he wants to make good the evil he has done; he resorts to bodily mortification. The notion arises spontaneously in his mind. All this belongs to the most elemental concept of the spiritual life."[82]

The degree of bodily mortification and particularly of fasting which is of obligation differs very much in individual cases and instances. Much depends on the temperament, the profession, condition and state of life, vocation. One who is leading a very hard life, filled with deprivations, and particularly any one who is weak physically or ill, is not obliged, at least not ordinarily, to perform any external acts of mortification. In fact, many such acts would even exceed the bounds of prudence and be unlawful. The religious, obliged by his very state to strive for perfection, has a greater obligation to practice penance than the layman. Anyone who is prone to the sensual is usually under a more serious obligation to practice mortification than the individual whom God has endowed with an even and tranquil temperament not so inclined to passion. Likewise there may be certain occasions or periods in life when there is greater need for severity of bodily discipline and mortification.

g. Sinful Mortification

If they exceed the bounds of moderation, penitential exercise and discipline cease to be virtue, for the acts of penance must always be acts of the virtue of temperance. Saint Jerome, himself given to austere practice of penance, says: "We do not enjoin immoderate and violent fasting. Through such acts weak bodies are ruined. And illness sets in before the foundation of holiness is laid down."[83] Thomas Aquinas repeats the words of warning attributed to Saint Jerome: "There is no difference if you bring about your death slowly throughout a long period of time or in a brief interval. He offers rapine to God in the guise of sacrifice who tortures himself excessively through vile food and insufficient nourishment or through lack of sleep."[84] Excessive mortification can readily lead to grave damage to one's health and, in consequence, may even result in moral disaster. Mortification must serve the higher purpose of the inner discipline of the will.

In his day Saint Paul was obliged to combat a pernicious principle regarding fasting and mortification in general. The Gnostics, and even more particularly the Manichaeans, looked upon the material world, and especially certain species of food, as impure and ungodly. Likewise the dietary prescriptions of the Jews were falsely understood by many Christian converts. Sharply the Apostle corrects this false attitude: "I know and am confident in the Lord Jesus that nothing is of itself unclean" (Rom 14:14). "You lay down the rules: Do not touch; nor taste; nor handle! . . . In this you follow the precepts and doctrines of men" (Col 2:20ff.). "For every creature of God is good, and nothing is to be rejected that is accepted with thanksgiving. For it is sanctified by the word of God and prayer" (1 Tm 4:4f.).

In India the prohibition of the slaughter and the eating of animals is primarily the result of the doctrine of the transmigration of souls, according to which the souls of men inhabit the bodies of animals. There has been a revival in our day of the ancient Gnostic and Manichaean concepts; this accounts for the prohibition of the eating of animal products by many vegetarian groups. The material thing and particularly flesh is viewed as the seat and source of evil. The vegetarian sect of the Mazdaznan prohibits the eating of meat because of a Zoroastrian dualistic bias. In this system temperance is the primary virtue as such, and self-redemption is sought through sex-hygiene, correct nourishment, and proper breathing technique. The power and value of love and the hazards of pride are not correctly grasped or are entirely ignored.[85]

An entirely different question arises regarding the influence of certain foods and drinks on the passions. It is the thought of Saint Thomas[86] that such influence is a determining factor in the ecclesiastical law of abstinence. Meat and animal products as such (particularly eggs) were thought to exercise a baneful influence on the sexual life. Obviously Saint Thomas does not hold that the eating of meat is in itself sinful or that it necessarily leads to sins against the sixth commandment. He merely suggests that excessive eating of meat, eggs, and so forth, reacts unfavorably on the passions, and therefore strict moderation and occasional abstinence are required and commanded. Ultimately, of course, we are here concerned with a question of fact which cannot readily be established scientifically. It should not be assumed that any ordinary food or drink directly excites the passions, though an indirect influence on the nervous system may occasion some moral dangers. Prudent spiritual directors always caution moderation in this matter.

Bodily mortification becomes sinful above all through evil motives on the part of the proud: for this reason the Lord rebuked the Pharisees who fasted in order to please and impress other men, disfiguring "their faces in order to appear to men as fasting" (Mt 6:16). The Christian does not rise to the heights of Christian virtue if he aims only at natural self-control in his mortification. Only if he seeks self-denial, the divine honor, true penance, and atonement for sin, imitation of the Crucified, does he practice true Christian virtue in bodily mortifications.

If it leads to neglect of higher things (love of neighbor, prayer, fulfillment of the duties of one's state of life or vocation) the external practice of acts of mortification may be immoderate and even sinful. Mortification must always remain the means to the end, which is disciplining the will for love of God and neighbor.

V. HUMILITY AS BASIC CHRISTIAN ATTITUDE

1. *Humility as a Christian Virtue*

Classical Greek and Roman thought had no concept of humility. The first meaning of such terms as *tapeinós* and *humilis* is petty, base, servile. In the Old Testament there are occasional passages which are profound exhortations to humility. We note for example Sirach 3:19ff. There are many prayers, notably in the Psalms, charged with the most beautiful sentiments of humility toward God. But the ideal of humility is revealed in its perfection only in the example and teaching of Christ.

There is a twofold tendency in the virtue of Christian humility: toward one's superiors, who are above us, and toward our equals and inferiors. The first tendency is inseparable from every truly religious attitude. Its sole prerequisite is living faith and genuine encounter with the personal God. Should anyone look upon himself as a portion of God or a manifestation of God, in a pantheistic sense, the very basis for humility toward the personal God above us is destroyed. Humility is first of all the virtue of the creature-status, the response of created being to Creator, recognition and affirmation of utter dependence on God. This aspect of humility as such is not yet typically or exclusively Christian, but rather something that Christianity has in common with every theistic religion. In Christianity, however, it occupies a pure position, and is given its purest and deepest expression.

On the contrary, the second aspect is peculiar to Christian humility as such: the humility of the superior toward the inferior, the gracious condescension springing from the rich inner source of grace. This God gave to us in Christ. Christian humility is the "inner spiritual imitation of the grand and unique movement of God in Christ in which He freely renounces His majesty and exaltation, dwells among men as one of them, in order to be the free and blessed servant of every man and of all creation."[87]

The Greeks knew only *Eros*, the love tending upward to the divine. The great manifestation of God is the *Agápe*, which from the very plenitude of glory stoops down and gives itself to creatures. The humility of man is his response to this manifestation of loving and humble condescension by which God bestows supernatural grace on undeserving creatures. It is at the same time participation of the creature in the divine act of condescension which empties itself in supreme service of love to men.

It is quite true that we do not usually list humility with the cardinal virtues as actually one of their number. But Christian thought and practice has always looked upon it as a fundamental virtue serving as the foundation for the whole edifice of Christian virtue. Unlike the four virtues which are usually listed as the four cardinal virtues, humility does not have its own limited sector in the area of virtue; it does not play the role of setting one single power of the soul in order. It rather regulates the entire order in the most essential of man's relations. It governs the most basic and characteristic status of man: the right subordination to God the Creator and the Bestower of grace. Humility of the child of God is filial response to the love of Creator and Saviour, whom he invokes by His own divine name. In this sense humility is a truly primordial attitude, a cardinal virtue.

2. *The Humility of Christ*

God has taught us humility in person. "Christ Jesus, who though he was by nature God, did not consider being equal to God a thing to be clung to, but emptied himself, taking the nature of a slave and being made like unto men" (PHIL 2:5ff.). It is the tremendous novelty of this revelation that humility does not spring from baseness or inferiority, but flows from the heights above, from the divine bounty to man. It derives from the "immensity" of the rich, glorious love of God. In the words of Saint Augustine, it is God "who descends from heaven by the weight of His charity" (*qui de coelo descendit pondere caritatis*).[88] God does not fear that He shall suffer loss if in His love He stoops down to His creatures. Only pride seeks presumptuous superiority (*rapina:* PHIL 2:6), a dignity insecurely clung to. "All pride is beggar's pride."[89] The truly great and noble follow the bold way of love for the little and the least. No bolder stroke of love is possible than the Incarnation of God and the call of sinful man to loving communion with God. The glory of God is the glory of love. The love of God manifests its glory, its entire height, depth, breadth in this condescension of God to man.

From His birth in the cave at Bethlehem, Christ gave us an example in humble living: in His debasement, in His exile and persecution, in His hidden and obscure life at Nazareth, in His perfect obedience to men, in respect and love for sinners and publicans, in a vocation of service toward mere man: "I am in your midst as he who serves" (LK 22:27). Incomparable is the mingling of humility with obedience, for humility and the spirit of obedience belong together. Rightly does Paul see the summit of the self-abasement, of the humility of Christ in His obedience unto death on the shameful tree of the cross (PHIL 2:8).

The *Magnificat,* recorded by Saint Luke, is filled with the thought of the awesome mystery of the divine humility in the Incarnation, flowing in ecstatic words from the bliss which filled Mary's heart. "He has regarded the lowliness of his handmaid; for, behold, henceforth all generations shall call me blessed . . . he has scattered the proud in the conceit of their heart. He has put down the mighty from their thrones and has exalted the lowly" (LK 1:48ff.).

3. *Our Humility in Relation to the Humility of Jesus*

In an incomparable manner the two tendencies just referred to are combined in the humility of Jesus: the humility which stoops lovingly to inferiors, and the humility which is profoundly conscious of the transcendence of superiors. The Incarnation is the very "humility" of God in condescension to man; all the acts of Jesus are acts of divine humility; but they are likewise the response of humility on the part of the humanity of Christ to the heavenly Father, the humility of the creature before His Creator, of the child toward the Father: "The Father is greater than I" (JN 14:28). His obedience unto the death of the cross is the humble submission of the human will of Christ to the higher will of the heavenly Father. The humility of Christ is incomparably greater than that of His disciples, both as to the height and depth of the condescension to those beneath Him and as to the obedient submission to the Father in heaven. But in a certain manner and degree the disciple can cooperate in this twofold movement of the humility of Jesus. By grace and the divine sonship, the disciple is elevated to participation in the divine nature; and by faith and love he is brought to some realization of the infinite distance which separates him from the Creator and Father. He can follow the path of the humility of Christ in loving service for the least of creatures and in obedience to the heavenly Father. The very providential visitations and dispositions which God imposes on His disciples through the basest of His creatures become the occasion of both humble service to men and perfect obedience to God.

In one point the humility of Christ is truly unique and utterly different from the humility of mere men: it is neither the humility of a mere creature nor the humility of a sinner. Thus it lacks the two most compelling motives which we possess. And yet it is supreme humility.

Christ is not pure creature as we are. And yet humility must be the primordial movement of submission of the creature, the most basic gesture of self-recognition in relation to the Creator. It must be the virtue which most rightly and properly suits the creature in his status as creature. Evidently the whole created human nature of Christ, which is raised to personal union with the uncreated Word, is moved to its very depth most mightily by this virtue-of-creature, humility before the Father, who is greater than He according to His human nature.

Christ is utterly sinless. Totally absent from Him is the second basis for the humility of the disciple. It is our sinfulness which infinitely widens and broadens the chasm separating us from God. Even though—or perhaps we should say, particularly because—we have been elevated from our depth of sinfulness to loving communion with the all-holy God, our grateful response must arise from the very pit of unworthiness in which we groveled and still grovel because of past sins and our ever-persisting sinfulness. Our loving response to the divine condescension and our elevation—even though we were sinners—cannot be true and genuine, if it is not the response of humility penetrating to the very depth of our being and yet filling us with jubilation.

From all this it is evident that the two most compelling motives for our humility are our own creature-status and our sinfulness. Nevertheless, it is evident from the humility of Christ, who is not mere creature or in any way stained by sin, that the actual dynamic force of humility, the force of "gravity" (to refer again to the thought of Augustine who speaks of the *pondus* or weight of charity) in humility is love.

Paradoxically Christ, though conscious of no sin and entirely free from sin, showed us sinners by His bloody sweat on Mount Olivet and His death on Calvary how the humility of sinners should be manifested. He bore the burden of sins which were not His own. For our sins, which He willingly bore for us, He was prostrated under the punishment which we and our sins deserved. If we are freed from the degradation of sin and elevated to the royal dignity of the kingdom of God through the humility of Christ, we have incurred the double debt of humility.

The Lord says to His disciples: "learn from me, for I am meek and humble of heart" (Mt 11:29). His humility is the foundation of our exaltation; imitation of His humility is the abiding basic condition on which the whole worth of our discipleship depends. Only if we possess the spirit of humility are we capable of learning from Christ and in some measure worthy to be taught by Christ. The greater the humility, the greater the docility, the more loving the condescending inspiration of the Holy Spirit. Humility is openness to the grace and truth of Christ. We can share in the wisdom and grace of Christ only in so far as we open our hearts in humility to Him.

4. *Essence and Requirements of Humility*

a. Humility Must Animate both Knowledge and Love

The humility of knowledge enables us to perceive our own true status in the presence of the all-holy God and to see ourselves as we really are in relation to our fellow men from this same standpoint. Therefore the first element in humility is the living confrontation with God: I, creature, sinner, in the face of the All-Holy! This consideration would not only dispose the creature to be humble. It would also discourage and depress him if another important truth were lost sight of: I, sinful man, have been raised up to God; God stoops down in incomprehensible love to me!

Thus humility turns her eyes from our own sinful baseness in the sight of God to ecstatic contemplation of the majesty of God. Only in humility can we rightly contemplate our own exaltation as flowing from the very "humility" of God. Precisely this consideration deepens our humility most of all. In humility man recognizes his own true place and God's infinite majesty. This recognition is perfect only if man rejoices in his total dependence on God and also gives glory to the majesty of God. Most efficaciously are we impelled to rejoice ecstatically in the glory of God—"we give Thee thanks for thy great glory"—by pondering the bounty of God who unselfishly shares His own great glory with us, His petty creatures.

b. The Hazard of False Perspectives

Humble self-knowledge and joyous realization of God's greatness is endangered by false (practically unbelieving) appraisal of our fellow men. Every comparison we make of ourselves with our neighbor without regard for the relation to God leads to false exaltation of ourselves and depreciation of our neighbor. Only if we view our fellow man in the light of his exaltation through God, and in our life and association with our fellow man always remain conscious of our own pettiness and sinfulness before God, can we really compare ourselves with our neighbor. Every confrontation with our fellow men must include God. We must confront God and our neighbor in the sight of God. Otherwise we cannot be truly humble. The humble man triumphs over every temptation to scorn his fellows by the thought of the love which God still bears for him and with which God still seeks him out even in his sin. Such temptation is overcome when it encounters the vivid horror which the humble man has for his own sinfulness in the sight of God.

Only the humble man is capable of a complete and just estimate of the good qualities and merits of his neighbor. The proud man sees his own merits in the light of his own self-exaltation and the merits of others in the light of his own advantage and prejudice. The humble man rejoices unselfishly over all good things for the sake of God who is their source. He can see nothing in the good qualities of his neighbor which could prove of prejudice to him because he sees all things in the joyous light of the glory they give to God.

c. "Humility Is Truth"

Humility realizes that pride is enslavement. In his estimation and consideration of things, the humble man does not assume that we can look upon ourselves and our achievements without the risk of pride. In true self-knowledge the humble man realizes that we are constantly assailed by pride, and accordingly he is always on guard against any unnecessary reflection on the faults of his neighbor. And he likewise shuns the studied reflection on his own good qualities. Of course, it is precisely the humble man who wishes to know and to acknowledge thankfully and joyfully the gifts he has received from God. But he must be on guard against "indulging" in the enjoyment of these good qualities and gifts. Only in regarding them as a gift (bestowed by God) and as a task (one's own obligations rest on the possession of good talents and capabilities) does the humble man dwell on himself, whereas without envy or prejudice he recognizes all the good qualities of his neighbor and rejoices over them. The height of his own election to grace the humble man gladly considers, but only to be astonished over the unheard-of condescension of God toward a miserable sinner. Grateful acknowledgement of our own dignity granted by God belongs essentially to Christian humility.

The Christian must be aware of his own talents. "But these talents appear as tasks and duties rather than as values which he possesses. Because of his responsibility and the realization that 'he is an unprofitable servant,' he cannot give himself over to an indulgent enjoyment of them.

The humble man will never have such a false sense of security as to believe that he can admire his own good qualities and analyze their value objectively as he would the gifts of others, without the risk of falling into the sin of pride. For the false sense of security itself is offspring of pride."[90] Only in eternity, when our humility is perfect, will this precaution be no longer necessary; for there we shall see and enjoy all, even our own good qualities, immediately in God and from God.

The humble man is not so much concerned with what he has already accomplished. He can, of course, show that he has made progress with the grace of God. But he realizes that it is entirely in accord with truth to attribute all that is good, not to himself, but to God. To himself alone he attributes all that is evil, all failure, all laxity or remissness in the use of the gifts of God. Therefore he looks to the good he has done as the "unprofitable servant" who thanks God for it. But the failure to do good, the remissness in virtue, he considers his very own. The further one progresses in love, the more exalted does the ideal and goal of love loom up before him as he strives for it, the greater the distance between his fidelity to God and God's true love for him.

The saints are altogether sincere in their humility when they call themselves ungrateful sinners or even the most vile of sinners. They do not mean to imply that they have committed the most heinous deeds which are objectively greater than the offenses of great sinners. But such is their humility that they are sincerely convinced that, if notorious sinners had received the same graces, they would have been more virtuous and filled with greater gratitude to God.

Humility is truth, because the humble man judges himself by the model which is truth and holiness itself, whereas the man who is haughty and conceited conforms himself to a miserable perversion of that ideal. "The proud man 'exalts himself' by perpetually gazing into the depths, with the result that he feels he is towering in the heights. As he actually sinks lower into the depths, he over-compensates for the loss by looking to still greater depths, so that he must fancy himself actually rising higher, though he is constantly falling. He does not realize that the abyss with its fatal fascination is gradually drawing him down as he continues his gaze, and in his illusion fancies that he is rising ever higher above it. Thus gradually the angel falls, lured into the pit by the pride of his gaze."[91]

The humble man looks aloft to the holiness of God in order to abase himself constantly, and by the very measure of his self-abasement God raises him up. This thought was expressed strikingly by Saint Augustine: "It is an essential element of humility that it directs the heart to what is above, but it is an essential element of self-exaltation that it depresses the heart. It is indeed paradoxical that pride is directed to that which is below us, humility to that which is exalted above us. But devout humility subordinates that which is higher. And nothing is higher than God. Therefore humility exalts us, for it makes God Himself subject."[92]

d. Humility Is Truth in Action

One would be totally lacking in truth and sincerity if he should confess before God that he is base and low, unworthy of grace, and not at the same time have the firm resolution to be subject to God in all his actions and to submit readily to the divine dispositions. To profess before God that one is worthy of punishment and dishonor and at the same time to rebel against every manifestation of contempt on the part of our fellow men is opposed to the spirit of sincerity and truth. Even though we may not merit the offensive criticism and contempt directed against us in particular instances, humility and truth should still compel us to admit that we have justly deserved them for much weightier reasons in other instances which passed by unnoticed. Of course, even the humble man must regret and deplore injustice wherever it occurs and not merely when it is directed against himself. He must deplore it above all for the simple reason that it offends God.

It is the part of humility above all to obey God and also men in so far as they manifest the will of God communicated to us through them. Holy obedience, the voluntary and joyful submission to the will of a human superior, is one of the Christian manifestations of humility and a most efficacious means of its cultivation. Humility is the will to serve. "Let him who is greatest among you become as the youngest, and him who is the chief as the servant" (Lk 22:26; Mt 20:25ff.). The humble man gladly forfeits undeserved honors. He is willing to bear scorn and shame in the following of the Crucified, in so far as this does not destroy the just minimum of honor which is customarily necessary for effective labor in the kingdom of God.

e. Humility the Manifestation of Love

Humility is both the result of love and its most perfect expression. "Humility is a form of love, whose warm bright rays thaw the icy anguish with which pride has rigged our empty hearts."[93] Only love gives to humility the clear insight into the good qualities of our neighbor. Thus love is in the service of humility, and humility in turn is altogether in the service of love. Only love of God can reveal to us the full depth of God's condescension and the unheard-of splendor of our elevation through grace. Only love imparts to humility the spirit and power of submission. Without love humility is at best self-abandonment. But through love humility is prepared to harken to the call from God to do great things for God. It would be a subtle form of pride to seek glory for one's self by confining one's efforts to petty things. Humility awaits the divine summons. When God summons to great works of love, when he invites to exalted sanctity, the humble man does not hesitate or cavil, but joyously abandons himself to God. "Because he who is mighty has done great things for me, and holy is his name" (Lk 1:49).

Truly great humility can flow only from great love. The measure of love corresponds to the measure of humility. The deeper the inner charity of man, the greater his humility. The more self-effacing his love, the more meritorious his humility of heart, the freer from every artifice and false constraint. But as long as love has not thawed our icy pride with the warmth of its rays, we must continue to struggle painfully to attain the virtue of humility.

f. Humility a Divine Gift

Humility is a gift from above which assures us of victory in our combat against evil. The struggle for humility is always painful for fallen man. Original sin and all other sins are due to pride. "Humility is the motion of a constant inward dying to ourselves, so that Christ may live in us."[94] Proud children of Adam that we are, we must ask for humility from God. The power to die to ourselves is a gift infused in the sacrament of baptism. It is given to us freely by God's grace. But it is not only a power; it is also a duty. Humility is always a gift and a task. "He must increase, but I must decrease" (Jn 3:30).

5. *The Fruits of Humility*

"Whoever humbles himself shall be exalted" (Mt 23:12). "God resists the proud, but gives grace to the humble" (1 Pt 5:5). Though divine grace is not strictly the result or fruit of humility, but of God's loving bounty, only the humble man is disposed to receive it. Without some measure of humility man will not attain to faith. Only the heart sufficiently humble to submit to the verdict of guilt which revelation and faith pronounce over the sinner, is truly open to the grace of faith. And the more profound the humility, the more profound the insight into the mysteries of faith. For the humble man never presumes to gauge the truth of divine revelation by the petty standard of self. He is altogether docile to the truth itself. He is willing to be taught. True humility gives insight into the inner value and beauty of the divine truth, whereas pride shuts itself out from every truth which does not serve one's own self and one's own self-glory. "I praise thee, Father, Lord of heaven and earth, that thou didst hide these things from the wise and prudent, and didst reveal them to little ones" (Mt 11:25).

Humility is prerequisite to true knowledge of self, to true sorrow and penance. Only the humble man has the courage to admit his own guilt constantly and steadfastly before God. Humility also opens the heart wide for the entry of love, of unselfish love for God and one's fellows. "To renounce self-love in order to serve a higher love, that is humility of heart."[95] "There is nothing loftier than the path of love, but only the humble man can follow it."[96] Humility even clears the vision of the sinner for the very values he has violated, for it is the "ointment of the eyes." It is indispensable for moral health of conscience.[97] If humility does not close the gap between knowledge and performance, between the ideal and its fulfillment, then pride will distort the knowledge of values we have disregarded. The gap will be filled, but through false conceptions. There will be a distortion of perspective. "Pride spoke to my memory: you could not have done this. Then memory yielded; hence I did not do it" (Nietzsche).[98]

Humility assures charity of the aloofness of reverence. Reverence and humility mutually demand and supplement each other. Through reverence the religious background of humility becomes most apparent. Just as humility ultimately rests in the encounter with God, so reverence always senses the glory of God in the thrill of all being.

6. Degrees of Pride in Opposition to Humility

As there are various steps and degrees of humility, so there are degrees of pride. In both pride and humility the degrees differ both in depth and in intensity. Under pride we list vanity, self-complacency, vainglory, ambition, and pride in the strict sense. Vanity delights in one's own petty qualities and passes over the values of a higher order. It is concerned with one's trifling merits, such as physical beauty, adornment in dress, parentage, and is really somewhat stupid and inoffensive. But the pride of self-esteem and self-complacency is odious and offensive. It is all the more offensive and insulting to God, the higher the good over which the self-complacent man exults. For the loftier the qualities we possess, the more they bear the character of gifts of divine grace and the more our vaunting offends the Giver who has bestowed them upon us. Even though the self-complacent man does not at all deny that he has received his good qualities from God, he actually vaunts them as though he himself were their sole source and cause.[99] Self-complacency is taken up with one's own good qualities and is usually allied with vainglory, which displays one's real or assumed excellence also for the admiration of others. Then follows ambition, which aims at excelling others in power and influence.

In all of these degrees there is pride. But pride strictly such is far more concerned with man himself as its center. The self-complacent man primarily views values as personal possession and adornment. But the proud man can no longer see the worth and beauty of the good which is in him; he sees only that which is prejudicial or profitable to himself. He is principally concerned with his independence of others. He cannot suffer depending on them or owing them a debt of gratitude. Pride may reach the extreme of arrogance and blind hostility to value. The arrogant man has a sharp eye for all that is good, but he senses that it accuses him, that it tends to topple him from his false throne. He sees the good with the view of ultimately perverting it and making a lie of it in his hateful resentment of it. He does not see the good reflecting the clear light of truth, nor does he feel the warmth of its power. When pride is total, it is satanic and can no longer endure dependence on God. The most extreme form of pride is the denial of God and the proclamation of the absolute autonomy of man. One given over entirely to pride scorns his fellow man. Not merely the sinner is object of his scorn, but also the religious man. He particularly scorns the religious man who submits to God and takes his rightful place in the human order in the spirit of obedience to God.

Above all, pride clashes with Christ, who is Himself humble and in His whole being and conduct invites us to humility. Frequently pride tolerates God from afar. But brought face to face with the humble figure of Christ, the God-man, it can only hate and resent His presence and His demand of loyalty. Many Fathers of the Church hold that the sin of the evil spirits was the pride of rebellion against this mystery of the Word Incarnate.

Each of these degrees of pride must be opposed by humility, which begins with modesty and reaches its perfection in the complete imitation of the humility of Christ. Modesty arises from a natural sense of spiritual shame and seeks to hide one's good qualities from the eyes of others. Nevertheless, though it is satisfied with an inferior position, modesty can be considered humility only if it is profoundly motivated. The humble man gladly forfeits all human honors, because in his gratitude he is filled with astonishment over all that God has bestowed upon him. He is astonished that God has raised him, despite all his unworthiness, to such heights of honor. True humility is the very antithesis of the pride which seeks the independence of man himself to the very point of denying God. Humility rests in the spirit of voluntary submission through obedience.

Center and hearth of all humility of man is the humility of Christ, tenderest and dearest model for humble souls. With Christ and for His sake, humility rejoices in humiliation, in the loss of honors truly merited, if only God can be glorified in this way. As Christ was subject to men, so the humble man must submit voluntarily to human authority in the state and in the civil order and, above all, in the Church and the religious sphere. Pride is at work in all heretics, who presume that their errors come directly from God, directly from Christ, in order to be able to close their ears to the voice of the Church.

The degrees of humility correspond exactly to the degrees of love, as the degrees of pride and arrogance correspond to the degrees of self-love. As humility conforms to true love, so do pride and arrogance of heart correspond to the selfishness of false love.

BIBLIOGRAPHY

ADAM, A. *The Primacy of Love*. Westminster, Md.: Newman, 1958.

———. *The Sixth Commandment*. Cork: (Ireland): Mercier, 1955.

ADNÈS, P. "L'humilité vertu spécifiquement chrétienne d'après saint Augustin," RAM, 28 (1952), 208–223.

ALLERS, R. *Sex Psychology in Education*. St. Louis: Herder, 1937.

BARBEAU, H. *Regards sur la chair et l'ésprit*. Bruges-Paris, 1947.

BEAUDENOM, CHAN. *Formation à la humilité*. Paris, 1953.

BÉLORGEY, G. *L'humilité benédictine*. Paris, 1948.

BENDER, L., OP. *Het recht. Rechtsphilosophische verhandelingen voor juristen en andere ontwikkelde personen*. Bussum, 1948.

BERGE, A. *L'éducation sexuelle et affective*. Paris, 1948.

BERNARD, R. "Apologie de la vertu de force," *VieSpir*, 68 (1943), 105–116.

──────. "Notre vocation à la vertu de force," *VieSpir*, 68 (1943), 212–221.

──────. "La vertu acquise et la vertu infuse," *VieSpirSupp* (1935), 25–53.

BLEIENSTEIN, H., S.J. "Sanctificate jejunium. Eine Sinndeutung christliche Fastens," *Geist-Leben*, 26 (1953), 8–19.

BONFILL AND BONFILL, J. "Humilidad ontólogica, humilidad personal, humilidad social," *Cristiandad*, 7 (1950), 108–119.

BOPP, L., O.S.B. "Die Demutsstufen der Benediktinerregel," *Benedictus, Vater des Abendlandes* (1947), 241–262.

BRAUNS, M., S.J. *Christelijke heldhaftigheid*. Antwerpen, 1951.

BREHM, B. *Ueber der Tapferkeit*. Wien, 1940.

*BRUNNER, E. *Divine Imperative*. Philadelphia: Westminster Press, 1947.

CAHIERS DE LA VIE SPIRITUELLE. *Christian Asceticism and Modern Man*. London: Blackfriars, 1955.

CAIAZZO, D. *L'idea della giustizia*. Roma, 1950.

CANICE, F., O.F.M. *Humility*. Westminster, Md., 1951.

CAPONE, D., C.SS.R. *Intorno alla veritá morale*. Excerpta ad diss. ad Lauream. Pontif. Univ. Gregoriana: Napoli, 1951.

CARLSON, S., O.P. *The Virtue of Humility*. Dubuque, 1953.

──────. "The Virtue of Humility," *Thomist* (1944), 363–414.

CARNOT, J. *Au service de l'amour*. Paris, 1939.

CASARES, T. D. *La justicia y el derecho*. Buenos Aires, 1935.

CATHREIN, V., S.J. *Die christliche Demut*. 2 Auflage. Freiburg (no date).

CHRETIEN, P. *De castitate. Tractatus ad usum confessariorum*. Metis, 1938.

──────. *De justitia*. Metz, 1947.

CLARKE, R. F. *Geduld*. Luzern, 1951.

COHAUSZ, O., S.J. "Stolze Selbsterhebung oder christlich-demuetige Selbstbescheidung," *ThPrQschr*, 89 (1936), 673–691.

──────. "Priesterliche Demut und Sanftmut," *ThPrQschr*, 90 (1937), 1–18.

CORTI, G., CASTELLI, C., etc. *Aspetti della purezza*. Milano, 1947.

DEL BON, D. "Sul concetto della giustizia," *Studium* (1947), 209ff.

DEMAN, TH., O.P. *S. Thomas d'Aquin, La prudence. Traduction française, notes et appendices*. 2e édition. Tournai, 1949.

DESCAMPS, A. *Les justes et la justice dans les évangiles et le christianisme primitif*. Louvain, 1950.

DEUTSCH, A. *Sex Habits of American Men*. A symposium on the Kinsey Report. New York: Prentice Hall, 1948.

DUYNSTEE, W. *Das sechste Gebot im modernen Leben*. Innsbruck, 1935.

EGENTER, R. "Ueber die Bedeutung der Epikie im christlichen Leben," *PhJahrb*, 53 (1940), 115–127.

──────. *Die Aszese des Christen in der Welt*. Ettal, 1957.

──────. *Von der Einfachheit*. Regensburg, 1947.

ENDRES, J., C.SS.R. "Ethos und Recht," *NO*, 3 (1948), 40–52.

ERASMI, B. "Die 'Unterscheidung der Geister' als Grundbedingung christlicher Muendigkeit," *GeistLeben*, 22 (1949), 204–216.

FEULING, D. "Diskretion," *BM* (1925), 240ff.

FICHTENAU, H. *Askese und Laster*. Wien, 1948.

FORCE CHRÉTIENNE. *Cahiers de la Vie Spirituelle*. Vol. I. Paris, 1943.

FUCHS, J., S.J. *Sexualethik des hl. Thomas von Aquin*. Koeln, Bachem, 1949.

GARRIGOU-LAGRANGE, R., O.P. "La prudence et la vie intérieure," *VieSpir*, 51 (1937), 24–41.

GATTERER, M. *Educating to Purity*. New York: Pustet, 1922.

GAUTHIER, R. A., O.P. "Magnanimité. L'idéal de la grandeur dans la philosophie païenne et dans la théologie chrétienne," *Bibliothèque Thomiste*, XXVII. Paris, 1951.

GEBSATTEL, V. R. VON. *Von der christlichen Gelassenheit*. Wuerzburg, 1940.

GERSTER, TH. VON. *Die Tugend der Reinheit*. Bregenz, 1934.

GILEN, L., S.J. "Die Demut des Christen nach dem Neuen Testament," *ZAM*, 13 (1938), 266–284.

GROSAM J. "Die soziale Gerechtigkeit im Sinne der Enz. *Quadragesimo anno*," *ThPrQschr*, 91 (1938), 258–271, 483–501.

GROUPE LYONNAIS D'ÉTUDES MÉDICALES. *Médicine et sexualité*. Paris, 1950.

GUARDINI, R. "Grundformen der Aszese," *Frankfurter Hefte*, 11 (1956), 40–45, 200–204.

GUILLAUME, P. *La formation des habitudes*. Paris, 1936.

GUITTON, J. *Essay on Human Love*. New York: Philosophical Library, 1952.

GUNDLACH, G., S.J. "Klugheit als Prinzip des Handelns," *Greg*, 23 (1942), 238–254.

HENGSTENBERG, H. E. *Christliche Aszese*. 2 Auflage. Regensburg, 1936.

HERING, H. "Quomodo solvendi sunt casus: recurrendo ad sola principia an etiam ad prudentiam?" *Ang* (1941), 311–335.

HEYLEN, V. *Tractatus de jure et justitia*. 5 editio. Mecheln, 1950.

HILDEBRAND, D. VON. *Liturgy and Personality*. New York: Longmans, 1943.

———. "Die rechtliche und sittliche Sphaere in ihrem Eigenwert und in ihrer Zusammenordnung," *Seitliches im Lichte des Ewigen* (Regensburg, 1932), 159–185.

HOEFFNER, J. *Soziale Gerechtigkeit und Liebe*. Saarbruecken, 1936. Cf. B. Mathis: "Um die soziale Gerechtigkeit," *ThPrQschr*, 89 (1936), 298–309.

HOFMANN, R. *Die heroische Tugend*. Muenchen, 1933.

HORNSTEIN, X., FALLER, A., and numerous experts: *Gesundes Geschlechtleben*. Olten, 1950.

HUGUENY, E., O.P. *Tempérance et chasteté*. Paris, 1941.

HUMMEL, E. L., C.M.M. *The Concept of Martyrdom According to St. Cyprian of Carthage*. Washington, 1946.

JENTGENS, G. *Die Gewohnheitshandlung. Eine moralpsychologische, paedagogische Studie*. Essen, 1940.

KAUSACK. *Max Scheler zur Krisis der Ehrfurcht*. Berlin, 1949.

KENNEDY, O. *De fortitudine christiana* (Dissertation). Gembloux, 1938.

KOLSKI, H. *Ueber die Prudentia in der Ethik des hl. Thomas* (Dissertation). Wuerzburg, 1934.

KRAUTWIG, N. "Der Leib im Kampf des Pneuma wider die Sárx," *ThG*, 39 (1949), 296–311.

———. "Die Tugend," *WissWeish* (1941), 120–129.

KUHAUPT, H. "Ueber die Dankbarkeit," *Seele* (Regensburg), 23 (1947), 197–202, 240–243, 261–263, 290–295.

KUNSENMUELLER, O. *Die Herkunft der platonischen Kardinaltugenden*. Erlangen, 1935.

LANG-HINRICHSEN, D. "Die Lehre von der Geduld in der Patristik und bei Thomas von Aquin," *GeistLeben*, 24 (1951), 209–223, 284–299.

LASANCE, F. X. *Patience*. New York, 1937.

LECLERCQ, J. *Wegbereitung fuer Gott. Die christliche Askese*. Luzern, 1956.

LEMAITRE, R. P. *Plaisirs permis, plaisirs défendus*. Avignon, 1951.

LIANG, K. W. *Het begrip deemoed in 1 Clemens. Bijdrage tot de geschiedenis van de oudchristelijke ethik*. Utrecht, 1951.

LINDWORSKY, J. *Psychology of Asceticism*. London: H. Edwards, 1936.

LORSON, P. *Le plaisir sanctifié. Pour une spiritualité des loisirs.* Colmar, 1952.

LOTTIN, O., O.S.B. "les vertus morales infuses dans l'école franciscaine au début du XIVe siècle," *RechThAncMéd,* 18 (1951), 106–127.

――――. *Psychologie et morale aux XIIe et XIIIe siècles.* III, 2 (1949), 459–535.

――――. "La connexion des vertus acquises, au dernier quart du XIIIe siècle," *RechThAnc-Méd,* 15 (1948), 107–151.

MARRES, P. H. *De justitia secundum doctrinam theologicam.* 2 Vols. Roermond, 1888.

MEILLE, J. *Die Bekaempfung des Alkoholismus in christlicher Schau.* Bueren, 1948.

MERKELBACH, B., O.P. *De castitate et luxuria.* 7 ed. Liège, 1950.

MERSCHMANN, H. *Die dreifache Gerechtigkeit.* Grundgedanken der scholastischen Gesellschaftslehre. Recklinghausen, 1946.

MOHR, R. *Ricerche sull' etica sessuale di alcune populazioni dell' Africa.* Firenze, 1940.

MONLEON, J. de, O.S.B. *Les XII degrés de l'humilité.* Paris, 1951.

MUELLER, J. *Das sexuelle Leben der Voelker.* 3 Auflage. Paderborn, 1935.

MUELLER, M. *Ethik und Recht in der Lehre von der Verantwortlichkeit. Ein Laengsschnitt durch die Geschichte der Moraltheologie.* Regensburg, 1932.

NEF, H. *Recht und Moral in der deutschen Rechtsphilosophie seit Kant.* St. Gallen.

NIEDERMEYER, A. *Das menschliche Sexualleben* (Handbuch der speziellen Pastoralmedizin I). Wien, 1949.

NOBLE, H. D. "Prudence," *DTC,* 13, 1023–1076.

――――. *Les passions dans la vie morale.* Paris, 1931–1932.

――――. "Mystique et continence," *EtCar* (1952).

NOLDIN, H. *De Castitate.* 32 Auflage. Innsbruck, 1948.

OBERLIN, S. *Direction et problèmes sexuels de l'adolescent.* Paris, 1946.

ODDONE, A., S.J. "Il piacere e l'asceticismo cristiano," *CC,* 100 (1949), 1, 379–392. Cf. 99 (1948), 4, 463–476.

OSENDE, V. *Sabiduría y eutrapelía. Para los que penan y para los que rien.* Villava, 1952.

OUDERZIJN, M. A. VAN DEN. *Der Tractat von den Tugenden der Seele.* Fribourg, 1942.

PETERSON, E. "Theologie des Kleides," *BM,* 16 (1934), 347–356. *Stimmen der kath. Welt,* 1 (1947), 311–321.

PFEIFFER, N. *Die Klugheit in der Ethik des Aristoteles und Thomas von Aquin.* Freiburg, 1943.

PIECHLER, TH., O.S.B. *Das Fasten bei Basilius dem Grossen und im antiken Heidentum.* Innsbruck, 1955.

PIEPER, J. *Ueber das christliche Menschenbild.* Leipzig, 1936.

――――. *Prudence.* New York: Pantheon, 1959.

――――. *Justice.* New York: Pantheon, 1955.

――――. *Fortitude and Temperance.* New York: Pantheon, 1954.

PREMM, M. "Von christlicher Demut," *ThPrQschr,* 99 (1940), 177–184.

PRIBILLA, M. "Klugheit und Gewissen," *StimmZeit,* 68 (1938), 205–216.

――――. *Tapferkeit und Christentum.* 2 Auflage. Hamburg, 1947.

――――. "Tapferkeit und Christentum," *StimmZeit,* 138 (1940/41), 1–5, 42–48.

PRZYWARA, E. "Vom Sinn der Geduld," *ZAM,* 15 (1940), 114–123.

RAHNER, K. "Zur Theologie der Entsagung," *Schriften zur Theologie,* III (Einsiedeln-Koeln, 1956), 61–72; "Passion und Aszese," 73–110.

RAITZ VON FRENTZ, E. *Selbstverleugnung.* Einsiedeln, 1936.

――――. "Selbstverleugnung oder selbstveredlung," *ZAM,* 15 (1940), 45–55.

RODIGHIERO, A. *L'uomo, l'istinto e la castità.* Vincenza, 1950.

ROSSI, A., C.M. *Sii forte. Dottrina e pratica della fortezza cristiana.* Milano, 1940.

RUIZ AMADA, R., S.J. *Educazione della castità.* 6 ed. Torino, 1942.

SAINT PIERRE, A. *La vertu chrétienne de témperance dans la vie religieuse*. Montreal, 1951.

SANCHEZ BORREGO, M. *Justicia social*. Zaragoza, 1945.

SCHAEUFELE, H. *Eucharistische Nuechternheit und Abendmesse nach dem geltenden Recht*. Karlsruhe, 1958.

SCHAMONI, W. *Die Gaben des Heiligen Geistes*. Paderborn, 1947.

SCHELER, M. *Vom Umsturz der Werte*. Leipzig, 1919. I/30.

———. "Zur Rehabilitierung der Tugend," *AbAuf*, I (Leipzig, 1915), 1–38.

SCHELSKY, H. "Die Moral der *Kinsey Report*. With comment by Albert Mitterer," *WW*, 9 (1954), 421–435.

SCHILLING, H. *Das Ethos der Mesotes*. Tuebingen, 1930.

SCHLATTER, A. *Jesu Demut, ihre Miszdeutung, ihr Grund*. Guetersloh, 1904.

SCHMIDT, H. *Organische Aszese*. 6 Auflage. Paderborn, 1952.

SCHOELLGEN, W. "Ueber den Sinn und die Bedeutung der Kardinaltugenden," *ThG*, 46 (1956), 26–39.

———. *Christliche Tapferkeit in Krankheit und Tod*. Wuerzburg, 1940.

SCHRATTENHOLZER, A. *Soziale Gerechtigkeit. Die Lehre von der natuerlichen Gemeinschaftsgerechtigkeit*. Wien-Graz, 1934.

SCHUHMACHER, H. "Zur Entwicklung der Askese in der Antike," *Festschrift fuer Tillmann* (Duesseldorf, 1950), 455–467.

SCHUSTER, J. B., S.J. "Das Verhaeltnis von *justitia legalis* und *distributiva* zur *justitia socialis* in *Quadragesimo anno* mit besonderer Beruecksichtigung der Lehre von H. Pesch," *Schol*, 11 (1936), 225–242.

SCHWER, W. "Recht und Liebe," *Der kath. Gedanke*, 42 (1929), 125–136.

SCHWERING, J. "Sittlichkeit und Recht," *StimmZeit*, 133 (1937/38), 9–17.

SERTILLANGES, A. D., O.P. "Le fondement spirituel: humilité," *VieSpir*, 48 (1936), 157–159; 49 (1936), 268–270.

SHERMAN, J. E. *The Nature of Martyrdom*. Paterson, N.J., 1942.

SNOECK, A., S.J., etc. "Sexual Problems of the Adolescent," *New Problems in Medical Ethics* (Dom Peter Flood, ed.), 1–44. Westminster, Md.: Newman, 1953.

SPICQ, C. "Bénignité, mansuétude, douceur, clémence," *Rb* (1947), 321–339.

STEINBUECHEL, TH. *Philosophische Grundlegung der kath. Sittenlehre*. 4 Auflage. 108–138.

———. *Die Ehrfurcht*. Stuttgart, 1947.

STELZENBERGER, J. "Die Ehrfurcht," *ThQschr*, 131 (1951), 1–16.

STÉVAUX, A. "Justice et charité," *RevDiocT*, 7 (1952), 211ff.

STOCKUMS, W. *Das christliche Tugenleben*. Freiburg, 1950.

SUAREZ, E. *Ueber die Lehrbarkeit der Tugend. Untersuchungen zum platonischen und nachplatonischen Problem des Lehrens und Lernens*. Wuerzburg, 1940.

TARASIEVITSCH, J. *Humility in the Light of St. Thomas*. Diss. Frib., 1935.

THIBON, G. "Le risque au service de la prudence," *EtCarm*, 24 (1939), I, 47–70.

THIEME, K. *Die christliche Demut*. Giessen, 1906.

TILLMANN, F. *Handbuch der kath. Sittenlehre*. 3 Auflage. III, 214ff.

UTZ, F., O.P. *Die Einheit und Geschlossenheit des sittlichen Lebens nach Thomas von Aquin, ZAM*, 15 (1940), 56–72.

VAISSIERE, J. DE LA, S.J. *Modesty*. A psychological study of its instinctive character. St. Louis: Herder, 1937.

VANDENBUNDER, A. "De clementia," *CollatBrug*, 46 (1950), 275–280.

———. "De mansuetudine," *CollatBrug*, 46 (1950), 107–113, 194–199.

———. "De vera humilitate," *CollatBrug*, 47 (1951), 210–214.

VECCHIO, G. DEL. *Justice*. An historical and philosophical essay. New York: Philosophical Library, 1954.

VEN, J. J. VAN DER. "Recht, Gerechtigkeit und Liebe," *Ho*, 47 (1955), 297–309.

VIGNON, H., S.J. *Adnotationes in tractatum de virtutibus infusis*. Romae, 1943.

VOEGTLE, A. *Tugend und Lasterkataloge im Neuen Testament*. Muenster, 1936.

WALTER, E. "Die Kraft wird in der Schwachheit vollendet. Zur paulinischen Theologie der Schwachheit," *GeistLeben*, 28 (1955), 248–255.

WANG TSCH'ANG-TCHE, J. S. *Augustin et les vertus des païens*. Paris, 1943.

WILDEMANN. *Ehe und Jungfraeulichkeit*. Karlsruhe, 1949.

WOLFF, P. *Vom Sinn der Ehrfurcht*. Muenchen, 1935.

WOLFSTEINER, W. *Die Demut nach der Lehre des hl. Benedikt*. Freiburg, 1922.

WULF, F., S.J. "Selbstverleugnung und Abtoetung als Uebung der Nachfolge Christi und als Kennzeichen des neuen Lebens in Christus,"*GeistLeben*, 25 (1952), 4–42.

Note also the bibliography on the rules of prudence and on casuistry in the second and third parts of this volume.

Additional Works in English

FLOOD, DOM P., O.S.B. (ed.). *New Problems in Medical Ethics*. Vol. I. Westminster, Md.: Newman, 1953. Cf. Sexual Problems of the Adolescent, pp. 1–44.

HILDEBRAND, D. VON. *In Defence of Purity*. New York: Sheed and Ward, 1935.
Man and His Happiness (Theology Library, Vol. 3). Chicago: Fides, 1956. Cf. pp. 177–228.

MEERSCH, E., S.J. *Love, Marriage and Chastity*. London: Sheed and Ward, 1939.

PERRIN, J., O.P. *Virginity*. Westminster, Md.: Newman, 1955.

PIERSE, G. *Virtues and Vices*. Milwaukee: Bruce, 1935.

SHEEDY, C. *The Christian Virtues*. Notre Dame, Ind.: N.D. Press, 1949.

Periodical Literature in English

CONNERY, J. R., S.J. "Prudence and Morality," *ThSt*, 13 (Dec. 1952), 564–82.

HARVEY, J. F. "Nature of the Infused Moral Virtues," *Proceedings Cath. Theol. Scty. Amer.* (1955), 172–217.

SMITH, R., O.P. "Virtue of Docility," *Thomist*, 15 (Oct., 1952), 572–623.

STEINMUELLER, J. E. "Holiness and the Cardinal Virtues," *HPR*, 51 (Oct., 1950), 39–44.

VAN ZELLER, H. "Humility," *ABR*, 8 (Winter, 1957), 324–49.

WELSH, M. S., O.P. "The Medium of Virtue," *AER*, 106 (Feb., 1942), 133–142.

NOTES

1. J. Mausbach, *Die Ethik des hl. Augustinus*, I, 48.
2. *Ibid.*, I, 47.
3. PL 140, 853 DC.
4. P. Galtier, "Satisfaction," in DTC XIV, 1165ff. Later Abelard vehemently opposed the penitential books and dealt a severe blow to the mechanical practice of penance. Cf. J. Hirschberger, *Geschichte der Philosophie* (Freiburg, 1949), I, 360. Abelard's decisive action was due to his own ethics of interior disposition (*Gessinungsethik*).
5. Bonaventure, *Prologue to the commentary on the Book of Sentences*, q. 3, Quarachi edition, I, 13.
6. *Prologue to the Summa*, I, q. 2.
7. *Prologue to the second part of the Summa*.
8. *Prologue to the third part of the Summa*.
9. It is particularly significant for the study of the Thomistic conception of virtue, that the concluding questions, 68–70, to this part deal with the gifts and fruits of the Holy Spirit.
10. I–II, q. 106, a. 1.
11. Critical edition by L. Gaude (Rome, 1905–1912; photomechanically reprinted in 1953).
12. J. Aertnys, C.SS.R. and C. A. Damen, C.SS.R., *Theologia moralis secundum doctrinam S. Alfonsi de Ligorio Doctoris Ecclesiae* (16th ed.; Rome, 1950).
13. Cf. the discussion of Sailer's moral teaching by Hirscher, *Theol. Quartalschrift*, 1 (1819), 242–269, 407–416. This outstanding study is still well worth reading today.
14. F. Probst, *Katholische Moraltheologie*, I, 125.
15. Cf. J. Zinkl, *Magnus Jocham. Ein Beitrag zur Geschichte der katholischen Theologie und Froemmigkeit im 19. Jahrhundert* (Freiburg, 1950).
16. M. Jocham, *Moraltheologie*, III, 7.
17. *Ibid.*, II, 24.
18. M. Deutinger, *Moralphilosophie*, 339.
19. *Ibid.*, 338.
20. *Ibid.*, 340.
21. Quoted by J. A. Endres, *Martin Deutinger* (Muenchen o.J.), 34.
22. K. Werner, *System der christlichen Ethik*, II, 222.
23. *Ibid.*, II, 232. Cf. P. Hadrossek, *Die Bedeutung des Systemgedankens fuer die Moraltheologie in Deutschland seit der Thomas-Renaissance*, 156f.
24. *Theol. Quartalschrift*, 53 (1871), 64–114, 221–277; 54 (1872), 3–49, 193–254.
25. *Ibid.*, 54 (1872), 45.
26. F. Friedhoff, *Moraltheologie*, I, 357.
27. *Ibid.*, I, 10.
28. P. Hadrossek, *op. cit.*, 239.
29. Th. Simar, *Lehrbuch de Moraltheologie* (3 ed.; Freiburg, 1867), 199.
30. Hadrossek, *op. cit.*, 252.
31. *Ibid.*, 297.
32. J. Mausbach, *Die katholische Moraltheologie* (7th ed.), I, 35.
33. A. Koch, *Lehrbuch der Moraltheologie* (3 ed.; Freiburg, 1910), 3.
34. *Ibid.*, 11.
35. *Ibid.*, 8.
36. The term as used here is phenomenological and is not intended to be understood in a metaphysical sense of essence or in a metaphysical sense of exigence.

37. Saint Bernard. *Liber de diligendo Deo,* Cap. XV. PL 182, 998. "Imprimis ergo diligit seipsum homo propter se. . . . Cumque videt per se non subsistere posse, Deum quasi sibi necessarium incipit per fidem inquirere et diligere. Diligit itaque in secundo gradu Deum, sed propter se, non propter ipsum. . . . Gustato quam suavis est Dominus transit ad tertium gradum, ut diligat Deum non jam propter se, sed propter ipsum. Sane in hoc gradu statur: et nescio, si a quoquam hominum quartus in hac vita perfecte apprehenditur, ut se scilicet diligat homo tantum propter Deum." But for Saint Bernard it is essential to "caritas" as a divine virtue at least to strive for this fourth degree of love. (Freely translated the words of Saint Bernard are as follows: "Therefore in the first place man loves himself for his own sake. . . . However, when he finds that he cannot subsist of himself alone, he begins the search for God as necessary for himself. He begins to inquire through faith and to love. Thereby he loves God in the second degree, but for himself, not for God's own sake. . . . But once having tasted how sweet God is he passes on to the third degree of love, so that he loves God no longer on account of himself, but for God's own sake. In this degree of love he remains, and I doubt if any one can be found in this life who has attained the fourth degree of love, so that he loves himself only on account of God.")

PART II

1. H. Conrad-Martius, "Seele und Leib," *Hochland,* 42 (1949), 67ff. Cf. W. Gruehn, *Religionpsychologie* (Breslau, 1920), 108.
2. Conrad-Martius, *loc. cit.,* 64.
3. Scheler in his later days, after he had lost his faith, frivolously (particularly in his work, *Der Mensch im Kosmos*) transferred this essential law which was valid for man in his body-soul composite, to the divine, thereby stamping the spirit as such with the stigma of impotence. It is not spirit as such, but only the human spirit which has need of body-soul urge and drive for its activity. And even man has no need of fulfillment of the sex urge for a vital and energetic moral life.
4. P. Siebeck, "Wissen und Glauben in der Medizin," *Universitas,* 5 (1950), 42.
5. I–II, qq. 22–48.
6. I–II, q. 24, a. 3.
7. As to the positive import of the principle of opposition to evil, the *agere contra,* compare Part Six, Chapter Fourteen, IV, 5: "Self-Denial."
8. A. Mager, *Psychologie der Mystik* (Salzburg, 1947).
9. E. Kretschmer, *Koerperbau und Character* (20th ed.; Berlin-Heidelberg, 1951); *idem., Medizinische Psychologie* (10th ed.; Stuttgart, 1950). This psychologist has not won acceptance among American authorities on the level with his recognition in Europe (Translator's note).
10. Compare Th. Muencker, *Die psychologischen Grundlagen der katholischen Sittenlehre* (3rd ed.; Duesseldorf, 1948), 82ff.
11. Cf. Saint Thomas, *De creaturis spiritualibus,* a. 8.
12. Cf. D. von Hildebrand, *Liturgy and Personality* (New York, Longmans, Green and Company, 1943).
13. E. Stein, *Jahrbuch fuer Philosophie und phaenomenologischen Forschung,* V (1922), 224.
14. *Ibid.,* 219.
15. *Ibid.,* 192.
16. Gerda Walther, *Jahrbuch fuer Philosophie und phaenomenologishe Forschung,* VI (1923), 107.

17. H. Bergson, *The Two Sources of Morality and Religion* (New York: Holt, 1935).
18. A. Delp, "Weltgeschichte und Heilsgeschichte," *Stimmen der Zeit,* 138 (1940/1941), 247.
19. *Ibid.*
20. If there are men today who are actually ignorant of this primordial historical fact, this very fact is a grave indictment of many other men. Such a condition would be impossible had there not been many erroneous and base decisions against Christ and His mission command to teach all mankind. In a very profound sense which in some way penetrates to the very depth of his being, anyone who does not know Christ as the historical Lord and Master of the whole temporal order is still influenced by Him. No position that he assumes is without its relation to Christ.
21. *Ibid.,* 254.
22. Ph. Dessauer, *Der Anfang und das Ende,* 114.
23. III, q. 65, a. 1.
24. "Ipse sibi causa est, ut aliquando frumentum, aliquando quidem palea fiat." Irenaeus, *Adversus haereses,* 4, 4. PG 7, 983.
25. Defectus gratiae prima causa est in homine. Cf. I–II, q. 79, a. 2; cf. I, q. 49, a. 2, ad 2.
26. Cf. D. von Hildebrand, *Sittlichkeit und ethische Werterkenntnis,* 34f.
27. Cf. what is said on cooperation in Volume Two.
28. In Existential philosophy, anxiety (*Angst*) arises from the extreme sensitiveness regarding one's own existence, which is at the same time the very abyss of peril to existence. Precisely human existence as being coming to itself in freedom bears the primordial stamp of anxiety, insofar as there is the ever-present, uncanny danger of sinking back into a state without freedom, into the loss, which is the "one," the impersonal life stream, the anonymous forces of the milieu. Only if existence in liberty is conscious that it is constantly granted anew through the grace of God and is ever hidden in this grace, can it enjoy the primordial possession of joy and security.
29. Cf. p. 63ff. (I. Man in His Totality, Body and Soul).
30. Granted the dangers of misuse of hypnotism in the hands of incompetent or wrongminded psychologists and the existence of serious purposes for its use, noted authors find in hypnotism much that is profitable both in its therapeutic use and in experimentation and research. "Hypnosis is used rather commonly by medical doctors, dentists, and psychologists in treating their patients. Psychiatrists and psychologists find it useful because of a heightened facility to recall which is valuable in discovering repressed experiences giving rise to conflicts and anxieties. Medical doctors and dentists find it useful in allaying fears of patients and as a simple type of anesthesia. . . . Merkelbach speaks of scientific investigation as a legitimate use of hypnosis, granted the skill of the hypnotist and the prudent selection of a subject. He does not say that a classroom demonstration on the college level is an instance of scientific investigation. The techniques and effects of hypnotism, however, are natural phenomena just as much as association and perception. Demonstration is a more effective pedagogical device than a simple lecture. Thus it would seem that the scientific interests of college students and the pedagogical requirements of the educational situation would justify such demonstrations. Obviously the many experiments for mere display of power and for entertainment are not on this serious level and cannot readily be justified." The above citations are from an article by John Fearon, O.P., in the *American Ecclesiastical Review* (November, 1956), pp. 309–312. Cf. Gerald Kelly, S.J., *Contemporary Moral Theology,* 1 (Westminster, Md.: The Newman Press, 1958), 299. Cf. also Dominic Pruemmer, O.P., *Handbook of Moral Theology* (New York: Kenedy, 1957), p. 437; Merkelbach, O.P., *Summa Theologiae Moralis,* 2 (Paris: Desclee, 1942), 348. (Translator's note.)
31. A. Niedermeyer, *Handbuch der speziellen Pastoralmedizin,* V, 76.

32. The classification and nomenclature of psychic and mental afflictions have changed over the course of the history of both psychiatry and psychology. Despite the adoption by the American Psychiatric Association in 1952 of a uniform diagnostic and statistical list of mental disorders, there is still considerable variation in names, classification, and description of the various disturbances that can upset the equilibrium of the person and his behavior. What is more, there are disconcerting differences between the American and the European classificatory systems. The text here has accordingly been freely adapted to the more familiar American usage. (Translator's note.)

33. Cf. the recent work by John C. Ford, S.J., and Gerald Kelly, S.J.. *Contemporary Moral Theology*, 1: *Questions in Fundamental Moral Theology* (Westminster, Md.: Newman, 1958). Chapters 10 and 13 study the problems of moral freedom and responsibility in the light of modern psychology and psychiatry. (Translator's note.)

34. Council of Trent, sess. 6, can. 5, D 815: "Can. 5. Si quis liberum hominis arbitrium post Adae peccatum amissum et extinctum esse dixerit, aut rem esse de solo titulo, immo titulum sine re, figmentum denique a satana invectum in Ecclesiam: A.S."

35. "Verbum non qualecumque, sed spirans amorem." I, q. 43, a. 5, ad 2.

36. K. Rahner, *Hoerer des Wortes* (Munich, 1941), 128.

37. J. Maritain, *Existence and the Existent* (New York: Pantheon, 1948), 84–85.

38. This sense of value (*Wertfuehlen*) is a kind of spiritual understanding, not at all an unspiritual sensation or mere feeling. But feeling and sensation also play their roles.

39. M. Scheler, *Materiale Wertethik*, 305. Scheler's word *"Begreifen,"* translated as "conceptualize," implies the philosophical capacity to express oneself about God.

40. Edith Stein, *Jahrbuch fuer Philosophie und phaenomenologische Forschung*, 5 (1922), 145.

41. D. von Hildebrand, "Ethische Werterkenntnis," *Jahrbuch fuer Philosophie und phaenomenologische Forschung*, 5 (1921), 492.

42. Cf. Barth-Goedekemeyer, *Die Stoa* (6th ed.; Stuttgart, 1946), *passim*.

43. Seneca, *Letter to Lucilius*.

44. Th. Schneider, "Der paulinische Begriff des Gewissens," *Bonner Zeitschrift* (1929), 207.

45. Hofmann, *loc. cit.*, 107f., with references to sources.

46. *Ibid.*, 108.

47. Cf. Odon Lottin, *Psychologie et morale aux XII et XIII siècles*, II, 347.

48. In preaching the word of God this psychological fact must not be overlooked: the stress of motive is not the same in the sermon aiming at the conversion of the sinner as in the sermon for those who are striving for perfection! The cry, "Save your soul!" is a summons, an alert, but it is not the content and substance of the Glad Tidings of the Law of God.

49. For a typical example of this view note the work of H. G. Stoker, *Das Gewissen* (Bonn, 1925). Otherwise this is an excellent book.

50. The possibility of conflict with the doctrinal decisions of the Church is treated in our tract on the theological virtue of faith in the subsequent volume. Cf. also Cartechini, S.J., *De Valore Notarum Theologicarum* (Romae: 1951), 126ff.

51. Typical of this manner of reaction is the remark of Max Scheler made shortly before his apostasy from the Church: "I cannot endure it any longer, to feel polluted" (D. von Hidebrand, "Max Schelers Stellung zur katholischen Gedankenwelt," *Der katholische Gedanke*, 1 [1928], 452). We do not have the slightest desire to condemn Scheler, no more than does his friend Dietrich von Hildebrand, despite the horrifying words he used in reference to himself in the fall of 1919: "A dreadful premonition warns me that God's patience will eventually be exhausted. He will not rescue me again, but permit me to sink into the abyss." *Ibid.*, 459. We hope it was only the abyss of dreadful errors, not the abyss of eternal reprobation!

52. John Henry Newman, *Apologia Pro Vita Sua* (New York: Modern Library, 1950), Part VI, p. 212.

53. Thomas Aquinas, *De veritate,* q. 17, a. 4. Cf. a. 5.

54. Cf. I–II, q. 19, a. 6, ad 3.

55. Even in noted Catholic writers we occasionally find the statement that Saint Thomas taught one must unconditionally follow one's conscience even though it is erroneous to such an extent as to demand apostasy from the Church. Note Karl Adam, *Una Sancta in katholischer Sicht* (Duesseldorf, 1948); English translation: *One and Holy* (New York: Sheed and Ward, 1951). Pages 104 and 115 refer only to the obligation of following one's conscience. O. Simmel, "Gewissen und Gewissenfreiheit," *Stimmen der Zeit,* 1952 (1953), 46–54; M. Laros, "Autoritaet und Gewissen," *Hochland,* 36 (1938–1939), 265–280. Laros cites (274) *De verit.,* q. 17, a. 4, objectio 4 together with the responsum ad 2, instead of ad 4. Thomas adduces with approval the conception of law, that a wife who has formed a probable judgment of consicence (*probabilis conscientia*) regarding the existence of a diriment impediment to her marriage, must follow her conscience even in the face of a threat of excommunication. But the response of Thomas clearly shows that the "probable conscience" does not mean an erroneous conscience or even a culpably erroneous conscience, but a demonstrable judgment of conscience. Nevertheless, regarding the culpably erroneous conscience, he clearly says in the very question referred to that it does not bind simply and in every instance. It does not simply forbid any and every contradictory act. In the background there is much rather the more original and correct dictate of conscience, which urges the correction of the guilty source and its error. Cf. Th. Deman, O.P., "The Dignity of Conscience," *Blackfriars,* 34 (1953), 115–119.

56. Cf. I–II, q. 19, a. 5.

57. Cf. II–II, q. 1, a. 4; q. 2, a. 1; q. 2, a. 9, ad 2.

58. Alphonse Liguori, *Theol. mor.,* liber 1, tr. I, n. 20, remark of Gaude.

59. The Vulgate translation *"discernit"* is incorrect. The Greek word *Diakrinesthai* found in other passages also means an attitude of vacillation and doubt (cf. Mk 11:23, Mt 21:21, Rom 4:20, Jas 1:6).

60. Saint Antonine, *Summa,* P. I, tit. III, cap. 10.

61. We propose the use of the term "rule of prudence" in order to indicate that a service is rendered in the order of prudence. And this fact plainly shows that the problems dealt with are as much in the domain of prudence as in the sphere of conscience.

62. Cf. I–II, q. 106, a. 1.

63. Cf. Thomas *De veritate,* q. 17, a. 4.

64. Our opinion in this matter, we freely concede, is not accepted by all the moral theologians of the later period. They hold that one is guilty of sin and of sinful imprudence only in the instance in which a universally and univocally preceptive or prohibitive law, binding the conscience, is broken as such. In the mind of these authorities the neglect of conformity with an ideal suited to the occasion or the call of grace is only a lack of magnanimity, an imperfection or an inadequacy in striving for self-perfection, but none of these is looked upon as sinful. Cf. the section on Prudence.

65. Probabilists admit the principle and this first application of it (has one actually recited the obligatory prayer?) only in case of negative doubt, not of positive doubt. Similarly, they dispute the obligation to pay a debt (certainly contracted) if there is a truly positive doubt (not a merely negative doubt) about its payment. (Translator's note.)

66. D 1154: "Ab infidelitate excusabitur infidelis non credens, ductus opinione minus probabili." (Condemned and prohibited, as stated, and at least as scandalous and pernicious in practice.)

67. This question is receiving more adequate treatment in current discussion. Some authors

might find the above position somewhat rigorous. Cf. Gerald Kelly, S.J., "Pius XII and the Principle of Totality," *Theological Studies,* 16 (1955), 385–91; Eugene Tesson, S.J., "Moral Reflection," in *Medical Experimentation on Man,* ed. by Dom Peter Flood, O.S.B. (Cork: Mercier Press, 1955), 101–15; John J. Shinners, *The Morality of Medical Experimentation on Living Human Subjects in the Light of Recent Papal Pronouncements* (Washington: Catholic University of America Press, 1958). The serious words of the Holy Father in his address to the First International Congress on the Histopathology of the Nervous System, September 13, 1952, make clear that the doctor "can take no measure or try no course of action without the consent of the patient," for he has "no other rights or power over the patient than those which the latter gives him, explicitly or implicitly and tacitly." The words of the Pontiff are equally emphatic in stressing the fact that the "patient has no right to involve his physical or psychic integrity" in mental experiments or research entailing serious evil to himself, such as the "permanent abolition and considerable and durable diminution of his freedom," or great moral evils. (AAS, 44, 779–89; see also footnote 125 in Part five). (Translator's note.)

68. D 1152: "Probabiliter existimo, iudicem posse iudicare juxta opinionem etiam minus probabilem." (Condemned and prohibited, as stated, and at least as scandalous and pernicious in practice.)

69. D 1153: "Generatim, dum probabilitate sive intrinsica sive extrinsica quamvis tenui, modo a probabilitatis finibus non exeatur, confisi aliquid agimus, semper prudenter agimus." (Condemned and prohibited, as stated, and at least as scandalous and pernicious in practice.)

70. D 1293: "Non licet sequi opinionem (probabilem) vel inter probabiles probabilissimam."

71. Alphonse Liguori, *Theol. mor.* (6th and 7th eds.), liber I, tr. I, n. 55, ed. Gaude, n. 54 nota marg.

72. *Ibid.,* n. 54.

73. *Ibid.,* n. 79.

74. *Ibid.*

75. *Ibid.*

76. D 1127: 'Si liber sit alicuius iunioris et moderni, debet opinio censeri probabilis, dum non constet, reiectam esse a Sede Apostolica tamquam improbabilem." (Condemned and prohibited as "at least scandalous.")

77. Cf. Damen, *Theol. mor.,* I, n. 95.

78. Decree of the S.C.R. of March 23, 1871, approved by Pius IX.

79. Alphonse Liguori, *op. cit.,* n. 82.

80. Cf. D. von Hildebrand, "Die Idee der sittlichen Handlung," *Jahrbuch fuer Philosophie und phaenomenologische Forschung,* 3, 226.

81. Cf. R. Scherer, *Christliche Weltverantwortung* (Freiburg, 1940).

82. *Jahrbuch fuer Philosophie und phaenomenologische Forschung,* 3, 249.

83. D. von Hildebrand, *loc. cit.,* 188.

84. Pfaender, *Psychologie der Gesinnung,* 352.

85. Augustine, *In epistolam Johannis ad Parthos,* tract. VII, 8. PL 35, 2033.

86. J. Mausbach, *Ethik des hl. Augustinus,* I, 48.

87. Augustinus, Sermo 72, 4. PL 38, 468: Muta cor et mutabitur opus.

88. Augustinus, *En. in psalm. 125,* 5, 7. PL 37, 1660–1662.

89. Augustinus, *De civ. Dei,* lib. 1, c. 18; c. 19, 3. PL 41, 31–34.

90. *Ibid.,* lib. 14, c. 7, PL 41, 410.

91. Cf. O. Lottin, *Psychologie et morale aux XII et XIII siècles,* II, 493–589.

92. Cf. W. Schoellgen, *Die Soziologischen Grundlagen der katholischen Sittenlehre* (Duesseldorf, 1953), 13, 91ff.

93. M. Weber, *Politik als Beruf* (1919), 56ff. in W. Schoellgen, *op. cit.*, 96.

PART III

1. A. Waibel, *Moraltheologie,* I, 308.

2. Thomas, *De veritate,* q. 23, a. 1.

3. I–II, q. 90, a. 4.

4. I–II, q. 93, a. 1.

5. I–II, q. 106, a. 1.

6. Cf. W. Schmidt, S.V.D., *Der Ursprung der Gottesidee* (Muenster, 1924–1953). English translation: *The Origin and Growth of Religion; facts and theories* (New York: Dial Press, 1931).

7. Cf. H. Junker, "Der altestestamentliche Bann gegen heidnische Voelker als moraltheologisches und offenbarungsgeschichtliches Problem," *Aus Theologie und Philosophie* (Duesseldorf, 1950), 164–179.

8. "It would be fundamentally wrong to resort to any explanation of the principles of the natural law which would divest them of their absolute binding power. This absolute character of their power to bind and oblige does not permit, if we may cite an example, of the explanation given by many scholastics to account for polygamy in the Old Testament. We may not follow the teaching of these authors who hold that God 'dispensed' from monogamy in the Old Testament." A. F. Utz, O.P., *Deutsche Thomasausgabe, Summa Theologica* (Heidelberg, 1953), 18, 440.

9. SCG, lib. 3, cap. 123.

10. D 408: "Nec ulli unquam licuit insimul plures uxores habere, nisi cui fuit divina revelatione concessum, quae mos quandoque, interdum etiam fas censetur, per quam sicut Jacob a mendacio, Israelitae a furto, et Samson ab homicidio, sic et Patriarchae et alii viri iusti, qui plures leguntur simul habuisse uxores, ab adulterio excusantur. Sane veridica haec sententia probatur etiam de testimonio Veritatis testantis in Evangelio: 'Quicunque dimiserit uxorem suam . . .' (Mt 19:9)."

11. Cf. I–II, q. 103, a. 4.

12. Cf. I–II, q. 104, a. 3. The entire Old Testament law with its threats and promises, the ceremonial, judicial, and moral law was abrogated by the death of Christ. These laws were dead, but not evil. Hence they could still be observed for a time, and continued in fact to be observed even by the Apostles. Only later when the separation between the Church and synagogue was complete and continuation of the observance would imply denial of Christ's all-sufficient sacrifice, was the law *evil, deadly.* Of course the precepts which belong to the law of nature itself could never be abrogated, nor the threats of eternal punishment for sin. Hence the moral precepts remained, but not as Old Testament law with Old Testament sanction. The Old Testament law as Old Testament law was abolished. For a more thorough discussion of this whole question, cf. Christian Pesch, S.J., *Praelectiones Dogmaticae,* vol. V, n. 506ff., particularly n. 511. (Translator's note.)

13. Trid. sess. 6, can. 21, D 831: "Si quis dixerit, Christum Jesum a Deo hominibus datum fuisse ut redemptorem, cui fidant, non etiam ut legislatorem, cui obediant: A.S."

14. Thomas Aquinas, *Commentary on 2 Cor.,* III lectio II.

15. Thomas Aquinas, *Commentary on Heb.*, VIII lectio II, last lines.

16. I–II, Q. 106, a. 1.

17. Augustine, *De spiritu et littera,* cap XXI. PL 44, 222.

18. Thomas Aquinas, *Commentary on Rom.*, 6 lectio III.

19. G. Siewerth, "Von der Bildung des Gewissens," *Herderkorr,* 6 (1952), 188ff.

20. G. Ermecke, *Theol. Quart.*, 131 (1951), 411.

21. Leo XIII, encyclical *Libertas,* ASS, 20, p. 597.

22. Bernard of Clairvaux, *De consideratione.* PL 182, 752ff.; I–II, q. 107, a. 4; cf. the reference to Augustine, Epist. 55. PL 33, 200.

23. Augustine, *De Spiritu et Littera,* cap. 19. PL 44, 221.

24. Cf. I–II, q. 106, a. 1.

25. H. Rommen, *Die ewige Wiederkehr des Naturrechts,* 217.

26. D 595: "Nullus est dominus civilis, nullus est praelatus, nullus est episcopus, dum est in peccato mortali." D 656: This proposition of John Huss condemned by Martin V and the Council of Constance is the same as the condemned proposition of Wyclif. Cf. D 595.

27. Cf. CIC, can. 87.

28. Cf. CIC, can. 18.

29. Thus for example, CIC, can. 5.

30. Aristotle, *Nicomachean Ethics,* V, 4; II–!I, q. 120.

31. Cf. CIC, can. 73ff.

32. Cf. CIC, can. 80ff.

33. D 899: "Etiam eas circumstantias in confessione explicandas esse, quae speciem peccati mutant (can. 7), quod sine illis peccata ipsa neque a poenitentibus integre exponantur, nec iudicibus innotescant, et fieri nequeat, ut de gravitate criminum recte censere possint et poenam, quam oportet, pro illis poenitentibus imponere." D 917: "Si quis dixerit, in sacramento poenitentiae ad remissionem peccatorum necessarium non esse iure divino confiteri omnia et singula peccata mortalia, quorum memoria cum debita et diligenti praemeditatione habeatur, etiam occulta, et quae sunt contra duo ultima decalogi praecepta, et circumstantias, quae peccati speciem mutant .•. . aut demum non licere confiteri peccata venialia: A.S."

34. Busenbaum, *Medulla theol. moralis,* IV, tr. 3, cap. 7.

35. Thinkers who are concerned with vitalizing our concept of substance by stressing the vital powers of the soul in act, should not be accused of actualism. Cf. B. Haering, *Das Heilige und das Gute,* 240ff.

36. Eberhard Griesbach, *Gegenwart, eine kritische Ethik* (Halle, 1928).

37. Cf. Steinbuechel, *Philosophische Grundlegung,* I, 237ff.

38. Karl Rahner, S.J., "Situationsethik und Suendenmystik," *Stimmen der Zeit,* 145 (1949–50), 336.

39. AAS, 28 (1936), 48.

40. John Climacus, *Scala Paradisi,* Gradus I. PG 47, 385.

41. Bernard, *Declamationes,* XXVII. PL 184, 456.

42. F. Tillmann, *Katholische Sittenlehre* (3 ed.), III, 199.

43. A. Waibel, *Moraltheologie* (Regensburg, 1839), I, 338.

44. K. Martin, *Lehrbuch der kath. Moral* (Mainz, 1855), 88.

45. *Ibid.,* 89, Cf. O. Schilling, *Handbuch der Moraltheologie* (1952), I, 166.

46. O. Zimmermann, *Lehrbuch der Aszetik* (Freiburg, 1932), 92, 260ff.

47. *Ibid.,* 92.

48. *Ibid.,* 93.

49. Cf. *Ibid.,* 262.

50. Cf. E. Hugueney, "Imperfection," DTC c. V I, 1286–1298.
51. Cf. M. Sanchez, "De Imperfectione morali," *Angelicum* 27 (1950), 73–80.
52. J. Lindworsky, S.J., *The Training of the Will* (Milwaukee: Bruce, 1929) 49ff., 76ff.
53. Muencker, *Die psychologischen Grundlagen der Moraltheologie* (3 ed.) 283f.
54. PL 37, 1592ff., 1682.
55. Augustine, *De vera religione,* cap. XVII. PL 34, 136.

PART IV

1. Cf. Trent, Sess. VI, c. 15, D 808: "Asserendum est, non modo infidelitate (can. 27), per quam et ipsa fides amittitur, sed etiam quocunque alio mortali peccato, quamvis non amittatur fides (can. 28), acceptam justificationis gratiam amitti: divinae legis doctrinam defendendo, quae a regno Dei non solum infideles excludit, sed et fideles quoque fornicarios, adulteros, molles, masculorum concubitores, fures, avares, ebriosos, maledicos, rapaces (1 Cor. 6:9ff.), ceterosque omnes, qui letalia committunt peccata, a quibus cum divinae gratiae adiumento abstinere possunt et pro quibus a Christi gratia separantur (can. 27)." D 837: "Can. 27. Si quis dixerit, nullum esse mortale peccatum nisi infidelitatis, aut nullo alio quantumvis gravi et enormi praeterquam infidelitatis peccato semel acceptam gratiam amitti: A.S."
2. The frequent use of the singular is noticeable; compare Kirchgaessner, *Erloesung und Suende,* 253ff.
3. *Confessions,* V. 10, 18; cf. Le Blond, *Les Conversions de S. Augustin,* 54, 63.
4. Kirchgaessner, *op. cit.,* 257.
5. Cf. *Ibid.,* 56ff.
6. Kittel, *Th. W. z. NT,* 317.
7. Grundmann, *Th. W. z. NT,* I, 312.
8. Linsenmann, *Moraltheologie,* 159.
9. D 838: "Can. 28. Si quis dixerit, amissa per peccatum gratia simul et fidem semper amitti, aut fidem, quae remanet, non esse veram fidem, licet non sit viva, aut eum, qui fidem sine caritate habet, non esse Christianum: A.S." Cf. also note 1, above.
10. I–II, q. 88, a. 1, and a. 5.
11. D 106: "Can. 6. Item placuit, quod ait S. Ioannes Apostolus: si dixerimus, quia peccatum non habemus, nos ipsos seducimus, et veritas in nobis non est (1 Jn 1:8): quisquis sic accipiendum putaverit, ut dicat propter humilitatem oportere dici, nos habere peccatum, non quia vere ita est, A S. . . . Cum ait: nos ipsos decipimus, et veritas in nobis non est: satis ostendit eum, qui se dixerit non habere peccatum, non verum loqui, sed falsum." D 106, D 107 are similar.
12. D 804: "Licet enim in hac mortali vita quantumvis sancti et justi in levia saltem et quotidiana, quae etiam venialia (can. 23) dicuntur, peccata quandoque cadant non propterea desinunt esse justi." D 899: "Nam venialia, quibus a gratia Dei non excludimur et in quae frequentius labimur, quamquam recte et utiliter citraque omnem praesumptionem in confessione dicantur (can. 7), quod piorum hominum usus demonstrat: taceri tamen citra culpam multisque aliis remediis expiari possunt."
13. D 833: "Can. 23. Si quis hominem semel iustificatum dixerit amplius peccare non posse, neque gratiam amittere, atque ideo eum, qui labitur et peccat, nunquam vere fuisse iustificatum; aut contra, posse in tota vita peccata omnia etiam venialia vitare, nisi ex speciali Dei privilegio, quemadmodum de beata Virgine tenet Ecclesia: A S."
14. D 804, (see note 12 above). D 835: "Can. 25. Si quis in quolibet bono opere iustum

saltem venialiter peccare dixerit, aut (quod intolerabilius est) mortaliter, atque ideo poenas aeternas mereri, tantumque ob id non damnari, quia Deus ea opera non imputet ad damnationem: A.S."

15. D 1020: "Nullum est peccatum ex natura sua veniale, sed omne peccatum meretur poenam aeternam."

16. D 899: (see note 12 above).

17. D 470: "Licet . . . de necessitate non sit, iterum eadem confiteri peccata, tamen, quia propter erubescentiam, quae magna est poenitentiae pars, ut eorundem peccatorum iteretur confessio, reputamus salubre: districte inungimus, ut Fratres (Praedicatores et Minores) ipsi confitentes attente moneant, et in suis praedicationibus exhortentur, quod suis sacerdotibus saltem semel confiteantur in anno, asserendo, id ad animarum profectum procul dubio pertinere." D 748: "Nullo modo praesumas confiteri peccata venialia, sed nec omnia mortalia, quia impossible est, ut omnia mortalia cognoscas. Unde in primitiva Ecclesia solum manifesta mortalia confitebantur." (This error of Martin Luther was condemned by Leo X in the bull, *Exsurge Domine.*) D 899 (see note 12 above).

18. For example, Cyprian, *Epistulae,* 55. PL 4, 359.

19. *De civ. Dei,* lib. 21, cap. 27, 5. PL 41, 750.

20. Landgraf, A., *Das Wesen der laesslichen Suende in der Scholastik bis Thomas von Aquin* (Bamberg, 1923), 199.

21. *Ibid.,* 198.

22. I–II, q. 89, a. 1; q. 88, a. 1, ad 1.

23. I–II, q. 88, a. 3.

24. I–II, q. 89, a. 1.

25. Zimmermann, *Laessliche Suende und Andachtsbeichte,* 59.

26. *Ibid.*

27. *De veritate,* q. 15, a. 5, ad 2.

28. I–II, q. 88, a. 2.

29. Cf. A. Landgraf, "Die Luege der Vollkommenen im Urteil der Fruehscholastik," *Divus Thomas,* 20 (1942), 67–71.

30. Cf. I–II, q. 88, a. 3.

31. D 899, 917 (see above, note 33, Part 3).

32. Cf. Aertnys-Damen, *Theol. mor.,* I, n. 229ff.

33. III, q. 80, a. 4.

34. I–II, q. 73, a. 8, ad 3.

35. II–II, q. 149, a. 3.

PART V

1. For evidence of this fundamental Apostolic attitude, cf. A. Kirchgaessner, *Suende und Erloesung im Neuen Testament* (Freiburg, 1950).

2. Cf. G. Quell, G. Staehlin, W. Grundmann, "hamartía," *Th. W. z. NT,* I, 267–320.

3. This point is brought out in various ways but particularly through the preference for the use of the singular form, especially in John and Paul. Cf. A. Kirchgaessner, *Suende und Erloesung,* 263ff.

4. For the entire discussion, compare R. Schnackenburg, "Typen der Metanoiapredigt im NT," *Muenchener Theol. Z.,* 1 (1950), 1–13; Behm and Wuerthwein, "metánoia," *Th. W. z. NT,* IV, 992–1001. Cf. also Aloys Dirksen, C.PP.S., *The New Testament Concept of Metánoia* (Carthagena, 1932).

5. M. T. L. Penido, *La conscience religieuse* (Paris, 1935), p. 123.

6. Cf. H. Pohlmann, *Die Metánoia als Zentralbegriff der christlichen Froemmigkeit* (Leipzig, 1938), 42.

7. K. L. Schmidt, "basileis," *Th. W. z. NT*, I, 573–595.

8. D 176: "Si quis invocatione humana gratiam Dei dicit posse conferri, non autem ipsam gratiam facere, ut invocetur a nobis, contradicit Isaiae Prophetae, vel Apostolo idem dicenti: Inventus sum a non quaerentibus me; palam apparui his, qui me non interrogabant' (Rom 10:20; Is 65:1)." D 177: "Si quis, ut a peccato purgemur, voluntatem nostram Deum expectare contendit, non autem, ut etiam purgari velimus, per Sancti Spiritus infusionem et operationem in nos fieri confitetur, resistit ipsi Spiritui Sancto per Salomonem dicenti: 'Praeparatur voluntas a Domino' (Prv 8:35) et Apostolo salubriter praedicanti: 'Deus est, qui operatur in vobis et velle et perficere pro bona voluntate' (Phil 2:13)." D 178: "Si quis, sicut augmentum, ita etiam initium fidei ipsumque credulitatis affectum, quo in eum credimus, qui iustificat impium, et ad regenerationem sacri baptismatis pervenimus, non per gratiae donum, id est per inspirationem Spiritus Sancti corrigentem voluntatem nostram ab infidelitate ad fidem, ab impietate ad pietatem, sed naturaliter nobis inesse dicit, Apostolicis dogmatibus adversarius approbatur, beato Paulo dicenti: 'Confidimus, quia qui coepit in vobis bonum opus, perficiet usque in diem Christi Iesu' (Phil 1:6); et illud: 'Vobis datum est pro Christo non solum, ut in eum credatis, verum etiam, ut pro illo patiamini' (Phil 1:29); et: 'Gratia salvi facti estis per fidem, et hoc non ex vobis: Dei enim donum est' (Eph 2:8)." These canons are from the second Council of Orange (529). Cf. also D 103ff. and 793ff.

9. Augustine, *Confessions*, lib. X, cap. 4, 4. PL 32, 781.

10. Augustine, *Sermo* 295. PL 38, 1349–50.

11. Augustine, *In Joannem*, tr. 49. PL 35, 1737.

12. Cf. Augustine, *Confessions*, lib. XI, cap. 9. PL 32, 813ff.; *Enarratio in psalmum 110*. PL 37, 1464.

13. D 897: "Contritio, quae primum locum inter dictos poenitentis actus habet, animi dolor ac detestatio est de peccato commisso, cum proposito non peccandi de cetero. Fuit autem quovis tempore ad impetrandam veniam peccatorum hic contritionis motus necessarius, et in homine post baptismum lapso ita demum praeparat ad remissionem peccatorum, si cum fiducia divinae misericordiae et voto praestandi reliqua coniunctus sit, quae ad rite suscipiendum hoc sacramentum requiruntur." D 898: "Docet praeterea, etsi contritionem hanc aliquando caritate perfectam esse contingat hominemque Deo reconciliare, priusquam hoc sacramentum actu suscipiatur, ipsam nihilominus reconciliationem ipsi contritioni sine sacramento voto, quod in illa includitur, non esse adscribendum. Illam vero contritionem imperfectam (can. 5), quae attritio dicitur . . . declarat . . . verum etiam donum Dei esse . . . Et quamvis sine sacramento poenitentiae per se ad justificationem perducere peccatorem nequeat, tamen eum ad Dei gratiam in sacramento . . . disponit."

14. III, q. 86, a. 6, ad 3.

15. *Ibid.*

16. D 894: "Fuit quidem poenitentia universis hominibus, qui se mortali aliquo peccato inquinassent, quovis tempore ad gratiam et iustitiam assequendam necessaria, illis etiam, qui baptismi sacramento ablui petivissent, ut perversitate abiecta et emendata tantam Dei offensionem cum peccati odio et pio animi dolore detestarentur."

17. Romano Guardini, in Wagner-Zaehringer, *Eucharistiefeier am Sonntag* (Erster liturgischer Kongress: Trier, 1951), 64.

18. Ed. Bonne Presse, 18.

19. *Ibid.*

20. E. Stakemeier, "Der Glaube des Suenders," *Theol. u. Glaube,* 27 (1935), 416–438. *Idem, Glaube und Rechtfertigung. Das Mysterium der christlichen Rechtfertigung aus dem Glauben, dargestellt nach den Verhandlungen und Lehrbestimmungen des Konzils von Trient* (Freiburg, 1937).

21. Cf. J. M. Le Blond, *Les conversions de Saint Augustin* (Paris, 1950).

22. Justin, *Dialogue with Trypho,* 14, 1.

23. Cf. Bietenhard, "onoma," *Th. W. z. NT,* V, 242ff.

24. III, q. 84, a. 6.

25. D 894 (see note 16 above).

26. Cf. III, q. 84, a. 10.

27. Cf. the *Shepherd* of Hermas; Ambrose, *De Paenitentia.* PL 16, 485–546; and under the works of Saint Ambrose, PL 17, 1059–1094.

28. D 895: "Ceterum hoc sacramentum multis rationibus a baptismo differre dignoscitur (can. 2). Nam praeterquam quod materia et forma, quibus sacramenti essentia perficitur, longissime dissidet: constat certe, baptismi ministrum iudicem esse non oportere, cum Ecclesia in neminem iudicium exerceat, qui non prius in ipsam per baptismi ianuam fuerit ingressus . . . Secus est de domesticis fidei, quos Christus Dominus lavacro baptismi sui corporis membra (1 Cor 12:13) semel effecit. Nam hos, si se postea crimine aliquo contaminaverint, non iam repetito baptismo ablui, cum id in Ecclesia catholica nulla ratione liceat, sed ante hoc tribunal tanquam reos sisti voluit, ut per sacerdotum sententiam non semel, sed quoties ab admissis peccatis ad ipsum poenitentes confugerint, possent liberari. Alius praeterea est baptismi, et alius poenitentiae fructus. Per baptismum enim Christum induentes (Gal 3:27) nova propsus in illo efficimur creatura, plenam et integram peccatorum omnium remissionem consequentes: ad quam tamen novitatem et integritatem per sacramentum poenitentiae, sine magnis nostris fletibus et laboribus, divina id exigente iustitia, pervenire nequaquam possumus, ut merito poenitentia 'laboriosus quidam baptismus' a sanctis Patribus dictus fuerit."

29. Cf. D 895 (see note 28 above). D 905: "Debent ergo sacerdotes Domini . . . pro qualitate criminum et poenitentium facultate, salutares et convenientes satisfactiones iniungere, ne . . . levissima quaedam opera pro gravissimis delictis iniungendo, alienorum peccatorum participes efficiantur (cf. 1 Tim 5:22). Habeant autem prae oculis, ut satisfactio, quam imponunt, non sit tantum ad novae vitae custodiam et infirmitatis medicamentum, sed etiam ad praeteritorum peccatorum vindictam et castigationem: nam claves sacerdotum non ad solvendum dumtaxat, sed et ad ligandum concessas . . . Nec propterea existimarunt, sacramentum poenitentiae esse forum irae vel poenarum; sicut nemo unquam catholicus sensit, ex hujusmodi nostris satisfactionibus vim meriti et satisfactionis Domini nostri Jesu Christi vel obscurari vel aliqua ex parte imminui; quod dum Novatores intelligere volunt, ita optimam poenitentiam novam vitam esse docent, ut omnem satisfactionis vim et usum tollant (can. 13)." D 906: "Docet praeterea, tantam esse divinae munificentiae largitatem, ut non solum poenis sponte a nobis pro vindicando peccato susceptis, aut sacerdotis arbitrio pro mensura delicti impositis, sed etiam (quod maximum amoris argumentum est) temporalibus flagellis a Deo inflictis et a nobis patienter toleratis apud Deum Patrem per Christum Iesum satisfacere valeamus (can. 13)."

30. D 896: "Sunt autem quasi materia huius sacramenti ipsius poenitentis actus, nempe contritio, confessio et satisfactio (can. 4). Qui quatenus in poenitente ad integritatem sacramenti, ad plenamque et perfectam peccatorum remissionem ex Dei institutione requiruntur, hac ratione poenitentiae partes dicuntur. Sane vero res et effectus huius sacramenti, quantum ad ejus vim et efficaciam pertinet, reconciliatio est cum Deo,

quam interdum in viris piis et cum devotione hoc sacramentum percipientibus conscientiae pax ac serenitas cum vehementi spiritus consolatione consequi solet." D 914: "Can. 4. Si quis negaverit, ad integram et perfectam peccatorum remissionem requiri tres actus in poenitente quasi materiam sacramenti poenitentiae, videlicet contritionem, confessionem et satisfactionem, quae tres poenitentiae partes dicuntur; aut dixerit, duas tantum esse poenitentiae partes, terrores scilicet incussos conscientiae agnito peccato, et fidem conceptam ex Evangelio vel absolutione, qua credit quis sibi per Christum remissa peccata: A.S."

31. Cf. D 896 (see note 30 above).

32. This means according to the beautiful explanation of Saint Thomas, that in the sacrament of Penance, "taking the place of matter there are the human acts, which flow from the interior inspiration (of the Holy Spirit), hence they are offered as matter not by the minister, but by the inner working of God Himself." (III, q. 84, a. 1, ad 2).

33. III, q. 49, a. 3, ad 2.

34. Cf. Schurr, "Das Sakrament der Busse in heutiger Sicht," *Paulus,* 22 (1950), 104.

35. III, q. 79, a. 3.

36. *Ibid.*

37. Thomas Aquinas, *Comment. in Joan.,* c. XI, lectio 6; I·I, q. 72, a. 7; III, q. 80, a. 4, ad 5.

38. *Suppl.,* q. 30, a. 1; *3 Sent.,* dist. XXII, q. 1, a. 2, sol. 1.

39. Theologians are still not in agreement regarding the source of this grave law. Does the divine law itself seriously oblige the sinner to submit his mortal sin to the power of the keys in the sacrament of penance before he approaches the Sacred Banquet? Or is the precept only of ecclesiastical origin? (Cf. DTC, XII, 1050). The problem has a very practical aspect in our appraisal of the weighty reasons which would dispense from this "positive" law.

40. Cf. Henri De Lubac, S.J., *Catholicisme, Les aspects sociaux du dogme* (4 ed.; Paris, 1947), particularly 56–83. English translation: *Catholicism, A Study of the Corporate Destiny of Mankind* (New York, 1958). G. N. Rus, *De munere sacramenti paenitentiae in aedificando Corpore Christi mystico* (Romae, 1944).

41. *Directoire episcopal,* n: 4; cf. n. 11, ed. Bonne Presse, 41ff.

42. The Church is not simply the kingdom of God as such. She is the "quasi-sacrament" of the kingdom of God in this temporal order.

43. Cf. CIC, can. 87.

44. "Le baptême entrée dans le peuple de Dieu," *La Maison-Dieu,* 32 (1952); J. B. Umberg, *Zum Kampfe geweiht, Vom Sinn der Firmung* (2 aufl.; Innsbruck, 1947).

45. Cf. P. Galtier, *De Paenitentia* (9 ed.; Rome, 1950); *Idem., L'Église et la rémission des péchés* (1932); B. Poschmann, *Busse und letzte Oelung. Handbuch der Dogmengeschichte,* Part IV, fasc. 3, with references to the literature.

46. Cf. A. Landgraf, "Suende und Trennung von der Kirche," *Scholastik,* 2 (1930), 210–248; cf. *L'Église et le pécheur, Cahiers de la Vie Spirituelle* (2nd ed.; Paris, 1948), 19.

47. Augustine, *Epist.,* 153. PL 33, 655.

48. Magister Martinus, cited in Landgraf, *loc. cit.,* 235.

49. Cf. E. Berbuir, "Theologie des Bussakramentes," *Wissenschaft und Weisheit* (1952), 81–97.

50. Pars III, "De expulsione publice paenitentium in feria IV. Cinerum"; "Reconciliatio paenitentium in feria V. Coenae Domini."

51. Directoire of the French Hierarchy, n. 1; cf. n. 10.

52. Cf. Brinktrine, "Das Amtspriestertum und das allgemeine Priestertum der Glaeubigen," *Divus Thomas,* 22 (1944), 295.

53. D 924: "Can. 14. Si quis dixerit, satisfactiones, quibus poenitentes per Christum Jesum peccata redimunt, non esse cultus Dei, sed traditiones hominum, doctrinam de gratia et verum Dei cultum atque ipsum beneficium mortis Christi obscurantes: A.S." D 905: (cf. note 29 above).

54. II–II, q. 24, a. 3, ad 2; cf. I–II, q. 69, a. 2.

55. Cf. B. Haering, "Seelenheil und Theozentrik in der Mission," *Paulus,* 20 (1948) Part 3, 3–15.

56. D 914 (cf. note 30 above).

57. M. Scheler, "Reue und Wiedergeburt," *Vom Ewigen im Menschen,* 21.

58. Augustine, *Epistola,* 118, 22. PL 33, 442.

59. Cf. P. Galtier, *De paenitentia* (9 ed.), p. 301; Augustine, *In epistolam Joannis ad Parthos,* tr. III, cap. II. PL 35, 2002; *Enchiridion,* cap. 80. PL 40, 270ff.; *De catechizandis rudibus,* cap. 25 PL 40, 343.

60. M. Scheler, *Vom Ewigen im Menschen,* 39ff.

61. Fulton Sheen, *Friede ohne Fragezeichen* (Regensburg, 1951), 286. English title: *Peace of Soul* (New York: Whittlesey House, 1949).

62. D 914 (cf. note 30 above).

63. Hermann Schuhmacher, "Die Stellung des Seelsorgers zu den Bemuehungen der Psychotherapie," *Anima,* 7 (1925), 300ff.

64. P. L. Beirnaert, S.J., "Sens du péché et fausse culpabilité," *Trouble et lumière* (Études Carmélitaines) (1949) 31. English translation: *Conflict and Light* (New York: Sheed and Ward, 1952).

65. Compare with what was stated regarding conscience, part 2, Chapter Four, III.

66. Compare with the antinomian attitude of the psychotherapeutist, Ernst Michel, to cite just one example. Note his works: *Der Partner Gottes, Glaeubige Existenz, Renovatio, Ehe.*

67. P. L. Beirnaert, *op. cit.,* 33.

68. M. Scheler, *Vom Ewigen im Menschen,* 41.

69. "The angels of God have the power to fix their entire future existence through one single interior act of their will," says Vladimir Soloviev. (This citation is from the German translation of *Russia and the Universal Church,* book III, chapter 5, of the *Complete Works,* Vol. III [Freiburg, 1954], 355).

70. Trent, sess. 14, D 897 (see note 13 above); cf. D 898 (see note 13 above); D 915: "Si quis dixerit, eam contritionem, quae paratur per discussionem, collectionem et detestationem peccatorum, qua quis recogitat annos suos in amaritudine animae suae (Is 38:15), ponderando peccatorum suorum gravitatem, multitudinem, foeditatem, amissionem aeternae beatitudinis, et aeternae damnationis incursum, cum proposito melioris vitae, non esse verum et utilem dolorem, nec praeparare ad gratiam, sed facere hominem hypocritam et magis peccatorem; demum illam esse dolorem coactum et non liberum ac voluntarium: A.S."

71. Trent, D 914: (see note 30 above).

72. Suppl., q. 3, a. 1.

73. Suppl., q. 3, a. 1. (English translation from the English Dominican translation [London: R. and T. Washbourne, 1917].)

74. Cf. I. Hausherr, *Penthos.*

75. Suppl. q. 3, a. 1 and 2; q. 4, a. 2.

76. D 897 (see note 13 above).

77. *Ibid.*

78. Max Scheler, "Reue und Wiedergeburt," *Vom Ewigen im Menschen* (Leipzig, 1921), 5–58.

79. *Ibid.,* 18.

80. *Ibid.*
81. *Ibid.,* 19.
82. *Ibid.*
83. *Ibid.,* 17f.
84. Von Hildebrand, *Die Umgestaltung in Christus* (3 aufl.; Einsiedeln, 1950), 36. For a somewhat different English version, cf. *Transformation in Christ,* New York, Longmans, Green & Company, 1948, p. 31.
85. Cf. D 819: "Can. 9. Si quis dixerit, sola fide impium iustificari, ita ut intelligat, nihil aliud requiri, quo ad iustificationis gratiam consequendam cooperetur, et nulla ex parte necesse esse, eum suae voluntatis motu praeparari atque disponi: A.S." D 829: "Can 19. Si quis dixerit, nihil praeceptum esse in Evangelio praeter fidem, cetera esse indifferentia, neque praecepta, neque prohibita, sed libera, aut decem praecepta nihil pertinere ad Christianos: A.S." D 830: "Can 20. Si quis hominem iustificatum et quantumlibet perfectum dixerit non teneri ad observantiam mandatorum Dei et Ecclesiae, sed tantum ad credendum, quasi vero Evangelium sit nuda et absoluta promissio vitae aeternae, sine conditione observationis mandatorum: A.S." Cf. D. 897 (see note 13 above). Cf. D 914 (see note 30 above).
86. M. Scheler, *loc. cit.,* 43.
87. *Ibid.,* 28.
88. *Ibid.,* 29.
89. Cf. J. B. Hirscher, *Die christliche Moral* (3 aufl.) II, 461ff.
90. D 798: "Disponuntur autem ad ipsam iustitiam (can. 7 et 9), dum excitati divina gratia et adiuti, fidem ex auditu (Rom 10:17) concipientes, libere moventur in Deum, credentes, vera esse, quae divinitus revelata et promissa sunt (can. 12 ad 14) atque illud in primis, a Deo iustificari impium per gratiam eius, 'per redemptionem, quae est in Christo Jesu' (Rom 3:24), et dum, peccatores se esse intelligentes, a divinae iustitiae timore, quo utiliter concutiuntur (can. 8) ad considerandum Dei misericordiam se convertendo, in spem eriguntur, fidentes, Deum sibi propter Christum propitium fore, illumque tanquam omnis iustitiae fontem diligere incipiunt ac propterea moventur adversus peccata per odium aliquod et detestationem (can. 9), hoc est, per eam poenitentiam, quam ante baptismus agi oportet (Act 2:38); denique dum proponunt suscipere baptismum, inchoare novam vitam et servare divina mandata." Cf. III, q. 85, a. 5.
91. D 1305: "Attritio, quae gehennae et poenarum metu concipitur, sine dilectione benevolentiae Dei propter se, non est bonus motus ac supernaturalis." (Error of the Jansenists, condemned by Alexander VIII.) D 1410: "Si solus supplicii timor animat poenitentiam, quo haec est magis violenta, eo magis ducit ad desperationem." (Error of Quesnel condemned by Clement XI.) D 1412: "Qui a malo non abstinet nisi timore poenae, illud committit in corde suo et iam est reus coram Deo." (Error of Quesnel condemned by Clement XI.) D 1525: "Doctrina, quae timorem poenarum generatim perhibet dumtaxat non posse dici malum, si saltem pertingit ad cohibendam manum; quasi timor ipse gehennae, quam fides docet peccato infligendam, non sit in se bonus et utilis, velut donum supernaturale ac motus a Deo inspiratus praeparans ad amorem iustitiae: falsa, temeraria, perniciosa, divinis donis iniuriosa, alias damnata (v.n. 746) contraria doctrinae Concilii Tridentini (v.n. 798, 898), tum et communi Patrum sententiae, opus esse, iuxta consuetum ordinem praeparationis ad iustitiam, ut intret timor primo, per quem veniat caritas: timor medicamentum, caritas sanitas."
92. Cf. A. Landgraf, "Reue," *Lexikon f. Theol. u. K.,* VII, 850.
93. Cf. J. Périnelle, O.P., *L'attrition d'après le concile de Trente et d'après saint Thomas* (Kain, 1927).
94. Cf. D 915 (see note 70 above).

95. D 1146: "Circa controversiam: an illa attritio, quae concipitur ex metu gehennae, excludens voluntatem peccandi, cum spe veniae, ad impetrandam gratiam in sacramento poenitentiae requirat insuper aliquem actum dilectionis Dei, asserentibus quibusdam, negantibus aliis, et invicem adversam sententiam censurantibus: . . . Sanctitas Sua . . . praecipit . . . ut . . . non audeant alicuius theologicae censurae . . . nota taxare alterutram sententiam, sive negantem . . . sive asserentem dictae dilectionis necessitatem, donec ab hac Sancta Sede fuerit aliquid hac in re definitum."

96. Cf. *Rit. Rom.*, tit. III, cap. I, n. 18.

97. Cf. the Rule and Constitutions of the Congregation of the Most Holy Redeemer, const. 130–132.

98. Max Scheler, *Vom Ewigen im Menschen*, 44.

99. Cf. I. Hausherr, 26.

100. Suppl. q. 2, a. 5.

101. I. Hausherr, 63, 186 *passim*.

102. Cf. I. Hausherr, 28.

103. A favorite figure of theological writers since the days of Origen.

104. Cf. III, q. 84, a. 8 and 9; Suppl., q. 4, a. 1.

105. Hugh of Saint Victor, tr. 6, *Summa Sent.* cap. 11, in Thomas Aquinas, Suppl. q. 4, a. 1.

106. Max Scheler, *Vom Ewigen im Menschen*, 52.

107. D 896 (see note 30 above).

108. D 895 (see note 28 above).

109. *Ibid.*

110. D 899, 917 (see note 33, Part three).

111. Cf. III, q. 84, a. 7. ad 2.

112. Hirscher, *Christliche Moral* (3 aufl.), II, 467.

113. A. Brunner, "Aus der Finsternis zum Licht. Ueber das Bekenntnis der Suenden," *Geist und Leben*, 23 (1950), 89.

114. *Ibid.*, 93.

115. *Ibid.*, 87.

116. *Ibid.*, 91.

117. "Personalisme catholique," *Esprit* (1940), 234.

118. Max Scheler, *Vom Ewigen im Menschen*, 21.

119. A. Brunner, *op. cit.*, 91.

120. "I sought refuge in science rather than in the sacrament: I confessed to the physician and received absolution from him, the only absolution which the world is able to give, namely the absolution of the psychiatrist, who does not acknowledge sin at all because there is no soul which can forsake God. And this absolution gave me that dreadful peace in which thousands live today, whose illness is nothing except their scorn for peace with God." (Gertrud von le Fort, *Das Schweisstuch der Veronika* (Munich, 1935), 349. English translation: *The Veil of Veronica* (New York: Sheed and Ward, 1935), p. 298 differs somewhat from the above.

121. Cf. DTC, XII, 996ff. A. Teetaert, *La confession aux laiques dans L'Eglise latine* (Louvain, 1926). R. Pettazoni, *La confessione dei peccati* (Bologna, 1935–1936), 3 Vols. R. Mohr, *Die christliche Ethik im Lichte der Ethnologie* (Munich, 1954), 26–37 and elsewhere.

122. Cf. D 899, 917 (see note 33, Part three). Cf. CIC, can. 901.

123. Fourth Council of the Lateran, D 437: "Omnis utriusque sexus fidelis, postquam ad annos discretionis pervenerit, omnia sua solus peccata saltem semel in anno fideliter confiteatur." (Fourth Council of the Lateran.) Confirmation by the Council of Trent: "Ceterum, quoad modum confitendi secreto apud solum sacerdotem, etsi Christus non

vetuerit, quin aliquis in vindictam suorum scelerum et sui humiliationem, cum ob aliorum exemplum tuum ob ecclesiae offensae aedificationem, delicta sua publice confiteri possit: non est tamen hoc divino praecepto mandatum, nec satis consulte humana aliqua lege praeciperetur, ut delicta, praesertim secreta, publica essent confessione aperienda (can. 6). Unde cum a sanctissimis et antiquissimis Patribus magno unanimique consensu secreta confessio sacramentalis, qua ab initio Ecclesia sancta usa est et modo etiam utitur, fuerit semper commendata, manifeste refellitur inanis eorum calumnia, qui eam a divino mandato alienam et inventum humanum esse, atque a Patribus in concilio Lateranensi congregatis initium habuisse, docere non verentur (can. 8); neque enim per Lateranense concilium Ecclesia statuit, ut Christi fideles confiterentur, quod iure divino necessarium et institutum esse intellexerat, sed ut praeceptum confessionis saltem semel in anno ab omnibus et singulis, cum ad annos discretionis pervenissent impleretur. Unde iam in universa Ecclesia cum ingenti animarum fructu observatur mos ille salutaris confitendi sacro illo et maxime acceptabili tempore Quadragesimae, quem morem haec sancta Synodus maxime probat et amplectitur tanquam pium et merito retinendum (can. 8; v.n. 437f.). Cf. CIC, Can. 906.

124. D 917 (see note 33, Part three).

125. Note the warning of the Holy Office in the "Normae de agendi ratione confessariorum circa sextum Decalogi praeceptum" of May 16, 1943 (norms of procedure for confessors in matters of the sixth commandment of the decalog). Cf. *Periodica de re Morali*, 33 (1944), 130–133. Cf. also T. L. Bouscaren, *Canon Law Digest* (Milwaukee: Bruce, 1953), III, 379–383. A detailed commentary can be found in J. Pistoni, *De agendi ratione confessariorum circa sextum Decalogi praeceptum juxta normas S. Officii* (Mutinae, 1944). Note that in his allocution of September 13, 1952, Pope Pius XII directs attention to the inviolable moral law which forbids all voluntary exciting of impure temptations, as is done, for instance, in the psychoanalytical disclosures. Even though there is a totally different procedure in the unburdening of conscience in the confessional from that of the universally hazardous psychoanalytical procedure according to Freud, still the general principle is equally valid for sacramental confession, that one must shun every unnecessary danger to temptation in this matter. Pius is stressing what has been constantly taught by moral theologians. Cf. A. Lehmkuhl, *Theologia moralis* (2 ed.), n. 437: "Si poenitens sibi timet, ne recogitando peccata, maxime luxuriae, misere in delectationem labatur: accuratiorem recogitationem omittere debet etiam cum periculo ab integritate deficiendi." (If the penitent fears that in pondering on his sins, especially the sins against purity, he will fall into sin by taking pleasure in them, he must omit a more detailed recollection of them even if there is danger that he fails to make an integral confession of his sins.) For the version in English of the message of the Pontiff (spoken in French, cf. *AAS*, 44 [1952], 779–89) directed to the First International Congress of the Histopathology of the Nervous System, held at Rome, cf. "Moral Limits of Medical Research and Treatment," *The Catholic Mind*, 51 (May, 1953), 305–13. The reader is also directed to the allocution of the same Pope given April 13, 1953. For this address (in French in the *AAS*, 45 [1953], 278–86) to the 5th International Congress of Psychotherapy and Psychology, see the English translation "Psychotherapy and Religion," *The Catholic Mind* (July, 1953), 428–35.

126. A species of moral science tainted with legal positivism sprang up and in part also a legalistic pastoral care. The result was a very resourceful moral casuistry which was often characterized by an astonishing rigorism wherever there was question of exact established statutes of law, whereas the broad norms of the order of creation and more particularly the norms of the order of grace which form the whole structure of the moral and spiritual life, though they may not be formulated in the precise or fixed

terms of statute law, were likely to be slighted or left to the tracts on ascetical theology.

127. Cf. L. Fanfani, *Manuale theol. mor.* (Romae, 1951), IV, 379. But note also Saint Alphonse, *Theol. moralis,* lib. IV, n. 478, and on the other hand also n. 477.

128. CIC, can. 903.

129. Nevertheless, the priest should not, except in cases of very urgent necessity, give general absolution, without having first petitioned his Ordinary for directives in the matter. Cf. *AAS,* 32 (1940), 571; 36 (1944), 155f. Cf. Bouscaren, O. C. 377ff.

130. Cf. D 1209: "Licet sacramentaliter absolvere dimidiate tantum confessos, ratione magni concursus poenitentium, qualis verbi gratia potest contingere in die magnae alicuius festivitatis aut indulgentiae." (Proposition condemned by Innocent XI.)

131. If the motive for the action is different in its species than the external action and is also gravely sinful, it is quite obvious that it must be stated in the confession. The law extends to all mortal sins according to number and species.

132. Trent, D 875: "Ergo Salvator noster . . . sacramentum hoc instituit . . . Sumi autem voluit sacramentum hoc tanquam spiritualem animarum cibum (MT 26:26), quo alantur et confortentur (can. 5) viventes vita illius, qui dixit: 'Qui manducat me, et ipse vivet propter me' (JN 6:58), et tanquam antidotum, quo liberemur a culpis quotidianis et a peccatis mortalibus praeservemur."

133. Cf. III, q. 79, a. 4.

134. III, q. 79, a. 5. Cf. D 887: "Can. 5. Si quis dixerit, vel praecipuum fructum sanctissimae Eucharistiae esse remissionem peccatorum, vel ex ea non alios effectus provenire: A.S."

135. III, q. 79, a. 5, ad 3; q. 79, a. 8.

136. Cf. D 917 (see note 33, Part three). Cf. D 1539: "Declaratio synodi de peccatorum venialium confessione, quam optare se ait non tantopere frequentari, ne nimium contemptibiles reddantur huiusmodi confessiones: temeraria, perniciosa, Sanctorum ac piorum praxi a sacro Concilio Tridentino probatae (v.n. 899) contraria." (Condemnation of the error of the Synod of Pistoia by Pius VI.) Cf. Encyclical, *Corporis mystici Christi,* AAS, 35 (1943), 235; *Mediator Dei,* AAS, 39 (1947), 505; III, q. 84, a. 2, ad 3.

137. Thomas Aquinas, *Sent.* 4, dist. 17, q. 3, a. 3, sol. 5, ad 4; *Suppl.* q. 8, a. 5, ad 4.

138. Cf. L. Fanfani, *Manuale theologiae moralis,* IV, 393; Alphonsus, *Th. mor.,* lib. VI, n. 477: "Potius piis meditationibus tempus impendat." (He should rather spend the time in pious meditation.)

139. "Actus quodammodo satisfactorius" (an act which is in some measure satisfactory), *Suppl.,* q. 4, a. 3.

140. Cf. III, q. 90, a. 2.

141. Cf. P. Galtier, "Satisfaction," in DTC, XIV, 1142f.

142. Cf. Leo the Great, Ep. 108, 2. PL 54, 1012 A.

143. Trent, sess. 14, cap. 8, D 904: "Neque vero securior ulla via in Ecclesia Dei unquam existimata fuit ad amovendam imminentem a Domino poenam, quam ut haec poenitentiae opera (MT 3:8, 4:17, 11:21, etc.) homines cum vero animi dolore frequentent. Accedit ad haec, quod, dum satisfaciendo patimur pro peccatis, Christo Jesu, qui pro peccatis nostris satisfecit (ROM 5:10; 1 JN 2:1f.), ex quo omnis nostra sufficientia est (2 COR 3:5), conformes efficimur, certissimam quoque inde arrham habentes, quod, si compatimur, et conglorificabimur, (cf. ROM 8:17). Neque vero ita nostra est satisfactio haec, quam pro peccatis nostris exsolvimus, ut non sit per Christum Jesum; nam qui ex nobis tanquam ex nobis nihil possumus, eo cooperante, qui nos confortat, omnia possumus (cf. PHIL 4:13). Ita non habet homo, unde glorietur; sed omnis gloriatio (cf. 1 COR 1:31; 2 COR 10:17; GAL 6:14) nostra in

Christo est, in quo vivimus, in quo movemur (cf. Acts 17:28) in quo satisfacimus, facientes fructus dignos poenitentiae (cf. Lk 3:8), qui ex illo vim habent, ab illo offeruntur Patri, et per illum acceptantur a Patre (can. 13f.)."

144. D 905 (see note 29 above).

145. In the theology of the Eastern Church, most particularly in the Russian Orthodox Church, the aspect of "salutariness" is placed in sharper focus. Cf. Galtier, "Satisfaction," 1449f.; A. Bukowski, *Die Genugtuung fuer die Suende nach der Auffassung der russischen Orthodoxie* (Paderborn, 1911).

146. D 904 (see note 143 above).

147. *Ibid.*

148. SCG, Lib. III, cap. 158. The translation is from *On the Truth of the Catholic Faith,* Book Three, part two, by Vernon Bourke, 257.

149. Cf. discussion on Historic Man, part two, chapter three, III.

150. Cf. Trent, D 904 (see note 143 above).

151. Albert the Great, *Sent.* 4, dist. 1, a. 12.

152. III, q. 52, a. 1, ad 2.

153. Thomas Aquinas, *Sent.* 4, dist. 18, q. 1, a. 3, sol. 3, ad 3; cf. *Suppl.* q. 18, a. 3, ad 3.

154. Cardinal Cajetan, Opusculum 15, *de indulgentiis,* cap. 8.

155. S. Bukowski, 107, 110.

156. Cf. III, q. 88, a. 1–4.

157. D 905 (see note 29 above). D 923: "Can. 13. Si quis dixerit, pro peccatis, quoad poenam temporalem, minime Deo per Christi merita satisfieri poenis ab eo inflictis et patienter toleratis vel a sacerdote iniunctis, sed neque sponte susceptis, ut ieiuniis, orationibus, eleemosynis vel aliis etiam pietatis operibus, atque ideo optimam poenitentiam esse tantum novam vitam: A.S."

158. The imposition of the penance belongs to the "juridical" consummation of the sacramental tribunal of grace and is demanded by the very nature of conversion; likewise the other expressly penitential works freely accepted by the penitent occupy a significant place in the whole context of penance. Not only do they manifest the inner spirit of penance, they have tremendous value in training and disciplining the penitent, and impart a truly penitential character to the "new life" and render it secure.

159. D 924 (see note 53 above).

160. Emil Brunner, *Gerechtigkeit,* 333.

161. Cf. D 906: "Docet praeterea, tantam esse divinae munificentiae largitatem, ut non solum poenis sponte a nobis pro vindicando peccato susceptis, aut sacerdotis arbitrio pro mensura delicti impositis, sed etiam (quod maximum amoris argumentum est) temporalibus flagellis a Deo inflictis et a nobis patienter toleratis apud Deum Patrem per Christum Iesum satisfacere valeamus (can. 13).

162. D 923 (see note 157 above).

163. Cf. Fanfani, *Manuale theologiae moralis,* IV, 400.

164. B. Poschmann, *Der Ablass in Lichte der Bussgeschichte* (Bonn, 1948). See also: K. Rahner, *Zeitschrift fuer Kath. Theologie,* 71 (1949), 481–490; and P. Galtier, "Les Indulgences," *Gregorianum,* 31 (1950), 258–274.

PART VI

1. Scheler, *Umsturz der Werte,* I, 13.

2. Augustine, *Retractiones,* I, 9. PL 32, 597.

3. W. Schamoni, "Hysterie und Heiligkeit," *Die Kirche in der Welt,* 3 (1950), 401. Cf.

J. Goldbrunner, *Heiligkeit und Gesundheit* (Freiburg i. Br., 1946); English translation: *Holiness Is Wholeness* (New York: Pantheon, 1955).

4. D 800: "Unde in ipsa iustificatione cum remissione peccatorum haec omnia simul infusas accipit homo per Iesum Christum, cui inseritur: fidem, spem et caritatem."

5. Even though we hold that the supernatural moral virtues are infused, we are not warranted to conclude that distinct habits (*habitus*) corresponding exactly to the traditional scheme of the four cardinal virtues are infused into the soul. Cf. P. De Vooght, O.S.B., "Y a-t-il des vertus morales infuses?" *ETL*, (1933), 232ff.

6. D 410: Innocent III states that some theologians hold that infants receive these virtues, others deny: "aliis asserentibus, per virtutem baptismi parvulis quidem culpam remitti, sed gratiam non conferri: nonnullis vero dicentibus, et dimitti peccatum, et virtutes infundi, habentibus illas quoad habitum, non quoad usum, donec perveniant ad aetatem adultam." (From the letter "Maiores Ecclesiae causas" to Ymbertus, Archbishop of Arles.) The doctrine that the moral virtues are infused seems to have been the certain and traditional teaching, though there was dispute about the time when the virtues were infused. Such is the implication of the statement of Innocent. (Cf. *Sacrae Theologiae Summa*, III, 711ff., I. A. Aldama, *De virtutibus infusis in seipsis*.)

7. D 483: "Nos autem . . . opinionem secundam, quae dicit, tam parvulis quam adultis conferri in baptismo informantem gratiam et virtutes, tanquam probabiliorem, et dictis Sanctorum et doctorum modernorum theologiae magis consonam et concordem, sacro approbante Concilio duximus eligendam." (Clement V.)

8. *The Tridentine Catechism*, p. II, c. 2, n. 51.

9. J. M. Sailer, *Handbuch der christlichen Moral*, I (1817), 433.

10. *Ibid.*, 428.

11. *Ibid.*, 429f.

12. Scheler, *Umsturz der Werte*, I, 14.

13. I. Kant, *Anthropologie in pragmatischer Hinsicht* (Cassirer), 8, 32.

14. Th. Steinbuechel, *Philosophische Grundlegung der katholischen Sittenlehre*, II, 136.

15. Scheler, "Zur Rehabilitierung der Tugend," *Umsturz der Werte*, I, 16.

16. H. Preisker, *Das urchristliche Ethos* (Guetersloh, 1949), 130ff. (on the Biblical expression *teleios*, "perfect").

17. Scheler, *Umsturz der Werte*, I, 14.

18. *Ibid.*, 15.

19. The following note is taken from the French edition of this work (*Loi du Christ*, 1, 283, note 20). As to this matter, Father de Couesnongle, O.P., holds that the notion of general virtue should be subjected to a renewed study. With the exception of prudence, he would like to see set down "in bold outlines the fundamental orientations of a Christian-motivated life. Confronted with the Nietzschean cult of force, the Christian, in relation to himself, must develop an appreciation for the *meaning of effort* (*'sens de l'effort'*) which is related to the virtue of magnanimity; in relation to others, he must be aware of the meaning of the *common good* (*'sens du bien commun,'* general justice) and thus recognize the legitimate aspirations of a community existence. In a world in danger of profanation by technical civilization, the sense of the sacred (*'sens du sacre,'* virtue of religion in general) helps man, confronted by a transcendent God, to discover himself" (*Lumiere et Vie*, 13 (1954), 133). Father Sertillanges had already followed a similar vein of thought. "To point out the conclusions reason must reach when confronted with the various situations in which our instincts come into play—the instinct of self-preservation, the sexual instinct, the religious instinct, properly understood—would be a definite achievement" (*La Philosophie morale de S. Thomas*, Nouv. edit. (1942), p. 158, note). Our special moral is inspired by a similar order, but from a fresh theological point of view. "If Saint Thomas did not follow

this logical division," says Father Sertillanges, "it is for reasons of tradition" (*ibid.*). These "traditional reasons" seem to be a determining factor in *L'Initiation théologique*, tome III, 1952. (Translator's note.)

20. Augustine, *De moribus Ecclesiae catholicae*, lib. I, cap. XV, 25. PL 32, 1322.

21. J. Pieper, *Traktat ueber die Klugheit*, 69. For a slightly different English version, cf. *Prudence*, New York, Pantheon, 1959, p. 65.

22. *Ibid.*, 18; *Prudence*, 18ff.

23. *Ibid.*, 30; *Ibid.*, 27.

24. *Ibid.*, 27; *Ibid.*, 27.

25. II–II, q. 51, a. 4; I–I', q. 57, a. 6, ad 3.

26. II–II, q. 47, a. 8.

27. II–II, q. 50.

28. II–II, q. 47, a. 10.

29. Cf. I–II, q. 57, a. 5, ad 1.

30. II–II, q. 47, a. 10.

31. II–II, q. 47, a. 6, ad 3.

32. II–II, q. 47, a. 8.

33. II–II, q. 49, a. 1.

34. II–II, q. 49, a. 2.

35. II–II, q. 49, a. 5.

36. II–II, q. 49, a. 3.

37. II–II, q. 49, a. 4.

38. II–II, q. 49, a. 6.

39. II–II, q. 49, a. 7.

40. II–II, q. 49, a. 8.

41. II–II, q. 47, a. 14.

42. *Ibid.*

43. D. Feuling, "Diskretion," *Benediktinische Monatschrift*, 7 (1925), 249.

44. II–II, q. 52.

45. I–II, q. 68, a. 1.

46. II–II, q. 53–55.

47. Pieper, *op. cit.*, 40; *Prudence*, pp. 28ff.

48. II–II, q. 53, a. 2.

49. II–II, q. 53, a. 6.

50. II–II, q. 55, a. 7.

51. II–II, q. 55, a. 3.

52. *Les quatre livres* (the four holy books) in French and Latin translation, by S. Couvreur, S.J. (Ho Kien Fou, 1895), p. 616. Cf. M. Heinrichs, *Die Bedeutung der Missionstheologie, aufgewiesen am Vergleich zwischen den abendlaendischen und chinesischen Kardinaltugenden* (The Meaning of Missiology in the Light of a Comparison between the Occidental Concept of the Cardinal Virtues and the Chinese Concept) (Muenster, 1954).

53. II–II, q. 58, a. 1.

54. II–II, q. 57, a. 1.

55. II–II, q. 58, a. 11.

56. II–II, q. 8, a. 5.

57. II–II, q. 8, a. 12.

58. Schrattenholzer, "Die Gemeinwohlgerechtigkeit," *Neues Abendland*, 2 (1947), 44.

59. N. Monzel, "Die christlichen Motive der Entproletarisierung," *Die neue Ordnung*, 3 (1949), 200ff.

60. In his definition and explanation of commutative justice, the author has in mind the

justice of exchange and trade (*Tausch und Verkehr*) which rests on private contract and agreement. In its fuller sense commutative justice is somewhat broader and goes beyond private contract or agreement. This is the *"ausgleichende Gerechtigkeit,"* which includes rights founded in the very nature of man (cf. Eberhard Welty, *Herders Sozial Katechismus,* 1, 244ff.). (Translator's note.)

61. II–II, q. 123, a. 6.
62. Ambrose, *De officiis* I, 35. PL 16, 75. Cf. J. Pieper, *Fortitude* (New York: Pantheon Books, 1954), 18ff.
63. II–II, q. 124, a. 3.
64. Pieper, *Fortitude,* 48.
65. *Ibid.,* 52.
66. *Ibid.* (quoted as to substance).
67. *Ibid.*
68. *Ibid.,* 63.
69. *De moribus ecclesiae,* lib. I, cap. XIX. PL 32, 1322.
70. Pieper, *Fortitude,* 82.
71. *Ibid.,* 67ff. Cf. II–II, q. 155, a. 4, ad 3.
72. *Ibid.,* 68. Cf. II–II, q. 155 and 156.
73. Cf. D 1258: "Crux voluntaria mortificationum pondus grave est et infructuosum, ideoque dimittenda." D 1259: "Sanctiora opera et poenitentiae, quas peregerunt Sancti, non sufficiunt ad removendam ab anima vel unicam adhaesionem." D. 1275: "Per hanc viam internam pervenitur, etsi multa cum sufferentia, ad purgandas et extinguendas omnes passiones, ita quod nihil amplius sentitur, nihil, nihil; nec ulla sentitur inquietudo, sicut corpus mortuum, nec anima se amplius commoveri sinit." D. 1276: "Duae leges et duae cupiditates (animae una, et amoris proprii altera) tamdiu perdurant, quamdiu perdurat amor proprius: unde quando hic purgatus est et mortuus, uti fit per viam internam, non adsunt amplius illae duae leges et duaè cupiditates, nec ulterius lapsus aliquis incurritur, nec aliquid sentitur amplius, ne quidem veniale peccatum." (These errors of Michael de Molinos were condemned by Innocent XI in 1687.)
74. C. Feckes, *Die Lehre vom christlichen Vollkommenheitsstreben,* 184.
75. *Ibid.,* S. 334.
76. AAS, 45 (1953), 15–24.
77. D 1258f. (see note 74 above).
78. DTC, V, 2147.
79. *De Servorum Dei beatificatione et de Beatorum canonizatione,* lib. III, cap. 28 s.
80. II–II, q. 147, a. 3, ad 1.
81. *Philothea,* 3, 23.
82. Moritz Meschler, S.J. (d. 1912), *Das Exerzitienbuch des hl. Ignatius von Loyola* (The Book of Spiritual Exercises of Saint Ignatius of Loyola) (Freiburg, 1925), I, 150f.
83. Saint Jerome, Ep. 130. PL 22, 1116.
84. II–II, q. 147, a. 1, ad 2. Cf. CIC, De consecrationibus, dist 5, cap, Non Immediocriter.
85. The reference here is to a sect founded by Otto Hanisch (1854–1936), a German immigrant to the United States. He dabbled in esoteric and strange cults and gave himself a Persian name and history. His sect is a pantheistic and naturalistic group which pretends to have descended from the ancient Mazdaism or Zoroastrianism. (Translator's note.)
86. II–II, q. 147, a. 8.
87. Scheler, *Umsturz der Werte,* I, 18.
88. Augustine, *De sancta virginitate,* 37f. PL 40, 417.

89. Scheler, *Umsturz der Werte*, I, 25.
90. D. von Hildebrand, *Transformation in Christ* (New York: Longmans, Green & Company, 1948), p. 144.
91. Scheler, *Umsturz der Werte*, I, 22f.
92. Augustine, *De civ. Dei*, lib. 14, cap. 13, 1. PL 41, 420.
93. Scheler, *Umsturz der Werte*, I, 24.
94. D. von Hildebrand, *Transformation in Christ*, p. 151.
95. Kleinadam, "Die Nachfolge Christi nach dem hl. Bernhard," *Amt und Sendung*, 442. (The Imitation of Christ According to Saint Bernard.)
96. Augustine, *Enarrationes in Psalmos*, 141, 7. PL 37, 1837.
97. Cf. the treatment on conscience in part two, chapter four, III.
98. Nietzsche's life is itself an appalling example of this confession.
99. Cf. D. von Hildebrand, *Transformation in Christ*, p. 139.

INDEX

A

Abelard, his opposition to penitential books, 563, n. 4

Abellan, 55

Abraham, 247; sacrifice of son, 227; tempted, 349

Absolution, general, consultation of ordinary, 580, n. 129; in emergencies, 461; of crowds, 580, n. 130; to unconscious dying, given conditionally, 454

Abulia, 116

Acedia, 381 f.

Act, commanded (*imperatus*), 108; determinants of morality of, 287 ff.; elicited, 104; external (*externus*), significance of, 192; external and inner disposition, 195 f ; essential elements according to modern phenomenology, 195; good, bad, or indifferent, 287; human, 108, 189; imputable, 108; indifferent, analysis of problem, 324 ff.; indifferent, teaching of scripture on, 328; individual, manifests whole man, 70 ff.; internal (*internus*), 189; internal, objects of law?, 277; intrinsically evil, 288; of man (*hominis*), 189; of penitent, essential parts of sacrament of penance, 421; of personal and objective value, 191 f.; possibly indifferent, (though voluntary) as lacking moral consciousness, 194 ff.; sins of, 373 f.; strictly human (*humanus*), 189 ff.; subject of moral value as human act, 108, 190 ff.

Actualistic system, 294

Adam, A., 213, 557; criticized for position on sins of impurity, 371

Adam, K., on erroneous conscience, 567, n. 55

Addict, drug, or alcohol, 118

Adiaphoristic controversy, 324

Adikia, sin, 346, 391

Adler, 426

Adnès, 557

Adultery, essentially evil, 288

Aertnys-Damen, xi, 22 f., 53, 563, 572

Affectation, 533

Agapè, 487, 546; of Eucharist, 415

Agere contra, counteract evil, 534

Agoraphobia, 159

Albert of Saxony, 15

Albert the Great, 581; notion of theology, 11; on conscience, 140 f.

Alcohol, morality in its use, 381

Aldama, 582

Alexander of Hales, notion of theology, 11; on conscience, 141

Alexander VII, contrition includes beginning of love?, 440

Alexander VIII, condemns distinction between theological and mere "philosophical sin," 345; Jansenists, 577, n. 91; rigorism, 186

Allers, 222, 478, 557

Allier, 478

Almsgiving as penance, 475 f.

Alphonse, St., xii, 8, 167, 168, 567, 568, 580; and equiprobabilism, 182; appraisal, 21 f.; authority, 188 f.; popular mission included preaching of *vita devota,* 441 f.

Alszechy, 53

Althaus, 328

Amann, 478

Ambition, 555

Ambrose, St., 6, 13, 574, 584; *De Officiis,* first casuistic theology, uses Cicero, Stoic concepts, comparison of pagan, Christian values, esteem of Old Testament morality, 7 ff.

Ambrosetti, 328

Amendment, contrition, 433 ff.

Amentia, 114

Ammer, 53

Anciaux, 478

Andersen, 213

Andrews, 53

Angel, totality in decision for good or evil, 429

Angelo Carletti di Chivasso, 16